A DIRECTORY OF AMERICAN SILVER,
PEWTER AND SILVER PLATE

By the same authors

DICTIONARY OF MARKS——POTTERY AND PORCELAIN

A DIRECTORY OF

AMERICAN SILVER, PEWTER AND SILVER PLATE

by Ralph M. & Terry H. Kovel

CROWN PUBLISHERS, INC. · NEW YORK

THIS BOOK IS DEDICATED TO
ISADORE
FOR HIS ENCOURAGEMENT,
AND TO
LEE AND KIM
WHO, AFTER ALL OUR WORK,
THINK THIS IS THE BEST
PAGE IN THE BOOK.

ACKNOWLEDGMENTS

We would like to thank those who helped us with research beyond the expected limits of their jobs: Mr. Legare Obear, The Library of Congress, Dr. Rawski and the entire staff of the Fine Arts Department of the Cleveland Public Library, Miss Bageley, Miss Lucy Buker, The Library of the Cleveland Museum of Art, Miss Ella Tallman, Miss Charlotte Van der Veer, Miss Elta Albaugh, The Metropolitan Museum of Art, Western Reserve University, Yale University, The Detroit Historical Society, International Silver Company, and Towle Silver Company.

A thank-you also to those who helped with the manuscript preparation: Teresa Costanzo, the illustrator; Mr. and Mrs. Raymond Grover, Mr. and Mrs. H. J. Horvitz, Miss Terri Kovel, Mr. and Mrs. Leon Lindheim, and Miss Janet Lucas.

Second Printing, April, 1963

CONTENTS

INTRODUCTION

Before trying to trace the maker, be sure the silver mark is American. The earliest silversmiths in the colonies used their initials. Many makers used the last name, or first initial and last name. Pseudo hallmarks were used by 1800. These were meant to mislead the buying public into the belief that the silver was of English origin. Many unmarked pieces of American silver were made and shipped to stores throughout the country by 1825. The store proprietor would then mark the silver with his name. By 1830 the words COIN, PURE COIN, DOLLAR, STANDARD, PREMIUM, or the letters C or D were placed on the silver to indicate that it was 900 out of 1000 parts silver. The word STERLING was frequently used by 1860. STERLING meant that 925 out of 1000 parts were silver. This is still the standard for sterling silver.

The makers of silver in Baltimore had a maker-date system from 1814 to 1830.

If the silver has several hallmarks, it might not be of American origin. The leopard's head indicates England. The lion passant refers to London. Silver made in Edinburgh was stamped with a thistle. The harp indicated the piece was made in Dublin. Glasgow silversmiths used a fish or tree. Ornate capital letters or the fleur-de-lis was used by French craftsmen. A hand indicates Antwerp, a spread eagle Germany or Russia. The word STERLING indicates Ireland as well as America. COIN, DOLLAR, and STANDARD were usually American terms, but some Irish makers also used them.

A single mark usually indicates that the piece of silver was made in America, although there are some known Irish and Scotch pieces with just the maker's name. Four or five marks indicate England. You should become familiar with the king's or queen's head mark as an indication of age.

The words quadruple, triple, double, EPNS, EPWM, all indicate that the ware is silver-plated.

If your piece is not American, refer to some of the many books written about English or Continental silver and pewter. If it seems to be American, look in the proper section of this book. Happy hunting!

The collection of American antiques is becoming increasingly important each day. They are now being collected by most museums and by many private collectors. It is important that the collector become acquainted with the best early American pieces of craftsmanship. When American silversmiths were first "discovered" in the early 1900's, most collectors felt that only the eighteenth-century makers were important. Now, years later, we have learned that fine American silver was also made during the nineteenth century.

The interest in the silver-plated wares has been growing. Most of it seems to be in poor taste by modern standards. It should be judged not by today's rules but by the styles popular in Victorian times when it was made. Many pieces were well designed and produced. There is no reason why this American product should not be collected in the same manner as Victorian china and other Victorian antiques. It is representative of a way of life now past.

Your collection will be only as good as your knowledge of the subject. This book is a guide or an indicator of where to look and what to seek. Learn to know good work by its shape, feel, and construction, then look up the maker and determine exact age and origin. We hope this book will make it easier for you to identify grandma's spoon or the pewter dish you found in the antique shop, but please remember that a mark is only the signature of the manufacturer, and can be easily copied.

NOTES ON THE USE OF THIS BOOK

This book is meant to be a guide for all collectors. We have included three sections (Silver, Silver Plate, and Pewter) because many pewter and silver-plate makers worked in all metals. When tracing a nineteenth-century pewterer, be sure to look at all sections; some silversmiths also made pewter and silver plate.

The information contained in this book is as accurate and complete as possible. Only the authoritative sources as indicated in our bibliography have been used. Many readers of our nationally syndicated newspaper column "Know Your Antiques," dealers, and collectors have helped furnish us with information heretofore not available.

There are several features that make this book entirely different from any existing book on American silver, pewter or silver plate. It is actually three books bound together for convenience. Each entry in the silver or pewter section is followed by a group of numbers ranging from 1 to 89. These numbers indicate the book or article that was used as a source of information. The bibliography list for each section is at the end of the book. The bibliography notation 89 refers to original research information obtained through our collection, talks with workers or relatives of silversmiths, and obscure unprinted material that was made available to us through local historical societies, museums, and collectors.

The bibliography is as complete as possible. Only technically accurate sources were included. We have omitted current articles from magazines and newspapers that are not devoted exclusively to antiques. We have also omitted some books which were glamorized biographies. Primary source material not available to the general public has been included under the 89 listing.

Numbers in parentheses are shown after each entry. The numbers refer to the birth or death dates of the craftsman or the most accurate working dates known. All of the dates used are based on information compiled in earlier studies and only the blatant errors have been corrected. For example: One silversmith was listed in many books as living to be 140 years old. This type of misinformation has been corrected. Many early books list information incorrectly and the later studies have been able to furnish more accurate information. If we were unable to prove that an error existed we listed all available information with no editorial comment. Because of this, you may find a silversmith listed as working in two cities during the same years. Some books list silversmiths, watchmakers, and jewelers separately. We have included all three as silversmiths because there is not enough evidence to differentiate their trades. Many later pieces of silver are marked with the jewelry store owner's name, not the maker's. It is impossible to determine which pieces were marked in this way.

Many of the entries are followed by an actual drawing of the mark used by the craftsman. In the silver section these marks are indicated in two ways: the complex mark was drawn by an artist but the marks which were comprised of just names or initials were set in type. The actual

mark on a piece of silver was incised or cut into the silver. Those appearing as an incised block are indicated by letters set in type surrounded by a line drawing of a box. Later marks were often incised letters indicated by simple letters set in type. The form of type, all capitals, or capitals and small letters, is an indication of how the original mark appeared. Those marks comprised of just initials have periods between the letters only if these appeared on the original mark on the silver. Pseudo hallmarks, the small symbols stamped separately from the maker's name, were not included. Symbols indicative of a specific city, such as the Baltimore assay marks or various city names, were not included. Unusual descriptive marks such as "OPPO THE POST OFFICE" or "JOYS BUILDING" are included in our listing.

The alphabetical organization of names makes this a simple book to use. A listing of all marks that are initials and may have been used by more than one maker is at the beginning of every letter. For example: If you have a piece of silver with the letters PM on it, you can immediately check the alphabetical listing at the beginning of the M section; it will refer to the names Francois Paul Malcher, Peter Martin, and Peter Mood, Sr.—all makers who used the initials P.M.

If your piece is marked with a name beginning with I or J look in the I and J sections, since these letters were frequently interchanged. There may be confusion when looking up makers whose last names begin with a vowel. For example: G. Eoff used a mark that might appear as GEOFF. Be sure always to check this possibility. All marks that contain the beginning M' are listed as Mc; consequently the name M'Donnell will appear in the listing for McDonnell.

During the past several hundred years the names of many cities have been changed. Wherever possible we have tried to use the most recent city name, but confusion still exists. For example, three settlements in Virginia were named Charleston.

The silver-plate marks listed were taken from company records, the Library of Congress, and other sources. We have frequently referred to the date 1902. This date indicates that a specific company was or was not working at that time. The latest source book we used was printed in 1902. It is not to be construed as an exact date for the closing of a factory.

PART ONE:
SILVER

The history of silver in America began in Boston, Massachusetts, with two men, Richard Sanderson (1608-1693) and John Hull (1624-1683). Sanderson was trained as a silversmith in England and arrived in the colonies in 1638. Hull had been trained by his half-brother, Richard Storer. Messrs. Hull and Sanderson worked together and made the earliest American silver pieces now known to exist. Collectors can still dream of the day when work made by Richard Storer or John Mansfield will be discovered. Both men are listed as silversmiths, but nothing made by them has ever appeared.

John Hull first gained fame when he was chosen to start the mint in Boston. England had forbidden the colonists to mint their own money, but in 1652 the general court of Massachusetts ordered the first silver money to be minted. There was a great need for coins to be used in local trading. Hull designed and made the now famous pine-tree shilling.

Very few families in seventeenth-century America had enough money or leisure to desire wares made from silver. Most of the early silver was made for the churches and were copies of English designs. The lines were simple and the pieces plain. New England (especially Boston), the state of New York (especially New York City), the state of Pennsylvania (especially Philadelphia), and later the states of Delaware and South Carolina, were the centers of the silversmithing trade. Each city developed its own designs and characteristics, which were influenced by the heritage of the new colonists. The silver design in Boston echoed the English, while the New York silversmiths received their inspiration from the Dutch.

More money and gracious living made the business of the silversmith a lucrative one by the eighteenth century. A law was passed in Boston in 1660 forbidding a maker to mark his silver work alone until he was twenty-one. The first American-born silversmith was Jeremiah Dummer, who was born in 1645. There were other rules, but the silversmiths in America were never controlled as rigidly as the English with their guilds which are still in existence.

It is interesting to note that there was little cheating and that few smiths ever got into trouble with their patrons or the law. The silversmith was usually a successful businessman and well respected in his community. He handled the wealth of his neighbors and was trusted to give a fair accounting of the amount of silver that was used.

It must be remembered that this was during a period when it was difficult to keep money safely hidden away. A family of means quickly learned that it was safer to have a silversmith melt their silver coins into a large teapot than it was to keep a box of money under the bed. Each teapot or sugar bowl was unique in design and marked by a maker so that it could be identified. A thief would have more trouble disposing of a teapot than a bag of coins.

Most silversmiths produced only the pieces of silver ordered by their customers. Most of his wealthy customers requested drinking vessels, which indicates the position of liquor in the daily living of our ancestors. Liquor was a part of the celebration for marriage, death, and business discussions. A silver tankard helped add to the enjoyment.

Coffee, tea, and chocolate became important beverages in the colonies by the early eighteenth century. Pots, then later sugar bowls, creamers, and other utensils, were made to fit this need. The design of these eating and drinking utensils changed to reflect the style or design of the period. Silver shapes changed from colonial to classical, then Federal, followed by Empire and Victorian. Silver was being made by machine by 1840. The age of fine handcrafted silver in the United States was ending. A few makers were still working by hand as they traveled west ahead of the machinery.

Victorian tastes and the machine age converted the simple silver designs to a mass of decoration by 1875. Handmade silver was no longer in demand. With the return of the simple lines of twentieth-century modern, the silversmith may again return to the early handcraft methods.

The history of silver in the colonies and the United States covers many years and many men. Families often passed their knowledge and skills on to future generations. Paul Revere was one of the most famous American silversmiths and was

one of the many men whose father and son were silversmiths. The Reveres, Burts, and Hurds of Boston, the Richardsons and Syngs of Philadelphia, the Faris family of Annapolis, the Ten Eyck family of Albany, the Moultons of Newburyport, and the Kirks of Baltimore, were all famous for their silversmiths. Silversmithing is an art that requires years of training, an inherent skill, and artistic talent. The silversmiths of America can be classed among the artists of the country, for they were true craftsmen.

The marks used by most American silversmiths were usually composed of the maker's name or initials. These letters or names were stamped inside the many characteristic shapes shown. The makers also used pseudo hallmarks and other marks, which were made to resemble the silver guild marks used by English silversmiths. Heads, birds, a hand, an arm, a star, or a letter often appeared in the pseudo marks, along with the maker's mark.

SILVER

Joseph Aaron (c. 1798)
Philadelphia, Pa.
Bibl. 3, 23, 36, 44

George Abbott (c. 1822)
Philadelphia, Pa.
Bibl. 3

J. S. Abbott
Location unknown
Bibl. 28, 29, 44

| J. S. ABBOTT |

John W. Abbott (b. 1790-d. 1850)
Portsmouth, N.H. (c. 1839)
Bibl. 3, 15, 23, 25, 28, 36, 44

| J ABBOT | J W ABBOTT

Robert K. Abel (c. 1840-1850)
Philadelphia, Pa.
Bibl. 3

John D. Abercrombie (c. 1823-1843)
Philadelphia, Pa.
Bibl. 3

Henry Abraham (c. 1844)
New York, N.Y.
Bibl. 23

F. W. (M.) Ackerly
(See Francis W. Ackley)

David Ackerman (c. 1818)
New York, N.Y.
Bibl. 23, 36, 44

E. Ackley (c. 1800)
Alexandria, Va.
Bibl. 24, 28

| E ACKLEY |

Francis W. Ackley (c. 1797-1800)
New York, N.Y.
Bibl. 15, 21, 23, 29, 36

| F.M.A | | F. ACKLEY |

Thad Ackley (c. 1840)
Warren, Ohio
Bibl. 89

George Acton (c. 1795)
New York, N.Y.
Bibl. 23, 36, 44

R. F. Adair
Paris, Ky. (to 1796)
Lexington, Ky. (after 1796)
Bibl. 32, 54

Charles Adam (b. 1848-d. 1925)
Alexandria, Va.
Bibl. 54

James Adam (b. 1755-d. 1798)
Alexandria, Va.
Bibl. 19, 54

John Adam (b. 1780-d. 1846)
Alexandria, Va. (c. 1799)
Bibl. 15, 19, 28, 29, 44, 54, 72, 78

John B. Adam (c. 1822)
New Orleans, La.
Bibl. 23, 36, 44

L. Adam (d. 1731)
Location unknown
Bibl. 28, 29

Robert L. Adam (c. 1846-1898)

Alexandria, Va.
Bibl. 54

William Wallace Adam (b. 1817-d. 1877)
Alexandria, Va. (c. 1846-   )
Charles Adam
Robert L. Adam
Bibl. 19, 54

Adams (c. 1800)
Location unknown
Bibl. 15

| ADAMS |

Adams & Buttre (c. 1836-   )
Elmira, N.Y.
Bibl. 20

Adams & Farnsworth
Location unknown
Bibl. 80

| ADAMS AND FARNSWORTH |

Benjamin F. Adams (c. 1845)
Troy, N.Y.
Bibl. 23

C. J. Adams (c. 1840)
Frankfort, Ky.
Bibl. 32

C. J. Adams & Co. (c. 1870)
Bowling Green, Ky.
Bibl. 54

Dunlap Adams (c. 1764)
Philadelphia, Pa.
Bibl. 3, 28

H. B. Adams (c. 1842)
Elmira, N.Y.
Adams & Buttre (c. 1836-   ) (?)
Hamilton & Adams (c. 1837-1842) (?)
Bibl. 20

Henry B. Adams (c. 1848)
Philadelphia, Pa.
Bibl. 3, 23

John Adams (c. 1829)
Alexandria, Va.
District of Columbia
Bibl. 23, 36

Jonathan Adams (c. 1783)
Philadelphia, Pa.
Bibl. 3, 23, 36, 44

Nathaniel Adams (c. 1797-1813)
Troy, N.Y.
Bibl. 20

Nathaniel W. Adams (c. 1842-
1844)
Buffalo, N.Y.
Sibley & Adams (c. 1847-1848)
Bibl. 20

Pygan Adams (b. 1712-d. 1776)
New London, Conn. (c. 1735)
Bibl. 15, 16, 22, 23, 28, 29, 36,
44, 54, 61, 72

R. Adams (c. 1800)
Location unknown
Bibl. 15, 44

Thomas F. Adams
Baltimore, Md. (c. 1804)
Petersburg, Va. (c. 1807)
Edenton, N.C. (c. 1809)
Bibl. 19, 21

Wesley Adams (c. 1849-1850)
Philadelphia, Pa.
Bibl. 3

William Adams (c. 1829-1859)
New York, N.Y.
Bibl. 4, 15, 22, 23, 28, 29, 35,
36, 44, 54, 79, 83

William L. Adams (c. 1842-
1850-   )
Troy, N.Y.

Bibl. 20, 23, 44

George Mitchell Addison
(c. 1798-1804, d. 1810)
Baltimore, Md.
Bibl. 23, 28, 44

William Addison (c. 1845-1850)
Philadelphia, Pa.
Bibl. 3

William Adgate (b. 1744-d.
1779)
Norwich, Conn.
Bibl. 16, 22, 23, 28, 36, 44

Duff Adolph (c. 1837)
Philadelphia, Pa.
Bibl. 3

Adriance & Cook (c. 1814-1815)
Poughkeepsie, N.Y.
John Adriance (?)
Harry Cook
Bibl. 20

Charles Platt Adriance (b.
1790-d. 1874)
Richmond, Va. (c. 1816-1832)
Bibl. 15, 19, 44

Edwin Adriance
Ithaca, N.Y. (c. 1832-1835)
St. Louis, Mo. (c. 1835-1870)
Mead, Adriance & Co. (c. 1831-
1832)
Mead & Adriance (c. 1838-
1842)
Bibl. 15, 20, 23, 25, 28, 36, 44,
54

John Adriance (c. 1814-1828)
Poughkeepsie, N.Y.
Adriance & Cook (c. 1814-
1815) (?)
Hayes & Adriance (c. 1816-
1826)
Bibl. 15, 20

William Adriance (c. 1835)
Natchez, Miss.
Bibl. 19

Thomas Agnis (c. 1761-1762)
Edenton, N.C.
Bibl. 21

Adolph Aherns (c. 1837)
Philadelphia, Pa.

Bibl. 3

Anthony Aigron (c. 1732-1745)
Charleston, S.C.
Bibl. 5

Charles G. Aiken (c. 1850)
Cleveland, Ohio
Bibl. 54

George Aiken (b. 1765-d. 1832)
Baltimore, Md. (w. 1787-c.
1823)
Bibl. 15, 23, 28, 29, 36, 39, 44,
50

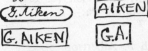

J. Aiken
(See John Aitken)

Michael Ainsworth (c. 1755)
Fredericks County, Va.
Winchester, Va.
Bibl. 3, 19, 23, 36, 44

John Aitken (Aitkin) (Aiken)
(c. 1785-1813)
Philadelphia, Pa.
Bibl. 3, 4, 22, 25, 28, 29, 36, 44

William Aitken (w. 1802)
Baltimore, Md.
Bibl. 38

William Aitken (c. 1825)
Philadelphia, Pa.
Bibl. 3, 22, 44

John Aitkin
(See John Aitken)

W. Aitkins (c. 1802)
Baltimore, Md.
Bibl. 23, 28, 36

Akerly & Briggs
Location unknown
Bibl. 15, 44

AKERLY & BRIGGS

John B. Akin (Brent Akin) (c.
1820-1860)
Danville, Ky.
Bibl. 25, 32, 44, 54, 68

J. B. AKIN   JOHN B. AKIN
STANDARD
JOHN B AKIN DANVILLE KY.

William Akin (d. 1824)
Danville, Ky. (c. 1812-1820)
Bibl. 32, 54, 68

Samuel Akins (c. 1841-1842)
Philadelphia, Pa.
Bibl. 3

John L. Albert
Shepherdstown, Va. (c. 1826)
Winchester, Va. (c. 1827)
George B. Graves
Bibl. 19

Anthony Albertson (c. 1848)
Philadelphia, Pa.
Bibl. 3

Joseph P. Albertson
New York, N.Y.
Cleveland, Ohio (c. 1849-1858)
Cowles & Albertson (c. 1849-1858)
Bibl. 54

Thomas F. Albright (c. 1835-1847)
Philadelphia, Pa.
Bibl. 3

Alcock & Allen (c. 1810)
Location unknown
Bibl. 28

ALCOCK & ALLEN

George Alcorn (c. 1830-1833)
Philadelphia, Pa.
Bibl. 3

Charles Aldis (c. 1814)
New York, N.Y.
Bibl. 15, 23, 25, 36, 44

C. ALDIS

Alexander
(See Brasher & Alexander)

Alexander & Riker (Riker & Alexander) (c. 1797-1798)
New York, N.Y.
———— Alexander
Peter Riker
Bibl. 44

A & RIKER

Alexander & Riter (c. 1797)
New York, N.Y.
Bibl. 25

A. Alexander (c. 1802)
Philadelphia, Pa.
Bibl. 3, 36, 44

Isaac Alexander (c. 1850)
New York, N.Y.
Bibl. 15, 23, 25, 44

I. ALEXANDER

Isaac B. Alexander (b. 1812-d. 1885)
Camden, S.C. (c. 1841)
Bibl. 5

Moses Alexander (c. 1851-1859)
York, S.C.
Bibl. 5

Philip Alexander
Location unknown
Bibl. 10

Robert Alexander (b. 1825-d. 1862)
Rochester, N.Y. (c. 1847-1850)
Bibl. 20, 41, 44

S. Alexander & A. Simmons (c. 1800)
Philadelphia, Pa.
Samuel Alexander
Anthony Simmons
Bibl. 22, 28, 44

S ALEXANDER

A. SIMMONS

Samuel Alexander (c. 1797-1808)
Philadelphia, Pa.
Wiltberger & Alexander (c. 1797-1808)
Simmon(s) & Alexander (c. 1798-1804)
S. Alexander & A. Simmons (c. 1800)
Bibl. 3, 4, 22, 25, 28, 29, 36, 44, 54

S. ALEXANDER

Samuel P. Alexander (b. 1810-d. 1900)
Charlotte, N.C.

Trotter & Alexander (c. 1837-1838)

Brem & Alexander (c. 1848)
Bibl. 21

Zenas Alexander (d. 1826)
Mecklenburg County, N.C. (c. 1805-1810)
(near Charlotte, N.C.)
Bibl. 21

Samuel Alford (c. 1759-1762)
Philadelphia, Pa.
Bibl. 3, 22, 28, 36

Samuel Alford (c. 1840)
Philadelphia, Pa.
Bibl. 44

Thomas Alford (c. 1762-1764)
Philadelphia, Pa.
Bibl. 3, 22, 23, 28, 36, 44

Samuel Allardice (d. 1798)
Philadelphia, Pa.
Bibl. 3

Allcock & Allen (c. 1810-1820)
New York, N.Y.
Bibl. 25, 44, 79

ALLCOCK & ALLEN

Allen
(See Allcock & Allen)
(See Evans & Allen)

Allen & Edwards (c. 1700-1707)
Boston, Mass.
John Allen
John Edwards
Bibl. 23, 25, 28, 29, 36, 44, 54

IA IE

A. C. Allen (c. 1836)
Cincinnati, Ohio
Bibl. 34

Alexander Allen (c. 1850)
Rochester, N.Y.
Bibl. 20

Cairns Allen (c. 1837-1848)
Philadelphia, Pa.
Bibl. 3

Caleb Allen (1836)
Cincinnati, Ohio
Bibl. 54

Charles Allen (c. 1760)
Boston, Mass.
Bibl. 25, 29, 36, 44

C ALLEN

G. W. Allen (c. 1836)
Batavia, N.Y.
Bibl. 20

J. T. Allen (c. 1832-1836)
Batavia, N.Y.
Bibl. 20

James Allen (c. 1720)
Philadelphia, Pa.
Bibl. 3, 4, 22, 23, 28, 36, 44

Jared T. Allen (c. 1844-1846)
Rochester, N.Y.
Bibl. 20, 41, 44

Joel Allen (b. 1755-d. 1825)
Middletown, Conn. (c. 1787)
Plantsville, Conn.
Southington, Conn.
Bibl. 16, 22, 23, 28, 36, 44

John Allen (b. 1671-d. 1760)
Boston, Mass.
Allen & Edwards (c. 1700-1707)
Bibl. 2, 15, 22, 23, 25, 28, 29,
44, 50, 54, 69

John Allen (c. 1814)
Philadelphia, Pa.
Bibl. 3, 23, 36, 44

L. C. Allen (c. 1850)
Utica, N.Y.
Bibl. 18, 20

Luther A. Allen (c. 1844-
1850-   )
Rochester, N.Y.
Bibl. 20

Oliver Allen (c. 1830)
Lyons, N.Y.
Bibl. 20

Philo Allen (c. 1844)
Buffalo, N.Y.
Chedell & Allen
Bibl. 20

Rhodes Allen & Co.
Cincinnati, Ohio
Bibl. 54

Richard Allen (c. 1816-1817)
Philadelphia, Pa.
Bibl. 3, 23, 36, 44

Richard Allen (c. 1850)
Auburn, N.Y.
Bibl. 20

Robert Allen (b. 1755-d. 1825)
Philadelphia, Pa. (c. 1787-1796)
Bibl. 3, 22, 28, 36, 44

Thomas Allen (c. 1758)
Boston, Mass.
Bibl. 22, 23, 28, 36, 44

William Allen (w. 1772)
Annapolis, Md.
Bibl. 38

Marc Alleoud (c. 1820)
Augusta, Ga.
Morand, Alleoud & Co.
Bibl. 17

W. A. Allibone (c. 1828-1833)
Philadelphia, Pa.
Bibl. 3

John Allies (w. 1782-1796, d.
1796)
Elkton, Md.
Bibl. 38

Peter Allison (c. 1791-1792)
New York, N.Y.
Bibl. 22, 23, 36, 44

William Allison (c. 1839)
Philadelphia, Pa.
Bibl. 3

William N. Allison
Albany, N.Y. (c. 1831-1834)
New York, N.Y. (c. 1834-1837)
Bibl. 15, 20

William Alloway (c. 1823)
Ithaca, N.Y.
Bibl. 20

J. N. Alrich & S. W. Warriner
(c. 1848)
Louisville, Ky.
Jacob N. Alrich
S. W. Warriner
Bibl. 32

Jacob N. Alrich (c. 1848)
Louisville, Ky.
J. N. Alrich & S. W. Warriner
Bibl. 32

Wessell Alrichs (b. 1670-d.
1734)
Salem, N.J. (c. 1719)
Delaware (after 1725)
Bibl. 30, 46, 54

Thomas Alsop (c. 1842-1850)
Philadelphia, Pa.
Bibl. 3

Jeromimus Alstyne (c. 1787-
1797)
New York, N.Y.
Bibl. 15, 22, 25, 28, 35, 36, 44,
83

Philo G. Alvord (b. 1812-d.
1878)
Utica, N.Y. (c. 1834)
Buffalo, N.Y. (c. 1837-1848)
Bibl. 18, 20

Fester Amant (c. 1794)
Philadelphia, Pa.
Bibl. 3

H. R. Ames & Co. (c. 1850)
Potsdam, N.Y.
Bibl. 20

Amory
Location unknown
Bibl. 28

Cornelius Amos (Armiss) (c.
1840)
Louisville, Ky.
E. C. Beard & Co. (c. 1831-
1852-   )
Bibl. 32

Martin Anatotte (c. 1818)
Philadelphia, Pa.
Bibl. 3

Adolph Ancker (c. 1806-1807)
Philadelphia, Pa.
Bibl. 3

Anderson
(See Buckley & Anderson,
Woolworth & Anderson)

———— Anderson
Greensboro, N.C.
Scott & Anderson (c. 1829)
Woolworth & Anderson (c. 1829
1830)
(might be James S. Anderson)
Bibl. 21

Anderson & Whitteker (c. 1831-
1835)
Charleston, Va.
Henry C. Anderson
———— Whitteker
Bibl. 19

Albert A. Anderson (c. 1837)
Philadelphia, Pa.
Bibl. 3

Alex Anderson (c. 1860-1868)
Danville, Ky.
Bibl. 54

Alexander J. Anderson (c. 1848)
Philadelphia, Pa.
Bibl. 3

Andrew Anderson (b. 1793-)
Danville, Ky. (c. 1814-1844)
Bibl. 32, 68

David Rush Anderson (b.
1795-d. 1855)
Cincinnati, Ohio (c. 1825)
Marietta, Ohio
Bibl. 34

Edward Anderson (c. 1854, d.
1886)
Laurens, S.C.

H. C. Anderson & Co.
(See next entry)
Bibl. 5

Henry C. Anderson
Charleston, Va. (c. 1828-1839)
Lewisburg, Va.
Anderson & Whitteker (c. 1831-
1835)
H. C. Anderson & Co. (c. 1839)
Bibl. 19

Stephen Anderson (c. 1802)
Philadelphia, Pa.
Bibl. 3

Thomas & William Anderson
(c. 1814-1817)
Philadelphia, Pa.
Bibl. 3

William Anderson (c. 1746)
New York, N.Y.
Bibl. 4, 15, 22, 23, 25, 28, 29,
35, 36, 44, 54, 83

W A

William S. Anderson (b. 1820-d.
1871)
Wilmington, N.C.
Brown & Anderson (c. 1850-
1871)
Bibl. 21

Andras & Co. (c. 1800)
New York, N.Y.
Bibl. 25, 44

ANDRAS & CO

Andras & Richard (c. 1797-
1799)
New York, N.Y.
Bibl. 15, 23, 25, 29, 36, 44

A&R

William Andras (c. 1795)
New York, N.Y.
Bibl. 23, 25, 29, 36, 44

ANDRAS

Abraham Andreas (c. 1780)
Bethlehem, Pa.
Bibl. 36, 44

Abraham Andrew(s) (c. 1795-
1796)
Philadelphia, Pa.
Bibl. 3, 23, 36, 44

John Andrew (b. 1747-d. 1791)
Salem, Mass.
Bibl. 2, 22, 23, 28, 29, 36, 44

I. ANDREW

J. Andrew

Elon Andrews (b. 1790-d.
1855)
Utica, N.Y.
Murdock & Andrews (c. 1822-
1826, c. 1838-1849)
James Murdock & Co. (c. 1826-
1838)
Bibl. 15, 18, 20

Henry Andrews (c. 1795-1800)
Philadelphia, Pa.
Bibl. 3, 22, 23, 25, 28, 29, 36, 44

H. A.

Henry Andrews (c. 1830-1847)
Boston, Mass.
Haddock & Andrews (c. 1838-
1847)
Bibl. 3, 6, 22, 23, 28, 44

H A

J. Andrews
Location unknown
Bibl. 28

J ANDREWS

Jeremiah Andrews (c. 1817)
New York, N.Y. (c. 1774)
Philadelphia, Pa. (c. 1776-1780)
Savannah, Ga. (c. 1788)
Norfolk, Va. (c. 1791-1817)
Bibl. 3, 17, 19, 22, 23, 36, 44,
50

J ANDREWS   I ANDREWS

J Andrews

Joseph Andrews (c. 1800)
Norfolk, Va.

Bibl. 23, 25, 29, 36, 44

.J.ANDREWS   J.ANDREWS

Jr. Andrews (c. 1746)
Philadelphia, Pa.
Bibl. 28, 44

N. Andrus & Co. (c. 1834-1837)
New York, N.Y.
Nelson Andrus
Bibl. 15, 25, 44

N ANDRUS & CO

Solomon Ange (c. 1827-1828)
New York, N.Y.
Bibl. 15

James Angram (c. 1835-1836)
Albany, N.Y.
Bibl. 20

William J. Angus (c. 1841)
New York, N.Y.
Bibl. 15

Isaac Aniston (c. 1785)
Philadelphia, Pa.
Bibl. 3

William F. Annelly (c. 1850)
Philadelphia, Pa.
Bibl. 3, 23

Robert M. Anners (c. 1824)
Philadelphia, Pa.
Bibl. 3

Annin & Dreer (c. 1837-1841)
Philadelphia, Pa.
John Annin
Ferdinand J. Dreer
Bibl. 3

Ansbey & McEuen (c. 1825)
Philadelphia, Pa.
George Ansbey
———— McEuen
Bibl. 3

George Ansbey (c. 1837-1850)
Philadelphia, Pa.
Ansbey & McEuen (c. 1825)
Bibl. 3

(Monsieur) Jean B. Anthiaume
(c. 1790)
Gallipolis, Ohio
Bibl. 34

Anthony & Carey (c. 1837)
(Carey & Anthony)
Cincinnati, Ohio
Bibl. 34

Edwin Anthony (c. 1835)
Troy, N.Y.
Bibl. 20

Isaac Anthony (b. 1690-d. 1773)
Swansea, Mass.
Newport, R.I.
Bibl. 15, 25, 28, 54, 56

I A   I ANTHONY

Isaac Anthony (c. 1807)
Augusta, Ga. (c. 1812)
Troy, N.Y.
Bibl. 17, 20, 29, 44

IA

J. Anthony (c. 1815)
Washington, Ga.
Bibl. 17

Joseph Anthony
(See next entry)

Joseph Anthony Jr. (b. 1762-d. 1814)
Philadelphia, Pa.
Bibl. 2, 3, 4, 15, 22, 23, 25, 28, 29, 36, 39, 44, 54, 81

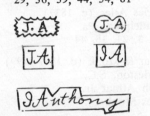

Joseph Anthony & Son (c. 1810-1814)
Philadelphia, Pa.
Bibl. 3, 4, 22, 23, 25, 28, 29, 36, 44

L. D. Anthony (c. 1805)
Providence, R.I.
Bibl. 22, 23, 36, 44

M. H. & T. Anthony (c. 1814)
Philadelphia, Pa.
Michael H. Anthony (?)
Thomas Anthony (?)
Bibl. 36

Michael H. Anthony (c. 1810-1814)
Philadelphia, Pa.
M. H. & T. Anthony (c. 1814) (?)
Michael H. & Thomas Anthony (c. 1816-1817)
Bibl. 3, 23, 36, 44

Michael H. & Thomas Anthony (c. 1816-1817)
Philadelphia, Pa.
Michael H. Anthony
Thomas Anthony
Bibl. 3, 23, 44

Thomas Anthony (c. 1810)
Philadelphia, Pa.
M. H. & T. Anthony (c. 1814) (?)
Michael H. & Thomas Anthony (c. 1816-1817)
Bibl. 23, 36, 44

William Anthony (c. 1800)
New York, N.Y.
Bibl. 22, 23, 36, 44

William Anthony (c. 1809-1810)
Ballston Spa, N.Y.
Bibl. 20

Charles Antrim (c. 1837-1847)
Philadelphia, Pa.
Bibl. 3

Kenrick Anwyl (b. 1748)
Baltimore, Md. (c. 1775)
Bibl. 23, 28, 36, 38, 44

Samuel App (c. 1837-1850)
Philadelphia, Pa.
Bibl. 3

George B. Appleton (c. 1850)
Salem, Mass.
Bibl. 15, 25, 44

APPLETON

William Applewhite
Columbia, S.C. (c. 1824-1828)
Camden, S.C. (c. 1828-1837)
Bibl. 5

John Arbuckle (c. 1843)
Philadelphia, Pa.
Bibl. 3

Joseph Arbuckle (c. 1847-1848)
Philadelphia, Pa.
Bibl. 3

John Archer (c. 1798)
Halifax, N.C.
Bibl. 21

Dumm Archibald (c. 1837)
Philadelphia, Pa.
Bibl. 3

John Archibald (c. 1843)
Philadelphia, Pa.
Bibl. 3

John Archie (c. 1759)
New York, N.Y.
Bibl. 22, 23, 28, 36, 44

D. P. Armer (c. 1850)
Richmond, Ky.
Bibl. 32, 54

George Armitage (c. 1800-1825)
Philadelphia, Pa.
Bibl. 3

Robert Armitage (c. 1797)
Charleston, S.C.
Bibl. 5

Nelson T. Arms (c. 1837-1850)
Albany, N.Y.
Bibl. 20, 44

T. N. Arms
(See preceding entry)
Bibl. 22, 23, 28

Allen Armstrong (c. 1806-1817)
Philadelphia, Pa.
Bibl. 3, 15, 23, 25, 28, 29, 36, 44, 54

A Armstrong

A ARMSTRONG

John Armstrong (c. 1810-1813)
Philadelphia, Pa.
Bibl. 3, 4, 22, 23, 28, 36

Thomas S. Armstrong (c. 1839-1840)
New York, N.Y.
Bibl. 15

William Armstrong (c. 1750) (d. 1775)
Philadelphia, Pa.
Bibl. 23, 36, 44

D. Arn
Delaware (?)
Bibl. 30

D. ARN

John Arnault (c. 1850)
New York, N.Y.
Bibl. 23

Cornelius Arniss
(See Cornelius Amos)

——— Arnold
(See Howell & Arnold)

G. Arnold (c. 1820)
Location unknown
Bibl. 24, 89

G: ARNOLD

H. B. Arnold (c. 1840-1844)
Rome, N.Y.
Bibl. 15, 20, 44

H. B. Arnold

Jacob Arnold (c. 1848)
Philadelphia, Pa.
Bibl. 3

Thomas Arnold (c. 1751-1828)
Newport, R.I.
Bibl. 22, 23, 29, 44, 54, 56

Sd   TA   T. ARNOLD
           ARNOLD

Thomas Arnold (c. 1760)
Philadelphia, Pa.
Bibl. 15, 25, 28, 36, 78

T ARNOLD
T A   ARNOLD

John Arrison (c. 1837)
Philadelphia, Pa.
Bibl. 3

William Arwin (c. 1837-1838)
Albany, N.Y.
Bibl. 20

Lawrence Ash (c. 1762-1763)
Baltimore, Md. (c. 1773)
Philadelphia, Pa.
Bibl. 3, 38

Ashburn & Shannon (c. 1841)
Philadelphia, Pa.
James C. Ashburn (?)
Robert Shannon
Bibl. 3

James C. Ashburn (c. 1841-
1850)
Philadelphia, Pa.

Ashburn & Shannon (c. 1841)
(?)
Clements & Ashburn (c. 1847)
Bibl. 3

John Ashburner (c. 1840-1841)
Philadelphia, Pa.
Bibl. 3

James Ashman (c. 1831-1841)
Philadelphia, Pa.
Bibl. 3

James J. Ashman (c. 1839-
1841)
Philadelphia, Pa.
Bibl. 3 .

William Ashmead (c. 1797)
Philadelphia, Pa.
Bibl. 3, 22, 23, 28, 36, 44

Isaac Ashton (c. 1790-1797)
Philadelphia, Pa.
Bibl. 3

William Ashton (c. 1845-1873,
d. 1873)
Charleston, S.C.
Bibl. 5

James Askew (1785)
Philadelphia, Pa.
Bibl. 44

James Askew (d. 1800)
Charleston, S.C. (c. 1776-1800)
Bibl. 5

Aspinwall & Griffing (c. 1831)
Oswego, N.Y.
C. B. Aspinwall
Edward Griffing
Bibl. 20

C. B. Aspinwall (c. 1831)
Oswego, N.Y.
Aspinwall & Griffing
Bibl. 20

Matthew Atherton (c. 1837-
1840)
Philadelphia, Pa.
Bibl. 3

Nathan Atherton Jr. (c. 1825-
1850)
Philadelphia, Pa.
Bibl. 3, 22, 23, 28, 36, 44

John H. Atkin (c. 1831-1838)
New York, N.Y.
Hinsdale & Atkin (c. 1830-
1838)
Bibl. 15

Alvin S. Atkins (c. 1850)
Rochester, N.Y.
Bibl. 20

Anne Maria Atkinson (c.
1790-1816)
Baltimore, Md.
Bibl. 38

Harrison Atkinson (c. 1823-
1824)
Philadelphia, Pa.
Bibl. 3

Isaac Atkinson (c. 1825-1833)
Philadelphia, Pa.
Bibl. 3, 23, 36, 44

Leroy Atkinson (w. 1824-1830)
Baltimore, Md.
Bibl. 38

Matthew & William Atkinson
(w. 1787)
Baltimore, Md.
Bibl. 38

William O. Atkinson (c. 1848)
Louisville, Ky.
Bibl. 32

Charles Atlee (c. 1837)
Philadelphia, Pa.
Bibl. 3, 23, 36, 44

Atmar & Monk (c. 1797-1799)
Charleston, S.C.
Ralph Atmar Jr.
James Monk
Bibl. 5

Ralph Atmar Jr. (c. 1793-1803)
Charleston, S.C.
Atmar & Monk (c. 1797-1799)
Bibl. 5

Edward W. Atmore (c. 1846-
1850)
Philadelphia, Pa.
Bibl. 3

J. A. Atterbury (c. 1799)
New Haven, Conn.
Bibl. 22, 23, 28, 36, 44

Marshall Attmore (c. 1821-
1837)
Philadelphia, Pa.
Bibl. 3

George E. Atwell (c. 1830-
1838)
Charleston, S.C.
Bibl. 5

David Austen (c. 1837-1839)
Philadelphia, Pa.
Bibl. 3, 23, 36, 44

——— Austin (before 1750)
Boston, Mass.
Bibl. 70

Austin & Boyer (c. 1750-1770)
Boston, Mass.
Josiah Austin
Daniel Boyer
Bibl. 25, 36, 44

Benjamin Austin (c. 1775)
Portsmouth, N.H.
Bibl. 22, 23, 28, 36, 44

Ebenezer Austin (b. 1733-d. 1818)
Hartford, Conn. (c. 1764)
New York, N.Y. (c. 1788)
Boston, Mass. (c. 1790)
Charlestown, Mass.
Bibl. 2, 16, 22, 23, 25, 28, 29, 36, 44, 61

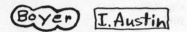

Isaac Austin (d. 1801)
Philadelphia, Pa. (c. 1781-1801)
Bibl. 3

James Austin (b. 1750)
Charlestown, Mass.
Bibl. 28, 44

John Austin (b. 1757-d. 1825)
Philadelphia, Pa. (c. 1802-1809)
Charleston, S.C. (c. 1809-1820)
Bibl. 3, 5, 23, 25, 36, 44

I. AUSTIN

John Austin (c. 1770)
Hartford, Conn.
Bibl. 28

Joseph Austin (c. 1740)
Hartford, Conn.
Bibl. 44

Josiah John Austin (b. 1719-d. 1780)
Boston, Mass. (c. 1760-1770)
Charlestown, Mass.
Austin & Boyer (c. 1750-1770)

Minott & Austin (c. 1760-1769)
Boyer & Austin (c. 1770)
Bibl. 2, 15, 22, 23, 25, 29, 36, 44, 50, 54, 69

I A   IA
J. AUSTIN

Nathaniel Austin (b. 1734-d. 1818)
Boston, Mass.
Charlestown, Mass.
Bibl. 15, 22, 23, 25, 28, 29, 36, 44

N A
AUSTIN

Seymour Austin
Hartford, Conn.
Geauga County, Ohio
Bibl. 34

Avery, Willis & Billis (c. 1820)
Salisbury, N.Y.
Bibl. 20, 23, 36

John Avery (b. 1732-d. 1794)
Preston, Conn. (c. 1762)
Bibl. 15, 16, 22, 23, 25, 28, 29, 36, 44, 61

I A
I. AVERY

JA

John Avery Jr. (b. 1755-d. 1815)
Preston, Conn. (c. 1776)
Bibl. 16, 22, 23, 28, 36, 44

Robert Staunton Avery (b. 1771-d. 1846)
Preston, Conn. (c. 1794)
Bibl. 16, 22, 23, 28, 36, 44

Samuel Avery (b. 1760-d. 1836)
Preston, Conn. (c. 1781)
Bibl. 15, 16, 22, 23, 25, 28, 36, 44, 61

S A
S AVERY

William Avery (b. 1765-d. 1798)
Preston, Conn. (c. 1786)
Bibl. 16, 22, 23, 28, 36, 44

W. & B. Avery (c. 1820)
Salisbury, N.Y.
Bibl. 20, 23, 36

Avice & Pottier (c. 1818)
Savannah, Ga.
Francis J. Avice
Francis Pottier
Bibl. 17

Avice & Raulin (c. 1818-1819)
Savannah, Ga.
Francis J. Avice
Anthony R. Raulin
Bibl. 17

Francis J. Avice (c. 1818-1820)
Savannah, Ga.
Avice & Pottier (c. 1818)
Avice & Raulin (c. 1818-1819)
Bibl. 17

Charles Avisse (w. 1812)
Baltimore, Md.
Bibl. 38

Ayers (c. 1839)
Penn Yan, N.Y.
Ayers & Dunning
Bibl. 20

Ayers & Badger (c. 1835)
Elmira, N.Y.
Socrates Ayers (?)
A. M. Badger
Bibl. 20

Ayers & Dunning (c. 1839)
Penn Yan, N.Y.
Bibl. 20

Ayers & Hall (c. 1800)
Newburgh, N.Y.
Ebenezer B. Ayers
George W. Hall (?)
Bibl. 20

B. Ayers (c. 1790)
Location unknown
Bibl. 24, 44

B. Ayers

Ebenezer B. Ayers (c. 1799-1800)
Newburgh, N.Y.
Ayers & Hall (c. 1800)
Bibl. 20

John Ayers (c. 1817-1819)
Philadelphia, Pa.
Bibl. 3

S. Ayers (c. 1805)
Lexington, Ky.
(May be Samuel Ayers)
Bibl. 23, 89

Socrates Ayers (c. 1845-after 1850)
Elmira, N.Y.
Ayers & Badger (c. 1835) (?)
Bibl. 20

Ayres & Beard (c. 1828-1831)
(Beard & Ayres)
Louisville, Ky.
Elias Ayres
Evans C. Beard
Thomas Jefferson Shepard
Bibl. 32, 54, 68

Ayres & Hiter (c. 1813)
Lexington, Ky.
Samuel Ayres
John G. Hiter
Bibl. 32

Ayres & Warden (c. 1817)
Philadelphia, Pa.
—— Ayres
—— Warden
Bibl. 3

E. Ayres & Company (c. 1816-1828)
Louisville, Ky.
Ebenezer Bryam Ayres
Bibl. 32, 54, 68

Ebenezer Bryam Ayres (c. 1816-1828)
Louisville, Ky.
E. Ayres & Company
Bibl. 32

Elias Ayres (b. 1791-d. 1842)
Louisville, Ky.
Ayres & Beard (c. 1828-1831)
Bibl. 32

Samuel Ayres (b. 1767-d. 1824)
Lexington, Ky. (c. 1790-1823)
Danville, Ky. (c. 1823-1824)
Ayres & Hiter (c. 1813)
Bibl. 25, 29, 32, 36, 44, 54, 84

S AYRES . LEX. K

Thomas R. J. Ayres (c. 1823-1861)
Danville, Ky.
Bibl. 29, 32, 44, 54, 68, 88

T AYRES

B. & C. (c. 1815)
Location unknown
Bibl. 24

B & C

B. & P. (c. 1800)
New York State
Bibl. 24, 72

B & P

P. B. & C. (c. 1815)
(See Pelletreau, Bennett, & Cook)
Bibl. 24

P B & C

R. J. B. & Co. (c. 1830)
Location unknown
Bibl. 89

R. J. B. & Co.

W. B. & T. (c. 1800)
Location unknown
Bibl. 24, 72

W. B. & T.

C. Babbitt (c. 1815)
Taunton, Mass.
Providence, R.I. (?)
Davis & Babbitt (c. 1815) (?)
Bibl. 15, 25, 44

C BABBITT

Babcock & Co. (c. 1831-1833)
Philadelphia, Pa.
Bibl. 3

Charles Babcock (c. 1832-1833)
Albany, N.Y.
Bibl. 20

Samuel Babcock (b. 1788-d. 1857)
Middletown, Conn. (c. 1812)
Saybrook, Conn.
Bibl. 16, 22, 23, 28, 29, 36, 44

Babcock

Thomas Bacall (c. 1836-1850)
Boston, Mass.
Pear & Bacall (c. 1850)
Bibl. 23, 36, 44

Valentine Bach (w. 1798)
Frederick, Md.
Bibl. 29, 38

Charles Bachelard (c. 1774)
Savannah, Ga.
Bibl. 17

Bachelder
Bachlader
Bachlander
(See Batchelder)

A. Bachman (c. 1848)
New York State
Bibl. 25, 44

John Peter Francis Backes (c. 1852-1858)
Charleston, S.C.
Bibl. 5

Delucine Backus (Bachus) (c. 1792)
New York, N.Y.
Cady & Backus (c. 1792-1796)
Bibl. 22, 23, 25, 28, 29, 36, 44

D. Backus

D. Backus

Simon Backus (d. 1805)
Burlington, Vt. (c. 1793)
Bibl. 54

Bacon & Smith (c. 1830)
Location unknown
Bibl. 28

BACON & SMITH

Samuel Bacon (w. 1752)
Annapolis, Md.
Bibl. 38

Badger & Lillie (c. 1837)
Elmira, N.Y.
A. M. Badger (?)
J. H. Lillie
Bibl. 20

A. M. Badger (c. 1836)
Elmira, N.Y.
Ayers & Badger (c. 1835)
Badger & Lillie (c. 1837) (?)
Bibl. 20

John Baen (c. 1849-1850)
Philadelphia, Pa.
Bibl. 3

William Baggs (c. 1850)
Philadelphia, Pa.
Bibl. 3, 23

Abbot G. Bagley (c. 1840)
Buffalo, N.Y.
Bibl. 20

Benjamin Bagnall (c. 1749-1753)
Philadelphia, Pa.
Bibl. 3

Benjamin Bagnall (c. 1770)
Boston, Mass.
Bibl. 3

Lewis Baielle (c. 1799)
Baltimore, Md.
Bibl. 22, 28, 36

Bailey & Brothers (c. 1846-1852)
Utica, N.Y.
James Bailey
Thomas Bailey
William Bailey
John J. Brown
Bibl. 18, 20

| BAILEY & BROTHERS |

Bailey & Co. (c. 1848-1850)
Philadelphia, Pa.
J. T. Bailey
Bibl. 3, 15, 25, 44, 79

| BAILEY & CO. |

Bailey & Kitchen (c. 1833-1846)
Philadelphia, Pa.
J. T. Bailey
Andrew B. Kitchen
Became Bailey & Co.
Bailey, Banks, & Biddle Co.
(before 1905)
Bibl. 3, 15, 28, 29, 39, 44, 72

| B & K |
| BAILEY & KITCHEN |

Bailey & Owen (c. 1848-1850)
Abbeville, S.C.
Edward S. Bailey
M. T. Owen
Bibl. 5

Bailey & Parker (c. 1845)
Owen, Vt.
Bibl. 23

Bailey & Parmenter (c. 1849)
Rutland, Vt.
Bibl. 23

B. M. Bailey (b. 1824-d. 1913)
New York, N.Y.
Ludlow, Vt. (c. 1848)

Rutland, Vt.
Bibl. 23, 25, 44

Benjamin Bailey (c. 1800-1820)
Boston, Mass.
Bibl. 22, 23, 28, 36, 44

E. E. Bailey (c. 1825)
Portland, Me.
E. E. & S. C. Bailey (c. 1825-1830)
Bibl. 15, 23, 25

| E. E BAILEY |

E. E. BAILEY & CO.

E. E. & S. C. Bailey (c. 1825-1830)
Portland, Me.
Claremont, N.H.
Bibl. 25, 28, 29, 36, 44

| EE & SC
BAILEY |

E. L. Bailey (c. 1835)
Claremont, Vt. (?)
Bibl. 25, 44

| E. L. BAILEY & CO. |

E. S. Bailey & Co. (c. 1854)
Newberry, S.C.
Bibl. 5

Edward Bailey (b. 1753)
Baltimore, Md. (c. 1774)
Bibl. 23, 28, 36, 38, 44

Edward S. Bailey
Abbeville, S.C. (c. 1847)
Newberry, S.C. (c. 1852-1860)
Bailey & Owen (c. 1848-1850)
E. S. Bailey & Co. (c. 1854)
Bibl. 5

Gamaliel Bailey
Mt. Holly, N.J. (c. 1807-1821)
Philadelphia, Pa. (c. 1828-1833)
Bibl. 3, 46, 54

Henry Bailey (c. 1780-1808)
Boston, Mass.

Bibl. 22, 25, 28, 36, 44, 72

| H B |

Hugh Bailey (b. 1830)
Utica, N.Y.
Bailey & Brothers (c. 1846-1852)
Bibl. 18, 20

I. Bailey
(See John Bailey)

J. T. Bailey (c. 1847)
Philadelphia, Pa.
Bailey & Kitchen (c. 1833-1846)
Bailey & Co. (c. 1848-1850)
Bibl. 3

James Bailey (b. 1825)
Utica, N.Y.
Bailey & Brothers (c. 1846-1852)
Bibl. 18, 20

John Bailey (Bayly) (Bayley)
Philadelphia, Pa. (c. 1754-1783)
New York, N.Y. (c. 1762)
Bibl. 3, 15, 22, 23, 28, 29, 36, 39, 44, 54

| J Bailey |

Loring Bailey (b. 1740-d. 1814)
Hingham, Mass. (b. 1780)
Hull, Mass.
Bibl. 22, 23, 28, 29, 36, 44, 54

| L B |

Robert (Rosewell) H. Bailey
(c. 1830)
Woodstock, Vt.
Bibl. 15, 23, 25, 28, 29, 36

| R. H. BAILEY |

S. P. Bailey (c. 1822-1863)
Woodstock, Vt. (c. 1845)
Bibl. 23

Simon (Simeon) A. Bailey
(c. 1789)
New York, N.Y.
Bibl. 22, 23, 28, 36, 44

T. A. Bailey (c. 1843-1845)
Philadelphia, Pa.
Bibl. 3

Thomas Bailey (b. 1826)
Utica, N.Y.

Bailey & Brothers (c. 1846-
   1852)
Bibl. 18, 20

T. BAILEY

Westcott E. J. Bailey (c. 1842)
Philadelphia, Pa.
Bibl. 3

William Bailey
(See William Baily)
(See William Baily Jr.)

William Bailey (b. 1818)
Utica, N.Y.
Bailey & Brothers (c. 1846-
   1852)
Bibl. 18, 20, 25, 44

W. BAILEY

John Baily (c. 1760)
Philadelphia, Pa.
Bibl. 25, 28

William Baily (Bailey) (c.
   1820-1850)
Philadelphia, Pa.
New York, N.Y. (c. 1810) (?)
Bibl. 3, 15, 29, 36, 44

W BAILY

W. BAILY

William Baily Jr. (Bailey)
   (c. 1816-1822)
Philadelphia, Pa.
Bibl. 3, 15, 44, 72

W. BAILY Jr.

Henry Bain (c. 1849)
Philadelphia, Pa.
Bibl. 3

——— Baird (c. 1805)
Raleigh, N.C.
Might be David Baird.
Bibl. 21

David Baird (c. 1804)
Raleigh, N.C.
Glass & Baird
Bibl. 21

Pleasant H. Baird
Paris, Ky. (c. 1813-1817)

Maysville, Ky. (c. 1817-1838)
Bibl. 32, 54, 68

Pleasant H. Baird (c. 1802)
Petersburg, Va.
Bibl. 19

Baker
(See Baldwin & Baker)
(See Knorr & Baker)

——— Baker (c. 1765)
Boston, Mass.
Bibl. 28, 44

Baker & Shriver (c. 1837-1841)
Philadelphia, Pa.
Edwin G. A. Baker
Thomas H. Shriver
Bibl. 3

Anson Baker (c. 1820-1837)
New York, N.Y.
Bibl. 15, 22, 23, 36, 44

Benjamin H. Baker (c. 1823-
   1825)
Philadelphia, Pa.
Bibl. 3

E. Baker
(See Eleazer Baker)

E. Baker (1740-1790)
New York, N.Y.
Bibl. 29

E. BAKER

Edwin G. A. Baker (c. 1837-
   1850)
Philadelphia, Pa.
Baker & Shriver (c. 1837-1841)
Bibl. 3

Eleazer Baker (b. 1764-d. 1849)
Ashford, Conn.
Bibl. 15, 23, 25, 36, 44, 54, 61

E BAKER

Elias Baker (b. 1815-d. 1874)
New Brunswick, N.J. (c. 1840)
Bibl. 46

George Baker
Providence, R.I. (c. 1825)
Salem, Mass.
Bibl. 15, 22, 23, 25, 28, 29, 36,
   44, 56

G. BAKER

George A. Baker (c. 1841-1843)
Philadelphia, Pa.
Bibl. 3

George M. Baker (c. 1840)
Philadelphia, Pa.
Bibl. 3

J. G. A. Baker (c. 1835)
Philadelphia, Pa.
Bibl. 3

J. M. S. Baker (c. 1828-1831)
Philadelphia, Pa.
Bibl. 3

James M. Baker (c. 1842)
Philadelphia, Pa.
Bibl. 3

L. Baker (c. 1821)
Batavia, N.Y.
Bibl. 20

L. Baker & Co. (c. 1826)
Auburn, N.Y.
Bibl. 20

Nehemiah Baker (c. 1816)
Philadelphia, Pa.
Bibl. 3

Nehemiah Baker (c. 1818)
Plattsburg, N.Y.
Bibl. 20

S. Baker (c. 1830-1840)
Location unknown
Bibl. 15

S BAKER

Samuel Baker (b. 1787-d. 1858)
New Brunswick, N.J. (c. 1822)
Bibl. 46, 54

Stephen Baker (c. 1817-1818)
Wilmington, N.C.
Bibl. 22

Stephen Baker (c. 1830)
New York, N.Y.
Bibl. 25, 44

S. BAKER

Balch & Fryer (c. 1784)
Albany, N.Y.
——— Balch
John W. Fryer
Bibl. 4, 20, 22, 23, 28, 36, 44

Ebenezer Balch (b. 1723-d.
   1808)
Hartford, Conn. (c. 1744)
Wethersfield, Conn.
Boston, Mass.
Bibl. 16, 22, 23, 25, 28, 29, 36,
   44, 61

E. BALCH

Baldwin
(See Cotton & Baldwin)
(See Downing & Baldwin)
(See Shinn & Baldwin)
(See Stiles & Baldwin)

Baldwin & Baker (c. 1817)
Providence, R.I.
Bibl. 22, 23, 28, 36, 44

Baldwin & Co. (c. 1830)
Newark, N.J.
New York, N.Y.
Bibl. 23, 25, 36, 44

Baldwin & Jones (c. 1813)
Boston, Mass.
Jabez L. Baldwin
John B. Jones
Bibl. 4, 15, 22, 23, 25, 28, 29,
    36, 44

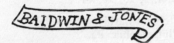

Baldwin & Storrs (c. 1792-
    1794)
Northampton, Mass.
Jedediah Baldwin
Nathan Storrs
Bibl. 41, 44, 84

Ebenezer Baldwin (c. 1810)
Hartford, Conn.
Bibl. 15, 23, 25, 36, 44

BALDWIN

Edgar Baldwin (c. 1848-
    1850-   )
Troy, N.Y.
Bibl. 20

H. E. Baldwin & Co. (c. 1825)
New Orleans, La.
Bibl. 15, 24, 44

Isaac Baldwin (c. 1825)
Newark, N.J.
Taylor & Baldwin (c. 1825)
Bibl. 54

J. & S. Baldwin
(possibly Jedediah & Storrs
    Baldwin)
Bibl. 15

J. & S. BALDWIN

Jabez L. Baldwin (b. 1777-d.
    1819)
Boston, Mass. (c. 1813)
Salem, Mass.
Baldwin & Jones (c. 1813)
Bibl. 22, 23, 25, 28, 29, 36, 44,
    54

J. BALDWIN

BALDWIN

Jedediah Baldwin (b. 1768-d.
    1849)
Northampton, Mass. (1791)
Norwich, Conn. (1791)
Hanner, N.H. (1793)
Fairfield, N.Y. (1811)
Monisville, N.Y. (1817-1820)
Rochester, N.Y. (1834-1844)
Stiles & Baldwin (c. 1791-1792)
Baldwin & Storrs (c. 1792-
    1794)
Bibl. 15, 20, 22, 23, 25, 28, 29,
    36, 41, 44, 84

J. BALDWIN

Jedediah & Storrs Baldwin
    (c. 1800)
Rochester, N.Y.
Bibl. 25

Jobey Baldwin (c. 1805)
Salem, Va.
Bibl. 19

Joseph Baldwin (c. 1823-1824)
Philadelphia, Pa.
Bibl. 3

Matthias Baldwin (c. 1819-
    1822)
Philadelphia, Pa.
Bibl. 3

S. Baldwin (c. 1810)
Boston, Mass.
Bibl. 22

S BALDWIN

Stanley S. Baldwin (c. 1820-
    1837)
New York, N.Y.
Bibl. 15, 23, 25, 29, 36, 44

STANLEY S BALDWIN

Ball
(See Jones, Low(s) & Ball)

Ball, Black & Co. (c. 1851-
    1876)
New York, N.Y.
Henry Ball
William Black
Bibl. 15, 23, 25, 44, 54, 78

BALL, BLACK & CO.

Ball & Heald (c. 1811-1812)
Baltimore, Md.
William Ball
J. S. Heald
Bibl. 15, 25, 29, 38

BALL & HEALD

Ball, Tompkins & Black
    (c. 1839-1851)
New York, N.Y.
Henry Ball
Erastus O. Tompkins
William Black
Bibl. 15, 22, 23, 36, 44, 78

Albert Ball (c. 1832-1835)
Poughkeepsie, N.Y.
Bibl. 20

Calvin S. Ball (b. 1798)
Pompey, N.Y. (c. 1825)
Bibl. 20

Calvin S. Ball Jr. (c. 1850)
Syracuse, N.Y.
Stone & Ball
Bibl. 20

Charles Ball (c. 1840-1842)
Poughkeepsie, N.Y.
Bibl. 20

David Ball (c. 1845-1846)
Rochester, N.Y.
Bibl. 20, 41, 44

Gideon I. Ball (c. 1832)
Buffalo, N.Y.
Bibl. 20

Henry Ball (c. 1833-1837)
New York, N.Y.
Marquand & Co. (c. 1834-1839)
Ball, Tompkins & Black
    (c. 1839-1851)

Ball, Black & Co. (c. 1851-
1876)
Bibl. 15, 23, 36, 44

John Ball
Philadelphia, Pa. (c. 1760)
Concord, Mass. (c. 1763-1767)
Boston, Mass. (c. 1770)
Bibl. 15, 22, 23, 25, 28, 29, 36,
44, 50

S. Ball (c. 1826)
Black Rock, N.Y.
Bibl. 20

S. S. Ball (w. 1838)
Boston, Mass.
John B. Jones & Co. (c. 1838)
Jones, Ball & Poor (c. 1840-
1846)
Bibl. 28, 44

Sheldon Ball (w. 1821-1836)
Buffalo, N.Y.
Bibl. 20, 25, 44

True M. Ball (b. 1815-d. 1890)
Boston, Mass.
Bibl. 28, 44

William Ball (b. 1729-d. 1810)
Philadelphia, Pa.
Bibl. 3, 4, 15, 22, 23, 25, 28, 29,
36, 39, 44

William Ball Jr. (b. 1763-d.
1815)
Baltimore, Md.
Johnson & Ball (c. 1785-1790)
Bibl. 4, 15, 22, 25, 28, 29, 38, 44

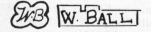

William H. Ball
Utica, N.Y.
Bingham, Ball & Co. (-1833)
Bibl. 18, 20

James Ballantine (c. 1772-1785)
Norfolk, Va.
Skinker & Ballantine (c.
1772-   )
Bibl. 19

Adrian Bancher
(See next entry)

Adrian Bancker (b. 1703-d.
1772)
New York, N.Y.
Bibl. 2, 4, 22, 23, 25, 28, 29, 35,
44, 54

Bangs
(See Dunbar & Bangs)

John J. Bangs (c. 1825-1829)
Cincinnati, Ohio
Bibl. 23, 24, 25, 34, 36, 44, 54

Benjamin B. Banker (c. 1834-
1836)
Albany, N.Y.
Bibl. 20

Joseph Banks (c. 1819)
Philadelphia, Pa.
Bibl. 3

John Banstein (c. 1791)
Philadelphia, Pa.
Bibl. 3

Edward Baptista (c. 1840)
New York, N.Y.
Bibl. 15

Jean Baptiste (c. 1807)
Charleston, S.C.
Bibl. 5

C. G. Barbeck (c. 1835)
Philadelphia, Pa.
Bibl. 3

J. C. Barber (c. 1844-1846)
Philadelphia, Pa.
Bibl. 3

James Barber (c. 1842-1850)
Philadelphia, Pa.
Bibl. 3

Lemuel D. Barber (c. 1850)
Syracuse, N.Y.
Bibl. 20, 23

William Barber (c. 1843)
Hartford, Conn.
Bibl. 23

Stephen Barbere (c. 1841)
Philadelphia, Pa.
Bibl. 3

Theon Barberet (c. 1822)
New Orleans, La.
Bibl. 23, 36, 44

G. Barbier (c. 1837-1842)
Philadelphia, Pa.
Bibl. 3

Peter Barbier (c. 1823-1824)
Philadelphia, Pa.
Bibl. 3, 23, 36, 44

Stephen Barbier (c. 1847)
Philadelphia, Pa.
Bibl. 3

Stephen P. Barbier (c. 1810-
1843)
Philadelphia, Pa.
Bibl. 3

Charles M. Barchett (c. 1824)
Clarksburg, Va.
Bibl. 19

James Barclay (c. 1848)
Philadelphia, Pa.
Bibl. 3

Orin Barclay (c. 1849)
Philadelphia, Pa.
Bibl. 3

Bard & Hoffman (Bird &
Hoffman) (c. 1837)
Philadelphia, Pa.
Conrad Bard (Bird)
Frederick Hoffman
Bibl. 3, 4, 22, 23, 36, 44

Bard & Lamont (c. 1841-1845)
Philadelphia, Pa.
Conrad Bard
Robert Lamont
Bibl 3, 4, 22, 23, 25, 28, 29,
44, 54

BARD & LAMONT

C. Bard & Son (c. 1850)
Philadelphia, Pa.
Bibl. 3, 4, 22, 23, 28, 44

Conrad Bard (Bird) (c. 1825-1850)
Philadelphia, Pa.
Bard & Hoffman (c. 1837)
Bard & Lamont (c. 1841-1845)
Bibl. 3, 15, 20, 23, 25, 29, 36, 44, 54

J. Bard (c. 1800)
Philadelphia, Pa.
Bibl. 22, 23, 36, 44

Connard Bardeer (c. 1830-1833)
Philadelphia, Pa.
Bibl. 3, 23, 36, 44

George Bardick (c. 1790-1802)
Philadelphia, Pa.
Bibl. 23, 25, 29, 36, 44

G B

John Bardick (c. 1805-1808)
Philadelphia, Pa.
Bibl. 3, 23, 36, 44

Stephen Bardon (c. 1785)
Philadelphia, Pa.
Bibl. 3, 23, 36, 44

Thomas Barge (w. 1848)
Philadelphia, Pa.
Bibl. 3

George Barger (w. 1844)
Philadelphia, Pa.
Bibl. 3

Willam Baria (c. 1805)
New York, N.Y.
Bibl. 23, 36, 44

Barker & Mumford (c. 1825)
Newport, R.I.
Bibl. 25, 28, 44

BARKER &
MUMFORD

James F. Barker (c. 1826)
Palmyra, N.Y.
Bibl. 20

J. Barklay (w. 1812-1824)
Baltimore, Md.
J. & S. Barklay (w. 1812-1816)
Bibl. 38

J. & S. Barklay (w. 1812-1816)
Baltimore, Md.
Bibl. 38

Edward C. Barlow (c. 1850)
Georgetown, Ky.
Bibl. 32, 54, 68

James Madison Barlow (c. 1812)
Lexington, Ky.
Bibl. 32, 54, 68

S. S. Barnaby (c. 1852-1853)
Utica, N.Y.
Bibl. 18

Barnard
(See Morrow & Barnard)

E. Barnard (c. 1834)
Geneva, N.Y.
Bibl. 20

Samuel Barnard (c. 1844-1845)
Utica, N.Y.
Bibl. 18, 20

Abraham Barnes (c. 1716)
Boston, Mass.
Bibl. 22, 23, 28, 36, 44

James Barnes (c. 1841-1844)
Philadelphia, Pa.
Bibl. 3

James M. Barnes (c. 1845-1850)
Philadelphia, Pa.
Bibl. 3

James P. Barnes (c. 1848-1869)
Louisville, Ky.
Bibl. 32, 54, 68

Moses D. Barnes (d. 1858)
Macon, Ga.
Bibl. 17

Archibald Barnet (w. 1781)
Baltimore, Md.
Bibl. 38

Joseph Barnett
(See Joseph Barrett)

Barney & Valentine (c. 1850)
Syracuse, N.Y.
———— Barney
Dennis Valentine
Bibl. 20

George Barney (c. 1850)
Syracuse, N.Y.
Bibl. 20

James Barney (c. 1840)
Syracuse, N.Y.
Bibl. 20

Robert Barnhill (c. 1776-1778)
Philadelphia, Pa.
Bibl. 3

Barnhurst & Walker (w. 1814)
Philadelphia, Pa.
Joseph Barnhurst
———— Walker
Bibl. 3

Joseph Barnhurst (c. 1813)
Philadelphia, Pa.
Bibl. 3

Laurent Baron (c. 1841-1850-)
Rochester, N.Y.
Bibl. 20

Louis (Lewis) Baron (b. 1792)
Rochester, N.Y. (c. 1841-1867)
Bibl. 11, 20, 44

John J. Barralet (w. 1794-1798)
Philadelphia, Pa.
Bibl. 3

Joseph J. Barras (w. 1833-1850)
Philadelphia, Pa.
Bibl. 3

Joshua L. Barrass (w. 1837)
Philadelphia, Pa.
Bibl. 3

James Barret (c. 1717)
Norwich, Conn.
Bibl. 23, 36, 44

J·B

James Barret(t) (c. 1805)
New York, N.Y.
Bibl. 22, 25, 28, 29, 36, 44

JB   ?

Robert Barret(t) (b. 1765-d. 1821)
Green County, Ky. (c. 1816-1818)
Greensburg, Ky.
Bibl. 32, 54, 68

Joseph Barrett (Barnett) (c. 1753)
Nantucket Island, Mass.
Bibl. 11, 14

J BARRETT

Samuel Barrett (c. 1760-1780)
Hingham, Mass.
Hull, Mass.
Nantucket, Mass. (?)
Providence, R.I. (?)
Bibl. 2, 12, 22, 23, 25, 28, 36, 44, 72

David Barriere (w. 1799-1817)
Baltimore, Md.
Bibl. 25, 29, 38, 44

George Barringer (c. 1842)
St. Louis, Mo.
Bibl. 54

Barrington & Davenport
　(c. 1806-1807)
Philadelphia, Pa.
————— Barrington
Robert Davenport
Bibl. 3, 23, 25, 29, 36, 44

Joseph Barrington
Dumfries, Va. (c. 1792)
Salisbury, N.C. (c. 1826)
Tarboro, N.C. (c. 1832)
Bibl. 19, 21

T. Barrington (c. 1839)
Tarboro, N.C.
Bibl. 21

Henry Barrow (c. 1833-1841)
New York, N.Y.
Bibl. 15

Samuel Barrow (c. 1771)
Philadelphia, Pa.
Bibl. 3

James Madison Barrows
　(b. 1809)
Tolland, Conn. (w. 1832)
Eddy & Barrows (c. 1832) (?)
Bibl. 15, 16, 22, 23, 25, 28, 29, 36, 44

| J. M. BARROWS |

Barrowss
(See Twedy & Barrowss)

Standish Barry (b. 1783-d.
　1844)
Baltimore, Md. (w. 1784-1810)
Rice & Barry (c. 1785-1787)
Bibl. 15, 22, 23, 25, 28, 29, 36, 38, 39, 44, 54, 72, 78

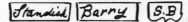

William Barry
Philadelphia, Pa. (c. 1801-1802)
Charleston, S.C. (c. 1809)
Bibl. 3, 5

Charles Barthe (c. 1750)
Detroit, Mich.
Bibl. 58

Charles Bartholomew (w. 1843-
　1846)
Philadelphia, Pa.
Bibl. 3

John Bartholomew (w. 1846-
　1848)
Philadelphia, Pa.
Bibl. 3

Joseph Bartholomew (w. 1818)
Philadelphia, Pa.
Bibl. 3

Joseph Bartholomew (w. 1833-
　1835)
Philadelphia, Pa.
Bibl. 3, 23, 36, 44

Leroux Bartholomew (1688-
　1713)

| B R |

(See Leroux, Bartholomew)
Roswell Bartholomew (b.
　1781-d. 1830)
Hartford, Conn.
Ward & Bartholomew (c. 1804-
　1809)
Ward, Bartholomew & Brainard
　(c. 1809-1830)
Bibl. 16, 22, 23, 25, 28, 36, 44

Israel Bartlet(t) (b. 1748-d.
　1838)
Haverhill, Mass.
Newbury, Mass.
Bibl. 15, 25, 44

Edward Bartlett (c. 1833)
Philadelphia, Pa.
Bibl. 23, 36

Edward M. Bartlett (w. 1843-
　1850)
Philadelphia, Pa.
Bibl. 3, 44

N. Bartlett (c. 1760)
Concord, Mass.
Bibl. 23, 25, 28, 29, 36, 44, 72

| N BARTLETT |

Samuel Bartlett (b. 1750-d.
　1821)
Boston, Mass.
Concord, Mass.
Bibl. 4, 15, 22, 23, 25, 28, 29, 36, 44, 54, 69

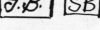

S. Bartley (c. 1841)
Philadelphia, Pa.
Bibl. 3, 23

Samuel Bartley (b. 1788, w.
　1801)
Baltimore, Md.
Bibl. 29, 38

Barton & Butler (c. 1831-1832)
Utica, N.Y.
Joseph Barton
————— Butler
Bibl. 15, 18, 20, 25, 44

Barton & Clark (c. 1826)
Utica, N.Y.
Joseph Barton
————— Clark
Bibl. 15, 18, 20, 25, 44

Barton & Porter (c. 1811-1816)
Utica, N.Y.
Joseph Barton

Joseph S. Porter
Bibl. 18, 20

 B & P

Barton & Smith (c. 1829-1831)
Utica, N.Y.
Joseph Barton
——— Smith
Bibl. 15, 18, 20, 25, 44

Benjamin Barton (d. 1816)
Alexandria, Va. (c. 1801- 1816)
Bibl. 15, 19, 44, 54

B BARTON

Benjamin Barton (2d)
 (c. 1821-1841)
Alexandria, Va.
Bibl. 19

Erastus Barton (d. 1823)
New York, N.Y.
Bibl. 23, 36, 44

Erastus Barton & Co. (1815
 1823)
New York, N.Y.
Erastus Barton
Isaac Marquand
Bibl. 25, 44

E B & CO

Joseph Barton (b. 1764-d. 1832)
Stockbridge, Mass. (c. 1764-
 1804)
Utica, N.Y. (c.1804-1832)
Barton & Porter (c. 1811-1816)
Barton & Clark (c. 1826)
Barton & Smith (c. 1829-1831)
Barton & Butler (c. 1831-1832)
Bibl. 15, 18, 20, 25, 44

Thomas Barton (c. 1816-1821)
Alexandria, Va.
Bibl. 19, 54

William Barton (Bartram)
 (c. 1769)
Philadelphia, Pa.
Bibl. 3, 22, 23, 25, 28, 36, 39, 44

W B

A. W. Bascom
Kentucky
Bibl. 54

Hiram B. Bascom (c. 1838-
 1842)
St. Louis, Mo.
Bibl. 54

Francis Basset(t)
Charlestown, Mass. (c. 1678-
 1715)
New York, N.Y. (c. 1764-1774)
Bibl. 23, 25, 28, 29, 36, 44

BASSETT

George Francis Basset (c. 1797)
Philadelphia, Pa.
Bibl. 3

John Francis Basset (c. 1798)
Philadelphia, Pa.
Bibl. 3

Bassett & Warford (c. 1800-
 1806)
Albany, N. Y.
Bibl. 15, 20, 23, 44

J. & W. H. Bassett
 (c. 1815-)
Cortland, N.Y.
Joshua Bassett
William H. Bassett (?)
Bibl. 20

Joshua Bassett (b. 1756-d. 1836)
Cortland, N.Y.
J. & W. H. Bassett
 (c. 1815-)
Bibl. 20

Nehemiah B. Bassett (w. 1795-
 1800, w. 1813-1819)
Albany, N.Y.
Bibl. 20

William H. Basset (d. 1834)
Cortland, N.Y. (w. 1828)
J. & W. H. Bassett (?)
Bibl. 20

——— Batchelder (Bachelder)
 (Bachlader) (Bachlander)
Boston, Mass. (c. 1850)
New York, N.Y. (?)
Palmer & Batchelder (c. 1850)
Bibl. 23, 24, 25, 28, 29, 36, 44

N. Batchellor (c. 1825)
New York, N.Y.
Bibl. 22, 23, 36, 44

William Bateman (c. 1774)
New York, N.Y.
Bibl. 28

Baton
(See Dubosq & Baton)

Augustine Baton Jr. (w. 1828-
 1837)
Philadelphia, Pa.
Bibl. 3

Augustus Baton (w. 1839-1845)
Philadelphia, Pa.
Bibl. 3

Charles Baton (w. 1833-1835)
Philadelphia, Pa.
Bibl. 3

A. T. Battel & Co. (1846-)
Utica, N.Y.
Albert T. Battel(s)
Bibl. 18, 20

Albert T. Battel(s) (Battle[s])
 (b. 1795)
Utica, N.Y.
Davies & Battel (1844-1850)
A. T. Battel & Co. (1846-)
Bibl. 18, 22, 23, 25, 28, 44

A. T. BATTEL

John Batterson (w. 1723)
Annapolis, Md.
Bibl. 38

Joseph Batting (w. 1850)
Philadelphia, Pa.
Bibl. 3

Battle(s)
(See Battel[s])

Jean Baptiste Baudry
 (w.c. 1750, d. 1755)
Detroit, Mich.
Bibl. 58

Valentine Baugh (c. 1800)
Abingdon, Va.
Bibl. 19

Bauman & Kurtzborn (c. 1850)
St. Louis, Mo.
Louis Bauman
——— Kurtzborn
Bibl. 54

Louis Bauman (b. 1843-d. 1870)
St. Louis, Mo.
Bauman & Kurtzborn (c. 1850)
Bibl. 54

Henry Baumford (w. 1806-
1807)
Philadelphia, Pa.
Bibl. 3

DeWitt Baxter (w. 1850)
Philadelphia, Pa.
Bibl. 3

A. S. Bay (w. 1786)
New York, N.Y.
Bibl. 22, 23, 36, 44

Bayeaux & Co. (1839-1842)
Troy, N.Y.
Bibl. 20

H. Bayeaux & Son (c. 1825-
1833)
Troy, N.Y.
Bibl. 20

Henry Bayeaux (c. 1801-1812)
Troy, N.Y.
Bibl. 20, 24, 25, 44

Henry F. Bayeaux (w. 1833-
1839) (d. 1839)
Troy, N.Y.
Bibl. 20

Bayley & Douglas(s) (c. 1798)
New York, N.Y.
Bibl. 4, 22, 23, 25, 28, 29, 36

D B & A D

Alexander Bayley (c. 1790)
New York, N.Y.
Bibl. 23, 36, 44

John Bayley
(See John Bailey)

S. H. Bayley (c. 1790)
New York, N.Y.
Bibl. 22, 36

Simeon and Alexander Bayley
(c. 1791)
New York, N.Y.
Bibl. 23, 36, 44

Simon A. Bayley (c. 1796)
New York, N.Y. (w. 1789-1796)
May be Simon A. Bailey.

Bibl. 15, 23, 25, 28, 29, 30, 35,
36, 44, 54

BAYLEY

Simeon C. Bayley (w. 1794)
Philadelphia, Pa.
Bibl. 3

J. Bayly
(See John Bailey)

Joseph Baysset (c. 1822)
New Orleans, La.
Bibl. 36, 44

Beach, Ives & Co. (c. 1820)
New York, N.Y.
Bibl. 23, 36, 44

Beach & Sanford (c. 1785-1788)
Hartford, Conn.
Miles Beach
Isaac Sanford
Bibl. 22, 23, 25, 28, 29, 36, 44,
74

B & S

Beach & Ward (c. 1790-1797)
Hartford, Conn.
Miles Beach
James Ward
Bibl. 15, 22, 23, 28, 29, 36, 44

B & W

A. Beach (c. 1823)
Hartford, Conn.
Bibl. 15, 23, 25, 29, 36, 44

A·BEACH

Isaac Beach (c. 1788-1794)
New Milford, Conn.
Noadiah Mygatt
Bibl. 16, 22, 23, 28, 36, 44

John Beach (c. 1813)
Hartford, Conn.
Miles Beach
Bibl. 15

Miles Beach (b. 1743-d. 1828)
Hartford, Conn. (c. 1780-1797,
c. 1813)
Goshen, Conn.
Litchfield, Conn.
Beach & Sanford (Sanford &
Beach) (c. 1785-1788)

Beach & Ward (c. 1790-1797)
Bibl. 5, 15, 22, 23, 25, 28, 29,
36, 44, 54, 61, 89

Caleb Beal (c. 1796)
Boston, Mass.
Hingham, Mass. (c. 1746-1801)
Bibl. 15, 22, 23, 28, 29, 35, 36,
44, 78

BEAL
C B

John J. Beal (c. 1845-1846)
Louisville, Ky.
Bibl. 32

Theodore L. Beal (c. 1845-
1846)
Louisville, Ky.
Bibl. 32

John Beale (b. 1749-d. 1837)
Baltimore, Md. (c. 1771)
Petersburg, Va. (c. 1791)
Lynchburg, Va. (c. 1793)
Alexandria, Va. (c. 1797)
Richmond, Va. (c. 1798-1808)
Bibl. 19, 54

Jacob Beam (c. 1821-1822)
Philadelphia, Pa.
Bibl. 3

Jacob C. Beam (c. 1818-1820)
Philadelphia, Pa.
Bibl. 3, 23, 36, 44

H. L. Bean (c. 1847-1850-   )
Skaneateles, N.Y.
Smith & Bean (c. 1844) (?)
H. L. Bean & Co. (c. 1846)
Bibl. 20

H. L. Bean & Co. (c. 1846)
Skaneateles, N.Y.
Bibl. 20

Henry Bean (c. 1848)
Philadelphia, Pa.
Bibl. 3

Jacob Bean (c. 1819-1822)
Philadelphia, Pa.
Bibl. 3

Bear & Conrad (c. 1846-1851)
Charlottesville, Va.
Harrisonburg, Va.
Luray, Va.

Jehu W. Bear
George Oliver Conrad
Bibl. 19

David S. Bear (c. 1847-1857)
Staunton, Va.
Bibl. 19

Jacob Bear (c. 1839)
Lexington, Va.
Philadelphia, Pa.
Bibl. 19

Jehu W. Bear (c. 1842-
1852-)
Harrisonburg, Va. (c. 1842)
Charlottesville, Va. (c. 1852)
Luray, Va.
Harry & Bear (c. 1842)
Bear & Conrad (c. 1846-1851)
Bibl. 19

Beard & Ayres (Ayres & Beard)
(c. 1828-1831)
Louisville, Ky.
Evans C. Beard
Elias Ayres
Thomas Jefferson Shepard
Bibl. 32, 54, 68

B. E. Beard (c. 1800)
Philadelphia, Pa.
Bibl. 15, 44

| B. E. BEARD |

Duncan Beard (d. 1797)
Appoquinimink Hundred, Del.
Bibl. 25, 30, 44

| D B |

E. Beard (c. 1800)
Philadelphia, Pa.
Bibl. 25

E. C. Beard & Co. (c. 1831-
1852-)
Louisville, Ky.
Evans C. Beard
Cornelius Amos (Arniss)
William Kendrick
George A. Zumar
Bibl. 32, 68

Evans C. Beard (c. 1824-1875)
Louisville, Ky.
Beard & Ayres (c. 1828-1831)
E. C. Beard & Co. (c. 1831-
1852-)
Bibl. 32, 54

Robert Beard (b. 1753, w. 1774)
Maryland
Bibl. 38

Beasley & Houston (c. 1886-
1890-)
Fayetteville, N.C.
Benjamin Franklin Beasley
J. C. Houston
Bibl. 21

Benjamin Franklin Beasley
Fayetteville, N.C.
Beasley & Houston (c. 1886-
1890-)
Bibl. 21

John M. Beasley (b. 1815-d.
1889)
Fayetteville, N.C.
(c. 1838-)
Bibl. 21

J. Beaton
(See James B. Eaton)

Albert L. Beatty (c. 1833)
Philadelphia, Pa.
Bibl. 3

G. Beatty
Location unknown
Bibl. 15, 44

John Anthony Beau
New York, N.Y. (c. 1770)
Philadelphia, Pa. (c. 1772)
Bibl. 3, 28, 44

J. Beauchamp (c. 1840-1850)
Bowling Green, Ky.
Bibl. 32, 54

Samuel Beauchamp (c. 1840-
1844)
Buffalo, N.Y.
Bibl. 20

Augustus Beauvais (c. 1850)
St. Louis, Mo.
R. & A. Beauvais
Bibl. 54

E. A. Beauvais (c. 1840)
St. Louis, Mo.
Bibl. 25, 44

| E·A·BEAVAIS |

R. & A. Beauvais (c. 1850)
St. Louis, Mo.
Rene Beauvais

Augustus Beauvais
Bibl. 54

Rene Beauvais (c. 1838-1898)
St. Louis, Mo.
R. & A. Beauvais (c. 1850)
Bibl. 25, 44, 89

| R BEAUVAIS |

Mathias Beaver (c. 1793)
Augusta, Ga.
Wittich & Beaver
Bibl. 17

———— Becham (c. 1740)
Location unknown
Bibl. 28, 29, 44

| BECHAM |

G. Bechler
(See G. Bichler)

Henry Bechtel (c. 1817)
Philadelphia, Pa.
Bibl. 3

Augustus Bechtler (b. 1813-d.
1846)
Rutherfordton, N.C.
(c. 1830-)
Bibl. 21

C. Bechtler & Son (c. 1857)
Spartanburg, S.C.
Bibl. 21

Christopher Bechtler (Sr.)
(b. 1780-d. 1842)
Philadelphia, Pa. (c. 1830-1831)
Rutherfordton, N.C. (c. 1832-
1842)
Bibl. 3, 21

Christopher Bechtler Jr.
(c. 1830-1857)
Rutherfordton, N.C.
Spartanburg, S.C. (c. 1857)
Sometimes confused with
Christopher Bechtler Sr.
Bibl. 5, 21

Henry Beck (c. 1837-1839)
Philadelphia, Pa.
Bibl. 3

John O. Beck (c. 1847)
Philadelphia, Pa.
Bibl. 3

Thomas Beck
Philadelphia, Pa. (c. 1773-1777)
Trenton, N.J. (c. 1784)
Bibl. 3, 23, 36, 44, 46, 54

Moses Beckel (c. 1848-1853)
Albany, N.Y.
Simpson & Beckel (c. 1848)
Bibl. 20

Albert Becker (c. 1850)
Syracuse, N.Y.
Bibl. 20

D. Becker & Co. (c. 1850)
Syracuse, N.Y.
Daniel Becker (?)
Bibl. 20

Daniel Becker (c. 1850)
Syracuse, N.Y.
D. Becker & Co. (?)
Bibl. 20

Fredrick Becker (c. 1736)
New York, N.Y.
Bibl. 23, 36, 44

Philip Becker (c. 1764)
Lancaster, Pa.
Bibl. 22, 23, 25, 28, 36, 44

| P B |

Beckwith & Brittain (c. 1858)
Charlotte, N.C.
Robert W. Beckwith
———— Brittain
Bibl. 21

Robert W. Beckwith
Raleigh, N.C. (c. 1840-1843)
Ramsay & Beckwith (c. 1840-
1843)
New Bern, N.C. (c. 1840-1843)
Tarboro, N.C. (c. 1850)
Charlotte, N.C. (c. 1858-1868)
Thomson & Beckwith (c. 1837-
1839)
Beckwith & Brittain (c. 1858)
Bibl. 21

E. Bedford (c. 1816)
Batavia, N.Y.
Bibl. 20

John Bedford (b. 1757-1834)
Fishkill, N.Y.
Bibl. 15, 20, 22, 23, 25, 28, 29,
30, 44

| 𝒥 B ed ford |

Morton Bedford (w. 1796)
Baltimore, Md.
Bibl. 38

Bedwell
(See Norman & Bedwell)

J. W. Beebe & Co. (c. 1844)
(James W. Beebe & Co.)
New York, N.Y.
Bibl. 15, 23, 25, 29, 44

| J. W. BEEBE & CO. |

James W. Beebe (c. 1835-1841)
New York, N.Y.
James W. & L. Beebe (c. 1836-
1840)
J. W. Beebe & Co. (c. 1844)
Bibl. 15, 23, 25, 29, 36, 44

| J W BEEBE |

James W. & L. Beebe (c. 1836-
1840)
New York, N.Y.
Bibl. 15

John O. Beebe (c. 1833-1835)
New York, N.Y.
Bibl. 15

Lemuel D. Beebe (c. 1850)
Syracuse, N.Y.
Bibl. 20

Samuel Beebe (d. 1819)
Onondaga, N.Y.
Bibl. 20

Stanton Beebe (c. 1818-1824)
Providence, R.I.
Gorham & Beebe (c. 1825-1831)
Bibl. 22, 23, 28, 36, 44

William Beebe (c. 1850)
New York, N.Y.
Bibl. 21, 23, 25, 44

| BEEBE |

Patrick Beech (c. 1773-1774)
Williamsburg, Va.
Bibl. 19

C. Beecher & Co. (c. 1820)
Meriden, Conn.
Clement Beecher
Bibl. 23, 36, 44

Clement Beecher (b. 1778-d.
1869)
Berlin, Conn.
Cheshire, Conn.
Meriden, Conn.
Clement Beecher & Co. (c.
1801-1820)
C. Beecher & Co. (c. 1820)
Bibl. 16, 22, 23, 25, 28, 30, 44

| C B |

| G·B |

Clement Beecher & Co. (c.
1801-1820)
Berlin, Conn.
Cheshire, Conn.
Meriden, Conn.
Bibl. 16

Isaac Beers (c. 1800)
New Haven, Conn.
Henry Dagget
Bibl. 23

J. B. Beers (c. 1838-1839)
Honeoye Falls, N.Y.
Bibl. 20

John Beesleyhaven (c. 1839-
1840)
Philadelphia, Pa.
Bibl. 3

Beggs & Smith (c. 1840?)
(Smith and Beggs)
Louisville, Ky.
William Beggs (?)
———— Smith
Bibl. 32, 54

William Beggs (c. 1841-1844)
Louisville, Ky.
Beggs & Smith (c. 1840?) (?)
McGrew & Beggs (c. 1850)
Bibl. 32, 54, 68

Julius Beidt (c. 1848)
Philadelphia, Pa.
Bibl. 3

Henry Beigel (c. 1816-1817)
Philadelphia, Pa.
Bibl. 3

Gilbert Belcher
Albany, N.Y. (1700's)
Massachusetts
Bibl. 54

Maxim Belgord (c. 1848)
Philadelphia, Pa.
Bibl. 3

Lewis Belin (c. 1818-1819)
Philadelphia, Pa.
Bibl. 3, 23, 36, 44

William Belk (c. 1797-1800)
Philadelphia, Pa.
Bibl. 3

Samuel Belknap (b. 1751-d.
1821)
Boston, Mass.
Bibl. 22, 23, 28, 36, 44

Stephen Belknap (Belnap) (c.
1818-1850)
Philadelphia, Pa.
Bibl. 3

Bell & Co. (c. 1825)
Location unknown
Bibl. 28

BELL & CO   S. BELL

Andrew Bell (b. 1712-d. 1752)
Beaufort, S.C.
Bibl. 5

J. Bell (c. 1817-1824)
New York, N.Y.
Perhaps Joseph Bell
Bibl. 15, 44

J BELL

J. & S. Bell (c. 1850)
San Antonio, Tex.
S. Bell
Bibl. 54

S. Bell (c. 1846)
San Antonio, Tex.
J. & S. Bell (c. 1850)
Bibl. 54

S. W. Bell (c. 1837)
Philadelphia, Pa.
Bibl. 3, 15, 25, 44

Thomas W. Bell
Philadelphia, Pa. (c. 1837)
Petersburg, Va. (c. 1838-1848)
Bibl. 3, 19

T. W. BELL

William Bell (c. 1805)
Philadelphia, Pa.
Bibl. 3

Francois Belliard (c. 1822)
New Orleans, La.
Bibl. 36, 44

Belloni & Durandeau (c. 1835-
1836)
New York, N.Y.
Louis J. Belloni
John Durandeau
Bibl. 15, 23, 36, 44, 72

BELLONI & DURAND

Louis J. Belloni (c. 1835)
New York, N.Y.
Belloni & Durandeau (c. 1835-
1836)
Bibl. 23, 36, 44

Stephen Belnap
(See Stephen Belknap)

B. Bement (c. 1810)
Pittsfield, Mass.
Bibl. 25, 44

B. BEMENT

———— Benedict (c. 1826-1828)
Auburn, N.Y.
Munger & Benedict
Bibl. 20

Benedict & Scudder (c. 1827-
1837)
New York, N.Y.
Andrew C. Benedict
Egbert Scudder
Bibl. 15, 79

Benedict & Son (c. 1840)
New York, N.Y.
Bibl. 23, 36, 44

Benedict & Squire (c. 1825-
1839)
New York, N.Y.
Martin Benedict
Bela S. Squire Jr.
Bibl. 15, 23, 25, 29, 36, 44

BENEDICT & SQUIRE

A. Benedict (c. 1835)
Syracuse, N.Y.
Bibl. 20

Andrew C. Benedict (c. 1827-
1840)
New York, N.Y.
Benedict & Scudder (c. 1827-
1837)
Bibl. 15, 23, 25, 29, 36, 44, 89

A. C. BENEDICT

Isaac H. Benedict (c. 1837-
1854, d. 1854)
Greenville, S.C.
Mr. Burns
Bibl. 5

J. Benedict (c. 1830)
New York, N.Y.
Bibl. 23, 36, 44

J. H. Benedict (c. 1830)
Skaneateles, N.Y.
Bibl. 20

Martin Benedict (c. 1823-1839)
New York, N.Y.
Benedict & Squire (c. 1825-
1839)
Bibl. 15, 89

Samuel Benedict (c. 1845)
New York, N.Y.
Bibl. 35, 83

Morris Benham (c. 1843)
Hartford, Conn.
Bibl. 23

Benjamin & Co.
New York, N.Y. (?)
Barzillai Benjamin (b. 1774-d.
1844)
Bibl. 15, 16, 23, 25, 28, 29, 36,
44

Benjamin & Ford (c. 1828-
1874?)
New Haven, Conn.
Everard Benjamin
George H. Ford
Bibl. 28

B. Benjamin
(See Benjamin Benjamin)

Barzillai Benjamin (b. 1774-d.
1844)
New Haven, Conn. (c. 1799)
Bridgeport, Conn.
Milford, Conn.
New York, N.Y.
Benjamin & Co.
Bibl. 15, 16, 23, 25, 28, 29, 36,
44

B BENJAMIN   B B

Benjamin Benjamin (c. 1825)
New Haven, Conn.
New York, N.Y.
Bibl. 15, 23, 29, 44

B BENJAMIN   B B

Everard Benjamin (b. 1807-
1874)
New Haven, Conn.
Benjamin & Ford (c. 1828-
1874?)
Bibl. 16, 23, 25, 28, 29, 36, 44

E BENJAMIN

Everard Benjamin & Co. (c.
1830-1840)
New Haven, Conn.

Bibl. 15, 44, 54, 61

E BENJAMIN & CO

E B & CO

John Benjamin (b. 1699-d.
1773)
Stratford, Conn.
Bibl. 25, 28, 44, 54, 61

J. B.

John Benjamin (b. 1730-d.
1796)
Stratford, Conn.
Bibl. 16, 23, 29, 36

Luther W. Benjamin (c. 1803)
Canandaigua, N.Y.
Thompson & Benjamin
Bibl. 20

Samuel C. Benjamin (c. 1801-
1831, c. 1819)
New Haven, Conn.
Bibl. 16, 23, 28, 36, 44

Solomon Benjamin (w. 1816-
1818)
Baltimore, Md.
Bibl. 23, 28, 36, 38, 44

Theodore Benjamin (c. 1823-
1824)
Philadelphia, Pa.
Bibl. 3

Whiteman Benner (c. 1818-
1824)
Philadelphia, Pa.
Bibl. 3

Bennet
(See Hall & Bennet)

Bennett (c. 1811)
Philadelphia, Pa.
Bibl. 3

Bennett & Caldwell (c. 1843-
1848)
Philadelphia, Pa.
——— Bennett
James E. Caldwell
Bibl. 3

Bennett & Cooke (c. 1820)
New York, N.Y.
Bibl. 78

Bennett, Cooke & Co. (c. 1823-
1827)
Charleston, S.C.
John Bennett Sr.
D. C. Cooke
Maltby Pelletreau,
Bibl. 5

Bennett & Fletcher (1830-1894)
(Fletcher & Bennett)
Louisville, Ky.
Philadelphia, Pa.
——— Bennett
Henry Fletcher
Bibl. 32, 54

Bennett, Fletcher & Co. (1830-
1894)
(Fletcher, Bennett & Co.)
Louisville, Ky.
Philadelphia, Pa.
Bibl. 32

Bennett, Lewis & Co. (c. 1856)
York, S.C.
Jordan Bennett
J. N. Lewis
Bibl. 5

Bennett & Thomas (c. 1812-
1819)
Petersburg, Va.
John Bennett
Ebenezer Thomas
John Warren Thomas
Bibl. 19

BENNETT & THOMAS

Bennett, Wilson & Co. (c. 1856)
York, S.C.
Jordan Bennett
D. W. Wilson
Bibl. 5

Alfred Bennett (c. 1837-1847)
Location unknown
Bibl. 3

Charles Fletcher Bennett (c.
1843-1848, d. 1876)
Louisville, Ky.
Bibl. 32, 54

J. D. Bennett (c. 1847)
J. D. Bennett & Co. (c. 1849)
Petersburg, Va.
Bibl. 19

Jacob Bennett (c. 1825-1850)
Philadelphia, Pa.
Bibl. 3, 23, 36, 44

James Bennett (c. 1769-1773)
New York, N.Y.
Bibl. 23, 36, 44

James Bennett (c. 1839)
Philadelphia, Pa.
Bibl. 3

John Bennett
Richmond, Va. (c. 1811-1812)
Petersburg, Va. (c. 1812-1827)
Bennett & Thomas (c. 1812-
1819)
John W. Thomas & Co. (c.
1819)
Bibl. 19

John Bennett Sr. (c. 1815-1827)
Charleston, S.C.
New York, N.Y.
Pelletreau, Bennett & Cooke (c.
1815-1827)
Bennett, Cooke & Co. (c. 1823-
1827)
Pelletreau, Bennett & Co. (c.
1827-1829)
Bibl. 5

Jordan Bennett (c. 1824-   )
York, S.C. (c. 1854-1856)
Chester, S.C.
J. N. Lewis & Co. (c. 1854)
(?)
Bennett, Lewis & Co. (c. 1856)
Bennett, Wilson & Co. (c.
1856)
Bibl. 5

L. M. Bennett (c. 1856-1860)
Utica, N.Y.
Leach & Bennett (c. 1856-1858)
Bibl. 18

Purden Bennett (c. 1837-1839)
Philadelphia, Pa.
Bibl. 3

Purnell Bennett (c. 1835-1843)
Philadelphia, Pa.
Bibl. 3

Robert H. Bennett (c. 1849-
1850)
Philadelphia, Pa.
Bibl. 3

Benneville
(See De Benneville)

Jonathan Benny (w. 1798)
Easton, Md.
Bibl. 38

Jean Baptiste Benoit (w. 1796)
Baltimore, Md.
Bibl. 38

G. L. Benson (c. 1818)
Cincinnati, Ohio
Bibl. 34

Thomas Bentley (b. 1764-d.
1804)
Boston, Mass.
Bibl. 4, 23, 25, 28, 29, 36, 44, 54

J. Benton (c. 1810)
Location unknown
Bibl. 24, 89

J. BENTON

Lucius Benton (c. 1850)
Cleveland, Ohio
Bibl. 54, 89

Peter Bentson (Bentzon) (c.
1817-1849)
Philadelphia, Pa.
Bibl. 3, 23, 36, 44

Eugene C. Benyard (c. 1839-
1849)
Philadelphia, Pa.
Bibl. 3

Hugh G. Benyard (c. 1841)
Philadelphia, Pa.
Bibl. 3

Ferdinand Bera (Bero) (c.
1839-1850)
Philadelphia, Pa.
Bibl. 3

Andrew Berard (c. 1797)
Philadelphia, Pa.
Bibl. 3, 23, 28, 36

E. Berard (c. 1800)
Philadelphia, Pa.
Bibl. 29, 36, 44

Samuel Berd (c. 1840)
Philadelphia, Pa.
Bibl. 3

Frederick Berenbroick (c. 1839-
1841)
New York, N.Y.

Frederick Berenbroick & Co.
(c. 1850)
Bibl. 15

Frederick Berenbroick & Co. (c.
1850)
New York, N.Y.
Bibl. 23

Peter W. Bergantz (c. 1848-
1852)
Louisville, Ky.
Bibl. 32

Joseph Berger (c. 1829-1833)
Philadelphia, Pa.
Bibl. 3

John Bering (c. 1790-1807)
Charleston, S.C.
Bibl. 5, 44, 54

I B

Charles H. Berkenbush (c.
1825)
New York, N.Y.
Bibl. 15, 23, 36, 44

A. & J. Berniard (c. 1806-1807)
Philadelphia, Pa.
Bibl. 3

Ferdinand Bero
(See Ferdinand Bera)

Peter Berrgant (c. 1829-1833)
Philadelphia, Pa.
Bibl. 3

A. & J. Berringer (c. 1834-1835)
Albany, N.Y.
Bibl. 20

Jacob Berringer (c. 1835-1843)
Albany, N.Y.
Bibl. 20

James Berry (w. 1803)
Easton, Md.
Bibl. 38

William Berry (c. 1805)
New York, N.Y.
Bibl. 23, 36, 44

Ferdinand Berstardus
(Besterdes) (1836-1840)
New York, N.Y.
Bibl. 15

George Bertie (c. 1808-1814)
Baltimore, Md.
Bibl. 38

Tousaint Bertrand (w. 1795-
1796)
Baltimore, Md.
Bibl. 38

John Besher (c. 1827-1832)
New York, N.Y.
Bibl. 15

Thauvet Besly (d. 1757)
New York, N.Y. (c. 1727-
1757)
Bibl. 4, 23, 25, 28, 29, 30, 35,
36, 44, 54

B

H. W. Bessac (c. 1823)
Hudson, N.Y.
Bibl. 15, 20, 44

H. W. Bessa

John Besselievre (c. 1825-
1840)
Philadelphia, Pa.
Bibl. 3

John A. Besselievre (c. 1841-
1850)
Philadelphia, Pa.
Bibl. 3

Thomas Besselievre (c. 1829-
1833)
Philadelphia, Pa.
Bibl. 3, 23, 36, 44

A. Besslievre (c. 1837)
Philadelphia, Pa.
Bibl. 3

B. Best & Co. (after 1850)
Louisville, Ky.
Bibl. 32, 54

John Best (c. 1794)
Lexington, Ky.
Shelby County, Ky.
Bibl. 32, 54

Joseph Best (c. 1723)
Philadelphia, Pa.
Bibl. 3, 23, 28, 36, 44

Robert Best (c. 1817)
Cincinnati, Ohio
Bibl. 34, 44

Samuel Best (c. 1793)
Cincinnati, Ohio
Bibl. 34

Besterdes
(See Berstardus)

W. J. Bettinger (c. 1853-1854)
Utica, N.Y.
Bibl. 18

Samuel Bettle (c. 1803)
Philadelphia, Pa.
Bibl. 3

Charles Betton (c. 1850)
Philadelphia, Pa.
Bibl. 3

Thomas W. Betton (c. 1830-1833)
Philadelphia, Pa.
Bibl. 3

Richard Bevan (w. 1803-1804)
Baltimore, Md.
Bibl. 23, 28, 36, 38, 44

William Bevans (c. 1810-1813)
Philadelphia, Pa.
Bibl. 3

John K. Bevin (c. 1786-1825)
Charleston, S.C.
Bibl. 5, 54

G. Bichler (Bechler) (b. 1807)
Utica, N.Y. (c. 1858-1860-   )
Bibl. 18

Francis Bicknell (c. 1818-1831)
Rome, N.Y.
Bibl. 15, 20, 25, 44

F. BICKNELL

Biddle
(See Krider & Biddle)

John S. Biddle (c. 1807)
Wheeling, Va.
Bibl. 19

Owen Biddle (d. 1799)
Philadelphia, Pa. (c. 1764-1770)
Bibl. 3

Henry Biegel (c. 1810-1813)
Philadelphia, Pa.
Bibl. 3

Henry Biershing (b. 1790-d. 1843)
Hagerstown, Md. (w. 1815-1843)
Bibl. 25, 29, 38, 44

H B

Bigelow (c. 1830)
Location unknown
Bibl. 54

BIGELOW

Bigelow & Bros. (c. 1840-1850)
Boston, Mass
John Bigelow
Abram O. Bigelow
Alanson Bigelow
Bibl. 15, 23, 25, 29, 36, 44

BIGELOW & BROS.

Bigelow Bros. & Kennard
(c. 1845)
Boston, Mass.
Bibl. 89

BIGELOW BROS. & KENNARD

Bigelow, Kennard & Co. (c. 1863)
Boston, Mass.
Bibl. 15

Bigelow, Kennard & Co., Inc.
(c. 1912)
Boston, Mass.
Bibl. 15

Abram O. Bigelow (c. 1830?)
Boston, Mass.
Bigelow & Bros. (c. 1840-1850)
Bibl. 23

Alanson Bigelow (c. 1832)
Boston, Mass.
Bigelow & Brothers (c. 1840-1850)
Bibl. 23

John Bigelow (c. 1830)
Boston, Mass.
Bigelow & Bros. (c. 1840-1850)
Bibl. 23, 25, 29, 36, 44

JOHN BIGELOW

Bigger & Clarke (c. 1783-1784)
Baltimore, Md. (1783-1784)
Philadelphia, Pa.
——— Bigger
Ambrose Clarke
Bibl. 3, 38

Gilbert Bigger (w. 1783-1816)
Baltimore, Md.
Bibl. 38

Joseph Biggs (c. 1827-1835)
New York, N.Y.
Bibl. 15, 23, 36, 44

S. Bigotut (c. 1800)
New York, N.Y.
Bibl. 23, 36, 44

Silvian A. Bijotal (c. 1795)
New York, N.Y.
Bibl. 23, 36, 44

Andrew Billings (b. 1743-d. 1808)
Preston, Conn.
Fishkill, N.Y.
Poughkeepsie, N.Y.
Bibl. 15, 20, 23, 25, 28, 29, 36, 44, 54

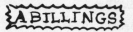

Daniel Billings (c. 1795)
New London County, Conn.
Preston, Conn.
Bibl. 16, 23, 25, 28, 29, 36, 44, 61

D. Billings

Joseph Billings (b. 1720)
Reading, Pa. (c. 1770)
Bibl. 3, 28

L. Billings (c. 1832)
Bloody Brook, Mass.
Bibl. 84

Billon & Co. (c. 1795-1797)
Philadelphia, Pa.
Charles Billon
Bibl. 3

Charles Billon (c. 1795-1819)
Philadelphia, Pa.
Billon & Co. (c. 1795-1797)
Bibl. 3

Charles Billon (c. 1860-   )
St. Louis, Mo.
Bibl. 25, 44, 54

C BILLON

Richard Bilton (w. 1800-1801)
Baltimore, Md.
Bibl. 38

Bingham, Ball & Co. (-1833)
Utica, N.Y.
George W. Bingham
William H. Ball
John D. Douglass
Bibl. 18, 20

Bingham & Breorbey (c. 1799)
Philadelphia, Pa.
Thomas Bingham
———— Breorbey
Bibl. 3

Flavel Bingham (c. 1802-1804)
Utica, N.Y.
Bibl. 18, 20

George W. Bingham
Utica, N.Y.
Bingham, Ball & Co.
(-1833)
Bibl. 18, 20

James Bingham (c. 1839-1850)
Philadelphia, Pa
Bibl. 3

John Bingham (c. 1678)
Boston, Mass.
Bibl. 4, 28

John Bingham (c. 1664)
Newark, N.J.
Bibl. 23, 36, 44

Thomas Bingham (c. 1797-
1811)
Philadelphia, Pa.
Bibl. 3

———— Bingley (c. 1790)
Connecticut (?)
Bibl. 28
BINGLEY

Theodore Binneau (c. 1820-
1822)
Philadelphia, Pa.
Bibl. 3, 23, 36, 44

John Bioren (c. 1829-1833)
Philadelphia, Pa.
Bibl. 3

Conrad Bird
(See Conrad Bard)

Albert G. Bird (c. 1829-1850)
Philadelphia, Pa.
Bibl. 3

John Stiles Bird (b. 1794-d.
1887)
Charleston, S.C. (c. 1820-1861)
Bibl. 5, 25, 44
J. S. B   J. S. Bird

Joseph Bird
Location unknown
Bibl. 15, 44
JOSEPH BIRD

Thomas Bird (c. 1791)
Alexandria, Va.
Bibl. 19, 54

William Bird (c. 1848-1850)
Philadelphia, Pa.
Bibl. 3

Lawrence Birnie (c. 1774-
1779)
Philadelphia, Pa.
Bibl. 3

Benjamin F. Bishop (c. 1846-
1847)
Philadelphia, Pa.
Bibl. 3

Edward Bishop (c. 1839)
Philadelphia, Pa.
Bibl. 3

Edwin Bishop (c. 1825-1833)
Philadelphia, Pa.
Bibl. 3

Erwin Bishop (c. 1835-1837)
Philadelphia, Pa.
Bibl. 3

Joachim Bishop (c. 1835)
Philadelphia, Pa.
Bibl. 3

Jodquin Bishop (c. 1837)
Philadelphia, Pa.
Bibl. 3

John Bishop (c. 1839-1851)
Wheeling, Va.
Bibl. 19

Joseph Bishop
Wilmington, N.C. (c. 1817-
1822)
Philadelphia, Pa. (c. 1829-
1833)
Bibl. 3, 21

Josiah Bishop (c. 1830)
Columbia, S.C.
Bibl. 5

Peter S. Bishop (c. 1837)
Philadelphia, Pa.
Bibl. 3

Thomas Bissbrown (c. 1788-
1790)
Albany, N.Y.
Bibl. 20, 23, 36, 44

Christian Bixler (c. 1784)
Easton, Pa.
Bibl. 25, 44

Black, Starr & Frost (c. 1876)
New York, N.Y.
Bibl. 15, 23, 72

I. Black (c. 1795-1822)
Philadelphia, Pa.
Perhaps James or John Black
Bibl. 15
I. BLACK

James Black (c. 1795-1822)
Philadelphia, Pa.
Bibl. 3, 23, 25, 29, 36, 44
I B   I BLACK

John Black (c. 1811-1819)
Philadelphia, Pa.
McMullin & Black (c. 1811)
Bibl. 3, 4, 23, 28, 36, 44

J B   I BLACK

John Black (c. 1839-1850)
Philadelphia, Pa.
Bibl. 3

William Black (c. 1833-1840)
New York, N.Y.
Ball, Tompkins & Black (c.
1839-1851)
Ball, Black & Co. (c. 1851-
1876)
Bibl. 15, 23, 36, 44

———— Blackburn (c. 1812)
Shelbyville, Ky.
Bibl. 32, 54, 68

F. S. Blackman & Co. (c. 1840)
Danbury, Conn.
Frederick Starr Blackman
Bibl. 15, 23, 25, 29, 36
F. S. B. & Co.

Frederick Starr Blackman (b.
1811-d. 1898)
Danbury, Conn. (c. 1832)
Bridgeport, Conn.

F. S. Blackman & Co. (c. 1840)
Bibl. 16, 23, 25, 28, 29, 36, 44

F. S. BLACKMAN

J. C. Blackman & Co. (c. 1835)
Bridgeport, Conn.
John Clark Blackman
Bibl. 15, 25

J. C. B. & Co

John Clark Blackman (b.
 1808-d. 1872)
Danbury, Conn. (c. 1829)
Bridgeport, Conn. (c. 1835)
J. C. Blackman & Co. (c. 1835)
Bibl. 15, 16, 23, 25, 36, 44

John Starr Blackman (b.
 1777-d. 1851)
Danbury, Conn.
Bibl. 16, 23, 25, 28, 29, 36, 44

J S B

Redman Blackwell (d. 1812)
Bethlehem Township, N.J.
Bibl. 46

Blackwood & Brooks (c. 1828-
 1830)
Utica, N.Y.
William Blackwood
Benjamin Franklin Brooks
Bibl. 18, 20

William Blackwood (c. 1836-
 1838)
Utica, N.Y.
Blackwood & Brooks (c. 1828-
 1830)
H. S. Bradley & Co. (c. 1836-
 1850)
Bibl. 18, 20

Daniel Blair
St. Louis, Mo. (c. 1817-1821)
Daggett & Blair (c. 1821)
Bibl. 54

Frederick Blake (c. 1840-1844)
Albany, N.Y.
Bibl. 20

George H. Blake (w. 1842-
 1849, d. 1849)
Troy, N.Y.
Bibl. 20

Isaac Blake (c. 1846-1850-   )
Troy, N.Y.
Bibl. 20

Peter Blake (c. 1807)
Charleston, S.C.
Bibl. 5

C. Blakeslee (c. 1820)
Vermont (?)
Bibl. 28

C BLAKESLEE

Blakesley
(See Willey & Blakesley)

Harper Blakesley (c. 1829)
Cincinnati, Ohio
Bibl. 54

Collins Blakley (c. 1845)
Troy, N.Y.
Bibl. 23

William Bla(c)kslee (b. 1795-d.
 1879)
Newtown, Conn.
Bibl. 16, 23, 28, 36, 44

Ziba (Zeba) Bla(c)kslee (b.
 1768-d. 1825)
Newtown, Conn.
Bibl. 23, 28, 36, 44

Lewis Blanc (c. 1810)
Philadelphia, Pa.
Bibl. 3

P. Blancan (c. 1811-1813)
Philadelphia, Pa.
Bibl. 3

Thomas Blanch (b. 1793, w.
 1827)
Baltimore, Md.
Bibl. 38

A. Blanchard (c. 1800)
Lexington, Ky.
Bibl. 30

Asa Blanchard (c. 1808-1838)
Lexington, Ky.
Bibl. 23, 25, 28, 29, 32, 36, 44,
 54, 68

A BLANCHARD   A. B

Joshua Blanchard (c. 1829)
Cincinnati, Ohio
Bibl. 54

Thomas Blanche (b. 1793, w.
 1805)
Baltimore, Md.
Bibl. 38

Peter Blancjour (c. 1838)
Richmond, Va.
Bibl. 19

Jurian Blanck Jr. (b. 1665)
New York, N.Y.
Bibl. 25, 44, 54

Samuel Bland (c. 1837-1850)
Philadelphia, Pa.
Bibl. 3

William Bland (c. 1845-1848)
St. Louis, Mo.
Bibl. 54

Victor G. Blandin (c. 1831-   )
Charlotte, N.C.
Bibl. 21

Charles Blank (c. 1850)
Philadelphia, Pa.
Bibl. 3

John Blank (c. 1837-1839)
Philadelphia, Pa.
Bibl. 3

Asa Blansett (c. 1795)
Dumfries, Va.
Bibl. 19

John Blatt (c. 1841)
Philadelphia, Pa.
Bibl. 3

John W. Blauvelt (c. 1831-
 1844)
New York, N.Y.
Bibl. 15, 23, 36, 44

Joseph Blauvelt (c. 1819)
New York, N.Y.
Bibl. 15

Spencer Blauvelt (c. 1839-
 1840)
New York, N.Y.
Bibl. 15

Bleasom & Reed (c. 1830)
Nassau, N.H.
Portsmouth, N.H.
Bibl. 23, 25, 29, 36, 44

BLEASOM & REED

Bliss
(See Hall & Bliss)

Jonathan Bliss
Middletown, Conn.
Hart & Bliss (c. 1803-1804)
Hughes & Bliss (c. 1806)
Bibl. 23, 25, 36, 44

William Bliss (c. 1812-1828)
Middletown, Conn.
Cleveland, Ohio
Bibl. 34, 54

George Blome (c. 1845)
Philadelphia, Pa.
Bibl. 3

Blondell (Blondel) & Descuret
(c. 1798-1799)
Philadelphia, Pa.
Anthony Blondell
Louis Descuret
Bibl. 3, 23, 36, 44

Anthony Blondell (Blondel)
Philadelphia, Pa. (c. 1797-1813)
Baltimore, Md. (w. 1814-1827)
Martinsburg, Va. (c. 1819-1840)
Blondell & Descuret (c. 1798-1799)
Bibl. 3, 19, 23, 28, 36, 38 44

John M. Blondell (Blondel) (c.
1814-1824)
Baltimore, Md.
Bibl. 19, 38

James & L. Bloodgood (c. 1805-1810)
Utica, N.Y.
James A. Bloodgood
Lynott Bloodgood
Bibl. 18, 20

Lynott Bloodgood (c. 1805)
Albany, N.Y.
Utica, N.Y.
James & L. Bloodgood (c. 1805-1810)
Bibl. 18, 20, 54

Charles Bloomer (c. 1850)
Syracuse, N.Y.
Bibl. 20

George Blowe (c. 1837-1850)
Philadelphia, Pa.
Bibl. 3

John Blowers (c. 1710-1748)
Boston, Mass.
Bibl. 2, 15, 23, 25, 28, 29, 36, 44, 54, 69, 70

I BLOWERS

Samuel Bluis (c. 1791)
Norfolk, Va.
Bibl. 19

Charles Blundy (d. 1766)
Charleston, S.C. (c. 1760)
Savannah, Ga. (c. 1766)
Bibl. 17

John Bochler (c. 1796-1820)
Savannah, Ga.
Bibl. 17

Joseph Bock (c. 1859-1891)
Charleston, S.C.
Bibl. 5, 44, 54

Jos. Bock

Daniel Bockius (Buckuis)
(Buckins) (c. 1792-1798)
Martinsburg, Va.
Young & Bockius (c. 1798)
Bibl. 19

William Bode (c. 1796-1798)
Philadelphia, Pa.
Bibl. 3

Lorenzo Rodnano (c. 1819)
Philadelphia, Pa.
Bibl. 3

Andreas W. Boehler (c. 1784)
New York, N.Y.
Bibl. 23, 36, 44

Charles Louis Boehme (b.
1774-d. 1868) (w. 1799-1812)
Baltimore, Md.
Bibl. 15, 23, 25, 28, 29, 36, 38, 44, 54, 78

Hendrik (Henricus) Boelen (b.
1684-d. 1755)
New York, N.Y.
Bibl. 2, 15, 23, 25, 28, 29, 30, 35, 36, 44, 54

Jacob Boelen (b. 1654-d. 1729)
New York, N.Y.
Bibl. 2, 4, 15, 23, 25, 28, 29, 30, 35, 36, 44, 54, 67

Jacob Boelen II (c. 1733-1786)
New York, N.Y.
Bibl. 15, 23, 25, 35, 36, 44, 67

Abraham Boemper (c. 1780-1792)
Bethlehem, Pa.
Bibl. 3, 23, 36, 44

Charles Bofenchen (c. 1854-1857)
Camden, S.C.
Bibl. 5

Everadus Bogardus (b. 1675)
New York, N.Y.
Bibl. 4, 15, 23, 25, 28, 29, 35, 36, 44

E B

Peter S. Bogardus (c. 1833-1834)
Albany, N.Y.
Bibl. 20

Albert Bogart (c. 1815-1836)
New York, N.Y.
Bibl. 15

Widow of Albert Bogart (c.
1834-1836)
New York, N.Y.
Bibl. 15

William Bogart (c. 1839-1847)
Albany, N.Y.
Bibl. 20

Boger & Wilson (c. 1846-1853)
Salisbury, N.C.
John E. Boger
William Rowan Wilson
Bibl. 21

John E. Boger (c. 1845-
1853-)
Salisbury, N.C.
Boger & Wilson (c. 1846-1853)
Bibl. 21

Albert Bogert (c. 1815-1830)
New York, N.Y.
Bibl. 15, 23, 25, 28, 29, 36, 44

Nicholas J. Bogert (Bogirt) (c.
1801)
New York, N.Y.
Bibl. 15, 23, 25, 28, 29, 36, 44

N. J. BOGERT   N. BOGERT

William Bogert (c. 1842)
Albany, N.Y.
Bibl. 23

Thomas Boggs (c. 1849)
Philadelphia, Pa.
Bibl. 3

Nicholas Bogirt
(See Nicholas Bogart)

Thomas H. Bogue & Co. (c.
1844)
Philadelphia, Pa.
Bibl. 3

L. T. Boland (c. 1844)
Columbia, S.C.
Bibl. 5

Bolland
(See Gottschalk & Bolland)

Bolles & Hasting (c. 1840)
Location unknown
Bibl. 89

Bolton & Horn (c. 1808)
Philadelphia, Pa.
William Bolton
Henry Horn
Bibl. 3

James Bolton (c. 1789)
New York, N.Y.
Bibl. 23, 28, 36, 44

William Bolton (Botton)
(Boulton) (c. 1797-1813)
Philadelphia, Pa.
Bolton & Horn (c. 1808)
Bibl. 3

John Bonaus (c. 1809)
Charleston, S.C.
Bibl. 5

C. Bond (c. 1840)
Location unknown

Bibl. 28

C BOND

W. Bond (c. 1765)
Location unknown
Bibl. 28, 29, 44

W. Bond

Boning & Co. (c. 1843)
Philadelphia, Pa.
William Boning
Bibl. 3

William Boning (c. 1844-1850)
Philadelphia, Pa.
Boning & Co. (c. 1843)
Holden & Boning (c. 1843)
Bibl. 3

Victor Bonjean (c. 1822)
New Orleans, La.
Bibl. 36, 44

———— Bonnaud (c. 1799)
Philadelphia, Pa.
Bibl. 3

James Bonnet (c. 1769)
New York, N.Y.
Bibl. 44

Bonsall & Jacot (c. 1849)
Philadelphia, Pa.
Edmund C. Bonsall
Julius Jacot
Bibl. 3

Bonsall & Scheer (c. 1845-1847)
Philadelphia, Pa.
Edmund C. Bonsall
John C. Scheer (?)
Bibl. 3

Edmund C. Bonsall (c. 1844-
1850)
Philadelphia, Pa.
Bonsall & Jacot
Bonsall & Scheer
Bibl. 3

Edward C. Bonsall (c. 1839-
1840)
Philadelphia, Pa.
Bibl. 3

Roswell Bontecou (Bonticou)
(Bounticou) (c. 1784-1805)
New Haven, Conn.
Augusta, Ga.

Gregory & Bontecou (c. 1802-
1805)
Bibl. 17

Timothy Bontecou (w. 1791-
1815)
Savannah, Ga.
Bibl. 89

Timothy Bontecou Sr. (b.
1693-d. 1784)
Hartford, Conn.
Stratford, Conn.
New York, N.Y.
Bibl. 15, 16, 23, 25, 28, 29, 36,
44, 61

T B   TB

Timothy Bontecou Jr. (b.
1723-d. 1789)
New Haven, Conn.
Stratford, Conn.
Bibl. 15, 16, 17, 23, 25, 28, 29,
36, 44, 61

TB

Boon
(See Webb & Boon)

Boon & Ormsby (c. 1832-1834)
Cortland, N.Y.
———— Boon
Daniel D. R. Ormsby
Bibl. 20

Michael Boon (c. 1840)
Philadelphia, Pa.
Bibl. 3

Sanford Boon (c. 1822-1844)
Hamilton, N.Y.
Bibl. 20

Jeremiah Boone (c. 1790-1796)
Philadelphia, Pa.
Bibl. 3, 23, 25, 29, 36, 44

J.BOONE

I BOONE

Ezra B. Booth (b. 1805-d.
1888)
Rochester, N.Y. (c. 1838-1888)
Vergennes, Vt.
Erastus Cook

Bibl. 20, 25, 41, 44

E. B. BOOTH

Thomas Booth (c. 1841)
Philadelphia, Pa.
Bibl. 3

Borde & Pettit (c. 1803)
Charleston, S.C.
Augustus Borde
——— Pettit
Bibl. 5

Augustine Bordeaux (c. 1798-1799)
Philadelphia, Pa.
Bibl. 3, 23, 36, 44

Christian Bordersen (c. 1850)
Russellville, Ky.
Bibl. 32, 54

Charles G. Borhek (c. 1829-1840)
Philadelphia, Pa.
Bibl. 3

Edward Borhek (c. 1835-1850)
Philadelphia, Pa.
Bibl. 3, 25, 44

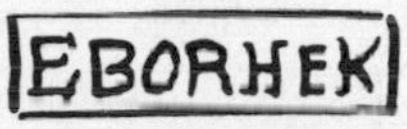

Frederick Bos(s)ardet (Boshardt) (Bussarec) (c. 1840-1847)
Philadelphia, Pa.
Bibl. 3

——— Bosier (c. 1811)
Philadelphia, Pa.
Bibl. 3

Boss & Kindell (c. 1794)
New York, N.Y.
Bibl. 23, 36, 44

Boss & Peterman (c. 1841)
Rochester, N.Y.
Philip Boss
Jefferson Peterman
Bibl. 20

James Boss (c. 1846-1847)
Philadelphia, Pa.
Bibl. 3

Philip Boss (c. 1841)
Rochester, N.Y.
Boss & Peterman
Bibl. 20

Peter Bossordet (c. 1847-1849)
Philadelphia, Pa.
Bibl. 3

Zalmon Bostwick (c. 1846-1852)
New York, N.Y.
Bibl. 15, 23, 25, 29, 44

Z. BOSTWICK

Samuel Bosworth (c. 1816-1837)
Buffalo, N.Y.
Bibl. 20, 23, 25, 29, 36, 44

BOSWORTH

Gideon B. Botsford (b. 1776-d. 1866)
Woodbury, Conn.
Bibl. 15, 16, 23, 25, 28, 29, 36, 44

G B BOTSFORD

J. S. Botsford (c. 1840-1849)
Schenectady, N.Y.
Troy, N.Y.
Bibl. 20

L. F. Botsford (c. 1830-1831)
Albany, N.Y.
Bibl. 20

Samuel N. Botsford (c. 1839-1842)
Norfolk, Va.
Bibl. 19

William Botton
(See William Bolton)

Joseph Boudar (c. 1800)
New York, N.Y.
Bibl. 23, 36, 44

Elias (Ellas) Boudinot (Buddinott) (b. 1706-d. 1770)
Philadelphia, Pa. (c.1733-1752)
Princeton, N.J. (c. 1753-1762)
Bibl. 3, 23, 25, 28, 29, 36, 44, 46, 54, 81

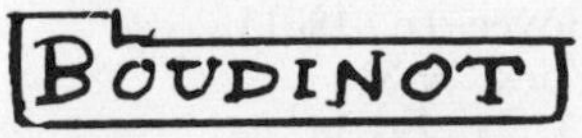

Heloise Boudo (c. 1827-1837, d. 1837)
Charleston, S.C.
Bibl. 5, 25, 44, 54

H BOUDO

Louis Boudo (b. 1786-d. 1829)
Charleston, S.C. (1819-1827)
Maurel & Boudo (c. 1810)
Bibl. 5, 15, 23, 25, 29, 36, 44, 54, 72

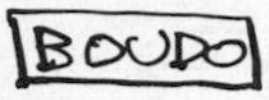

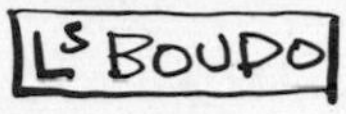

Joseph Bouju (w. 1812-1849)
St. Louis, Mo.
Bibl. 54

J BOUJU

——— Boullien (c. 1811)
Philadelphia, Pa.
Bibl. 3

Mousier Boullien (c. 1811)
Philadelphia, Pa.
Bibl. 23, 36, 44

William Boulton
(See William Bolton)

Bounticou
(See Bontecou)

Stephen Bourdet(t) (c. 1730)
New York, N.Y.
Bibl. 4, 23, 25, 28, 35, 36, 44, 83

Phelix Bourge (w. 1804)
Baltimore, Md.
Bibl. 38

Francis Bourgeois (c. 1799)
Philadelphia, Pa.
Bibl. 3

Mary Bourgeois (c. 1801)
Charleston, S.C.
Bibl. 5

Joseph Bourreus (c. 1820)
Charleston, S.C.
Bibl. 5

Lewis Charles Boute (c. 1839)
Philadelphia, Pa.
Bibl. 3

James Boutelle (c. 1783-1787)
Worcester, Mass.
Bibl. 23, 28, 36, 44

(Widow) Boutier (c. 1824-
1826)
New York, N.Y.
Bibl. 15

John Boutier (c. 1805-1824)
New York, N.Y.
Bibl. 15, 23, 25, 29, 36, 44, 72

J BOUTIER

Joseph Bouvar (c. 1797)
Philadelphia, Pa.
Bibl. 3, 23, 36, 44

Daniel Bouvier (c. 1816)
Putnam, Ohio
Bibl. 34, 44

Bowdle & Needles (w. 1798)
Easton, Md.
James Bowdle
William Needles
Bibl. 38

James Bowdle (c. 1790-1798)
Easton, Md.
Bowdle & Needles (c. 1798)
Bibl. 38

John Bowen (c. 1809)
Philadelphia, Pa.
Bibl. 3

Joseph Morgan Bowene and Mr.
Prentice (w. 1788)
Baltimore, Md.
Bibl. 38

C. Bower (c. 1828-1833)
Philadelphia, Pa.
Bibl. 3, 23, 25, 36, 44

BOWER

Michael Bower (c. 1799)
Philadelphia, Pa.
Bibl. 3

George Bowers (c. 1850)
Philadelphia, Pa.
Bibl. 3

Daniel Bowler (c. 1815)
Providence, R.I.
Bibl. 28

Bowles & Phelps (c. 1828-1829)
Albany, N.Y.
Bibl. 20

Elias Bowman (c. 1834)
Rochester, N.Y.
Bibl. 15, 20, 25, 41, 44

E. BOWMAN

Samuel Bowne (c. 1780-1819)
New York, N.Y.
Bibl. 4, 15, 23, 25, 28, 29, 35,
36, 44, 83

S BOWNE

(Widow) Samuel Bowne (c.
1825-1826)
New York, N.Y.
Bibl. 15

Boyce & Jones (c. 1825-1830)
New York, N.Y.
Geradus Boyce
William Jones (?)
Bibl. 15, 23, 25, 29, 36, 44, 66

B & J   BOYCE & JONES

Geradus (Gheradus) (Jared)
Boyce (c. 1814-1841)
New York, N.Y.
Boyce & Jones (c. 1825-1830)
Bibl. 4, 15, 23, 25, 28, 29, 35,
36, 44

G. BOYCE   G B

James Boyce (c. 1825-1841)
New York, N.Y.
James Boyce & Co. (c. 1836-
1838)
Bibl. 15, 23, 36

James Boyce (c. 1849)
Philadelphia, Pa.
Bibl. 3

James Boyce & Co. (c. 1836-
1838)
New York, N.Y.
Bibl. 15

Jared Boyce
(See Geradus Boyce)

John Boyce (c. 1801)
New York, N.Y.
Bibl. 23, 25, 29, 36, 44

J B

Joseph Boyce (c. 1802-1810)
Philadelphia, Pa.
Bibl. 3

William Boyce (w. 1806)
Baltimore, Md.
Bibl. 38

Boyd & Hoyt (c. 1830-1842)
Albany, N.Y.
William Boyd
George B. Hoyt
Bibl. 20, 23, 25, 28, 36, 44

Boyd & Mulford (c. 1832-1842)
Albany, N.Y.
William Boyd
John H. Mulford
Bibl. 20, 23, 25, 28, 36, 44

BOYD & MULFORD

Boyd & Richards (c. 1808)
Philadelphia, Pa.
Thomas Boyd
———— Richards
Bibl. 3

Ezekiel C. Boyd (c. 1830-1833)
Philadelphia, Pa.
Coats & Boyd (c. 1831) (?)
Bibl. 3

Joseph W. Boyd (c. 1820)
New York, N.Y.
Bibl. 23, 25, 29, 36, 44

J W B

Thomas Boyd (c. 1807-1809)
Philadelphia, Pa.
Boyd & Richards (c. 1808)
Bibl. 3

William Boyd (b. 1775-d. 1840)
Albany, N.Y. (c. 1809-1840)
Shepard & Boyd (c. 1810-1830)
Boyd & Hoyt (c. 1830-1842)
Boyd & Mulford (c. 1832-1842)
Bibl. 20, 23, 28, 36, 44

Boyden & Fenno
Location unknown
Bibl. 54

———— Boyer (c. 1748)
Boston, Mass.
Bibl. 4

Boyer & Austin (c. 1770)
Boston, Mass.
Daniel Boyer
Josiah Austin
Bibl. 25, 44

Daniel Boyer (c. 1726-1779)
Boston, Mass.
Austin & Boyer (c. 1750-1770)

Boyer & Austin (c. 1770)
Bibl. 2, 15, 23, 25, 28, 29, 36,
    44, 54, 69

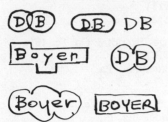

James Boyer (c. 1700-1741)
Boston, Mass.
Bibl. 2, 23, 44, 70

E. Boylston (c. 1789)
Stockbridge, Mass.
Bibl. 28, 44

Edward Boylston (b. 1765-d.
    1836)
Catskill, N.Y.
Manlius, N.Y.
Bibl. 20

Daniel Boyter (c. 1803)
Poughkeepsie, N.Y.
Bibl. 20

Isaac Brabant (d. 1764)
Savannah, Ga.
Bibl. 17, 23, 36, 44

Brackett, Crosby & Brown
    (c. 1850)
Boston, Mass.
Jeffrey R. Brackett
Samuel T. Crosby
—— Brown
Bibl. 28

Jeffrey R. Brackett (c. 1815-
    1876)
Boston, Mass.
Brackett, Crosby & Brown
    (c. 1850)
Bibl. 25, 28, 44

JEFFREY BRACKETT

Francis Braconnier (c. 1826)
New York, N.Y.
Bibl. 15

Bradbury & Brother (c. 1810)
Newburyport, Mass.
Bibl. 23, 28, 36, 44

Edward Bradbury (c. 1819-
    1822)
Philadelphia, Pa.
Bibl. 3

Capt. Phineas Bradbury
    (c. 1779)
New Haven, Conn.
Bibl. 28

Theophilus Bradbury (c. 1815)
Newburyport, Mass.
Moulton & Bradbury (c. 1830)
Bibl. 15, 23, 25, 28, 29, 36, 44

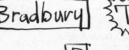

Charles H. Bradford
Westerly, R.I.
Bibl. 28, 44

Joseph Bradford (c. 1842-1843)
Philadelphia, Pa.
Bibl. 3

O. C. Bradford (c. 1841)
Binghamton, N.Y.
Bibl. 20

Simon Bradford (b. 1797)
Lexington, Ky (c. 1814-1819)
Bibl. 32, 54, 68

John Bradier (c. 1802-1804)
Philadelphia, Pa.
Bibl. 3

—— Bradley
Hartford, Conn.
Bradley & Bunce (1830-1835)
Bibl. 16, 23, 36, 44

Bradley & Bunce (c. 1830-1835)
Hartford, Conn.
—— Bradley
—— Bunce
Bibl. 16, 23, 36, 44

Bradley & Merriman (c. 1826-
    1847)
New Haven, Conn.
Zebul Bradley
Marcus Merriman Jr.
Bibl. 16, 23, 25, 28, 29, 36, 44

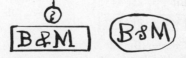

Aner Bradley (b. 1753-d. 1824)
New Haven, Conn.
Watertown, Conn.
Bibl. 16, 23, 25, 28, 29, 36,
    44, 54

A BRADLEY

G. C. Bradley
Binghamton, N.Y. (c. 1841)
Kingston, N.Y. (c. 1842-1843)
Bibl. 20

Gustavus Bradley (c. 1848)
New Haven, Conn.
Zebul Bradley & Son
Bibl. 16, 23

H. G. Bradley (c. 1810)
Mantua, Ohio
Bibl. 34, 44, 88

H. S. Bradley & Co. (c. 1836-
    1850)
Utica, N.Y.
Horace S. Bradley
William Blackwood (c. 1836-
    1838)
Bibl. 18, 20

Horace P. Bradley (c. 1832-
    1841)
Utica, N.Y.
Storrs & Cooley (c. 1831-1839)
Tanner & Cooley (c. 1840-1842)
Bibl. 18, 20

Horace S. Bradley (b. 1805)
Utica, N.Y. (c. 1828-1850)
Leach & Bradley (c. 1832-1835)
H. S. Bradley & Co. (c. 1836-
    1850)
Bibl. 18

Luther Bradley (c. 1772-1830)
New Haven, Conn.
Bibl. 15, 23, 25, 28, 36, 44, 61

Phineas Bradley (c. 1745-1797)
New Haven, Conn.
Bibl. 15, 16, 23, 25, 28, 29, 36,
    39, 44

P B

Richard Bradley (b. 1787-d.
    1867)
Hartford, Conn. (c. 1825-1828)
Bibl. 16, 23, 28, 36, 44

Zebul Bradley (b. 1780-d. 1859)
New Haven, Conn.
Marcus Merriman & Co.
    (c. 1806-1817)

Merriman & Bradley (c. 1817-
1820)
Bradley & Merriman (c. 1826-
1847)
Zebul Bradley & Son (c. 1848)
Bibl. 15, 16, 23, 25, 28, 29, 36,
44, 61

Zebul Bradley & Son (c. 1848)
New Haven, Conn.
Zebul Bradley
Gustavus Bradley
Bibl. 16, 23

William Bradshaw (c. 1809-
1810)
Philadelphia, Pa.
Bibl. 3

E. Brady (c. 1825)
New York, N.Y.
Bibl. 23, 25, 29, 36, 44

John Brady (c. 1835)
Philadelphia, Pa.
Bibl. 3

William Brady (c. 1835)
New York, N.Y.
Bibl. 4, 28

William V. Brady (c. 1834-1841)
New York, N.Y.
Bibl. 15, 23, 36, 44

Frederick Adolphus Brahe
(d. 1892)
Albany, N.Y. (c. 1840-1844)
Augusta, Ga. (c. 1845)
Bibl. 17

F A BRAHE

C. Brainard & Son (1830)
Hartford, Conn.
Charles Brainard
Charles H. Brainard
Bibl. 16, 25, 28, 36, 44

Charles Brainard (b. 1787-d.
1850)
Hartford, Conn.
Ward, Bartholomew & Brainard
(c. 1809-1830)
C. Brainard & Son (Charles H.)
Bibl. 16, 23, 28, 36, 44

Barnet Brakman (c. 1840)
Philadelphia, Pa.
Bibl. 3

E. Braman (c. 1830)
Location unknown
Bibl. 24

E. Braman

S. Bramhall (c. 1863)
Plymouth, Mass.
Bibl. 23, 25, 28, 29, 36, 44

S BRAMHALL

Bartlett M. Bramhill (c. 1820)
Boston, Mass.
Davis, Watson & Co.
Bibl. 25, 28, 29

C. Brand (c. 1820)
Philadelphia, Pa. (?)
Bibl. 89

Thomas Brand (c. 1837-1842)
Troy, N.Y.
Bibl. 20

Charles Branda
Philadelphia, Pa. (c. 1817)
Norfolk, Va. (c. 1818-1829)
Bibl. 19

C. BRANDA

James Brander (c. 1813)
Charleston, S.C.
Bibl. 5

Brandt & Mathey (c. 1795-1799)
Philadelphia, Pa.
————— Brandt
Lewis Mathey
Bibl. 3

Brandt (Brant), Brown &
Lewis (c. 1795-1796)
Philadelphia, Pa.
Bibl. 3

Aime Brandt (c. 1816-1831)
Philadelphia, Pa.
Aime & Charles Brandt
(c. 1800-1814)
Bibl. 3

Aime & Charles Brandt (c.
1800-1814)
Philadelphia, Pa.
Bibl. 3, 25, 44, 54

A & C BRANDT

Charles Brandt
Philadelphia, Pa.

Aime & Charles Brandt
(c. 1800-1814)
Charles Brandt & Co. (c. 1816-
1818)
Bibl. 3

Charles Brandt & Co. (c. 1816-
1818)
Philadelphia, Pa.
Bibl. 3

Barnet Brannan (c. 1840)
Philadelphia, Pa.
Bibl. 3

Bernard Brannan (c. 1842-1848)
Philadelphia, Pa.
Bibl. 3

Rees Branson (b. 1771)
Martinsburg, Va. (c. 1802-1809)
Bibl. 19

Brasher & Alexander (c. 1800)
New York, N.Y.
Bibl. 23, 36, 44

Amable Brasher (c. 1790-1840)
New York, N.Y.
(See Amable Brasier)
Bibl. 23, 25, 29, 36, 44

A. BRASHER

E. Brasher & Co. (c. 1790)
New York, N.Y.
Ephraim Brasher
Bibl. 23, 36, 44

E B & Co

Ephraim Brasher (b. 1744-d.
1810)
New York, N.Y.
E. Brasher & Co. (c. 1790)
Bibl. 4, 15, 23, 25, 28, 29, 30,
35, 36, 44, 54

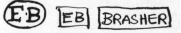

Amable Brasier (c. 1794-1828)
Philadelphia, Pa.
(See Amable Brasher)
Bibl. 3, 15, 28, 29, 72, 78, 79

A BRASIER

Francis Brasier (c. 1824)
Philadelphia, Pa.
Bibl. 3

John Brassington (c. 1820-   )
Alexandria, Va.
Bibl. 19

Henry Bray (c. 1799-1813)
Philadelphia, Pa.
Bibl. 3, 23, 36, 44

Thomas Bray (c. 1799)
Augusta, Ga.
Bibl. 17

C. L. Bready (c. 1808)
Philadelphia, Pa.
Bibl. 3

John Breans (c. 1825)
Philadelphia, Pa.
Bibl. 3

James Brearley (c. 1795-1822)
Philadelphia, Pa.
Bibl. 3

Louis Brechémin (c. 1816-1850)
Philadelphia, Pa.
Laret & Brechémin (c. 1816-
   1818)
Bibl. 3

Joseph Hunt Breck (c. 1789-
   1801, d. 1801)
New England
Bibl. 84

John Breed (b. 1752-d. 1803)
Colchester, Conn.
Bibl. 16, 23, 28, 36, 44

William Breed (c. 1750)
Boston, Mass.
Bibl. 15, 23, 25, 28, 29, 36, 44, 69

Lamon Brees (c. 1837)
Wellsburg, Va.
Bibl. 19

L. Breidenbauch (c. 1807)
Philadelphia, Pa.
Bibl. 3

Brelet, Wearer & Co. (c. 1825)
Augusta, Ga.
Francis Brelet
William Wearer
John Guimarin
Bibl. 17

Francis Brelet (c. 1824-   )
Augusta, Ga.
Guimarin & Brelet (c. 1824)
Brelet, Wearer & Co. (c. 1825)
Bibl. 17

Brem & Alexander (c. 1848)
Charlotte, N.C.
——— Brem
Samuel P. Alexander
Bibl. 21

Barnabas Brennan (c. 1843)
Philadelphia, Pa.
Bibl. 3

Brenno & Co. (c. 1818)
Philadelphia, Pa.
John Brenno
Bibl. 3

John Brenno (c. 1824)
Philadelphia, Pa.
Brenno & Co. (c. 1818)
Bibl. 3

Benjamin Brenon (b. 1686-d.
   1740)
Newport, R.I.
(See next entry)
Bibl. 54

B B

Benjamin Brenton (b. 1695 or
   1710?—c. 1731)
Newport, R.I.
(See preceding entry)
Bibl. 15, 23, 25, 28, 29, 36,
   44, 56, 72

B B   B B

——— Breorbey (c. 1799)
Philadelphia, Pa.
Bingham & Breorbey
Bibl. 3

John Breslin (c. 1828-1833)
Philadelphia, Pa.
Bibl. 3

John Brevoort (b. 1715-d.
   1775)
New York, N.Y.
Bibl. 4, 15, 23, 25, 28, 29, 35,
   36, 44, 54

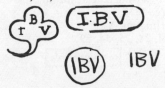

Brewer & Mann (c. 1803-1805)
Middletown, Conn.
Charles Brewer
Alexander Mann
Bibl. 16, 23, 28, 36, 44

C. Brewer & Co. (c. 1810)
Middletown, Conn.
Bibl. 15, 23, 25, 36

C. BREWER & CO.

Charles Brewer (b. 1778-d.
   1860)
Middletown, Conn.
Hart & Brewer (c. 1800-1803)
Brewer & Mann (c. 1803-1805)
Bibl. 15, 16, 25, 28, 29, 36,
   61, 78

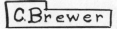

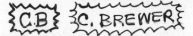

Charles Brewer (c. 1824)
New York, N.Y.
Moore & Brewer (c. 1824-1844)
Bibl. 15, 44

N. Alexander F. Brewer
   (c. 1842-1847)
Charlotte, N.C.
Lawing & Brewer (c. 1842-
   1843)
Bibl. 5, 21

Thomas A. Brewer (c. 1830-
   1850)
Philadelphia, Pa.
Bibl. 3

William Brewer (c. 1774-1824)
Philadelphia, Pa.
Bibl. 3

——— Brewington (c. 1711)
Charleston, S.C.
Bibl. 5

Abel Brewster (b. 1775, c. 1797-
   1805)
Canterbury, Conn.
Norwich, Conn.
Bibl. 16, 23, 25, 28, 36, 44

BREWSTER

Samuel Bricknall (c. 1817)
Philadelphia, Pa.
Bibl. 3

Benjamin Bridge (c. 1797)
Rutland, Vt.
Bibl. 54

John Bridge (b. 1723, c. 1751)
Boston, Mass.
Bibl. 2, 4, 15, 23, 25, 28, 29, 36,
44

Joseph Brier (c. 1849-1850)
Philadelphia, Pa.
Bibl. 3, 23

Robert Brier (c. 1848)
Philadelphia, Pa.
Bibl. 3, 23

Thomas Brigan (c. 1832)
Louisville, Ky.
Bibl. 32, 54

C. Brigden (c. 1770)
Boston, Mass.
Bibl. 23, 29, 36, 44

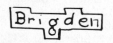

Timothy Brigden (Brigdon)
    (c. 1774-1819)
Albany, N.Y.
Bibl. 15, 20, 23, 25, 28, 36,
    44, 54

Zachariah Brigden (b. 1734-d.
    1787)
Boston, Mass.
Bibl. 2, 15, 23, 25, 28, 29, 36,
    39, 44, 54, 72

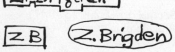

C. Brigdens (c. 1770)
Boston, Mass.
Bibl. 4, 28

C. B

Brigdon
(See Timothy Brigden)

Briggs
(See Akerly & Briggs)

Briggs & Harlow
Location unknown
Bibl. 89

Daniel Briggs (c. 1836)
New York, N.Y.
Bibl. 15

William W. Briggs (c. 1834-
    1836)
New York, N.Y.
Bibl. 15

John Brigham (c. 1678)
Location unknown
Bibl. 28

Anthony Bright (d. 1749)
Philadelphia, Pa. (c. 1739)
Bibl. 3, 23, 28, 36, 44

Abraham Brindsmaid (c. 1815)
Burlington, Vt.
Bibl. 44

A BRINDSMAID

———— Bringhurst (c. 1850)
Maine or New Hampshire
Bibl. 28

BRINGHURST

Joseph Bringhurst (c. 1813)
Philadelphia, Pa.
Bibl. 3

William Brinkley (c. 1802)
New York, N.Y.
Bibl. 28, 36

William Brinkley (c. 1802-
    1810)
New York, N.Y.
Bibl. 23, 44

Brin(d)smaid & Hildreth
    (c. 1830)
Burlington, Vt.
Bibl. 24, 25, 54, 89

B & H   BRINSMAID'S

Brinsmaid's
(See Brin[d]smaid & Hildreth)
(See Pangborn & Brinsmaid)

Henry Brinsmaid (c. 1847-
    1850-   )
Rochester, N.Y.
Bibl. 20

Brinton, Gordon & Quick
    (Quirk) (c. 1780)
Boston, Mass.
Bibl. 23, 28, 36, 44

F. Brintzinghoffer (c. 1804)
Philadelphia, Pa.
Bibl. 3

Brittain
(See Beckwith & Brittain)

Isaac Britton (Brittin) (c. 1811-
    1816)
Philadelphia, Pa.
Bibl. 3, 23, 36, 44

Jacob Britton (Brittin)
    (c. 1807-1850)
Philadelphia, Pa.
Bibl. 3, 23, 36, 39, 44

Thomas Britton (Brittin)
    (c. 1848-1850)
Philadelphia, Pa.
Bibl. 3

James Broadbridge (c. 1806-
    1832)
Newburgh, N.Y.
Bibl. 20

Samuel Broadhurst (c. 1724)
New York, N.Y.
Bibl. 4, 23, 28, 36, 44

Charles P. Brocha (c. 1833)
Philadelphia, Pa.
Bibl. 3

Charles Brochet (c. 1819-1822)
Philadelphia, Pa.
Bibl. 3

Charles B. Brochett (c. 1831)
Philadelphia, Pa.
Bibl. 3

John Brock (c. 1831-1841)
New York, N.Y.
Bibl. 4, 15, 23, 25, 28, 29, 36, 44

72 CHATHAM ST

J.B   J. BROCK

L. Brock (c. 1830)
New York, N.Y.
(May be John Brock)
Bibl. 23, 25, 29, 36, 44

[L. BROCK]

F. C. Brockman (c. 1821-1844)
Cincinnati, Ohio
Bibl. 34

John Brodnox (b. 1668-d. 1719)
Williamsburg, Va.
Bibl. 19

John Bronaugh (c. 1817-1827)
Richmond, Va.
Bibl. 19, 54

[BRONAUGH]

Robert Brookhouse (b. 1778-d.
   1866)
Salem, Mass. (c. 1750)
Bibl. 15, 23, 25, 28, 29, 36, 44

(R·B)

Brooks
(See Trott & Brooks)

Brooks & Griswold (c. 1832)
Utica, N.Y.
Benjamin Franklin Brooks
Joab Griswold
Bibl. 18, 20

Brooks & Hone (c. 1858)
Utica, N.Y.
Benjamin Franklin Brooks
———— Hone
Bibl. 18, 20

Brooks & Van Voorhis
   (c. 1843)
Utica, N.Y.
Benjamin Franklin Brooks
———— Van Voorhis
Bibl. 18, 20

Brooks & Warrock (c. 1795-
   1796-   )
Norfolk, Va.
Samuel Brooks
William Warrock
Bibl. 19

   BROOKS & WARROCK

B. F. Brooks & Co. (c. 1829-
   1831)
Utica, N.Y.

Benjamin Franklin Brooks
Gaylord Griswold
Bibl. 18, 20

B. F. Brooks & Son (c. 1855)
Utica, N.Y.
Benjamin Franklin Brooks
Bibl. 18, 20

Benjamin Franklin Brooks
   (c. 1828-1858)
Utica, N.Y.
Blackwood & Brooks (c. 1828-
   1830)
B. F. Brooks & Co. (c. 1829-
   1831)
Brooks & Griswold (c. 1832)
Brooks & Van Voorhis
   (c. 1843)
B. F. Brooks & Son (c. 1855)
Brooks & Hone (c. 1858)
Bibl. 18, 20

Charles V. Brooks (c. 1834-
   1838)
Utica, N.Y.
B. F. Brooks & Co.
Bibl. 18, 20

Nicholas Brooks (1775)
Philadelphia, Pa.
Bibl. 44

Samuel Brooks
Philadelphia, Pa. (c. 1790)
Norfolk, Va. (c. 1794)
Richmond, Va. (c. 1803-1820)
Brooks & Warrock (c. 1795-
   1796-   )
Bibl. 3, 19, 23, 25, 29, 36, 44

{ Brooks }

Brookway & Bacon (c. 1836)
Louisville, Ky.
Bibl. 32

Broom & Clement (c. 1837)
Philadelphia, Pa.
William Broom (?)
James W. Clement (?)
Bibl. 3

William Broom (c. 1833-1837)
Philadelphia, Pa.
Broom & Clement (c. 1837) (?)
Bibl. 3

William Broom Jr. (c. 1835)
Philadelphia, Pa.
Bibl. 3

Lewis R. Broomall (c. 1846-
   1850)
Philadelphia, Pa.
Bibl. 3

William Broome (c. 1825-1850)
Philadelphia, Pa.
Bibl. 3

Peter S. Broshey (c. 1829-1831)
Philadelphia, Pa.
Bibl. 3

Michael Brothe(a)rs (c. 1772-
   1773)
Philadelphia, Pa.
Bibl. 3, 23, 36, 44

T. Brothers (c. 1830-1835)
Philadelphia, Pa.
Bibl. 3

George Brougham (w. 1774)
Maryland
Bibl. 38

Brower & Rusher (c. 1834)
New York, N.Y.
Bibl. 23, 25, 28, 29, 35, 36, 44,
   83

[B & R]

B. D. Brower & Son (c. 1850)
Albany, N.Y.
Bibl. 23

J. H. Brower (c. 1848-1849)
Albany, N.Y.
Bibl. 20

S. & B. Brower (c. 1810-1850)
Albany, N.Y.
Bibl. 23, 25, 29, 36, 44

[S & B BROWER]

S. Douglas Brower
Troy, N.Y. (c. 1832-1836)
New York, N.Y. (c. 1834)
Albany, N.Y. (c. 1837-1850)
Brower & Rusher (c. 1834)
Hall, Hewson & Co. (c. 1836-
   1842)
Hall, Brower & Co. (c. 1836-
   1842)
Hall & Hewson (c. 1842-1847)
Hall, Hewson & Brower
   (c. 1847-1850)
Hall and Brower (c. 1852-1854)
Bibl. 20, 23, 25, 28, 36, 44

Walter S. Brower (c. 1850-
   1898)

Albany, N.Y.
Bibl. 23, 29, 44

Brown
(See Crosby & Brown)
(See Davis & Brown)
(See Leavenworth Brown & Co.)
(See Packard & Brown)
(See Shreve, Brown & Co.)
(See Watson & Brown)

Brown & Anderson (c. 1850-
1871)
Wilmington, N.C.
Thomas William Brown
William S. Anderson
Bibl. 21

Brown & Dart
Location unknown
Bibl. 89

Brown(e) & Houlton (c. 1799)
Baltimore, Md.
John Houlton
Liberty Brown
Bibl. 39

Brown & Kirby (c. 1850)
New Haven, Conn.
Bibl. 25, 44

Brown & Mann (c. 1805)
Connecticut
Bibl. 28

Brown & Stout
(c. 1811)
Philadelphia, Pa.
Bibl. 3, 46

Alexander Brown (c. 1840-
1847)
Philadelphia, Pa.
Bibl. 3, 23, 36, 44

Chancey Brown (c. 1845)
Philadelphia, Pa.
Bibl. 3

Charles Brown (c. 1829-1833)
Philadelphia, Pa.
Bibl. 3

Charles C. Brown (b. 1827-d.
1871)
Rochester, N.Y.
Bibl. 20, 41, 44

D. Brown (c. 1811)
Philadelphia, Pa.
Bibl. 15, 23, 25, 28, 29, 36, 44

| D BROWN |

E. Brown
(See John Eden Brown)

Ebenezer Brown (c. 1773-1816)
Boston, Mass.
Bibl. 23, 28, 36, 44

Edward Brown (c. 1816-1830)
Baltimore, Md. (c. 1807-1808)
Liberty, Va. (c. 1817)
Lynchburg, Va. (c. 1824)
Bibl. 19, 54

| BROWN | | E BROWN |

Elnathan C. Brown (18th
century)
Westerly, R.I.
Bibl. 28, 44, 56

Francis Brown (c. 1837-1844)
New York, N.Y.
Jared L. Moore & Co.
Bibl. 15

George Brown (c. 1830)
Barnesville, Ohio
Bibl. 34

Henry Brown (c. 1777)
(Henry Brown Guest)
Philadelphia, Pa.
Bibl. 3, 23, 36, 44

Henry S. Brown (c. 1850)
New York, N.Y.
Bibl. 23

Henry S. Brown (b. 1833)
Syracuse, N.Y. (c. 1851-1852)
Utica, N.Y. (c. 1853-1860)
Bibl. 18, 20

Isaac C. Brown (c. 1844)
Philadelphia, Pa.
Bibl. 3, 23

James Brown (c. 1785)
Philadelphia, Pa.
Bibl. 3; 23, 36, 44

James Brown (w. 1792)
Baltimore, Md.
Bibl. 38

James Brown (c. 1800)
Detroit, Mich.
Bibl. 58

| I B | ?

James Brown (c. 1772-1808)
Fredericksburg, Va.
Bibl. 19

Jesse Brown (c. 1813-1817)
Baltimore, Md. (w. 1819)
Philadelphia, Pa.
Bibl. 3, 23, 36, 38, 44

John Brown (c. 1785-1824)
Philadelphia, Pa.
Baltimore, Md. (1799) (?)
Bibl. 3, 23, 25, 28, 29, 36, 38, 44

| J. B |

John Brown (c. 1777)
Port Royal, Va.
Bibl. 19

John Eden Brown (w. 1810-
1816)
Baltimore, Md.
Bibl. 38

John J. Brown (c. 1848-1852)
Utica, N.Y.
Bailey & Brothers (c. 1846-
1852)
Bibl. 18, 20

L. Brown (c. 1838)
Rochester, N.Y.
Bibl. 20, 41, 44

L. S. F. Brown (c. 1872)
Wilmington, N.C.
T. W. Brown & Sons
Bibl. 21

Lester Brown (c. 1843)
Cazenovia, N.Y.
Clark & Brown
Bibl. 20

Levi Brown (c. 1866)
Detroit, Mich,
Chauncey S. Payne
Bibl. 58

Liberty Brown (c. 1801)
Philadelphia, Pa.
Bibl. 36, 44

| LBrown |

Liberty Brown(e) (c. 1801-
1819)
Baltimore, Md.
Philadelphia, Pa.
Brown & Houlton (c. 1799)
Browne & Seale (c. 1810-
1811)

Bibl. 3, 15, 23, 25, 39, 44

M. S. Brown & Co. (c. 1835)
Shepherdstown, Va.
Bibl. 19

Martin S. Brown
Winchester, Va. (c. 1827)
Shepherdstown, Va. (c. 1829-
1838)
Bibl. 19

Philip Brown (c. 1841)
Philadelphia, Pa.
Bibl. 3

R. Brown & Son (c. 1830)
Baltimore, Md.
Bibl. 24

R. BROWN & SON

R. J. Brown & Son (c. 1833)
Boston, Mass.
Bibl. 25, 44

Robert Brown (c. 1774)
Savannah, Ga.
Pinkerd & Brown
Bibl. 17

Robert Brown (c. 1827-1831)
Baltimore, Md.
Bibl. 15, 23, 24, 29, 36, 38

R BROWN

Robert Brown & Son
(1833-   )
Baltimore, Md.
Bibl. 29, 38

R BROWN & SON

Robert Johnson Brown (c.
1813)
Boston, Mass.
Bibl. 25, 44

ROBERT J. BROWN

S. Brown (c. 1815-1834)
New York, N.Y.
Bibl. 15, 28, 44, 54

S BROWN   S BROWN

S. D. Brown (1834)
Albany, N.Y.
Bibl. 44

Samuel C. Brown (c. 1820-
1850)
New York, N.Y.
Bibl. 15, 23, 24, 25, 29, 36, 44

S. BROWN

Seth E. Brown
Location unknown
Bibl. 15, 44

T. J. Brown (c. 1835)
Location unknown
Bibl. 28

T. J. BROWN

T. W. Brown & Sons (c. 1872)
Wilmington, N.C.
Thomas William Brown
L. S. F. Brown
E. F. Story
Bibl. 21

Theodore G. Brown (after
1825)
New York, N.Y.
Bibl. 23

Theodore G. Brown & Son (c.
1840)
New York, N.Y.
Bibl. 23

Thomas Brown (c. 1827-1835)
New York, N.Y.
Bibl. 15

Thomas William Brown (b.
1803-d. 1872)
Wilmington, N.C.
Brown & Anderson (c. 1850-
1871)
T. W. Brown & Sons (c. 1872)
Bibl. 21

William Brown (c. 1810)
Baltimore, Md.
Bibl. 15, 25, 44

WM BROWN

William Brown (c. 1845-1849)
Albany, N.Y.

Bibl. 23, 25, 28, 44, 54

W. BROWN

William Brown (c. 1823-1847)
Philadelphia, Pa.
Bibl. 3

William H. Brown (c. 1848-
1849)
Philadelphia, Pa.
Bibl. 3

William S. Brown (c. 1849-
1850)
Philadelphia, Pa.
Bibl. 3

Brown(e) & Kirby (c. 1825)
Philadelphia, Pa.
Bibl. 24

BROWN & KIRBY

Browne & Seale (c. 1810-1811)
Philadelphia, Pa.
Liberty Brown(e)
William Seal(e) (Jr.)
Bibl. 3, 15, 23, 24, 25, 28, 36,
39, 44, 72

Hiram Brownson (c. 1841-1842)
Troy, N.Y.
Bibl. 20

Robert Bruce (c. 1772-1774)
Williamsburg, Va.
Bibl. 19

Thaddeus Bruder (c. 1837)
Philadelphia, Pa.
Bibl. 3

Charles Oliver Bruff (b. 1731-d.
1787)
Elizabeth, N.J. (c. 1760-1765)
New York, N.Y. (c. 1765-
1776)
Nova Scotia (c. 1783-1787)
Bibl. 3, 15, 23, 24, 25, 28, 29,
44, 46, 50, 54

James Bruff (d. 1780)
Elizabeth, N.J. (c. 1748-1765)
New York, N.Y. (c. 1766)
Bibl. 46, 54

Joseph Bruff (b.c. 1730-1785)
Easton, Md. (w. 1750-1785)
Bibl. 3, 15, 24, 25, 29, 44

I. BRUFF   I B

Joseph Bruff (b.c. 1770-d.
1803)
Easton, Md. (w. 1790-1800)
Chestertown, Md. (w. 1800-
1803)
Bibl. 29, 38

I. BRUFF

Joseph Bruff (c. 1767)
Philadelphia, Pa.
Bibl. 23, 28, 36

Thomas Bruff (b. 1760-d.
1803)
Easton, Md. (c. 1785-1791)
Chestertown, Md. (c. 1791-
1803)
Bibl. 25, 29, 44

T. BRUFF   T BRUFF

———— Bruleman (c. 1760)
Philadelphia, Pa.
Bibl. 3

Paul Bruneau (c. 1819)
Philadelphia, Pa.
Bibl. 3

Bruno & Virgins (c. 1840-1849)
Columbus, Ga.
Macon, Ga.
———— Bruno
Samuel Stanley Virgin(s)
Bibl. 17

George Bruns (b. 1839-d. 1920)
Columbia, S.C. (c. 1855-1914)
Bibl. 5

Isaac Brunson (c. 1800)
Detroit, Mich.
Bibl. 58

I B

Edward Brush (c. 1774)
New York, N.Y.
Bibl. 23, 36, 44

James Bryan (19th century)
Kentucky (?)

Bibl. 32

JAMES BRYAN

John Bryan (c. 1749)
Williamsburg, Va.
Bibl. 19

Philip Bryan (c. 1802)
Philadelphia, Pa.
Bibl. 24

Phil(l)ip Bryan (c. 1802-1803)
Philadelphia, Pa.
Bibl. 3, 12, 23, 25, 29, 44

BRYAN

Butler Bryant (c. 1838-1848)
Frankfort, Ky.
Louisville, Ky.
Bibl. 32

Edward (Edmund) A. Bryson
(c. 1841-1848)
Louisville, Ky.
Bibl. 32

Charles W. Buard (c. 1849)
Philadelphia, Pa.
Bibl. 3

Stanton Bube (c. 1805)
Providence, R.I.
George C. Clark
Bibl. 28

Peter Buche(z) (c. 1795-1797)
New York, N.Y.
Bibl. 23, 36, 44

John B. Buchey (c. 1818-1819)
Philadelphia, Pa.
Bibl. 3

I. R. Buchoz
(See next entry)

L. R. Buchoz (c. 1835)
New York, N.Y.
Bibl. 23, 36, 44

Azariah Buck (c. 1847-1850)
Rochester, N.Y.
Bibl. 20, 41, 44

Solomon Buck (c. 1827-1828)
Glen Falls, N.Y.
Bibl. 20

Buckhey & Anderson (c. 1804)
Philadelphia, Pa.
Bibl. 3, 44

Daniel Buckins
(See Bockius)

Daniel Buckius
(See Bockius)

Buckley & Anderson (c. 1804)
Philadelphia, Pa.
J. B. Buckley
———— Anderson
Bibl. 23, 36, 44

J. B. Buckley (c. 1807)
Philadelphia, Pa.
Buckley & Anderson
Bibl. 3, 23, 24, 25, 36, 44

BUCKLEY

Samuel Buckley (c. 1811)
Philadelphia, Pa.
Bibl. 3

George Buckman (w. 1802)
Baltimore, Md.
Bibl. 38

Samuel Bucknell (c. 1825)
Philadelphia, Pa.
Bibl. 3

Buddinott
(See Boudinot)

Daniel Buddy (c. 1769)
Philadelphia, Pa.
Bibl. 3, 23, 36, 44

Buel & Greenleaf (c. 1798)
New Haven, Conn.
Abel Buel(l)
———— Greenleaf
Bibl. 23, 25, 36, 44

Buel & Mix (c. 1783)
New Haven, Conn.
Abel Buel
———— Mix
Bibl. 23, 28, 36, 44

Abel Buel(l) (b. 1742-d. 1825)
New Haven, Conn. (c.-1783,
c. 1798)
Hartford, Conn.
Killingworth, Conn.
Buel & Mix (c. 1783)
Buel & Greenleaf (c. 1798)
Ebenezer Chittenden
Bibl. 2, 15, 16, 23, 24, 25, 28,
29, 36, 44, 47, 54, 61

D. H. Buel (c. 1763 ? 1825 ?)
Hartford, Conn.
Bibl. 23, 36, 44

John Buel (b. 1744-d. 1783)
Derby, Conn.
New Haven, Conn.
Bibl. 16, 23, 28, 36, 44

Samuel Buel(l) (b. 1742-d. 1819)
Middletown, Conn. (c. 1777)
Hartford, Conn. (c. 1780)
Bibl. 15, 16, 23, 24, 25, 28, 29, 44, 61

S B

William Buel
Rupert, Vt. (c. 1787-1790)
Fair Haven, Vt. (c. 1790-1796)
Bibl. 54

C. I. Buel (c. 1846)
Saratoga Springs, N.Y.
Bibl. 20

Charles I. Buel (c. 1849)
Schenectady, N.Y.
Bibl. 20

Lewis Buichle (c. 1798-1802)
Baltimore, Md.
Bibl. 25, 29, 38, 44

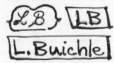

Bull & Morrison (c. 1780)
Hartford, Conn.
Caleb Bull
Norman Morrison
Bibl. 23, 36, 44

Caleb Bull (b. 1746-d. 1797)
Hartford, Conn.
Bull & Morrison (c. 1780)
Bibl. 16, 23, 28, 36, 44

Epaphras Bull (c. 1813)
Boston, Mass.
Bibl. 23, 36, 44

G. W. Bull (c. 1840)
Farmington, Conn.
Bibl. 23, 25, 29, 36, 44

G. W. BULL

Martin Bull (b. 1744-d. 1825)
Farmington, Conn.
Thomas Lee
Bibl. 16, 23, 28, 36, 44

Bulles & Childs (c. 1840)
Hartford, Conn.
Bibl. 25, 44

John Buly (c. 1778)
Philadelphia, Pa.
Bibl. 3, 44

Bumm & Shepper (c. 1818-1823)
Philadelphia, Pa.
Peter Bumm (?)
John D. Shepper
Bibl. 3, 4, 23, 25, 28, 36, 44

John S. Bumm (c. 1837-1850)
Philadelphia, Pa.
Bibl. 3

Peter Bumm (c. 1814-1833)
Philadelphia, Pa.
Whartenby and Bumm (c. 1816-1818) (?)
Bumm & Shepper (c. 1818-1823) (?)
Bibl. 3, 23, 36, 44

———— Bunce
Hartford, Conn.
Bradley & Bunce (c. 1830-1835)
Bibl. 16, 23, 36, 44

H. Bunce (c. 1801)
Augusta, Ga.
Bibl. 17

Benjamin Bunker (b. 1751-d. 1842)
Nantucket Island, Mass.
Bibl. 12, 15, 25, 44

Benjamin Bunker (c. 1810)
Providence, R.I.
Bibl. 23, 28, 36

Francis Bunnell (c. 1850)
Syracuse, N.Y.
Bibl. 20

Daniel Bunting (c. 1844)
Philadelphia, Pa.
Bibl. 3

Buntz
(See Bradford & Buntz)

A. F. Burbank (c. 1845)
Worcester, Mass.
Bibl. 25, 44

A. F. BURBANK

A. F. B.

Albert Burd (c. 1823-1824)
Philadelphia, Pa.
Bibl. 3

Charles Burd (c. 1850)
Philadelphia, Pa.
Bibl. 3

Burdick & Burritt (c. 1816-1819)
Ithaca, N.Y.
William P. Burdick
Joseph Burritt
Bibl. 20

William P. Burdick (c. 1815)
Ithaca, N.Y.
Burdick & Burritt (c. 1816-1819)
Bibl. 20

William S. Burdick (c. 1810-1814)
New Haven, Conn.
Ufford & Burdick (c. 1812-1814-   )
Bibl. 16, 23, 28, 36, 44

George Burdock (Bordick) (c. 1790-1811)
Philadelphia, Pa.
Bibl. 3, 23, 36, 44

Nicholas Burdock (c. 1797)
Philadelphia, Pa.
Bibl. 3, 23, 25, 28, 29, 36, 44, 72

N. B

J. P. Burgalie (c. 1799)
New York, N.Y.
Bibl. 23, 36, 44

Frederick Burge (c. 1766)
Bound Brook, N.J.
Bibl. 54

Burger & Prichard (c. 1776)
New York, N.Y.
Bibl. 35, 83

David I. Burger (c. 1805-1835)
New York, N.Y.
Bibl. 15, 23, 24, 25, 29, 36, 44

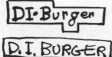

John Burger (c. 1786-1807)
New York, N.Y.
Bibl. 4, 15, 23, 24, 25, 28, 29, 35, 36, 39, 44, 54, 72, 83

Joseph Burger (c. 1830-1831)
Philadelphia, Pa.
Bibl. 3

Thomas Burger (c. 1805)
New York, N.Y.
Bibl. 15, 23, 24, 25, 35, 36, 44, 83

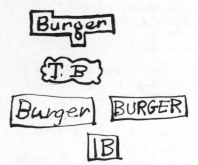

Thomas & John Burger (c. 1805)
New York, N.Y.
Bibl. 15, 25

Leonard G. Burgess (c. 1831-1850)
Albany, N.Y.
Bibl. 20

Frederick Burgi (c. 1766-1776)
Bound Brook, N.J.

Hurtin & Burgi
Bibl. 46

Robert Burham (Burnham) (c. 1790)
New York, N.Y.
Bibl. 23, 36, 44

Charles Burk (c. 1848)
Philadelphia, Pa.
Bibl. 3

———— Burke (c. 1790)
Location unknown
Bibl. 24

BURKE

E. K. Burke (c. 1842)
St. Louis, Mo.
Bibl. 54

Edmund K. Burke (c. 1841)
Louisville, Ky.
Bibl. 32

Samuel Burkelow (Burkloe) (c. 1790-1813)
Philadelphia, Pa.
Bibl. 3, 23, 36, 44

Thomas F. Burkhand (c. 1837-1843)
Philadelphia, Pa.
Bibl. 3

Trubert Burkhart (c. 1839-1846)
Philadelphia, Pa.
Bibl. 3

Burkloe
(See Burkelow)

John Burn (c. 1823-1824)
Philadelphia, Pa.
Bibl. 3

Daniel Burnap (b. 1760-d. 1838)
Coventry, Conn.
East Windsor, Conn.
Bibl. 16, 23, 28, 36, 44

Ela Burnap
Boston, Mass. (c. 1810)
New York (c. 1817)
Hartford, Conn. (c. 1813)
Eatonton, Ga. (c. 1821)
Rochester, N.Y. (c. 1827-1844)
Bibl. 15, 17, 20, 25, 28, 41, 44

E Burnap

Burnet(t) & Ryder (c. 1795)
Philadelphia, Pa.
Bibl. 23, 24, 25, 29, 36

Aaron Lee Burnet (c. 1820)
Charleston, S.C.
Bibl. 5

Samuel Burnet (c. 1796)
Newark, N.J.
Philadelphia, Pa.
Burnet(t) & Rider (Ryder) (c. 1795)
Bibl. 23, 36, 44

Smith Burnet (b. 1770-d. 1830)
Newark, N.J. (c. 1793-1830)
Bibl. 16, 54

B. L. Burnett
Milledgeville, Ga. (c. 1847-1848)
Macon, Ga. (c. 1847-1857)
Lexington, Ky. (c. 1857)
C. K. Wentworth & Co. (c. 1847)
Bibl. 17, 32, 54, 68

Charles A. Burnett (c. 1785-1849)
Georgetown, D.C.
Alexandria, Va.
Bibl. 15, 19, 23, 24, 25, 28, 29, 36, 44, 46, 54

C A B   C A BURNETT

Lawrence Burney (Birnie) (c. 1774-1779)
Philadelphia, Pa.
Bibl. 3

Charles E. Burnham
Utica, N.Y. (c. 1853-1854)
Binghamton, N.Y. (c. 1857)
Bibl. 18, 20

E. B. Burnham (c. 1821)
Salisbury, N.C.
Elliott & Burnham
Bibl. 21

John Burnham (c. 1776)
Brattleboro, Vt.
Bibl. 54

P. B. Burnham (c. 1856)
Greenville, S.C.
P. B. Burnham & Co.
Bibl. 5

P. B. Burnham & Co. (c. 1860)
Greenville, S.C.
Bibl. 89

Robert Burnham
(See Robert Burham)

(Miss) Burns (c. 1810)
Washington, Ga.
Bibl. 17

(Mr.) Burns (c. 1837-1854)
Greenville, S.C.
Isaac H. Benedict
Bibl. 5

Andrew Burns (c. 1796)
Louisville, Ga.
Bibl. 17

Anthony Burns (c. 1785)
Philadelphia, Pa.
Bibl. 3, 23, 36, 44

Hugh Burns (c. 1809-1811, d.
1812)
Philadelphia, Pa.
Bibl. 3

James Burns (c. 1784-1799)
(See James Byrne)

James Burns (c. 1810)
Philadelphia, Pa.
Bibl. 23, 36, 44

John H. Burns (c. 1834-1841)
New York, N.Y.
Bibl. 15, 23, 36, 44

Andrew Burot (o. 1819-1827)
Baltimore, Md.
Bibl. 4, 23, 28, 36, 38, 44

Burr & Lee (c. 1815)
Providence, R.I.
Samuel W. Lee
Ezekiel Burr
Bibl. 23, 25, 36, 41, 48

Albert Chapin Burr (b. 1806-d.
1832)
Providence, R.I. (c. 1815-1825)
Rochester, N.Y. (c. 1826-1832)
Bibl. 15, 20, 24, 25, 28, 36, 41,
44

Alexander Jay Burr (b. 1810-d.
1838)
Rochester, N.Y. (c. 1832-1838)
Bibl. 20, 41, 44

C. A. Burr & Co. (before 1863)
Rochester, N.Y.

Cornelius A. Burr
John T. Fox
Bibl. 15, 20, 23, 36, 41, 44

C. A. BURR & CO.

Christopher Burr (c. 1800-d.
1825)
Providence, R.I.
George C. (G.) Clark (c. 1813-
1824)
Bibl. 15, 23, 25, 28, 29, 36, 44,
56

Cornelius A. Burr (b. 1816-d.
1863)
Rochester, N.Y. (c. 1838-1850)
Brooklyn, N.Y. (before 1863)
C. A. Burr & Co. (before 1863)
Bibl. 20, 25, 41, 44

E. & W. Burr (c. 1793)
Providence, R.I.
Ezekiel Burr
William Burr
Bibl. 36, 44

Ezekiel Burr (b. 1764-d. 1846)
Providence, R.I.
E. & W. Burr (c. 1793)
Burr & Lee (c. 1815)
Bibl. 23, 24, 25, 29, 36, 44, 54,
56

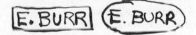

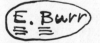

Ezekiel & William Burr (c.
1793)
Providence, R.I.
Bibl. 23

Nathaniel Burr (b. 1698-d.
1784)
Fairfield, Conn.
Bibl. 24, 25, 44, 61

N B

William Burr (c. 1792)
Providence, R.I.

E. & W. Burr (c. 1793)
Bibl. 15, 23, 25, 28, 36, 44, 55,
56

W. BURR

John Burrage (w. 1769)
Annapolis, Md.
Bibl. 38

Burrel
(See Burrill)

Burrett
(See Rice & Burrett)

———— Burrill
Augusta, Ga.
Huntington & Burrill (c. 1817-
1819)
Bibl. 17

Burrill & Beebe (c. 1836)
New York, N.Y.
George Burrill
Bibl. 15

George Burrill (c. 1837)
New York, N.Y.
Burrill & Beebe (c. 1836)
Bibl. 15

Joseph Burrill (c. 1823)
Boston, Mass.
Bibl. 23, 28, 36, 44

Samuel Burrill (Burrell) (c.
1704-1770)
Boston, Mass.
Bibl. 4, 15, 23, 24, 25, 28, 29, 36,
44, 50, 80

Samuel Burrill Jr. (c. 1829)
Boston, Mass.
Bibl. 23, 36, 44

Theophilus Burrill (c. 1717-
1739, d. 1739)
New London, Conn.
Boston, Mass.
Bibl. 16, 23, 28, 36, 44

J. Burritt & Son (c. 1838-1862)
Ithaca, N.Y.
Joseph Curtiss Burritt
Bibl. 20

Joseph Burrltt
Ithaca, N.Y.
Burdick & Burritt (c. 1816-1819)
Bibl. 20

Joseph Curtiss Burritt (b.
1817-d. 1889)
Ithaca, N.Y.
J. Burritt & Son (c. 1838-1862)
Bibl. 20

Bardon Burrow (c. 1829-1833)
Norfolk, Va.
Bibl. 19

William Burrows (c. 1829-1837)
Philadelphia, Pa.
Bibl. 3, 23, 36, 44

Benjamin Burt (c. 1729-1805)
Boston, Mass.
Bibl. 2, 15, 23, 24, 25, 28, 29,
36, 44, 50, 54

John Burt (b. 1691-d. 1745)
Boston, Mass.
Bibl. 2, 4, 15, 23, 24, 25, 28,
29, 44, 50, 54

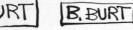

M. Burt (c. 1860)
Cleveland, Ohio
Bibl. 89

Samuel Burt (b. 1724-d. 1754)
Boston, Mass.
Bibl. 2, 15, 23, 24, 25, 28, 29,
36, 44, 54

William Burt (b. 1726-d. 1752)
Boston, Mass.
Bibl. 2, 4, 23, 24, 25, 28, 29, 36,
39, 44, 54

W BURT   W BURT

Jacob Burton (c. 1839)
Philadelphia, Pa.
Bibl. 3, 23, 36

Burtt
(See Durgin & Burtt)

Burwell & Winship (c. 1855)
Norfolk, Va.
F. W. Burwell
——— Winship
Bibl. 19

F. W. Burwell (c. 1846-1855)
Norfolk, Va.
Burwell & Winship (c. 1855)
Bibl. 15, 19

F. W. BURWELL

Fitch Burwell (c. 1841-1843)
Norfolk, Va. (c. 1843-1844)
Portsmouth, Va.
J. M. Freeman & Co. (c. 1843-
1844)
Bibl. 19

M. Busches (c. 1810)
Philadelphia, Pa.
Bibl. 3

Francis A. Bush (b. 1834)
Utica, N.Y. (c. 1852-1857)
Bibl. 18

G. Bush
Location unknown
Bibl. 15, 44

G. Bush

John H. Bush (b. 1830)
Utica, N.Y. (c. 1848-1859)
Bibl. 18, 20

Philip Bush Jr. (b. 1765-d.
1807)
Winchester, Va. (c. 1787)
Frankfort, Ky. (?)
Bibl. 19, 32

John Bushea (c. 1808-1809)
Philadelphia, Pa.
Bibl. 3

Phineas Bushnell (b. 1741-d.
1836)
Guilford, Conn.

Saybrook, Conn.
Bibl. 16, 23, 28, 36, 44

Francis Bushwry (Busshwry)
(c. 1798-1799)
Philadelphia, Pa.
Bibl. 3

Bussarec
(See Bos[s]ardet)

Benjamin Bussey (b. 1757-d.
1842)
Dedham, Mass.
Bibl. 2, 23, 24, 25, 28, 29, 36, 44

B B

Thomas D. Bussey (b. 1773-d.
1804)
Baltimore, Md. (w. 1792-1804)
Bibl. 15, 23, 25, 28, 36, 38, 44

JD Bussey

Busshwry
(See Bushwry)

Jason Buswell (c. 1839)
Portsmouth, N.H.
Bibl. 23, 36, 44

Isaac Butaud (c. 1813-1818)
Philadelphia, Pa.
Bibl. 3

Butler & DeBerard (c. 1807-
1815)
Utica, N.Y.
Nathaniel Butler
Charles J. J. DeBerard
Bibl. 18, 20

Butler & Keim (c. 1843)
Philadelphia, Pa.
William H. Butler (?)
Alexander Keim
Bibl. 3, 23

Butler & Little (c. 1759-1765)
Portland, Me.
John Butler
Paul Little
Bibl. 23, 36, 44

Butler & McCart(h)y (c. 1850)
Philadelphia, Pa.
Bibl. 4, 15, 23, 25, 28, 44

BUTLER & M'CARTY

Butler & Osborn (c. 1805-1807)
Utica, N.Y.
Nathaniel Butler

John Osborn
Bibl. 18, 20

Butler, Wise & Co. (c. 1842)
Philadelphia, Pa.
Bibl. 3, 23, 25, 44

B W & Cº

Butler, Wise & Keim (c. 1850)
Philadelphia, Pa.
William H. Butler
George K. Wise
Alexander Keim
Bibl. 3, 23

Charles Paxton Butler (b.
1765-d. 1858)
Charleston, S.C.
Bibl. 5, 25, 44, 54

C P B

Courtland Butler (c. 1843-1845)
Philadelphia, Pa.
Bibl. 3

Franklin Butler (c. 1846-1850)
Philadelphia, Pa.
Bibl. 3

Henry W. Butler (c. 1833-1850)
Philadelphia, Pa.
Bibl. 3, 17, 23, 36, 44

James Butler (c. 1713-1776)
Boston, Mass.
Bibl. 23, 24, 25, 28, 29, 36, 44

J BUTLER

I B

James F. Butler (c. 1850)
Utica, N.Y.
Bibl. 18, 20

John Butler (b. 1732-d. 1827)
Portland, Me.
Butler & Little (c. 1759-1765)
Bibl. 15, 23, 28, 36, 44

Lewis A. Butler (c. 1850)
Binghamton, N.Y.
Bibl. 20

N. H. Butler (c. 1837)
Philadelphia, Pa.
Bibl. 3, 23, 36, 44

Nathaniel Butler (b. 1760-d.
1829)
Savannah, Ga. (c. 1790-1797)
Utica, N.Y.
Butler & Osborn (c. 1805-1807)
Butler & DeBerard (c. 1807-
1815)
Truman Smith (c. 1815)
Bibl. 17, 18, 20, 23, 28, 36, 44

N BUTLER

Thomas R. Butler (c. 1820-
1822)
Philadelphia, Pa.
Bibl. 3

William H. Butler (c. 1842-
1843)
Philadelphia, Pa.
Butler & Keim (c. 1843) (?)
Butler, Wise & Keim (c. 1850)
Bibl. 3, 23

Henry Buttercase (c. 1853-
1854-   )
Utica, N.Y.
Bibl. 18

Buttre
(See Adams & Buttre)

J. L. Buzell (c. 1750)
Location unknown
Bibl. 28, 29, 44

J. L. BUZELL

Columbus Buzzel (c. 1837)
Philadelphia, Pa.
Bibl. 3

———— Bwistrand (c. 1844)
New York, N.Y.
Van Ness & Bwistrand
Bibl. 23

William Byrd (Burd) (b.
1774-d. 1813)
Augusta, Ga. (c. 1796)
Charleston, S.C. (c. 1802)
Savannah, Ga. (?)
Bibl. 17, 44

W B

William Byrd (Burd) (c. 1802)
Charleston, S.C.
Bibl. 5

W B

James Byrne (Burns)
Philadelphia, Pa. (c. 1784)
New York State (c. 1789-1797)
Elizabeth, N.J. (c. 1799)

James Byrne & Co. (c. 1799)
Bibl. 3, 15, 23, 24, 25, 28, 29,
35, 36, 39, 44, 46, 54

J. Byrne

JByrne

James Byrne & Co. (c. 1799)
Elizabeth, N.J.
Bibl. 46

John Byrne (c. 1835-1846)
Lexington, Ky.
Bibl. 54, 68

John Byrne (c. 1846-1859)
Lexington, Ky.
Bibl. 32

Thomas Byrnes (c. 1766-1798)
Wilmington, Del.
Woodcock & Byrnes (c. 1793)
Bibl. 25, 30, 39, 44

T BYRNES

C. C. & Co. (c. 1810-1830)
Location unknown
Bibl. 89

Charles Cable (c. 1816-1818)
Philadelphia, Pa.
Bibl. 3

Jean Cabos (b. 1757, c. 1804-
1806)
Charleston, S.C.
Bibl. 19

Felix Ferjeux Cachot (Cashot)
(c. 1813-1839)
Bardstown, Ky.
Bibl. 32, 68

Jay Cadwell (c. 1850)
Philadelphia, Pa.
Bibl. 3

Cady & Backus (Bachus) (c.
1792-1796)
New York, N.Y.
Samuel Cady
Delucine Backus
Bibl. 23, 28, 36, 44

Samuel Cady (c. 1792-1796)
New York, N.Y.
Cady & Backus
Bibl. 23, 28, 36, 44

Michael Cagger (c. 1832-1838)
Albany, N.Y.
Finch & Cagger (c. 1832-1838)
Bibl. 20

Abraham Cahn (c. 1850)
Philadelphia, Pa.
Bibl. 3

———— Caijol (w. 1795)
Baltimore, Md.
Bibl. 38

Cain & Clements (c. 1817)
Petersburg, Va.
Claiborn W. Cain
Sampson Clements
Bibl. 19

Claiborn W. Cain (c. 1817-
1824)
Petersburg, Va.
Cain & Clements (c. 1817)
Bibl. 19

Michael Cain (c. 1831-1832)
Albany, N.Y.
Bibl. 20

John Cairns (c. 1827)
Rochester, N.Y.
Bibl. 20, 41, 44

Oliver Calame
Charles Town, Va. (c. 1821)
Frederick Town, Md. (c. 1819)
Harpers Ferry, Va. (c. 1820)
Bibl. 19, 38

Calder & Co. (c. 1830)
Albany, N.Y.
Troy, N.Y.
Bibl. 23, 28, 36, 44

Andrew Calderwood (c. 1800-
1822)
Philadelphia, Pa.
Bibl. 3

Caldwell
(See Zadek & Caldwell)

Caldwell & Co. (c. 1850)
Philadelphia, Pa.
James E. Caldwell
Bibl. 3

E. Caldwell (c. 1800)
New York, N.Y.
Bibl. 23, 36, 44

J. E. Caldwell & Co. (c. 1848-
present)
Philadelphia, Pa.
Bibl. 15, 44, 78

James E. Caldwell (c.
1840-   )
Philadelphia, Pa. (c. 1840-
1850)
Bennett & Caldwell (c. 1842-
1848)
J. E. Caldwell & Co. (c. 1848-
present)
Caldwell & Co. (c. 1850)
Filley, Mead & Caldwell (c.
1850) (?)
Bibl. 3, 15, 44

Samuel Caldwell (c. 1825)
Philadelphia, Pa.
Bibl. 3

Benjamin Callender (c. 1784)
Boston, Mass.
Bibl. 28

T. G. Calvert (c. 1815-1850)
Lexington, Ky.
Bibl. 54, 68

Joseph Camain
(See Camoia)

Alexander Cameron (Camman)
(Cammon) (c. 1813-1834)
Albany, N.Y.
Bibl. 4, 20, 23, 24, 25, 28, 29,
36

[A C]

Samuel Cameron (c. 1828-
1830)
Philadelphia, Pa.
Bibl. 3

Alexander Camman or
Cammon
(See Alexander Cameron)

William Cammer (c. 1839-
1842)
Philadelphia, Pa.
Bibl. 3

Joseph Camoia (Camain,
Camoin) (w. 1803-1806)
Baltimore, Md.
Bibl. 38

———— Camoin (c. 1797)
Philadelphia, Pa.
Bibl. 3, 23, 28, 36, 44

Elias Camp (c. 1825-1827)
Bridgeport, Conn.

George Kippen (c. 1827)
Bibl. 23, 24, 25, 36, 44

Campbell & Meredith (c. 1850)
Winchester, Va.
Thomas Boyle Campbell
James Meredith
Bibl. 19

[CAMPBELL] [J. MEREDITH]

Campbell & Polk (c. 1850-1858)
Winchester, Va.
Thomas Boyle Campbell
Robert I. W. Polk
Bibl. 19

[CAMPBELL] [POLK]

Campbell & Prior (c. 1834-
1836)
Fayetteville, N.C.
John Campbell
Warren Prior
Bibl. 21, 25

Alexander Campbell (b. 1775,
c. 1793-1798)
Fayetteville, N.C.
Bibl. 21

Alexander Campbell (c. 1798-
1799)
Philadelphia, Pa.
Bibl. 3

Alexander H. Campbell
(c. 1849)
Marion, Va.
Bibl. 19

Andrew Campbell (c. 1835-
1854)
Baltimore, Md.
R. & A. Campbell
Bibl. 15, 23

Andrew Campbell (c. 1829-
1842)
Philadelphia, Pa.
Bibl. 3

Archibald Campbell (w. 1827-
1837)
Baltimore, Md.
Bibl. 38

C. Campbell (c. 1827)
Greenville, S.C.
Bibl. 5

Charles Campbell (c. 1794-
1803)
Philadelphia, Pa.
Bibl. 3

Christopher Campbell (c. 1808-
1812
New York, N.Y.
Bibl. 5, 15, 23, 25, 29, 36, 44

{ CAMPBELL }

Isaac Campbell (c. 1813-1824)
Philadelphia, Pa.
Bibl. 3

J. Campbell (c. 1835)
Cheraw, S.C.
Bibl. 5

James Campbell (c. 1817)
Steubenville, Ohio
Bibl. 34

John Campbell (c. 1828-1831)
Philadelphia, Pa.
Bibl. 3

John Campbell (b. 1803)
Fayetteville, N.C. (c. 1834-
1836)
Cheraw, S.C. (1836-   )
Nashville, Tenn. (1836-   )
Selph & Campbell (c. 1827-
1829)
Campbell & Prior (c. 1834-
1836)
Bibl. 21, 25, 44

John W. Campbell (c. 1814-
1819)
New York, N.Y.
Bibl. 15, 23, 36, 44

R. & A. Campbell (c. 1835-
1854)
Baltimore, Md.
Robert Campbell
Andrew Campbell
Bibl. 4, 15, 23, 24, 25, 28, 29, 44

    R. & A.C.   R & A CAMPBELL

Robert Campbell (b. 1799-d.
1872)
Baltimore, Md. (w. 1819-1835)
Richards & Campbell (c. 1819)
R. & A. Campbell (c. 1835-
1854)
Bibl. 4, 23, 24, 25, 28, 29, 36, 44

R.C

Robert E. Campbell (c. 1818-
1830)
Ravenna, Ohio
Cincinnati, Ohio
Bibl. 34

Thomas Campbell (c. 1770)
New York, N.Y.
Bibl. 23, 24, 29, 36, 44

T CAMPBELL

Thomas Campbell (c. 1800-
1833)
New York, N.Y.
Philadelphia, Pa.
Bibl. 3, 25

Thomas Campbell
New York, N.Y. (c. 1800)
Philadelphia, Pa. (c. 1828-
1833)
Bibl. 3, 25

Thomas Boyle Campbell (b.
1796-d. 1858)
Winchester, Va.
Campbell & Polk (c. 1850-1858)
Campbell & Meredith (c. 1850)
Bibl. 19

T B C   CAMPBELL

W. Campbell (c. 1765)
Philadelphia, Pa.
Bibl. 23, 28, 36

William Campbell (c. 1765)
Carlisle, Pa.
Bibl. 3, 44

William L. Campbell (b. 1759-d.
1815)
Winchester, Va. (c. 1785-1816)
Bibl. 19

CAMPBELL

Can & Dunn Charters
(See Charters, Cann & Dunn)

Anton Canavillo (Candevalo)
(c. 1819-1835)
New York, N.Y.
Bibl. 15, 23, 36, 44

S. Canavillo (c. 1825)
New York, N.Y.
Bibl. 23, 36, 44

John H. Canby (c. 1797)
Alexandria, Va.
Bibl. 19

Candee & McEwan (c. 1858)
Edgefield, S.C.
Bibl. 5

L. B. Candee & Co. (c. 1830)
Woodbury, Conn.
Lewis Burton Candee
Bibl. 24, 44

L B CANDEE & CO

Lewis Burton Candee
(b. 1806-d. 1861)
Woodbury, Conn. (c. 1825)
Curtis(s) & Candee (c. 1826-
1831)
L. B. Candee & Co. (c. 1830)
Curtis(s), Candee & Stiles
(c. 1831-1835)
Bibl. 16, 23, 25, 28, 36, 44

Charles Candell (c. 1795-1800)
New York, N.Y.
Bibl. 23, 24, 25, 29, 36, 44, 54

C C

Anton Candevalo
(See Canavillo)

Canfield & Brother (c. 1830)
Baltimore, Md.
Ira B. Canfield
William B. Canfield
Bibl. 23, 36, 44

Canfield Bro. & Co. (c. 1850)
Baltimore, Md.
Ira B. Canfield
William B. Canfield
Bibl. 4, 28

Canfield & Foot(e) (c. 1795-
1799)
Middletown, Conn.
Samuel Canfield
William Foote
Bibl. 16, 23, 28, 36, 44

Canfield & Hall (c. 1790-1805)
Middletown, Conn.
Samuel Canfield
Bibl. 24, 25, 44, 61

Ira B. Canfield (c. 1834)
Baltimore, Md.
North Haddam, Conn.
Bibl. 83

L. Canfield (c. 1849)
Binghamton, N.Y.
Bibl. 20

L CANFIELD

Lewis Canfield (c. 1845)
Rochester, N.Y.
Bibl. 20

Samuel Canfield (c. 1780-1807)
Middletown, Conn.
Canfield & Hall (c. 1790-1805)
Canfield & Foote (c. 1795-1799)
Bibl. 16, 23, 24, 25, 28, 29,
    36, 44

CANFIELD

William B. Canfield
Baltimore, Md.
Canfield & Brother (c. 1830)
Canfield Bro. & Co. (c. 1850)
Bibl. 4, 23, 28, 36, 44

William Canfield (c. 1843-1846)
Troy, N.Y.
Bibl. 20

Cann
(See Kidney, Cann & Johnson)

John Cann (1834-1850)
New York, N.Y.
Dunn & Cann (c. 1834-1838)
Charters, Cann & Dunn
    (c. 1850)
Bibl. 4, 15, 23, 28, 36, 44

George Cannon (Canon)
    (b. 1767-d. 1835)
Warwick, R.I. (c. 1800)
Nantucket Island, Mass.
    (c. 1825-1835)
Bibl. 12, 15, 24, 25, 44

G C   G CANNON

G CANON

William Cannon (c. 1738)
Philadelphia, Pa.
Bibl. 3

James Canoll (c. 1839-1845)
Albany, N.Y.
Bibl. 20

John W. H. Canoll (c. 1824-
    1848)
Albany, N.Y.
Bibl. 20

Godfrey Cant (c. 1796)
New York, N.Y.
Bibl. 23, 28, 36, 44

John Porter Capelle (c. 1848-
    1868)
Wilmington, Del.
St. Louis, Mo.
Bibl. 24, 25, 44, 54

CAPELLE   J. P. CAPELLE

Marcus Eugene Capelle
    (c. 1875-1879)
St. Louis, Mo.
Bibl. 54

Michael Capper (c. 1798-1800)
Philadelphia, Pa.
Bibl. 3

George Washington Cappuck
    (c. 1825)
Mt. Holly, N.J.
Bibl. 54

Pierce Caralin (c. 1804-1808)
New York, N.Y.
Bibl. 23, 28, 36, 44

Theodorus (Theodore) Carbin
    (Karbin) (c. 1758-1759)
Philadelphia, Pa.
Bibl. 3, 23, 36, 44

Joseph Carels (c. 1817-1818)
Philadelphia, Pa.
Bibl. 3

Carey & Anthony (c. 1837)
(Anthony & Carey)
Cincinnati, Ohio
Bibl. 34

———— Cargill
Location unknown
Bibl. 28

Michael Cario (c. 1728-1748)
New York, N.Y. (c. 1728)
Philadelphia, Pa. (c. 1734)
Bibl. 3, 23, 28, 44

William Cario
Boston, Mass. (c. 1738)
New York, N.Y. (c. 1742)
Portsmouth, N.H. (before 1748)
Newmarket, N.H. (c. 1790)
Newfields, N.H. (c. 1809)

W CARIO   W CARIO

W. Cario

Bibl. 15, 23, 24, 25, 29, 36, 44,
    70

———— Cariolle (c. 1822)
New Orleans, La.
Bibl. 23, 36, 44

Hugh Carland (c. 1840)
Macon, Ga.
Bibl. 17

Carleton & Co. (c. 1800)
Location unknown
Bibl. 28, 29

CARLETON & CO.

Carleton & Kimball
Location unknown
Bibl. 15, 44

CARLETON & KIMBALL

George Carleton (c. 1810)
New York, N.Y.
Bibl. 15, 24, 25, 44

CARLETON

Abraham Carlisle (Carlile)
    (c. 1780-1794)
Philadelphia, Pa.
Bibl. 3, 15, 23, 24, 25, 29, 36,
    44, 54, 68, 81

A. Carlisle

A.C.

John Carman
Philadelphia, Pa. (c. 1771)
Kingston, N.Y. (c. 1774-1776)
Bibl. 20, 23, 24, 25, 36, 44

I C

John Carman (c. 1800)
New York, N.Y.
Bibl. 23, 36

Samuel Carman (b. 1784,
    c. 1807-1815)
New York, N.Y.
Bibl. 15, 23, 36, 44

J. Carmichael (c. 1840)
Owego, N.Y.
Bibl. 20

John Carnan (c. 1774)
Baltimore, Md.
Bibl. 3

John Carnan (c. 1771-1777)
Baltimore, Md. (c. 1773-1774)
Philadelphia, Pa.
Christopher Hughes & Co.
(c. 1773-1774)
Bibl. 3, 28, 38

Nicholas Caron (1718)
New York, N.Y.
Bibl. 44

Carondolet
(See Wm. Lawler, Carondolet &
Marion)

Benjamin R. Carpenter
(c. 1850)
Syracuse, N.Y.
Bibl. 20

Charles Carpenter
Norwich, Conn. (c. 1790)
Boston, Mass. (c. 1807)
Bibl. 15, 25, 28, 44

C C

Joseph Carpenter (b. 1747-d.
1804)
Norwich, Conn. (c. 1775)
Canterbury, Conn. (c. 1797)
Bibl. 15, 16, 23, 24, 25, 28, 36,
44, 61, 78

I. C.   I C

Lumen Carpenter (c. 1845-
1847)
Oswego, N.Y.
Bibl. 20

Carr
(See Steele & Carr)

B. D. Carr (c. 1845-1846)
Philadelphia, Pa.
Bibl. 3

Daniel Carrell (c. 1804-1806)
Philadelphia, Pa.
Bibl. 3, 23, 36

David S. Carr (c. 1841-1845)
Troy, N.Y.
Bibl. 20

Thomas Carr Jr. (c. 1835)
Philadelphia, Pa.
Bibl. 3

Daniel Carrel(l)
Philadelphia, Pa. (c. 1790)
Charleston, S.C. (c. 1790-1801)
John & Daniel Carrel(l)
(c. 1785)
Bibl. 5, 44, 54

John Carrel (c. 1790-1794)
Philadelphia, Pa.
John & Daniel Carrel(l)
(c. 1785)
Bibl. 3

John & Daniel Carrel(l)
(c. 1785)
Philadelphia, Pa.
Bibl. 3, 23, 24, 25, 29, 36, 44

CARRELL   CARREL

Peter Carribec (Carribee)
(c. 1745-1796)
Philadelphia, Pa.
Bibl. 3, 23, 36, 44

Peter Carribee
(See Peter Carribec)

Jacob Carrigan (c. 1825-1829)
Philadelphia, Pa.
Bibl. 3

J. Carrigan Jr. (c. 1830-1835)
Philadelphia, Pa.
Bibl. 3

Daniel Noble Carrington
(c. 1793)
Danbury, Conn.
Eli Mygatt
Najah Taylor
Bibl. 28

William Carrington (c. 1830)
New York, N.Y.
Charleston, S.C.
Carrington, Thomas & Co.
W. Carrington & Co.
James Eyland & Co.
Bibl. 5, 28, 44, 54

W CARRINGTON

James Carrol(l)
New York, N.Y. (c. 1825)
Albany, N.Y. (c. 1834)
Bibl. 4, 23, 28, 36, 44

John Carroll (c. 1825)
New York, N.Y.
Bibl. 15

John Carrow (c. 1839-1850)
Philadelphia, Pa.

Dubosq & Carrow (c. 1839-
1843)
Dubosq, Carrow & Co.
(c. 1844-1850)
Bibl. 3

John Carrows (c. 1837)
Philadelphia, Pa.
Bibl. 3

Carson & Hall (c. 1810-1818)
Albany, N.Y.
Thomas Carson
Green Hall
Bibl. 4, 15, 20, 23, 25, 28, 36, 44

CARSON & HALL

T. C & H   (?)

Allen Carson (c. 1849)
Philadelphia, Pa.
Bibl. 3, 23

David Carson (c. 1842-1850)
Albany, N.Y.
Bibl. 20, 23, 28, 44

Thomas Carson (c. 1810-1850)
Albany, N.Y.
Carson & Hall (c. 1810-1818)
Bibl. 20, 23, 25, 28, 36, 44

T C

Thomas H. Carson (c. 1838-
1843)
Albany, N.Y.
Bibl. 20

Joseph Sayre Cart (b. 1767-d.
1822)
Charleston, S.C. (c. 1792)
Augusta, Ga. (c. 1802)
Bibl. 5, 17, 44

CART

Vernal Cart (c. 1797-1829)
Charleston, S.C.
Bibl. 54

Carter & Morrell
Gonzales, Tex.
Bibl. 54

C. W. Carter (c. 1840)
Location unknown
Bibl. 89

George M. Carter (c. 1839)
Philadelphia, Pa.
Bibl. 3

J. H. Carter
Location unknown
Bibl. 89

Jacob Carter (c. 1806-1808)
Philadelphia, Pa.
Bibl. 3

Thomas Carter (c. 1823-1824)
Philadelphia, Pa.
Bibl. 3

William Carter (c. 1683,
    d. 1738)
Philadelphia, Pa.
Bibl. 3

William Carter (c. 1844-1847)
Philadelphia, Pa.
Bibl. 3

David N. Carvalho (b. 1787-d.
    1860)
Charleston, S.C. (c. 1815-1822)
Baltimore, Md. (c. 1828)
Philadelphia, Pa.
Bibl. 5

D. N. Carvalks (c. 1846)
Philadelphia, Pa.
Bibl. 3

Franklin L. Carver (c. 1818)
Philadelphia, Pa.
Bibl. 3

G. Carver (c. 1797)
Philadelphia, Pa.
Bibl. 3

Jacob Carver (c. 1785-1833)
Philadelphia, Pa.
Bibl. 3

Samuel Carver (c. 1814)
Philadelphia, Pa.
Bibl. 3

I. H. Cary & Co.
Boston, Mass.
Bibl. 15, 44

I H CARY & CO.

Lewis Cary (b. 1798-d. 1834)
Boston, Mass. (c. 1815-1820)
Bibl. 2, 4, 15, 23, 25, 28, 29,
    36, 44

George Case (c. 1779)
East Hartford, Conn.
Bibl. 16, 23, 28, 36, 44

Philemon N. Case (d. 1852)
Hamilton, N.Y. (c. 1849-1852)
Bibl. 20

Gideon Casey (b. 1726-d. 1786)
Newport, R.I.
South Kingston, R.I.
Samuel Casey (c. 1753)
Bibl. 2, 15, 23, 24, 25, 28, 29,
    36, 44, 54, 56

G. CASEY   G. C.

Samuel Casey (b. 1723-d. 1773)
Newport, R.I. (c. 1753)
South Kingston, R.I.
    (c. 1753)
Boston, Mass.
Little Rest, R.I.
Gideon Casey (c. 1753)
Bibl. 2, 15, 24, 25, 28, 29, 36,
    44, 54

R. Cashell (w. 1811)
Baltimore, Md.
Bibl. 38

R. H. Cashell (c. 1819)
Winchester, Va.
Bibl. 19

Randall H. Cashell (c. 1807-
    1811)
Philadelphia, Pa.
Bibl. 3, 44

Felix Ferjeux Cashot
(See Cachot)

B. W. Caskell
Philadelphia, Pa.
Bibl. 54

Randall Caskell
Philadelphia, Pa.
Bibl. 54

Samuel Caskell (19th century)
Louisville, Ky.
Bibl. 32, 54

William Cassaday (Cassiday)
    (Cassedy)

Philadelphia, Pa. (c. 1846-1850)
Bibl. 3

Abraham Cassal (c. 1840)
Philadelphia, Pa.
Bibl. 3

Andrew Cassedy (c. 1840)
Philadelphia, Pa.
Bibl. 3, 23, 36, 44

William Cassiday
(See Cassaday)

Stephen Castan (c. 1818)
Philadelphia, Pa.
Bibl. 3

Stephen Castan & Co. (c. 1819)
Philadelphia, Pa.
Bibl. 3, 15, 25, 44

S C & Co

J. M. Castens (c. 1810)
Washington, Ga.
Bibl. 17

Castle & Morrell (c. 1840-1844)
Buffalo, N.Y.
Daniel B. Castle
Joseph Morrell
Bibl. 20

Daniel B. Castle (c. 1837-1848)
Buffalo, N.Y.
Castle & Morrell (c. 1840-1844)
Bibl. 20

Francoise Caston (c. 1804)
New York, N.Y.
Bibl. 23, 28, 36, 44

Samuel Caswell (d. 1878)
Louisville, Ky. (c. 1838-1850)
Bibl. 32, 68

John Catlett (d. 1811)
South Carolina (c. 1766)
Augusta, Ga. (c. 1790)
Bibl. 17

Charles Catlin (c. 1841)
Athens, Ga.
Bibl. 17

Charles Catlin
Athens, Ga. (c. 1842)
Augusta, Ga. (c. 1845-1860)
Bibl. 17

C CATLIN

J. & W. Catlin (c. 1823)
Augusta, Ga.

Joel Catlin
Willys Catlin
Bibl. 17

Joel Catlin (c. 1822-1829)
Augusta, Ga.
J. &. W. Catlin (c. 1823)
Bibl. 17

Willys Catlin (c. 1823)
Augusta, Ga.
J. & W. Catlin
Bibl. 17

W. CATLIN

John Cauchais (c. 1816)
Philadelphia, Pa.
Bibl. 3

B. Caulette (c. 1828-1833)
Philadelphia, Pa.
Bibl. 3

Richard Cauthorn III
 (b. 1743-d. 1790)
Ephesus Springs, Va.
Bibl. 19

Joseph Cave (c. 1837-1847)
Philadelphia, Pa.
Bibl. 3

Nich (Nicholas) Cavenaugh
 (c. 1829-1833)
Philadelphia, Pa.
Bibl. 3

Antoine Cayon (w. 1800-1801)
Baltimore, Md.
Bibl. 38

Peter Cazelle
Baltimore, Md. (w. 1803)
Bibl. 38

Peter Cazelles (c. 1818)
Cincinnati, Ohio
Bibl. 34

Charles Cecil (c. 1808-1809)
Philadelphia, Pa.
Bibl. 3

John Cellers (c. 1814)
Chillicothe, Ohio
Bibl. 34

Jacobi Cembuhler
(See Jacob Sandbuhler)

Cerneau & Co. (c. 1811)
New York, N.Y.
Bibl. 23, 36

John Cerneau (c. 1823)
New York, N.Y.
Bibl. 23, 36, 44

Joseph Cerneau (c. 1807)
New York, N.Y.
Bibl. 23, 36, 44

George Certier (c. 1845-1850)
Philadelphia, Pa.
Bibl. 3

Thomas Chadwick (c. 1809-
 1825)
Philadelphia, Pa.
Bibl. 3, 23, 44

Thomas Chadwick & Heims
 (c. 1815)
Albany, N.Y.
Bibl. 25

T C & H

Samuel Chadwick Jr. (c. 1839)
Buffalo, N.Y.
Bibl. 20

Chaffee
(See Root & Chaffee)

James Chalmers, Sr. (c. 1749-
 1780)
Annapolis, Md.
Baltimore, Md. (1766-1768)
Bibl. 25, 28, 29, 38, 44

I C

John Chalmers (b.c. 1750-
 d.c. 1819, c. 1770-c. 1791)
Annapolis, Md.
Bibl. 25, 29, 38, 44

I C

Chamberlain
(See Smith & Chamberlain)

Charles Chamberlain (c. 1833-
 1839)
Philadelphia, Pa.
Bibl. 3

Lewis Chamberlain
Elkton, Md. (1824)
Philadelphia, Pa. (c. 1829-1842)
Bibl. 3, 38

Wilson Chamberlain (c. 1839)
Providence, R.I. (c. 1824)
Portsmouth, N.H. (c. 1839)
Bibl. 23, 36, 44

Lewis Chamberlin (c. 1831-
 1840)
Philadelphia, Pa.
Bibl. 3

John Champlin (b. 1745-
 d. 1800)
New London, Conn. (c. 1768-
 1800)
Bibl. 15, 16, 23, 24, 25, 28, 36,
 44, 61

I C

Lewis C. Champney (c. 1845-
 1850-)
Troy, N.Y.
Fisher & Champney (c. 1846-
 1847)
Bibl. 20

W. & G. Chance
Charleston, S. C.
James Eyland & Co. (c. 1820-
 1827)
Bibl. 89

William Chanceaulone (b. 1785,
 w. 1801)
Baltimore, Md.
Bibl. 38

(Goldsmith) Chandlee
 (d. 1821)
Winchester, Va. (c. 1775)
Bibl. 19

Chandlee & Holloway (w. 1818-
 1823)
Baltimore, Md.
Benjamin Chandlee
Robert Holloway
Bibl. 38

Benjamin Chandlee (d. 1745)
Wilmington, Del. (c. 1710-1745)
Philadelphia, Pa.
Bibl. 3, 38

Benjamin Chandlee (c. 1763)
Chester County, Pa.
Bibl. 3

Benjamin Chandlee (w. 1814-
 1823)
Baltimore, Md.
Bibl. 3, 38

Chandler & Darrow (c. 1843-
 1861)
New York, N.Y.
Bibl. 35

James Chandler (c. 1827-1832)
Schenectady, N.Y.
Bibl. 20

James Chandler (c. 1831)
Troy, N.Y.
James Chandler & Co.
Bibl. 20

James Chandler & Co. (c. 1831)
Troy, N.Y.
Bibl. 20

John Chandler (w. 1774)
Maryland
Bibl. 38

Stephen Chandler (c. 1817-1819)
New York, N.Y.
Bibl. 15, 23, 24, 25, 36, 44

CHANDLER

William Chandless (c. 1836-1838)
New York, N.Y.
Bibl. 4, 15, 23, 28, 44

Claudius Chap
(See Claudius Chat)

H. Chapel (c. 1845-1846)
Louisville, Ky.
Bibl. 32

Chapell & Roberts (c. 1850)
Hartford, Conn.
Hiram F. Chapell
L. D. Roberts
Bibl. 23

Henry Chapell (c. 1848)
St. Louis, Mo.
Bibl. 54

Hiram F. Chapell (c. 1845-1850)
Hartford, Conn.
Chapell & Roberts (c. 1850)
Bibl. 23

Aaron Chapin (b. 1753-d. 1838)
Hartford, Conn.
Bibl. 16, 23, 28, 36, 44

Alexander Chapin (c. 1846)
Hartford, Conn.
Bibl. 23, 36, 44

E. Chapin (c. 1850)
Perry, N.Y.
Bibl. 20

Edwin G. Chapin (c. 1836)
Buffalo, N.Y.
Bibl. 20

Edwin G. Chapin (c. 1838-1839)
Little Falls, N.Y.
Bibl. 20

Otis Chapin (c. 1820)
Morrisville, N.Y.
Bibl. 20

S. Chapin
Location unknown
Bibl. 15, 44

S. CHAPIN

S. & A. Chapin (c. 1834)
South Hadley, Mass.
Bibl. 84

Alonzo Chapman (c. 1835-1836)
Troy, N.Y.
Bibl. 20

Charles Chapman (c. 1838-1839)
Troy, N.Y.
Bibl. 20

David W. Chapman (c. 1834-1841)
Rochester, N.Y.
Bibl. 20, 41, 44

Henry Chapman (b. 1744)
Charleston, S.C. (c. 1774)
Bibl. 5, 28

William Chapman (c. 1849)
Charleston, S.C.
Bibl. 5

Lewis Charles (c. 1837)
Philadelphia, Pa.
Bibl. 3

Charters, Cann & Dunn
(c. 1850)
New York, N.Y.
James Charters
John Cann
David Dunn
Bibl. 4, 25, 28, 29, 44

C C & D

James Charters (c. 1844-1850)
New York, N.Y.
Charters, Cann & Dunn
(c. 1850)
Bibl. 4, 23, 28, 44

Chase
(See Moffatt & Chase)

Chase & Easton (c. 1837)
Brooklyn, N.Y.
Bibl. 23, 36, 44

Chase & Vaughn (c. 1842)
Buffalo, N.Y.
Thomas B. Chase
George C. Vaughn (?)
Bibl. 20

George W. Chase
Utica, N.Y. (c. 1842-1844)
Troy, N.Y. (c. 1845-1847)
Bibl. 18, 20, 23

J. D. Chase (c. 1820)
New York, N.Y.
Bibl. 23, 36, 44

Thomas B. Chase (c. 1839-1848)
Buffalo, N.Y.
Chase & Vaughn (c. 1842)
Bibl. 20

Chasley (1764)
Boston, Mass.
Bibl. 44

André D. Chastant (c. 1822)
New Orleans, La.
Bibl. 23

Claudius Chat (Chap) (c. 1793-1798)
Philadelphia, Pa.
Bibl. 3, 23, 36

Easton Chat (1793)
Philadelphia, Pa.
Bibl. 44

Le Sieur Chat (c. 1790)
New York, N.Y.
Bibl. 28, 44

Chaudron (c. 1798)
Philadelphia, Pa.
Bibl. 54

Chaudron & Co. (c. 1810)
Philadelphia, Pa.
Bibl. 25, 28, 46

Chaudron(s) & Rasch (c. 1812-
1820)
Philadelphia, Pa.
———— Chaudron
Anthony Rasch
Bibl. 3, 15, 23, 24, 25, 28, 36,
39, 44, 54, 72

Edward Chaudron (Chadron)
(c. 1816)
Philadelphia, Pa.
Bibl. 3

J. Chaudron (c. 1798)
Philadelphia, Pa.
Bibl. 3

P. Chaudron (c. 1797)
Philadelphia, Pa.
Bibl. 3

Simon Chaudron (c. 1798-1814)
Philadelphia, Pa.
Bibl. 3, 15, 23, 36, 44, 54

Simon Chaudron & Co. (c.
1807-1811)
Philadelphia, Pa.
Bibl. 3, 23, 24, 25

S C & Co

S. Chaudrons & Co. (c. 1807)
Philadelphia, Pa.
Bibl. 36, 44

Deruisseau Chaulotte (w.
1801)
Baltimore, Md.
Bibl. 38

Frederick Chaulotte (w. 1802)
Baltimore, Md.
Bibl. 38

Charles Chaysenholder (c.
1814)
Philadelphia, Pa.
Bibl. 3

Cheadell & Co. (before 1850)
Auburn, N.Y.
Bibl. 20

John Hatch Cheadell (b. 1806-d.
1875)
Auburn, N.Y. (c. 1827)
Bibl. 20

Cheavins & Hyde (c. 1810)
New York State
Bibl. 46

Chedell & Allen (c. 1844)
Buffalo, N.Y.
Philo Allen
Charles H. Chedell
Bibl. 20

Charles H. Chedell (c. 1844)
Buffalo, N.Y.
Chedell & Allen
Bibl. 20

John Hatch Chedell (b. 1806-d.
1875)
Auburn, N.Y. (c. 1827)
Bibl. 25, 44

CHEDELL

Chelius (c. 1840)
Location unknown
Bibl. 28

Daniel Chene (c. 1786)
New York, N.Y.
Bibl. 4, 23, 28, 36, 44

James Cherry (c. 1824)
Philadelphia, Pa.
Bibl. 3, 23, 36

James Cherry (c. 1849-1850)
Philadelphia, Pa.
Bibl. 3, 44

Chevalier & Tanguay (c. 1816-
1819)
Philadelphia, Pa.
Clement E. Chevalier
———— Tanguay (Tanguy)
Bibl. 3, 23, 36, 44

Clement E. Chevalier (c. 1816-
1833)
Philadelphia, Pa.
Chevalier & Tanguay (c. 1816-
1819)
Bibl. 3, 23, 36, 39, 44

Henry T. Child (c. 1840-1842)
Philadelphia, Pa.
Bibl. 3

John Child (c. 1813-1847)
Philadelphia, Pa.
Bibl. 3

S. T. & T. T. Child (c. 1848-
1850)
Philadelphia, Pa.
Samuel T. Child
Thomas T. Child
Bibl. 3

Samuel T. Child (c. 1843-1848)
Philadelphia, Pa.
S. T. & T. T. Child (c. 1848-
1850)
Bibl. 3

Thomas T. Child (c. 1845)
Philadelphia, Pa.
S. T. & T. T. Child (c. 1848-
1850)
Bibl. 3

Childs
(See Bulles & Childs)

O. & A. K. Childs (c. 1847-
1861)
Athens, Ga.
Otis Childs
Asaph King Childs
Bibl. 17

Childs & Chamberlain (c. 1852-
1861)
Milledgeville, Ga.
Otis Childs
Asaph King Childs
Bibl. 17

Asaph King Childs (b. 1820-d.
1902)
Athens, Ga.
O. & A. K. Childs (c. 1847-
1861)
Childs & Chamberlain (c. 1852-
1861)
Bibl. 17

Ezekiel Childs (c. 1830-1835)
Philadelphia, Pa.
Bibl. 3

George K. Childs (c. 1828-
1850)
Philadelphia, Pa.
Bibl. 3, 4, 15, 23, 25, 28, 36, 44

Otis Childs (b. 1811-d. 1899)
Milledgeville, Ga. (c. 1836-
1845)
Athens, Ga. (c. 1846-1861)
Newton, Mass. (c. 1872)
O. & A. K. Childs (c. 1847-
1861)
Childs & Chamberlain (c. 1852-
1861)
Bibl. 17

Peter Chitrey
(See Peter Chitry)

Edward Chitry (c. 1827-1832)
New York, N.Y.
Bibl. 15

F. Chitry (c. 1840)
Owego, N.Y.
Bibl. 20

Peter Chitry (Chitrey)
(Chittery) (c. 1814-1832)
New York, N.Y.
Philadelphia, Pa.
Bibl. 3, 4, 15, 24, 28, 29, 30, 36,
39, 44, 79

P. CHITRY   P. CHITRY

Beriah Chittenden (b. 1751-d.
1827)
New Haven, Conn. (c. 1787)
Milford, Conn.
Salisbury, Conn.
Kinderbrook, N.Y.
Middlebury, Ohio
Bibl. 16, 23, 34, 36, 44, 61

B C

Ebenezer Chittenden (b. 1726-d.
1812)
Madison, Conn.
New Haven, Conn. (c. 1747-
1765)
East Guilford, Conn.
Abel Buel(l)
Bibl. 15, 16, 23, 24, 25, 28, 29,
36, 44, 61

E C   E C
E. CHITTENDEN

Peter Chittery
(See Peter Chitry)

Chitty & Forbes (c. 1800's)
New York, N.Y.
Bibl. 74

Robert W. Choate (c. 1829-
1837)
Philadelphia, Pa.
Bibl. 3

Stephen D. Choate (c. 1841-
1852-   )
Louisville, Ky.
Bibl. 32, 68

John B. Chollot (c. 1816-1819)
Philadelphia, Pa.
Bibl. 3

Christensen
Location unknown
Bibl. 15

CHRISTENSEN

George W. Christian (c. 1850)
Utica, N.Y.
Bibl. 18, 20

Nathan M. Christian (c. 1840-
1851)
Utica, N.Y.
Tanner & Cooley (c. 1840-
1842)
Bibl. 18, 20

William N. Christian (c. 1846-
1847)
Utica, N.Y.
Bibl. 18, 20

———— Christofle
Cincinnati, Ohio
Bibl. 34

Thomas Christy (c. 1794)
Lexington, Ky.
Bibl. 32, 68

William Chrystler (c. 1828-
1835)
Philadelphia, Pa.
Bibl. 3

E. Chubbuck & Son (c. 1850)
Lockport, N.Y.
Bibl. 20

Samuel W. Chubbuck (b.
1799-d. 1875)
Utica, N.Y.
Morrisville, N.Y.
Storrs & Chubbuck (c. 1847-
1849-   )
Bibl. 18, 20

Charles L. Chur (c. 1837)
Staunton, Va.
Bibl. 19

Church & Metcalf (c. 1842)
Providence, R.I.
Bibl. 23

Church & Rogers (c. 1825-1828)
Hartford, Conn.
Joseph Church
Joseph Rogers
William Rogers
Bibl. 23, 24, 25, 28, 36, 44

CHURCH & ROGERS

C. C. Church (c. 1819-1830)
Batavia, N.Y.
Bibl. 20

John Church (b. 1756-d. 1806)
Savannah, Ga.
Philadelphia, Pa.
Bibl. 17

Joseph Church (b. 1794-d.
1876)
Hartford, Conn.
New Haven, Conn.
Church & Rogers (c. 1825-
1828)
Bibl. 15, 16, 23, 25, 28, 36

J. CHURCH

Ralph Church (c. 1832-1848)
Buffalo, N.Y.
Bibl. 20, 23, 36, 44

Churchill & Treadwell (c.
1805-1813)
Boston, Mass.
Jesse Churchill
———— Treadwell
Bibl. 4, 24, 25, 28, 29, 36, 44

CHURCHILL &
TREADWELL

Jesse Churchill (c. 1773-1819)
Boston, Mass.
Churchill & Treadwell (c.
1805-1813)
Bibl. 2, 4, 15, 23, 24, 25, 28, 29,
36, 44

CHURCHILL   I. CHURCHILL

Charles Churchwell (c. 1781)
Philadelphia, Pa.
Bibl. 3, 23, 36, 44

Andrew S. Clackner (c. 1847-
1850-   )
Rochester, N.Y.
Bibl. 20

John S. Clackner
Troy, N.Y. (c. 1833-1837)
Rochester, N.Y. (c. 1838-1848)
Bibl. 20

Claland
(See Cleland)

Clapp
(See Palmer & Clapp)

Clapp & Riker (c. 1802-1808)
New York, N.Y.
Philip Clapp
Peter Riker
Bibl. 4, 15, 23, 28, 36, 44

A. L. Clapp (c. 1802)
New York, N.Y.
Bibl. 25, 44

A. L. CLAPP

Philip Clapp (c. 1802-1819)
New York, N.Y.
Clapp & Riker (c. 1802-1808)
Bibl. 15, 23, 36, 44

(Widow) Philip Clapp (c. 1825-1826)
New York, N.Y.
Bibl. 15

Joseph Clarico (d. 1828)
Norfolk, Va. (c. 1813-1828)
Bibl. 19, 21

J CLARICO

I. CLARICO

Clark
(See Reeve & Clark, Yates & Clark)

——— Clark (c. 1837)
Circleville, Ohio
Bibl. 34

Clark & Anthony (c. 1790)
New York, N.Y.
Bibl. 23, 24, 25, 28, 29, 36, 44

CLARK & ANTHONY

Clark & Brother (c. 1825)
Norwalk, Conn.
Bibl. 24, 25, 36, 44

CLARK & BRO.

Clark & Brown (c. 1843)
Norwalk, Conn.
Bibl. 24, 25, 36, 44

Clark & Brown (c. 1843)
Cazenovia, N.Y.
Lester Brown
Jehiel Clark Jr.
Bibl. 20

Clark & Coit (c. 1820)
Norwich, Conn.
——— Clark

Thomas Chester Coit
Bibl. 23, 36, 44

Clark & Hartley (c. 1839-1841)
Philadelphia, Pa.
——— Clark
Samuel Hartley
Bibl. 3

C & P

Clark & Pelletreau (c. 1819)
New York, N.Y.
Curtis H. Clark
Maltby Pelletreau
Bibl. 15, 25

Clark, Pelletreau & Upson (c. 1823)
Charleston, S.C.
Gregory Clark Jr. (c. 1822)
——— Upson
Pelletreau (?)
Bibl. 5, 25, 44

C P & U

Clark, Rackett & Co. (c. 1840-1852)
Augusta, Ga.
Horace Clark
George Rackett
Bibl. 17

C R & Co

CLARK R. & CO

Clark & Turner (c. 1820-1823)
Cheraw, N.C.
Fayetteville, N.C.
Wadesboro, N.C.
Charles Clark
Franklin Turner
Bibl. 21

Alexander C. Clark (c. 1850)
Syracuse, N.Y.
Bibl. 20

Andrew Clark (c. 1744)
New York, N.Y.
Fredericksburg, Va.
Bibl. 3, 19, 23, 44, 36

Benjamin & Ellis Clark (c. 1811-1840)
Philadelphia, Pa.
Bibl. 3

Benjamin W. Clark (c. 1791-1848)

Philadelphia, Pa.
Bibl. 3

C. & G. Clark (c. 1833)
Boston, Mass.
Bibl. 23, 28, 44

Charles Clark (c. 1798)
New Haven, Conn.
Boston, Mass.
Bibl. 23, 28, 36, 44

Charles Clark (c. 1809-1814)
Philadelphia, Pa.
Ephraim & Charles Clark (c. 1806-1811)
Bibl. 3

Charles Clark (c. 1821)
Fayetteville, N.C.
Clark & Turner (c. 1820-1823)
Bibl. 21

Curtis Clark (c. 1823)
New York, N.Y.
Bibl. 23, 36, 44

Edward Clark (c. 1809-1814)
Philadelphia, Pa.
Bibl. 3

Elias Clark (c. 1802)
Philadelphia, Pa.
Bibl. 3

Ellis Clark (c. 1816-1848)
Philadelphia, Pa.
Bibl. 3

Ephraim Clark (d. 1822)
Philadelphia, Pa. (c. 1780-1811)
Ephraim & Charles Clark (c. 1806-1811)
Bibl. 3

Ephraim & Charles Clark (c. 1806-1811)
Philadelphia, Pa.
Bibl. 3

F. Clark & Co. (c.   -1822)
Augusta, Ga.
Francis C. Clark
Bibl. 17

F. H. Clark & Co. (c. 1850)
Memphis, Tenn.
Bibl. 15, 25, 44, 54

F. H. CLARK & CO

F. & H. Clark (c. 1830-1840)
Augusta, Ga.
Francis C. Clark

62

Horace Clark
Bibl. 17

Francis C. Clark (c. 1816-1860)
Augusta, Ga.
F. Clark & Co. (c.   -1822)
F. & H. Clark (c. 1830-1840)
Bibl. 17

Frederick Clark (c. 1827)
Rochester, N.Y.
Bibl. 20, 41

Gabriel D. Clark (b. 1813-d.
1896)
Baltimore, Md. (w. 1830-1896)
Foxcroft & Clark (c. 1831-
1839)
Bibl. 23, 24, 25, 38, 44

| G. D. CLARK |

George Clark (c. 1842-1843)
Philadelphia, Pa.
Bibl. 3

George C. (G.) Clark (c. 1813-
1824)
Providence, R.I.
Christopher Burr (c. 1800-1825)
Henry (G.) (B.) Mumford (c.
1813)
Jabez Gorham (c. 1813-1847)
William Hadwen (c. 1816-1828)
Bibl. 23, 24, 25, 28, 29, 36, 44,
56

| G. C. CLARK |

George D. Clark (c. 1826)
Baltimore, Md.
Bibl. 23, 24, 29, 44

| G. D. CLARK |

George R. Clark (c. 1827-
1846)
Auburn, N.Y. (c. 1827)
Rome, N.Y.
Utica, N.Y.
Jenkin(s) & Clark (c. 1827)
Bibl. 18, 20

Gregory Clark Jr. (c. 1822)
Charleston, S.C.
Clark, Pelletreau & Upson (c.
1823)
Bibl. 5

Henry Clark (c. 1813-1824)
Philadelphia, Pa.
Bibl. 3, 23, 36, 44

Horace Clark (c. 1854)
Augusta, Ga.

F. & H. Clark (c. 1830-1840)
Clark, Rackett & Co. (c. 1840-
1852)
Bibl. 17

Horatio Clark (c. 1795-1806)
Bennington, Vt.
Hunt & Clark (c. 1795-1803)
Bibl. 54

Humphrey Clark (c. 1798-
1819-   )
Auburn, N.Y.
Manlius, N.Y.
Onondaga, N.Y.
Troy, N.Y.
Bibl. 20

I. (J.) Clark (c. 1754)
Boston, Mass.
Salem, Mass.
Bibl. 2, 15, 23, 24, 25, 28, 29, 36,
44, 54, 56, 72

| I·G | | CLARK |

| I. CLARK | | I.C. |

I. & H. Clark (c. 1821)
Portsmouth, N.H.
Bibl. 2, 24, 25, 28, 29, 36, 44

| I. & H. CLARK |

J. Clark
(See I. Clark)

J. A. Clark (c. 1835-   )
Batavia, N.Y.
Bibl. 20

J. H. Clark (c. 1812-1815)
Portsmouth, N.H.
New York, N.Y.
Bibl. 15, 23, 24, 25, 29, 36, 44

| J. H. CLARK |

Ⓒ

Jehiel Clark (c. 1808)
Pompey, N.Y.
Bibl. 20

Jehiel Clark Jr. (c. 1843)
Cazenovia, N.Y.
Clark & Brown
Bibl. 20

Jesse Clark (c. 1809-1814)
Philadelphia, Pa.
Bibl. 3

John Clark (c. 1837-1840)
Philadelphia, Pa.
Bibl. 3

John J. Clark
Cambridge, Md. (c. 1833-   )
Portsmouth, Va. (c. 1842-1845)
Bibl. 19

John L. Clark (c. 1837-1838)
Utica, N.Y.
Bibl. 18, 20

John L. Clark
Laurens, S.C. (c. 1856)
Hodges Depot, S.C. (c.
1857-   )
Bibl. 5

Jonas C. Clark (c. 1837-1841)
Watertown, N.Y. (c. 1836-
1837)
Utica, N.Y. (c. 1839-1840)
Albany, N.Y.
L. W. & J. C. Clark (c. 1836-
1837)
Bibl. 20

Joseph Clark (c. 1791-1817)
Danbury, Conn.
Newburgh, N.Y.
Died in Alabama in 1821.
Bibl. 15, 16, 20, 24, 25, 28, 29,
36, 44

| J C | | CLARK |
| I C |

Joseph Clark (c. 1800)
Portsmouth, N.H.
Bibl. 28

L. W. & J. C. Clark
Watertown, N.Y. (c. 1836-
1837)
Utica, N.Y. (c. 1837)
Lewis W. Clark
Jonas C. Clark
Bibl. 20

Levi Clark (b. 1801-d. 1875)
Norwalk, Conn.
Bibl. 15, 16, 24, 25, 28, 29, 36,
44, 61

| CLARK |

Lewis W. Clark (c. 1832-1838)
Utica, N.Y. (c. 1837)
Watertown, N.Y. (c. 1836-
1837)
L. W. & J. C. Clark (c. 1836-
1837)

Bibl. 15, 18, 20, 25, 44

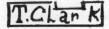

Metcalf B. Clark (c. 1835)
Boston, Mass.
Bibl. 23, 28, 36, 44

Patrick F. Clark (c. 1842-1843)
Philadelphia, Pa.
Bibl. 3, 23

Peter G. Clark (c. 1810)
New Haven, Conn.
Bibl. 16, 23, 28, 36, 44

Philip Clark (c. 1837-1843)
Albany, N.Y.
Bibl. 20

Richard Clark (c. 1765)
Philadelphia, Pa.
May & Clark
Bibl. 3

Richard Clark (c. 1795)
New York, N.Y.
Bibl. 23, 36, 44

Samuel Clark (b. 1659-d.
1705)
Boston, Mass.
Bibl. 4, 15, 23, 28, 36, 44

Thomas Clark (c. 1725-1783,
d. 1783)
Boston, Mass.
Bibl. 15, 23, 24, 25, 28, 29, 44

T.C.

Thomas W. Clark (c. 1830-
1850)
Philadelphia, Pa.
Bibl. 3

William Clark (b. 1750-d.
1798)
New Milford, Conn.
Bibl. 16, 23, 24, 25, 28, 29, 36,
44

W C

William Clark (c. 1831-1833)
Philadelphia, Pa.
Bibl. 3

William Barton Clark (c. 1817-
1834-   )

Utica, N.Y.
Bibl. 18, 20

Clarke & Hutchinson (c. 1813)
Philadelphia, Pa.
Bibl. 3

Ambrose Clarke (b. 1757-d.
1810, w. 1783-c. 1790)
Baltimore, Md. (c. 1783-1784)
Philadelphia, Pa.
Bigger & Clarke (c. 1783-1784)
Bibl. 3, 38

James Clarke (1734)
Newport, R.I.
Bibl. 44

Jonathan Clarke (b. 1705-d.
1770)
Newport, R.I. (c. 1734)
Providence, R.I.
Bibl. 2, 23, 24, 25, 29, 36, 44,
54, 56, 69, 72, 80

IC   J CLARKE
I CLARKE   J Clarke

Claude & French (c. 1783-1785)
Annapolis, Md.
Abraham Claude
James Ormsby French
Bibl. 38

Claude & Jacob (Jacob &
Claude) (c. 1772-1774)
Annapolis, Md.
Abraham Claude
Charles Jacob
Bibl. 38

Abraham Claude (c. 1750-
1800)
Annapolis, Md.
Claude & Jacob (c. 1772-1774)
Claude & French (c. 1783-1785)
Bibl. 38

Chat Claude
(See Claudius Chat)

Clausen & Maull (c. 1830-1833)
Philadelphia, Pa.
——— Clausen

Joseph E. Maull (?)
Bibl. 3

Clayland
(See Cleland)

Barns Clayton (c. 1850)
Philadelphia, Pa.
Bibl. 3

Elias B. Clayton (c. 1848-1850)
Philadelphia, Pa.
Bibl. 3

Richard Clayton (c. 1821-1844)
Cincinnati, Ohio
Bibl. 34

Clealand
(See Cleland)

William Cleaveland
(See William Cleveland)

John Clein (c. 1830-1833)
Philadelphia, Pa.
Bibl. 3

John Cleland (Clealand)
(Claland) (Clayland) (c.
1745-1770-   )
Edenton, N.C.
Bibl. 21

Clement & Broom
Clement & Browne
(See Broom & Clement)

James W. Clement (c. 1833-
1850)
Philadelphia, Pa.
Broom & Clement
(c. 1837) (?)
Bibl. 3

Clements & Ashburn (c. 1847)
Philadelphia, Pa.
James Clements
James C. Ashburn
Bibl. 3

James Clements (c. 1847)
Philadelphia, Pa.
Clements & Ashburn
Bibl. 3

Sampson Clements (c. 1817)
Petersburg, Va.
Cain & Clements
Bibl. 19

Isaac Clemmons (c. 1775)
Boston, Mass.
Bibl. 28

Benjamin Clench (c. 1813-   )
Albany, N.Y.
Truax & Clench
Bibl. 20

Cleveland & Post (c. 1799? or
    1816?)
Norwich, Conn.
William Cleveland
Samuel Post
Bibl. 23, 24, 25, 28, 29, 36, 39,
    44

Aaron Cleveland (c. 1820)
Norwich, Conn.
Bibl. 23, 24, 25, 28, 29, 36, 44

Benjamin Cleveland (c. 1760)
Norwich, Conn.
Bibl. 24, 29, 36

Benjamin Cleveland (b. 1767-d.
    1837, c. 1790-1830)
Newark, N.J.
New Jersey
Bibl. 15, 23, 25, 44, 46, 54

William Cleveland (Cleaveland)
    (b. 1770-d. 1837)
Norwich, Conn. (c. 1791, c.
    1816)
New London, Conn. (c.
    1792-   )
Putnam, Ohio (c. 1808)
Salem, Mass. (c. 1812)
Worthington, Mass.
Zanesville, Ohio
Trott & Cleveland (c.
    1792-   )
Cleveland & Post (c. 1816)
Bibl. 15, 16, 23, 24, 28, 29, 34,
    36, 44, 61

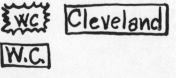

Josiah Clift (b. 1818-d. 1893)
Portsmouth, Va. (c. 1833)
Easton, Md. (c. 1834)
Centerville, Md. (c. 1834)
Norfolk, Va. (c. 1842)
Baltimore, Md. (c. 1846-1852)
Lynchburg, Va. (c. 1857-1862)
Silverthorn & Clift (c. 1857-
    1860-   )
Bibl. 19, 54

Cline & Curtz (c. 1819-1822)
Philadelphia, Pa.
Bibl. 3

B. Cline (c. 1858-1859)
Utica, N.Y.
Bibl. 18

C. & P. Cline (c. 1842-1847)
Philadelphia, Pa.
Charles Cline (?)
Philip Cline (?)
Bibl. 3

Charles Cline (c. 1829-1850)
Philadelphia, Pa.
C. & P. Cline (c. 1842-1847)
    (?)
Bibl. 3, 23, 36, 44

Charles Cline Jr. (c. 1849)
Philadelphia, Pa.
Bibl. 3

J. Cline (c. 1857-1865)
Utica, N.Y.
W. & J. Cline (c. 1857-1860)
Bibl. 18

Philip Cline (c. 1819-1847?)
Philadelphia, Pa.
C. & P. Cline (c. 1842-1847)
    (?)
Bibl. 3

W. & J. Cline (c. 1857-1860)
Utica, N.Y.
Walter Cline
J. Cline
Bibl. 18

Walter Cline (b. 1825)
Utica, N.Y. (c. 1857-1861)
W. & J. Cline (c. 1857-1860)
Bibl. 18

Thomas B. Cloutman (c. 1837)
Buffalo, N.Y.
Bibl. 20

John Cluet (c. 1725)
Albany, N.Y.
Kingston, N.Y.
Van Sanford & Cluet
Bibl. 25, 44

Matthew Cluff
Norfolk, Va. (c. 1803-1816)
Elizabeth City, N.C. (c. 1817-
    1819)
Ott & Cluff (c. 1803-1806)
Bibl. 19

Isaac D. Cluster (c. 1850)
St. Louis, Mo.
Bibl. 24, 25, 44

C. E. Coan (Coen) & Co. (c.
    1810)
New York, N.Y.
Bibl. 24, 25, 44

Charles Coan (c. 1814-   )
Cooperstown, N.Y.
Ernst & Coan
Bibl. 20

Isaac Coates (c. 1835-1839)
Philadelphia, Pa.
Bibl. 3

William Coates (c. 1835-1839)
Buffalo, N.Y.
Bibl. 20

Coats & Boyd (c. 1831)
Philadelphia, Pa.
A. W. Coats (?)
Ezekiel C. Boyd (?)
Bibl. 3

A. W. Coats (c. 1831-1837)
Philadelphia, Pa.
Coats & Boyd (c. 1831) (?)
Bibl. 3

Ephraim Cobb (b. 1708-d.
    1775)
Boston, Mass. (c. 1729)
Plymouth, Mass. (c. 1735)
Bibl. 2, 4, 15, 23, 24, 25, 28,
    29, 44, 72

George Cobham (c. 1834)
New York, N.Y.
Bibl. 15

John Coburn (b. 1725-d. 1803)
Boston, Mass. (c. 1750)
Bibl. 2, 4, 15, 23, 24, 25, 29, 36,
44, 50, 54, 69, 70, 72

J. COBURN

J C   J. C

William D. Cochran
Albany, N.Y. (1830-1836)
Troy, N.Y. (c. 1832-1833)
Schenectady, N.Y. (c. 1841)
Bibl. 20

Cochrane (c. 1820)
Location unknown
Bibl. 24

COCHRANE

George Cockman (c. 1818-
1822)
Philadelphia, Pa.
Bibl. 3

James Cockrell (c. 1843-1850)
Philadelphia, Pa.
Bibl. 3

John Coddington (b. 1690-d.
1743)
Newport, R.I.
Bibl. 2, 15, 23, 24, 25, 28, 29,
36, 44, 56

Willard Codman (c. 1839)
Boston, Mass.
Bibl. 23, 36, 44

John Codner (c. 1754-1782)
Boston, Mass.
Bibl. 28, 44

Coe & Upton (c. 1840)
New York, N.Y.
———— Coe
———— Upton
H. L. Sawyer
Bibl. 23, 24, 25, 28, 29, 36, 44

COE & UPTON

H. H. Coe (c 1840)
Location unknown
Bibl. 24

L. P. Coe (c. 1819?)
New York, N.Y.

Bibl. 15, 44

L. P. COE

C. Coen
(See C. E. Coan)

Daniel Bloom Coen (Coan) (c.
1787-1805)
New York, N.Y.
Bibl. 4, 23, 24, 25, 28, 29, 35, 36,
44, 54

D. C

D. COEN   D COEN

William Coffman (c. 1839-1850)
Philadelphia, Pa.
Bibl. 3, 23, 36, 44

George Cogswell (c. 1834-1835)
Albany, N.Y.
Bibl. 20

H. Co(g)gswell (c. 1760)
Boston, Mass.
Bibl. 23, 24, 28, 29, 36

H. COGSWELL   H COGSWELL

Henry Cogswell (c. 1846-1853)
Salem, Mass.
Bibl. 25, 44

H. COGSWELL

Cohen & Levy (w. 1819)
Baltimore, Md.
Bibl. 38

Cohen & Stevens (c. 1808)
Petersburg, Va.
Thomas Cohen
Robert Stevens
Bibl. 19

Albert Cohen (c. 1848)
St. Louis, Mo.
Bibl. 54

Albert Cohen

Barrow A. Cohen (c. 1825)
New York, N.Y.
Bibl. 15, 23, 36, 44

M. A. Cohen (c. 1840-1843)
Philadelphia, Pa.
Bibl. 3

Thomas Cohen
Petersburg, Va. (c. 1808)
Lynchburg, Va. (c. 1809-1814)
Chillicothe, Ohio (c.
1814-   )

Cohen & Stevens (c. 1808)
Bibl. 19, 25, 34, 44, 54

T COHEN

William Cohen (c. 1833-1838)
Alexandria, Va.
District of Columbia
Bibl. 19, 23, 36, 44, 54

Louis Coignard (c. 1805)
New York, N.Y.
Bibl. 23, 36, 44

Coit & Mansfield (c. 1816-1819)
Norwich, Conn.
Thomas Chester Coit
Elisha Hyde Mansfield
Bibl. 16, 23, 24, 25, 28, 29, 36,
44

C & M

E. Coit (d. 1839)
Norwich, Conn. (c. 1825)
Bibl. 23, 24, 25, 29, 36, 44, 61

E. COIT

Thomas Chester Coit (b.
1791-d. 1841)
Norwich, Conn. (c. 1812-1820)
Natchez, Miss.
Coit & Mansfield (c. 1816-
1819)
Clark & Coit (c. 1820)
Bibl. 16, 23, 24, 25, 28, 29, 36,
44

John Coke (b. 1704-d. 1767)
Williamsburg, Va. (c. 1724-
1760)
Bibl. 19

Samuel Coke (d. 1773)
Williamsburg, Va. (c. 1760-
1773)
Bibl. 19

George Colden (c. 1832-1833)
New York, N.Y.
Bibl. 15

Cole & Van Court (c. 1850)
New York, N.Y.
Bibl. 23

Albert Cole (c. 1844)
New York, N.Y.
(See Albert & Coles)

Bibl. 4, 23, 24, 25, 28, 29, 35, 44, 88

Ebenezer Cole (c. 1818-1826)
New York State
Benjamin B. Wood
Bibl. 15, 23, 25, 36, 44, 54

E. COLE

Jacob Cole (c. 1785)
Philadelphia, Pa.
Bibl. 3, 23, 36, 44

John Cole (c. 1686)
Boston, Mass.
Bibl. 23, 28, 36, 44

John A. Cole (c. 1844)
New York, N.Y.
Bibl. 23

William Groat Cole (b. 1815-d. 1898)
Utica, N.Y.
Bibl. 18, 20

Coleman
(See Decker & Coleman)

Alvan Coleman (c. 1847-1849)
Troy, N.Y.
Bibl. 20

Benjamin Coleman (c. 1785)
Burlington, N.J.
Bibl. 15, 23, 24, 25, 29, 36, 44

B COLEMAN

Benjamin Coleman Jr. (c. 1802)
Sag Harbor, N.Y.
Bibl. 20

C. C. Coleman (c. 1835)
Burlington, N.J.
Bibl. 23, 25, 36, 44

C C COLEMAN

James Coleman (c. 1833)
Philadelphia, Pa.
Bibl. 3

John Coleman (c. 1814)
New York, N.Y.
Bibl. 23, 36, 44

John Coleman (c. 1848)
Philadelphia, Pa.
Bibl. 3

John F. Coleman (c. 1850)
Philadelphia, Pa.
Bibl. 3

Joseph Coleman (b. 1839-d. 1900)
Massillon, Ohio
Bibl. 34

Nathaniel Coleman (b. 1765-d. 1842)
Burlington, N.J.
Bibl. 15, 23, 24, 25, 28, 29, 36, 39, 44, 46, 54

N. C

N. COLEMAN

Samuel Coleman (b. 1761-d. 1842)
Burlington, N.J. (c. 1805)
Trenton, N.J.
Bibl. 15, 23, 24, 25, 29, 36, 44, 46, 54

S. COLEMAN

William Coleman (w. 1783-1793?)
Baltimore, Md.
Bibl. 38, 44

Albert Coles & Co. (c. 1851-1875)
New York, N.Y.
Bibl. 15

Albert Coles (c. 1836-1838)
New York, N.Y.
(See Albert Cole)
Bibl. 15, 28, 44, 89

John A. Coles (c. 1850)
New York, N.Y.
Bibl. 28, 29, 44

C

Lambert Colette (Collette) (c. 1835-1848)
Buffalo, N.Y.
Bibl. 20, 23, 36, 44

Samuel Coley
New York, N.Y.
Bibl. 89

Simeon Coley (c. 1766)
New York, N.Y.
William & Simeon Coley
Bibl. 23, 24, 25, 28, 36, 44

William & Simeon Coley (c. 1766)
New York, N.Y.
Bibl. 15, 25, 44

William Coley (w. 1766, c. 1801-1815)
New York, N.Y.
Van Voorhis & Coley (c. 1786)
Bibl. 4, 15, 23, 24, 25, 28, 29, 36, 44, 54

Thomas Colgan (c. 1760-1771)
New York, N.Y.
Bibl. 25, 35

J. B. Collet (c. 1805)
New York, N.Y.
Bibl. 23, 36, 44

Collette
(See Colette)

Peleg Collings (1836-1850)
Cincinnati, Ohio
May be same man as Peley Collins
Bibl. 54

Francis Collingwood (c. 1817-1845)
Elmira, N.Y.
Bibl. 20

Collins
(See Colton & Collins)
(See Hazen & Collins)
(See Shipp & Collins)

Arnold Collins (c. 1690-1735, d. 1735)
Newport, R.I.
Bibl. 2, 15, 23, 24, 25, 28, 29, 36, 44, 50, 56

Blakely Collins (c. 1846-1850-)
Troy, N.Y.
Bibl. 20

Patrick Collins (c. 1839-1844)
Albany, N.Y.
Bibl. 20

Peley Collins (c. 1824)
Cincinnati, Ohio
(See Peley Collings)
Bibl. 34

Selden Collins Jr. (b. 1819-d. 1885)
Utica, N.Y.
James Murdock & Co. (c. 1837)
Murdock & Andrews (c. 1838-1849)
Murdock & Collins (c. 1849-1850)
Bibl. 18, 24, 25, 44

S. COLLINS

W. A. Collins (c. 1840-1841)
Troy, N.Y.
Bibl. 20

William & L. Collins (c. 1831-1835)
New York, N.Y.
Colton & Collins (c. 1825-1835)
Bibl. 15, 23, 36, 44

David W. Collom (c. 1846-1850)
Philadelphia, Pa.
Bibl. 3

John Colnenn (c. 1825-1833)
Philadelphia, Pa.
Bibl. 3

John Colner (c. 1818)
New York, N.Y.
Bibl. 23, 36, 44

John Colonel (c. 1804-1822)
Philadelphia, Pa.
Bibl. 3, 23, 36, 44

Abraham Colser (c. 1845-1846)
Albany, N.Y.
Bibl. 20, 23

Colton & Baldwin (c. 1819-1822)
Philadelphia, Pa.
Bibl. 3, 23, 36, 44

Colton & Collins (c. 1825-1835)
New York, N.Y.
Levi Colton
William & L. Collins
Bibl. 15, 23, 25, 36, 44

Demas Colton Jr. (c. 1826-1829)
New York, N.Y.
Bibl. 15, 25, 44

D. COLTON JR.

Levi Colton (c. 1825)
New York, N.Y.
Colton & Collins (c. 1825-1835)
Bibl. 15, 23, 36, 44

Noah Colton (c. 1770)
Rhode Island
Bibl. 54

Oren Colton (c. 1818-1822)
Philadelphia, Pa.
Bibl. 13, 44

Colwell & Lawrence (c. 1850)
Albany, N.Y.
Bibl. 4, 23, 28, 44

William Commel (c. 1837)
Philadelphia, Pa.
Bibl. 3

William Compton (c. 1844-1846)
Rochester, N.Y.
Bibl. 20

A. Conery (c. 1838-1854)
Frankfort, Ky.
Bibl. 32

John Coney (b. 1655-d. 1722)
Boston, Mass.

Bibl. 2, 7, 15, 23, 24, 25, 28, 29, 36, 44, 50, 54

T. Conlyn (c. 1845)
Philadelphia, Pa.
Bibl. 15, 25, 44

T. CONLYN

John Connell (c. 1831-1833)
Philadelphia, Pa.
Bibl. 3

M. Connell (c. 1800)
Philadelphia, Pa. (?)
Bibl. 28, 29, 44, 72

M: CONNELL

Patrick Connelly (c. 1834-1836)
Albany, N.Y.
Bibl. 20

William Conner
(See William J. Connor)

James Conning (b. 1813-d. 1872)
New York, N.Y. (c. 1840)
Mobile, Ala. (c. 1842-1872)
Bibl. 24, 25, 28, 29, 44, 54

J CONNING

William A. Conning (b. 1834)
Mobile, Ala. (c. 1850)
Bibl. 54

Patrick Connolly (c. 1837-1848)
Buffalo, N.Y.
Bibl. 20

Connor & Stickles (c. 1837)
New York, N.Y.
Bibl. 15

John H. Connor (c. 1833-1838)
New York, N.Y.
Eoff & Conner (c. 1833-1835)
Bibl. 15, 23, 24, 25, 28, 36, 44

John W. Connor (1836)
Norwalk, Conn.
Bibl. 29, 44

William J. Connor (Conner)
   (c. 1855)
Charleston, S.C.
Bibl. 5

G. Conrad Jr. (c. 1830)
Philadelphia, Pa.
Bibl. 3

George Conrad (c. 1839-1843)
Philadelphia, Pa.
Bibl. 3

George Oliver Conrad
   (b. 1823-d. 1907, c. 1846-
   1854)
Charlottesville, Va.
Harrisonburg, Va.
Luray, Va.
Bear & Conrad (c. 1846-1851)
Bibl. 19

Godfrey Conrad (c. 1831-1848)
Philadelphia, Pa.
Bibl. 3

Osborn Conrad (c. 1841-1850)
Philadelphia, Pa.
Bibl. 3

Robert Conway (w. 1794)
Baltimore, Md.
Bibl. 38

Thomas A. Conway (1819-
   1824)
Baltimore, Md.
Bibl. 38

Thomas A. Conway (c. 1824)
Cincinnati, Ohio
Bibl. 34

Joseph Conyers (c. 1700)
Boston, Mass.
Bibl. 23, 28, 36, 44, 50

I. C

Richard Conyers (c. 1688-
   1708, d. 1708)

Boston, Mass.
Bibl. 15, 23, 25, 28, 29, 36, 44

Cook
(See Morgan & Cook)

Cook & Co. (c. 1797-1805)
New York, N.Y.
John Cook
Bibl. 23, 36, 44

Cook & Co. (c. 1849)
Syracuse, N.Y.
Bibl. 20, 25

Cook & Stillwell (c. 1847-1859)
Rochester, N.Y.
Erastus Cook
Mortimer F. Stillwell
Bibl. 20, 41

A. H. Cook (c. 1838)
Hudson, N.Y.
Bibl. 20

Benjamin E. Cook (b. 1803,
   c. 1827-1885)
Amherst, Mass. (c. 1827-1833)
Northampton, Mass. (c. 1827-
   1833)
Troy, N.Y.
Storrs & Cook (c. 1827-1833)
B. E. Cook (c. 1833-1885)
B. E. Cook & Son (c. 1885)
Bibl. 15, 20, 25, 44, 84

B. E. COOK
NORTHAMPTON

Charles L. Cook (c. 1843-1850)
Philadelphia, Pa.
Bibl. 3

Erastus Cook (b. 1793-d. 1864)
Rochester, N.Y. (c. 1815-1859)
Madison, Wis. (c. 1859-1864)
Ezra B. Booth
Cook & Stillwell (c. 1847-1859)
Bibl. 20, 25, 41, 44

F. B. Cook (c. 1820)
Location unknown
Bibl. 24

F. B. COOK

G. E. Cook & Co.
Kentucky (?)
Bibl. 54

H. Cook (c. 1810)
Location unknown
Bibl. 24

H. T. Cook (c. 1840)
Location unknown
Bibl. 89

H. T. COOK

Harry Cook (c. 1815-1817)
Poughkeepsie, N.Y.
Adriance & Cook (c. 1814-1815)
Bibl. 20

J. Cook (c. 1820)
Portland, Mo. (?)
Bibl. 28, 72

J. COOK

John Cook
New York, N.Y. (c. 1795)
Boston, Mass. (c. 1813)
Cook & Co. (c. 1797-1805)
Bibl. 23, 24, 25, 29, 36, 44

     J. COOK

COOK

Joseph Cook(e) (c. 1785-1795)
Philadelphia, Pa.
Bibl. 25, 36

William G. Cook (w. 1817-
   1824)
Baltimore, Md.
Bibl. 38

Cooke & Co. (c. 1785)
Philadelphia, Pa.
Bibl. 3, 23, 36, 44

Cooke & Son (c. 1833-1838)
Petersburg, Va.
William Cooke
William A. Cooke
Bibl. 19

Cooke & White (c. 1833)
Norfolk, Va.
William A. Cooke
Andrew White
Bibl. 19

COOKE & WHITE

D. C. Cooke
Charleston, S.C.
New York, N.Y.
Pelletreau, Bennett & Cooke
(c. 1815-1827)
Bennett, Cooke & Co.
(c. 1823-1827)
Bibl. 5

John Cooke (c. 1804)
New York, N.Y.
Bibl. 28

John B. Cooke (c. 1838-1843)
Petersburg, Va.
Bibl. 15, 19, 44

J. B. COOKE

J. B. COOKE

Joseph Cooke (c. 1785-1796)
Philadelphia, Pa.
Bibl. 3, 4, 15, 23, 28, 44

William Cooke
Petersburg, Va.
Cooke & Son (c. 1833-1838)
Bibl. 19, 89

William A. Cooke
Petersburg, Va. (c. 1826-1834)
Norfolk, Va. (c. 1834)
White & Cooke (c. 1829-1833)
Cooke & White (c. 1833)
William A. Cooke & Co. (c.
1833-1834)
Cooke & Son (c. 1833-1838)
Bibl. 19

W. A. COOKE

William A. Cooke & Co. (c.
1833-1834)
Norfolk, Va.
Bibl. 19

Henry P. Cooley
Troy, N.Y. (c. 1842-1843)
Cooperstown, N.Y. (c. 1843-
1846)
Bibl. 20

Oliver B. Cooley (d. 1844)
Utica, N.Y.
Storrs & Cooley (c. 1831-1839)
Tanner & Cooley (c. 1840-
1842)
Bibl. 18, 20, 25, 44

O. B Cooley   COOLEY

Joseph Coolidge Jr. (b. 1747-d.
1821)
Boston, Mass.

Bibl. 2, 15, 23, 24, 25, 28, 29,
36, 44

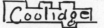

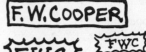

Jeremiah (Jerry) Coon (c.
1846)
Cleveland, Ohio
Bibl. 54

John W. Coon (Coom) (c.
1840-1846)
Cleveland, Ohio
Bibl. 23, 34

———— Cooper (c. 1816)
Philadelphia, Pa.
Bibl. 3, 23, 36, 44

Cooper & Fisher (c. 1850)
New York, N.Y.
Bibl. 24, 25, 44

COOPER & FISHER
131 AMITY ST. N.Y.

Cooper & Gaither (c. 1855)
Greenville, S.C.
Joseph Cooper
J. W. Gaither
Bibl. 5

Cooper & Yongue (c. 1852)
Columbia, S.C.
Joseph Cooper
Robert A. Yongue
Bibl. 5, 44

COOPER & YONGUE

Archibald Cooper
Louisville, Ky. (c. 1838-1848)
Frankfort, Ky. (c. 1842)
William & Archibald Cooper
(c. 1838-1844)
Bibl. 32, 68

B. Cooper (c. 1814)
New York, N.Y.
Bibl. 36, 44

B. & J. Cooper (c. 1810-1830)
New York, N.Y.
Bibl. 23, 25, 28, 36, 44

David Cooper (c. 1829-1833)
Philadelphia, Pa.
Bibl. 3

Francis W. Cooper (c. 1846-
1851)
New York, N.Y.
Bibl. 4, 15, 23, 25, 28, 44

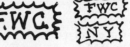

G. Cooper (c. 1800)
Location unknown
Bibl. 28, 29

G. COOPER

John Cooper (c. 1814)
New York, N.Y.
Bibl. 23, 36, 44

Joseph Cooper (c. 1770)
New York, N.Y.
Bibl. 23, 36, 44

Joseph Cooper
Columbia, S.C. (c. 1843-1854,
c. 1856-1860)
Greenville, S.C. (c. 1855)
Cooper & Gaither
Bibl. 5

Joseph B. Cooper (c. 1842-
1846)
Philadelphia, Pa.
Bibl. 3

Robert H. Cooper (c. 1850)
Philadelphia, Pa.
Bibl. 3

Samuel B. Cooper (c. 1840)
Philadelphia, Pa.
Bibl. 3

W. & A. Cooper
(See William & Archibald
Cooper)

William Cooper
Louisville, Ky. (c. 1838-1844)
Frankfort, Ky. (c. 1842)
William & Archibald Cooper
(c. 1838-1844)
Bibl. 32

William Cooper (c. 1844)
Philadelphia, Pa.
Bibl. 3, 23

William & Archibald Cooper
(W. & A. Cooper)
Louisville, Ky. (c. 1838-1844)
Frankfort, Ky. (c. 1842)
Bibl. 32, 54, 68

John Cope (c. 1792)
Richmond, Va.
Bibl. 19

John Copeland (d. 1773)
Edenton, N.C. (c. 1769)
Bibl. 21

Robert Copeland (w. 1796)
Baltimore, Md.
Bibl. 38

Robert Copeland (c. 1850)
New York, N.Y.
Bibl. 23

Joseph Copp (b. 1732)
New London, Conn.
(c. 1757-1776)
Bibl. 15, 16, 24, 25, 28, 36, 44,
61

N. P. Copp (c. 1827)
Georgetown, Ohio
Bibl. 34

Nathaniel P. Copp
Troy, N.Y. (c. 1832-1835)
Albany, N.Y. (c. 1844-1845)
Bibl. 4, 20, 23, 28, 36, 44

Frederick Coppock
Palmyra, N.Y. (c. 1830)
Buffalo, N.Y. (c. 1832)
W. R. & F. Coppock (c. 1830)
Bibl. 20

George F. Coppock (c. 1847-
1848)
Utica, N.Y.
Bibl. 18, 20

W. R. & F. Coppock (c. 1830)
Palmyra, N.Y.
William R. Coppock
Frederick Coppock
Bibl. 20

William R. Coppock (c. 1831)
Palmyra, N.Y.
W. R. & F. Coppock (c. 1830)
Bibl. 20

George Washington Coppuck
(b. 1804-d. 1882)
Mt. Holly, N.J.
Bibl. 46

John Copson (c. 1720)
Philadelphia, Pa.
Bibl. 3

Corbett
Location unknown
Bibl. 15

J. Corbett
Location unknown
Bibl. 15, 44

John Corbett (c. 1800)
Whitingham, Vt.
Bibl. 54

John Corby (c. 1806)
Philadelphia, Pa.
Bibl. 3

Frankland & Cordell (c. 1882)
Warrenton, Va.
————— Frankland
William B. Cordell (?)
Bibl. 19

Presley Cordell (c. 1799-1837)
Leesburg, Va.
Bibl. 19

William B. Cordell
Warrenton, Va. (c. 1814-1820)
Charles Town, Va. (c.
1810-   )
Frankland & Cordell (c. 1822)
(?)
Bibl. 19

Ferdinand Corew (c. 1837)
Philadelphia, Pa.
Bibl. 3

William Corey (c. 1828-1833)
Philadelphia, Pa.
Bibl. 3

Arthur Corgee (c. 1823-1824)
Philadelphia, Pa.
Bibl. 3

John Cork (c. 1837-1850)
Philadelphia, Pa.
Bibl. 3

William Corky (c. 1811)
New York, N.Y.
Bibl. 23, 36

William Corley (1811)
New York, N.Y.
Bibl. 44

Cornelius Cornelison (c. 1712)
New York, N.Y.
Bibl. 4, 23, 28, 36, 44

Christian Cornelius (c. 1810-
1819)
Philadelphia, Pa.
Bibl. 3, 15, 23, 24, 25, 29, 36, 44

Walter Cornell (c. 1780-1800)
Providence, R.I.
Bibl. 15, 23, 24, 25, 29, 36,
44, 56

Edward Corner (w. 1811)
Easton, Md.
Bibl. 38

N. Cornwell (Corwell)
(b. 1776-d. 1837)
Danbury, Conn.
Bibl. 24, 44

Nathaniel Cornwell (c. 1816-
1817)
Hudson, N.Y.
Bibl. 20

Josiah Corrin (c. 1823-1824)
Philadelphia, Pa.
Bibl. 3, 23, 36, 44

Jacques W. Cortelyou
(b. 1781-d. 1822)
New Brunswick, N.J. (c. 1805)

Bibl. 15, 25, 44, 46, 54

J. W. CORTELYOU

Edward Corvazier (c. 1846)
Philadelphia, Pa.
Bibl. 3

N. Corwell
(See N. Cornwell)

Coryton & Lynn (c. 1795-1796)
Alexandria, Va.
Josiah Coryton
Adam Lynn
Bibl. 19

Josiah Coryton (c. 1795-1797)
Alexandria, Va.
Coryton & Lynn (c. 1795-1796)
Bibl. 19

Cosby & Hopkins (c. 1846-
1847)
Cosby, Hopkins & Co. (c. 1846-
1847)
Petersburg, Va.
Thomas E. Cosby
Thomas R. Hopkins
Bibl. 19

T. E. Cosby & Co. (c. 1846)
Petersburg, Va.
Thomas E. Cosby
Bibl. 19

Thomas E. Cosby (c. 1815-
1858)
Petersburg, Va.
T. E. Cosby & Co. (c. 1846)
Cosby & Hopkins (c. 1846-
1847)
Cosby, Hopkins & Co. (c. 1846-
1847)
Bibl. 19

Ezekiel Costen (c. 1845-1850)
Philadelphia, Pa.
Bibl. 3

Abel Cottey (c. 1712)
Philadelphia, Pa.
Bibl. 3

Cotton
(See Hayes & Cotton)

Hilaire Courcelle (c. 1822)
New Orleans, La.
Bibl. 23, 36, 44

Pierre Louis Couret (w. 1805)
Baltimore, Md.
Bibl. 38

James Alexander Courtonne
(b. 1720-d. 1793)
Charleston, S.C. (c. 1751-1784)
Philadelphia, Pa. (?)
Bibl. 5, 54

William Courts (w. 1829)
Baltimore, Md.
Bibl. 38

John B. Couvertier (w. 1810-
1812)
Baltimore, Md.
Bibl. 38

L. Couvertie (Louis Couvertie)
(c. 1822)
New Orleans, La.
Bibl. 15, 23, 24, 25, 29, 44

L'COUVERTIE

Couzens
(See Cozens)

Covell & Higgins (c. 1850)
Syracuse, N.Y.
William W. Covell (?)
George E. Higgins
Bibl. 20

William W. Covell (c. 1850)
Syracuse, N.Y.
Covell & Higgins (?)
Bibl. 20

John Coverley (c. 1750-1800)
Boston, Mass. (c. 1766)
Newburyport, Mass.
Bibl. 15, 25, 44, 88

I. COVERLEY

Thomas Coverly (b. 1750-d.
1800)
Newburyport, Mass.
Newport, R.I.
Bibl. 15, 23, 25, 28, 29, 36, 44,
50, 56

T. COVERLY

William Cowan (b. 1779-d.
1831)
Fredericksburg, Va. (c. 1803)
Richmond, Va. (c. 1803-1831)
McCay & Cowan (c. 1805-1807)
Bibl. 19

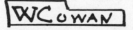

William D. Cowan (Cowen)
(c. 1808-1814)
Philadelphia, Pa.
Bibl. 3, 15, 23, 24, 25, 29, 36, 44

W. COWAN

Charles Cowdrick (c. 1833-
1839)
Philadelphia, Pa.
Bibl. 3

Charles H. Cowdrick (c. 1840-
1850)
Philadelphia, Pa.
Bibl. 3

John Cowell (c. 1728)
Boston, Mass.
Bibl. 70

Robert Cowell (c. 1777)
Philadelphia, Pa.
Bibl. 3

William Cowell (b. 1682-d.
1736)
Boston, Mass.
Bibl. 2, 15, 23, 24, 25, 28, 29,
36, 39, 44, 54

William Cowell Jr. (b. 1713-d.
1761)
Boston, Mass.
Bibl. 2, 15, 23, 25, 28, 36, 44, 69

W COWELL

W C

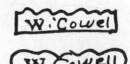

William D. Cowen
(See William D. Cowan)

Cowles & Albertson (c. 1849-
1858)
Cleveland, Ohio
Royal Cowles
Joseph P. Albertson
Bibl. 54

Ralph Cowles (c. 1840-1850)
Cleveland, Ohio
Bibl. 23, 24, 25, 29, 34, 44

Royal Cowles (c. 1849-1858)
Cleveland, Ohio
Cowles & Albertson
Bibl. 54

`COWLES`

C. J. Cowperthwait (c. 1846-
1849)
Philadelphia, Pa.
Bibl. 3

Albion Cox (d. 1795)
Philadelphia, Pa.
Bibl. 3

Benjamin Cox (c. 1809-1813)
Philadelphia, Pa.
Bibl. 3

J. & I. Cox (c. 1817-1853)
New York, N.Y.
John & James Cox
Bibl. 15, 24, 28, 29, 44

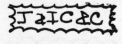

J. & J. Cox & Clark (c. 1831-
1833)
New York, N.Y.
John & James Cox
————— Clark
Bibl. 15, 25, 44

John Cox (c. 1818)
Philadelphia, Pa.
Bibl. 3, 23, 36, 44

John & James Cox
(See J. & I. Cox)
Bibl. 25

William Cox (c. 1825-1837)
Fredericksburg, Va.
Bibl. 19

J. B. Cozens (Couzens)
(c. 1823-1829)
Philadelphia, Pa.
Bibl. 3

Jacob B. Cozens (Couzens)
(c. 1818)
Philadelphia, Pa.
Bibl. 3

Josiah B. Cozens (Couzens)
(c. 1819-1824)
Philadelphia, Pa.
Bibl. 3

Jared Crab (c. 1823)
Elkton, Ky.
Bibl. 32, 54, 68

Stephen Crafts (c. 1815)
New York, N.Y.
Bibl. 15, 23, 36, 44

James Craig (d. 1794)
Williamsburg, Va. (c. 1746-
1774)
Bibl. 19, 23, 36

Richard Cram (c. 1845-1848)
Rochester, N.Y.
Bibl. 20

Benjamin Crandall (Crandell)
(c. 1824)
Providence, R.I.
Bibl. 23, 28, 36, 44

Benjamin Crandall (c. 1839)
Portsmouth, N.H.
Bibl. 23, 36

BENJ F CRANE

Benjamin F. Crane & Co.
(c. 1842-1861)
St. Louis, Mo.
Benjamin F. Crane
Prince H. Jones
Bibl. 54

Benjamin F. Crane (c. 1842-
1861)
St. Louis, Mo.
Benjamin F. Crane & Co.
Bibl. 54

Stephen M. Crane (c. 1813)
New York, N.Y.
Bibl. 23, 36, 44

Samuel Cranston (b. 1659-d.
1727)
Newport, R.I.
Bibl. 23, 28, 36, 44

V. Craup (c. 1816)
Philadelphia, Pa.
Bibl. 3

Alfred Craven (c. 1843)
Philadelphia, Pa.
Bibl. 3

Alfred Craven (c. 1851)
York, S.C.
Bibl. 5

John Crawford (c. 1815-1835,
c. 1837-1843)
New York, N.Y. (c. 1815-1835)
Philadelphia Pa. (c. 1837-1843)
Bibl. 3, 4, 15, 23, 24, 25, 28, 29,
35, 44, 54, 83

`J. CRAWFORD`

C. Crawley (c. 1829-1833)
Philadelphia, Pa.
Bibl. 3

Edmond Crawley (c. 1817-
1824)
Philadelphia, Pa.
Bibl. 3

Edmund T. Crawley (c. 1824)
Philadelphia, Pa.
Bibl. 3

John Crawley
(See John Crowley)

George Creamer (c. 1850)
Poughkeepsie, N.Y.
Bibl. 20

Credon
(See C. Redon)

V. Crepu (c. 1820-1822)
Philadelphia, Pa.
Bibl. 3

Victor Crepu (c. 1830)
Augusta, Ga.
Bibl. 17

James Creswell (c. 1795-1799)
Philadelphia, Pa.
Bibl. 3

S. J. Creswell (c. 1840)
Philadelphia, Pa.
Bibl. 3

Benjamin Creuse (c. 1772)
Philadelphia, Pa.
Bibl. 3

John T. Crew (c. 1830-1850)
Albany, N.Y.
Bibl. 20, 23, 28, 44

Peter Crider (c. 1845)
Philadelphia, Pa.
Bibl. 3

Elnathan F. Crissey (c. 1847)
Rochester, N.Y.
Dunning & Crissey
Bibl. 20

Charles Crittenden
Canfield, Ohio (c. 1816)
Cleveland, Ohio (c. 1820)
Talmadge, Ohio (c. 1830)
Bibl. 34

Newton E. Crittenden
Leroy, N.Y. (c. 1824)
Cleveland, Ohio (c. 1826-1872)
Bibl. 15, 20, 23, 25, 34, 36,
    44, 54, 89

N. E. CRITTENDEN

Crawford (c. 1815)
New York State
Bibl. 54

John G. Crocker (c. 1832-1834)
Utica, N.Y.
Bibl. 18, 20

William Crocker (c. 1837)
Philadelphia, Pa.
Bibl. 3

Frederick Crocks (Crox)
    (Croix) (Crooks)
    (c. 1835-1850)
Philadelphia, Pa.
Bibl. 3

Croix
(See Crocks)

Barclay Croker (c. 1808)
Petersburg, Va.
Bibl. 19

William S. Croker (c. 1839)
Harpers Ferry, Va.
Bibl. 19

———— Cromwell (c. 1844)
Poughkeepsie, N.Y.
Van Vliet & Cromwell
Bibl. 20

Henry Crone (c. 1780)
Lancaster, Pa.
(not Cleveland, Ohio)
Bibl. 23, 36, 44

T. Cronsberry (c. 1848)
Location unknown
Bibl. 3

Crooks
(See Crocks)

Crosby
(See Higbie & Crosby)

Crosby & Brown (c. 1849-1850)
Boston, Mass.
Samuel T. Crosby
———— Brown
Bibl. 23

C. A. W. Crosby (c. 1850)
Location unknown
Bibl. 89

Charles Crosby (c. 1835)
Angelica, N.Y.
Bibl. 20

Jonathan Crosby (b. 1743,
    c. 1796)
Boston, Mass.
Bibl. 4, 23, 24, 25, 28, 29, 36, 44

(J.C.)

Samuel T. Crosby (c. 1849-
    1850)
Boston, Mass.
Crosby & Brown (c. 1849-1850)
Brackett, Crosby & Brown
    (c. 1850)
Bibl. 23, 28, 44

———— Cross (c. 1695)
Boston, Mass.
Bibl. 4, 28

William Cross (b. 1658, c. 1695)
Boston, Mass.
Bibl. 15, 24, 25, 29, 44

Alexander Crouckeshanks
    (c. 1768)
Boston, Mass.
Bibl. 28, 44

Victoire Crouss (c. 1817)
Philadelphia, Pa.
Bibl. 3

George Crow (c. 1788)
New Castle County, Del.
Bibl. 30

Thomas Crow (c. 1770-1782)
Wilmington, Del.
Bibl. 3

David B. Crowell (c. 1849-1850)
Philadelphia, Pa.
Bibl. 3

Crowley & Farr (c. 1823-1825)
Philadelphia, Pa.
John Crowley
John C. Farr (?)
Bibl. 3, 54

E. Crowley (c. 1833)
Philadelphia, Pa.
Somers & Crowley (c. 1828-
    1833) (?)
Johnson & Crowley (c. 1830-
    1833)
Bibl. 3

John Crowley (Crawley)
    (c. 1803-1825)
Philadelphia, Pa.
Crowley & Farr (c. 1823-1825)
Bibl. 3, 54

Henry Crown (b. 1731)
Maryland (w. 1774)
Bibl. 38

Crox
(See Crocks)

Henry Crump (c. 1848)
Philadelphia, Pa.
Bibl. 3

Thomas Crumpton (c. 1823-
    1824)
Philadelphia, Pa.
Bibl. 3

William Crumpton (c. 1811-
    1822)
Philadelphia, Pa.
Bibl. 3

John Cullen (c. 1840-1841)
Leesburg, Va.
Bibl. 19

Hugh Cullin (c. 1844)
Louisa Court House, Va.
Bibl. 19

David B. Cumming(s)
  (c. 1811)
Philadelphia, Pa.
Bibl. 3, 4, 23, 28, 36, 44

George Cummings (c. 1843)
Hartford, Conn.
Bibl. 23

Henry Cummings (c. 1849-
1850)
Philadelphia, Pa.
Bibl. 3

John Cummings (c. 1837)
Philadelphia, Pa.
Bibl. 3

John B. Cummings (c. 1841-
1850)
Philadelphia, Pa.
Bibl. 3

William Cummings (c. 1841-
1850)
Philadelphia, Pa.
Bibl. 3

A. J. Cunningham (c. 1830-
1835)
Charleston, S.C.
Bibl. 5

Robert Cunningham (c. 1844-
1845)
Louisville, Ky.
Bibl. 32

T. D. Curbier (c. 1800)
Philadelphia, Pa. (?)
Bibl. 89

T. D. CURBIER

Jule F. Cure (c. 1839-1840)
Philadelphia, Pa.
Bibl. 3

Lewis Cure (c. 1811-1819)
Philadelphia, Pa.
Bibl. 3

I. B. Curran & Co. (c. 1839)
Ithaca, N.Y.
I. B. Curran
Bibl. 20, 25

I. B. Curran (c. 1835-1839)
Ithaca, N.Y.
I. B. Curran & Co. (c. 1839)
Bibl. 20, 25

I B CURRAN

James Curran (c. 1843-1850)
Philadelphia, Pa.
Bibl. 3

Currier & Trott (c. 1836)
Boston, Mass.
——— Currier

John Proctor Trott
Bibl. 23, 24, 25, 29, 33, 44

  Currier & Trott

A. S. Currier
Location unknown
Bibl. 15, 44

A. S. Currier

Edmund M. Currier (c. 1830)
Salem, Mass.
Bibl. 25, 44, 54

James W. Currin (c. 1843-1850)
Philadelphia, Pa.
Owens & Currin (c. 1846-1850)
Bibl. 3

Joseph Currin (c. 1829)
Philadelphia, Pa.
Bibl. 23, 36, 44

——— Curry (c. 1849)
Newburgh, N.Y.
Curry & Preston
Bibl. 20

Curry & Preston (c. 1825-1831)
Philadelphia, Pa.
John Curry
——— Preston
Bibl. 3, 15, 23, 24, 25, 29, 36, 44

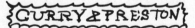

Curry & Preston (c. 1849)
Newburgh, N.Y.
——— Curry
Stephen L. Preston
Bibl. 20

John Curry (c. 1825-1850)
Philadelphia, Pa.

Curry & Preston (c. 1825-1831)
Bibl. 3, 4, 15, 23, 24, 25, 28, 29,
36, 44

J CURRY

Curtis(s) & Candee (c. 1826-
1831)
Woodbury, Conn.
Lewis Burton Candee
Daniel Curtis(s)
Bibl. 16, 23, 36, 44

Curtis(s), Candee & Stiles
  (c. 1831-1835)
Woodbury, Conn.
Daniel Curtis(s)
Lewis Burton Candee
Benjamin Stiles
Bibl. 15, 16, 23, 24, 25, 28, 29,
36, 44

C C & S

CURTISS CANDEE & STILES

Curtis(s) Clarke & Co.
Connecticut
(See Curtis Clark)

Curtis & Dunning (c. 1828)
Woodbury, Conn.
Daniel Curtis (?)
——— Dunning
Bibl. 23, 24, 25, 29, 36, 44

CURTIS & DUNNING

Curtis(s) & Stiles (c. 1835)
Woodbury, Conn.
Daniel Curtis(s)
Benjamin Stiles
Bibl. 15, 16, 23, 24, 25, 36, 44

CURTISS & STILES

D. Curtis (c. 1820)
Lexington, Ky.
Bibl. 32, 44, 68

Daniel Curtis (c. 1816)
Fredericksburg, Va.
Bibl. 19, 44

Daniel Curtis(s) (b. 1801-d.
1878)
Woodbury, Conn.
Curtis(s) & Candee (c. 1826-
1831)

Curtis (s), Candee & Stiles
(c. 1831-1835)
Bibl. 16, 19, 23, 28, 36

Francis Curtis (c. 1845)
Woodbury, Conn.
Bibl. 23

Joel Curtis (b. 1786, c. 1810-
1825)
Wolcott, Conn.
Cairo, N.Y.
Bibl. 16, 23, 28, 36, 44

Lewis Curtis (b. 1774-d. 1845)
Farmington, Conn.
St. Charles, Mo. (c. 1820)
Hazel Green, Wis. (c. 1845)
Bibl. 16, 23, 25, 28, 29, 36, 44

| L. CURTIS |

Solomon Curtis (c. 1793,
d. 1793)
Philadelphia, Pa.
Bibl. 3

Thomas Curtis (c. 1831-1837)
New York, N.Y.
Bibl. 15, 23, 36, 44

Daniel Curtiss
(See Daniel Curtis)

Isaac Cushman (c. 1823)
Boston, Mass.
Bibl. 23, 36, 44

Isaac D. Custer (c. 1847-1854)
St. Louis, Mo.
Bibl. 54

| I D CUSTER |

Cutler, Silliman, Ward & Co.
(c. 1767)
New Haven, Conn.
Richard Cutler
Hezekiah Silliman
Ambrose Ward
Bibl. 16, 28, 36, 44

A. Cutler (c. 1820-1850)
Boston, Mass.
Bibl. 15, 23, 24, 25, 28, 29, 36,
44, 54

| A. CUTLER |
| A CUTLER |

Eben Cutler (c. 1820-1846)
New Haven, Conn.
Boston, Mass.

Bibl. 23, 24, 25, 29, 36, 44

| E CUTLER |

John N. Cutler (c. 1829-1850)
Albany, N.Y.
Bibl. 20, 23, 28, 44

Richard Cutler (b. 1736-d.
1810)
New Haven, Conn. (c. 1760)
Cutler, Silliman, Ward & Co.
(c. 1767)
Richard Cutler & Sons (c. 1800-
1810)
Bibl. 16, 23, 28, 36, 44

Richard Cutler Jr. (b. 1774-d.
1811)
New Haven, Conn. (c. 1800-
1810)
Richard Cutler & Sons
Bibl. 16, 23, 28, 44

Richard Cutler & Sons (c. 1800-
1810)
New Haven, Conn.
Richard Cutler
Richard Cutler Jr
William Cutler
Bibl. 16, 23, 36, 44

William Cutler (b. 1785-d.
1817)
New Haven, Conn. (c. 1800-
1810)
Connecticut
Richard Cutler & Sons (c. 1800-
1810)
Bibl. 16, 23, 28, 44

William Cutler (c. 1823)
Portland, Me.
Bibl. 23, 36, 44

A. Cuyler (c. 1740)
Albany, N.Y.
Bibl. 54

A C

Jacob Cuyler (b. 1741)
Albany, N.Y. (c. 1765)
Bibl. 54

I C   ?

Stanislas Czekayski (c. 1822-
1824)
Philadelphia, Pa.
Bibl. 3

Willson Dabrall
(See Wilson Dalziel)

Louis H. Dadin (c. 1849-1852)
Charleston, S.C.
Bibl. 5

Thomas Daft (c. 1775)
Philadelphia, Pa.
Bibl. 3

Henry Dagget (b. 1741-d. 1830)
New Haven, Conn.
Isaac Beers (c. 1800)
Bibl. 16, 23, 28, 36, 44

Daggett & Blair (c. 1821)
St. Louis, Mo.
John C. Daggett
Daniel Blair
Bibl. 54

John C. Daggett
St. Louis, Mo. (c. 1817-1821)
Massachusetts
Daggett & Blair (c. 1821)
Bibl. 54

Henry Dagon (c. 1847-1850)
Philadelphia, Pa.
Bibl. 3

John Dallon (c. 1791)
Philadelphia, Pa.
Bibl. 3, 23, 36, 44

Dally & Halsey (c. 1787-1789)
New York, N.Y.
Philip Dally
Jabez Halsey
Bibl. 23, 28, 36, 44

Philip Dally (c. 1779-1789)
New York, N.Y.
Dally & Halsey (c. 1787-1789)
Bibl. 23, 24, 25, 35, 36, 44, 54

| P D |

John Dalton (c. 1790)
Philadelphia, Pa.
Bibl. 3

Wilson Dalziel (Willson
Dabrall)
(b. 1749-d. 1781)
Georgetown, S.C. (c. 1774-
1781)
Bibl. 5, 28

Dana & Maynard (c. 1841)
Utica, N.Y.
——— Dana
Thomas Maynard
Bibl. 18

E. B. Dana & Co. (c. 1832)
Elmira, N.Y.
Bibl. 20

Peyton Dana (b. 1795-d. 1849)
Providence, R.I.
Bibl. 15, 25, 28, 44, 80

George Dane (c. 1797-1826)
London, England
Macon, Ga.
Bibl. 17

Thomas Dane (c. 1724-1796)
Boston, Mass. (c. 1745)
Bibl. 15, 23, 24, 25, 28, 29, 36,
    44, 54, 69, 78

Anthony D'Angen (Dangen)
    (Dangin)
(See Antoine Danjen)

George C. Daniel (c. 1829)
Elizabeth City, N.C.
Halifax, Nova Scotia
Bibl. 21

James H. Daniel (c. 1830-1850)
Philadelphia, Pa.
Bibl. 3

Joshua Daniel (c. 1830-1850)
Philadelphia, Pa.
Bibl. 3

Perry O. Daniel (c. 1830)
Boston, Mass.
Bibl. 29, 44

PERRY O. DANIEL

Charles W. Daniels (c. 1836-
    1838)
Troy, N.Y.
Bibl. 20, 23, 36, 44

G. L. Daniels (c. 1840-1843)
Rome, N.Y.
Bibl. 20

Danjean
(See next entry)

Antoine Danjen (D'Angen)
    (Dangln) (Danjean)
    (Anthony Dangen)
    (b. 1781-d. 1827)
St. Louis, Mo.
Bibl. 54

A D

Danul
(See Daniel)

John Darby (c. 1801-1831)
Charleston, S.C.
Bibl. 5, 25, 44

J. DARBY

DARBY

William Darby (c. 1790-1797)
Charleston, S.C.
Bibl. 5, 44

John Dargee (c. 1810-1815)
New York, N.Y.
Bibl. 23, 36, 44

John Darragh (c. 1785)
Philadelphia, Pa.
Bibl. 3

Frederick Darrigrand (b. 1826)
Utica, N.Y. (c. 1854-1865)
Bibl. 18

David Darrow (c. 1825)
New York, N.Y.
Bibl. 24, 44

DARROW

Edmund Darrow (c. 1843-1861)
New York, N.Y.
Bibl. 15, 35, 44, 83

DARROW

DARROW

John F. Darrow (c. 1818)
Catskill, N.Y.
Bibl. 15, 20, 25, 44

Victoire Daubayson (c. 1820-
    1822)
Philadelphia, Pa.
Bibl. 3, 23, 36, 44

Simon Dauce (c. 1798-1819)
Philadelphia, Pa.
Bibl. 3, 23, 36, 44

Simon Dauci (c. 1823-1833)
Philadelphia, Pa.
Bibl. 3

E. J. Daumont & Co. (c. 1820)
Lexington, Ky.
Bibl. 32

Edmund J. Daumont
Louisville, Ky.
E. J. Daumont & Co. (c. 1820)
James I. Lemon & Co. (c. 1859-
    1861)
Bibl. 32

Peter Daumont (c. 1843-1846)
Louisville, Ky.
Richard Ewing Smith (c. 1821-
    1849)
Bibl. 32

Jules D'Autel
Augusta, Ga. (c. 1841)
Athens, Ga. (c. 1845)

Davane, Davanne
(See Daverne)

John Davenport (b. 1753-d.
    1842)
Portsmouth, N.H. (c. 1773)
Bibl. 54

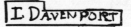

I D

Jonathan Davenport (d. 1801)
Baltimore, Md. (c. 1789-1793)
Philadelphia, Pa. (c. 1793-1796)
Bibl. 15, 29, 38, 44, 54

I D   I DAVENPORT

Robert Davenport (c. 1806-
    1822)
Philadelphia, Pa.
Barrington & Davenport
    (c. 1806-1807)
Bibl. 3, 23, 36, 44

Samuel Davenport (b. 1720-d.
    1793)

Milton, Mass.
Bibl. 23, 28, 36, 44

John Daverne (Davane)
(Davanne)
Baltimore, Md. (c. 1766-1801)
Bibl. 5, 23, 28, 36, 38, 44

David & Dupuy (c. 1792-1805)
Philadelphia, Pa.
John David
John David (Jr.)
Daniel Dupuy
Bibl. 23, 36, 44

Henry David (c. 1844)
New York, N.Y.
Bibl. 23

John David (b. 1736-d. 1794
or 1798?, c. 1763-1777)
Philadelphia, Pa.
New York, N.Y.
David & Dupuy (c. 1792-1805)
Bibl. 2, 3, 15, 23, 24, 25, 28, 29,
30, 36, 39, 44, 50, 54, 81

John David (Jr.) (d. 1805)
Philadelphia, Pa. (c. 1792-1805)
David & Dupuy
Bibl. 3, 4, 15, 23, 24, 25, 29, 36,
44, 81

Lewis A. David (c. 1823-1840)
Philadelphia, Pa.
Bibl. 3, 4, 23, 36, 44

Marquis David (c. 1855-1859)
Charleston, S.C.
I. Epstein (?)
Bibl. 5

Peter David (b. 1691-d. 1755)
Philadelphia, Pa. (c. 1738)

Bibl. 2, 3, 15, 23, 24, 25, 28, 29,
36, 39, 81

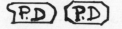

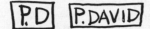

Barzillai (Brazillai) Davidson
(See Barzillai Davison)

Charles Davidson
(See Charles Davison)

Samuel Davidson (c. 1774)
Baltimore, Md.
Bibl. 38

Adam Davie
(See Davy)

Davies & Battel (c. 1843-1847)
Utica, N.Y.
Thomas Davies
Albert T. Battel(s)
Bibl. 18, 20

Davies & Taylor (c. 1851-1852)
Utica, N.Y.
Thomas Davies
William S. Taylor
Bibl. 18

B. F. & T. M. Davies
(c. 1858-   )
Utica, N.Y.
Benjamin F. & Thomas M.
Davies
Bibl. 18

Benjamin F. Davies (b. 1830)
Utica, N.Y.
Thomas Davies (c. 1853-1855)
Thomas Davies & Sons (c. 1856-
1858)
B. F. & T. M. Davies
(c. 1858-   )
Bibl. 18, 20

Thomas Davies (b. 1801,
c. 1823-1858)
Utica, N.Y.
Storrs & Davies (c. 1829-1830)
Leach & Davies (c. 1835-1840)
Davies & Battel (c. 1843-1850)
Davies & Taylor (c. 1851-1852)
Benjamin F. Davies (c. 1853-
1855)
Thomas Davies & Sons (c. 1856-
1858)
Bibl. 18, 20

Thomas Davies & Sons (c. 1856-
1858)
Utica, N.Y.
Thomas Davies
Thomas M. Davies
Benjamin F. Davies
Bibl. 18

Thomas M. Davies (b. 1833-d.
1882)
Utica, N.Y.
Thomas Davies & Sons (c. 1856-
1858)
B. F. & T. M. Davies
(c. 1858-   )
Bibl. 18

William A. Davies (b. 1828)
Utica, N.Y.
Davies & Battel (c. 1844-1847)
Bibl. 18, 20

Davis
(See Mosher & Davis)

Davis & Babbitt (c. 1815)
Providence, R.I.
Samuel Davis (?)
C. Babbitt (?)
Bibl. 23, 28, 36, 44

Davis & Brown (c. 1802-1820)
Boston, Mass.
Bibl. 15, 23, 24, 25, 29, 44, 78

| DAVIS & BROWN |

Davis, Palmer & Co. (c. 1841-
1846)
Boston, Mass.
Bibl. 2, 15, 23, 24, 25, 28, 29, 44

| Davis Palmer & Co. |
| Davis Palmer & Co. |

Davis & Watson (c. 1815)
Boston, Mass.
Samuel Davis
Edward E. Watson
Bibl. 15, 23, 24, 25, 29, 36, 44

Davis, Watson & Co. (c. 1820)
Boston, Mass.
Samuel Davis
Edward E. Watson
Bartlett M. Bramhill
Bibl. 25, 28, 29

| DAVIS WATSON & CO. |

Aaron Davis (c. 1811-1818)
Philadelphia, Pa.
Bibl. 3

Caleb Davis (b. 1769-d. 1834)
Woodstock, Va. (c. 1792)
Clarksburg, Va. (c. 1824)
Bibl. 19

Edward Davis (d. 1781)
   (c. 1770)
Newburyport, Mass.
Bibl. 2, 15, 23, 24, 25, 28, 29,
   44, 50, 54, 72

E D | E DAVIS

Elias Davis (c. 1805-1825)
Boston, Mass.
Newburyport, R.I. (c. 1775)
Bibl. 15, 23, 25, 36, 44

Elias Davis

George Davis (c. 1832-1836)
Albany, N.Y.
Bibl. 20

John Davis (c. 1818)
Philadelphia, Pa.
Bibl. 3

John D. (W.?) Davis
Newburyport, Mass.
Moulton & Davis (c. 1824-1830)
Bibl. 15, 23, 25, 36, 44

Joshua G. Davis (c. 1796-1840)
Boston, Mass.
Bibl. 4, 15, 23, 24, 25, 28, 29,
   36, 44, 72

Richard Davis (c. 1837)
Philadelphia, Pa.
Bibl. 3

Riley A. Davis (c. 1850)
New Bern, N.C.
Bibl. 22

Sampson Davis (c. 1772-1806)
Woodstock, Vt.
Bibl. 54

Samuel Davis (c. 1801-1842)
Boston, Mass.
Plymouth, Mass.
Providence, R.I.
Davis & Babbitt (c. 1815) (?)
Davis & Watson (c. 1815)
Davis, Watson & Co. (c. 1820)
Bibl. 23, 24, 25, 28, 29, 44

DAVIS | S DAVIS

Samuel B. Davis (c. 1837-1850)
Philadelphia, Pa.
Bibl. 3

T. W. Davis (c. 1857)
Greenville, S.C.
Bibl. 5

Thomas Aspinwall Davis
   (c. 1824-1830)
Boston, Mass.
Bibl. 4, 15, 23, 24, 25, 28, 29,
   36, 44

T. A. DAVIS

W. M. Davis (c. 1825)
Morrisville, N.Y.
Bibl. 20

William Davis
Boston, Mass. (c. 1823)
Philadelphia, Pa. (c. 1843)
Bibl. 3, 23, 28, 36

Barzillai (Brazillai) Davison
   (Davidson) (b. 1740-d. 1828)
Norwich, Conn.
Bibl. 16, 23, 28, 44

Charles Davison (c. 1803-1806)
Norwich, Conn.
Norfolk, Va.
Bibl. 19, 23, 24, 25, 29, 36, 44

C DAVISON

Clement Davison (c. 1819-1838)
New York, N.Y.
Bibl. 15, 28, 44

C. DAVISON

Jesse G. Davison (c. 1849-1850)
Richmond, Va.
Bibl. 19

John G. Davison (c. 1842-1843)
Utica, N.Y.
Bibl. 18, 20

Peter I. Davison (b. 1786-d.
   1873)
Sherburne, N.Y. (c. 1815-1860)
Bibl. 20

Adam Davy (Davie) (c. 1795-
   1798)
Philadelphia, Pa.
Bibl. 3, 23, 28, 36, 44

Dawe & McIver (c. 1785)
Alexandria, Va.
Philip Dawe
Colin (?) McIver
Bibl. 19, 54

Philip Dawe (c. 1771-1806)
Alexandria, Va. (c. 1785)
Dumfries, Va.
Dawe & McIver (c. 1785)
Bibl. 19

Robert Dawes (c. 1767-   )
Boston, Mass.
Bibl. 2, 54

Simon Dawes (c. 1829-1833)
Philadelphia, Pa.
Bibl. 3

William Dawes (c. 1719-1802)
Boston, Mass.
Bibl. 23, 28, 36, 44

Henry Dawkins (c. 1754-1776)
New York, N.Y.
Philadelphia, Pa.
Bibl. 3, 28

R. Daws (c. 1800)
Location unknown
Bibl. 28, 29, 44

R DAWS

John Dawson (c. 1767)
New York, N.Y.
Bibl. 23, 28, 36, 44

Jonas (James) Dawson
   (c. 1813-1824)
Philadelphia, Pa.
Bibl. 3

William Dawson (c. 1793-1797)
Philadelphia, Pa.
Bibl. 3, 23, 36, 44

Day
(See Eolles & Day)

George Day (c. 1794-1806)
Charleston, S.C.
John Lowe (?)
Bibl. 5

Israel Day (c. 1807)
Baltimore, Md.
Bibl. 38

John Day
Philadelphia, Pa. (?) (c. 1815-1820)
Boston, Mass. (c. 1820-1825)
Bibl. 15, 25, 44

Sidney B. Day (c. 1847-1850-   )
Macon, Ga.
Bibl. 17

Edward Deacon (c. 1836-1838)
New York, N.Y.
Bibl. 15

Samuel R. Deacon (c. 1823-1824)
Philadelphia, Pa.
Bibl. 3

Thomas Deaderick (b. 1765-d. 1831)
Winchester, Va.
Nashville, Tenn. (?)
Bibl. 19

Reuben Dean (b. 1759-d.1811)
Windsor, Vt.
Bibl. 54

James Deane (b. 1726)
New York, N.Y. (c. 1760)
Bibl. 23, 36, 44

D. Deardorff (c. 1840)
Dayton, Ohio
Bibl. 34

David Deas (c. 1829-1833)
Philadelphia, Pa.
Bibl. 3, 23, 36, 44

Philip Deas (c. 1837)
Philadelphia, Pa.
Bibl. 3

N. De Benneville (c. 1820-1822)
Philadelphia, Pa.
Bibl. 3

Charles J. J. DeBerard
(DeBerad) (c. 1807-1834)
Utica, N.Y. (c. 1807-1815)
Onondaga, N.Y. (c. 1819)
Butler & DeBerard (c. 1807-1815)
Lewis W. Clark (c. 1832-1838)
Bibl. 18, 20

Abraham DeBour (c. 1805)
Philadelphia, Pa.
Bibl. 3

John Debrot (c. 1819)
Philadelphia, Pa.
Bibl. 3

Michael Samuel Debruhl
(c. 1798-1806)
Charleston, S.C.
Abbeville, S.C. (?)
Mary Matilda Dunseth
(c. 1804)
Bibl. 5

Joseph Decatrell (c. 1816-1822)
Philadelphia, Pa.
Bibl. 3

Decker & Coleman (c. 1847-1849)
Troy, N.Y.
Bibl. 20

James Decker (c. 1830-1848)
New York, N.Y. (c. 1830)
Troy, N.Y.
Bibl. 20, 23, 24, 25, 36, 44

J. DECKER

Leonard Decker (c. 1845-1849)
Troy, N.Y.
Bibl. 20

DeForest & Co. (c. 1827-1828)
New York, N.Y.
Bibl. 15, 25, 44

D & Cº

DeForest & Fowler (c. 1827-1828)
New York, N.Y.
———— DeForest
Gilbert Fowler (?)
Bibl. 15

William C. Defrees (Defriez)
(c. 1848)
St. Louis, Mo.
Kentucky

Bibl. 54

WILLIAM C. DEFREES
W C Defriez

Michael Deganny (c. 1819)
Baltimore, Md.
Bibl. 38

Godfrey DeGilse (c. 1837)
Columbus, Ga.
Bibl. 17

Philip H. Delachaux (c. 1820-1822)
Philadelphia, Pa.
Bibl. 3

William DeLacy (c. 1815)
Norfolk, Va.
Bibl. 19

Andrew Delagrow (c. 1795)
Philadelphia, Pa.
Bibl. 3, 23, 36, 44

Emanuel De La Motta
(b. 1761-d. 1821)
Savannah, Ga. (c. 1784)
Bibl. 17

Jebez Delano (b. 1763-d. 1848)
New Bedford, Mass. (c. 1784)
Bibl. 15, 23, 25, 28, 36, 44

Charles Delaplace (c. 1795-1800-   )
Augusta, Ga.
Bibl. 17

John Delarue (Delaroux)
(c. 1882)
New Orleans, La.
Bibl. 23, 24, 25, 36, 44, 54

Jean Delauney (c. 1805)
New York, N.Y.
Bibl. 23, 36, 44

John Delauney (c. 1816)
Philadelphia, Pa.
Bibl. 3

Stephen Deleane (b. 1786)
Baltimore, Md. (c. 1803)
Bibl. 38

Delleker & Richardson
  (Richardson & Delleker)
  (c. 1819)
Philadelphia, Pa.
Samuel Delleker
John Richardson
Bibl. 3

Samuel Delleker (c. 1819-1825)
Philadelphia, Pa.
Delleker & Richardson
  (c. 1819)
Young & Delleker (c. 1823-
1824)
Bibl. 3

Nicolas Delonguemare (Jr.)
  (d. 1711)
Charleston, S.C. (1699-1711)
Bibl. 5

Francis Deloste (c. 1812-1851)
Baltimore, Md.
Suire & Deloste (c. 1822-1826)
Bibl. 38

Andrew Demilt (c. 1805)
New York, N.Y.
Bibl. 15, 23, 24, 25, 29, 44, 89

| DEMILT |

Thomas & Benjamin Demilt
  (c. 1810)
New York, N.Y.
Bibl. 28, 46

| DEMILT |

John Demmock (c. 1798)
Boston, Mass.
Bibl. 23, 28, 36, 44

Jean Demorsy (c. 1822)
New Orleans, La.
Bibl. 23, 36, 44

John Demort (c. 1810)
New York, N.Y.
Bibl. 23, 36, 44

Lucien Demort (c. 1810)
New York, N.Y.
Bibl. 23, 36, 44

D. C. Denham
New York, N.Y.
Bibl. 15, 44

John Denham (c. 1848)
Philadelphia, Pa.
Bibl. 3

John DeNise (c. 1698)
Philadelphia, Pa.
Bibl. 29, 33, 44

John Denise (Johan Nys)
  (c. 1798)
New York, N.Y.
Bibl. 24, 25, 29, 33, 44

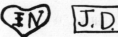

John & Tunis Denise
Kingston, R.I. (c. 1770)
New York, N.Y. (c. 1798)
Bibl. 4, 23, 24, 25, 28, 29, 35,
  36, 44, 83

| J & T D |

T. Denison (c. 1790)
New York, N.Y.
Bibl. 28, 29, 44, 72

| T DENISON | | T DENISON |

Henry Dennery (c. 1819)
New York, N.Y.
Bibl. 15

John Denning (c. 1833-1835)
Philadelphia, Pa.
Bibl. 3.

Dennis & Fitch (c. 1835-1839)
Troy, N.Y.
Bibl. 15, 20, 23, 25, 36, 44

| DENNIS & FITCH |

Augustus Dennis (c. 1831-1833)
Troy, N.Y.
Bibl. 20

Ebenezer Dennis (b. 1753-d.
  1785)
Hartford, Conn.
Bibl. 16, 23, 28, 36, 44

George Dennis Jr. (b. 1753, c.
  1770)
Norwich, Conn.
Bibl. 16, 23, 28, 36, 44

Johannis Dennis
(See Johannis Nys)

Stephen A. Dennis (c. 1839-
  1845)
Troy, N.Y.
Bibl. 20

De Noys
(See Johannis Nys)

Conway Dentz (c. 1850)
Philadelphia, Pa.
Bibl. 3

De Parisien
De Perrizang
(See Parisien)

De Peyser
(See De Pryster)

L. DePoorter (c. 1829-1830)
Charleston, S.C.
Bibl. 5

William De Pryster
  (De Peyser) (c. 1733)
New York, N.Y.
Bibl. 4, 23, 28, 36, 44

DeRiemer & Mead (c. 1830-
  1831)
Ithaca, N.Y.
Cornelius Brouwer DeRiemer
Adriance Mead
Edward Edmund Mead (?)
Bibl. 20, 23, 28, 36, 44 ·

C. B. DeRiemer & Co.
  (c. 1831-1833)
Auburn, N.Y.
Bibl. 20

Cornelius Brouwer DeRiemer
  (b. 1804-d. 1872)
Auburn, N.Y. (c. 1840)
Ithaca, N.Y.
DeRiemer & Mead (c. 1830-
  1831)
Bibl. 20, 23, 36, 44

Jacob Roome DeRiemer
  (b. 1805-d. 1863)
New York, N.Y. (c. 1830)
Bibl. 23, 36, 44

Peter DeRiemer (b. 1738-d.
  1814)

New York, N.Y. (c. 1763-1796)
Bibl. 4, 23, 24, 25, 28, 29, 35,
36, 54

John Derr (c. 1825-1848)
Philadelphia, Pa.
Bibl. 3

Francis Deschamps (c. 1846-
1849)
Philadelphia, Pa.
Bibl. 3

Louis Descuret (Desuret)
(Desueret)
Philadelphia, Pa. (c. 1799-1811)
Blondell & Descuret (c. 1798-
1799)
Bibl. 3, 23, 36, 44

Daniel Deshon (b. 1698-d.
1781)
New London, Conn.
Bibl. 15, 16, 23, 24, 25, 28, 29,
36, 44, 61

Pierre-Jean Desnoyers
(b. 1772-d. 1846) (c. 1790-
1835)
Gallipolis, Ohio (c. 1790)
Detroit, Mich. (c. 1796)
Pittsburgh, Pa.
Jean-Baptiste Piquette (c. 1803-
1805)
Bibl. 58

Desquet & Tanguy (c. 1805)
Philadelphia, Pa.
Bibl. 3, 23, 36, 44

Desueret, Desuret
(See Descuret)

Jacob Deterle (c. 1829-1831)
Cincinnati, Ohio
Bibl. 34

Deterley
(See Woodruff & Deterley)

G. Deuconer (c. 1817)
Philadelphia, Pa.
Bibl. 3

Augustus Deuschler (b. 1822)
Utica, N.Y. (c. 1858-1859)

Bibl. 18

(Monsieur) Joseph De Vacht
(c. 1790)
Gallipolis, Ohio
Bibl. 34

J. & M. Develin (Devlin)
(c. 1848-1850)
Philadelphia, Pa.
Bibl. 3

John Deverell (c. 1764-1813)
Boston, Mass.
Bibl. 23, 24, 25, 28, 29, 36, 44

Deverell

James Devine (c. 1848-1849)
Philadelphia, Pa.
Bibl. 3

Charles Devit(t) (c. 1844-1846)
Philadelphia, Pa.
Bibl. 3, 23

Devlin
(See Develin)

Daniel DeWald (c. 1823-1827)
Canton, Ohio
Bibl. 34

Dwight Dewey (c. 1840)
Ravenna, Ohio
Bibl. 34

Francis Dewing (c. 1716)
Boston, Mass.
Bibl. 28

Abram Henry Dewitt (c. 1847)
Columbus, Ga.
Bibl. 17

Garrit Dewitt
Sparta, Ga. (c. 1823-1827)
Bibl. 17

Zachariah De Witt (c. 1821)
Hamilton, Ohio
Bibl. 34

B. Dexter
Location unknown
Bibl. 54

John Dexter (b. 1735-d. 1800)
Dedham, Mass.
Marlboro, Mass.
Bibl. 23, 28, 36, 44

Minerva Dexter (b. 1785)
Middletown, Conn. (c. 1810)
Bibl. 16, 28

W. W. Dexter (c. 1843-1846)
Earlville, N.Y.
Bibl. 20

John Dey (c. 1846)
Philadelphia, Pa.
Bibl. 3

E. De Young & Co.
(See next entry)

Elias De Young & Co. (c. 1836-
1839-   )
Louisville, Ky.
Bibl. 32, 54

Michael De Young (c. 1816-
1836)
Baltimore, Md.
Bibl. 25, 29, 38, 44

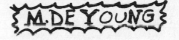

Dibble & Jacks (c. 1842)
Savannah, Ga.
Oscar J. H. Dibble
Pulaski Jacks
Bibl. 17

Henry E. Dibble (o. 1847)
Columbus, Ga.
Bibl. 17

Oscar J. H. Dibble (c. 1835-
1849)
Savannah, Ga. (c. 1842)
Columbus, Ga. (c. 1845)
Dibble & Jacks (c. 1842)
Bibl. 17

O J H DIBBLE

H. Dickerson & Co. (c. 1815)
Philadelphia, Pa.
Bibl. 23, 36, 44

John Dickerson (b. 1755-d.
1828)
Philadelphia, Pa. (c. 1778)
Morristown, N.J. (c. 1778-1796)
Not in Massachusetts c. 1797.
Bibl. 3, 4, 23, 28, 36, 44, 46, 54

Dickinson & Hannum (c. 1843)
Syracuse, N.Y.
Pliny Dickinson
John Hannum
Bibl. 20, 84

Dickinson & Henry (c. 1793)
Philadelphia, Pa.
Bibl. 39

Dickinson (Dickson) (Dixon)
& Robeson (Robinson)
Philadelphia, Pa. (c. 1796-
1797)
D. L. Dickinson (Dickson)
(Dixon)
———— Robeson
Bibl. 3, 23, 36, 44

Anson Dickinson (c. 1800)
Litchfield, Conn.
New York, N.Y.
Bibl. 28

Charles Dickinson (c. 1812)
Zanesville, Ohio
Bibl. 34

D. L. Dickinson (Dickson)
(Dixon)
Philadelphia, Pa. (c. 1796-
1797)
Portsmouth, Va. (c. 1806)
Dickinson & Robeson (1796-
1797)
Bibl. 19

G. W. Dickinson
Location unknown
Bibl. 89

John Dickinson (c. 1822-
1825)
Philadelphia, Pa.
Bibl. 3

Jonathan Dickinson (c. 1794-
1796)
Philadelphia, Pa.
Bibl. 3, 23, 36, 44

P. Dickinson & Co. (c. 1837-
1842)
Syracuse, N.Y.
Bibl. 20

Pliny Dickinson (c. 1828-1847)
Syracuse, N.Y.
Dickinson & Hannum (c. 1843)
Bibl. 20, 84

Richard Dickinson (c. 1768)
Mt. Holly, N.J.
Bibl. 3

William Dickinson (c. 1843-
1845)
Philadelphia, Pa.
Bibl. 3

Dickson
(See D. L. Dickinson)

Dickson, White & Co. (c. 1837)
Philadelphia, Pa.
Bibl. 3, 54

Henry Dickson (b. 1774-d.
1854)
Paintsville, Ky.
Bibl. 32, 54, 68

Pierre & Jacques Didier (c.
1821)
St. Louis, Mo.
Bibl. 54

Philip Diehr (c. 1840-1850)
Philadelphia, Pa.
Bibl. 3

Gerhard Diercks (d. 1886)
Columbia, S.C. (c. 1855-1880)
Bibl. 5

Bernard Gregory Dietz (c. 1848)
Cleveland, Ohio
Bibl. 34, 54

Dikeman
(See Wetmore & Dikeman)

Aaron Dikeman (c. 1824-1837)
New York, N.Y.
Bibl. 15, 25, 44, 54

A. DIKEMAN

Burr Dikeman (c. 1845-1855)
St. Louis, Mo.
Bibl. 54

Henry A. Dikeman (c. 1845-
1855)
St. Louis, Mo.
Bibl. 54

Rene Dikeman (c. 1845-1855)
St. Louis, Mo.
Bibl. 54

D. Dilling (c. 1760)
Location unknown
Bibl. 28

D DILLING

John Dimmock (c. 1801)
New York, N.Y.
Bibl. 23, 36, 44

Dimond & Gurnee (c. 1831-
1832)
New York, N.Y.
Bibl. 15

Isaac M. Dimond (c. 1828-
1838)

New York, N.Y.
Bibl. 15, 23, 36, 44

James Dinwiddie (b. 1820-d.
1885)
Lynchburg, Va. (c. 1840-1868)
Bibl. 19, 54

JAMES DINWIDDIE

G. E. Disbrow (c. 1825)
New York, N.Y.
Bibl. 24, 25, 44

G E DISBROW

Dix
(See Woodbury, Dix, &
Hartwell)

Joseph Dix (c. 1769)
Philadelphia, Pa.
Bibl. 3

Dixon
(See D. L. Dickinson)

A. Dixon (c. 1800)
Location unknown
Bibl. 28

Isaac Dixon (c. 1843-1850)
Philadelphia, Pa.
Bibl. 3, 15, 25, 44

I DIXON

Basil Dixwell (c. 1711-1746)
Boston, Mass.
Bibl. 2, 15, 23, 28, 36, 44

John Dixwell (b. 1680-d. 1725)
Boston, Mass.
Bibl. 2, 4, 10, 15, 23, 24, 25, 28,
29, 36, 44, 69, 70

ID   ID

John Doane (b. 1733-d. 1801?)
Boston, Mass.
Bibl. 15, 28

I DOANE

Joshua Doane (c. 1720-1753,
d. 1753)
Providence, R.I.
Bibl. 15, 23, 24, 25, 28, 29, 36,
44, 56

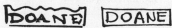

Alexander M. Dobbie
Utica, N.Y. (c. 1844-1849)
Troy, N.Y. (c. 1845-1846)
Bibl. 18, 20, 23

Adam Dobbs
New York, N.Y. (c. 1788)
Philadelphia, Pa. (c. 1813)
Bibl. 28, 36, 44

Frederick Dobleman (c. 1813-
1818)
Philadelphia, Pa.
Bibl. 3, 23, 36, 44

F. F. G. Doblenar (c. 1810)
Philadelphia, Pa.
Bibl. 23, 36

———— Dodd
Hartford, Conn.
Goodwin & Dodd (c. 1812)
Bibl. 89

Dodge
(See Longley & Dodge)

Abraham Dodge Jr (c. 1825)
Ithaca, N.Y.
Munger & Dodge (c. 1824-
1825)
Bibl. 20

Benjamin Dodge (c. 1836)
Boston, Mass.
Bibl. 23, 36, 44

Daniel H. Dodge (c. 1816-
1824)
Philadelphia, Pa.
Wood & Dodge (c. 1816-1817)
Bibl. 3

E. Dodge (c. 1828-1833)
Philadelphia, Pa.
Bibl. 3

E. S. Dodge (c. 1845-   )
Batavia, N.Y.
Bibl. 20

Ezekiel Dodge (c. 1792-1793)
New York, N.Y.
Bibl. 15, 23, 25, 36, 44

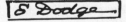

E ☆ DODGE

Ezra W. Dodge (c. 1766-1798)
New London, Conn.
Bibl. 16, 23, 28, 36, 44

Ezra W. Dodge (c. 1821)
Wheeling, Va.
Bibl. 19

John Dodge
New York, N.Y. (c. 1790-
1817)
Catskill, N.Y. (c. 1818-1819)
Bibl. 15, 20, 23, 24, 25, 29, 36,
44

J DODGE

Nehemiah Dodge (c. 1790-
1824)
Providence, R.I.
Pitman & Dodge (c. 1790)
Bibl. 15, 23, 24, 25, 28, 29, 36,
39, 44, 54, 56

N. DODGE

S. M. Dodge (c. 1840)
New York State (?)
Bibl. 89

Seril Dodge (b. 1765-d. 1802)
Providence, R.I. (c. 1795)
Bibl. 23, 24, 25, 28, 29, 36, 39,
44, 56

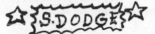

S. DODGE

Joseph Doerflinger (c. 1845-
1850)
Richmond, Va.
Bibl. 19

Philip Doflein (c. 1845-1850)
Philadelphia, Pa.
Bibl. 3

Victor Dohet (c. 1790-1817)
Savannah, Ga.
Bibl. 17

Daniel N. Dole
Portsmouth, N.H. (c. 1805)
Newburyport, Mass. (c. 1811)
Bibl. 15, 24, 25, 28, 29, 89

D N DOLE

E. G. Dole (c. 1820)
Portsmouth, N.H.
Bibl. 28, 29, 44

E G DOLE

Daniel Doler (c. 1765)
Boston, Mass.
Bibl. 23, 28, 36, 44

Dolfinger & Hudson (c. 1855-
1858)
(Hudson & Dolfinger)
Louisville, Ky.
Jacob Dolfinger
Henry Hudson
Bibl. 54

Jacob Dolfinger (b. 1820-d.
1892)
Louisville, Ky. (c. 1848-1861)
Dolfinger & Hudson (c. 1855-
1858) (Hudson & Dolfinger)
Hirshbuhl & Dolfinger (c. 1859-
1861)
Bibl. 32, 54

J. Doll (c. 1820-1830)
New York, N.Y.
Bibl. 15, 25, 44

J. DOLL

W. H. Doll (c. 1845-1850)
New York, N.Y.
Bibl. 15, 44

W. H. Doll

Bernhardus Dominick (c. 1775)
Philadelphia, Pa.
Bibl. 3

Frederick Dominick (c. 1768-
1777)
Philadelphia, Pa.
Bibl. 3

Nathaniel Dominy (c. 1804)
Easthampton, N.Y.
Bibl. 20

Gothard Domuth (c. 1734?)
Savannah, Ga.
Bibl. 17

Alexander Don (c. 1815-1817)
Albany, N.Y.
Bibl. 20

Joseph Donald (c. 1828)
Buffalo, N.Y.
Bibl. 20

John W. Donalon (Donaldson)
(c. 1823)
Boston, Mass.
Bibl. 23, 36, 44

Abel Done (c. 1818-1819)
Philadelphia, Pa.
Bibl. 3

Donleavy
(See Dunlevy)

A. Donnaud (c. 1816)
Philadelphia, Pa.
Bibl. 3

Charles Donnelly (c. 1847-
1848)
Philadelphia, Pa.
Bibl. 3, 23

William Donovan (c. 1784-
1785)
Philadelphia, Pa.
Bibl. 3, 23, 28, 29, 36, 44

C. Dontremei (c. 1805)
Philadelphia, Pa.
Bibl. 3, 23, 36, 44

G. Dontremei
(Same as C. Dontremei)

Amos Doolittle (b. 1754-d.
1832)
New Haven, Conn.
New Hampshire
Bibl. 15, 16, 23, 24, 25, 28, 29,
36, 44, 61

Enos Doolittle (c. 1781)
Hartford, Conn.
Bibl. 16, 23, 28, 36, 44

John Doran (c. 1826)
Cincinnati, Ohio
Bibl. 23, 34, 36, 44, 54

A. M. Doret (c. 1831)
Charleston, S.C.
Bibl. 5

Joseph Dorflinger (c. 1837)
Philadelphia, Pa.
Bibl. 3

Peter Dorgy (c. 1816-1817)
Philadelphia, Pa.
Bibl. 3, 23, 36, 44

George Dorie (c. 1845)
Philadelphia, Pa.
Bibl. 3, 23

C. W. Dorn (c. 1847-1848)
Philadelphia, Pa.
Bibl. 3

———— Dorrance (c. 1795-
1800)
Providence, R.I.
Pitman & Dorrance
Bibl. 15, 44

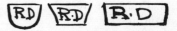

Dorsey
(See Garrow & Dorsey)

Henry C. Dorsey (c. 1845-
1846)
Louisville, Ky.
Bibl. 32, 54, 68

John Dorsey (c. 1793-1794)
Philadelphia, Pa.
Bibl. 3, 36

Joshua Dorsey (c. 1793-1804)
Philadelphia, Pa.
Bibl. 3, 4, 15, 23, 24, 25, 29, 39,
54

Samuel Dorsey (c. 1804)
Philadelphia, Pa.
Bibl. 3, 23, 36, 44

Simon Dorsey (c. 1820-1822)
Philadelphia, Pa.
Bibl. 3, 23, 36, 44

Joshua Dorson (c. 1802)
Philadelphia, Pa.
Bibl. 23, 36

Dorwig
(See Dowig)

Michael Doster (c. 1831-1850)
Philadelphia, Pa.
Bibl. 3, 23, 36, 44

George Doty (c. 1835)
Buffalo, N.Y.
Bibl. 20

John F. Doty (c. 1813-1823)
Albany, N.Y.
Bibl. 20

John W. Doty (c. 1844)
Rochester, N.Y.
Bibl. 20

William Gaylord Doud (b.
1820-d. 1841, c. 1839-1841)
Middletown, Conn.
Utica, N.Y. (1841)
Tanner & Cooley (c. 1840-
1842)
Stephens & Doud (c.
1841-   )
Bibl. 18, 20

E. Doughty
Location unknown
Bibl. 89

Alexander Douglas (c. 1792)
New York, N.Y.
Bibl. 23, 36, 44

Cantwell Douglas
(See Douglass)

Henry Douglas (c. 1837-1838)
New York, N.Y.
Bibl. 15

James W. Douglas (c. 1791)
Philadelphia, Pa.
Bibl. 29, 44

Robert Douglas (c. 1740-1776)
New London, Conn.
Bibl. 16, 23, 24, 25, 28, 36, 44,
61

Douglass & Heckman (c. 1837)
Philadelphia, Pa.
Bibl. 3, 23, 36, 44

Cantwell Douglass (Douglas)
(c. 1772-1807)
Savannah, Ga.
Baltimore, Md.
Bibl. 17, 23, 28, 36, 38, 44

James Douglass (c. 1800-1802)
New York, N.Y.
Bibl. 23, 36

Jeremott William Douglass (c. 1790-1793)
Philadelphia, Pa.
Bibl. 3, 23, 24, 25, 36, 44

John Douglass (c. 1840-1842)
Philadelphia, Pa.
Bibl. 3, 23, 36, 44

John D. Douglass (c. 1833)
Utica, N.Y.
Bingham, Ball & Co.
   (-1833)
Bibl. 18, 20

James Doull (c. 1823-1849)
Philadelphia, Pa.
Bibl. 3

Doumoutet
(See John Baptiste Dumoutet)

Gille (Cule) Doutiemer (c. 1791)
Philadelphia, Pa.
Bibl. 3, 23, 36, 44

Henrick Douty (c. 1774)
Philadelphia, Pa.
Bibl. 3

Joseph Dover (c. 1820-1822)
Philadelphia, Pa.
Bibl. 3

Burrows Dowdney (c. 1768-1771)
Philadelphia, Pa.
Bibl. 3

William Dowdney (c. 1773-   )
Alexandria, Va.
Bibl. 19, 54

George G. Dowell (c. 1843-1847)
Philadelphia, Pa.
Dunlevy & Dowell (c. 1843-1846)
Bibl. 3, 23

Christopher Dowig
George Dowig
(See next entry)

George Christopher Dowig (b. 1724-d. 1807)
(Dorwig) (Drewrey)

(Drewry)
Philadelphia, Pa. (c. 1765-1773)
Baltimore, Md. (c. 1773-1795)
Bibl. 3, 4, 23, 24, 25, 28, 29, 36, 38, 44, 54

J. Downes (c. 1770)
Philadelphia, Pa.
Bibl. 23, 24, 28, 29, 36, 44

David Downie (c. 1817)
Augusta, Ga.
Bibl. 17

Downing & Baldwin (c. 1832-1837)
New York, N.Y.
Bibl. 15, 25, 44

Downing & Phelps
Newark, N.J. (c. 1815)
New York, N.Y. (c. 1825)
George R. Downing
Silas Phelps
Bibl. 15, 24, 25, 28, 29, 36, 44, 46, 54

George R. Downing (c. 1810-1825)
Newark, N.J. (c. 1815)
New York, N.Y. (c. 1825)
Downing & Phelps
Bibl. 25, 28, 29, 36, 44, 46, 54

Samuel P. Downing (c. 1817)
Canandaigua, N.Y.
Bibl. 20

John Draper (c. 1844)
Cincinnati, Ohio
Bibl. 34

Joseph Draper
Wilmington, Del. (c. 1816-1832)
Cincinnati, Ohio (c. 1849)
Hopkinsville, Ky.
Bibl. 15, 24, 25, 30, 32, 44, 54

J. Dray (c. 1846)
Portsmouth, Va.
Bibl. 19

R. Dreden (c. 1839)
Philadelphia, Pa.
Bibl. 3

Dreer & Hayes (c. 1842-1850)
Philadelphia, Pa.
Ferdinand J. Dreer
George Hayes
Bibl. 3

Ferdinand Dreer (c. 1837-1840)
Philadelphia, Pa.
Bibl. 3

Ferdinand J. Dreer (c. 1837-1850)
Philadelphia, Pa.
Amin & Dreer (c. 1837-1841)
Dreer & Hayes (c. 1842-1850)
Bibl. 3

George Drewr(e)y
(See George Christopher Dowig)

Dreyfous & Bro. (c. 1820-1822)
Philadelphia, Pa.
Bibl. 3

Dreyfous Fils Aime (c. 1819)
Philadelphia, Pa.
Bibl. 3

Joseph Dreyfous (c. 1825)
Philadelphia, Pa.
Bibl. 3

Simon Dreyfous (c. 1825-1837)
Philadelphia, Pa.
Bibl. 3

John Drinker (c. 1835-1838)
New York, N. Y.
Bibl. 15, 23, 36, 44

M. A. Dropsie (c. 1842-1849)
Philadelphia, Pa.
Bibl. 3

Dross
(See Droz)

Benjamin Drown(e) (c. 1759-
1793)
Portsmouth, N.H.
Bibl. 23, 25, 36, 44

B DROWNE

Samuel Drown(e) (b. 1749-d.
1815)
Portsmouth, N.H.
Bibl. 15, 23, 24, 25, 28, 29, 36,
39, 44, 72

S+D

T. P. Drown(e) (c. 1790-1816)
Boston, Mass.
Newbury, Mass.
Portsmouth, N.H.
Bibl. 14, 23, 28, 29, 36

T P DROWN

Shem Drowne (b. 1683-d.
1774)
Boston, Mass.
Bibl. 23, 28, 29, 36, 44, 72

S.D　　S.D.

Droz & Son (c. 1806-1814)
Philadelphia, Pa.
Bibl. 3

Charles A. Droz (Dross) (c.
1811-1841)
Philadelphia, Pa.
Bibl. 3

Hannah Droz (Dross) (c.
1842-1850)
Philadelphia, Pa.
Bibl. 3

Hymbert (Lambert) Droz
(Dross) (c. 1793-1811)
Philadelphia, Pa.
Bibl. 3

John Droz (c. 1824)
Cincinnati, Ohio
Bibl. 34

Arnold Druding (c. 1843-1850)
Philadelphia, Pa.
Bibl. 3

Francis Druding (c. 1847-1850)
Philadelphia, Pa.
Bibl. 3

Antoine Drumont (c. 1808)
New York, N.Y.
Bibl. 23, 36, 44

Arnold Drunnin (c. 1837)
Philadelphia, Pa.
Bibl. 3

William Drysdale (c. 1816-
1850)
Philadelphia, Pa.
Bibl. 3

William Drysdale Jr. (c. 1842-
1845)
Philadelphia, Pa.
Bibl. 3

Edward Dubasee (c. 1847-
1850)
Philadelphia, Pa.
Bibl. 3

Dubois & Co. (c. 1803)
Philadelphia, Pa.
New York, N.Y. (?)
Bibl. 3, 23, 36, 44

Abraham Dubois (d. 1807)
Philadelphia, Pa. (c. 1777-
1802)
New York, N.Y. (c. 1803)
Bibl. 3, 4, 15, 23, 24, 25, 28,
29, 36, 39, 44, 54

Abraham Dubois Sr. & Jr. (c.
1803-1807)
Philadelphia, Pa.
Bibl. 3, 15, 23, 36

B. T. Dubois (c. 1830)
Philadelphia, Pa. (?)
Bibl. 89

Francis Dubois (c. 1831-1833)
Philadelphia, Pa.
Bibl. 3

George Dubois (c. 1841)
Philadelphia, Pa.
Bibl. 3

Henry Dubois (c. 1825-1833)
Philadelphia, Pa.
Bibl. 3

James Dubois (c. 1827-1831)
Albany, N.Y.
Bibl. 20

John Dubois (c. 1831-1833)
Philadelphia, Pa.
Bibl. 3

Joseph Dubois (c. 1790-1797)
New York, N.Y.
Bibl. 4, 15, 23, 24, 25, 28, 29,
30, 35, 36, 44, 72

J DUBOIS　I DUBOIS

Peter Dubois (c. 1841-1843)
Philadelphia, Pa.
Bibl. 3

Philo Dubois (c. 1842-1848)
Buffalo, N.Y.
Bibl. 15, 20, 25, 44

P. DUBOIS BUFFALO

Thomas Dubois (c. 1849)
Philadelphia, Pa.
Bibl. 3

Tunis D. Dubois (c. 1797-
1799)
New York, N.Y.
Bibl. 15, 23, 24, 25, 28, 29, 35,
36, 44, 72, 83

T. D. D.　T. D. DUBOIS

Dubosq
(See Richards & Dubosq)

———— Dubosq (c. 1829-1830)
Philadelphia, Pa.
Bibl. 3

Dubosq & Baton (c. 1835-
1841)
Philadelphia, Pa.
Bibl. 3

Dubosq, Baton & Co. (c. 1839-
1840)
Philadelphia, Pa.
Bibl. 3

Dubosq & Carrow (c. 1839-
1843)
Philadelphia, Pa.
George Dubosq (?)
John Carrow
Bibl. 3

Dubosq, Carrow & Co. (c.
1844-1850)
Philadelphia, Pa.
George Dubosq (?)

John Carrow
Bibl. 3

Dubosq & Jardella (c. 1833)
Philadelphia, Pa.
Bibl. 3

Dubosq & Scheer (c. 1849-
1850)
Philadelphia, Pa.
——— Dubosq
John C. Sheer (?)
Bibl. 3

Francis P. Dubosq (c. 1837-
1850)
Philadelphia, Pa.
Bibl. 3

George Dubosq (c. 1839-1850)
Philadelphia, Pa.
Dubosq & Carrow (c. 1839-
1843) (?)
Dubosq, Carrow & Co. (c.
1844-1850) (?)
Bibl. 3

H. & W. Dubosq (c. 1846-
1850)
Philadelphia, Pa.
Bibl. 3, 23

Henry Dubosq Jr. (c. 1818-
1850)
Philadelphia, Pa.
Bibl. 3

Peter Dubosq (c. 1835-1850)
Philadelphia, Pa.
Bibl. 3

Philip L. Dubosq (c. 1837-
1850)
Philadelphia, Pa.
Bibl. 3

Theodore Dubosq (c. 1829-
1850)
Philadelphia, Pa.
Bibl. 3

William Dubosq (c. 1835-1837)
Philadelphia, Pa.
Bibl. 3

William A. Dubosq (c. 1839)
Philadelphia, Pa.
Bibl. 3

Benne R. Duché
(See Rene Rock Duché)

Duche & Donnand (c. 1820-
1822)

Philadelphia, Pa.
Bibl. 3, 23, 36, 44

Rene Rock Duché (c. 1795-
1805)
New York, N.Y.
Bibl. 15, 23, 28, 36, 44

R. R. Duchi (c. 1823-1824)
Philadelphia, Pa.
Bibl. 3

A. L. Ducomman (c. 1795-
1798)
Philadelphia, Pa.
Bibl. 3

Henry Ducommun (c. 1818-
1850)
Philadelphia, Pa.
Bibl. 3

Henry Ducommun Jr. & Co. (c.
1843-1844)
Philadelphia, Pa.
Bibl. 3

Lewis Ducray (c. 1771)
Philadelphia, Pa.
Bibl. 3

——— Dudley (c. 1784)
Philadelphia, Pa.
Bibl. 3

Benjamin Dudley (c. 1768)
Birmington, Ga.
Savannah, Ga.
Bibl. 17, 23, 36, 44

George Duff (c. 1837)
Philadelphia, Pa.
Bibl. 3

George C. Duff (c. 1846)
New Bern, N.C.
Bibl. 22

——— Duffee (c. 1785)
Location unknown
Bibl. 28

DUFFEE

James Duffel (b. 1761-d. 1835)
Georgetown, S.C. (c. 1790-
1800)
New York, N.Y. (c. 1801)
Fredericksburg, Va. (c. 1802-
1807)
Lynchberg, Va. (c. 1810-1828)
Bibl. 15, 29, 36, 44, 54

| I Duffel | J D | J. DUFFEL |

| I Duffel |

George Hurd Duffey (b.
1800-d. 1855)
Alexandria, Va.
Bibl. 19, 54

John Duffey (c. 1790-1809)
Alexandria, Va.
Bibl. 19, 54

Major George Nelson Duffey
(b. 1820-d. 1896)
Alexandria, Va.
Bibl. 19, 54

Edward Duffield (c. 1756-
1775, d. 1803)
Philadelphia, Pa.
Bibl. 3, 28

Duhme (c. 1839)
Cincinnati, Ohio
Bibl. 54

Duhme & Co. (c. 1839-1887)
Cincinnati, Ohio
(not St. Louis, Mo.)
Bibl. 24, 25, 44, 54

DUHME

John Dulty Sr. (c. 1807)
Zanesville, Ohio
Bibl. 34

Anthony Dumesnil(l) (d.
1833)
Lexington, Ky. (c. 1818-1833)
Bibl. 32, 44

Jeremiah Dummer (Dunner)
(b. 1645-d. 1718)
Boston, Mass.
Bibl. 2, 8, 15, 23, 24, 25, 28, 29,
36, 44, 54

P. Dumont (c. 1844-1846)
Louisville, Ky.
Bibl. 32

Dumontot, Dumorte
(See Dumoutet)

Joseph Dumourier (c. 1814-
1816)
Philadelphia, Pa.
Bibl. 3, 23, 36, 44

Elizabeth Dumoutet (c. 1817-1822)
Philadelphia, Pa.
Bibl. 3

John Baptiste Dumoutet (Doumoutet) (Dumontot) (Dumorte) (Dymotit) (Doumouet) (c. 1793-1816)
Philadelphia, Pa.
Charleston, S.C.
Bibl. 3, 5, 15, 23, 24, 25, 28, 29, 36, 39, 44, 46, 54

Dunbar & Bangs (c. 1850)
Worcester, Mass.
Bibl. 15, 25, 44, 89

DUNBAR & BANGS | FINE
WORCESTER

John Dunbar (c. 1796)
Baltimore, Md.
Bibl. 38

R. D. Dunbar
Worcester, Mass. (?)
Bibl. 15, 44

R. D. DUNBAR

William Henry Duncan (c. 1850)
Shelby County, Ky.
Springfield, Ky.
Washington County, Ky.
Bibl. 32, 54, 68

Pratt Dundas (c. 1837)
Philadelphia, Pa.
Bibl. 3, 23, 36, 44

R. Dunham
Location unknown
Bibl. 28, 29

R DUNHAM

George Dunkerley (c. 1844-1847)
Philadelphia, Pa.
Bibl. 3

Joseph Dunkerly (c. 1787)
Boston, Mass.
Bibl. 23, 28, 36, 44

Dunlevy
(See Shaw & Dunlevy)

Robert Dunlev(e)y (c. 1787)
Philadelphia, Pa.
Bibl. 28

Robert Dunlev(e)y (Donleavy) (c. 1830-1837)
Philadelphia, Pa.
Bibl. 3, 4, 23, 36, 44

Dunlevy & Dowell (c. 1843-1846)
Philadelphia, Pa.
Robert Dunlevy Jr.
George G. Dowell
Bibl. 3, 23

Dunlevy & Wise (c. 1847-1850)
Philadelphia, Pa.
Robert Dunlevy Jr.
George K. Wise (?)
Bibl. 3, 23

Robert Dunlevy Jr. (Donleavy) (c. 1839-1850)
Philadelphia, Pa.
Dunlevy & Dowell (c. 1843-1846) (?)
Dunlevy & Wise (c. 1847-1850)
Bibl. 3, 23

James Dunlop (c. 1784)
Bennington, Vt.
Bibl. 54

Dunn
(See Kidney & Dunn)

Dunn & Cann (c. 1834-1838)
New York, N.Y.
David Dunn
John Cann
Bibl. 15, 44

Dunn & Son (c. 1787-1791)
New York, N.Y.
Bibl. 23, 36, 44

Cary Dunn (c. 1765-1787)
Underhill, Vt. (c. 1765)
Morristown, N.J. (c. 1778)
Newark, N.J. (c. 1782)
New York, N.Y.
Bibl. 4, 15, 23, 24, 25, 28, 29, 30, 35, 36, 46, 54, 83

C DUNN

David Dunn (c. 1834-1850)
New York, N.Y.
Dunn & Cann (c. 1834-1838)

Charters, Cann & Dunn (c. 1850)
Bibl. 15, 23, 36, 44

John Dunn (c. 1823-1824)
Philadelphia, Pa.
Bibl. 3

Jeremiah Dunner
(See Dummer)

Dunning
(See Curtis & Dunning)

——— Dunning (c. 1839)
Penn Yan, N.Y.
Ayers & Dunning
Bibl. 20

Dunning & Crissey (c. 1847)
Rochester, N.Y.
Elnathan F. Crissey
Julius N. Dunning
Bibl. 20

Julius N. Dunning (c. 1847)
Rochester, N.Y.
Dunning & Crissey
Bibl. 20

Dennis Dunscomb (c. 1765)
New York, N.Y.
Bibl. 23, 36, 44

Mary Matilda Dunseth (c. 1804)
Charleston, S.C.
Michael Samuel Debruhl (c. 1798-1806)
Bibl. 5

H. Duon (c. 1819)
Baltimore, Md.
Not a silversmith but a lace maker.
Bibl. 23, 36, 38, 44

John Baptiste Duplat (c. 1809-1820)
Charleston, S.C.
Bibl. 5

Rose Duplat (c. 1806)
Charleston, S.C.
Bibl. 5

Dupuy & Sons (c. 1784)
Philadelphia, Pa.
Daniel Dupuy
David Dupuy
John Dupuy
Bibl. 23, 24, 29, 36, 44

Andrew Dupuy (d. 1743)
Charleston, S.C.
Bibl. 5, 54

Bernard Dupuy (c. 1828-1844)
Raleigh, N.C.
Bibl. 21, 25, 44

| B. DUPUY |

Daniel Dupuy (b. 1719-d.
1807)
New York, N.Y. (c. 1719)
Reading, Pa. (c. 1777)
Philadelphia, Pa. (c. 1784-
1790)
Dupuy & Sons (c. 1784)
Daniel Dupuy & Sons (c. 1784)
David & Dupuy (c. 1792-1805)
Bibl. 3, 4, 15, 23, 24, 25, 28,
29, 36, 39, 44, 54, 81

Daniel Dupuy Jr. (b. 1753-d.
1826)
Philadelphia, Pa. (c. 1782-
1813)
John & Daniel Dupuy Jr. (c.
1783-1785)
Bibl. 3, 15, 23, 25, 28, 36, 44

| D. DuPuY |

Daniel Dupuy & Sons (c. 1784)
Philadelphia, Pa.
Daniel Dupuy
John Dupuy
Bibl. 25

John Dupuy (b. 1747-d. 1838)
Reading, Pa. (c. 1777)
Philadelphia, Pa. (c. 1784)
John & Daniel Dupuy Jr. (c.
1783-1785)
Dupuy & Sons (c. 1784)
Daniel Dupuy & Sons (c. 1784)
Bibl. 3, 36, 44

John & Daniel Dupuy Jr. (c.
1783-1785)
Philadelphia, Pa.
Bibl. 3, 15, 23, 36, 44

Odean Dupuy (c. 1735)
Philadelphia, Pa.
Bibl. 3

Cyrus Durand (b. 1787-d.
1868)
Newark, N.J.
Bibl. 28

John Durand (c. 1835)
New York, N.Y.
Bibl. 15, 23, 36

Louis Durand (c. 1834)
New York, N.Y.
Bibl. 15

John Durandeau (c. 1833-1836)
New York, N.Y.
Belloni & Durandeau (c. 1835-
1836)
Bibl. 15, 23, 36, 44

Elihu Durfee (c. 1828)
Palmyra, N.Y.
Bibl. 20

Durgin & Burtt (c. 1859)
St. Louis, Mo.
Freeman A. Durgin
——— Burtt
Bibl. 54

DURGIN & BURTT

Freeman A. Durgin (c. 1859-
1911)
St. Louis, Mo.
Durgin & Burtt (c. 1859)
Bibl. 54

William B. Durgin (c. 1850)
Concord, N.H.
Bibl. 24, 25, 44

| WM B DURGIN |

Dusenberry (c. 1800)
Location unknown
Bibl. 28

DUSENBERRY

William C. Dusenberry (c.
1819-1835)
New York, N.Y.
Bibl. 15, 24, 25, 44, 79

| W. C. DUSENBERRY |

Pierre Eugene Du Simitiere (c.
1776, d. 1784)
Philadelphia, Pa.
Bibl. 3

Dutens (Duteus) & Harper (c.
1755-1756)
Philadelphia, Pa.
Charles J. Dutens

David Harper
Bibl. 3, 23, 36, 44

Charles J. Dutens (Duteus)
Philadelphia, Pa. (c. 1751-
1757)
Dutens & Harper (c. 1755-1756)
Bibl. 3, 23, 36, 44

——— Duvalier (c. 1800)
Location unknown
Bibl. 28, 29, 44

| DUVALIER |

Daniel Duyckinck (c. 1790-
1800)
New York, N.Y.
Bibl. 23, 25, 28, 36, 44

| D. DUYCKINCK |

Timothy Dwight (b. 1654-d.
1691)
Boston, Mass.
Bibl. 2, 4, 25, 29, 36, 44, 54, 66

William Dye
Fayetteville, N.C.
Bibl. 21

A. S. Dygert (c. 1830)
Location unknown
Bibl. 24

| A. S. DYGERT |

Dymotit
(See Dumotet)

Eagles & Morrie (c. 1799)
New York, N.Y.
Bibl. 23, 36, 44

Samuel Eakins (c. 1837)
Philadelphia, Pa.
Bibl. 3

Joseph Ealer (c. 1838-1842)
St. Louis, Mo.
Bibl. 54

Joshua Eames (d. 1722)
Boston, Mass. (c. 1700)
Bibl. 23, 28, 36, 44

Alfred Earnshaw (c. 1846-
1849)
Troy, N.Y.
Bibl. 20

George Easley (c. 1838)
Lexington, Ky.
Bibl. 32, 68

Easman
(See next entry)

Benjamin Eastman (Easman)
    (c. 1777-1790)
Pasquotank County, N.C.
Bibl. 21

Moses Eastman (b. 1794-d.
    1850)
Savannah, Ga. (c. 1826)
J. Penfield & Co. (c. 1820-
    1828)
Bibl. 17

M EASTMAN

Seth Eastman (c. 1820)
Concord, N.H.
Bibl. 15, 25, 44

 SETH EASTMAN

Easton
(See Chase & Easton)

Easton & Sanford (c. 1830-
    1838)
Nantucket Island, Mass.
James Easton
Frederick C. Sanford
Bibl. 12, 23, 24, 25, 28, 29, 36,
    44

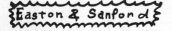 Easton & Sanford

E&S

James Easton (2d) (b. 1807-d.
    1903)
Nantucket, Mass.
Easton & Sanford (c. 1830-
    1838)
Bibl. 12, 23, 24, 25, 28, 36, 44

 J.EASTON

NANTUCKET

J. EASTON 2nd

PURE COIN

Nathaniel Easton (c. 1780-
    1815)
Nantucket Island, Mass.
Bibl. 12, 23, 24, 25, 36, 44

 N. EASTON

Thomas Eastwick (c. 1743)
Boston, Mass.
Bibl. 23, 36, 44

(Captain) James B. Eaton (d.
    1829)
Charleston, S.C. (c. 1829) (?)
Boston, Mass. (c. 1805)
Macon, Ga.
Bibl. 5, 15, 17, 25

J. B. EATON

Timothy Eaton (c. 1793-1794)
Philadelphia, Pa.
Bibl. 3, 15, 23, 25, 36, 44

T EATON

W. Eaves & A. Falize (c. 1842)
Lexington, Ky.
Bibl. 32

W. T. Eaves (c. 1845-1848)
St. Louis, Mo.
Bibl. 54

Eayas
Eayers
(See next entry)

Thomas Stevens Eayres
    (Eayas) (Eayers) (c. 1760-
    1803)
Boston, Mass. (c. 1785)
Worcester, Mass. (c. 1791-
    1793)
Bibl. 15, 23, 24, 28, 29, 36, 44,
    69

T.E   EAYRES

John Eberman Jr. (c. 1771-
    1772)
Lancaster, Pa.
Bibl. 3

D. Eccleston (c. 1805)
Lancaster, Pa.
Bibl. 3

John Eckart (c. 1848-1850)
Camden, N.J.
Bibl. 3

Alexander Perry Eckel (b.
    1821-d. 1906, c. 1845)
Greensboro, N.C.
Front Royal, Va. (?)
Jefferson County, Tenn. (?)
Bibl. 22

Andrew Eckel (c. 1837-1840)
Philadelphia, Pa.
Bibl. 3

David Eckerman (c. 1819)
Philadelphia, Pa.
Bibl. 3

Valentine Eckert (c. 1839)
Philadelphia, Pa.
Bibl. 3

Adam Eckfeldt (c. 1800-1850)
Philadelphia, Pa.
Bibl. 3

Charles Eckfeldt (c. 1839-
    1843)
Philadelphia, Pa.
Bibl. 3

Jacob Eckfield (c. 1783, d.
    1818)
Philadelphia, Pa.
Bibl. 3

John Eckart (c. 1845)
Philadelphia, Pa.
Bibl. 3

Lewis Ecuyer (b. 1829, c.
    1851-1854)
Utica, N.Y.
Bibl. 18

Eddy & Barrows (c. 1832)
Tollard, Conn.
——— Eddy
James Madison Barrows (?)
Bibl. 28

John Edgar (c. 1807)
New York, N.Y.
Bibl. 23, 36, 44

Charles Edler (c. 1844-1846)
Philadelphia, Pa.
Bibl. 3

J. C. Edler (c. 1841)
Philadelphia, Pa.
Bibl. 3

Claude Edmechat (c. 1790)
New York, N.Y.
Bibl. 23, 28, 36, 44

T. Edmond (c. 1800)
Location unknown
Bibl. 24

William Edmond (c. 1848)
Philadelphia, Pa.
Bibl. 3

B. F. Edmunds (19th century)
Location unknown
Bibl. 15, 44

B. F. EDMUNDS

Oliver Edson (c. 1804-1810)
Ballston Spa, N.Y.
Bibl. 20

Abraham Edwards (c. 1763)
Ashby, Mass.
Bibl. 28, 44

Andrew Edwards (c. 1763-
1798)
Boston, Mass.
Bibl. 4, 23, 28, 36, 44

Calvin Edwards (b. 1698, c.
1710)
Ashby, Mass.
Bibl. 23, 28, 36, 44

Gage D. Edwards (c. 1827-
1836)
Athens, Ga.
Bibl. 17

John Edwards (b. 1671-d.
1746)
Annapolis, Md. (c. 1735)
Bucks County, Pa. (c. 1778)
Boston, Mass.
Bibl. 2, 3, 15, 23, 25, 28, 29,
36, 44, 50, 54, 66, 69, 70

John Edwards & John Allen (c.
1699-1707)
Boston, Mass.
(See Allen & Edwards [c. 1700-
1707])
Bibl. 80

Joseph Edwards Sr. (b. 1707-d.
1777)
Boston, Mass.
Bibl. 23, 24, 29, 36, 44

Joseph Edwards Jr. (b. 1737-d.
1783)
Boston, Mass.
Bibl. 2, 15, 23, 25, 28, 29, 36,
44, 54, 69

I Edwards

I E

Peter Edwards (c. 1850)
Philadelphia, Pa.
Bibl. 3

Samuel Edwards (b. 1705-d.
1762, c. 1729)
Boston, Mass.
Natick, Mass.
Bibl. 2, 15, 23, 24, 25, 28, 29,
36, 39, 49, 54, 66, 69

Thomas Edwards (b. 1701-d.
1755)
Boston, Mass. (c. 1725)
New York, N.Y. (c. 1731)
Bibl. 2, 4, 15, 23, 24, 25, 28, 36,
44, 70

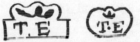

Robert Egan (c. 1772)
Williamsburg, Va.
Bibl. 19

Jacob Ege (b. 1754-d. 1795)
Richmond, Va.
Bibl. 19

James L. Ege & Co. (c. 1832)
Fredericksburg, Va.
Bibl. 19

Edward Egg (c. 1860-1880)
Columbia, S.C.
Bibl. 5

Edward Elder (c. 1812)
Lexington, Ky.
Bibl. 32

William Elder (c. 1841)
Philadelphia, Pa.
Bibl. 3

Elderkin & Staniford (c. 1790-
1792)

Windham, Conn.
Alfred Elderkin
John Staniford
Bibl. 23, 36, 44

Alfred Elderkin (b. 1759-d.
1833)
Windham, Conn. (c. 1790-
1792)
Killingsworth, Conn.
Red Hook, N.Y.
Elderkin & Staniford (c. 1790-
1792)
Bibl. 15, 16, 23, 25, 28, 36, 44

Elisha Elderkin (b. 1753-d.
1822)
Killingworth, Conn.
New Haven, Conn.
Bibl. 16, 23, 28, 36, 49

Jacob H. Eler (c. 1829-1833)
Philadelphia, Pa.
Bibl. 3

Jeremiah Elfreth Jr. (c. 1723-
1765)
Philadelphia, Pa. (c. 1752)
Bibl. 25, 44, 54, 81

J E
I E   J E

H. P. Elias (c. 1840)
Location unknown
Bibl. 89

Peter Elleson (c. 1796)
New York, N.Y.
Bibl. 28

Joseph Ellicott (c. 1778)
Bucks County, Pa.
Bibl. 3

George Elliot(t) (c. 1810-1852)
Wilmington, Del.
Bibl. 25, 30, 44

G. ELLIOT

H. Elliot (19th century)
Location unknown
Bibl. 15, 28, 44

H ELLIOT

——— Elliott (c. 1818-1822)
Philadelphia, Pa.
Bibl. 3

Elliott & Burnham (c. 1821)
Salisbury, N.C.
Zebulon Elliott
E. B. Burnham
Bibl. 21

Benjamin P. Elliott (c. 1843-1850)
Philadelphia, Pa.
Bibl. 3

James Elliott (c. 1804)
Philadelphia, Pa.
Bibl. 3

James Elliott (b. 1773-d. 1865)
Winnsboro, S.C. (c. 1807)
Bibl. 5, 44

J. E

John Aaron Elliott (b. 1788-d. 1857)
Sharon, Conn. (c. 1815)
Michigan
New York State
Bibl. 15, 16, 23, 25, 28, 36

A E

Joseph Elliott (c. 1768)
New Castle County, Del.
Bibl. 3, 23, 30, 36, 44

Zebulon Elliott
New York, N.Y. (c. 1814-1821)
Salisbury, N.C. (c. 1821)
Elliott & Burnham (c. 1821)
Bibl. 22

Benjamin Ellis (c. 1829-1833)
Philadelphia, Pa.
Bibl. 3

George Ellis (c. 1850)
Philadelphia, Pa.
Bibl. 3

Hugh Ellis (c. 1810-1825)
Philadelphia, Pa.
Bibl. 3

Lewis W. Ellis (c. 1837)
Philadelphia, Pa.
Bibl. 3, 23, 36, 44

Samuel (S. O.) Ellis (c. 1839-1847)
Philadelphia, Pa.
Bibl. 3

Peter Elliston (Ellison) (c. 1791-1800)
New York, N.Y.

Bibl. 23, 24, 25, 36, 44

ELLISTON

David Ellsworth (b. 1742-d. 1821)
Windsor, Conn. (c. 1772-1792)
Bibl. 16, 23, 28, 36, 44

Thomas Elmes (c. 1841)
Philadelphia, Pa.
Bibl. 3

Ormond Elsbre (d. 1801)
Augusta, Ga.
Bibl. 17

Hermann Elson (c. 1843-1848)
Philadelphia, Pa.
Bibl. 3

Julius Elson (c. 1842-1844)
Philadelphia, Pa.
Bibl. 3

Francis Eltheridge (c. 1749)
Annapolis, Md.
Bibl. 38

A. D. Elton (c. 1841-   )
Geneva, N.Y.
Hall & Elton
Bibl. 20

Thomas Eltonhead (c. 1835)
Baltimore, Md.
Bibl. 23, 36, 44

William D. Eltonhead (c. 1849-1850)
Philadelphia, Pa.
Bibl. 3

William Elvins (c. 1796-1808)
Baltimore, Md.
Bibl. 38

———— Embree (c. 1790)
Location unknown
Bibl. 28, 29, 44

EMBREE

Albert Emerick (c. 1847-1850)
Philadelphia, Pa.
Bibl. 3, 23

Augustus Emerick (c. 1825-1829)
Philadelphia, Pa.
Bibl. 3

Emery & Co. (c. 1798)
Boston, Mass.
New York, N.Y.

Stephen Emery
Bibl. 23, 28, 36, 44

Stephen Emery (b. 1725-d. 1801)
Boston, Mass.
Emery & Co. (c. 1798)
Bibl. 4, 15, 23, 24, 25, 28, 29, 36, 39, 54, 72

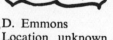

Thomas Knox Emery (b. 1781-d. 1815)
Boston, Mass.
New York, N.Y.
Bibl. 4, 15, 23, 24, 25, 28, 29, 36, 44, 54, 72

D. Emmons
Location unknown
Bibl. 89

D. EMMONS

L. Emmons
Location unknown
Bibl. 15

L. EMMONS

Samuel Emmons (c. 1831-1833)
Philadelphia, Pa.
Bibl. 3

Thomas Emond (c. 1802-1819)
Petersburg, Va.
Bibl. 19

T. EMOND

Thomas Emond (c. 1806-1821)
Raleigh, N.C.
Bibl. 21

Theobald Endt (c. 1742)
Philadelphia, Pa.
Bibl. 3

Samuel Engard (c. 1837-1842)
Philadelphia, Pa.
Bibl. 3

George England (c. 1800)
New York, N.Y.
Bibl. 4, 23, 36

James England (d. 1830)
Charleston, S.C. (c. 1801-1806)
Baltimore, Md. (c. 1807-1830)
Bibl. 5, 38

William England (c. 1717)
Philadelphia, Pa.
Bibl. 3, 4, 23, 28, 36, 44

C. W. Englebert (c. 1839)
Philadelphia, Pa.
Bibl. 3

Charles M. Englehart (c. 1839-
1850)
Philadelphia, Pa.
Bibl. 3

M. Englehart (c. 1837)
Philadelphia, Pa.
Bibl. 3

John English (c. 1819-1828)
Philadelphia, Pa.
Bibl. 3

J. Enno & Hale (c. 1830)
Bangor, Me.
Bibl. 89

J. ENNO & HALE

———— Ensign (c. 1800)
Location unknown
Bibl. 28, 29, 44

ENSIGN

Charles Ensign (c. 1842-
1850-   )
Troy, N.Y.
Bibl. 20

John Ent (c. 1763-1794, d.
1794)
Philadelphia, Pa.
Bibl. 3

Eoff & Connor (c. 1833-1835)
New York, N.Y.
Garret Eoff
John H. Connor
Bibl. 15, 23, 24, 25, 28, 36, 44

J. H. CONNOR   &   G. EOFF

J H CONNOR & G EOFF

Eoff & Howell (c. 1805-1810)
New York, N.Y.
Garret Eoff
Paul Howell
Bibl. 15, 23, 24, 25, 28, 29, 36,
44, 54

EOFF & HOWELL   E & H

Eoff & Moore (c. 1835)
New York, N.Y.
Garret Eoff
John C. Moore
Bibl. 15, 23, 24, 25, 36, 44

G. EOFF   J. C. MOORE

Eoff & Phyfe (c. 1844-1850)
New York, N.Y.
Garret Eoff
William Phyfe
Bibl. 4, 15, 23, 24, 25, 29, 35

E & P

Eoff & Shepherd (c. 1850)
New York, N.Y.
Garret Eoff (?)
———— Shepherd
Bibl. 15, 25, 28, 29, 44

E & S

Edgar M. Eoff (b. 1785-d.
1858)
New York, N.Y. (c. 1850)
Bibl. 15, 23, 24, 25, 44

E. M. E.

Garret Eoff (b. 1785-d. 1858)
New York, N.Y.
Eoff & Howell (c. 1805-1810)
Eoff & Connor (c. 1833-1835)
Eoff & Moore (c. 1835)
Eoff & Phyfe (c. 1844-1850)
Bibl. 4, 23, 24, 25, 28, 29, 35,
36, 39, 54, 79

G. EOFF   G. Eoff

Mortimer E. Eoff (c. 1850)
New York, N.Y.
Bibl. 23, 25

Eolles & Day (c. 1825)
Hartford, Conn.
Bibl. 24, 25, 44

EOLLES & DAY
HARTFORD

EOLLES & DAY
HARTFORD

John Eppelsheimer (c. 1845)
Philadelphia, Pa.
Bibl. 3

Ashman Epps (c. 1848)
Philadelphia, Pa.
Bibl. 3

Ellery Epps (c. 1808)
Boston, Mass.
Bibl. 23, 28, 36, 44

Equer & Aquimac (c. 1816)
New York, N.Y.
Bibl. 23, 36, 44

John Erens (c. 1845-1846)
Louisville, Ky.
Bibl. 32

Ernst & Coan (c. 1814)
Cooperstown, N.Y.
John Frederick Ernst Jr. (?)
Charles Coan
Bibl. 20

Henry B. Ernst (c. 1830-1836,
c. 1844-1845)
Cooperstown, N.Y.
Bibl. 20

John Frederick Ernst Jr. (c.
1808-d. 1830)
Cooperstown, N.Y.
Ernst & Coan (c. 1814) (?)
Bibl. 20

John Ervan (Erwin) (c. 1815)
New York, N.Y.
Bibl. 15, 23

Andrew Erwin (c. 1837)
Philadelphia, Pa.
Bibl. 3, 23, 36, 44

Henry Erwin (c. 1795-1842)
Philadelphia, Pa.
John McMullen (c. 1796)
Bibl. 3, 15, 23, 24, 29, 36, 39,
44, 54

H.ERWIN

H.ERWIN

Henry Erwin & John
McMullen (McMullin)
Philadelphia, Pa. (c. 1796)
Bibl. 54

James Erwin
Baltimore, Md. (c. 1809)
New York, N.Y. (c. 1815)
Bibl. 44

J. ERWIN

John Erwin (c. 1809-1819)
Baltimore, Md.
New York, N.Y.
Bibl. 15, 24, 28, 29, 36, 38

J. ERWIN

John Erwin (c. 1816)
Philadelphia, Pa.
Lownes & Erwin
Bibl. 3

Thomas M. Erwin (d. 1889)
Louisville, Ky. (c. 1845-1846)
Bibl. 32

William C. Erwin (c. 1850)
Rochester, N.Y.
Bibl. 20

Jacob Esler (c. 1829-1833)
Philadelphia, Pa.
Bibl. 3

Charles Esslinger (c. 1840-
1848)
Buffalo, N.Y.
Bibl 20

Robert Estep (c. 1812-1818)
Paris, Ohio
Bibl. 34

Esterle Sons
Louisville, Ky.
Bibl. 54

Jacob R. Esterle (b. 1814-d.
1868)
Louisville, Ky. (c. 1832-1868)
Bibl. 32, 54

Hayacinth Esteva (c. 1804-
1808)
New York, N.Y.
Bibl. 23, 36

George Eter (Etter) (Ettris)
(1833-1850)
Philadelphia, Pa.
Bibl. 3

John E. Ethridge (d. 1894,
c. 1838-1848)
Louisville, Ky.
Bibl. 32, 54

Ettenheimer (c. 1850)
Ohio (?)
Bibl. 89

    Ettenheimer

B. Etter (c. 1780)
Location unknown
Bibl. 28, 29, 44

B. ETTER

Benjamin Etting (c. 1769)
New York, N.Y.
Bibl. 2, 4, 23, 36

Eubank & Jeffries (Jeffries &
Eubank) (c. 1805-1841)
Glasgow, Ky.
———— Eubank
James Jeffries
Bibl. 32, 68

James Eubank (c. 1816-1855)
Glasgow, Ky.
Savage & Eubank (c. 1805-
1820)
James & Joseph Eubank
(1834-1841)
Bibl. 32

James & Joseph Eubank
(c. 1834-1841)
Glasgow, Ky.
Bibl. 32, 54, 68

J. & J. EUBANK

Joseph Eubank (c. 1829-1855)
Glasgow, Ky.
James and Joseph Eubank
(c. 1834-1841)
Bibl. 32, 54, 68

Evans & Allen (c. 1850)
Binghamton, N.Y.
Bibl. 20

Evans & Manning (c. 1850)
New York, N.Y.
Bibl. 89

EVANS & MANNING

Alfred J. Evans (c. 1831-1854)
Binghamton, N.Y.
H. & A. J. Evans (c. 1836-
1841)
Bibl. 20

A J EVANS

David Evans
Philadelphia, Pa. (before 1773)

Baltimore, Md. (c. 1773-1795)
Bibl. 3, 38

Edwin T. Evans (c. 1836-1841)
Binghamton, N.Y.
Bibl. 20

H. & A. J. Evans
Binghamton, N.Y. (c. 1836-
1841)
Horatio Evans
Alfred J. Evans
Bibl. 20

Henry Evans (c. 1820)
New York, N.Y.
Bibl. 23, 24, 25, 28, 29, 44

HENRY EVANS

Horatio Evans (c. 1841)
Binghamton, N.Y.
H. & A. J. Evans (c. 1836-1841)
Bibl. 20

James Evans (c. 1821)
Chenango Point, N.Y.
Bibl. 20

John Evans (c. 1816-1830)
New York, N.Y.
Bibl. 4, 23, 24, 28, 29, 36, 44, 78

EVANS

Oliver Evans (c. 1833)
Philadelphia, Pa.
Bibl. 3

R. C. Evans (c. 1811)
Norwich, N.Y.
Bibl. 20, 54

Robert Evans (c. 1768, d. 1812)
Boston, Mass.
Bibl. 4, 15, 23, 24, 25, 28, 29,
44, 54, 72

Roger Evans (c. 1815)
Waterford, N.Y.
Bibl. 20

Thomas Evans & Sons
(b. 1834)
Binghamton, N.Y.
Bibl. 20

W. R. Evans (c. 1850)
Covington, Ky.
Bibl. 32, 54, 89

W. R. EVANS

William M. Evans (c. 1813-
1848)
Philadelphia, Pa.
Bibl. 3

C. E. Evard & Brother
(c. 1849-   )
Staunton, Va.
Charles Eugene Evard
Charles Edward Evard
Bibl. 19

Charles A. Evard (c. 1847-
1849)
Lynchburg, Va.
Bibl. 19

Charles C. Evard (c. 1837)
Philadelphia, Pa.
Bibl. 3

Charles Edward Evard
(b. 1825-d. 1906)
Leesburg, Va. (c. 1846-1867)
Staunton, Va. (c. 1849-1850)
C. E. Evard & Brother
(c. 1849-   )

C. E. E.

Charles Eugene Evard
(d. 1857)
Philadelphia, Pa. (c. 1837)
Lynchburg, Va. (c. 1840-1844)
Winchester, Va. (c. 1842,
c. 1848)
Staunton, Va. (c. 1849-   )
C. E. Evard & Brother
(c. 1849-   )
Bibl. 19, 54

EVARD

Cornelius Everest (c. 1847-
1850)
Philadelphia, Pa.
Bibl. 3

Jesse Everite (Everitt)
(c. 1811-1819-   )
New York, N.Y.
Bibl. 3, 15, 36, 44

John Evertsen (Evertson)
(Eversten) (c. 1813-1822)
Albany, N.Y.
Bibl. 4, 20, 23, 36, 44

John Ewan (b. 1786-d. 1852)
Charleston, S.C. (c. 1823-1852)
P. Mood & Co. (c. 1823-1834)
Mood & Ewan (c. 1824)
Bibl. 5, 15, 23, 25, 28, 29, 36,
39, 44, 54

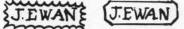

JOHN EVAN

William H. Ewan (c. 1849-
1859)
Charleston, S.C.
Bibl. 5, 15, 25, 44, 54

Wm H. Ewan

John Ewet (c. 1832)
New York, N.Y.
Bibl. 15

John Ewing (b. 1755)
Lancaster, Pa. (c. 1789-
1806?)
Bibl. 3, 54

Warren B. Ewing (c. 1840-
1876)
Shelbyville, Ky.
Sharrard and Ewing (c. 1840)
Bibl. 32, 44, 68

Eyland & Hayden (c. 1832-
1835)
Charleston, S.C.
James Eyland
Nathaniel Hayden
Bibl. 5

James Eyland (b. 1795-d.
1835)
Charleston, S.C. (c. 1819-1835)
James Eyland & Co. (c. 1820-
1827)
Eyland & Hayden (c. 1832-
1835)
Bibl. 5, 25, 44, 54

J EYLAND

James Eyland & Co. (c. 1820-
1827)
Charleston, S.C.
James Eyland
W. & G. Chance
Bibl. 5, 44

J EYLAND & CO.

Matthias Eyre (c. 1775)
Philadelphia, Pa.
Bibl. 3

Simon Eytinge (c. 1829-1831)
Philadelphia, Pa.
Bibl. 3

Faber & Hoover (c. 1837)
Philadelphia, Pa.
William Faber (c. 1828-1850)
Joseph E. Hoover (c. 1837-
1841)
Bibl. 3, 4, 23, 28, 36, 44

W. Faber & Sons
Philadelphia, Pa. (?)
Bibl. 89

W Faber & Sons

William Faber (c. 1828-1850)
Philadelphia, Pa.
Faber & Hoover (c. 1837)
Bibl. 3, 4, 23, 28, 36, 44

H. Fabian
Chester, S.C. (c. 1853)
Lancaster, S.C. (c. 1853)
Bibl. 5

Augustus P. Faff (c. 1837)
Philadelphia, Pa.
Bibl. 3

George M. Fagaler (c. 1808)
Philadelphia, Pa.
Bibl. 23, 36, 44

B. Fagan (c. 1845)
Cassville, Ga.
Bibl. 17

George M. Fagley (c. 1806)
Philadelphia, Pa.
Bibl. 3

Fairchild & Taylor (c. 1838)
Wheeling, Va.
Artemas O. Fairchild
———— Taylor
Bibl. 19

Artemas O. Fairchild (c. 1839-
1851)
Wheeling, Va.
Fairchild & Taylor (c. 1838)
Bibl. 1

A. O. FAIRCHILD

C. Fairchild (c. 1830-1831)
Waterloo, N.Y.
Bibl. 20

James L. Fairchild (c. 1824-
1838)
New York, N.Y.
Bibl. 15, 23, 36, 44

Joseph Fairchild (c. 1824)
New Haven, Conn.
Bibl. 5, 16, 23, 25, 28, 36, 44

Robert Fairchild (b. 1703-d.
1794)
Durham, Conn. (c. 1739)
Stratford, Conn. (c. 1747)
New Haven, Conn. (c. 1772)
New York, N.Y. (c. 1780-1794)
Bibl. 15, 16, 17, 25, 29, 36, 44,
54

Fairman, Draper & Co.
(c. 1823-1825)
Philadelphia, Pa.
Gideon Fairman
—————— Draper
Bibl. 3

Gideon Fairman (b. 1774-d.
1827, c. 1800-1822)
New London, Conn.
Albany, N.Y.
Philadelphia, Pa. (c. 1823-1825)
Fairman, Draper & Co.
(c. 1823-1825)
Bibl. 3, 28, 44

George Gustavus Fakes
(c. 1807)
Baltimore, Md.
Bibl. 38

I. Fales (19th century)
Location unknown
Bibl. 15, 44

Charles Faris (b. 1764-d. 1800)
Annapolis, Md. (c. 1785-1800)
Not in Boston, Mass.

Bibl. 15, 23, 24, 25, 28, 29, 36,
38, 44

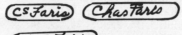

Hyram Faris (b. 1769-d. 1800)
Annapolis, Md. (c. 1790-1800)
Bibl. 15, 38

William Faris (b. 1728-d. 1804)
Annapolis, Md. (c. 1760-1780)
Bibl. 15, 19, 22, 25, 29, 38, 39,
44, 54

William Faris Jr. (b. 1762)
Annapolis, Md. (c. 1782)
Norfolk, Va. (c. 1786)
Havana, Cuba (c. 1792-1794)
Edenton, N.C. (c. 1798-1803)
Bibl. 15, 19, 38

Charles Farley (c. 1812-1830)
Portland, Me. (c. 1828-1830)
Ipswich, Mass.
Wyer & Farley (c. 1828-1830)
Bibl. 15, 23, 24, 25, 28, 36, 44

| C FARLEY | | FARLEY |

Farnam & Ward (c. 1810,
c. 1816)
Norwich, Conn. (c. 1810)
Boston, Mass. (c. 1816)
Rufus Farnam
—————— Ward
Bibl. 23, 24, 25, 28, 29, 36, 44

| FARNAM & WARD |

C. H. Farnam
Location unknown
Bibl. 28, 29

| C H FARNAM |

Henry Farnam (b. 1773,
c. 1798-1833)
Boston, Mass.
Bibl. 4, 15, 3, 24, 25, 28, 29, 36,
44, 54

| H. Farnam |

Rufus Farnam (b. 1771,
c. 1799-1833)
Boston, Mass. (c. 1799-1830)
Hanover, N.H. (c. 1833)

Norwich, Conn. (c. 1810)
Farnam & Ward (c. 1810,
c. 1816)
Bibl. 15, 23, 24, 25, 28, 29, 36,
44, 54, 72

| R. FARNAM | | R. F. |

Rufus & Henry Farnam
(c. 1800-1807)
Boston, Mass.
Hanover, N.H.
Bibl. 2, 15, 25, 28, 29, 36, 44

| R. & H. FARNAM |

Thomas Farnam (c. 1825-1836)
Boston, Mass.
Bibl. 24, 25, 28, 29, 36, 44

| Th FARNAM |

Farnham & Owen (c. 1810)
Location unknown
Bibl. 29, 44

| FARNHAM & OWEN |

Samuel H. Farnham (b. 1813)
Oxford, N.Y. (c. 1840-1845)
Bibl. 20

J. C. Farnsworth
Location unknown
Bibl. 28

J. C. Farnsworth

Farnum
(See Farnam)

Farr
(See Crowley & Farr)

Farr & Co. (c. 1837-1850)
Philadelphia, Pa.
Bibl. 3

Farr & Gilbert (c. 1813-1814)
Manlius, N.Y.
Joseph Farr
—————— Gilbert
Bibl. 20

Bela Farr (c. 1829)
Norwich, N.Y.
Bibl. 20

John Farr (c. 1834)
Utica, N.Y.
Bibl. 20

John C. Farr (c. 1812)
Boston, Mass.

Bibl. 23, 24, 29, 36, 39

| JOHN C FARR |

John C. Farr (c. 1824-1840)
Philadelphia, Pa.
Bibl. 3, 25, 44, 54

| J.C.FARR |

John S. Farr (c. 1834-1837)
Norwich, N.Y.
Bibl. 20

John S. Farr (c. 1849)
Elmira, N.Y.
Bibl. 20

Joseph Farr (c. 1775-d. 1845)
Manlius, N.Y. (c. 1813-1845)
Farr & Gilbert (c. 1813-1814)
Bibl. 20

Farrington & Hunnewell
   (c. 1835-1850)
Boston, Mass.
John Farrington
George W. Hunnewell
Bibl. 4, 23, 24, 25, 28, 29, 36, 44

| FARRINGTON & HUNNEWELL |
| F & H |

John Farrington (c. 1833)
Boston, Mass.
Farrington & Hunnewell
   (c. 1835-1850)
Bibl. 3, 4, 28, 44

John H. Fasbender
Charleston, S.C. (before 1804)
Richmond, Va. (c. 1804-
   1819-   )
Bibl. 19

Fassett & Follet (c. 1793-1795)
Bennington, Vt.
——— Fassett
Timothy Follet
Bibl. 54

Fatman Brothers (c. 1843)
Philadelphia, Pa.
Bibl. 3

Fatton & Co. (c. 1840-1841)
Philadelphia, Pa.
Bibl. 3

Frederick Fatton (c. 1830-1839)
Philadelphia, Pa.
Bibl. 3

John W. Faulkner (c. 1835)
New York, N.Y.
Bibl. 24, 25, 44

John James Favre (c. 1797)
Philadelphia, Pa.
Bibl. 3

Fay & Fisher (c. 1841)
Troy, N.Y.
Henry C. Fay
George Fisher
Bibl. 20

George H. Fay (b. 1830)
Utica, N.Y. (c. 1853-1857)
Bibl. 18

Henry C. Fay (c. 1842-1843)
Troy, N.Y.
Fay & Fisher (c. 1841)
Bibl. 20

August Feckhart (c. 1849-
   1850)
Rochester, N.Y.
Bibl. 20, 41, 44

Fellette
(See Fillette)

Abraham Fellows (b. 1786-d.
   1851)
Troy, N.Y. (c. 1810-1819,
   c. 1829-1835, c. 1844-1850)
Newport, R.I. (c. 1826)
New York, N.Y. (c. 1837-1838)
Albany, N.Y. (c. 1841-1844)
Buffalo, N.Y. (c. 1851)
Fellows & Storm (c. 1839-1844)
Bibl. 15, 20, 24, 25, 28, 29, 36,
   44, 56

| FELLOWS |

Fellows, Cargill & Co.
   (c. 1838)
New York State
Bibl. 21

Fellows & Green (c. 1825)
Maine (?)

Bibl. 28, 29, 44

| FELLOWS & GREEN |

Fellows & Storm (c. 1839-1844)
Albany, N.Y.
New York, N.Y.
Abraham Fellows
Abraham G. Storm
Bibl. 23, 24, 25, 29, 36, 44

| FELLOWS & STORM |

Ignatius W. Fellows
(See next entry)

I. W. & J. K. Fellows (c. 1834)
Lowell, Mass.
Ignatius W. Fellows
James K. Fellows
Bibl. 15, 25, 44

| I. W. & J. K. FELLOWS |

J. Fellows & Co. (c. 1810-1813)
Troy, N.Y.
James Fellows
Bibl. 20

J. C. Fellows (c. 1844-1847)
Albany, N.Y.
Bibl. 20

James Fellows (c. 1810)
Troy, N.Y.
J. Fellows & Co. (c. 1810-1813)
Bibl. 20

James K. Fellows (c. 1832-
   1834)
Lowell, Mass.
I. W. & J. K. Fellows (c. 1834)
Bibl. 15, 25, 44

| J. K. FELLOWS |

John F. Fellows (c. 1824)
Portsmouth, N.H.
Werner & Fellows
Bibl. 23, 36

Louis Strite Fellows (c. 1845)
New York State
Bibl. 21

Philip M. Fellows (c. 1839-
   1841)
Troy, N.Y.
Bibl. 20

J. S. Felt (c. 1825)
Portland, Me.
Bibl. 14, 25, 28

| J. S. FELT |

Robert Felton (c. 1683)
Philadelphia, Pa.
Bibl. 3

Alexander Fenlester (c. 1807)
Baltimore, Md.
Bibl. 38

Jason Fenn (c. 1820)
Lancaster, Ohio
Bibl. 34

Fenno & Hale (c. 1840)
Bangor, Me.
Bibl. 25, 44

FENNO & HALE

J. Fenno (c. 1825)
Location unknown
Bibl. 28, 29, 44

J. Fenno

Charles Edward Ferguson
    (b. 1752)
Williamsburg, Va. (c. 1778-
1781)
Richmond, Va. (c. 1782)
Bibl. 19

Elijah Ferguson (c. 1833-1850)
New Bern, N.C.
Bibl. 21

George Ferguson (c. 1820-
1822)
Philadelphia, Pa.
Bibl. 3

John Ferguson (c. 1801-1810)
Philadelphia, Pa.
Moore & Ferguson (c. 1801-
1805)
Bibl. 3, 23, 36, 39, 44

Louis Ferit (Ferret) (c. 1819-
1825)
Philadelphia, Pa.
Bibl. 3

Mathew Fernbach (c. 1819)
Norfolk, Va.
Bibl. 19

Ferret
(See Ferit)

John F. Ferrette (c. 1821)
Charleston, S.C.
Bibl. 5

Lewis Ferrey (c. 1837)
Philadelphia, Pa.
Bibl. 3

John Ferrier (c. 1822)
New Orleans, La.
Bibl. 23, 38, 44

Ferris & McElwee (c. 1813)
Philadelphia, Pa.
Benjamin Ferris (?)
James McElwee
Bibl. 3

Benjamin Ferris (c. 1802-1811)
Philadelphia, Pa.
Ferris & McElwee (c. 1813)
    (?)
Bibl. 3

Benjamin Ferris (c. 1808-1824)
Albany, N.Y. (c. 1816)
New York, N.Y.
Bibl. 15, 20, 23, 28, 36

Benjamin Ferris (c. 1811)
Waterford, N.Y.
Bibl. 20

Edward B. Ferris (c. 1846-1848)
Philadelphia, Pa.
Bibl. 3

R. Ferris (c. 1850)
Location unknown
Bibl. 44

R. FERRIS

Ziba Ferris b. 1786-d. 1875)
Wilmington, Del. (c. 1810-
1860)
Bibl. 25, 30, 44

ZIBA FERRIS

William Ferriss (c. 1813)
Glens Falls, N.Y.
Bibl. 20

William Ferriss (c. 1836-1839)
Buffalo, N.Y.
Bibl. 20

Jacob (J. W.) Fertig
    (c. 1810-1811)
Philadelphia, Pa.
Bibl. 3

——— Fessenden (c. 1845)
Newport, R.I.
Bibl. 23, 24, 44

FESSENDEN

John Fessler Sr. (b. 1757-d.
1820, c. 1785-1820)
Frederick, Md.
Lancaster, Pa.
Bibl. 38

John Fessler Jr. (c. 1800-
1820-   )
Frederick, Md.
Bibl. 38

Fest & Bro. (c. 1850)
Philadelphia, Pa.
Bibl. 3

Alfred Fest (c. 1850)
Philadelphia, Pa.
Bibl. 3

Edwy Fest (c. 1842-1850)
Philadelphia, Pa.
Bibl. 3

Peter Feurt (c. 1703-1737,
    d. 1737)
Boston, Mass.
New York, N.Y.
Bibl. 2, 25, 28, 29, 44, 69

Godfrey Ficher (c. 1811-1813)
Philadelphia, Pa.
Bibl. 3

James B. Fidler (c. 1850)
Philadelphia, Pa.
Bibl. 3

Field
(See Henderson, Field & Co.)

Field & Halliwell (c. 1806-
1813)
Poughkeepsie, N.Y.
John Field
George Halliwell
Bibl. 20

Field & Monger (c. 1805-1806)
Poughkeepsie, N.Y.
John Field
Benjamin Monger
Bibl. 20

——— Field (c. 1817)
Auburn, N.Y.
Bibl. 20

Charles Field (c. 1835-1850)
Philadelphia, Pa.
Bibl. 3

David E. Field (c. 1840-1848)
Cleveland, Ohio
Bibl. 34, 54

George Field (c. 1840)
Philadelphia, Pa.
Bibl. 3

John Field (d. 1821)
Poughkeepsie, N.Y. (c. 1799-1806)
Field & Monger (c. 1805-1806)
Field & Halliwell (c. 1806-1813)
Bibl. 20

John H. Field (c. 1811)
Batavia, N.Y.
Bibl. 20

Peter Field
Hudson, N.Y. (c. 1785)
Albany, N.Y. (c. 1795-1800)
Bibl. 20

Peter Field (Jr.)
New York, N.Y. (c. 1805-1837)
Newburgh, N.Y. (c. 1807-1810)
Bibl. 15, 20, 25, 44

P. FIELD JR

Peter W. Field
May be Peter Field Jr.
Bibl. 89

Samuel Field(s) (c. 1816-1829)
Philadelphia, Pa.
Steel & Field (c. 1814-1825)
Henderson, Field & Co.
(c. 1816)
Bibl. 3, 23, 36, 44

George Fielding
New York, N.Y. (c. 1731-1750)
Albany, N.Y. (c. 1765)
Bibl. 4, 15, 23, 25, 28, 29, 35, 36,
44, 54, 72

John S. Fifield (18th century)
Westerly, R.I.
Bibl. 28, 44

File
(See Pheil)

Francis Fillette (Fellette)
(b. 1791-d. 1838)
Charleston, S.C. (w. 1807-1838)

———— Pineau
Bibl. 5

Filley, Mead & Caldwell
(c. 1850)
Philadelphia, Pa.
———— Filley
John O. Mead
James E. Caldwell (?)
Bibl. 3

Finch & Cagger (c. 1832-1838)
Albany, N.Y.
Hiram Finch
Michael Cagger
Bibl. 20

Hiram Finch (c. 1829-1840)
Albany, N.Y.
Finch & Cagger (c. 1832-1838)
Bibl. 4, 20, 23, 28, 36, 44

Peter Finch (c. 1826)
Georgetown, S.C.
John Hawkins
Bibl. 5

The Rev. James Findley
(c. 1810)
Zanesville, Ohio
Bibl. 34

Samuel Finefield
Troy, N.Y. (c. 1834-1835)
Buffalo, N.Y. (c. 1835-1836)
New York, N.Y. (?) (c. 1835)
Bibl. 20, 23

Samuel Finewall (c. 1835)
New York, N.Y.
Bibl. 36, 44

———— Finlayson (c. 1782)
Charleston, S.C.
Bibl. 5, 44, 54

Henry Finlayson (d. 1788)
Savannah, Ga. (c. 1775)
Bibl. 17, 28

Francis Finney (c. 1844)
Philadelphia, Pa.
Bibl. 3, 23

John Finney (c. 1754)
Charlestown, Md.
Bibl. 38

John P. Fireng (Firing)
Burlington, N.J. (c. 1810-1830)
Philadelphia, Pa. (c. 1823-1833)
Bibl. 3, 23, 24, 25, 28, 29, 36, 44

J. P. FIRENG

Jean B. Fischesser (c. 1857)
Walhalla, S.C.
Bibl. 5

Isaac Fish Jr. (c. 1843-1850)
Utica, N.Y.
Bibl. 18, 20
ISAAC FISH

Willson Fish (c. 1838)
Rochester, N.Y.
Bibl. 20

Fisher
(See Cooper & Fisher)

Fisher & Champney (c. 1846-1847)
Troy, N. Y.
George Fisher
Lewis C. Champney
Bibl. 20

George Fisher & Co. (c. 1842-1844)
Troy, N.Y.
Bibl. 20

George Fisher (c. 1837-1846)
Troy, N.Y.
Fay & Fisher (c. 1841)
George Fisher & Co. (c. 1842-1844)
Fisher & Champney (c. 1846-1847)
Bibl. 20

Henry Fisher (c. 1849-1850)
Philadelphia, Pa.
Bibl. 3

James Fisher (c. 1821-1832)
New York, N.Y.
Bibl. 15, 23, 36, 44

John Fisher (c. 1790)
York, Pa.
Bibl. 3

John P. Fisher (c. 1820-1822)
Philadelphia, Pa.
Bibl. 3

Martin Fisher (c. 1798-1799)
Philadelphia, Pa.
Bibl. 3

Robert Y. Fisher (c. 1824)
Philadelphia, Pa.
Bibl. 3

Thomas A. Fisher
Philadelphia, Pa. (c. 1797)
Baltimore, Md. (c. 1803)

Easton, Md. (c. 1803-1807)
Bibl. 3, 15, 23, 24, 25, 28, 29, 36, 38, 44

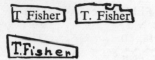

William Fisher (c. 1841-1845)
Charleston, Va.
Bibl. 19

R. Fiske (19th century)
Location unknown
Bibl. 89

R. Fiske

Amon Fister (c. 1794)
Philadelphia, Pa.
Bibl. 3

Fitch & Hobart (c. 1811-1813)
New Haven, Conn.
New Bern, N.C.
Joshua Hobart
Allen Fitch
Bibl. 21, 23, 28, 36, 44

Fitch
(See Dennis & Fitch)

Allen Fitch (b. 1785)
New Haven, Conn. (c. 1808-   )
New Bern, N.C. (c. 1811-1826-   )
Fitch & Hobart (c. 1811-1813)
Bibl. 16, 21, 23, 28, 36, 44

David Fitch (c. 1835)
Philadelphia, Pa.
Bibl. 3

Dennis M. Fitch (c. 1840-1850)
Troy, N.Y.
Not New Haven, Conn.
Bibl. 20, 23, 24, 25, 36, 44

D M FITCH

James Fitch (d. 1826)
Auburn, N.Y. (c. 1816-1821)
Graves & Fitch (c. 1816-1821)
Bibl. 20, 25

John Fitch (b. 1743-d. 1798)
Trenton, N.J. (c. 1769-1776)
New York, N.Y. (c. 1782)

East Windsor, Conn.
East Hartford, N.J.
Kentucky
Bibl. 3, 23, 24, 25, 29, 36, 44, 46, 54, 61

J F   J. FITCH

William Fitch (c. 1831)
Batavia, N.Y.
Keyes & Fitch
Bibl. 20

John Fite (b. 1783-d. 1818)
Baltimore, Md. (c. 1807-1818)
Bibl. 15, 24, 25, 29, 38, 44

I. FITE   J F

Enoch Fithian (c. 1771-1776)
Greenwich, N.J.
Bibl. 46, 54

James Fitzer (c. 1849)
Camden, N.J.
Bibl. 3

George (G. K.) R. Fitzgerald
(c. 1841-1848)
Philadelphia, Pa.
Bibl. 3, 23

James Fitzgerald (c. 1841-1846)
Philadelphia, Pa.
Bibl. 3, 23

R. Fitzgerald & Co. (c. 1827)
Plattsburg, N.Y.
Bibl. 20

George W. Flach (b. 1818-d. 1877)
Charleston, S.C. (c. 1840-1870)
Bibl. 5

Josiah Flagg (c. 1713-1765)
Boston, Mass.
Bibl. 4, 23, 25, 28, 36, 44

J. F

Josiah Flagg Jr. (b. 1738)
Boston, Mass. (c. 1810)
Bibl. 28, 44

S. Flagg (c. 1825)
Location unknown
Bibl. 15, 44

S FLAGG

Edward Flaig (c. 1830)
Danville, Ky.
Bibl. 32

James Flanagan (c. 1833)
Philadelphia, Pa.
Bibl. 3

Henry Flatcher (c. 1818)
Lexington, Ky.
Bibl. 54

George Fleegal (c. 1819-1824)
Philadelphia, Pa.
Bibl. 3

Flere & Harris (c. 1767)
Charleston, S.C.
Thomas Flere
Charles Harris
Bibl. 44

Thomas Flere (c. 1767)
Charleston, S.C.
Flere & Harris (c. 1767)
Bibl. 5

L. H. Flersheim (c. 1839)
Buffalo, N.Y.
Bibl. 20

Fletcher & Bennett (Bennett & Fletcher) (c. 1830-1894)
Fletcher, Bennett & Co.
Louisville, Ky.
Philadelphia, Pa.
Henry Fletcher
——— Bennett
Bibl. 3, 23, 32, 36, 44, 54, 68

FLETCHER & BENNETT

Fletcher & Gardiner
Boston, Mass. (c. 1810)
Philadelphia, Pa. (c. 1815-1822)
Charles Fletcher
Thomas Fletcher
Baldwin Gardiner
Sidney Gardiner
Bibl. 3, 4, 15, 23, 24, 25, 28, 29, 36, 39, 44, 54

F. & G.

C. & G. Fletcher (c. 1819-1824)
Philadelphia, Pa.
Bibl. 3

Charles Fletcher (c. 1810-1833)
Philadelphia, Pa.
Fletcher & Gardiner (c. 1810, c. 1815-1822)
Bibl. 3, 23, 36, 44

Francis C. Fletcher (c. 1833-
1834)
Troy, N.Y.
Bibl. 20

George Fletcher (c. 1821-1831)
Philadelphia, Pa.
Bibl. 3

Henry Fletcher
Lexington, Ky. (c. 1818-1830)
Louisville, Ky. (c. 1830-1866)
Bibl. 32, 54, 68

Leonard Fletcher (c. 1819)
Philadelphia, Pa.
Bibl. 3

Samuel Fletcher (c. 1804)
Philadelphia, Pa.
Bibl. 3

T. Fletcher & T. Bailey (c.
1830)
Philadelphia, Pa.
Bibl. 54

Thomas Fletcher
Boston, Mass. (c. 1810)
Philadelphia, Pa. (c. 1813-
1830)
Fletcher & Bennett
Fletcher & Gardiner
Bibl. 3, 15, 23, 24, 25, 28, 29,
36, 39, 44, 72

T. FLETCHER   PHILAD.

John Flexion (c. 1837)
Philadelphia, Pa.
Bibl. 3

Daniel Fling (c. 1809-1822)
Philadelphia, Pa.
Bibl. 3

George Fling (c. 1749)
Philadelphia, Pa.
Bibl. 23, 28, 36, 44

James Flood (c. 1839-1850)
Philadelphia, Pa.
Bibl. 3

William Flood (c. 1837)
Philadelphia, Pa.
Bibl. 3

Simon Flootron (c. 1838)
St. Louis, Mo.
Bibl. 54

William Floto (c. 1849)
Philadelphia, Pa.
Bibl. 3

Lewis Flott(e) (c. 1814-1818)
Baltimore, Md.
Bibl. 23, 28, 36, 38, 44

John Flot(t)ard & Co. (c. 1793)
Charleston, S.C.
———— Flot(t)ard (c. 1793)
Bibl. 5

———— Flot(t)ard (c. 1793)
Charleston, S.C.
John Flot(t)ard & Co.
Bibl. 5

Jacob Flournoy (b. 1663)
Williamsburg, Va. (c. 1700-
1712)
Bibl. 19

Henry Flower (c. 1753-1755)
Philadelphia, Pa.
Bibl. 3

Joseph Flower (c. 1844)
Philadelphia, Pa.
Bibl. 3, 23

Charles Fobes (c. 1850)
Philadelphia, Pa.
Bibl. 3

Jacob Fogle (b. 1803-d. 1867)
Milledgeville, Ga. (c. 1825-
1837)
Columbus, Ga. (c. 1835)
Foster & Fogle (c. 1835-1837)
Bibl. 17

George Foley (c. 1823)
Canton, Ohio
Bibl. 34

William Folkrod (c. 1849-1850)
Philadelphia, Pa.
Bibl. 3

Timothy Follet (d. 1803)
Bennington, Vt. (c. 1784-1801)
Fassett & Follet (c. 1793-1795)
Bibl. 54

A. A. Folloppe (c. 1808-1810)
Boston, Mass.
New York, N.Y.
Bibl. 23, 36, 44

John Folson (Folsom) (c.
1781)
Albany, N.Y.
Bibl. 20, 23, 28, 36, 44

Folwell & Haines (c. 1844)
Philadelphia, Pa.
John T. Folwell (?)
Imlah Haines (?)
Bibl. 3

Folwell, Shadforth & Co. (c.
1791)
Richmond, Va.
Petersburg, Va.
———— Folwell
Whitaker Shadforth
Bibl. 19

Godfrey G. Folwell (c. 1832-
1845)
Philadelphia, Pa.
Bibl. 3

John T. Folwell (c. 1847-1850)
Philadelphia, Pa.
Folwell & Haines (c. 1844) (?)
Bibl. 3

Samuel Folwell (c. 1788-1793)
Philadelphia, Pa.
Bibl. 3

Louis H. Fontenay (c. 1840)
Charleston, S.C.
Bibl. 5

William Foote (Foot) (b.
1772, c. 1797)
Middletown, Conn. (c. 1795-
1799)
East Haddam, Conn. (c. 1796-
1799?)
Colchester, Conn.
Glastonbury, Conn.
Michigan
Canfield & Foote (c. 1795-
1799)
Bibl. 16, 23, 28, 36, 44

Abraham Gerritze Forbes (c.
1769-1795)
New York, N.Y.
Bibl. 15, 16, 23, 24, 25, 28, 29,
35, 36, 44

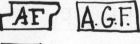

Benjamin G. Forbes (c. 1817-
1837)
New York, N.Y.
Fordham & Forbes (c. 1826-
1828)

Bibl. 4, 15, 23, 28, 36, 44
B. G. Forbes

C. & I. W. Forbes (c. 1810-1825)
New York, N.Y.
Colin & John W. Forbes
(not Garret Forbes)
Bibl. 15, 23, 25, 36, 44

[C & I W FORBES]

Colin & John W. Forbes (c. 1825)
New York, N.Y.
C. & I. W. Forbes
Bibl. 15, 23, 25, 36, 44

Colin V. G. Forbes (c. 1808-1825)
New York, N.Y.
Bibl. 4, 15, 23, 25, 28, 29, 36, 44

[C FORBES]   [C V G F]

Colin V. G. Forbes & Son (c. 1826-1838)
New York, N.Y.
Bibl. 15, 23, 24, 25, 29, 36, 44

[FORBES & SON]
[FORBES & SON]

Garret Forbes (c. 1808-1833)
New York, N.Y.
Bibl. 4, 15, 23, 25, 28, 29, 35, 36, 44, 83

[G. FORBES]

J. W. Forbes & Co. (c. 1819)
New York, N.Y.
John W. Forbes
Bibl. 15

John W. Forbes (c. 1808-1838)
New York, N.Y.
J. W. Forbes & Co. (c. 1819)
Bibl. 2, 4, 15, 23, 24, 25, 28, 29, 30, 35, 39, 54, 83

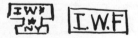   [I.W.F]

L. Forbes & Co. (c. 1845-1865)
St. Louis, Mo.
Leonard Forbes
Bibl. 54

William G. Forbes (b. 1752-d. 1840)
New York, N.Y. (w. 1773-1830)
Bibl. 4, 15, 23, 24, 25, 28, 29, 30, 35, 36, 39, 44, 50, 54, 83

[W. G. Forbes]   [W.F]

[N·YORK]

[W·G·FORBES]

[W G Forbes]

[W. FORBES]

[W.G FORBES]

Jabez W. Force (c. 1819-1839)
New York, N.Y.
Wood & Force (c. 1839-1841)
Bibl. 15, 23, 24, 25, 29, 36, 44

[J W FORCE]   [FORCE]

——— Ford (c. 1879)
New Haven, Conn.
Bibl. 2

Ford & Brother (c. 1847)
Oswego, N.Y.
Bibl. 20

[FORD & BROTHER]

Asa R. Ford (c. 1827)
Sackets Harbor, N.Y.
Bibl. 20

George H. Ford
New Haven, Conn.
Benjamin & Ford (c. 1828-1874?)
Bibl. 28

James 'M. Ford (19th century)
Location unknown
Bibl. 28

Samuel Ford
Philadelphia, Pa. (c. 1797)
Baltimore, Md. (c. 1802-1803)
Bibl. 3, 4, 23, 24, 25, 28, 36, 38, 44

[S F]

William Ford (c. 1848)
Philadelphia, Pa.
Bibl. 3

William Forde (c. 1820-1828)
Philadelphia, Pa.
Bibl. 3

Fordham & Forbes (c. 1826-1828)
New York, N.Y.
Merrit Fordham
Benjamin G. Forbes
Bibl. 15

Merrit Fordham (c. 1827-1833)
New York, N.Y.
Fordham & Forbes (c. 1826-1828)
Bibl. 15

Alexander Forest (c. 1802)
Baltimore, Md.
Bibl. 23, 36, 44

Benoni B. Forman
Albany, N.Y. (c. 1813-1815, c. 1834-1846)
Troy, N.Y. (c. 1846-1848)
Bibl. 20, 23, 28, 36, 44

[B. B. FORMAN]

Alexander (Alex) Forrest (c. 1802-1803)
Baltimore, Md.
Bibl. 4, 28, 38, 44

Christian Forrey (c. 1773)
Lancaster, Pa.
Bibl. 3

J. Silas Fors (c. 1839-1851)
Wheeling, Va.
Bibl. 19

O. C. Forsyth (c. 1810)
Location unknown
Bibl. 24

George H. Forsythe (c. 1843-1848)
Louisville, Ky.
Bibl. 32, 54, 68

Anthony Fortune (c. 1767)
Philadelphia, Pa.
Bibl. 3, 23, 36, 44

——— Foss
Boston, Mass.
Lincoln & Foss (c. 1850)
Haddock, Lincoln & Foss (c. 1850-1865)

Foster
(See Phillips & Foster)

Foster & Fogle (c. 1835-1837)
Milledgeville, Ga. (c. 1835-1837)
Columbus, Ga.
W. Foster
Jacob Fogle
Bibl. 17

Foster & Purple (c. 1844-1845)
Columbus, Ga.
W. Foster
Samuel B. Purple
Bibl. 17

Foster & Richards (c. 1815)
New York, N.Y.
John Foster
Thomas Richards
Bibl. 24, 25, 44

J. F.   T. RICHARDS

Foster & Ward (c. 1840)
Columbus, Ga.
W. Foster
———— Ward
Bibl. 17

Abraham Foster (b. 1778)
Philadelphia, Pa. (c. 1800-1816)
Boston, Mass.
Bibl. 3, 23, 28, 36, 39, 44

Carl Foster (c. 1831-1833)
Philadelphia, Pa.
Bibl. 3

Chandler Foster (c. 1832-1840)
Albany, N.Y.
Bibl. 20

George B. Foster (c. 1838-1854)
Boston, Mass.
Salem, Mass.
Bibl. 23, 25, 28, 36, 44, 72

GEORGE B FOSTER

G FOSTER

Henry Foster (c. 1841)
Savannah, Ga.
Bibl. 17

Hiram Foster (c. 1817-1818)
Philadelphia, Pa.
Bibl. 3, 23, 36

Jeremiah Foster (b. 1791-d. 1823)
Hopkinsville, Ky.
Bibl. 32, 54, 68

John Foster
New York (c. 1811-1817)
Winchester, Va. (c. 1817-1825-   )
Woodstock, Va. (c. 1825)
Martinsburg, Va. (c. 1827-1835)
Foster & Richards (c. 1815)
Phillips & Foster (c. 1817)
Bibl. 15, 19, 23, 24, 25, 29, 36, 44

J. FOSTER

Joseph Foster (b. 1760-d. 1839)
Boston, Mass.
Bibl. 2, 4, 15, 23, 24, 25, 28, 36, 44, 54, 72, 80

FOSTER

I. FOSTER

Nathaniel & Thomas Foster (c. 1820-1860)
Newburyport, Mass.
Bibl. 14, 15, 23, 25, 28, 36, 44

N & T. FOSTER

M & T. FOSTER

Samuel Foster (c. 1676-1702)
Boston, Mass.
Bibl. 23, 28, 36, 44

Thomas Foster (c. 1823)
Newburyport, Mass.
Bibl. 15, 24, 25, 28, 29, 36, 44

T. FOSTER

W. Foster (c. 1835-1845)
Columbus, Ga.
Foster & Fogle (c. 1835-1837)
Foster & Ward (c. 1840)
Foster & Purple (c. 1844-1845)
Bibl. 17

———— Fournier (c. 1796)
Philadelphia, Pa.
Bibl. 3

Fourniquet & Wheatley (c. 1815)
New York, N.Y.
Louis Fourniquet
Frederick G. Wheatley
Bibl. 15, 23, 36, 44

Louis Fourn(i)(e)quet (c. 1795-1823)
New York, N.Y.

Bibl. 15, 23, 24, 25, 28, 29, 35, 36, 44, 54, 72

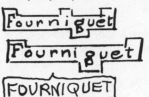

Fowle & Kirkland (c. 1828-1833)
Northampton, Mass.
Nathaniel Fowle
Samuel W. Kirkland
Bibl. 84

Nathaniel Fowle
Northampton, Mass. (c. 1819-1820, c. 1833-1850)
Fowle & Kirkland (c. 1828-1833)
Bibl. 84

Gilbert Fowler (c. 1825-1830)
New York, N.Y.
Bibl. 15, 23, 36, 44

Andrew W. Fox (c. 1843)
Hartford, Conn.
Bibl. 23

Asa Fox
Buffalo, N.Y. (c. 1811)
Leroy, N.Y. (c. 1815)
Bibl. 20

DeForest Fox (c. 1846-1850-   )
Troy, N.Y.
Bibl. 20

John Fox (c. 1809)
Philadelphia, Pa.
Bibl. 3

John T. Fox (c. 1841-1850-   )
Rochester, N.Y.
Brooklyn, N.Y. (?)
C. A. Burr & Co. (c. 1863)
Bibl. 20, 41

Foxcroft & Clark (c. 1831-1839)
Baltimore, Md.
James A. Foxcroft
Gabriel D. Clark
Bibl. 83

James A. Foxcroft (c. 1822-1839)
Baltimore, Md.

Foxcroft & Clark (c. 1831-1839)
Bibl. 38

G. F. Foy & Co. (c. 1850)
Location unknown
Bibl. 89

G. F. FOY & CO.

Thomas Fradgley (c. 1797)
New York, N.Y.
Bibl. 23, 36, 44

Basil Francis (c. 1766-1768)
Baltimore, Md.
Bibl. 3, 38

Edward Francis (c. 1828-1837)
Leesburg, Va.
Bibl. 15, 19, 44

E. FRANCIS

Julius C. Francis (b. 1785-d. 1862)
Middletown, Conn.
Hughes & Francis (c. 1807-1809)
Bibl. 16, 23, 28, 36, 44

Justus Francis (c. 1850)
Hartford, Conn.
Bibl. 23

Nathaniel Francis (c. 1805-1828)
New York, N.Y.
Bibl. 15, 23, 24, 25, 28, 29, 30, 35, 36, 44

N. FRANCIS

FRANCIS

Thomas Francis (c. 1841-1848)
Philadelphia, Pa.
Bibl. 3

George Franciscus Sr. (c. 1776-1791, d. 1791)
Baltimore, Md.
Bibl. 15, 23, 25, 29, 36, 38, 44

G. FRANCISCUS

George Franciscus Jr. (c. 1810-1818)
Baltimore, Md.

Bibl. 15, 25, 28, 38, 44

G. FRANCISCUS

Jacob Frank(s) (c. 1785-1794)
Philadelphia, Pa.
Bibl. 3, 24, 25, 36, 44

J. FRANK

Franklin & Cordell (c. 1822)
Warrenton, Va.
Bibl. 19

J. & S. Franks (c. 1850)
Philadelphia, Pa.
Bibl. 3

Jacob Franks (c. 1845-1849)
Philadelphia, Pa.
Bibl. 3

William Franks (c. 1839)
Philadelphia, Pa.
Bibl. 3, 36, 44

William Fran(c)ks (c. 1839-1840)
Philadelphia, Pa.
Bibl. 3, 23

William Fraser (c. 1738)
Philadelphia, Pa.
Bibl. 3, 23, 28, 36, 44

William Fraser (c. 1825-1833)
Philadelphia, Pa.
Bibl. 3

Alexander Frazer (Frazier)
Paris, Ky. (c. 1799)
Lexington, Ky. (c. 1803-1810)
Phillips & Frazer (c. 1799)
Bibl. 32, 54, 68

H. N. Frazer (c. 1839)
Vienna, N.Y.
Bibl. 20

Robert Frazer (Frazier) (b. 1769-d. 1851)
Paris, Ky. (c. 1799)
Lexington, Ky. (c. 1799-1851)
Phillips & Frazer (c. 1799)
Bibl. 32, 54, 68

Robert Frazer Jr. (c. 1838-1851)
Lexington, Ky.
Bibl. 32

ROBERT FRAZER JR

Samuel Frazier (c. 1822-1824)
Baltimore, Md.
Bibl. 38

William Frazier (c. 1824)
Philadelphia, Pa.
Bibl. 3

Frear & Halliwell (c. 1813-1816)
Poughkeepsie, N.Y.
John B. Frear (?)
George Halliwell
Bibl. 20

John B. Frear (d. 1821)
Poughkeepsie, N.Y. (c. 1816-1821)
Frear & Halliwell (?) (c. 1813-1816)
Bibl. 20

Daniel Frederick (c. 1847-1850)
Philadelphia, Pa.
Bibl. 3

John H. Frederick (c. 1823-1850)
Philadelphia, Pa.
Bibl. 3

K. L. Frederick (c. 1835)
Philadelphia, Pa.
Bibl. 3

Daniel Fredericks (c. 1841)
Philadelphia, Pa.
Bibl. 3

Fredline
(See Friedlein)

N. Freeborn (c. 1800)
Location unknown
Bibl. 28, 29, 44

N. FREEBORN

Freeman & Pollard (c. 1832-1834)
Norfolk, Va.
Joseph M. Freeman
Lewis R. Pollard
Bibl. 19

FREEMAN & POLLARD

Freeman & Wallin (c. 1839-1840)
Philadelphia, Pa.
William Freeman

Robert Wallin
Bibl. 15, 25, 44

FREEMAN & WALLIN

J. M. Freeman(s) & Co.
(c. 1843-1844)
Norfolk, Va.
Joseph M. Freeman (?)
Fitch Burwell
Bibl. 19, 28, 29, 44

J. M. FREEMAN & CO

J. M. FREEMAN & CO.

J. N. Freeman (c. 1860)
Augusta, Ga.
Bibl. 17

J. N. FREEMAN

Joseph M. Freeman (b. 1806-d.
1882)
Norfolk, Va. (c. 1831-1856)
Freeman & Pollard (c. 1832-
1834)
J. M. Freeman & Co. (c. 1843-
1844) (?)
Bibl. 15, 19, 24

FREEMAN

J. M. FREEMAN

N. A. Freeman (c. 1850)
Richmond, Va.
Bibl. 89

N. A. FREEMAN

Thomas W. Freeman (d. 1853)
Augusta, Ga.
Bibl. 17

William Freeman (c. 1839-
1840)
Philadelphia, Pa.
Bibl. 3, 23, 36, 44

Freemans
(See J. M. Freeman & Co.)

Robert Freeston (c. 1818-1833)
Philadelphia, Pa.
Bibl. 3

Meyer Freide (c. 1848)
St. Louis, Mo.
Bibl. 54

Meyer Freide

Freidline
(See Friedlein)

James Ormsby French (c.
1771)
Annapolis, Md. (c. 1783-1785)
Baltimore, Md.
Claude & French (c. 1783-
1785)
Bibl. 38

Matthew French (c. 1814-1823)
Baltimore, Md.
Bibl. 38

C. R. Fricke (c. 1820)
Philadelphia, Pa. (?)
Bibl. 89

C. R. Fricke

Henry Friedeberg (c. 1849-
1850)
Philadelphia, Pa.
Bibl. 3

John L. Friedlein (c. 1835-
1850)
Philadelphia, Pa.
Bibl. 3

J. Fries (c. 1850)
Location unknown
Bibl. 15, 24, 44, 79

J. FRIES

J. & P. Fries (c. 1837)
Philadelphia, Pa.
Bibl. 3

John Fries (c. 1830-1850)
Philadelphia, Pa.
Bibl. 3

P. Fries (c. 1837)
Philadelphia, Pa.
Bibl. 3

James Frith (Frinth) (c. 1840-
1850)
Philadelphia, Pa.
Bibl. 3, 23, 36, 44

C. Fritz (c. 1848-1850)
Philadelphia, Pa.
Bibl. 3

Benjamin C. Frobisher (b.
1792-d. 1862)
Boston, Mass. (c. 1834)
Stodder & Frobisher (c. 1816-
1825) (?)

Bibl. 4, 15, 23, 24, 25, 28, 29,
36, 44

B. C. Frobisher

FROBISHER

James Frodsham (c. 1845)
St. Louis, Mo.
Bibl. 54

Charles Froeligh (c. 1857-
1860-)
Utica, N.Y.
Bibl. 18

Frost & Mum(n)ford (c. 1810)
Providence, R.I.
——— Frost
Henry (G.) (B.) Mumford (?)
Bibl. 23, 24, 25, 28, 29, 36, 44

F & M

Ebenezer Frothingham
(Frotheringham) (b. 1756-d.
1814)
Boston, Mass.
Bibl. 23, 28, 36, 44, 54

E F

C. Fry (c. 1837-1857)
Canton, Ohio
Bibl. 34

N. L. Fry (c. 1844-1848)

Philadelphia, Pa.
Titlow & Fry (c. 1844-1847)
Bibl. 3, 23

John W. Fryer (c. 1784-1813)
Albany, N.Y.
Balch & Fryer (c. 1784)
Bibl. 20, 23, 28, 36, 44

Peter Fryer
Albany, N.Y. (c. 1824-1825)
Norwich, N.Y. (c. 1828-1830,
1838-1840)
Bibl. 20

Daniel Christian Fueter
(c. 1754-1805)
New York, N.Y.
Bibl. 4, 15, 24, 25, 28, 29, 36,
44, 54

David Fueter (c. 1789)
New York, N.Y.
Bibl. 4, 28, 44

Lewis Fueter (c. 1770-1775)
New York, N.Y.
Bibl. 4, 15, 23, 24, 25, 29, 35,
    36, 44, 54

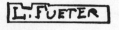

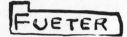

Alexander Fuller (c. 1811)
New York, N.Y.
Bibl. 23, 36, 44

Asa C. Fuller (c. 1834-   )
Utica, N.Y.
Bibl. 18, 20

David Fuller (c. 1854-1855)
Utica, N.Y.
Bibl. 18

F. A. Fuller (c. 1850)
Jamestown, N.Y.
Bibl. 20

George W. Fuller (c. 1829-
    1844)
Lewisburg, Va. (c. 1829-1832)
Staunton, Va.
Bibl. 19

David C. Fulton (c. 1838-1841)
Louisville, Ky.
Bibl. 32, 54

James Fulton (c. 1838-1861)
Louisville, Ky.
Bibl. 32

Thomas G. Funston (c. 1850)
Philadelphia, Pa.
Bibl. 3, 23

———— Furer (c. 1759)
New York, N.Y.
Bibl. 28

Lewis Furis (c. 1810)
New York, N.Y.
Bibl. 24, 44

Philip H. Furman (c. 1821-
    1842)

Schenectady, N.Y.
Bibl. 20

Charles Furnace (c. 1837-
    1838)
Albany, N.Y.
Bibl. 20

Roger Fursden (Fursdon)
    (c. 1784)
Charleston, S.C.
Bibl. 5, 44

Moritz Furst (c. 1807-1833)
Philadelphia, Pa.
Bibl. 3

Peter Furt (d. 1737)
New York, N.Y. (c. 1720-1727)
Boston, Mass. (c. 1727-1737)
Bibl. 23, 36

John W. Fury (c. 1850)
Philadelphia, Pa.
Bibl. 3

Fuselli & Hilburn (c. 1866-
    1873)
Bowling Green, Ky.
Peter Fuselli
Jonas Jacob Hilburn
Bibl. 54

Fuselli & McGoodwin
    (c. 1873-1885)
Bowling Green, Ky.
Peter Fuselli
I. D. McGoodwin
Bibl. 54

Fuselli & Valenti (late 19th
    century)
Bowling Green, Ky.
Peter Fuselli
Philip Valenti
Bibl. 54

Peter Fuselli (c. 1850-1880)
Bowling Green, Ky.
Fuselli & Valenti
Fuselli & Hilburn (c. 1866-
    1873)
Fuselli & McGoodwin (c. 1873-
    1885)
Bibl. 54

Fusselli
(See McLure & Fusselli)

Joseph Gaddy (c. 1772)
Halifax, N.C.
Bibl. 21

Henry L. Gadeken (c. 1845-
    1850)
Philadelphia, Pa.
Bibl. 3

Gaely
(See Geley)

John Gaffney (c. 1827-1829)
Charleston, S.C.
Bibl. 5

J. Gafkins (c. 1832)
Providence, R.I.
Bibl. 23, 36, 44

W. B. Gainey (c. 1859)
Pendleton, S.C.
Bibl. 5

Greenbury Gaither (c. 1822-
    1834)
Washington, D.C.
Bibl. 23, 25, 36, 44, 72

John Gaither (c. 1811)
Alexandria, Va.
Griffith & Gaither
    (c. 1809-   ) (?)
Bibl. 19

J. W. Gaither (c. 1855)
Greenville, S.C.
Cooper & Gaither
Bibl. 5

———— Galbard (19th century)
Philadelphia, Pa. (?)
Bibl. 89

Galbard

Patrick Galbraith (Gilbraith)
Philadelphia, Pa. (c. 1794-1817)
Bibl. 3

Gale & Hayden (c. 1848)
New York, N.Y.
Charleston, S.C.
William Gale
———— Hayden
Bibl. 4, 15, 23, 24, 25, 28, 29, 44

Gale & Moseley (c. 1828-1833)
New York, N.Y.
William Gale
Joseph Moseley
Bibl. 5, 23, 24, 25, 28, 29, 36, 44

Gale & Stickler (c. 1823)
New York, N.Y.
William Gale
John Stickler
Bibl. 23, 24, 25, 29, 36, 44

G & S

Gale & Willis (c. 1840)
New York, N.Y.
William Gale
——— Willis
Bibl. 23, 24, 25, 28, 36, 44

GALE & WILLIS

Gale, Wood & Hughes (c. 1833-
1844)
New York, N.Y.
William Gale
Jacob Wood
Jasper W. Hughes
Bibl. 4, 15, 23, 24, 25, 28, 29,
36, 44

G. W & H

J. L. & O. W. Gale (c. 1826)
New York, N.Y.
John L. Gale
O. W. Gale
Bibl. 15

John L. Gale (c. 1816-1837)
New York, N.Y.
Heyer & Gale (c. 1800-1807)
J. L. & O. W. Gale (c. 1826)
Bibl. 4, 15, 23, 28, 29, 36, 44

J. GALE   J. L. G.

J. L. GALE

John S. Gale (c. 1825)
New York, N.Y.
Bibl. 15, 23, 36, 39

J. GALE

Joseph Gale (c. 1788-1799)
Fayetteville, N.C.
Lord & Gale (c. 1792)
Bibl. 21

O. W. Gale
New York, N.Y.
J. L. & O. W. Gale (c. 1826)
Bibl. 15

William Gale (b. 1799-d. 1867)
New York, N.Y.
Gale & Stickler (c. 1823)
Gale & Moseley (c. 1828-1833)
Gale, Wood & Hughes (c. 1833-
1844)

Gale & Willis (c. 1840)
Gale & Hayden (c. 1848)
Bibl. 4, 15, 23, 25, 28, 29, 35,
36, 44, 54

W. G.   W G

William Gale Jr. (b. 1825,
c. 1844-1850)
New York, N.Y.
Bibl. 23, 25, 29, 36, 44

WM. GALE JR.

William Gale & Son (c. 1823-
1850)
New York, N.Y.
Bibl. 24, 25, 28, 29, 35, 36, 39,
44, 78, 83

W. GALE & SON

W. G.   G & S   W. G & S

Gallard & Co. (c. 1811-1822)
Philadelphia, Pa.
Peter Gallard (?)
Bibl. 3

Peter Gallard (Gillard)
(c. 1807-1811)
Philadelphia, Pa.
Gallard & Co. (c. 1811-1822)
(?)
Bibl. 3

C. Gallome (c. 1819)
Baltimore, Md.
Bibl. 38

Christopher Gallup (Gallop)
(Gullup) (b. 1764-d. 1849)
North Groton (Ledyard),
Conn.
Bibl. 16, 23, 28, 36, 44

James Galt (b. 1741-d. 1800)
Richmond, Va. (c. 1766-1771)
Bibl. 19

James Galt (c. 1801-1827)
Alexandria, Va.
Bibl. 19

Peter Galt (b. 1777-d. 1830)
Baltimore, Md. (c. 1800-1825)
Bibl. 38

Samuel Galt (b. 1700-d. 1761)
Mill Creek, Va. (c. 1738)
Hampton, Va. (c. 1749-1751)
Williamsburg, Va. (c. 1751-
1759)
Bibl. 19, 23, 36, 44

Stirling Galt (c. 1802-1830)
Baltimore, Md.
Bibl. 38

William Galt (b. 1723)
Yorktown, Va. (c. 1751)
Alexandria, Va. (c. 1791)
Williamsburg, Va.
Bibl. 19

Charles Gamble (c. 1847-1849)
Philadelphia, Pa.
Bibl. 3

James Gamble & Son (c. 1852)
Gamble & Son
Charleston, S.C.
James Gamble
Richard J. Gamble
Bibl. 5

Richard J. Gamble (c. 1849-
1852)
Charleston, S.C.
James Gamble & Son
Gamble & Son
Bibl. 5

Hugh Ganley (c. 1842-1847)
Utica, N.Y.
Bibl. 18, 20

Aaron Gannet (c. 1842-1844)
Troy, N.Y.
Bibl. 20

John Garde (c. 1849-1850)
Philadelphia, Pa.
Bibl. 3, 23

Francis Garden (c. 1745)
Boston, Mass.
Bibl. 28

B. Gardiner & Co. (c. 1840)
New York, N.Y.
Bibl. 23, 24, 25, 29, 36, 44, 83

B. G. & Co

B GARDINER & CO

Baldwin Gardiner
Philadelphia, Pa. (c. 1814-1817)
New York, N.Y. (c. 1827-1838)
Fletcher & Gardiner (c. 1815-
1822)
Bibl. 3, 4, 15, 23, 24, 28, 29,
35, 44, 54, 83

B GARDINER   B. G

J. & A. Gardiner (c. 1853-1861)
St. Louis, Mo.
Bibl. 54

John Gardiner (Gardner)
Boston, Mass. (?) (c. 1730-
1776)
New London, Conn. (c. 1734-
1776)
Bibl. 2, 15, 16, 23, 24, 25, 28,
29, 36, 44, 61, 69

I G

J. GARDINER   J: GARDNER

Sidney Gardiner (Gardner)
Boston, Mass. (before 1810)
Philadelphia, Pa. (c. 1810-1825)
Fletcher & Gardiner
Bibl. 3, 23, 28, 36, 44

Barzillai Gardner (b. 1778)
Charlotte, N.C. (c. 1807-   )
McBride & Gardner (c. 1807)
Bibl. 22

Benjamin F. Gardner (c. 1817)
Nantucket Island, Mass.
Bibl. 12, 44

George Gardner (c. 1841-1842)
Philadelphia, Pa.
Bibl. 3

John Gardner
(See John Gardiner)

Samuel Gardner (c. 1826-1840)
Syracuse, N.Y.
Bibl. 20

Sidney Gardner
(See Sidney Gardiner)

William W. Gardner (c. 1858-
1859)
Utica, N.Y.
Bibl. 18

Garland & Menard (c. 1828-
1829)
Macon, Ga.
John R. Garland
Alexander Menard
Bibl. 17

John R. Garland
Greenville, S.C. (c. 1826-1828)
Macon, Ga. (c. 1828-1829)
Greensboro, N.C. (c. 1843)
Charlotte, N.C.
Garland & Menard (c. 1828-
1829)
Rockwell & Garland (c. 1829)
Bibl. 5, 17, 21

William Garland (19th
century)
Location unknown
Bibl. 15, 44

W GARLAND

Shavelier Garllow (c. 1813)
Philadelphia, Pa.
Bibl. 3, 23, 36

Garner & Stewart (c. 1850)
Lexington, Ky.
Eli C. Garner Sr.
George W. Stewart
Bibl. 32, 54

Garner & Winchester (c. 1838-
1861)
Lexington, Ky.
Eli C. Garner Sr.
———— Winchester
Bibl. 32, 54

Edwin T. Garner (c. 1842-
1843)
Utica, N.Y.
Bibl. 18, 20

Eli C. Garner (Sr.?)
(b. 1817-d. 1878)
Lexington, Ky. (c. 1838-1864)
Garner & Winchester (c. 1838-
1861)
Garner & Stewart (c. 1850)
Bibl. 32 54, 68

G. G. Garner (c. 1808)
Fincastle, Va.
Bibl. 19

George Garner (c. 1850)
Lexington, Ky.
Bibl. 32

John Garner (c. 1825-1830)
Cincinnati, Ohio
Bibl. 23, 34, 36, 44, 54

———— Garnsey
Location unknown
Bibl. 28

David Garnsey (c. 1810)
Frankfort, Ky.
Bibl. 32, 54, 68

S. Garre (c. 1825)
New York, N.Y.
Bibl. 24, 25, 44

S G   S GARRE

Anthony Garren (Gerren)
(c. 1811-1814)
Philadelphia, Pa.
Bibl. 3, 23, 36, 44

Philip Garret(t) (c. 1801-1835)
Philadelphia, Pa.
Bibl. 3, 15, 23, 24, 25, 28, 29,
36, 39, 44, 46

P. GARRETT

Eliakim Garretson (c. 1785-
1800)
Wilmington, Del.
Bibl. 25, 30, 44

E. GARRETSON   E G

Garrett & Hartley (c. 1837)
Philadelphia, Pa.
———— Garrett
Samuel Hartley
Bibl. 3, 23

Garrett & Haydock (c. 1837-
1840)
Philadelphia, Pa.
Bibl. 3

Everard Garrett (c. 1760-
1777-   )
Chowan County, N.C.
Bibl. 21

Philip Garrett & Son (c. 1828-
1835)
Philadelphia, Pa.
Bibl. 3

Thomas C. Garrett (c. 1829-
1840)
Philadelphia, Pa.
Bibl. 3, 24, 25, 44

T C GARRETT

Thomas C. Garrett & Co.
(c. 1841-1850)
Philadelphia, Pa.
Bibl. 3, 23, 29, 36, 44

T. C. GARRETT & CO.

Jacob J. Garrigues (c. 1837)
Philadelphia, Pa.
Bibl. 3

———— Garrington (19th
century)
Location unknown
Bibl. 54

John Garrison (c. 1825-1826)

New York, N.Y.
Bibl. 15, 23, 36, 44

Joseph Garrison (c. 1836-1838)
New York, N.Y.
Bibl. 15

A. Garroch
Location unknown
Bibl. 15, 44

Garrow & Dorsey (c. 1800)
Baltimore, Md.
Philadelphia, Pa.
Bibl. 3, 23, 36, 44

William Garton (c. 1753)
Annapolis, Md.
Bibl. 38

——— Gaskins
Location unknown
Bibl. 21

James Gaskins (c. 1804-1830)
Norfolk, Va.
Portsmouth, Va.
Bibl. 15, 19, 25, 28, 29, 39, 44,
   72

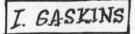

W. W. Gaskins (c. 1806)
Norfolk, Va.
Bibl. 23, 24, 25, 29, 36, 44

W W G

Gates
(See Goetes)

James Gates (c. 1815)
Chillicothe, Ohio
Bibl. 34

Benjamin Gatfield (c. 1826)
New York, N.Y.
Bibl. 15

Gatham
(See William Gethen)

G. Gatther (c. 1825)
(probably Greenbury Gaither)
Bibl. 24

G. GATTHER

Peter Gaudechaud
   (Goudchaud) (Gudichaud)
   (Godichew)
Philadelphia, Pa. (c. 1814-1833)
Bibl. 3

Gaultier
(See Gottier)

Gotleib Gause (c. 1840-1841)
Philadelphia, Pa.
Bibl. 3

J. B. Gaushier (c. 1835)
Philadelphia, Pa.
Bibl. 3

Benjamin Gautier (c. 1812-
   1815)
Norfolk, Va.
Bibl. 19

Nicholas Gautier
Norfolk, Va. (c. 1768-   )
Portsmouth, Va. (c. 1776-1778)
Bibl. 19

Gavett
(See Ward & Govett)

William P. Gaw (c. 1816-1822)
Philadelphia, Pa.
Widdifield & Gaw (c. 1820-
   1822)
Bibl. 3

Charles Gay (c. 1779)
Baltimore, Md.
Bibl. 23, 36, 44

Charles H. Gay (c. 1837)
Athens, Ga.
Bibl. 17

Nathaniel Gay (b. 1643-d.1713)
Boston, Mass.
Bibl. 23, 28, 36, 44

S. Gayhart (c. 1846-1849)
Camden, N.J.
Bibl. 3

——— Gaylord (c. 1822-   )
Batavia, N.Y.
Sargent & Gaylord
Bibl. 20

S. Gazlay (19th century)
Location unknown
Bibl. 15, 44

S. GAZLAY

Gealey
(See Geley)

James Geddes
(See James Geddy)

Charles Geddes (c. 1778)
New York State
Bibl. 3

James Geddy (Geddes)
   (b. 1731-d. 1807)
Petersburg, Va. (c. 1783-1807)
Williamsburg, Va.
James Geddy & Sons (c. 1790)
Bibl. 15, 19, 25, 44

I. G   I G   J G

James Geddy Jr. (c. 1789-1803)
Petersburg, Va.
James Geddy & Sons (c. 1790)
Bibl. 19

James Geddy & Sons (c. 1790)
Petersburg, Va.
James Geddy
James Geddy Jr.
William Waddill Geddy
Bibl. 19

William Waddill Geddy
   (c. 1790-1811)
Petersburg, Va.
James Geddy & Sons (c. 1790)
Bibl. 19

W W G

Joseph Gee (c. 1788)
Philadelphia, Pa.
Bibl. 3, 4, 23, 25, 28, 36, 44, 72

G E E

Nicholas Geffroy (b. 1761-d.
   1839)
Newport, R.I.
Bibl. 24, 25, 28, 29, 36, 44,
   54, 56, 72

N. GEFFROY

GEFFROY   N. GEFFROY

John G. Gehring (c. 1827-1831)
Baltimore, Md.
Bibl. 38

John Ulrich Geissendanner
  (c. 1737)
Charleston, S.C.
Bibl. 54

Peter Geley (Gealey) (Geyley)
  (Gaely) (Gilley) (d. 1815)
Philadelphia, Pa. (c. 1793-1814)
Bibl. 3, 23, 28, 36, 44

Gelston & Co. (c. 1837)
New York, N.Y.
George S. Gelston
Bibl. 4, 23, 24, 25, 28, 35, 36,
  44, 83

GELSTON & CO

Gelston & Gould (c. 1816-1820)
Baltimore, Md.
Hugh Gelston
James Gould
Bibl. 23, 36, 38, 44

Gelston, Ladd & Co. (c. 1840)
New York, N.Y.
George S. Gelston
———— Ladd
Bibl. 23, 24, 25, 28, 29, 36, 44

GELSTON LADD&CO

Gelston & Treadwell (c. 1836)
New York, N.Y.
George S. Gelston
———— Treadwell
Bibl. 23, 25, 28, 35, 36, 44, 83

George P. Gelston (c. 1824-
  1830)
Boston, Mass.
Walcott & Gelston (c. 1824)
Bibl. 28

George S. Gelston (c. 1833)
New York, N.Y.
Gelston & Treadwell (c. 1836)
Gelston & Co. (c. 1837)
Gelston, Ladd & Co. (c. 1840)
Bibl. 4, 23, 24, 28, 29, 36, 44

GELSTON   G. S. GELSTON

Henry Gelston (c. 1828)
Boston, Mass.
Bibl. 28

Hugh Gelston (b. 1794-d. 1873)
Baltimore, Md.
Gelston & Gould (c. 1816-1820)
Bibl. 25, 28, 29, 38, 44

H U.   GELSTON   GELSTON

Maltby Gelston (d. 1828)
Boston, Mass.
Walcott & Gelston (c. 1824)
Bibl. 28

Welles Gelston
(See Welles & Gelston)

W. T. & T. V. Gendar (c. 1850)
Location unknown
Bibl. 15, 44

W. T. & T. V. GENDAR

Gennet & James (c. 1849-1866)
Richmond, Va.
Charles Gennet Jr.
Joseph H. James
Bibl. 19

GENNET & JAMES

A. Gennet (c. 1850)
Binghamton, N.Y.
Bibl. 20

Charles Gennet Jr. (b. 1807-d.
  1887)
Richmond, Va. (c. 1837-
  1866-   )
Gennet & James (c. 1849-1866)
Bibl. 19

C. GENNET   C. GENNET JR.

W. Gennett (c. 1850-   )
Watertown, N.Y.
Bibl. 20

Georgeon (Gorgeon) & Philipe
  (c. 1794)
Philadelphia, Pa.
Bernard Georgeon
———— Philipe
Bibl. 3, 23, 36

Bernard Georgeon (c. 1795-
  1798)
Philadelphia, Pa.
Bibl. 3, 28, 36, 44

Isaac Gere (b. 1771-d. 1812)
Northampton, Mass. (c. 1793)
Bibl. 84

Gerg
(See Gery)

Geriung
(See Guerin)

Michael Germain (b. 1752-d.
  1806)
Savannah, Ga.
Bibl. 17

Joseph German (c. 1819)
Baltimore, Md.
Bibl. 23, 36, 38

Greenberry D. Germon
  (c. 1813-1833)
Philadelphia, Pa.
Bibl. 3, 4, 23, 28, 36

John D. Germon (German)
  (c. 1785-1825)
Philadelphia, Pa.
Bibl. 3, 4, 15, 23, 24, 25, 28,
  29, 36, 39, 44

Germon   I. G.

Francis Gero (c. 1818)
Philadelphia, Pa.
Bibl. 3, 23, 36

Gerren
(See Garren)

A. Gerrish (c. 1800-1810)
Location unknown
Bibl. 15, 44

A. GERRISH

Gerrish & Pearson (c. 1800)
New York, N.Y.
Bibl. 24, 25, 44

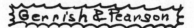

Timothy Gerrish (b. 1753-d.
  1813)
Portsmouth, N.H.
Bibl. 15, 23, 24, 25, 28, 29,
  36, 44

Frederick Gerstaecker
  (c. 1828)
Cincinnati, Ohio
Bibl. 3

Herman Gery (Gerg) (c. 1848-
  1850)
Philadelphia, Pa.
Bibl. 3

Christian Gessler (c. 1841-
  1850)
Philadelphia, Pa.
Bibl. 3

Getham
(See William Gethen)

John W. Gethen (c. 1811-1814)
Philadelphia, Pa.
Bibl. 3, 15, 19, 23, 36, 44

I W G

William Gethen (Getham)
    (Gatham) (c. 1797-1808)
Philadelphia, Pa.
Bibl. 3, 23, 24, 25, 29, 44

W GETHEN

James Getty (c. 1772)
(perhaps James Geddy)
Williamsburg, Va.
Bibl. 23, 36, 44

Peter Getz (c. 1782-1792)
Lancaster, Pa.
Bibl. 3, 23, 24, 25, 29, 36, 39, 44

P Getz

Geyley
(See Geley)

Cesar Ghiselin (Gisling)
    (Griselm) (b. 1670-d. 1734)
Philadelphia, Pa. (c. 1700-1715)
Annapolis, Md. (c. 1715-1728)
Bibl. 3, 23, 24, 25, 28, 29, 36,
    38, 44, 54, 81

William Ghiselin (Gisling)
    (c. 1782?)
Philadelphia, Pa. (c. 1751-
    1762)
Bibl. 3, 15, 23, 24, 25, 28, 29,
    36, 39, 44, 81

W G   w g   GHISELIN

Thomas Gibbons (c. 1750-1752)
Philadelphia, Pa.
Bibl. 3

Daniel Gibbs (c. 1716)
Boston, Mass.
Bibl. 23, 28, 36, 44

Eli M. Gibbs (c. 1820-1829)
Norwich, N.Y.
Bibl. 20

Eliza Gibbs (widow of John)
    (c. 1798)
Providence, R.I.
Bibl. 25

James Gibbs (c. 1847)
Philadelphia, Pa.
Bibl. 3

John Gibbs (d. 1797)
Providence, R.I.
Bibl. 15, 23, 24, 25, 28, 29,
    36, 44, 54, 56

John F. Gibbs (b. 1784)
Providence, R.I. (c. 1803)
Bibl. 23, 36, 44

William Giberson (c. 1823-
    1825)
Philadelphia, Pa.
Bibl. 3

Gibney & Reade (c. 1847)
New York, N.Y.
Michael Gibney
———— Reade
Bibl. 23

Michael Gibney (c. 1836-1845)
New York, N.Y.
Bibl. 15, 23, 25, 28, 44

Gibson
(See Morgan & Gibson)

Luther R. Gibson (c. 1851)
Norfolk, Va.
Bibl. 19

Peter Gibson (c. 1702)
Yorktown, Va.
Bibl. 19

Thomas Gibson (c. 1797-1800)
Philadelphia, Pa. (c. 1797-1800)
Charleston, S.C.
James Jack(s) & Co.
Bibl. 5

William Gibson (c. 1845-1849)
Philadelphia, Pa.
Bibl. 3, 23, 24, 25, 44

GIBSON

Samuel Gideon (c. 1770)
Rhode Island
Bibl. 54

John Ulrich Giessendanner
    (c. 1737)
Charleston, S.C.
Bibl. 5, 44

Giffing & Sweeney (c. 1809-
    1814)
Geneva, N.Y.
William Giffing Jr.
John Sweeney (?)
Bibl. 20

Christopher Giffing (c. 1815-
    1835)
New York, N.Y.
Bibl. 15, 25, 28, 29, 36, 44

C GIFFING   C Giffing

William Giffing Jr. (c. 1809-
    1814)
Geneva, N.Y.
Giffing & Sweeney
Bibl. 20

Clifton C. Gifford (c. 1850)
Rochester, N.Y.
Bibl. 20

E. Gifford (c. 1825)
Fall River, Mass.
Bibl. 15, 25, 44

E Gifford

S. K. Gifford (c. 1836)
Camden, S.C.
Bibl. 5

C. Gigon & Bros. (c. 1839)
Philadelphia, Pa.
Bibl. 3

Gustavus Gigon (c. 1845-1847)
Philadelphia, Pa.
Bibl. 3

Z. & G. Gigon (c. 1842-1850)
Philadelphia, Pa.
Bibl. 3

———— Gilbert (c. 1813-1814)
Manlius, N.Y.
Farr & Gilbert
Bibl. 20

Gilbert & Cunningham
(c. 1839-1840)
New York, N.Y.
Bibl. 4, 15, 23, 28, 36, 44

Charles Gilbert (c. 1835-1837)
Philadelphia, Pa.
Bibl. 3

Henry Gilbert (c. 1850)
Mt. Morris, N.Y.
Bibl. 20

John Gilbert (c. 1828-1833)
Philadelphia, Pa.
Bibl. 3

Philo B. Gilbert (c. 1839)
New York, N.Y.
Bibl. 15, 23

Samuel Gilbert (c. 1798)
Hebron, Conn.
Bibl. 2, 16, 23, 24, 25, 28, 29,
36, 44

S G

William W. Gilbert (c. 1772,
d. 1818)
New York, N.Y.
Bibl. 4, 15, 23, 24, 25, 28, 29,
35, 36, 44, 54, 83

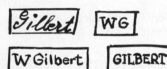

Gilbraith
(See Galbraith)

Edward Giles (c. 1841)
Philadelphia, Pa.
Bibl. 3

Caleb Gill (b. 1774-d.1855)
Hingham, Mass.
Bibl. 23, 24, 25, 28, 29, 36, 44

GILL

John Gill (b. 1798)
New Bern, N.C. (c. 1814-
1843-   )
Bibl. 21

Leavitt Gill (b. 1789-d. 1854)
Hingham, Mass.
Bibl. 28, 36, 44

Gillard
(See Gallard)

John Gillaspie (Gillispie)
(c. 1845-1846)
Louisville, Ky.
Bibl. 32, 54, 68

Samuel Gillespie (c. 1848-1849)
Louisville, Ky.
Bibl. 32

Joab Gillett (c. 1810-1833)
Cazenovia, N.Y.
Bibl. 20

Gilley
(See Geley)

Gillispie
(See Gillaspie)

Benjamin Clark Gilman
(b. 1763-d. 1835)
Exeter, N.H.
Bibl. 15, 25, 28, 44, 54

B C G

John Ward Gilman (b. 1771-d.
1823)
Exeter, N.H. (c. 1792)
Bibl. 15, 24, 25, 28, 29, 36, 44

I W G

Gilpin & Taylor (c. 1837-1842)
Philadelphia, Pa.
Bibl. 3

J. S. Gilpin
Location unknown
Bibl. 54

Vincent C. Gilpin (c. 1837-
1843)
Philadelphia, Pa.
Bibl. 3

John B. Ginochio (c. 1837-
1854)
New York, N.Y.
Bibl. 15, 22, 25, 44

J B GINOCHIO

John B. F. Giquel (c. 1822)
New Orleans, La.
Bibl. 23, 36, 44

Francis Girard (c. 1817)
Philadelphia, Pa.
Bibl. 3, 23, 36, 44

Henry Giraud (Girrad)
(c. 1805)
New York, N.Y.
Bibl. 23, 36, 44

William F. Gird (c. 1799-1806)
Alexandria, Va.
Bibl. 19

Girrad
(See Giraud)

Stephen Girreaun (c. 1785)
Philadelphia, Pa.
Bibl. 3, 23, 36, 44

Gisling
(See Ghiselin)

John Gistner (c. 1794-1796)
Philadelphia, Pa.
Bibl. 3

Thomas Giude (b. 1751)
New York, N.Y. (c. 1774)
Bibl. 28

A. Givan (c. 1849)
Albany, N.Y.
May be G. A. Given
Bibl. 23, 28, 44

G. A. Given (c. 1848-1849)
Albany, N.Y.
Bibl. 20

Glass & Baird (c. 1804)
Raleigh, N.C.
David Glass
David Baird
Bibl. 21

David Glass (c. 1803-
1856-   )
Raleigh, N.C.
Glass & Baird (c. 1804)
Bibl. 21

Thomas Glass (c. 1771-1801)
Raleigh, N.C.
Hanover, Va.
Norfolk, Va.
Bibl. 19, 21

Glaze & Radcliff(e) (c. 1848-
1851)
Columbia, S.C.
William Glaze
Thomas W. Radcliffe
Bibl. 5, 44

GLAZE & RADCLIFF

William Glaze (c. 1838-1882)
Columbia, S.C.
Veal & Glaze (c. 1838-1841)
Glaze & Radcliffe (c. 1848-
1851)
Bibl. 5

SPOONS

The dating of spoons is simple, because the shape and method of construction has changed through the years. Prior to 1800 most spoons were made from two pieces: a bowl, and a straight piece that formed the handle. After 1800 spoons were usually made from one piece of silver. The design of the bowl changed from fig-shaped to elliptical, then to the narrow oval shape used today. The early handle was straight, but by 1730 the tip was bent down, and about 1830 the tip was turned upward.

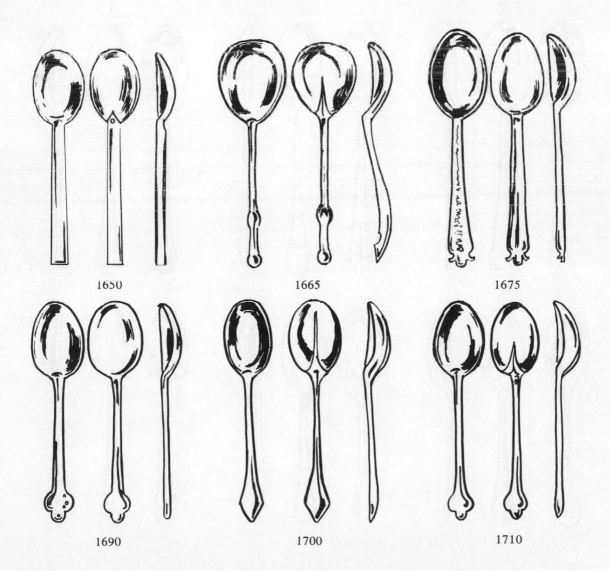

1650   1665   1675

1690   1700   1710

SPOONS

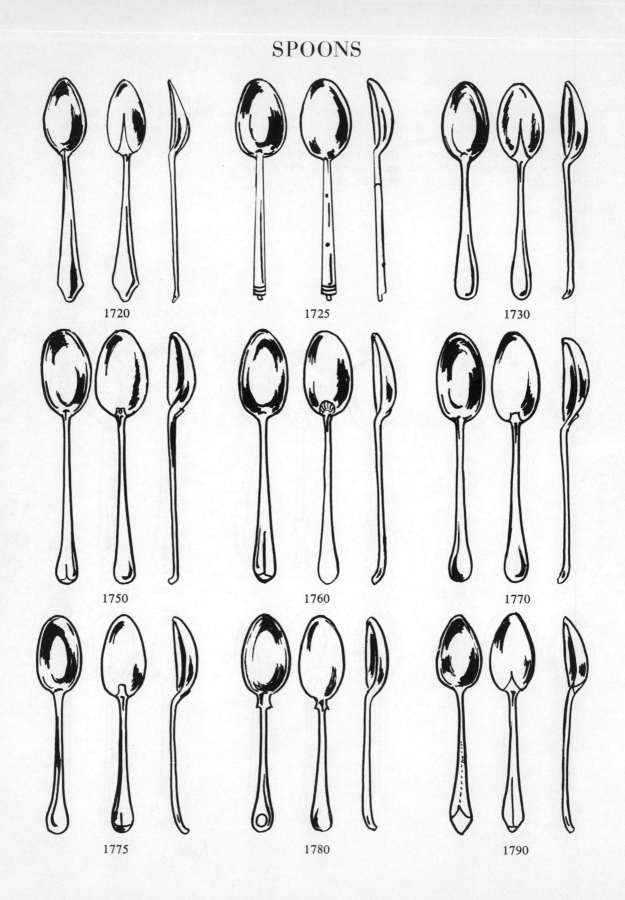

1720   1725   1730

1750   1760   1770

1775   1780   1790

SPOONS

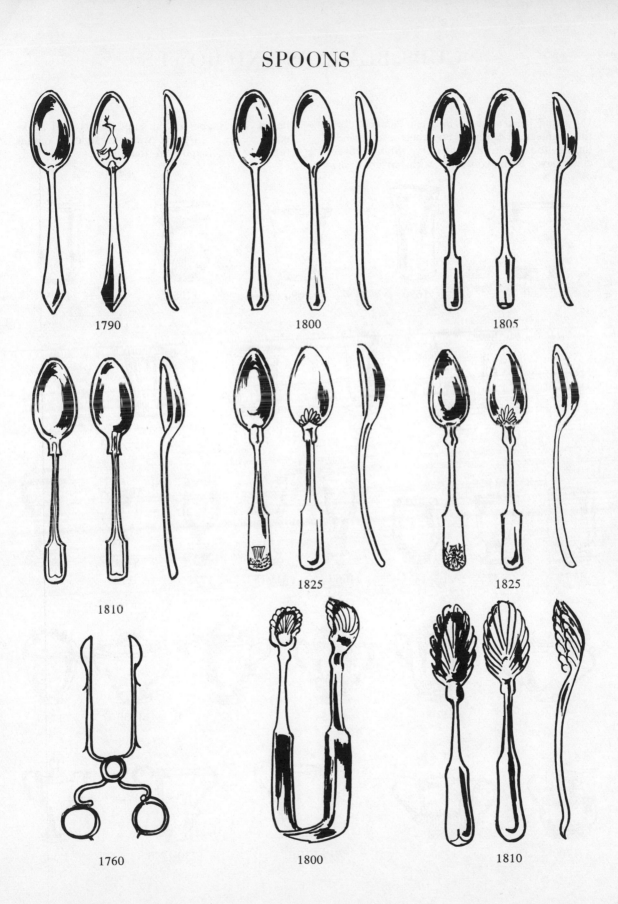

1790

1800

1805

1810

1825

1825

1760

1800

1810

CUPS, BEAKERS AND BOWLS

Cups and beakers were in great demand during the eighteenth century, but their use dwindled during the nineteenth century. Many covered cups have been confused with covered sugar bowls. The shapes of the cups, bowls, and beakers were in accordance with the style of design used for the teapots of the time.

| 1660 | 1690 | 1690 | 1705 | 1715 |

| 1740 | 1760 | 1775-1795 | 1800 |

| 1775 | 1775 | 1833 | 1660 | 1725-1825 | 1775 | 1720 | 1780 |

| 1695 | 1700 | 1725 | 1725 | 1730 | 1740 |

| 1700 | 1700 | 1710 | 1730-1740 | 1740 |

Gleason & Hovey (c. 1846-
1848)
Rome, N.Y.
F. A. Gleason
J. S. Hovey
Bibl. 20

F. A. Gleason (c. 1848)
Rome, N.Y.
Gleason & Hovey (c. 1846-
1848)
Bibl. 20

John W. Gleaves (c. 1850)
Philadelphia, Pa.
Bibl. 3

George Glenford (c. 1848)
Philadelphia, Pa.
Bibl. 3

William Glenn (c. 1811)
Philadelphia, Pa.
Bibl. 3

Joseph Glidden (b. 1707-d.
1780)
Boston, Mass.
Bibl. 23, 36, 44

Edwin Glover (c. 1843-1869)
Fayetteville, N.C.
Bibl. 21

Christian Gobrecht (Gobright)
(c. 1819-1844)
Philadelphia, Pa.
Bibl. 3

Gobright
(See preceding entry)

———— Goddard (c. 1810)
Location unknown
Bibl. 24

GODDARD

Benjamin Goddard
Location unknown
Bibl. 89

Benj Goddard

D. Goddard & Co. (c. 1845-
1850)
Worcester, Mass.
Bibl. 15, 25

D. Goddard & Cº

D. Goddard & Son (c. 1845)
Worcester, Mass.
Bibl. 23, 24, 25, 29, 44

D. GODDARD & SON

L. Goddard & Son (c. 1830)
Massachusetts
Bibl. 89

L GODDARD & SON

Nicholas Goddard (b. 1773-d.
1823)
Rutland, Vt. (c. 1807-1810)
Lord & Goddard (c. 1797-1810)
Bibl. 54

M. T. Godfrey (c. 1845)
Cambridge, Mass.
Bibl. 23

Godichew
(See Gaudechaud)

Godley & Johnson (Johnson &
Godley) (c. 1843-1849)
Albany, N.Y.
Richard Godley
———— Johnson
Bibl. 23, 28, 44

Richard Godley
Albany, N.Y.
Johnson & Godley (c. 1843-
1849)
Bibl. 20

Jacob Godschalk (c. 1771)
Philadelphia, Pa.
Bibl. 3

Philip Goelet (b. 1701-d. 1748)
New York, N.Y.
Bibl. 2, 4, 15, 23, 24, 25, 28, 30,
36, 39, 44, 54

P.G   P.G

Peter Goetes (Gates) (c. 1813-
1844)
Bardstown, Ky.
Bibl. 32, 54, 68

Jeremiah Goforth (c. 1700)
Philadelphia, Pa.
Bibl. 3, 23, 36, 44

Thomas Goldsmith (c. 1842-
1850-   )
Troy, N.Y.
Bibl. 20

B. Goldstone (c. 1839)
Philadelphia, Pa.
Bibl. 3

Joseph Goldthwaite (b. 1706-d.
1780)

Boston, Mass.
Bibl. 2, 15, 23, 24, 25, 28, 29,
36, 44, 70

James L. Goman (c. 1847-
1848)
Utica, N.Y.
Bibl. 18, 20

John Gombach (c. 1802)
Philadelphia, Pa.
Bibl. 3, 23, 36, 44

Gooch & Hequembourg
(c. 1845)
St. Louis, Mo.
Bibl. 54

Henry Gooddy (c. 1767)
Philadelphia, Pa.
Bibl. 3

L. Goode (c. 1835)
Location unknown
Bibl. 24, 28

L. GOODE

Goodfellow & Son (c. 1799)
Philadelphia, Pa.
Bibl. 3

William Goodfellow (c. 1793-
1818)
Philadelphia, Pa.
Bibl. 3

D. T. Goodhue (c. 1840)
Boston, Mass.
Bibl. 15, 25, 44

D T GOODHUE   D T G

John Goodhue (c. 1822-1855)
Salem, Mass.
Bibl. 15, 23, 24, 25, 28, 29, 36,
44

J. GOODHUE

Henry Gooding (c. 1820-1854)
Boston, Mass.
Bibl. 4, 15, 23, 24, 25, 28, 29,
36, 44

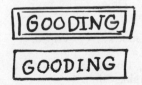

Joseph Gooding (c. 1861)
Boston, Mass.
Bibl. 23, 25, 36, 44

Josiah Gooding (c. 1841-1859)
Boston, Mass.
Bibl. 15, 25, 28, 29, 44

| Josiah Gooding |

———— Goodrich (c. 1850)
Philadelphia, Pa.
Smith & Goodrich
Bibl. 3

C. W. Goodrich (c. 1816-1866)
New Orleans, La.
Hyde & Goodrich
Bibl. 54

Erastus H. Goodrich (c. 1837-
1848)
Buffalo, N.Y.
Bibl. 20

Goodwin & Dodd (c. 1812)
Hartford, Conn.
Horace Goodwin
———— Dodd
Bibl. 16, 23, 25, 28, 36, 44

| G & D |

Allyn Goodwin (b. 1797-d.
1869)
Hartford, Conn.
H. &. A. Goodwin (c. 1811-
1852)
Bibl. 16, 23, 28, 36, 44

Benjamin Goodwin (b. 1732-d.
1792)
Boston, Mass.
Easton, Mass.
Bibl. 15, 23, 25, 28, 29, 36, 44

| B Goodwin |

H. & A. Goodwin (c. 1811-
1852)
Hartford, Conn.
Horace & Allyn Goodwin
Bibl. 16, 23, 24, 25, 28, 29, 36,
44, 61

| GOODWIN |

Homer Goodwin (c. 1857)
Cleveland, Ohio
Bibl. 65

Horace Goodwin (b. 1787-d.
1864)
Hartford, Conn. (c. 1811-1852)
New Britain, Conn.

Vermont
H. & A. Goodwin (c. 1811-
1852)
Bibl. 16, 23, 28, 36, 44

Ralph Goodwin (b. 1793-d.
1856)
Hartford, Conn.
Bibl. 16, 23, 28, 36, 44

Samuel Goodwin (c. 1820-
1822)
Philadelphia, Pa.
Bibl. 3

Daniel Gookin (b. 1682)
Boston, Mass. (c. 1696)
Bibl. 54

Gordon & Co. (c. 1849)
Boston, Mass.
Bibl. 4, 23, 28, 44

A. & J. Gordon (c. 1798)
New York, N.Y.
Alexander S. Gordon
James Gordon
Bibl. 4, 23, 28, 36, 44

Alexander S. Gordon (c. 1795-
1800)
New York, N.Y.
A. & J. Gordon (c. 1798)
Bibl. 15, 23, 24, 25, 29, 35, 36,
44, 54

Andrew Gordon (c. 1796)
New York, N.Y.
Bibl. 28, 44

| GORDON |

George Gordon (c. 1795-1840)
Newburgh, N.Y.
New York, N.Y.
Bibl. 20, 23, 24, 25, 29, 36,
44, 78

| G Gordon |

George Gordon (c. 1847-1850)
Philadelphia, Pa.
Bibl. 3

George Clinton Gordon
(c. 1847)
Augusta, Ga.
Bibl. 17

G. C. Gordon (c. 1845)
Edgefield, S.C.
Bibl. 5

James Gordon (c. 1795-1798)
New York, N.Y.
A. & J. Gordon (c. 1798)
Bibl. 15, 23, 36, 44

James Gordon (c. 1813)
Savannah, Ga.
Bibl. 17

James Samuel Gordon (c. 1769-
1771)
Philadelphia, Pa.
Bibl. 3, 23, 28, 36, 44

John Gore (c. 1832-1835)
New York, N.Y.
Bibl. 15

Gorgeon
(See Georgeon)

Gorham & Beebe (c. 1825-
1831)
Providence, R.I.
Jabez Gorham
Stanton Beebe
Bibl. 25

Gorham Manufacturing Co.
(19th century)
Providence, R.I.
Jabez Gorham
Bibl. 89

Gorham Silver (c. 1831)
Providence, R.I.
Bibl. 89

Gorham & Son (c. 1842)
Providence, R.I.
Jabez Gorham
John Gorham
Bibl. 23

Gorham & Thurber (c. 1850)
Providence, R.I.
Bibl. 23, 24, 25, 44

| Gorham & Thurber |

Gorham & Webster (c. 1831-
1841)
Providence, R.I.
Jabez Gorham
Henry L. Webster

Bibl. 15, 23, 24, 25, 28, 29, 36, 44, 56

Gorham & Webster

Gorham, Webster & Price (c. 1835)
Providence, R.I.
Jabez Gorham
Henry L. Webster
——— Price
Bibl. 15, 25, 44

Gorham Webster & Price

J. (Jabez) Gorham & Son (c. 1842-1847)
Providence, R.I.
Jabez Gorham
John Gorham
Bibl. 15, 23, 24, 25, 28, 29, 44

J Gorham & Son

Jabez Gorham (b. 1792)
Providence, R.I. (c. 1813-1847)
George C. (G.) Clark (c. 1813-1824)
William Hadwen (c. 1016-1828)
Gorham & Beebe (c. 1825-1831)
Gorham & Webster (c. 1831-1841)
Gorham & Son (c. 1842)
J. Gorham & Son (c. 1842-1847)
Gorham Manufacturing Co.
Bibl. 15, 23, 24, 25, 28, 36, 44

J GORHAM

John Gorham (c. 1814)
New Haven, Conn.
Bibl. 16, 23, 28, 36

John Gorham (b. 1820)
Providence,, R.I. (c. 1842)
Gorham & Son (c. 1842)
J. (Jabez) Gorham & Son (c. 1842-1847)
Bibl. 15, 23, 28, 44

Jonathan Gorham (c. 1816)
Nantucket Island, Mass.
Bibl. 12

Miles Gorham (b. 1757-d. 1847)
New Haven, Conn.
Bibl. 16, 23, 24, 25, 28, 29, 36, 44, 61, 69

M G   M GORHAM

Richard Gorham (b. 1775-d. 1841)
New Haven, Conn.
Shethear & Gorham (c. 1806-   )
Bibl. 16, 23, 28, 36, 44

William Gorrie (c. 1816)
Charleston, S.C.
Bibl. 5

John Goshea (Gosher) (c. 1824-1833)
Philadelphia, Pa.
Bibl. 3

Gott
(See George Ott)

Francis Gottier (Gaultier) (d. 1784)
Charleston, S.C. (c. 1741-1783)
Bibl. 5, 44, 54

Gottschalk & Bolland (c. 1848)
St. Louis, Mo.
Bibl. 54

Goudchaud
(See Gaudechaud)

Jesse W. Gouge & Co. (c. 1828)
Philadelphia, Pa.
Bibl. 3

James Gough (c. 1769-1795)
New York, N.Y.
Bibl. 23, 24, 25, 28, 36, 39, 44

J. G   J.G

Mel Gouiran
Location unknown
Bibl. 22

Michael Gouiran (Gowran) (c. 1820-1833)
Philadelphia, Pa.
Bibl. 3

Gould, Stowell & Ward (c. 1855-1858)
Baltimore, Md.
James Gould
A. Stowell Jr.
William H. Ward
Bibl. 23, 36, 38, 44

Gould & Ward (c. 1850)
Baltimore, Md.
James Gould
William H. Ward

Bibl. 24, 25, 36, 38, 44

GOULD & WARD

Edwin F. Gould
Utica, N.Y. (c. 1842-1844)
Cortland, N.Y. (c. 1846-1847)
Bibl. 18, 20

Ezra B. Gould (c. 1841)
Rochester, N.Y.
Bibl. 20

James Gould (b. 1795-d. 1874)
Baltimore, Md.
Boston, Mass.
Gelston & Gould (c. 1816-1820)
Gould, Stowell & Ward (c. 1855-1858)
Gould & Ward (c. 1850)
Bibl. 23, 24, 25, 29, 36, 38, 44

J. GOULD   J. GOULD

John Gould (c. 1831-1833)
New York, N.Y.
Bibl. 15

John H. Gould (c. 1840-1850)
Philadelphia, Pa.
Bibl. 3, 23, 36, 44

Govert
(See James Govett)

Govett (Gavett)
(See Ward & Govett [Gavett])

George Govett (c. 1811-1850)
Philadelphia, Pa.
Bibl. 3

James Govett (Govert) (c. 1802-1813)
Philadelphia, Pa.
Bibl. 3, 23, 44

John & William Gowdey (c. 1757-1795)
Charleston, S.C.
Bibl. 44

William Gowdey (d. 1798)
Charleston, S.C. (c. 1757-1795)
John & William Gowdey
Bibl. 5, 25, 54

William Gowen (b. 1749-d. 1803)
Medford, Mass. (c. 1777)
Charlestown, Mass.
Bibl. 23, 24, 25, 28, 29, 36, 44

W GOWEN   W G

Gowran
(See Gouiran)

Gragg & Thayer (c. 1808-1809)
Troy, N.Y.
Hugh Gragg
Amos Thayer (?)
Bibl. 20

Hugh Gragg (c. 1808-1809)
Troy, N.Y.
Gragg & Thayer
Bibl. 20

Graham
(See Oliver & Graham)

———— Graham (c. 1803)
Portsmouth, Va.
Bibl. 19

Dr. Christopher Columbus
 Graham (b. 1787)
Springfield, Ky. (c. 1812)
Bibl. 20, 32, 54

Daniel Graham (b. 1764)
West Suffield, Conn. (c. 1789)
Bibl. 16, 28, 36, 44

John Graham (c. 1837-1840)
Philadelphia, Pa.
Bibl. 3

Mitchell Graham (c. 1837)
Philadelphia, Pa.
Bibl. 3

Samuel Graham (c. 1825)
Philadelphia, Pa.
Bibl. 3

William Graham (c. 1733)
Philadelphia, Pa.
Bibl. 3

Christian Grammer (c. 1800)
Baltimore, Md.
Bibl. 38

Grant & Smith (Smith &
 Grant) (c. 1827-1831)
Louisville, Ky.
William Grant (?)
Richard Ewing Smith
Bibl. 54

Israel Boone Grant (c. 1817-
 1820)
St. Louis, Mo.
Bibl. 54

James Grant (c. 1789)
Albany, N.Y.
Bibl. 20

John Grant (b. 1793-d. 1817)
Savannah, Ga.
Bibl. 17

Thomas Grant (b. 1731-d.
 1804)
Marblehead, Mass.
Bibl. 15, 23, 24, 25, 28, 29, 36,
 44, 72

T GRANT

William Grant (Jr.) (b.
 1766-d. 1809)
Marblehead, Mass.
Bibl. 3, 4, 23, 24, 25, 28, 29,
 36, 44

W G   W G
W. Grant

William Grant (c. 1808)
Lexington, Ky.
Grant & Smith (?)
Bibl. 32

Gerard Graval (c. 1807)
Philadelphia, Pa.
Bibl. 3

Gravelle
(See Le Fevre & Gravelle)

Louisa M. Gravelle (c. 1820-
 1830)
Philadelphia, Pa.
Bibl. 3

Rene L. Gravelle (c. 1811-
 1831)
Philadelphia, Pa.
Lefevre & Gravelle (c. 1811)
Bibl. 3, 23, 36, 44

Gerrit Graverat (c. 1772)
Detroit, Mich.
Bibl. 58

Graves & Fitch (c. 1816-1821)
Auburn, N.Y.
Samuel Graves (?)
James Fitch
Bibl. 20, 25

Graves & Nichols (c. 1809-
 1816)
Cooperstown, N.Y.
Bibl. 20

Graves & Thompson (c. 1844)
Winchester, Va.
George B. Graves
William Thompson
Bibl. 19

George B. Graves (c. 1840)
Winchester, Va.
Graves & Thompson (c. 1844)
John L. Albert (c. 1827)
Bibl. 19

George W. Graves (c. 1848)
Winchester, Va.
Bibl. 19

Jesse Graves (c. 1804-1847)
Cooperstown, N.Y.
Bibl. 20

Samuel Graves (c. 1816-1823)
Auburn, N.Y.
Graves & Fitch (c. 1816-
 1821) (?)
Bibl. 20

Samuel Graves (c. 1824)
Batavia, N.Y.
Bibl. 20

Thomas Graves (c. 1828)
Cincinnati, Ohio
Bibl. 34, 36

Thomas Graves (c. 1828-1830)
Cincinnati, Ohio
Bibl. 23, 44

Nicholas Gravier (c. 1822)
New Orleans, La.
Bibl. 23, 36, 44

———— Gray (c. 1850)
Cleveland, Ohio
Bibl. 65

Gray & Libby (c. 1850)
Location unknown
Bibl. 28

Charles Gray (b. 1749)
Maryland (c. 1774)
Bibl. 28, 38

G. Gray (c. 1839)
Portsmouth, N.H.
Bibl. 23, 24, 25, 28, 29, 36, 44

G. GRAY

Henry A. Gray (c. 1854)
Edgefield, S.C.
Bibl. 5

John Gray (b. 1692-d. 1720)
New London, Conn.
Boston, Mass.

Bibl. 4, 16, 23, 24, 25, 28, 29, 36,
44, 50, 70

John Gray (c. 1811)
Philadelphia, Pa.
Bibl. 3

Robert Gray (d. 1850)
Portsmouth, N.H. (c. 1830)
Bibl. 15, 23, 24, 25, 28, 29, 36,
44

Samuel Gray (b. 1684-d. 1713)
New London, Conn.
Boston, Mass.
Bibl. 15, 16, 23, 24, 25, 28, 29,
36, 44, 54, 61

Thomas Gray (c. 1818-1820)
Lexington, Ky.
Bibl. 32, 54, 68

William Gray (b. 1772-d. 1803)
Charleston, S.C. (c. 1800)
Bibl. 5

William H. Gray (c. 1845-
1846)
Philadelphia, Pa.
Bibl. 3

Green
(See Fellows & Green)
(See Lincoln & Green)

Green(e)
(See Whitaker & Green[e])

——— Green (c. 1843)
Hartford, Conn.
Bibl. 23

Bartholomew Green (c. 1697-
1738-   )
Boston, Mass.
Bibl. 15, 28

B: GREEN

Benjamin Green(e) (b. 1712-d.
1776)
Boston, Mass.

Bibl. 15, 24, 28, 29, 36

B: GREEN

Edward Green (c. 1826)
Fairfax, Va.
Bibl. 19

Glover Green (c. 1844)
Philadelphia, Pa.
Bibl. 3

J. Green (c. 1797-1798)
Albany, N.Y.
Bibl. 20

James Green (c. 1764)
Savannah, Ga.
Bibl. 17

James Green (c. 1805)
New York, N.Y.
Bibl. 23, 36, 44

John Green (c. 1794-1796)
Philadelphia, Pa.
Bibl. 3

John N. Green (c. 1822-1842)
Baltimore, Md.
Bibl. 38

Josiah B. Green (c. 1847-1850)
Leesburg, Va.
Bibl. 19

Rufus Green(e) (b. 1707-d.
1777)
Boston, Mass.
Bibl. 2, 4, 15, 23, 24, 25, 28, 29,
36, 44, 54, 69, 70

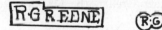

William Greenawalt
Halifax, N.C.
Bibl. 21

Gaither Greenburg (c. 1820)
Washington, D.C.
May be Greenberg Gaither.
Bibl. 44

Greene & Bros. (c. 1835-1837)
Philadelphia, Pa.
Bibl. 3

William Greene (c. 1837-1841)
Philadelphia, Pa.
Bibl. 3

William Greene & Co. (c. 1815)
Providence, R.I.
Bibl. 23, 28, 36, 44

Max Greener (19th century)
Shelbyville, Ky.
Bibl. 32, 54

Benjamin Greenleaf (d. 1780)
Newburyport, Mass. (c. 1756)
Bibl. 15

David Greenleaf (b. 1737-d.
1800)
Hartford, Conn.
Norwich, Conn.
Boston, Mass.
Bibl. 15, 16, 23, 24, 25, 29, 36,
44

David Greenleaf Jr. (b. 1765-d.
1835)
Hartford, Conn.
Frederick Oakes
Bibl. 15, 16, 23, 25, 28, 29, 36,
44, 61

G. Greenleaf (b. 1790-d.
1850)
(George Greenleaf)
Newburyport, Conn.
Bibl. 54

Joseph Greenleaf (d. 1798)
New London, Conn. (c. 1778-
1798)
Bibl. 15, 16, 23, 28, 44

Daniel Greenough (c. 1710-
1714)
Newcastle, N.H.
Portsmouth, N.H.
Bibl. 28, 54

Charles F. Greenwood (b.
1858-d. 1904)
Norfolk, Va.
C. F. Greenwood & Bro. (c.
1851)

Bibl. 19

C. F. GREENWOOD

C. F. Greenwood & Bro. (c. 1851)
Norfolk, Va.
Charles F. Greenwood
Frederick Greenwood
Bibl. 19

John Greer (d. 1774)
Carlisle, Pa.
Bibl. 3

Peter Greffin (c. 1801)
Philadelphia, Pa.
Bibl. 3, 23, 36, 44

——— Gregg (b. 1751-d. 1820)
Savannah, Ga.
Bibl. 17

Gregg & Hayden (Hayden & Gregg) (c. 1832-1846)
Charleston, S.C.
Bibl. 44, 54, 89

Gregg & Hayden

Gregg, Hayden & Co. (Hayden, Gregg & Co.) (c. 1846-1852)
Charleston, S.C.
William Gregg
H. Sidney Hayden
Nathaniel Hayder.
Bibl. 24, 25, 44

GREGG, HAYDEN & CO.

Gregg, Hayden & Whilden (c. 1855)
Charleston, S.C.
William Gregg
H. Sidney Hayden (?)
William G. Whilden
Bibl. 54

Jacob Gregg (b. 1766-d. 1832)
Alexandria, Va.
Bibl. 19

William Gregg (b. 1800-d. 1867)
Lexington, Ky. (c. 1818-1821)
Petersburg, Va. (c. 1821-1824)
Columbia, S.C. (c. 1824-1831)
Charleston, S.C. (c. 1838-1855)
Gregg & Hayden (Hayden & Gregg) (c. 1832-1846)
Gregg, Hayden & Co. (Hayden, Gregg & Co.) (c. 1846-1852)

Gregg, Hayden & Whilden (c. 1855)

Bibl. 5, 19, 32, 44, 54

W. GREGG

Gregory
Location unknown
Bibl. 15

Gregory

Gregory & Bontecou (Bonticou) (c. 1802-1805)
New Haven, Conn.
Augusta, Ga.
Levi Gregory
Roswell Bontecou (Bonticou)
Bibl. 17

Gregory & Shuber (c. 1837)
Philadelphia, Pa.
James Gregory
——— Shuber
Bibl. 3

James Gregory (c. 1837)
Philadelphia, Pa.
Bibl. 3

Levi Gregory (c. 1802-1805)
Augusta, Ga.
Gregory & Bontecou (Bonticou)
Bibl. 17

George W. Greiner (d. 1891)
Waynesboro, Va. (c. 1837-1843)
Bibl. 19

Michael Gretter (b. 1785-d. 1868)
Richmond, Va. (c. 1806-1813-   )
Lynchburg, Va. (c. 1814)
Baltimore, Md.
Bibl. 19

ML. GRETTER

Griffee
(See George F. Griffith)

Griffen & Hoyt (c. 1819-1832)
New York, N.Y.
Peter Griffen
Walter B. Hoyt
Bibl. 15, 23, 24, 25, 29, 36, 44

GRIFFEN & HOYT
GRIFFEN & HOYT

Griffen & Son (c. 1832-1837)
Albany, N.Y. (c. 1832)
New York, N.Y.
Peter Griffen
William Griffen
Bibl. 15, 25, 44

C. B. Griffen (Griffin)
Troy, N.Y. (c. 1827-1829)
Little Falls, N.Y. (c. 1833-1834)
G. M. & C. B. Griffen (c. 1827-1829)
Bibl. 20

G. M. & C. B. Griffen (c. 1827-1829)
Troy, N.Y.
George M. Griffen
C. B. Griffen
Bibl. 20

George M. Griffen
Troy, N.Y. (c. 1827-1829)
Athens, Ga. (c. 1839)
Savannah, Ga. (c. 1850-1855)
G. M. & C. B. Griffen (c. 1827-1829)
Bibl. 17, 20

Isaiah Griffen (c. 1802-1823)
Hudson, N.Y.
Bibl. 20

John Griffen
Staunton, Va. (c. 1773-1794)
Germantown, N.C. (c. 1794-1803)
Bibl. 21

Peter Griffen (c. 1815-1840)
Albany, N.Y. (c. 1832)
New York, N.Y. (c. 1819-1832)
Griffen & Hoyt (c. 1819-1832)
Griffen & Son (c. 1832-1837)
Bibl. 15, 23, 24, 25, 36, 44

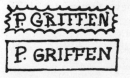

David Griffeth (d. 1779)
Portsmouth, N.H. (c. 1763)
Bibl. 25, 54

Nathaniel Griffeth (b. 1740-d.
  1771)
Portsmouth, N.H.
Bibl. 54

Samuel Griffeth (b. 1729-d.
  1773)
Portsmouth, N.H. (c.
  1757-   )
Bibl. 54

Griffin
(See C. B. Griffen)

Edward Griffin (c. 1828-   )
Utica, N.Y.
Bibl. 18, 20

George Griffin (c. 1841-1852)
Louisville, Ky.
Bibl. 32, 54, 60

Isaiah Griffin (c. 1802)
Location unknown
Bibl. 28

John Griffin
Staunton, Va. (before 1794 and
  after 1803)
Germantown, N.C. (c. 1794-
  1803)
Bibl. 19

Griffing
(See Giffing)

Edward Griffing (c. 1831)
Oswego, N.Y.
Aspinwall & Griffing
Bibl. 20

Griffith & Gaither (c.
  1809-   )
Alexandria, Va
Greenberry Griffith
John Gaither(?)
Bibl. 19

David Grif(f)ith (c. 1798)
Boston, Mass.
Bibl. 23, 28, 36

C. Greenberry Griffith
Baltimore, Md. (c. 1816-1818)
Washington, D.C. (c. 1830)
Riggs & Griffith (c. 1816-
  1818) (?)
Bibl. 15, 38

Edward Griffith (d. 1805)
Savannah, Ga. (c. 1785-1786)
Augusta, Ga. (c. 1801-1802)

Thompson & Griffith (c. 1785-
  1786)
Bibl. 17

Edward Griffith (c. 1847)
Albany, N.Y.
Bibl. 20

George F. Griffith (Griffee)
  (c. 1841-1850)
Philadelphia, Pa.
Bibl. 3

Greenberry Griffith (b. 1787-d.
  1848)
Alexandria, Va.
Griffiith & Gaither (c.
  1809-   )
(See C. Greenberry Griffith)
Bibl. 19

G. G

Henry Griffith (c. 1816-1818)
Baltimore, Md.
Riggs & Griffith (?)
Bibl. 15, 38

L. Griffith (c. 1842-1843)
Philadelphia, Pa.
Bibl. 3

Samuel Griffith (c. 1847)
Philadelphia, Pa.
Bibl. 3

James Griffiths (c. 1836)
Glens Falls, N.Y.
Bibl. 20

John Griffiths (c. 1855)
Greenville, S.C.
Bibl. 5

C. Grifing (c. 1825)
New York, N.Y.
Bibl. 23

William Grigg (c. 1760-1795)
Albany, N.Y. (c. 1770-1778)
Bibl. 4, 15, 20, 23, 24, 25, 28,
  29, 30, 35, 36, 44, 54

Benjamin(e) Grignon (17th
  century)
Charleston, S.C.
Bibl. 5

Benjamin(e) Grignon (c. 1685)
Boston, Mass.
Oxford, Mass.
Bibl. 2, 23, 28, 36, 44

René Grignon (d. 1715)
Oxford, Mass. (c. 1691, c.
  1699)
Boston, Mass. (c. 1696)
Norwich, Mass. (c. 1708)
Bibl. 2, 15, 16, 23, 24, 25, 28,
  29, 36, 69

John Paul Grimke (b. 1713-d.
  1791)
Charleston, S.C. (c. 1740-1772)
Bibl. 5, 23, 36, 44, 54

George Griscom (c. 1791)
Philadelphia, Pa.
Bibl. 3, 23, 36, 44

Caesar Griselm (c. 1700)
Philadelphia, Pa.
(See Cesar Ghiselin)
Bibl. 36, 44

A. B. Griswold & Co. (1866)
New Orleans, La.
Bibl. 54

Chauncey D. Griswold (c.
  1838-1839)
Troy, N.Y.
Bibl. 20

Francis A. Griswold (c. 1838-
  1839)
Louisville, Ky.
Bibl. 32

Gaylord Griswold (b. 1807)
Utica, N.Y. (c. 1831)
B. F. Brooks & Co. (c. 1829-
  1831)
Bibl. 18, 20

Gilbert Griswold (c. 1810-
  1825)
Middletown, Conn.
Portland, Me.
Bibl. 16, 23, 28, 36, 44

H. A. Griswold (c. 1850)
Whitehall, N.Y.
Bibl. 20

J. Griswold (c. 1805)
Salem, N.Y.
Bibl. 20

Joab Griswold (c. 1832-1835)
Buffalo, N.Y.
Utica, N.Y.
Brooks & Griswold (c. 1832)
Bibl. 18, 20

William Griswold (c. 1820)
Portland, Me.
Middletown, Conn. (?)
Bibl. 15, 23, 24, 25, 29, 44

W. GRISWOLD

Jacob Marius Groen
(Morrisgreen) (d. 1750)
New York, N.Y. (c. 1701)
Bibl. 44

J. R. Groff (c. 1841-1850)
Philadelphia, Pa.
Bibl. 3, 23

J. L. Gropengiesser (c. 1841-
1850)
Philadelphia, Pa.
Bibl. 3

Grosjean
(See Woodward & Grosjean)

Francis J. Gross (c. 1841-
1850)
Philadelphia, Pa.
Bibl. 3

William Grout (c. 1816)
Philadelphia, Pa.
Bibl. 3

George Gruber (c. 1840)
Berryville, Va.
Bibl. 19

Gudichaud
(See Gaudechaud)

Victor A. Gue (b. 1800)
Charleston, S.C. (c. 1831-1835)
Bibl. 5

A. Guelberth (c. 1838-1848)
St. Louis, Mo.
Bibl. 54, 89

A. GUELBERTH
- St. Louis -

Dominick Guercy (c. 1795-
1798)
New York, N.Y.
Bibl. 23, 36, 44

Anthony Guerin (Gurine)
(Geriung) (Gurnine)
(Guirna)
Philadelphia, Pa. (c. 1791-
1814)
Bibl. 3, 23, 28, 36, 44

Isaac Guernsey (c. 1765-1767,
d. 1767)
Northampton, Mass.
Bibl. 84

Theodore Guesnard
(Guesmard) (c. 1818-1822)
Philadelphia, Pa.
Bibl. 3

Henry Brown Guest
(See Henry Brown)

E. Guey (c. 1820)
Location unknown
Bibl. 24

E GUEY

James S. Guignard
Columbia, S.C.
Radcliffe & Guignard (c. 1856-
1858)
Bibl. 5

John Guild (Guile) (c. 1818-
1825)
Philadelphia, Pa.
Bibl. 3

Noah Guille (c. 1701)
Boston, Mass.
Bibl. 23, 28, 36, 44, 72

Guimarin & Brelet (c. 1824)
Augusta, Ga.
John Guimarin
Francis Brelet
Bibl. 17

John Guimarin (c. 1815-1825)
Augusta, Ga.
Guimarin & Brelet (c. 1824)
Brelet, Wearer & Co. (c. 1825)
Bibl. 17

Frederick Edward Guinand
(Guinaud)
Baltimore, Md. (c. 1814-1827)
Bibl. 15, 25, 38, 44

F E. GUINAND

Joseph Guingan (c. 1837-1838)
Albany, N.Y.
Bibl. 20

Jacob Guinguigner (b. 1795-d.
1853)
Utica, N.Y. (c. 1840-
1853-)
Bibl. 18, 20

——— Guion
New York, N.Y.
Howe & Guion (c. 1839-1840)
Bibl. 15, 24

Rence Guiot (b. 1793)
Baltimore, Md. (c. 1803)
Bibl. 38

Guirna
(See Guerin)

Calvin Guiteau (c. 1828-1845)
Watertown, N.Y.
Bibl. 20

Nathan Gulick (b. 1777-d.
1826) (c. 1818-1826)
Maysville, Ky.
Easton, Pa.
New Jersey
Bibl. 32

Nathan & Elizabeth Gulick (c.
1818-1826)
Maysville, Ky.
Bibl. 32

N. & E. G.

Gullup
(See Gallup)

Henry Guluger (c. 1817)
St. Louis, Mo.
Bibl. 54

Gunn & Mitchell (c. 1832)
New York, N.Y.
Henry Mitchell (c. 1837-1841)
(?)
——— Gunn
Bibl. 15

——— Gunn
New York, N.Y.
Gunn & Mitchell (c. 1832)
Bibl. 15

Enos Gunn (b. 1770)
Waterbury, Conn. (c. 1792)
Bibl. 16, 23, 24, 25, 28, 29, 36,
44

ENOS GUNN   E. GUNN

John P. Gurau (c. 1797-1819)
Savannah, Ga.
Bibl. 17

Gurine
(See Guerin)

William Gurley (b. 1764)
Norwich, Conn. (c. 1804)
Bibl. 16, 23, 24, 25, 28, 29, 36, 44

| W. G |

The Rev. William Gurley (c.
    1810-1812)
Zanesville, Ohio
Bibl. 34

Gurnee & Co. (c. 1835)
New York, N.Y.
Benjamin Gurnee
Bibl. 23, 25, 36, 44

Gurnee & Stephen (c. 1833-
    1837)
New York, N.Y.
Benjamin Gurnee (?)
——— Stephen (Stevens)
Bibl. 15

B. & S. Gurnee (c. 1833)
New York, N.Y.
Benjamin Gurnee (?)
S. Gurnee
Bibl. 4, 23, 28, 36, 44

Benjamin Gurnee (c. 1824-
    1840)
New York, N.Y.
Benjamin Gurnee & Co. (c.
    1826-1828)
Gurnee & Co. (c. 1835)
Bibl. 15, 23, 25, 36, 44

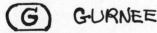

Benjamin Gurnee & Co. (c.
    1826-1828)
New York, N.Y.
Bibl. 15

Daniel Gurnee (c. 1850)
New York, N.Y.
Bibl. 23

S. Gurnee
New York, N.Y.
B. & S. Gurnee (c. 1833)
Bibl. 4, 23, 28, 36, 44

Gurnine
(See Guerin)

Guthre & Jefferis (c. 1840)
Wilmington, Del.
James Guthre
Emmor Jefferis
Bibl. 25, 44

James Guthre (b. 1796-d. 1877)
Wilmington, Del.
Philadelphia, Pa.
Guthre & Jefferis (c. 1840)
Bibl. 15, 25, 30, 44

| J. GUTHRE |

Philip Ranard Guyeon & Yver
    (c. 1796)
Philadelphia, Pa.
Bibl. 3

Benjamin Guyer (c. 1848)
Philadelphia, Pa.
Bibl. 3

John Gyles (b. 1781-d. 1822)
Charleston, S.C. (c. 1808-1822)
Bibl. 5

James A. Haas (c. 1846-1849)
Philadelphia, Pa.
Bibl. 3

N. Haas (c. 1846-1850)
Philadelphia, Pa.
Bibl. 3

Joseph Hacker (c. 1831-1850)
Philadelphia, Pa.
Bibl. 3

William Hacker (c. 1848-1849)
Philadelphia, Pa.
Bibl. 3

Charles Hackett (c. 1790-1806)
Easton, Md.
Bibl. 38

William Hackle (c. 1763-1772)
Baltimore, Md.
Bibl. 3, 23, 28, 29, 36, 38, 44

William Hadder (c. 1837)
Philadelphia, Pa.
Bibl. 3

Haddock & Andrews (c. 1838-
    1847)
Boston, Mass.

Henry Haddock
Henry Andrews
Bibl. 4, 23, 28, 36, 44

Haddock, Lincoln & Foss (c.
    1850-1865)
Boston, Mass.
Henry Haddock
A. L. Lincoln
——— Foss
Bibl. 28, 44

HADDOCK, LINCOLN & FOSS

Henry Haddock (c. 1836-1850)
Boston, Mass.
Haddock & Andrews (c. 1838-
    1847)
Haddock, Lincoln & Foss (c.
    1850-1865)
Bibl. 4, 23, 28, 36, 44

William Hadwen (b. 1791-d.
    1862, c. 1816-1828)
Nantucket Island, Mass.
Providence, R.I.
George C. (G.) Clark
Jabez Gorham
Bibl. 12, 23, 24, 25, 28, 36, 44

HADWEN ★

W. HADWEN

Haes
(See George Hays)

John Hafline (d. 1804)
Philadelphia, Pa. (c. 1785-
    1803)
Bibl. 3

Elias Hager (c. 1841-1844)
Rochester, N.Y.
Bibl. 20, 41, 44

Wolfgung Haggan (c. 1752)
Reading, Pa.
Bibl. 44

J. H. Haggenmacher & Co. (c.
    1836)
Philadelphia, Pa.
Bibl. 3, 23, 36, 44

John Hague (c. 1831-1835)
New York, N.Y.
Bibl. 15

C. G. Hahn (c. 1798)
Philadelphia, Pa.
Bibl. 3

Haight & Leach (c. 1850)
Auburn, N.Y.
John W. Haight
Leonard D. Leach
Bibl. 20

Haight & Leonard (c. 1847)
Newburgh, N.Y.
Nelson Haight
D. Gillis Leonard
Bibl. 20

Haight & Sterling (c. 1841-
1843)
Newburgh, N.Y.
Nelson Haight
——— Sterling
Bibl. 20

John W. Haight (c. 1838-   )
Auburn, N.Y.
Haight & Leach (c. 1850)
Bibl. 20

Nelson Haight (c. 1839-1852)
Newburgh, N.Y.
Haight & Sterling (c. 1841-
1843)
Haight & Leonard (c. 1847)
Bibl. 15, 20, 25, 44

  N. Haight

Holme Haike (Haikes)
  (Hakes)
Paris, Ky. (c. 1840)
Bibl. 32, 54, 68

Moses Haine (c. 1775)
Philadelphia, Pa.
Bibl. 3

Abraham Haines (c. 1801)
New York, N.Y.
Bibl. 23, 36, 44

Imlah Haines (c. 1829-1833)
Philadelphia, Pa.
Folwell & Haines (c. 1844) (?)
Bibl. 3

Joshua J. Hair (c. 1848)
Louisville, Ky.
Bibl. 32

Hakes
(See Haike)

Hale
(See J. Enno & Hale)

J. J. Hale
Kentucky
Bibl. 54

J. R. Hale
Location unknown
Bibl. 15, 44

J. R. HALE

Henry Halewood (c. 1788)
Richmond, Va.
Bibl. 19

Haley & Haley (c. 1850)
Paris, Ky.
P. Haley
G. W. Haley
Bibl. 32
G. W. Haley (c. 1850)
Paris, Ky.
Haley & Haley
Bibl. 32

P. Haley (c. 1850)
Paris, Ky.
Haley & Haley
Bibl. 32

William Halfpenny (c. 1835)
Philadelphia, Pa.
Bibl. 3

Hall & Bennet (c. 1840?)
New York State
Bibl. 89

HALL & BENNET

Hall & Bliss (c. 1816-1818)
Albany, N.Y.
Bibl. 15, 20, 44

HALL & BLISS

Hall & Brower (c. 1852-1854)
Albany, N.Y.
Green Hall
S. Douglas Brower
Bibl. 4; 20, 23, 28, 36, 44

Hall, Brower & Co. (c. 1836-
1842)
Albany, N.Y.
Green Hall
S. Douglas Brower
Bibl. 23, 36, 44

Hall & Elton (c. 1841)
Geneva, N.Y.
Abraham B. Hall
A. D. Elton
Bibl. 20, 25, 44

Hall & Hewson (c. 1842-1847)
Albany, N.Y.
Green Hall
John D. Hewson
S. Douglas Brower
Bibl. 4, 20, 23, 24, 28, 29, 36

H & H

Hall, Hewson & Brower (c.
1847-1850)
Albany, N.Y.
Green Hall
John D. Hewson
S. Douglas Brower
Bibl. 4, 15, 20, 23, 28, 44

Hall, Hewson & Co. (c. 1839-
1842, 1847-1850)
Albany, N.Y.
Green Hall
John D. Hewson
S. Douglas Brower
Thomas V. Z. Merrifield
Bibl. 4, 20, 28

Hall, Hewson & Merrifield (c.
1840)
Albany, N.Y.
Green Hall
John D. Hewson
Thomas V. Z. Merrifield
Bibl. 4, 23, 28, 36, 44

Hall & Merriman
New Haven, Conn. (c. 1825)
Albany, N.Y.
Bibl. 24, 25, 29, 44

  H & M

Hall & Sanger (c. 1840?)
Location unknown
Bibl. 89

Hall & Sanger

Hall & Snow (c. 1835)
Cleveland, Ohio
Ransom E. Hall
William H. Snow
Bibl. 54, 65, 89

A. B. Hall
Location unknown
(May be Abraham H. Hall)
Bibl. 28

Abijah Hall
Albany, N.Y. (c. 1813)
New York, N.Y. (c. 1830-1835)
Bibl. 20, 23, 28, 36, 44

Abraham B. Hall (c. 1806-
1839)
Geneva, N.Y.
Hall & Elton (c. 1841)
Bibl. 20, 44

Asa Hall (b. 1760-d. 1819)
Washington, Ga. (c. 1811-
1819)
Raynham, Mass.
Bibl. 17, 20

C. Hall (c. 1815)
Ovid, N.Y.
Bibl. 20

Charles Hall (b. 1742, c. 1755-
1780)
Lancaster, Pa.
Bibl. 3, 15, 23, 36, 44, 46, 54, 62
| C Hall | | C H |

David Hall (d. 1779)
Philadelphia, Pa. (c. 1760-
1777)
Burlington, N.J. (c. 1777-1778)
Bibl. 3, 15, 23, 24, 25, 28, 29,
36, 39, 44, 46, 54, 81

Drew Hall (c. 1789-1805)
New York, N.Y.
Bibl. 4, 23, 28, 36, 44

George Hall (c. 1823-1842)
Philadelphia, Pa.
Bibl. 3

George W. Hall (c. 1840)
Newburgh, N.Y.
Ayers & Hall (c. 1800) (?)
Bibl. 20

Green Hall (d. 1863)
Albany, N.Y. (c. 1810-1827)
Carson & Hall (c. 1810-1818)

Hall & Brower (c. 1852-1854)
Hall, Brower & Co. (c. 1836-
1842)
Hall, Hewson & Merrifield (c.
1840)
Hall & Hewson (c. 1842-1847)
Hall, Hewson & Brower (c.
1847-1850)
Hall, Hewson & Co. (c. 1836-
1842)
Bibl. 20, 23, 28, 36, 44

Ivory Hall (b. 1780-d. 1870)
Concord, Mass. (c. 1801)
Bibl. 23, 36, 44

J. & A. B. Hall (c. 1813)
Geneva, N.Y.
Bibl. 20

John Hall (c. 1804-1840)
Philadelphia, Pa.
Bibl. 3

John Hall (c. 1848)
Louisville, Ky.
Bibl. 32

Joseph Hall (c. 1781)
Albany, N.Y.
Bibl. 15, 20, 23, 24, 25, 28, 29,
36, 44
| I. Hall | | J Hall |

Peter Hall (c. 1818-1824)
Philadelphia, Pa.
Bibl. 3

Ransom E. Hall (c. 1829-
1836)
Cleveland, Ohio (c. 1835)
Detroit, Mich.
Geneva, N.Y.
Hall & Snow (c. 1835)
Bibl. 20, 54, 65

Alonzo Corwin Hallack
(Halleck)
Paris, Ky. (c. 1840-1853)
L. Matthews (c. 1852)
Bibl. 32
| A C HALLACK |

John Hallam (c. 1752-1800)
New London, Conn.
Bibl. 16, 23, 28, 36, 44

Halleck
(See Hallack)

——— Haller (Hiller) (c.
1837)

Circleville, Ohio
Bibl. 34

Elias H. Halliday (c. 1828-
1833)
Philadelphia, Pa.
Bibl. 3

Hiram Halliday (c. 1834-1844)
Albany, N.Y.
Bibl. 20

James H. Halliday (c. 1841-
1843)
Philadelphia, Pa.
Bibl. 3, 23

George Halliwell (c. 1813-
1817)
Poughkeepsie, N.Y.
Field & Halliwell (c. 1806-
1813)
Frear & Halliwell (c. 1813-
1816)
Bibl. 20

Charles Halsel (c. 1839)
Philadelphia, Pa.
Bibl. 3

Jabez Halsey (b. 1762-d. 1820)
New York, N.Y. (c. 1787-
1796)
Dally & Halsey (c. 1787-1789)
Bibl. 15, 23, 24, 28, 29, 30, 35,
36, 44, 71, 78
| I. HALSEY | | HALSEY |

Halstead & Son (c. 1799)
New York, N.Y.
Bibl. 23, 36, 44

Benjamin Halsted (Halstead)
New York State (c. 1764-1766,
1786-1806)
Elizabeth, N.J. (c. 1766-   )
Philadelphia, Pa. (c. 1783-
1785)
Benjamin & Matthias Halsted
(c. 1766-1769)
Bibl. 3, 4, 23, 24, 25, 28, 29, 30,
36, 44, 46, 54

Benjamin & Matthias Halsted
(c. 1766-1769)
Elizabeth, N.J.
Bibl. 46

Joseph Halstrick (b. 1815-d.
1886)
Boston, Mass.
Stanwood & Halstrick (c. 1850)
Bibl. 4, 23, 44,

William S. Halstrick
Location unknown
Bibl. 28

George Ham (c. 1810)
Portsmouth, N.H.
Bibl. 23, 28, 36, 44

William Hamelin (b. 1772)
Middletown, Conn. (c. 1791)
Bibl. 39

Hamersly
(See Hammersley)

Hamill & Co. (c. 1817-1819)
New York, N.Y.
James Hamill
Bibl. 15, 23, 36, 44

James Hamill
New York, N.Y. (c. 1810-
1816)
Portsmouth, Ohio (c. 1820)
Hamill & Co. (c. 1817-1819)
Bibl. 15, 23, 24, 25, 28, 29, 34,
36, 44

Hamilton & Adams (c. 1837-
1842)
Elmira, N.Y.
Daniel S. Hamilton
H. B. Adams (?)
Bibl. 20

Charles Hamilton (c. 1761)
Poughkeepsie, N.Y.
Bibl. 54

Daniel S. Hamilton (c. 1848)
Elmira, N.Y.
Hamilton & Adams (c. 1837-
1842)
Bibl. 20

James Hamilton (c. 1766)
Annapolis, Md.
Bibl. 23, 28, 36, 44

James Hamilton (c. 1776-1771)
Fredericksburg, Va.
Bibl. 19

James Hamilton (c. 1848)
Philadelphia, Pa.
Bibl. 3

John Hamilton (c. 1798)
New York, N.Y.
Bibl. 23, 36, 44

R. J. Hamilton (c. 1837-1846)
Philadelphia, Pa.
Bibl. 3

Samuel Hamilton (c. 1837)
Philadelphia, Pa.
Bibl. 3

Cyrus Hamlin (b. 1810-d.
1900)
Portland, Me. (w. 1831)
Bibl. 23, 28, 36, 44

William Hamlin (b. 1772-d.
1869?)
Middletown, Conn.
Providence, R.I.
Bibl. 15, 16, 23, 24, 25, 28, 29,
36, 44, 56

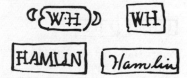

Crosby Hamman (Hammond)
(c. 1823-1825)
Philadelphia, Pa.
Bibl. 3

Peter Hamman (Hammond)
(c. 1817)
Philadelphia, Pa.
Bibl. 3

Thomas Hammersley
(Hammersly) (Hamersly)
(b. 1727-d. 1781)
New York, N.Y. (c. 1756)
Bibl. 15, 23, 24, 29, 30, 35, 36,
44, 72

Richard Hammett (c. 1844-
1845)
Troy, N.Y.
Bibl. 20

Crosby Hammond
(See Hamman)

Eleazer Hammond (c. 1837-
1838)
Troy, N.Y.
Bibl. 20

Peter Hammond
(See Hamman)

Seneca Hammond (c.
1804-   )
Utica, N.Y.
Osborn & Hammond
Bibl. 20

Hampton & Palmer (c. 1830-
1832)
Salisbury, N.C.
James Brandon Hampton
John C. Palmer
Bibl. 21

Henry Hampton (c. 1835)
Richmond, Va.
Bibl. 19

James Brandon Hampton (c.
1801-1832)
Salisbury, N.C.
Hampton & Palmer (c. 1830-
1832)
Bibl. 21

John Hancock (b. 1732-d.
1784)
Talbot County, Md.
Boston, Mass.
Charlestown, Mass.
Providence, R.I.
Bibl. 2, 15, 23, 24, 28, 29, 36,
38, 44, 56, 72

Robert Hancock (c. 1793-
1794)
Philadelphia, Pa.
Bibl. 3

J. Hand (c. 1837)
Philadelphia, Pa.
Bibl. 3

Joseph S. K. Hand (c. 1833-
1850)
Philadelphia, Pa.
Spencer & Hand (c. 1843)
Bibl. 3

John Handle (c. 1839-1848)
Philadelphia, Pa.
Bibl. 3, 23, 36, 44

A. Hanford (c. 1820-1830)
Location unknown
Bibl. 15, 44

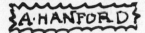

Abraham Hanis (c. 1840)
Charleston, S.C.
Bibl. 5

Benjamin Hanks
Windham, Conn. (c. 1777-
1779)
Litchfield, Conn. (c. 1783)
Ashford, Conn. (c. 1790)
Bibl. 16, 23, 28, 36, 44

C. A. Hanna
Location unknown
Bibl. 89

George Hannah (c. 1720)
Boston, Mass.
Bibl. 70

William W. Hannah (c. 1840-
1850)
Albany, N.Y.
Hudson, N.Y.
Bibl. 15, 20, 23, 25, 28, 29, 36,
44

W W HANNAH

George Hanners (b. 1696-d.
1740)
Boston, Mass.
Bibl. 2, 15, 23, 24, 28, 29, 36,
44, 50, 54, 72

George Hanners Jr. (b. 1721-d.
1760)
Boston, Mass.
Bibl. 2, 15, 23, 28, 29, 44, 54

G. H

John Hannum (c. 1837-1849)
Northampton, Mass.
Syracuse, N.Y.
Dickinson & Hannum (c. 1843)
Bibl. 20, 84

Hano & Co. (c. 1848)
Philadelphia Pa.
Bibl. 3

L. Hano (c. 1849)
Philadelphia, Pa.
Bibl. 3

Hamlet Hansbrough (c. 1800-
1839)
Lexington, Ky.
Bibl. 32

James Hansell (c. 1816-1850)
Philadelphia, Pa.
Valley Forge, Pa.
Bibl. 3, 25, 44

Robert Hansell (c. 1823)
Boston, Mass.
Bibl. 23, 28, 36, 44

Benjamin Hanson (c. 1822-
1840)
Albany, N.Y.
Bibl. 20

Pierre Harache (c. 1691)
Williamsburg, Va.
Bibl. 23, 36, 44

Harbottle & Smith (c. 1850)
Auburn, N.Y.
George Harbottle
Charles A. Smith
Bibl. 20

George Harbottle (c. 1850)
Auburn, N.Y.
Harbottle & Smith
Bibl. 20

W. Hardeman (1838)
Lexington, Ky.
Bibl. 54

James Harden (c. 1818-1824)
Philadelphia, Pa.
Bibl. 3

C. H. Harding (c. 1850)
Location unknown

Bibl. 28

C. H. HARDING

N. Harding & Co. (c. 1830-
1860)
Boston, Mass.
Bibl. 23, 24, 25, 28, 36, 39, 44

N. & C. Harding (c. 1830)
New York, N.Y.
Bibl. 36

Newell Harding (b. 1796-d.
1862)
Boston, Mass.
Haverhill, Mass.
Bibl. 4, 15, 23, 24, 25, 28, 29,
36, 44, 72

Jacob N. Hardman (c. 1845-
1849)
Louisville, Ky.
Bibl. 32

William Hardman (c. 1838-
1840)
Lexington, Ky.
Bibl. 32, 68

W HARDMAN

Hardwood
(See John Harwood)

J. H. Hardy (c. 1820)
Lexington, Ky.
Bibl. 32, 54

Stephen Hardy (b. 1781-d.
1843)
Portsmouth, N.H.
Bibl. 23, 24, 25, 28, 29, 36, 44

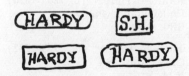

William Harker (c. 1850)
Philadelphia, Pa.
Bibl. 3

Willis Harker (c. 1845)
Philadelphia, Pa.
Bibl. 3

James Harkins (c. 1840-1847)
Philadelphia, Pa.
Bibl. 3

Thomas Harland (b. 1735-d.
1807)
Norwich, Conn.
Bibl. 16, 23, 24, 25, 28, 29, 36,
44, 54

HARLAND

Thomas Harland Jr. (c. 1781-
1806)
Norwich, Conn.
Bibl. 16, 23, 28, 36, 44

Alexander Harman (c. 1835)
Philadelphia, Pa.
Bibl. 3

Reuben Harmon (b. 1750-d.
1806)
Rupert, Vt.
New York, N.Y. (?)
Van Voorhis & Coley (c. 1786)
Bibl. 28, 54

Thomas W. Harpel (c. 1813)
Philadelphia, Pa.
Bibl. 23, 36, 44

Alexander Harper (c. 1819)
Philadelphia, Pa.
Bibl. 3, 23, 36, 44

Benjamin Harper (c. 1843)
Philadelphia, Pa.
Bibl. 3

David Harper (c. 1755-1756)
Philadelphia, Pa.
Dutens & Harper
Bibl. 3, 23, 36, 44

George W. Harper (c. 1832-
1835)
New York, N.Y.
Bibl. 15, 23

John M. Harper (c. 1841-1850)
Philadelphia, Pa.
Bibl. 3

Thomas Harper (c. 1773-1782)
Charleston, S.C.
Bibl. 5, 54

Thomas E. Harper (c. 1847-
1850)
Philadelphia, Pa.
Bibl. 3

Thomas W. Harper
Philadelphia, Pa. (c. 1813-
1817)
New York, N.Y. (c. 1825-
1835)
Bibl. 3, 15, 23, 36, 44

William W. Harpur (c. 1839-
1850)
Philadelphia, Pa.
Bibl. 3

Francis Harrall (c. 1828-1830)
Philadelphia, Pa.
Bibl. 3

Marquand Harriman & Co.
(See Marquand, Harriman &
Co.)

Samuel Harrington (c. 1842-
1845-   )
Amherst, Mass.
Prevear & Harrington (c. 1841-
1842)
Bibl. 84

William Harrington (c. 1849-
1850)
Philadelphia, Pa.
Bibl. 3

Harris & Co. (c. 1771-1777)
Charleston, S.C.
Charles Harris
James Mortimer Harris
Bibl. 5

Harris & Co. (c. 1850)
New York, N.Y.
George Harris
Bibl. 23

Harris & Hoyt
Kentucky
Bibl. 54

Harris & Kendrick (c. 1831-
1832)
Louisville, Ky.
John C. Harris (?)
William Kendrick
Bibl. 32, 54, 68

Harris & Stanwood (c. 1835)
Boston, Mass.
—— Harris

Henry B. Stanwood
Bibl. 23, 24, 29, 36, 44

HARRIS & STANWOOD

(H) (&) (S)

Harris, Stanwood & Co. (c.
1845)
Boston, Mass.
—— Harris
—— Stanwood
Bibl. 4, 15, 25, 28

HARRIS, STANWOOD & CO.

Harris & Wilcox
Albany, N.Y. (c. 1844)
Troy, N.Y. (c. 1847-1850)
—— Harris
Alanson D. Wilcox (?)
Bibl. 4, 20, 25, 28, 29

HARRIS & WILCOX

Charles Harris (c. 1767-1798)
Charleston, S.C.
Flere & Harris (c. 1767)
Harris & Co. (c. 1771-1777)
Bibl. 5, 44

Edward Harris (c. 1848)
Philadelphia, Pa.
Bibl. 3, 23

George Harris
New York, N.Y. (c. 1802,
c. 1850)
Pittsburgh, Pa. (c. 1815)
Harris & Co. (c. 1850)
Bibl. 23, 36, 44

H. Harris (c. 1820)
Albany, N.Y.
Bibl. 23, 36, 44

Heman Harris (c. 1833-1847)
Troy, N.Y.
Bibl. 20

James Mortimer Harris (c.
1771-1782)
Charleston, S.C.
Charles Harris (c. 1767-1798)
Bibl. 5

John C. Harris (c. 1831-1836)
Louisville, Ky.
Harris & Kendrick (c. 1831-
1832) (?)
Bibl. 32

Thomas Harris (c. 1818-1822)
Philadelphia, Pa.
Bibl. 3

Harry & Bear (c. 1842)
Harrisonburg, Va.
Jehu W. Bear
Bibl. 19

Jacob Harsen
Detroit, Mich. (c. 1760)
Bibl. 52

Hart & Bliss (c. 1803-1804)
Middletown, Conn.
Judah Hart
Jonathan Bliss
Bibl. 16, 23, 28, 36, 44

Hart & Brewer (c. 1800-1803)
Middletown, Conn.
Judah Hart
Charles Brewer
Bibl. 16, 23, 24, 25, 28, 36

Hart & Smith (c. 1814-1816)
Baltimore, Md.
William Hart
John Smith
Bibl. 15, 24, 25, 28, 29, 38, 44

[IIART & SMITH]   [H & S]

Hart & Wilcox (Willcox)
Norwich, Conn. (c. 1805-1807)
Judah Hart
Alvan Wilcox
Bibl. 16, 23, 24, 25, 28, 29, 36, 44

[HART & WILCOX]   [H & W]

Eliphaz Hart (b. 1789-d. 1866)
New Britain, Conn.
Norwich, Conn.
Bibl. 15, 16, 23, 24, 25, 28, 29, 36, 44

[E IIART]   [E H]

John Hart (c. 1776)
Philadelphia, Pa.
Bibl. 3, 23, 36, 44

John I. (J.) Hart (c. 1820-1826)
New York, N.Y.
Bibl. 15, 23, 36, 44

Jonathan Hart (c. 1815)
Canandaigua, N.Y.
Bibl. 25

Judah Hart (1777-1824)
Berlin, Conn. (c. 1803)
Middletown, Conn. (c. 1803-1804)
Norwich, Conn. (c. 1805-1807)
Griswald, Md. (c. 1816)

Brownsville, Ohio (c. 1822)
Hart & Brewer (c. 1800-1803)
Hart & Bliss (c. 1803-1804)
Hart & Wilcox (c. 1805-1807)
Bibl. 15, 16, 23, 24, 25, 28, 29, 36, 44, 61

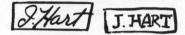

Walter Hart (c. 1849-1850)
Philadelphia, Pa.
Bibl. 3, 23

William Hart (c. 1810-1824)
Philadelphia, Pa.
Baltimore, Md. (c. 1814-1816)
Hart & Smith (c. 1814-1816)
Bibl. 3, 15, 23, 24, 29, 36, 38, 44

[W. HART]

George Hartford (c. 1794)
Philadelphia, Pa.
Bibl. 3, 23, 36, 44

Hartin & Bargi (c. 1766)
Bound Brook, N.J.
Bibl. 23, 36

Harting & Koesning
Kentucky
Bibl. 54

Jeremiah Hartley (c. 1837-1850)
Philadelphia, Pa.
Bibl. 3

Samuel Hartley
Philadelphia, Pa. (c. 1818-1825, c. 1837-1850)
New York, N.Y. (c. 1827-1828)
Albany, N.Y. (c. 1828-1838)
Garrett & Hartley (c. 1837)
Clark & Hartley (c. 1839-1841)
Bibl. 3, 15, 20, 23, 36, 44

Thomas Hartley (c. 1827-1828)
Location unknown
Bibl. 15

Philip Hartman (c. 1813-1814)
Philadelphia, Pa.
Bibl. 3, 23, 36, 44

Jonathan Hartt (c. 1810-1815)
Canandaigua, N.Y.
Bibl. 20

Hartwell
(See Woodbury, Dix, & Hartwell)

Samuel S. Hartwell (c. 1842)
Philadelphia, Pa.
Bibl. 3

Lewis Harvey
(See Harvey Lewis)

John Harward (c. 1816)
Philadelphia, Pa.
Bibl. 44

Harwell
(See Randle & Harwell)

— Harwood
Location unknown
Bibl. 28, 29

[HAR WOOD]

Benjamin Harwood (c. 1819)
Philadelphia, Pa.
Bibl. 3

John Harwood
(Hardwood) (c. 1816-1821)
Philadelphia, Pa.
Robinson & Harwood (c. 1814-1819)
Bibl. 3, 23, 36

Alexander R. Hascy (c. 1831-1850)
Albany, N.Y.
Bibl. 15, 20, 25, 28, 44

[HASCY]

Nelson Hascy (c. 1843-1849)
Albany, N.Y.
Bibl. 20, 23, 28, 44

Samuel Hascy (c. 1819-1829)
Albany, N.Y.
Samuel Hascy & Son (c. 1829-1831)
Bibl. 20

Samuel Hascy & Son (c. 1829-1831)
Albany, N.Y.
Bibl. 20

Haselton & Co.
Location unknown

Bibl. 15, 44

Haselton & Co.

Ira Haselton (c. 1821-1825)
Portsmouth, N.H.
Bibl. 25, 44

George W. Haselwood
(c. 1848)
Philadelphia, Pa.
Bibl. 3

William Haselwood (c. 1848-
1850)
Philadelphia, Pa.
Bibl. 3

Alexander Hasey
(See Alexander R. Hascy)

Barnabas Haskell (c. 1833)
Boston, Mass.
Bibl. 4, 23, 28, 36, 44

V. W. Haskell
Location unknown
Bibl. 15, 44

V. W. HASKELL

Haskin & Martin (c. 1830)
Location unknown
Bibl. 24

James Hasle (c. 1748)
Maryland (c. 1774)
Bibl. 38

Charles Hassan
(See Charles Hassell)

Moses Hassan (Hessen)
(c. 1848-1852)
Louisville, Ky.
Bibl. 32

Charles Hassell (Hassan)
(c. 1837-1842)
Philadelphia, Pa.
Bibl. 3

John Hastier (b. 1691?-d. 1791)
New York, N.Y.
Bibl. 2, 4, 15, 23, 24, 25, 28, 29,
30, 35, 36, 44, 54, 83

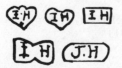

Marguerite Hastier (c. 1771)
New York, N.Y.

Bibl. 15, 23, 24, 25, 28, 29, 36,
39, 44

M H

Hasting
(See Bolles [Holles] & Hasting)

B. B. Hastings (c. 1830-1846)
Cleveland, Ohio
Bibl. 15, 23, 24, 25, 28, 34, 36,
44, 54

HASTINGS   HASTINGS

D. B. Hastings
Boston, Mass.
Bibl. 79

H. Hastings (c. 1815)
New York, N.Y.
Ohio(?)
Bibl. 24, 25, 34, 44

H HASTINGS

B. B. Hatch (c. 1836-1840)
Cleveland, Ohio
Bibl. 34

Israel (I. A.) Hatch (c. 1844-
1845)
Philadelphia, Pa.
Bibl. 3

John Hatch (c. 1831)
Portsmouth, Ohio
Bibl. 34

Haterick
(See James Hattrick)

James L. Hathway (c. 1842)
Norfolk, Va.
Bibl. 19

Hattrick & Shannon (c. 1844)
Philadelphia, Pa.
James Hattrick
Robert Shannon
Bibl. 3

Hattrick & Smith (c. 1837)
Philadelphia, Pa.
James Hattrick
——— Smith
Bibl. 3

James (J. R.) Hattrick
(Haterick)
Philadelphia, Pa. (c. 1839-1850)
Hattrick & Smith (c. 1837)
Hattrick & Shannon (c. 1844)
Bibl. 3

Samuel Haugh
(See Samuel Hough)

John Haushall (c. 1816-1817)
Philadelphia, Pa.
Bibl. 3

William Haverstick (c. 1781-
1798)
Lancaster, Pa.
Philadelphia, Pa.
Bibl. 3, 23, 24, 25, 36, 44

W H

Hawes & Co. (c. 1850)
Location unknown
Bibl. 24

James Hawkins (c. 1841)
Philadelphia, Pa.
Bibl. 3

John Hawkins (c. 1826)
Georgetown, S.C.
Peter Finch
Bibl. 5

Hawley
(See Tracy & Hawley)

Hawley, Fuller & Co. (c. 1850)
Utica, N.Y.
Horace H. Hawley
——— Fuller
Bibl. 18

Hawley & Leach (c. 1853-1856)
Utica, N.Y.
Horace H. Hawley
Almon Leach
George Leach
Bibl. 18

H. H. Hawley & Co. (c. 1850)
Utica, N.Y.
Horace H. Hawley
Bibl. 18

H. & H. H. Hawley (c. 1850)
Utica, N.Y.
Horace H. Hawley
Bibl. 18

Horace H. Hawley (b. 1818)
Utica, N.Y. (c. 1837-1856)
H. H. Hawley & Co. (c. 1850)
Hawley, Fuller & Co. (c. 1850)
H. & H. H. Hawley (c. 1850)
Hawley & Leach (c. 1853-1856)
Bibl. 18

John Dean Hawley (b. 1821-d.
1913)

Syracuse, N.Y. (c. 1844-1851)
Cazenovia, N.Y.
Willard & Hawley (c. 1844-
1851)
Bibl. 20

Noah Hawley (c. 1810-1816)
New York, N.Y.
Bibl. 23, 24, 36, 44

O. A. Hawley (c. 1850-   )
Cazenovia, N.Y.
Bibl. 20

T. S. Hawley (c. 1837)
Canajoharie, N.Y.
Bibl. 20

John Haws (c. 1837)
Philadelphia, Pa.
Bibl. 3, 23, 36, 44

John Hay (c. 1830-1850?)
New York State (?)
Bibl. 89

Hayden, Brothers & Co.
(c. 1852-1855)
Charleston, S.C.
Nathaniel Hayden
Bibl. 5, 44

HAYDEN BROTHER & CO.

Hayden & Gregg (c. 1832-1846)
New York, N.Y.
Charleston, S.C.
Nathaniel Hayden
William Gregg
Bibl. 23, 24, 25, 28, 29, 36, 54

HAYDEN & GREGG

Hayden, Gregg & Co. (Gregg,
Hayden & Co.) (c. 1846-
1852)
Charleston, S.C.
H. Sidney Hayden
Nathaniel Hayden
William Gregg
Bibl. 5, 44

Hayden & Whilden (c. 1855-
1863)
Charleston, S.C.
H. Sidney Hayden (?)
William G. Whilden (?)
Bibl. 5

HAYDEN & WHILDEN

H. Sidney Hayden
Charleston, S.C.

Hayden, Gregg & Co. (c. 1846-
1852)
Gregg, Hayden & Whilden
(c. 1855) (?)
Hayden & Whilden (c. 1855-
1863) (?)
Bibl. 5, 44, 54

J. Hayden (c. 1840)
Columbus, Ga.
Bibl. 17

Jesse Hayden (c. 1811-1845)
Martinsburg, Va.
Bibl. 19

Nathaniel Hayden (b. 1805-d.
1875)
Charleston, S.C. (c. 1832-1843)
Hayden & Gregg (c. 1832-1846)
Hayden, Gregg & Co. (c. 1846-
1852)
Hayden, Brothers & Co.
(c. 1852-1855)
Bibl. 5, 44

N. HAYDEN

William H. Hayden (d. 1853)
Martinsburg, Va. (c. 1845-
1851)
Bibl. 19

Eden Haydock (c. 1839-1850)
Philadelphia, Pa.
Bibl. 3

James B. Haydock (c. 1846-
1849)
Location unknown
Bibl. 3

Thomas O. Haydock (c. 1850)
Philadelphia, Pa.
Bibl. 3

Hayes & Adriance (c. 1816-
1826)
Poughkeepsie, N.Y.
Peter P. Hayes
John Adriance
Bibl. 15, 20, 25, 44

HAYES & ADRIANCE
H & ADRIANCE

HAYES&ADRIANCE

Hayes & Cotton (c. 1831)
Newark, N.J.
Bibl. 23, 28, 36, 44

C. B. Hayes & Co. (c. 1845)
Poughkeepsie, N.Y.
Bibl. 20

Edmund M. Hayes (c. 1842-
1843)
Poughkeepsie, N.Y.
Bibl. 20

George Hayes (c. 1842-1850)
Philadelphia, Pa.
Dreer & Hayes
Bibl. 3

Peter P. Hayes (b. 1788-d.
1842)
Poughkeepsie, N.Y.
Hayes & Adriance (c. 1816-
1826)
Bibl. 15, 20, 25, 44

P. P. HAYES

Peter P. Hayes & Son (c. 1841-
1842)
Poughkeepsie, N.Y.
Bibl. 20

W. Hayes (c. 1780)
Connecticut (?)
Bibl. 28, 29, 44

W. Hayes   W H

David Haynes (c. 1835-
1850-   )
Troy, N.Y.
D. Haynes & Son (c. 1842-
1845) (?)
Bibl. 20

D. Haynes & Son (c. 1842-
1845)
Troy, N.Y.
David Haynes (?)
Bibl. 20

J. R. Haynes (c. 1851)
Cincinnati, Ohio
Bibl. 54

Lafayette Haynes (c. 1836-
1837)
Troy, N.Y.
Bibl. 20

Hays & Myers (c. 1770)
New York, N.Y.
Andrew Hays
Myer Myers
Bibl. 2, 15, 23, 24, 25, 28, 29,
35, 36, 44, 83

H & H   HAYS & MYERS

Andrew Hays (c. 1769-1770)
New York, N.Y.
Hays & Myers (c. 1770)
Bibl. 4, 15, 23, 28, 36, 44

George Hays (Haes) (b. 1819)
Utica, N.Y. (c. 1849-1859)
Bibl. 18

Hazen & Collins (c. 1846)
Cincinnati, Ohio
N. L. Hazen (c. 1836-1850) (?)
———— Collins
Bibl. 54

N. L. Hazen (c. 1829-1830)
Troy, N.Y.
Bibl. 20, 24

N. L. Hazen (c. 1836-1850)
Cincinnati, Ohio
Hazen & Collins (c. 1846) (?)
Bibl. 54

Joseph Head (c. 1798)
Philadelphia, Pa.
Bibl. 3, 23, 25, 36, 44

William Headington (c. 1806-1807)
Frankfort, Ky.
Bibl. 32

William Headman (c. 1828-1850)
Philadelphia, Pa.
Bibl. 3

J. S. Heald (c. 1810)
Baltimore, Md.
Ball & Heald (c. 1811-1812)
Bibl. 24, 25, 38, 44

J. S. HEALD

William Healey (Heyley)
(Helly) (c. 1785-1799)
Philadelphia, Pa.
Bibl. 3

Samuel Healy (d. 1773)
Boston, Mass.
Bibl. 28, 36, 38

R. Hearn
Location unknown
Bibl. 28

R. HEARN

Samuel Heasley (c. 1847-1852)
Winchester, Ky.
Bibl. 32, 54

John Heath (c. 1760-1763)
New York, N.Y.
Bibl. 4, 15, 23, 24, 25, 28, 29, 35, 36, 44, 54

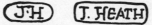

Ralph Heath (c. 1807-1815)
Cambridge, Ohio
Chillicothe, Ohio
Bibl. 34, 44

John J. Hebard (c. 1831-1832)
Poughkeepsie, N.Y.
Bibl. 20

Hebbard & Co. (c. 1850)
New York, N.Y.
Bibl. 23

H. Hebberd (c. 1847)
New York, N.Y.
Bibl. 4, 23, 28, 44

HEBBERD

Benjamin Hebrank (c. 1812)
Zanesville, Ohio
Bibl. 34

John David Hechstetter
(c. 1796)
Philadelphia, Pa.
Bibl. 3

Ludwig Lewis Heck (c. 1760-1780)
Lancaster, Pa.
Bibl. 3, 23, 24, 25, 29, 36, 44, 50, 54

L H

Heckman
(See Douglass & Heckman)

Archimedes Heckman (c. 1839-1840)
Philadelphia, Pa.
Bibl. 17

John Hector (c. 1774)
Charleston, S.C.
Bibl. 5, 44

Hedden & Heydorn (c. 1810)
New Jersey
Bibl. 46

Richard B. Hedden (c. 1824-1826)
New York, N.Y.
Bibl. 15

George Hedge(s) (Hedger)
Waterford, N.Y. (c. 1819)
Buffalo, N.Y. (c. 1828-1848)
Bibl. 15, 20, 28, 44

HEDGES

Daniel (David) Hedges Jr.
(b. 1779-d. 1856)
Easthampton, N.Y.
Bibl. 20, 23, 24, 25, 29, 36, 44

HEDGES

A. Judson Heffron (c. 1859-1860)
Utica, N.Y.
Bibl. 18

James Hegeman (c. 1829-1850-)
Troy, N.Y.
Bibl. 20

John Heilig (Helig) (c. 1801-1850)
Philadelphia, Pa.
Bibl. 3

Gottlieb Heimberg (c. 1842-1847)
St. Louis, Mo.
Bibl. 54

Daniel Heineman (c. 1837)
Philadelphia, Pa.
Bibl. 3

George Heineman (c. 1847-1849)
Philadelphia, Pa.
Bibl. 3

L. C. (L. G.) Heineman
(c. 1849-1850)
Philadelphia, Pa.
Bibl. 3

Frederick Heisley (c. 1786-1816)
Fredericktown, Md.
Bibl. 38

James P. Heiss (c. 1849-1850)
Philadelphia, Pa.
Bibl. 3

Henry Helge(r)fort (c. 1849)
Philadelphia, Pa.
Bibl. 3, 23

Helig
(See Heilig)

Jacob Heller (c. 1837-1850)
Philadelphia, Pa.
Bibl. 3

John Heller (c. 1837)
Philadelphia, Pa.
Bibl. 3

Helly
(See Healey)

Christian Helm (c. 1802-1804)
Philadelphia, Pa.
Bibl. 3

Thomas Helm (c. 1835-1850)
Philadelphia, Pa.
Bibl. 3

Nathaniel Helme (c. 1761-
  1789)
South Kingston, R.I.
Bibl. 24, 25, 28, 29, 44, 56

Henry Helwich (c. 1815-1817)
New York, N.Y.
Bibl. 15

George Hemburgh (c. 1845)
St. Louis, Mo.
Bibl. 54

Thomas Heming (c. 1764)
New York (?), N.Y.
Bibl. 28

Alexander Hemphill (c. 1741)
Philadelphia, Pa.
Bibl. 3, 23

Thomas J. Hemphill (c. 1836-
  1841)
Philadelphia, Pa.
Bibl. 3

Daniel B. Hempsted (b. 1784-d.
  1852)
New London, Conn.
Daniel B. Hempsted & Co.
  (c. 1821) (?)
Bibl. 44

Daniel B. Hempsted & Co.
  (c. 1821)
Eatonton, Ga.
Daniel B. Hempsted
Nathaniel Saltonstall
Bibl. 17

E. Hempsted (c. 1820)
Location unknown
Bibl. 28

Hemstead & Chandler (c. 1811-
  1815-   )
New York, N.Y.
——— Hemstead
Stephen Chandler
Bibl. 23, 36, 44

Daniel Henchman (b. 1730-d.
  1775)
Boston, Mass.
Bibl. 2, 15, 23, 24, 25, 28, 29,
  36, 44, 54, 69

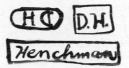

Henderson & Lossing (c. 1835)
Poughkeepsie, N.Y.
Adam Henderson (?)
Benson John Lossing
Bibl. 20

A. A. Henderson (c. 1835-
  1837)
Philadelphia, Pa.
Bibl. 3, 15, 24, 25, 44

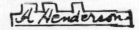

Adam Henderson (c. 1846)
Poughkeepsie, N.Y.
Henderson & Lossing
  (c. 1835) (?)
Bibl. 20, 25, 44

Henderson Field & Co.
  (c. 1816)
Philadelphia, Pa.
Bibl. 23

Henderson, Field & Co.
  (c. 1816)
Philadelphia, Pa.
Stephen Henderson
Samuel Field
Bibl. 3

Logan Henderson (c. 1767)
Charleston, S.C.
Oliphant & Henderson
  (c. 1767)
Bibl. 5

Stephen Henderson (c. 1803-
  1816)
Philadelphia, Pa.
Henderson, Field & Co.
  (c. 1816)
Bibl. 3

William Henderson (c. 1770)
Appoquinimink, Del.
New Castle, Del.
Bibl. 3

John Hendrick (c. 1835-1836)
Albany, N.Y.
Bibl. 20

Ahasuerus Hendricks (d. 1727)
New York, N.Y.
  (c. 1678-   )
Bibl. 2, 4, 15, 23, 24, 25, 28,
  29, 30, 36, 44, 54

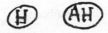

John Hendricks (c. 1848)
Philadelphia, Pa.
Bibl. 3, 23

Hendrickse
(See Hendricks)

William Hendrickson (c. 1848-
  1850)
Philadelphia, Pa.
Bibl. 3, 23

John A. Henneman (b. 1835-d.
  1889)
Chester, Pa. (c. 1854)
Spartanburg, S.C. (c. 1859-
  1889)
Norfolk, Va.
Bibl. 5

Henry
(See Dickinson & Henry)

——— Henry (c. 1793)
Philadelphia, Pa.
Dickinson & Henry
Bibl. 3

Felix Henry (c. 1815)
New York, N.Y.
Bibl. 15, 23, 36, 44

Samuel Hensley (c. 1829-1833)
Mt. Sterling, Ky.
Bibl. 32, 54, 68

Frederick Hepton (c. 1785)
Philadelphia, Pa.
Bibl. 3

Charles Hequembourg (Jr.)
New Haven, Conn. (c. 1804)
New York, N.Y. (c. 1827-
1829)
Buffalo, N.Y. (c. 1835-1842)
Hartford, Conn.
Bibl. 15, 16, 20, 23, 24, 25,
28, 36, 44, 61

Charles Louis Hequembourg
(c. 1845-1856)
St. Louis, Mo.
Bibl. 54

Theodore Hequembourg
(c. 1845-1856)
St. Louis, Mo.
Bibl. 54

Theodore Hequembourg
(c. 1835-1842)
Buffalo, N.Y.
Bibl. 20

A. Herbel (c. 1821-1853)
St. Louis, Mo.
Bibl. 54

Lawrence Herbert (c. 1748-
1751)
Philadelphia, Pa.
Bibl. 3, 28

Matthew Herbert (b. 1710-d.
1746)
Saint Marys County, Md.
(c. 1732-1746)
Bibl. 38

Timothy B. Herbert (c. 1824-
1829)
New York, N.Y.
Bibl. 15, 23, 36, 44

Widow of Timothy Herbert
(c. 1831-1832)
New York, N.Y.
Bibl. 15

Francis Herils (Herrils)
(c. 1804-1833)
Philadelphia, Pa.
Bibl. 3, 23, 36, 44

Charles Heringer (c. 1844-
1850)
Philadelphia, Pa.
Bibl. 3

John C. Heringer (c. 1849-
1850)
Philadelphia, Pa.
Bibl. 3

Erskine Heron (c. 1762-1765)
Charleston, S.C.
Bibl. 5, 54

Isaac Heron
Philadelphia, Pa. (c. 1763)
Bound Brook, N.J. (c. 1764)
Middlesex City, N.J. (c. 1764)
New York, N.Y. (c. 1766-1780)
Bibl. 3, 23, 28, 36, 44, 46, 54

Heroy
(See Reeve & Heroy)

———— Heroy (c. 1813-1815)
Newburgh, N.Y.
Reeve & Heroy
Bibl. 20

Isaac Heroy (c. 1823-1824)
Troy, N.Y.
Bibl. 20

Herrils
(See Herils)

William Herrington (c. 1850)
Syracuse, N.Y.
Philadelphia, Pa.
Bibl. 3, 20

Stephen Hesler (c. 1801)
Baltimore, Md.
Bibl. 38

Hessen
(See Moses Hassan)

Jacob Hester (c. 1823)
Philadelphia, Pa.
Bibl. 3

John M. Hetzel (c. 1795)
Newton, N.J.
Bibl. 46, 54

John Heughan (c. 1772)
Schenectady, N.Y.
Bibl. 28

William Heurtin (b. 1703-d.
1765)
Newark, N.J.
New York, N.Y.
Bibl. 4, 23, 24, 25, 34, 44, 46, 54

Archill Hevitt (Huet) (c. 1804)
Baltimore, Md.
Bibl. 38

Abram Hewes (c. 1823)
Boston, Mass.
Bibl. 28

C. W. Hewit (c. 1850-   )
Utica, N.Y.
Bibl. 18, 20

A. Hews Jr. (c. 1823-1850)
Boston, Mass.
Bibl. 23, 24, 25, 28, 29, 36, 44

A HEWS JR

John D. Hewson (c. 1815-
1817)
Albany, N.Y.
Hall, Newson & Co. (c. 1839-
1842, 1847-1850)
Hall, Brower & Co. (c. 1836-
1842)
Hall, Hewson & Merrifield
(c. 1840)
Hall & Hewson (c. 1842-1847)
Hall, Hewson & Brower
(c. 1847-1850)
Bibl. 20, 23, 28, 36, 44

William Hewson (c. 1818-1822)
Albany, N.Y.
Bibl. 20

Charles Heyde (c. 1839-1840)
Philadelphia, Pa.
Bibl. 3

Charles W. Heydon (c. 1841-
1845)
Portsmouth, Va.
Bibl. 19

Heydorn
(See Hedden & Heydorn)

Heydorn & Imlay (c. 1810)
Hartford, Conn.
Bibl. 24, 25, 44, 46, 61

Heyer & Gale (c. 1800-1807)
New York, N.Y.
William B. Heyer
John L. Gale
Bibl. 23, 24, 25, 30, 35, 36, 44

William B. Heyer (c. 1798-
1827)
New York, N.Y.
Heyer & Gale (c. 1800-1807)
Bibl. 4, 15, 23, 24, 28, 29, 30,
35, 36, 39, 44, 74, 83

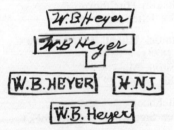

Widow of William B. Heyer
(c. 1831-1832)
New York, N.Y.
Bibl. 15

Heyley
(See Healey)

Moses Hiams (b. 1751)
Philadelphia, Pa. (c. 1775)
Bibl. 28

Andrew Hibben (c. 1764,
d. 1784)
Charleston, S.C.
Bibl. 5

John Hickman
Louisville, Ky. (1832-1850)
Taylorsville, Ky. (c. 1850-
1862)
Bibl. 32, 54, 68

Joseph Hicks (c. 1798-1823)
Harrisonburg, Va.
Bibl. 19

Higbie & Crosby (w. 1829)
Boston, Mass.
Bibl. 23, 24, 25, 29, 36, 44

HIGBIE & CROSBY

Thomas Higginbotham
(c. 1829-1830)
Augusta, Ga.
Sparta, Ga.
Bibl. 17

Abraham Higgins (c. 1738-
1763)
Eastham, Mass.
Bibl. 28

George E. Higgins (c. 1850)
Syracuse, N.Y.
Covell & Higgins
Bibl. 20

Samuel Higginson (c. 1771-
1775)
Annapolis, Md. (c. 1774)
St. Marys County, Md.
Whetcroft & Higginson
(c. 1774)
Bibl. 38

Christian Hight (c. 1819-
1822)
Philadelphia, Pa.
Bibl. 3

Jonas Jacob Hilburn (c. 1857-
1877)
Bowling Green, Ky.
Fuselli & Hilburn (1866-1873)
Bibl. 54

Hildeburn & Bros. (c. 1849-
1850)
Philadelphia, Pa.
Bibl. 3

Hildeburn & Watson (c. 1833-
1849)
Philadelphia, Pa.
Bibl. 3

Samuel Hildeburn (c. 1810-
1837)
Philadelphia, Pa.
Bibl. 3, 36, 44, 54

HILDEBURN

Woolworth Hildeburn (c. 1816-
1819)
Philadelphia, Pa.
Bibl. 3

———— Hill (c. 1782)
(May have been Richard Hill)
Petersburg, Va.
Hill & Waddill
Bibl. 19

Hill & Johnson (c. 1849)
Richmond, Va.
John Hill
W. M. Johnson
Bibl. 19

Hill & Waddill (c. 1780-1782)
Petersburg, Va.
Noel Waddill
Bibl. 19, 23, 36, 44

Arundel Hill (c. 1829)
Steubenville, Ohio
Bibl. 34

Benjamin Hill (c. 1687-   )
Boston, Mass.
Bibl. 54

Charles Hill (c. 1816)
Canandaigua, N.Y.
Bibl. 20

E. Hill (c. 1821-1844)
Cincinnati, Ohio
Bibl. 34

E. H. Hill (18th century)
Kentucky (?)
Bibl. 54

Hugh Hill
Norfolk, Va. (before 1770)
Williamsburg, Va. (after 1770)
Bibl. 19

James Hill (c. 1770)
Boston, Mass.
Bibl. 15, 23, 25, 36, 44

J. HILL

John Hill (c. 1818-1850)
Richmond, Va.
Hill & Johnson (c. 1849)
Bibl. 19

Nobel S. A. Hill (c. 1795)
Bennington, Vt.
Bibl. 54

William F. Hill (c. 1815-1817)
New York, N.Y.
Bibl. 15, 25, 44

W. F. Hill

Thomas Hilldrup (c. 1795,
d. 1804)

Hartford, Conn.
Bibl. 16, 23, 28, 36, 44

————— Hiller
(See Haller)

Benjamin Hiller (b. 1687)
Boston, Mass. (until 1745)
Bibl. 2, 15, 24, 28, 29, 33,
   36, 44, 69

Joseph Hiller (b. 1721-d. 1758)
Boston, Mass.
Charlestown, Mass.
Bibl. 23, 28, 36, 44

Major Joseph Hiller (c. 1748-
   1814)
Salem, Mass.
Bibl. 28

Christopher Hilliard (b. 1802-d.
   1871)
Hagerstown, Md.
Bibl. 38

George W. Hilliard (c. 1823)
Fayetteville, N.C.
Bibl. 21

William Hilliard (c. 1801-1810)
Fayetteville, N.C.
Bibl. 21

C. F. Hills (c. 1850)
Hartford, Conn.
Bibl. 23

Frederick Hillworth (c. 1844-
   1849)
Philadelphia, Pa.
Bibl. 3

Philip Hillyartiner (c. 1844)
Philadelphia, Pa.
Bibl. 3

William Hilton (c. 1814)
Philadelphia, Pa.
Bibl. 3, 23, 36, 44, 54

Richard Hinckley (c. 1839-
   1841)
Philadelphia, Pa.
Bibl. 3

Robert H. Hinckley (c. 1839-
   1841)
Philadelphia, Pa.
Bibl. 3

John Hind (d. 1775)
Philadelphia, Pa.
Bibl. 3, 23, 36, 44

D. B. Hindman & Co.
   (Hinman) (c. 1833-1837)
Philadelphia, Pa.
Bibl. 3, 15, 25, 44

Robert Hines (c. 1848-1850)
Philadelphia, Pa.
Bibl. 3

Benjamin Hinkin (c. 1837)
Philadelphia, Pa.
Bibl. 3

Benjamin Hinkle (c. 1840-1850)
Philadelphia, Pa.
Thirion & Hinkle (c. 1850)
Bibl. 3

John P. Hinkle (c. 1824)
Philadelphia, Pa.
Bibl. 3

Hinlton
(See John Holton)

Hinman
(See Hindman)

Hinsdale & Atkin (c. 1830-
   1838)
New York, N.Y.
Horace Hinsdale
John H. Atkin
Bibl. 15, 24, 25, 44

HINSDALE & ATKIN

E. Hinsdale & Co. (before
   1810)
Newark, N.J.
Epaphras Hinsdale
John Taylor
Bibl. 46

Epaphras (Epahras) Hinsdale
   (b. 1769-d. 1810)
Newark, N.J. (c.   -1810)
New York, N.Y.
E. Hinsdale & Co. (before
   1810)
Bibl. 23, 24, 28, 29, 36,
   44, 46, 54

HINSDALE

Horace Hinsdale (c. 1815-
   1842)

Newark, N.J.
New York, N.Y. (c. 1815,
   c. 1830-1838)
Palmer & Hinsdale (c. 1815)
Hinsdale & Atkin (c. 1830-
   1838)
Bibl. 15, 23, 25, 28, 44

William M. Hinton (b. 1830)
Paris, Ky. (c. 1844-1847,
   c. 1854)
Shelbyville, Ky. (c. 1847-1854)
Bibl. 32, 54, 68

Hirshbuhl & Dolfinger (c. 1859-
   1861)
Louisville, Ky.
————— Hirshbuhl
Jacob Dolfinger
Bibl. 32

Daniel Hitchborn (c. 1752-
   1828)
Boston, Mass.
Bibl. 23, 36, 44

Eliakim Hitchborn
(See Hitchcock)

Samuel Hitchborn (c. 1752-
   1828)
Boston, Mass.
Bibl. 36, 44, 79

Hitchcock
(See Sigburney & Hitchcock)

Eliakim Hitchcock (Hitch-
   born) (b. 1726-d. 1788)
Cheshire, Conn.
New Haven, Conn.
Bibl. 15, 16, 23, 24, 25, 28, 29,
   36, 44, 54, 61

E H

John G. Hiter (c. 1813-1819)
Lexington, Ky.
Ayres & Hiter (c. 1813)
Bibl. 32, 54

Joshua Hobart(h) (c. 1811-
   1813)
New Haven, Conn.
New Bern, N.C.
Fitch & Hobart (c. 1811-1813)
Bibl. 16, 21, 23, 24, 25, 28, 29,
   36, 44

J. HOBART

Nathan Hobbs (b. 1792-d.
   1868)
Boston, Mass.

Bibl. 4, 15, 23, 24, 25, 28, 29,
36, 44

HOBBS

N HOBBS

Joseph Hocker (c. 1829-1833)
Philadelphia, Pa.
Bibl. 3

Willis Hocker (c. 1846-1849)
Philadelphia, Pa.
Bibl. 3

Hocknell
(See Steele & Hocknell)

John Hodge (c. 1775-1800)
Hadley, Mass.
Bibl. 3, 23, 24, 29, 36, 44

J HODGE

T. Hodgman
Location unknown
Bibl. 28

William Hodgson (c. 1785)
Philadelphia, Pa.
Bibl. 3

Daniel Hodkins (c. 1840-1841)
Albany, N.Y.
Bibl. 20

———— Hodsdon
Location unknown
Bibl. 28

Edward Hoell (1830-1873)
New Bern, N.C.
Greenville, N.C. (c. 1830-
1847)
Pitt County, N.C. (c. 1873)
Washington, N.C.
Bibl. 21

Augustus E. Hofer (c. 1841-
1843)
Albany, N.Y.
Bibl. 20

George Frederick Hoff
(b. 1810)
Lancaster, Pa.
Bibl. 3

George W. Hoff (c. 1850)
Auburn, N.Y.
Hyde & Hoff
Bibl. 20

John Hoff (c. 1776, d. 1818)
Lancaster, Pa.
Bibl. 3

Frederick Hoffman
New York, N.Y. (c. 1819-
1820)
Philadelphia, Pa. (1820-1849)
Bard & Hoffman (Bird &
Hoffman) (c. 1837)
Bibl. 3, 23, 36, 44

James M. Hoffman (c. 1804-
1820)
Philadelphia, Pa.
Bibl. 23, 24, 25, 29, 36, 44

J. M. HOFFMAN

John H. Hoffman (c. 1848-
1850)
Philadelphia, Pa.
Bibl. 3

Henry Hoffner (c. 1791)
Philadelphia, Pa.
Bibl. 3

John Hoffner (c. 1818)
Philadelphia, Pa.
Bibl. 3

Hogan & Wade (c. 1850)
Cleveland, Ohio
Bibl. 89

Hogan & Wade

Augustus F. Hoguet (Hognet)
Philadelphia, Pa. (c. 1814-
1833)
Bibl. 3

Holden & Boning (c. 1843)
Philadelphia, Pa.
Eli Holden
William Boning
Bibl. 3

Eli Holden (c. 1843-1850)
Philadelphia, Pa.
Holden & Boning (c. 1843)
Bibl. 3

E HOLDEN

A. A. Holdredge (c. 1841)
Glens Falls, N.Y.
Bibl. 20

Julius Holister (Hollister)
(c. 1843)
Hartford, Conn.
Seymour & Holister
Bibl. 23

J. HOLISTER

Littleton Holland (b. 1770-d.
1847)
Baltimore, Md. (c. 1800-1847)
Bibl. 15, 23, 24, 25, 28, 29, 36,
38, 39, 44, 54, 78, 80

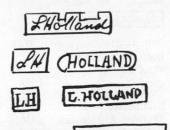

Nelson Holland (c. 1827-1828)
Northampton, Mass.
Phelps & Holland
Bibl. 84

Holles (Bolles) & Hasting
(c. 1840)
Location unknown
Bibl. 89

A. Hollinger (c. 1839)
Philadelphia, Pa.
Bibl. 3

John Hollingshead (c. 1768)
Philadelphia, Pa.
Bibl. 3, 23, 36, 44

Morgan Hollingshead (c. 1775)
Moorestown, N.J.
Bibl. 3

William Hollingshead
(c. 1754-1785)
Philadelphia, Pa.
Bibl. 3, 15, 23, 24, 25, 28, 29,
36, 44, 54, 81

Jacob Hollinshead (c. 1768-
1772)
Salem, N.J.
Bibl. 3

Joseph Hollinshead (c. 1740-
1765)
Burlington, N.J.
Bibl. 46, 54

Julius Hollister
Hartford, Conn.

(See Holister)

Julius Hollister (b. 1818-d.
1905)
Owego, N.Y.
Bibl. 15, 20, 25, 44

J. HOLLISTER

Robert Holloway (c. 1822)
Baltimore, Md.
Bibl. 38

D. Holman
Baltimore, Md.
Munroe & Holman (c. 1826-
1829)
Bibl. 38

Holmes & Rowan (c. 1847-
1850)
Philadelphia, Pa.
Bibl. 3

Adrian B. Holmes (c. 1801-
1849)
New York, N.Y.
Bibl. 15, 23, 24, 25, 29, 36, 44

A. HOLMES

George H. Holmes (c. 1840-
1850)
Philadelphia, Pa.
Bibl. 3

Israel Holmes (b. 1768-d.
1802)
Greenwich, Conn.
Waterbury, Conn.
Bibl. 16, 23, 28, 36, 44

J. Holmes (c. 1816)
New York, N.Y.
Bibl. 23, 36, 44

J. Holmes (c. 1842)
Philadelphia, Pa.
Bibl. 3

William Holmes (c. 1801)
New York, N.Y.
Bibl. 23, 36, 44

William Holmes
William Holmes Jr.
Boston, Mass.
(See Homes)

E. Holsey (c. 1820)
Philadelphia, Pa.
Bibl. 24, 25, 44

E HOLSEY

Holsted
(See Myers & Holsted)

David Holt Jr. (c. 1831-1833)
Harpers Ferry, Va.
Bibl. 19

David Holton (c. 1804)
Baltimore, Md.
Bibl. 23, 28, 36, 44

John Holton (Houlton)
(Hinlton)
Philadelphia, Pa. (c. 1794-
1798)
Bibl. 23, 36, 44

Jacob Holtzbaum (c. 1790-
1793)
Fredericktown, Md.
Koontz & Holtzbaum (c. 1793)
Bibl. 38

Edward Holyoke (c. 1817)
Boston, Mass.
Bibl. 23, 24, 25, 28, 36, 44

HOLYOKE

Charles Holzaphel (c. 1846)
New York, N.Y.
Bibl. 23

William Homes (Holmes)
(b. 1717-d. 1783)
Boston, Mass.
Bibl. 2, 15, 23, 24, 25, 28, 29,
36, 39, 44, 50, 54

HOMES   HOMES
W. HOMES   W H

William Homes Jr. (Holmes)
(b. 1742-d. 1825)
Boston, Mass.
Bibl. 2, 15, 23, 24, 25, 28, 29,
36, 44

W H   HOMES

Samuel D. Honeyman (c. 1841)
Charleston, Va.
Bibl. 19

Hood & Tobey (c. 1848-1849)
Albany, N.Y.
Bibl. 15, 20, 23, 24, 25, 28, 29,
44

HOOD & TOBEY

Benjamin L. Hood (c. 1841-
1844)
Buffalo, N.Y.

Rochester, N.Y.
Bibl. 20

Harry O. Hood (c. 1842-1844)
Buffalo, N.Y.
Bibl. 20

Henry O. Hood (c. 1841)
Rochester, N.Y.
Bibl. 20

Jacob Hood (c. 1825)
Philadelphia, Pa.
Bibl. 3

Frederick Hoofman (c. 1819)
New York, N.Y.
Bibl. 15

Hooker & Morgan (c. 1813)
Pine Plains, N.Y.
Bibl. 20

William Hooker (c. 1813-1814)
Philadelphia, Pa.
Bibl. 3

William Hookey (d. 1812)
Newport, R.I.
Bibl. 6, 23, 28, 44

Jacob Hoop (c. 1823-1824)
Philadelphia, Pa.
Bibl. 3

William W. Hooper (c. 1832-
1833)
Macon, Ga.
Milledgeville, Ga.
Bibl. 17

Henry Hoover (c. 1816,
c. 1822)
Philadelphia, Pa.
Bibl. 3, 23, 36, 44

Joseph E. Hoover (c. 1837-
1841)
Philadelphia, Pa.
Faber & Hoover (c. 1837)
Bibl. 3, 23, 36, 44

Constantine Hope (c. 1805-
1809-   )
Savannah, Ga.
Bibl. 17

Henry Hopkins (c. 1831-1833)
Philadelphia, Pa.
Bibl. 3

James E. Hopkins (c. 1828-
1830)

Westfield, N.Y.
Bibl. 20

Jesse Hopkins (b. 1766)
Waterbury, Conn.
Bibl. 16, 23, 28, 36, 44

Joseph W. Hopkins (b. 1730-d.
1801)
Waterbury, Conn.
Bibl. 16, 23, 24, 25, 28, 36, 44,
61

HOPKINS

Lawrence Hopkins (c. 1836-
1837)
New York, N.Y.
Bibl. 15

Robert Hopkins (c. 1833)
Philadelphia, Pa.
Bibl. 3

Stephen Hopkins (b. 1721-d.
1796)
Waterbury, Conn.
Bibl. 16, 23, 24, 25, 28, 44

S. H

Thomas R. Hopkins (d. 1869)
Petersburg, Va.
Cosby & Hopkins (c. 1846-
1847)
Bibl. 19

Benjamin C. Hopper (c. 1844-
1850)
Philadelphia, Pa.
Bibl. 3

Joseph (J. M.) Hopper
(c. 1816-1841)
Philadelphia, Pa.
Bibl. 3

Samuel M. Hopper (c. 1835-
1850)
Philadelphia, Pa.
Bibl. 3, 23, 36, 44

Hugh Horah (b. 1760-d. 1822)
Salisbury, N.C.
Wilkinson & Horah (c. 1820-
1821)
Bibl. 21

James Horah (b. 1826-d. 1864)
Salisbury, N.C. (c. 1849)
Bibl. 21

William Henry Horah
(b. 1788-d. 1863)

Salisbury, N.C.
Bibl. 21

Horn & Kneass (c. 1811-1837)
Philadelphia, Pa.
Henry Horn
William Kneass
Bibl. 3

E. B. Horn (c. 1847)
Boston, Mass.
Bibl. 23, 28, 44

Henry Horn (c. 1809-1840)
Philadelphia, Pa.
Bolton & Horn (c. 1808)
Horn & Kneass (c. 1811-1837)
Bibl. 3

George Horner (c. 1848)
Camden, N.J.
Bibl. 3

Horton & Rikeman (c. 1850-
1856)
Savannah, Ga.
M. P. Horton
———— Rikeman
Bibl. 17, 89

HORTON & RIKEMAN

H. P. Horton (c. 1850)
Savannah, Ga.
Horton & Rikeman (c. 1850-
1856)
Bibl. 17

H P HORTON

H. V. Horton (c. 1848)
Louisville, Ky.
Bibl. 32

Harley Hosford (c. 1820)
New York, N.Y.
Bibl. 23, 24, 25, 36, 44

HOSFORD

Samuel Hoskins (c. 1835)
Philadelphia, Pa.
Bibl. 3

Hotchkiss & Co. (c. 1847-1848)
Buffalo, N.Y.
John W. Hotchkiss
Bibl. 20

Hotchkiss & Norton (c. 1841)
Palmyra, N.Y.
David Hotchkiss
Benjamin R. Norton
Bibl. 20

Hotchkiss & Schreuder
(Schroeder)
Syracuse, N.Y. (after 1850)
David Hotchkiss
Andrew B. Schreuder
Bibl. 20, 24, 28, 29

H & S

David Hotchkiss (c. 1841-1855)
Palmyra, N.Y. (c. 1841)
Syracuse, N.Y. (c. 1849-   )
Hotchkiss & Norton (c. 1841)
Norton & Hotchkiss
(c. 1849-   )
Hotchkiss & Schreuder
(after 1850)
Bibl. 15, 20, 25, 49

D. HOTCHKISS

Hezekiah Hotchkiss (d. 1761)
New Haven, Conn.
Bibl. 16, 23, 28, 36, 44

John Hotchkiss (c. 1850)
Rochester, N.Y.
Bibl. 20

John W. Hotchkiss (c. 1847)
Buffalo, N.Y.
Hotchkiss & Co. (c. 1847-1848)
Bibl. 20

William Hotchkiss (b. 1744,
w. 1775)
Maryland
Bibl. 38

Frederick Houck (c. 1834-1839)
Harpers Ferry, Va.
Bibl. 19

John E. S. Hough (c. 1846-
1852)
Leesburg, Va.
Bibl. 19

Samuel Hough (c. 1675-1717)
Boston, Mass.
(See Samuel Haugh)
Bibl. 2, 15, 23, 24, 25, 28,
29, 44, 54

S H

Houlton
(See John Holton)

Houlton & Brown(e) (Brown
& Houlton)
Baltimore, Md. (c. 1794-1798)
John Houlton

Liberty Brown
Bibl. 15, 25, 38, 44

HOULTON
& BROWNE

Houlton, Otto & Falk
(c. 1797)
Philadelphia, Pa.
John Houlton
———— Otto
———— Falk
Bibl. 25, 44

John Houlton (Holton)
(c. 1794-1801)
Baltimore, Md. (c. 1794-1798)
Philadelphia, Pa.
Houlton & Brown(e)
(c. 1794-1798)
(Brown & Houlton)
Bibl. 3, 4, 15, 24, 28, 29, 36,
38, 44

HOULTON

A. House
Location unknown
Bibl. 15, 44

A. HOUSE

Weddell (Wenddell) House
(c. 1845)
(See P. M. Weddell)
Cleveland, Ohio
Not a silversmith but a hotel.
Bibl. 23, 89

George Smith Houston
(c. 1802-1808-   )
Augusta, Ga.
George Smith Houston & Co.
Bibl. 17

George Smith Houston & Co.
(c. 1802-1808)
Augusta, Ga.
George Smith Houston
Bibl. 17

Henry Houston (d. 1799)
Philadelphia, Pa.
Bibl. 3

J. C. Houston
Fayetteville, N.C.
Beasley & Houston (c. 1886-
1890-   )
Bibl. 21

Jacob Houtzell (c. 1801-1808)
Philadelphia, Pa.
Bibl. 3, 23, 36, 44

J. R. Hovey (c. 1817)
Norwich, N.Y.
Bibl. 20

J. S. Hovey (c. 1848)
Rome, N.Y.
Gleason & Hovey (c. 1846-
1848)
Bibl. 20

Hovy (c. 1800)
Location unknown
Bibl. 24, 28

HOVY

David How (b. 1745)
Castine, Me.
Boston, Mass. (w. 1805)
Bibl. 23, 28, 36, 44

William How (Howe) (c. 1842-
1846)
Philadelphia, Pa.
Bibl. 3, 23

Howard & Co. (c. 1866)
New York, N.Y.
Bibl. 35, 54, 78, 83

Abram (Abraham) Howard
(c. 1810)
Salem, Mass.
Bibl. 23, 28, 36, 44

John Howard (c. 1819-1822)
Philadelphia, Pa.
Bibl. 3, 23, 36, 44

John Howard (c. 1824)
New York, N.Y.
Bibl. 15

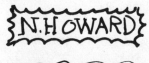

N. Howard
Location unknown
Bibl. 15, 44

Thomas Howard (c. 1620)
Jamestown, Va.
Not Philadelphia, Pa.
Bibl. 23, 36, 44

Thomas Howard (c. 1775-1791)
Philadelphia, Pa.
Bibl. 3

William Howard (b. c. 1720,
w. 1749-1775?)
Pickawaxon, Md.
Bibl. 38

William Howard (c. 1800-
1823)
Boston, Mass.
Bibl. 23, 28, 36, 44

Nathaniel Howcott (c. 1828)
Edenton, N.C.
Bibl. 21

Howe & Guion (c. 1839-1840)
New York, N.Y.
George C. Howe
———— Guion
Bibl. 15, 24

HOWE & GUION

George C. Howe (c. 1810-
1843)
New York, N.Y.
George C. Howe & Co.
(c. 1837-1838)
Stebbins & Howe (c. 1830-
1832) (?)
Bibl. 15, 23, 24, 25, 29, 35, 36,
44, 83

GEORGE C. HOWE

GEO. C. HOWE

George C. Howe & Co.
(c. 1837-1838)
New York, N.Y.
Bibl. 15, 23, 25, 36, 44

GEO. C. HOWE & CO.

Otis Howe (c. 1788-1825)
Sackets Harbor, N.Y. (c. 1816-
1817)
Boston, Mass.
Portsmouth, N.H.
Albany, N.Y.
Watertown, N.Y.
Putney & Howe (c. 1816-1817)
Bibl. 20, 28, 36, 44

William Howe
(See How)

Howell & Arnold (c. 1797-
1798)
Albany, N.Y.
Silas White Howell

——— Arnold
Bibl. 20, 23, 36, 44, 46

Howell & Hall (c. 1801)
Albany, N.Y.
Silas White Howell
——— Hall
Bibl. 20

Benjamin H. Howell(s)
   (c. 1837-1848)
Buffalo, N.Y.
Bibl. 20

Benoni H. Howell(s)
   (c. 1835-1848)
Buffalo, N.Y.
Newburgh, N.Y.
Bibl. 15, 20, 44

HOWELL

C. (S.) (G.) W. Howell
   (c. 1790)
Location unknown
Bibl. 28, 29, 36

G W Howell

James Howell (c. 1800-1812)
Philadelphia, Pa.
James Howell & Co. (c. 1802-
1810)
Bibl. 2, 3, 4, 15, 23, 24, 25, 28,
  29, 36, 39, 44, 54, 72

James Howell & Co. (c. 1802-
1810)
Philadelphia, Pa.
Bibl. 24, 25, 39, 79

J Howell & Co

John Howell (c. 1776-1794)
Augusta, Ga.
Bibl. 17

John Howell (b. 1785-d. 1815)
Savannah, Ga. (c. 1806)
Bibl. 17

Paul Howell (c. 1810-1812)
New York, N.Y.
Eoff & Howell (c. 1805-1810)

Bibl. 15, 23, 24, 25, 29, 36, 44

P. HOWELL   P Howell

S. Howell (c. 1800)
Philadelphia, Pa.
(Could be James Howell's
  mark)
Bibl. 15

S Howell

Silas White Howell (b. 1770,
  c. 1793-1801)
New Brunswick, N.J.
Albany, N.Y.
Howell & Arnold (c. 1797-
1798)
Bibl. 20, 23, 25, 29, 36, 44, 46,
54

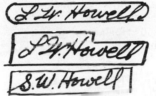

William Howell (c. 1841)
Philadelphia, Pa.
Bibl. 3, 23

John (J. L.) Howland
  (c. 1828-1833)
Philadelphia, Pa.
Bibl. 3

Hoyt & Kippen (c. 1830)
Albany, N.Y.
George Kippen
George B. Hoyt
Bibl. 25

Hoyt
(See Harris & Hoyt)
(See Whitney & Hoyt)

F. Hoyt & Co. (c. 1850-1851)
Sumter, S.C.
Freeman Hoyt
Charles T. Mason
Bibl. 5

Freeman Hoyt (b. 1805-d.
  1869)
Sumter, S.C. (c. 1831-1869)
F. Hoyt & Co. (c. 1850-1851)
Bibl. 5

George A. Hoyt (c. 1822-1844)
Albany, N.Y.
George A. Hoyt & Co.
  (c. 1829-1833)

George A. Hoyt & Son
  (c. 1845-1846)
Bibl. 20

George A. Hoyt & Co.
  (c. 1829-1833)
Albany, N.Y.
Bibl. 20

George A. Hoyt & Son
  (c. 1845-1846)
Albany, N.Y.
Bibl. 20, 23, 36

George B. Hoyt (c. 1827-1850)
Albany, N.Y. (c. 1830-1842)
Middletown, Conn.
Troy, N.Y. (?)
Hoyt & Kippen (c. 1830)
(G. Kippen & Hoyt)
Boyd & Hoyt (c. 1830-1842)
Bibl. 20, 23, 24, 25, 28, 29, 44

GEO B HOYT

Henry Hoyt (c. 1828-1836)
Albany, N.Y.
Bibl. 20

Henry E. Hoyt (c. 1820)
New York, N.Y.
Bibl. 23, 24, 25, 29, 36, 44

H E HOYT

HENRY HOYT

James A. Hoyt (c. 1838-
  1850-   )
Troy, N.Y.
Bibl. 20

Jonathan Perkins Hoyt
  (b. 1805, c. 1847-1871)
Clarksville, Ga. (1847-1849)
Laurens, S.C. (1852-1871)
Bibl. 5, 17

S. Hoyt & Co. (c. 1842)
New York, N.Y.
Seymour Hoyt
Bibl. 23, 24, 25

S. HOYT & CO.

Seymour Hoyt (c. 1817-1850)
New York, N.Y.
S. Hoyt & Co. (c. 1842)
Bibl. 15, 23, 24, 25, 29, 36, 44

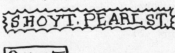

Walter B. Hoyt (c. 1819-1832)
New York, N.Y.
Griffen & Hoyt
Bibl. 15

William Hubbal(1) (c. 1834)
Washington, D.C.
Bibl. 23, 36, 44

Addison T. Hubbard (c. 1870)
Cleveland, Ohio
Bibl. 65

John Hubbs (c. 1830-1837)
Philadelphia, Pa.
Bibl. 3

Henry Huber Jr. (c. 1818-1824)
Philadelphia, Pa.
Bibl. 3

John L. Hubert (c. 1848)
Philadelphia, Pa.
Bibl. 3

Lafayette Hubert (c. 1846-1850)
Philadelphia, Pa.
Bibl. 3

Samuel Huckel (c. 1818-1829)
Philadelphia, Pa.
Bibl. 3

Henry Huddy (c. 1843-1844)
Philadelphia, Pa.
Bibl. 3

William M. Huddy (c. 1835)
Philadelphia, Pa.
Bibl. 3

Hudson & Dolfinger (c. 1855-1858)
(Dolfinger & Hudson)
Louisville, Ky.
Henry Hudson
Jacob Dolfinger
Bibl. 54

Henry Hudson (d. 1888)
Louisville, Ky. (c. 1841-1856)
Hudson & Dolfinger (c. 1855-1858)
Bibl. 32, 54, 68

Jonathan Hudson (b. 1834)
Geneva, N.Y.
Bibl. 20

William Huertin (d. 1771)
New York, N.Y. (c. 1731)

Bibl. 15, 28, 29

W H

W H

James Hues (c. 1808)
Wilmington, N.C.
Bibl. 21

Huet
(See Hevitt)

Christopher Huges & Co.
(See Christopher Hughes & Co.)

Joseph Huggins (c. 1837)
Philadelphia, Pa.
Bibl. 3

Hughes & Bliss (c. 1806)
Middletown, Conn.
Edmund Hughes
Jonathan Bliss
Bibl. 16, 23, 28, 36, 44

Hughes & Francis (c. 1807-1809)
Middletown, Conn.
Edmund Hug(h)es
Julius C. Francis
Bibl. 16, 23, 28, 36, 44

Hughes & Hall (c. 1840)
Location unknown
Bibl. 15, 24, 44

HUGHES & HALL

Charles Hughes (c. 1849)
Philadelphia, Pa.
Bibl. 3, 23

Christopher Hughes (b. 1744-d. 1824)
Baltimore, Md. (c. 1771-1790)
Christopher Hughes & Co. (c. 1773-1774)
Bibl. 3, 24, 25, 29, 38, 44

C. H   C H

Christopher Hughes (Huges) & Co.
Baltimore, Md. (c. 1773-1774)
Christopher Hughes
John Carnan
Bibl. 4, 23, 28, 36, 38

Edmund Hughes
Hampton, Conn. (c. 1804)
Middletown, Conn. (c. 1806-1809)
Ward & Hughes (c. 1806)

Hughes & Bliss (c. 1806)
Hughes & Francis (c. 1807-1809)
Bibl. 15, 16, 23, 25, 28, 36, 44

E. HUGHES

George W. Hughes (c. 1829-1833)
Philadelphia, Pa.
Bibl. 3

Henry Hughes (b. 1756)
Baltimore, Md. (c. 1774-1781)
Bibl. 23, 28, 36, 38, 44

J. Hughes (c. 1798)
Middletown, Conn.
Bibl. 23, 24, 36

J HUGHES

Jasper W. Hughes (c. 1827-1840)
New York, N.Y.
Gale, Wood & Hughes (c. 1833-1844)
Wood & Hughes (c. 1845)
Bibl. 15

Jeremiah Hughes (b. 1783-d. 1848)
Annapolis, Md. (c. 1805-1820)
Bibl. 25, 29, 38, 44

J. HUGHES

William Hughes (b. 1744-d. 1791)
Baltimore, Md. (c. 1785-1791)
Bibl. 25, 29, 38, 44

W. H

John Hughs (c. 1768)
Norfolk, Va.
Bibl. 19

Tubehill Hughs (c. 1768)
Norfolk, Va.
Bibl. 19

Charles T. Huguenail (c. 1799)
Philadelphia, Pa.
Bibl. 3

C. A. Huguenin (c. 1820-1825)
Philadelphia, Pa.
Bibl. 3

Charles Frederick Huguenin
Philadelphia, Pa. (c. 1797-1802)
Fayetteville, N.C.
Halifax, N.C.
Bibl. 3, 21

Davis L. Hugunin (c. 1830-1833)
Philadelphia, Pa.
Bibl. 3

Philip Hulbeart (d. 1764)
Philadelphia, Pa. (c. 1750-1764)
Bibl. 3, 15, 23, 25, 36, 44, 81

Daniel S. Hulett (c. 1833-1849)
Schenectady, N.Y.
Bibl. 20

Alexander Huling (c. 1837)
Philadelphia, Pa.
Bibl. 3

Hull & Sanderson (c. 1652-1683)
Boston, Mass.
John Hull
Robert Sanderson
Bibl. 4, 23, 24, 25, 28, 29, 36, 44, 54

Hull & Sanger (after 1800)
Location unknown
Bibl. 28

Hull & Smith (c. 1815-1816)
Batavia, N.Y.
William Hull
—— Smith
Bibl. 20

Benjamin Hull (b. 1649-d. 1678)
Boston, Mass.
Bibl. 54

John Hull (b. 1624-d. 1683)
Boston, Mass.
Hull & Sanderson
Bibl. 9, 15, 23, 24, 25, 28, 29, 36, 44

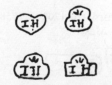

William Hull (c. 1816)
Batavia, N.Y.
Hull & Smith (c. 1815-1816)
Bibl. 20

August (Augustus) Humbert (c. 1818-1819)
New York, N.Y.
Bibl. 15, 23, 36, 44

Widow of August Humbert (c. 1824-1826)
New York, N.Y.
Bibl. 15

Michael Humble
Louisville, Ky.
Bibl. 54

David Humphrey(s) (c. 1789-1793)
Lexington, Ky.
Bibl. 32, 54, 84

Richard Humphrey(s) (c. 1771-1796)
Wilmington, Del.
Philadelphia, Pa.
Bibl. 3, 15, 23, 24, 25, 28, 29, 30, 36, 39, 44, 54, 81

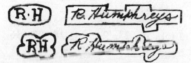

Joshua Humphreys (b. 1743-d. 1823, c. 1775-1785)
Lexington, Ky.
Richmond, Va.
Bibl. 19, 32

Thomas B. Humphreys (c. 1809-1850)
Philadelphia, Pa. (1809-1814)
Baltimore, Md. (w. 1829-1835)
Louisa Court House, Va. (1831-1836)
Richmond, Va. (1831-1850)
Thomas B. Humphreys & Son (c. 1849)
Bibl. 3, 4, 19, 23, 28, 36, 38, 44

T B Humphreys

Thomas B. Humphreys & Son (c. 1849)

Richmond, Va.
Thomas B. Humphreys
Thomas F. Humphreys
Bibl. 15, 19, 44

T. B. Humphreys & Son

Thomas F. Humphreys (c. 1849-1869)
Richmond, Va.
Thomas B. Humphreys & Son (c. 1849)
Bibl. 19

Bouman Hunlock (c. 1752)
Philadelphia, Pa.
Bibl. 3, 23, 36, 44

George W. Hunnewell (c. 1836)
Boston, Mass.
Farrington & Hunnewell (c. 1835-1850)
Bibl. 23, 36, 44

Smith Hunsicker (c. 1832-1835-   )
Shepherdstown, Va.
Bibl. 19

Hunt & Clark (c. 1795-1803)
Bennington, Vt
Jonathan Hunt
Horatio Clark
Bibl. 54

Edmund Hunt (c. 1700s)
Philadelphia, Pa.
Bibl. 54

Edward Hunt (c. 1717-1718)
Philadelphia, Pa.
Bibl. 3, 4, 23, 28, 36, 44

H. B. Hunt
Location unknown
Bibl. 89

H. B. Hunt

John T. Hunt (c. 1819-1840)
Lynchburg, Va.
Bibl. 19, 54

Jonathan Hunt (c. 1795-1803)
Bennington, Vt.
Hunt & Clark
Bibl. 54

William Hunt (c. 1819)
Boston, Mass. (?)
Bibl. 44

William Hunt (c. 1819-1822)
Philadelphia, Pa.
Bibl. 3, 23, 36, 44

William I. Hunt (c. 1815-1816)
Albany, N.Y.
Bibl. 20

Hunter & Pearse (c. 1831-1832)
New York, N.Y.
William H. Hunter
———— Pearse
Bibl. 15

Daniel Hunter (c. 1785)
Newport, R.I.
Bibl. 28

George Hunter (c. 1761)
Portsmouth, N.H.
Bibl. 54

John Hunter (c. 1835-1847)
Albany, N.Y.
Bibl. 20, 24

William H. Hunter (c. 1832-1833)
New York, N.Y.
Hunter & Pearse (c. 1831-1832)
Bibl. 15

Huntington & Burrill (c. 1817-1819)
Augusta, Ga.
Bibl. 17

Huntington & Lynch (c. 1834)
Hillsboro, N.C.
John Huntington
Lemuel Lynch
Bibl. 21

Huntington & Packard (c. 1811)
Springfield, Mass.
Jonathan Packard
Richard Huntington
Bibl. 11

Huntington & Wynne (c. 1827-1828)
Salisbury, N.C.
John Huntington
Robert Wynne
Bibl. 21

Asa Huntington (b. 1792-d. 1857)
Rochester, N.Y. (c. 1821-1822)
Pittsford, N.Y. (c. 1853-1857)
Bibl. 20, 41

John Huntington (d. 1855)
Oxford, N.C. (c. 1824)
Salisbury, N.C. (c. 1827-1828)
Charlotte, N.C. (c. 1828-1832)
Hillsboro, N.C. (c. 1834)
William & John Huntington (c. 1824)
Huntington & Wynne (c. 1827-1828)
Trotter & Huntington (c. 1828-1832)
Huntington & Lynch (c. 1834)
Bibl. 21

M. P. Huntington & Co. (c. 1819)
Milton, N.C.
Martin Palmer Huntington
William Huntington
Bibl. 21

Martin Palmer Huntington (c. 1815-1832)
Milton, N.C. (c. 1819)
Hillsboro, N.C.
M. P. Huntington & Co. (c. 1819)
Bibl. 21

Phil(ip) Huntington (b. 1770-d. 1825)
Norwich, Conn.
Bibl. 16, 23, 24, 25, 28, 29, 36, 44

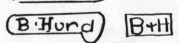

Richard Huntington (b. 1786)
Utica, N.Y. (c. 1823-1850)
Bibl. 18, 20, 24, 25, 44

Huntington

Richard Huntington (c. 1811)
Springfield, Mass.
Huntington & Packard
Bibl. 41

Roswell Huntington (b. 1763-d. 1836, c. 1784)
Norwich, Conn.
Hillsboro, N.C.
Bibl. 16, 21, 23, 28, 36, 44

S. Huntington (c. 1850)
Portland, Me.

Bibl. 24, 25, 28, 44

S HUNTINGTON

William Huntington (b. 1792-d. 1874)
Hillsboro, N.C. (c. 1815-1824)
Milton, N.C. (c. 1819)
Oxford, N.C. (c. 1824)
William Huntington & Co. (c. 1816-1820)
M. P. Huntington & Co. (c. 1819)
William & John Huntington (c. 1824)
Bibl. 21

William Huntington & Co. (c. 1816-1820)
Hillsboro, N.C.
William Huntington
John Van Hook Jr.
Bibl. 21

William & John Huntington (c. 1824)
Oxford, N.C.
William Huntington
John Huntington
Bibl. 21

Jacob Hupp (c. 1828-1833)
Philadelphia, Pa.
Bibl. 3

John H. Huquenele (c. 1839-1842)
Philadelphia, Pa.
Bibl. 3

Benjamin Hurd (b. 1739-d. 1781)
Boston, Mass.
Roxbury, Mass.
Bibl. 15, 23, 24, 25, 27, 28, 29, 36, 44

Isaac Hurd (c. 1754)
Boston, Mass.
Bibl. 23, 36

Jacob Hurd (b. 1702-d. 1758)
Boston, Mass.

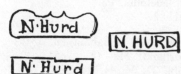

Bibl. 15, 23, 24, 27, 28, 29, 36, 44, 54

Nathaniel Hurd (b. 1729-d. 1777)
Boston, Mass.
Bibl. 15, 23, 24, 25, 27, 28, 29, 36, 44

Philip Hurlbeart (d. 1764)
Philadelphia, Pa. (c. 1761)
Bibl. 24, 28, 29

Hurm & Co. (c. 1796)
Charleston, S.C.
Bibl. 5

P. Hurm (c. 1797)
Charleston, S.C.
Bibl. 5

Henry Hurst (b. 1665-d. 1717)
Boston, Mass.
Bibl. 2, 15, 23, 24, 25, 28, 29, 36, 44, 69

John Hurt (Hurtt) (c. 1839-1842)
Philadelphia, Pa.
Bibl. 3

Hurtin & Burgi (c. 1766-1776)
Bound Brook, N.J.
William Hurtin
Frederick Burgi
Bibl. 28, 44, 46

Christian Hurtin (c. 1792-1793)
Goshen, N.Y.
Bibl. 20

Joshua Hurtin (b. 1738-d. 1780)

Newark, N.J.
Bibl. 46, 54

William Hurtin (c. 1766-1776)
Bound Brook, N.J.
Hurtin & Burgi
Bibl. 46, 54

William Hurtin Jr. (c. 1776)
Newark, N.J.
New York State
Bibl. 46

John Husband (c. 1795-1796)
Philadelphia, Pa.
Bibl. 3, 23, 28, 36, 44

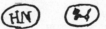

Stephen Hussey (c. 1818-1830)
Easton, Md.
Bibl. 24, 25, 29, 38, 44

James Huston (c. 1799)
Baltimore, Md.
Bibl. 28, 36, 38, 44

William Huston (c. 1767-1771)
Philadelphia, Pa.
Bibl. 3

Jacob Hutchins (c. 1774)
New York, N.Y.
Bibl. 23, 24, 25, 29, 36, 44

HUTCHINS

Nicholas Hutchins (b. 1777-d. 1845)
Baltimore, Md. (c. 1810-1830)
Bibl. 24, 25, 29, 38, 44

Hutchinson
(See Clarke & Hutchinson)

Charles Hutchinson (c. 1847)
Warrenton, Va.
Bibl. 19

J. Hutchinson (c. 1820-1850)
Location unknown
Bibl. 28, 72

J HUTCHINSON

James Hutchinson (c. 1823-1832)

Martinsburg, Va.
Bibl. 19

John Hutchinson (c. 1820-1821)
Fredericksburg, Va.
Bibl. 19

Samuel Hutchinson (c. 1828-1839)
Philadelphia, Pa.
Bibl. 3, 15, 25, 44

S. HUTCHINSON

Thomas Hutchinson (c. 1773)
Lancaster, Pa.
Bibl. 3

Thomas Hutchinson (c. 1816-1824, d. 1820)
Philadelphia, Pa.
Bibl. 3

John Hutt (c. 1774)
New York, N.Y.
Bibl. 28

Hutton
(See Jones & Hutton)

George Hutton (b. 1729-d. 1806)
Albany, N.Y.
Isaac & George Hutton (c. 1799-1815)
Bibl. 20, 23, 24, 28, 36, 44

G·H

Isaac Hutton (b. 1767-d. 1855)
Albany, N.Y. (c. 1790-1815)
Isaac & George Hutton (c. 1799-1815)
Bibl. 15, 20, 23, 24, 25, 28, 29, 30, 36, 39, 44, 54, 72

IH   HUTTON

Isaac & George Hutton (c. 1799-1815)
Albany, N.Y.
Bibl. 20, 23, 36, 44

John Strangeways Hutton (b. 1684-d. 1792)
New York, N.Y. (c. 1720)
Philadelphia, Pa.

Bibl. 3, 4, 23, 24, 25, 28, 29, 30, 35, 36, 44, 83

Samuel Hutton (c. 1850)
Philadelphia, Pa.
Bibl. 3, 23

George Huyler (c. 1819-1833)
New York, N.Y.
Bibl. 15, 25, 44

HUYLER ?

Francis Hycorn (w. 1822, d. 1834)
Baltimore, Md.
Bibl. 38

Hyde
(See Cheavins & Hyde)

———— Hyde (c. 1730?)
Newport, R.I.
Bibl. 28, 44

HYDE

Hyde & Goodrich (c. 1816-1866)
New Orleans, La.
James N. Hyde
C. W. Goodrich
Bibl. 23, 24, 25, 28, 29, 36, 44

HYDE & GOODRICH

HYDE & GOODRICH

Hyde & Hoff (c. 1850)
Auburn, N.Y.
James Hyde
George W. Hoff
Bibl. 20

Hyde & Nevins (c. 1798-1819)
New York, N.Y.
J. N. Hyde
Rufus Nevins
Bibl. 15, 23, 24, 25, 28, 29, 36, 44

Hyde & Nevins

HYDE & NEWINS   H & N

Charles L. Hyde (c. 1842)
Philadelphia, Pa.
Bibl. 3

J. N. Hyde
New York, N.Y.

Hyde & Nevins (c. 1798-1819)
Bibl. 15, 23, 24, 25, 28, 29, 36, 44

James Hyde (c. 1850)
Auburn, N.Y.
Hyde & Hoff
Bibl. 20

James N. Hyde (c. 1816)
New Orleans, La.
Hyde & Goodrich (c. 1816-1866)
Bibl. 54

Hyman & Co. (c. 1845-1846)
Richmond, Va.
Lewis Hyman
Bibl. 19

H. Hyman (c. 1818-1819)
Philadelphia, Pa.
Bibl. 3

Henry W. Hyman
Lexington, Ky. (c. 1800)
Richmond, Va. (c. 1845-1846)
Bibl. 15, 19, 25, 32, 44, 54, 68, 89

H HYMAN   RHD

H HYMAN R.N.D

Lewis Hyman (c. 1845-1846)
Richmond, Va.
Hyman & Co.
Bibl. 19

William Hymas (c. 1818-1822)
Philadelphia, Pa.
Bibl. 3

Thomas Hynes (c. 1822-1827, c. 1847-1853)
Baltimore, Md.
May be father and son.
Bibl. 38

Henry Iagol(e) (b. 1716-d. 1761)
New York, N.Y.
Bibl. 23, 36

G. P. H. Illig (Ilig) (c. 1836)
Louisville, Ky.
Bibl. 32, 54, 68

———— Ilsley (c. 1830)
Location unknown
Bibl. 28

ILSLEY

Imlay
(See Heydorn & Imlay)

John Inch (b. 1720-d. 1763)
Annapolis, Md. (c. 1741-1763)
Bibl. 25, 29, 38, 44

FI

Charles Inglehart (c. 1840)
Philadelphia, Pa.
Bibl. 3

Henry Ingraham (c. 1829-1833)
Philadelphia, Pa.
Bibl. 3

Joseph H. Ingraham (d. 1818)
Portland, Me. (c. 1785)
Bibl. 23, 36, 44

Charles W. Ingram (c. 1835-1846)
Philadelphia, Pa.
Bibl. 3

James Ingram
Albany, N.Y. (c. 1837-1842)
Troy, N.Y. (c. 1843-1850)
Bibl. 20

Benjamin Inman (c. 1814-1819)
Philadelphia, Pa.
Bibl. 3, 23, 36, 44

William Ireland (before 1803)
Charleston, S.C.
Bibl. 5

Matt Irion
Louisville, Ky.
Bibl. 32

David Irving (c. 1848-1850)
Philadelphia, Pa.
Bibl. 3

Mason T. Irwin (c. 1838-1839)
Louisville, Ky.
Bibl. 32

Thomas M. Irwin (c. 1832-1850)
Louisville, Ky.
Bibl. 54, 68

Michael Isaac(k)s (c. 1765)
New York, N.Y.
Bibl. 23, 36, 44

Lester Isadore (c. 1807-1830)
Rochester, N.Y.
Bibl. 54

LESTER ISADORE

Isbell & Co.
Cincinnati, Ohio
Bibl. 34

B. Ivers (c. 1800)
Location unknown
Bibl. 28, 29, 44, 89

B·Ivers

David Ives
Location unknown
Bibl. 28

L. Ives
Location unknown
Bibl. 28

John Izabell (c. 1818)
Lexington, Ky.
Bibl. 32, 54

Jaccard & Co. (c. 1830-1860)
St. Louis, Mo.
D. C. Jaccard
Bibl. 24, 25, 29, 44, 54, 89

JACCARD & CO

D. C. Jaccard (c. 1830-1860)
St. Louis, Mo.
Jaccard & Co.
Bibl. 54

Eugene Jaccard (c. 1850)
St. Louis, Mo.
E. Jaccard & Co. (c. 1830-
1860)
Bibl. 54

E. (Eugene) Jaccard & Co. (c.
1830-1860)
St. Louis, Mo.
Eugene Jaccard
Bibl. 54

Louis Jaccard (Jackard) (c.
1829-1860)
St. Louis, Mo.
Bibl. 54, 89

  L. Jaccard

James Jack(s) (d. 1822)
Charleston, S.C. (c. 1784-
1797)

Philadelphia, Pa. (c. 1797-
1800)
Charleston, S.C. (c. 1800-1822)
James Jack(s) & Co. (c. 1797-
1800)
Bibl. 3, 5, 23, 36, 44

James Jack(s) & Co. (c. 1797-
1800)
Philadelphia, Pa.
James Jacks
Thomas Gibson
Bibl. 5

Jackard
(See Louis Jaccard)

Richard D. Jackman (c. 1822)
Wellsburg, Va.
Bibl. 19

Pulaski Jacks (c. 1842)
Savannah, Ga.
Dibble & Jacks
Bibl. 17

William Jacks (c. 1798-1800)
Philadelphia, Pa.
Bibl. 3, 23, 36, 44

Jackson & McConky (c. 1808-
1809)
Savannah, Ga.
William Jackson
David Marion McConky
Bibl. 17

Jackson
(See Zahm & Jackson)

A. Jackson (c. 1840)
Norwalk, Conn.
Bibl. 25, 44

Charles Jackson (c. 1816)
Schenectady, N.Y.
Bibl. 20

Clement Jackson (b. 1741-d.
1777)
Portsmouth, N.H. (c. 1762)
Bibl. 54

C I

Daniel Jackson (c. 1782-1790)
New York, N.Y.
Bibl. 15, 23, 24, 25, 29, 36, 44

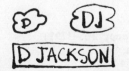

Ephraim Jackson (c. 1813-
1817)
Philadelphia, Pa.
Bibl. 3

George Jackson (c. 1827)
Baltimore, Md.
Bibl. 38

James Jackson (b. 1756)
Maryland (c. 1775)
Bibl. 23, 28, 38, 44

James Jackson
Troy, N.Y. (c. 1840-1842)
Syracuse, N.Y. (c. 1850)
Bibl. 20

John Jackson (c. 1726)
Nantucket Island, Mass.
Bibl. 12

John Jackson (c. 1731)
New York, N.Y.
Bibl. 4, 23, 25, 28, 29, 35, 36,
44, 54, 89

JACKSON

Joseph Jackson
Baltimore, Md. (c. 1803-1813)
Richmond, Va. (c. 1813-1818)
Bibl. 19, 23, 24, 28, 29, 36, 38,
44

I Jackson   25
I Jackson   28

Low Jackson (d. 1753)
Nansemond County, Va.
Bibl. 54

Richard Jackson (c. 1804-
1812)
East Springfield, Ohio
Bibl. 34

Robert Jackson (c. 1752)
Fredericksburg, Va.
Bibl. 19

Thomas Jackson (c. 1837-1849)
Philadelphia, Pa.
Bibl. 3

William Jackson (c. 1808-1809)
Savannah, Ga.
Jackson & McConky
Bibl. 17

Jacob & Claude (Claude &
Jacob) (c. 1772-1774)

Annapolis, Md.
Charles Jacob
Abraham Claude
Bibl. 38

Celestin Jacob (c. 1840)
Philadelphia, Pa.
Bibl. 3

Charles Jacob
Annapolis, Md. (c. 1772-1777)
Port Tobacco, Md. (c. 1778)
Jacob & Claude (c. 1772-1774)
Bibl. 38

George Jacob(s) (b. 1775-d.
  1846
Baltimore, Md. (c. 1802-1846)
Bibl. 4, 23, 24, 28, 29, 36, 38,
  44

| G. JACOB | G JACOBS |

Moses Jacob(s) (b. 1753)
Philadelphia, Pa. (c. 1775)
Bibl. 3, 23, 28, 36, 44

Jacobi & Jenkins (c. 1894-
  1908)
Baltimore, Md.
William F. Jacobi
Talbot Jenkins
Bibl. 89

A. Jacobi (1879)
Baltimore, Md.
Bibl. 89

William F. Jacobi
Baltimore, Md.
Jacobi & Jenkins (c. 1894-
  1908)
Bibl. 89

A. Jacobs (c. 1800)
New York, N.Y.
Bibl. 28

| A Jacobs |

A. Jacobs & Co. (c. 1820)
Philadelphia, Pa.
Abel Jacobs (?)
Bibl. 24, 25, 44

| A J & Co |

Abel Jacobs (c. 1816)
Philadelphia, Pa. (c. 1820)
Baltimore, Md. (?)
A. Jacobs & Co. (c. 1820) (?)
Bibl. 15, 23, 24, 25, 29, 36, 44

| A. JACOBS |

D. Jacobs (c. 1852)
Charleston, S.C.
Bibl. 5

George Jacobs
(See George Jacob)

George W. Jacobs (c. 1839-
  1846)
Philadelphia, Pa.
Bibl. 3

John M. Jacobs (c. 1839-1844)
Warrenton, Va.
Bibl. 19

Moses Jacobs
(See Moses Jacob)

Henry W. Jacot (c. 1841-1850)
Philadelphia, Pa.
Bibl. 3

Julius Jacot (c. 1848-1850)
Philadelphia, Pa.
Bonsall & Jacot (c. 1849)
Bibl. 3

James
(See Musgrave & James)

Jacob S. James (c. 1837)
Philadelphia, Pa.
Bibl. 3

Joseph H. James (c. 1849)
Richmond, Va.
Gennet & James (c. 1849-
  1866)
Bibl. 19

John D. Jameson (c. 1823)
Trenton, N.J.
Kentucky
Bibl. 32

Jean Baptiste Jamin (c. 1796)
Baltimore, Md.
Bibl. 38

Jacques Joseph Jamme (b.
  1793, c. 1816)
Charleston, S.C.
Bibl. 5

Jange (c. 1825)
Location unknown
Bibl. 24

| •JANGE• |

Joshua Janney (c. 1791)
Alexandria, Va.
Bibl. 19, 54

January & Nutman (c. 1818)
Lexington, Ky.
Andrew McConnell January
————— Nutman
Bibl. 32, 54

Andrew McConnell January
  (b. 1794-d. 1877)
Lexington, Ky. (c. 1812-1818)
January & Nutman (c. 1818)
Bibl. 32, 54

Lewis Janvier (January) (d.
  1748)
Charleston, S.C. (c. 1734-1748)
Bibl. 5, 23, 36, 44, 54

Daniel Jaques (b. 1785-d.
  1818)
Charleston, S.C. (c. 1813-1818)
Bibl. 5

————— Jardella (c. 1833)
Philadelphia, Pa.
Dubosq & Jardella
Bibl. 3

Munson Jarvis (b. 1742-d.
  1825)
New Brunswick, Canada
St. Johns, Canada
Stamford, Conn.
Bibl. 2, 15, 16, 23, 24, 25, 28,
  29, 36, 44, 61

| M J | M I |

Henry J. Javain (d. 1838)
Charleston, S.C. (c. 1835-1838)
Bibl. 5, 25, 44

| JAVAIN |

Thomas Jeanes (c. 1835-1837)
Philadelphia, Pa.
Bibl. 3

John Jeangu (c. 1804)
Philadelphia, Pa.
Bibl. 3

Theophilus H. Jeanneret (c.
  1818)
Philadelphia, Pa.
Bibl. 3

————— Jeannert (c. 1850)
Philadelphia, Pa.
Sleeper & Jeannert
Bibl. 3

Jeannert
(See Sleeper & Jeannert)

David H. Jefferies (c. 1846-
1850)
Philadelphia, Pa.
Bibl. 3

E. Jefferies (c. 1837-1839)
Philadelphia, Pa.
Bibl. 3

Emmor Jefferis (b. 1804-d.
1892)
Wilmington, Del.
Guthre & Jefferis (c. 1840)
Bibl. 25, 30, 44

E. JEFFERIS

Ephraim Jefferson (b. 1788-d.
1844)
Smyrna, Del. (c. 1810)
Bibl. 25, 30, 44

E. JEFFERSON

Samuel Jeffreys (c. 1771-1778)
Philadelphia, Pa.
Bibl. 3

Jeffries & Eubank (Eubank &
    Jeffries) (c. 1805-1841)
Glasgow, Ky.
James Jeffries
———— Eubank
Bibl. 54

James Jeffries (c. 1820-1860)
Glasgow, Ky.
Jeffries & Eubank (c. 1805-
1841)
Bibl. 32, 54

Smith Jeffries (c. 1825-1835)
Winchester, Ky.
Bibl. 32, 54, 68

Jenckes & Co. (c. 1798)
Providence, R.I.
John C. Jenckes
Bibl. 23, 36, 44

John Jenckes & Co. (c. 1798)
Providence, R.I.
John C. Jenckes
Bibl. 25

John C. Jenckes (b. 1777-d.
1852)
Providence, R.I. (c. 1795)
Jenckes & Co. (c. 1798)
John Jenckes & Co. (c. 1798)

Bibl. 15, 23, 24, 25, 28, 29, 36,
56

J C JENCKES

J JENCKES

Jenkin(s) & Clark (c. 1827)
Auburn, N.Y.
Benjamin R. Jenkins (?)
George R. Clark
Bibl. 20

Jenkins & Jenkins (c. 1850)
Baltimore, Md.
Bibl. 23

Jenkins & Jenkins (1908-1923)
Baltimore, Md.
Bibl. 89

Benjamin R. Jenkins (c. 1827)
Auburn, N.Y.
Jenkin(s) & Clark (?)
Bibl. 20, 24, 89

B. R. Jenkins

Edward J. Jenkins (c. 1843-
1850)
Philadelphia, Pa.
Bibl. 3

Harman (Herman?) Jenkins (c.
1817-1823)
Albany, N.Y.
I. & H. Jenkins (c. 1815-1816)
Bibl. 20, 24

I. & H. Jenkins (c. 1815-1816)
Albany, N.Y.
(Not Baltimore, Md.)
Ira Jenkins
Harman Jenkins
Bibl. 15, 20, 25, 44

I & H Jenkins

Ira Jenkins (c. 1813)
Albany, N.Y.
I. & H. Jenkins (c. 1815-1816)
Bibl. 20

James Jenkins (c. 1794)
Philadelphia, Pa.
Bibl. 3

John Jenkins (b. 1777-d. 1796)
Philadelphia, Pa.
Bibl. 3, 23, 24, 25, 28, 36, 39,
44

I J

John Jenkins (c. 1844-1848)
Philadelphia, Pa.
Bibl. 3

Josias Jenkins (b. 1794)
Baltimore, Md. (c. 1811)
Bibl. 38

Martin J. Jenkins (c. 1847-
1848)
Troy, N.Y.
Bibl. 20

Talbot Jenkins
Baltimore, Md.
Jacobi & Jenkins (c. 1894-
1908)
Bibl. 89

B. Jenner (c. 1846)
Philadelphia, Pa.
Bibl. 3

Jenning(s) & Lander (c. 1848-
1851)
New York, N.Y.
Bibl. 15, 25, 44

JENNING & LANDER

Jacob Jennings (b. 1729-d.
1817)
Norwalk, Conn. (c. 1763)
Bibl. 16, 23, 24, 25, 28, 36, 44,
61

I. I

Jacob Jennings Jr. (b. 1779)
Norwalk, Conn. (c. 1810)
Bibl. 16, 23, 28, 36, 44

Thomas Jennings (c. 1837)
Philadelphia, Pa.
Bibl. 3

Chauncey Jerome (c. 1846-
1849)
Philadelphia, Pa.
Bibl. 3

David Jesse (Jess) (b. 1670-d.
1705)
Boston, Mass. (c. 1695)
Bibl. 2, 15, 23, 24, 25, 28, 29,
36, 44, 70

Steven C. Jett (c. 1848-1860)
St. Louis, Mo.

Bibl. 54

S. C. JETT

Charles E. Jeuneret (c. 1817)
St. Louis, Mo.
Bibl. 54

John Job (c. 1819)
Philadelphia, Pa.
Bibl. 3

John M. Johannes (b. 1799-d.
1883)
Baltimore, Md. (c. 1828-1850)
Bibl. 23, 36, 38, 44

———— John (c. 1760)
Location unknown
Bibl. 36

JOHN

Johnsohn
Location unknown
Bibl. 15

JOHNSOHN

Johnson
(See Kidney, Cann & Johnson)

———— Johnson (c. 1810)
Burton, Ohio
Bibl. 34

Johnson & Ball (c. 1785-1790)
Baltimore, Md.
William Ball, Jr.
Israel H. Johnson (?)
Bibl. 23, 25, 29, 36, 38, 44

Johnson & Crowley (c. 1830-
1833)
Philadelphia, Pa.
———— Johnson
E. Crowley
Bibl. 3

Johnson & Godley (Godley &
Johnson) (c. 1843-1849)
Albany, N.Y.
———— Johnson
Richard Godley
Bibl. 4, 20, 23, 28, 44

Johnson & Lewis (c. 1837-1842)
Philadelphia, Pa.
———— Johnson

John M. Lewis (?)
Bibl. 3

Johnson & Reat (c. 1810-1815)
Baltimore, Md.
Portland, Me. (?)
Richmond, Va.
Reuben Johnson
James Reat
Bibl. 15, 19, 23, 24, 25, 28, 29,
36, 38

JOHNSON & REAT

J+R

Johnson & Riley (c. 1786)
Baltimore, Md.
Israel H. Johnson (?)
———— Riley
Bibl. 24, 25, 29, 38, 44

J+R

Alonzo W. Johnson (c. 1831-
1838)
Albany, N.Y.
C. & A. W. Johnson
Bibl. 20

B. Johnson (c. 1840)
Richmond, Va.
Bibl. 19

C. & A. W. Johnson (c. 1831-
1838)
Albany, N.Y.
Chauncey Johnson
Alonzo W. Johnson
Bibl. 20

Chauncey Johnson (c. 1824-
1831, c. 1838-1841)
Albany, N.Y.
C. & A. W. Johnson (c. 1831-
1838)
Bibl. 15, 20, 23, 25, 28, 36,
44, 72

C. JOHNSON

Daniel B. Johnson (b. 1817)
Utica, N.Y. (c. 1834-1858)
Bibl. 18, 20

E. J. Johnson (c. 1842)
Macon, Ga.
Bibl. 88

Edward Johnson (b. 1754)
Maryland (c. 1774)
Bibl. 38

Elisha Johnson (c. 1841)
Greensboro, N.C.
Bibl. 21

Israel H. Johnson
Baltimore, Md. (c. 1786-
1790-   )
Easton, Md. (c. 1793)
Johnson & Ball (c. 1785-1790)
(?)
Johnson & Riley (c. 1786) (?)
Bibl. 38

J. Johnson (c. 1827)
Weedsport, N.Y.
Bibl. 20

James R. Johnson (b. 1808-d.
1855)
Fredericksburg, Va. (c. 1829)
Norfolk, Va. (c. 1829-1838,
c. 1851-1852)
Richmond, Va. (c. 1832)
Clarksburg, Va. (c. 1840-1846)
Bibl. 19

John Johnson (c. 1815)
Pittsburgh, Pa.
Bibl. 23, 36, 44

Maycock W. Johnson (c. 1815)
Albany, N.Y.
Bibl. 4, 20, 23, 24, 25, 28, 29,
36, 44

M. W. JOHNSON

MW JOHNSON

N. B. Johnson (c. 1838)
Watertown, N.Y.
Bibl. 20

Reuben Johnson (b. 1782-d.
1820)
Richmond, Va.
Johnson & Reat (c. 1810-1815)
Bibl. 19

Robert Johnson (Johnston)
(c. 1823-1850)
Philadelphia, Pa.
Bibl. 3

Samuel Johnson (c. 1780-1796,
d. 1796)
New York, N.Y.

Bibl. 4, 23, 24, 25, 28, 29, 35,
36, 44, 54, 83

S. J

JOHNSON

Samuel Johnson
Winchester, Va. (c. 1827-1829)
Harpers Ferry, Va. (c. 1830)
Bibl. 19

Samuel Johnson (c. 1834)
Albany, N.Y.
Bibl. 20

Samuel W. Johnson (c. 1836-
1844)
(Simeon)
Louisville, Ky.
Bibl. 32

W. M. Johnson (c. 1849)
Richmond, Va.
Hill & Johnson
Bibl. 19

William Johnson (c. 1799)
Boston, Mass.
Bibl. 28

William Johnson (c. 1829)
Charlottesville, Va.
Bibl. 19

William E. Johnson (c. 1841)
Philadelphia, Pa.
Bibl. 3

A. Johnston (c. 1830)
Philadelphia, Pa.
Bibl. 24, 25, 44

A JOHNSTON

Edmund J. Johnston (c. 1845-
1849-1870?)
Macon, Ga.
W. B. Johnston & Bro. (c. 1845-
1849)
Bibl. 17

James Johnston (c. 1812-1843)
Louisville, Ky.
Bibl. 32, 54, 68

W. B. Johnston & Brother
(c. 1845-1849)
Macon, Ga.
William Blackstone Johnston
Edmund J. Johnston
Bibl. 17

William Johnston (c. 1826-
1827)

Winchester, Va. (c. 1827)
Woodstock, Va.
Meredith & Johnston (c. 1827)
Bibl. 19

William B. Johnston & Co.
(c. 1839-1842)
Macon, Ga.
William Blackstone Johnston
Bibl. 17

William Blackstone Johnston
(b. 1832-d. 1881)
Macon, Ga.
William B. Johnston & Co.
(c. 1839-1842)
W. B. Johnston & Bro. (c. 1845-
1849)
Bibl. 17

Johonnot & Tuells (c. 1809)
Windsor, Vt.
William B. Johonnot
Bibl. 54

William D. Johonnot (b. 1766-d
1849)
Middletown, Conn. (c. 1787)
Windsor, Vt. (c. 1792, c. 1809)
Johonnot & Tuells (c. 1809)
Bibl. 16, 23, 24, 25, 28, 36,
44, 54

John Jolineth (c. 1841-1843)
Philadelphia, Pa.
Bibl. 3

John Jolivet (c. 1829-1850)
Philadelphia, Pa.
Bibl. 3

Joseph Jonas (c. 1817)
Philadelphia, Pa.
Bibl. 3

Joseph Jonas (c. 1817-1824)
Cincinnati, Ohio
Bibl. 34

Francis Jonckheere (c. 1807-
1824)
Baltimore, Md.
Bibl. 38

Jones
(See Newland & Jones)
(See Ward & Jones)

Jones, Ball & Co. (c. 1850-
1852)

Boston, Mass.
John B. Jones
S. S. Ball
Bibl. 15, 23, 25, 28, 36, 44

JONES, BALL & CO.

Jones, Ball & Poor (c. 1840-
1846)
Boston, Mass.
John B. Jones
S. S. Ball
Bibl. 15, 23, 24, 25, 28, 36, 44,
72

JONES, BALL & POOR

Jones & Hutton (c. 1840-1862?)
Wilmington, Del.
Philip Jones (?)
——— Hutton
Bibl. 25, 30, 44

Jones & Hutton   P. Jones

Jones, Low(s) & Ball (c. 1839)
Boston, Mass.
John B. Jones
——— Low
——— Ball
Bibl. 15, 24, 25, 28, 44, 72

JONES LOWS & BALL

JONES LOW & BALL

Jones & Peirce
Location unknown
Bibl. 15, 44

JONES & PEIRCE

Jones, Shreve, Brown & Co.
(c. 1854)
Boston, Mass.
John B. Jones
Benjamin Shreve
——— Brown
Bibl. 15

Jones & Ward (c. 1809)
Boston, Mass.
Richard Ward
John B. Jones
Bibl. 15, 23, 24, 25, 28, 36, 44

JONES & WARD

Jones & Wood (c. 1846)
Syracuse, N.Y.
J. F. Jones (?)
——— Wood
Bibl. 20

A. Jones
Location unknown
Bibl. 15, 44

A. JONES

C. H. Jones & Co. (c. 1854)
Georgetown, S.C.
Bibl. 5

Caleb Jones (c. 1818)
Plattsburg, N.Y.
Bibl. 20

Christopher Jones (c. 1847)
St. Louis, Mo.
Bibl. 54

Daniel Jones (d. 1822)
Wellsburg, Va. (c. 1821)
Bibl. 17

E. Jones (c. 1820)
Baltimore, Md.
Bibl. 23, 36

Elisha Jones (c. 1827-1833)
New York, N.Y.
Bibl. 15, 25, 44

E. JONES ?

G. W. Jones (c. 1838)
Savannah, Ga.
Bibl. 17

George B. Jones (b. 1815-d.
1875)
Boston, Mass.
Bibl. 23, 28, 36, 44

George W. Jones (c. 1840-
1841)
Philadelphia, Pa.
Bibl. 3

Griffith (William) G. Jones
(c. 1824-1827)
Baltimore, Md.
Bibl. 38

H. Jones (c. 1816)
Painesville, Ohio
Bibl. 34

Harlow Jones (c. 1811)
Canandaigua, N.Y.
Swift & Jones (c. 1810) (?)
Bibl. 20

Isaac Jones (d. 1805)
Charleston, S.C. (c. 1800)
Bibl. 5

J. F. Jones (c. 1850)
Syracuse, N.Y.

Jones & Wood (c. 1846) (?)
Bibl. 20

J. Walter Jones (c. 1842)
Troy, N.Y.
Bibl. 20

Jacob Jones (c. 1817-1818)
Baltimore, Md.
Bibl. 38

James Jones (d. 1815)
Philadelphia, Pa.
Bibl. 3, 15, 23, 36, 44

J. JONES 57 MARKET ST.

James M. Jones (c. 1825-1850)
Savannah, Ga.
Spear & Jones (c. 1841)
Bibl. 17

John Jones (d. 1768)
Philadelphia, Pa. (c. 1750)
Bibl. 3, 23

John Jones (c. 1784)
Staunton, Va.
Bibl. 3, 19, 23

John B. Jones (b. 1782-d. 1854)
Boston, Mass.
Jones & Ward (c. 1809)
Baldwin & Jones (c. 1813)
John B. Jones & Co. (c. 1838)
Jones, Low(s) & Ball (c. 1839)
Jones, Ball & Poor (c. 1840-
1846)
Jones, Ball & Co. (c. 1850-
1852)
Jones, Shreve, Brown & Co.
(c. 1854)
Bibl. 4, 15, 23, 24, 25, 28,
29, 36, 44, 54, 78

J JONES

J. B. JONES

John B. Jones & Co. (c. 1838)
Boston, Mass.
John B. Jones
S. S. Ball
Bibl. 15, 25, 28, 44

J B JONES & CO

John W. Jones & Son (19th
century)
Mt. Sterling, Ky.
Bibl. 32, 54

Levi Jones (c. 1845-1846)
Philadelphia, Pa.
Bibl. 3

Philip Jones (c. 1843)
Wilmington, Del.
Jones & Hutton (c. 1840-
1862?) (?)
Bibl. 25, 44

P. JONES

Prince H. Jones (c. 1842-1861)
St. Louis, Mo.
Benjamin F. Crane & Co.
Bibl. 54

Robert E. Jones (c. 1837-1838)
Utica, N.Y.
Bibl. 18, 20

Rowland Jones (c. 1837-1838)
Utica, N.Y.
Bibl. 18, 20

Samuel G. Jones (c. 1799-1829)
Baltimore, Md. (c. 1799-1815)
Philadelphia, Pa.
(c. 1804-1814)
Patton & Jones (c. 1799-1815)
Bibl. 38

Samuel S. Jones (c. 1844)
Philadelphia, Pa.
Bibl. 3

Samuel W. Jones (c. 1792-
1802?)
Augusta, Ga.
Bibl. 17

Thomas L. Jones
Location unknown
Bibl. 15, 44

THOS. L. JONES

William Jones (b. 1694-d. 1730)
Marblehead, Mass. (c. 1715)
Bibl. 2, 15, 23, 25, 28, 36, 44,
66, 69

William Jones (c. 1820-1823)
New York, N.Y.
Boyce & Jones (c. 1825-
1830) (?)
Bibl. 23, 36

William E. Jones (b. 1826)
Rochester, N.Y. (c. 1847)
Bibl. 20, 41, 44

William G. Jones (c. 1837)
Philadelphia, Pa.
Bibl. 3

William H. Jones (c. 1837-
1841)
Charleston, S.C.
Bibl. 5

William Talbot Jones
(c. 1796?)
Savannah, Ga.
Bibl. 17

Peter Jordan (c. 1823)
Philadelphia, Pa.
Bibl. 23, 36, 44

R. Jordan (c. 1819)
Richmond, Va.
Bibl. 19

Samuel Jordan (c. 1807)
Baltimore, Md.
Bibl. 38

Peter Joubert (Jubart)
(c. 1807-1830)
Philadelphia, Pa.
Bibl. 3, 23, 36, 44

Peter Jourdan (c. 1823-1824)
Philadelphia, Pa.
Bibl. 3

Michael Journot (c. 1809-1810)
Philadelphia, Pa.
Bibl. 3

Thomas E. Joyce (c. 1820-
1825)
Philadelphia, Pa.
Bibl. 3

Jubart
(See Joubert)

———— Judah (c. 1774)
New York, N.Y.
Bibl. 28, 36, 44

Benjamin Judd (c. 1812)
Burton, Ohio
Bibl. 34

Judson & Lawrence (c. 1803)
Stillwater, N.Y.
Bibl. 20

C. H. Judson (c. 1846)
Syracuse, N.Y.
Bibl. 20

Hiram Judson (c. 1824-1854)
Syracuse, N.Y.
Bibl. 15, 20, 25, 44

H. JUDSON

Thomas W. Judson (c. 1850)
Syracuse, N.Y.
Bibl. 20

Cadmus Julian (c. 1840)
Philadelphia, Pa.
Bibl. 3

Joseph J. Justice (c. 1844-1848)
Philadelphia, Pa.
Bibl. 3

Swan Justice (Justis) (c. 1818-
1819)
Richmond, Va.
Bibl. 19

S JUSTIS

J. Kadmus (c. 1839)
St. Louis, Mo.
Bibl. 54

William Kahmer (c. 1843-
1850)
Philadelphia, Pa.
Bibl. 3

H. Q. Kakle (c. 1838-1848)
St. Louis, Mo.
Bibl. 54

William Kanapauge
(Kannapaux)
Charleston, S.C. (c. 1809-1819)
Bibl. 5

———— Kanot (c. 1781)
Alexandria, Va.
Bibl. 54

Karbin
(See Carbin)

J. N. Karl (c. 1810)
Philadelphia, Pa.
Bibl. 3

A. L. Karn (c. 1809-1810)
Philadelphia, Pa.
Bibl. 3

C. Karner (Karrar) (c. 1809-
1811)
Philadelphia, Pa.
Bibl. 3

Am(os) Kay (c. 1725)
Boston, Mass.
Bibl. 23, 28, 29, 36, 44

A K

Kayser
(See Lohse & Kayser)

B. Kayton (c. 1847)
Fredericksburg, Va.
Bibl. 19

John W. Kean (c. 1837-1850)
Philadelphia, Pa.
Bibl. 3

———— Keating (c. 1840-1843)
Philadelphia, Pa.
Warner & Keating
Bibl. 3

Lambert Keatting Jr. (c. 1831-
1843)
Philadelphia, Pa.
Bibl. 3

J. Kedzie & Co. (c. 1847-1848)
Rochester, N.Y.
John Kedzie
Bibl. 20, 41, 44

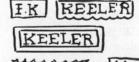

John Kedzie (b. 1809-d. 1889)
Rochester, N.Y. (c. 1838-1868)
(not Philadelphia, Pa.)
J. Kedzie & Co. (c. 1847-1848)
Bibl. 20, 25, 41, 44

J KEDZIE

John Keel (c. 1835-1837)
Philadelphia, Pa.
Bibl. 3

A. Keeler (c. 1800)
New London, Conn.
Norwalk, Conn.
Bibl. 23, 24, 36

KEELER

Joseph Keeler (b. 1786-d. 1824)
Norwalk, Conn. (c. 1810)
Bibl. 15, 16, 23, 24, 25, 28, 29,
36, 44, 89

I.K KEELER

KEELER

KEELER IK

Thad(d)eus Keeler (Keller)
New York, N.Y. (c. 1805-1813)
Boston, Mass. (c. 1823?)
Bibl. 15, 23, 24, 25, 28, 29, 35,
36, 44, 54, 83, 89

T. KEELER T. K

George Keesee (c. 1831-1846)
Richmond, Va.
Bibl. 19

G. KEESEE

G. H. Keeve (c. 1848-1849)
Louisville, Ky.
Bibl. 32

Joseph Keiff (c. 1828-1833)
Philadelphia, Pa.
Bibl. 3, 23, 36, 44

Alexander Keim (c. 1841-1850)
Philadelphia, Pa.
Butler & Keim (c. 1843)
Butler, Wise & Keim (c. 1850)
Bibl. 3, 23

John Keim (c. 1777)
Reading, Pa.
Bibl. 3

T. & W. Keith (c. 1805)
New York, N.Y.
Bibl. 23, 29, 36, 44

Timothy Keith (c. 1800-1805)
Boston, Mass.
Bibl. 25, 28

T.   Keith

T. KEITH

Timothy & W. Keith (c. 1829)
Worcester, Mass.
Bibl. 23, 25, 36, 44

T & W KEITH

Grael Keley (Kelley) (c. 1823)
Boston, Mass.
Bibl. 23, 28, 36, 44

Charles Keller (c. 1841)
Philadelphia, Pa.
Bibl. 3

George Keller (c. 1846)
Philadelphia, Pa.
Bibl. 3

Thaddeus Keller
(See Thadeus Keeler)

David Kelley (c. 1806-1816)
Philadelphia, Pa.
Bibl. 3

E. G. & J. S. Kelley (c. 1820-
1842)
Nantucket, Mass.
Providence, R.I.
Edward G. Kelley

James S. Kelley
Bibl. 23, 28, 36, 44

E & J. Kelley

Edward G. Kelley (b. 1818)
Nantucket Island, Mass.
(c. 1840)
E. G. & J. S. Kelley (c. 1820-
1842)
Bibl. 12

Grael Kelley
(See Grael Keley)

H. A. & E. G. Kelley (before
1842)
Nantucket, Mass.
Henry A. Kelley
Edward G. Kelley
Bibl. 44

H. A. & E. G. Kelley

Henry A. Kelley (c. 1815-1869)
Nantucket Island, Mass.
Bibl. 12, 44

H A KELLEY

James S. Kelley (b. 1820-d.
1900)
Nantucket Island, Mass.
(c. 1838-1856)
New Bedford, Mass. (1856)
E. G. & J. S. Kelley (c. 1820-
1842)
Bibl. 12, 44

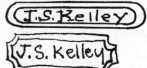

Royal T. Kelley (c. 1835-1836)
Buffalo, N.Y.
Bibl. 20

John V. Kellinger (c. 1837)
Philadelphia, Pa.
Bibl. 3

Allen Kell(e)y (c. 1810-1825)
Nantucket Island, Mass.
Providence, R.I.
Bibl. 12, 23, 28, 36, 44

Robert Kelly (c. 1843-1844)
Philadelphia, Pa.
Bibl. 3

Thomas Kelvey (c. 1817-1831)
Cincinnati, Ohio

West Union, Ohio
Bibl. 34

Kenab
(See next entry)

Charles Kendal(l) (Kendle)
(Kindle) (Kenab)
New York, N.Y. (c. 1780-1797)
Bibl. 15, 23, 25, 28, 36, 44

C. KENDALL

James Kendall (b. 1768-d.
1808) (c. 1790-1800)
Wilmington, Del.
Philadelphia, Pa.
Bibl. 15, 25, 30, 44

J. KENDALL   J. K

S. Kendall
Location unknown
Bibl. 15, 44

S KENDALL

Kendle
(See Kendal)

Kendrick
(See Hendricks)

William Kendrick (b. 1810-d.
1880)
Louisville, Ky. (c. 1824-1880)
Harris & Kendrick (c. 1831-
1832)
Lemon & Kendrick (c. 1831-
1842)
E. C. Beard & Co. (c. 1831-
1852-   )
Bibl. 23, 24, 25, 29, 32, 36, 44,
54, 68, 89   W. KENDRICK
W KENDRICK   LOUISVILLE

Kennedy
(See Morgan & Kennedy)

Hugh Kennedy (c. 1837-1850)
Philadelphia, Pa.
Bibl. 3

John Kennedy (b. 1823,
c. 1839)
Charleston, S.C.
Bibl. 5

Matthew Kennedy (c. 1825)
Philadelphia, Pa.
Bibl. 23, 36, 44

Nathan Kennedy (c. 1825)
Philadelphia, Pa.
Bibl. 3

Patrick Kennedy (c. 1795-1801)
Philadelphia, Pa.
Bibl. 3

Kenney
(See Kinney)

Anwyl Kenrick (c. 1775)
Maryland
Bibl. 36, 44

William Kensell (c. 1835)
Philadelphia, Pa.
Bibl. 3

Kent
(See Yates & Kent)

Luke Kent (c. 1817-1841)
Cincinnati, Ohio
Bibl. 34

Thomas Kent (c. 1821-1844)
Cincinnati, Ohio
Bibl. 34

Samuel Keplinger (b. 1770-d.
1849)
Baltimore, Md. (c. 1812-1849?)
Bibl. 25, 29, 38, 44

| S KEPLINGER |

William Keplinger (c. 1829-
1831)
Baltimore, Md.
Bibl. 38

Alexander Kerr (d. 1738)
Williamsburg, Va. (c. 1734)
Bibl. 19

| A K |

Robert M. Kerrison (c. 1842-
1850)
Philadelphia, Pa.
Bibl. 3

Kersey & Pearce (c. 1845-1850)
Richmond, Va.
Edward Kersey
Hamett A. Pearce
Bibl. 19

Edward Kersey (c. 1845-1878)
Richmond, Va.
Kersey & Pearce (c. 1845-1850)
Bibl. 19

| E. KERSEY |

Robert Kersey (c. 1793)
Easton, Md.
Bibl. 38

John Kershaw (c. 1789-1791)
Charleston, S.C.
Bibl. 5

John Kessler Jr. (c. 1806-1807)
Philadelphia, Pa.
Bibl. 3

Ketcham
(See James Ketchum)

Joseph Ketcham (c. 1815-1826)
New York, N.Y.
Bibl. 15

James Ketchum (Ketcham)
(c. 1807-1849)
New York, N.Y.
Utica, N.Y.
Bibl. 18, 20, 23, 24, 25, 36, 44

| I KETCHAM |

L. A. Ketchum & Co. (c. 1840-
1842)
Buffalo, N.Y.
Lewis A. Ketchum
Bibl. 20

Lewis A. Ketchum (c. 1837-
1840)
Buffalo, N.Y.
L. A. Ketchum & Co. (c. 1840-
1842)
Bibl. 20

Thomas Kettel(l) (b. 1760-d.
1850)
Charlestown, Mass. (c. 1784)
Bibl. 23, 25, 28, 29, 36, 44

| T. K. | | T + K |

George Kew (c. 1840)
Philadelphia, Pa.
Bibl. 3

Key & Sons (c. 1850)
Philadelphia, Pa.
F. C. Key
Bibl. 3

F. C. Key (c. 1848-1850)
Camden, N.J.
Philadelphia, Pa.
Key & Sons (c. 1850)
Bibl. 3

Keyes & Fitch (c. 1831)
Batavia, N.Y.
S. C. Keyes

William Fitch
Bibl. 20

Keyes & Stocking (c. 1831)
Batavia, N.Y.
S. C. Keyes
Reuben Stocking
Bibl. 20

S. C. Keyes (c. 1830-1834)
Batavia, N.Y.
Keyes & Fitch (c. 1831)
Keyes & Stocking (c. 1831)
Bibl. 20, 24

Joseph Keyser (c. 1828-1833)
Philadelphia, Pa.
Bibl. 3

William Keyser (c. 1850)
Philadelphia, Pa.
Bibl. 3, 23

John Keywood (c. 1851)
Wheeling, Va.
Bibl. 19

Robert Keyworth (c. 1830-
1833)
Washington, D.C.
Bibl. 23, 24, 25, 29, 36, 44

| R. KEYWORTH |

P. Kibbe
Location unknown
Bibl. 54

Kidney, Cann & Johnson
(c. 1850-1853)
New York, N.Y.
Bibl. 4, 23, 24, 25, 28, 29, 44, 54

| K. C. & J. |

Kidney & Dunn (c. 1844)
New York, N.Y.
Bibl. 23, 24, 25, 29, 44

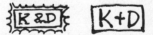

Kierstead
Kiestede
(See next entry)

Cornelius Kierstede (Kierstead) (Kiestede) (b. 1674-d.
1757, c. 1702-1729)
New Haven, Conn.
New York, N.Y.

Bibl. 2, 4, 15, 16, 23, 25, 28,
29, 36, 44, 54, 61

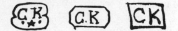

John Killingsworth (c. 1812)
Raleigh, N.C.
Bibl. 21

Kimball
(See Carleton & Kimball)

J. Kimball (c. 1785)
Location unknown
Bibl. 28

J. KIMBALL

Kimball
(See Woodford & Kimball)

Lewis A. Kimball (c. 1837-
1842)
Buffalo, N.Y.
Bibl. 15, 25, 44

L. KIMBALL

O. Kimball (c. 1842-1843)
Elmira, N.Y.
Yates & Kimball
Bibl. 20

William H. Kimberly
(b. 1780-d. 1821, c. 1805-
1821)
Baltimore, Md.
New York, N.Y.
Bibl. 15, 23, 24, 25, 29, 36,
38, 44

W. K   Kimberly
KIMBERLY

William H. Kimberly (c. 1842)
St. Louis, Mo.
Bibl. 54

Jane Kind (b. 1624-d. 1710)
Boston, Mass.
Bibl. 28

Kindle
(See Kendal)

—— King (c. 1817)
Warren, Ohio
Bibl. 34

G. W. King (c. 1790)
Location unknown

Bibl. 24

G. W. KING

George King (c. 1834-1844)
New York, N.Y.
Bibl. 15, 23

Gilbert King (c. 1845)
Rochester, N.Y.
Bibl. 20

Henry King (c. 1830)
Troy, N.Y.
Bibl. 20

John King (c. 1817-1819)
Philadelphia, Pa.
Bibl. 3

Joseph King (c. 1770-1807)
Middletown, Conn.
Bibl. 16, 23, 28, 36, 44

R. King (c. 1820)
Philadelphia, Pa. (?)
Bibl. 15, 44

R KING

Solomon King (c. 1808)
Baltimore, Md.
Wheeling, Va.
Bibl. 19

Thomas King (c. 1840)
Leesburg, Va.
Bibl. 19

Thomas R. King (c. 1819-1831)
Baltimore, Md.
Bibl. 25, 29, 38, 44

T R KING

Walter King (c. 1817)
Warren, Ohio
Bibl. 34, 88

William King (c. 1806-1816)
Philadelphia, Pa.
Bibl. 3

William King (c. 1838)
Charleston, S.C.
Bibl. 5

John Kingston (c. 1775-1795)
New York, N.Y.
Bibl. 4, 23, 28, 36, 44

James Kinkead (c. 1765-1774)
Christiana, Del.
Philadelphia, Pa.
Bibl. 3

A. Kinley (c. 1841)
Philadelphia, Pa.
Bibl. 3, 23

Kinne
(See Thomas Kinney)

Thomas Kinne Jr. (c. 1836)
Cortland, N.Y.
Bibl. 20

Thomas Kinney (Kenney)
(Kinne) (c. 1786-1836)
Norwich, Conn.
Cortland, N.Y.
Bibl. 16, 23, 24, 25, 28, 36,
44, 61

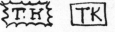

William & Jesse Kinsel
(c. 1837-1839)
Philadelphia, Pa.
Bibl. 3

Kinsey
(See Scovil & Kinsey)

David I. Kinsey (c. 1817-
1860)
Cincinnati, Ohio
Edward & David Kinsey
(c. 1836-1850)
Bibl. 15, 23, 24, 25, 29, 34,
44, 54

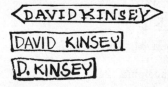

Edmund Kinsey (c. 1845)
Jamaica, N.Y.
Bibl. 20

Edward Kinsey (c. 1834-1845)
Newport, Ky.
Cincinnati, Ohio
Edward & David Kinsey
(c. 1836-1850)
Bibl. 32, 34, 54, 72

E. KINSEY

Edward & David Kinsey
(c. 1836-1850)
Newport, Ky.
Cincinnati, Ohio

Edward Kinsey
David I. Kinsey
Bibl. 15, 23, 24, 25, 29, 32,
44, 54, 89

E & D KINSEY

F. Kinsey (c. 1837)
Cincinnati, Ohio
Bibl. 34

John Kinzie (c. 1804, d. 1828)
Chicago, Ill.
Detroit, Mich.
St. Joseph, Mich.
Maumee, Ohio
Bibl. 58

Benjamin Kip (c. 1702)
New York, N.Y.
Bibl. 4, 23, 28, 36, 44

Jesse Kip (b. 1660-d. 1722)
Newtown, N.Y.
New York, N.Y.
Bibl. 25, 54

I K

William Kip (c. 1825-1850)
Kinderhook, N.Y.
Bibl. 20

R. M. Kipp (c. 1833)
Wheeling, Va.
Stocking & Kipp
Bibl. 19

George Kippen (b. 1790-d.
1845)
Bridgeport, Conn. (c. 1827)
Albany, N.Y. (c. 1830)
Middletown, Conn.
G. Kippen & Hoyt (c. 1830)
(Hoyt & Kippen)
Elias Camp (c. 1825-1827)
Bibl. 15, 16, 23, 24, 25, 28, 29,
36, 44, 61

G. KIPPEN

Kirby
(See Brown(e) & Kirby)

William Kirby (c. 1783)
New York, N.Y.
Bibl. 23, 36, 44

J. H. Kirchoff (c. 1805)
Philadelphia, Pa.
Bibl. 3

E. H. Kirckhaff (c. 1803)
Philadelphia, Pa.
Bibl. 3

Kirk & Smith (c. 1818-1823)
Baltimore, Md.
Samuel Kirk
John Smith
Bibl. 15, 23, 24, 25, 28, 36,
38, 44, 86

KIRK & SMITH

K & S

Abdiel Kirk (c. 1835)
Albany, N.Y.
Bibl. 20

Henry Child Kirk (b. 1827-d.
1894)
Baltimore, Md.
Samuel Kirk & Son (c. 1846-
1861)
Samuel Kirk & Sons (c. 1861-
1868)
Bibl. 15, 23

Henry Child Kirk Jr. (c. 1900-
1901)
Baltimore, Md.
Samuel Kirk & Sons, Inc.
Bibl. 89

Joshua Kirk (c. 1848-1849)
Philadelphia, Pa.
Bibl. 3

Robert Sherman Kirk
(b. 1800-d. 1874, c. 1827-
1833)
Baltimore, Md.
Philadelphia, Pa.
Bibl. 3, 38

S. Kirk & Son (c. 1846-   )
Baltimore, Md.
Bibl. 54

Samuel Kirk (b. 1793-d. 1872,
c. 1815-1822)
Baltimore, Md.
Doylestown, Pa.
Kirk & Smith (c. 1818-1823)
S. Kirk & Son (c. 1846-   )
Samuel Kirk & Son (c. 1846-
1861)
Samuel Kirk & Sons (c. 1861-
1868)
Samuel Kirk, Son & Co.
(c. 1898)
S. Kirk, Sons, Co. Inc.

Bibl. 4, 15, 23, 24, 25, 28, 29, 36,
39, 44, 86

Samuel Kirk & Son (c. 1846-
1861)
Baltimore, Md.
Samuel Kirk
Henry Child Kirk
Bibl. 15, 23, 28, 72, 86

S KIRK & SON

Samuel Kirk, Son & Co.
(c. 1898)
Baltimore, Md.
Bibl. 86

Samuel Kirk & Sons (c. 1861-
1868)
Baltimore, Md.
Samuel Kirk
Charles D. Kirk
Clarence E. Kirk
Henry Child Kirk
Bibl. 15, 86

Samuel Kirk & Sons, Inc.
(c. 1900-1901)
Baltimore, Md.
Henry Child Kirk Jr.
Bibl. 15

J. Kirkham (c. 1840)
Location unknown
Bibl. 24

Samuel W. Kirkland (c. 1828-
1835)
Northampton, Mass.
Fowle & Kirkland (c. 1828-
1833)
Bibl. 84

E. M. Kirkpatrick (c. 1856-
1861)
York, S.C.
Bibl. 5

Peter Kirkwood
Chestertown, Md. (c. 1790-
1795)
Annapolis, Md. (c. 1799-1801)
Bibl. 25, 29, 38, 44

P K

Warner Kirthright (c. 1802)
Baltimore, Md.
Bibl. 38

Joseph P. Kirtland (b. 1770,
w. 1796)
Middletown, Conn.
Bibl. 16, 23, 28, 36, 44

Andrew B. Kitchen (c. 1835-
1837)
Philadelphia, Pa.
Bailey & Kitchen (c. 1833-
1846)
Bibl. 3, 23, 36, 44

Kitts & Stoy (c. 1851-1852)
Louisville, Ky.
John Kitts
David C. Stoy
Bibl. 32

Kitts & Werne (c. 1865-1874)
Louisville, Ky.
John Kitts
Joseph Werne
Bibl. 32, 54, 68

John Kitts (c. 1836-1878)
Louisville, Ky.
Smith & Kitts (c. 1844-1845)
Kitts & Stoy (c. 1851-1852)
John Kitts & Co. (c. 1859-1878)
Kitts & Werne (c. 1865-1874)
Bibl. 25, 32, 44, 54, 68

J. KITTS

John Kitts & Co. (c. 1859-1878)
Louisville, Ky.
Bibl. 32

John Klauer (c. 1842)
St. Louis, Mo.
Bibl. 54

John Klein (c. 1828-1850)
Philadelphia, Pa.
Bibl. 3

John A. Klein (c. 1833-1837)
Leesburg, Va.
Bibl. 19

Jacob Kleiser (Kleizer)
(c. 1822-1824)
Philadelphia, Pa.
Bibl. 3

B. Kline & Co. (c. 1837)
Philadelphia, Pa.
Bartholomew Kline
Bibl. 3, 4, 23, 28, 36, 44

Bartholomew Kline (c. 1837-
1850)
Philadelphia, Pa.

B. Kline & Co. (c. 1837)
Bibl. 3, 23, 36

F. S. Kline & Co. (c. 1850)
Lyons, N.Y.
Foster S. Kline (?)
Bibl. 20

Foster S. Kline (c. 1850)
Syracuse, N.Y.
F. S. Kline & Co. (c. 1850) (?)
Bibl. 20

Peter Kline (c. 1835)
Philadelphia, Pa.
Bibl. 3

Philip Kline
(See Cline)

Joseph Klingle (c. 1823-1825)
Philadelphia, Pa.
Bibl. 3

John J. Klink (d. 1900)
Louisville, Ky. (c. 1841-1859)
Bibl. 32

John Kloebner (c. 1845-1850)
Richmond, Va.
Bibl. 19

B. T. Kluth (c. 1850)
Louisville, Ky.
Bibl. 32

J. Knapp
Location unknown
Bibl. 15, 44

J KNAPP

William Knapp (c. 1764-1768)
Annapolis, Md.
Bibl. 38

Philip Knappe (c. 1839-1841)
Philadelphia, Pa.
Bibl. 3

Christian Kneass (c. 1811-1837)
Philadelphia, Pa.
Bibl. 3

William Kneass (c. 1805-1842)
Philadelphia, Pa.
Horn & Kneass (c. 1811-1837)
Bibl. 3

Joseph I. Kneeland (b. 1698-d.
1760)
Boston, Mass.

Bibl. 2, 4, 15, 23, 24, 25, 28, 29,
36, 44, 60

I. Kneeland

Benjamin Knight (c. 1822)
Painesville, Ohio
Bibl. 34

John W. Knight (c. 1845)
Rochester, N.Y.
Bibl. 20

Philip Knipe (c. 1829-1833)
Philadelphia, Pa.
Bibl. 3

Julius Knock (c. 1845-1850)
Philadelphia, Pa.
Bibl. 3

Knorr & Baker (c. 1830)
Philadelphia, Pa.
James Knorr
————— Baker
Bibl. 3

James Knorr (c. 1828-1829)
Philadelphia, Pa.
Knorr & Baker (c. 1830)
Bibl. 3

Knowles & Ladd (c. 1850)
Location unknown
Bibl. 24

John Knowles (c. 1784)
Philadelphia, Pa.
Bibl. 3

Ebenezer B. Knowlton
(c. 1848)
Cazenovia, N.Y.
Bibl. 20

Henry Knox (c. 1848)
Louisville, Ky.
Bibl. 32

Augustus Koch (c. 1850)
Philadelphia, Pa.
Bibl. 3

Carl Koch (c. 1846-1848)
Philadelphia, Pa.
Bibl. 3

H. Kock (c. 1838-1845)
St. Louis, Mo.
Bibl. 54

Henry Kocksperger (c. 1837)
Philadelphia, Pa.
Bibl. 3

Koesning
(See Harting & Koesning)

Peter Kolb (c. 1829-1850)
Philadelphia, Pa.
Bibl. 3

John Kolby (c. 1807-1808)
Philadelphia, Pa.
Bibl. 3

Abraham I. Kolster (c. 1850)
Syracuse, N.Y.
Bibl. 20

Koontz & Holtzbaum (c. 1793)
Fredericktown, Md.
Henry Koontz Jr.
Jacob Holtzbaum
Bibl. 38

Henry Koontz Jr. (c. 1781?-
1793-   )
Fredericktown, Md.
Koontz & Holtzbaum (c. 1793)
Bibl. 38

Henry Kopke (c. 1850)
New York, N.Y.
Bibl. 23

William Kramer (c. 1848)
Philadelphia, Pa.
Bibl. 3

John Samuel Krause
(w. 1805, d. before 1815)
Bethlehem, Pa.
Bibl. 3, 23, 36, 44

Peter Krebs (c. 1844)
New York, N.Y.
Bibl. 23

Krider & Biddle (c. 1850)
Philadelphia, Pa.
Peter L. Krider
——— Biddle
Bibl. 25, 28, 29, 44

Peter L. Krider (c. 1850)
Philadelphia, Pa.
Krider & Biddle

Bibl. 4, 23, 24, 25, 28, 44, 54
P. L. K.

Jacob Kucher (Kuchler)
(c. 1806-1833)
Philadelphia, Pa.
Bibl. 3, 23, 24, 25, 28,
29, 36, 44
I. KUCHER

O. Kuchler (c. 1850)
New Orleans, La.
Bibl. 15, 25, 44
O. KUCHLER

M. H. Kum (c. 1820)
Location unknown
Bibl. 24

William Kumbel (c. 1780-
1786-   )
New York, N.Y.
Bibl. 23, 36, 44

Henry Kunsman
Fredericksburg, Va. (c. 1819)
Richmond, Va. (c. 1820)
Raleigh, N.C. (c. 1823)
Salisbury, N.C. (c. 1823)
Savage & Kunsman (c. 1823)
Bibl. 19, 21

——— Kurtzborn
(See Bauman & Kurtzborn)

John Kurtz (c. 1823-1824)
Philadelphia, Pa.
Bibl. 3

Francis Labacoone (before
1773)
Georgetown, S.C.
Bibl. 5

Augustus LaBlanc (c. 1819)
Philadelphia, Pa.
Bibl. 3

John Lacey (c. 1819-1825)
Philadelphia, Pa.
Bibl. 3

Peter Lachaise (c. 1794-1808)
New York, N.Y.
Bibl. 23, 36, 44

Henry Lackey (c. 1808-1811)
Philadelphia, Pa.
Bibl. 3

Ladd
(See Knowles & Ladd)

H. H. Ladd (c. 1800)
Location unknown
H. H. Ladd & Co. (c. 1830)
Bibl. 28

H. H. Ladd & Co. (c. 1830)
Location unknown
Bibl. 89
H. H. LADD & CO.

William F. Ladd (c. 1830)
New York, N.Y.
Bibl. 29, 36, 44, 79
WM F. LADD   WM F. LADD

Jacob Ladomus (c. 1843-1850)
Philadelphia, Pa.
Bibl. 3, 15, 25, 44
J. LADOMUS

Lewis Ladomus (c. 1830-1850)
Philadelphia, Pa.
Bibl. 3, 24

John Joseph Lafar (b. 1781-d.
1849)
Charleston, S.C. (c. 1805-1849)
Bibl. 5, 25, 44
LAFAR

Joseph David Lafar (b. 1786-d.
1818)
Charleston, S.C. (c. 1816)
Bibl. 5

Peter X. Lafar (b. 1779-d.
1814)
Charleston, S.C. (c. 1805-1814)
Bibl. 5, 44
L'AFAR

Laforme & Brother (c. 1850)
Boston, Mass.
Bibl. 23

Antoine Laforme (c. 1836)
Boston, Mass.
Bibl. 23, 36, 44

Bernard Laforme (c. 1836)
Boston, Mass.
Bibl. 23, 36

F. J. Laforme (c. 1835)
Boston, Mass.
Bibl. 4, 23, 28, 36, 44

Vincent Laforme (c. 1850)
Boston, Mass.
Bibl. 4, 23, 25, 28, 29, 44
V. LAFORME

Vincent Laforme & Brother
(c. 1850-1855)
Boston, Mass.
Bibl. 15, 25, 44

V. L. & B   V. L & Bro

Lagazze & Sonnier (c. 1814-1816)
Philadelphia, Pa.
John Lagazze
Joseph Sonnier
Bibl. 3

John Lagazze
Philadelphia, Pa.
Lagazze & Sonnier (c. 1814-1816)
Bibl. 3

J. C. La Grange
Charlottesville, Va.
Staunton, Va.
A. Robinson & Co. (c. 1839-1842)
Bibl. 89

Stephen Lain(e)court (c. 1800-1805-   )
New York, N.Y.
Bibl. 23, 36, 44

Ebenezer Knowlton Lakeman
(b. 1799-d. 1857)
Salem, Mass. (c. 1819-1830)
Stevens & Lakeman (c. 1825)
Bibl. 15, 23, 25, 28, 29, 36, 39, 44

E. K. LAKEMAN

John Lalande (Lalarde)
(c. 1844-1850)
Philadelphia, Pa.
Bibl. 3

Benjamin Lamar
(See Benjamin Lemaire)

Matthias Lamar (Lemaire)
(Lemar) (c. 1781-1797)
Philadelphia, Pa.
Bibl. 3, 4, 23, 24, 25, 28, 29, 36, 44, 81

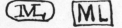

Anthony Lamb (c. 1760)
New York, N.Y.
Bibl. 28

John Lamb (c. 1756)
New York, N.Y.
Bibl. 28

John Lambe (c. 1787)
Baltimore, Md.
Bibl. 23

E. J. Lambers (c. 1821)
Philadelphia, Pa.
Bibl. 3, 23

D. Lambertoz (d. 1817)
Wilmington, N.C. (c. 1795)
Savannah, Ga. (c. 1799)
Bibl. 17, 21

Mathias Lamer
(See Matthias Lamar)

Peter Lamesiere (c. 1811)
Philadelphia, Pa.
Bibl. 3, 23, 36, 44

Lewis Lammel (c. 1843-1850)
Philadelphia, Pa.
Bibl. 3

A. Lamoine
(See A. Lemoine)

Robert Lamont (c. 1842-1845)
Philadelphia, Pa.
Bard & Lamont (c. 1841-1845)
Bibl. 3, 23

Pierre Lamothe (c. 1822)
New Orleans, La.
Pierre Lamothe & Son
Bibl. 23, 24, 25, 29, 36, 44

Pierre Lamothe & Son (c. 1822)
New Orleans, La.
Bibl. 23, 36

Pierre Lamothe & Son

La Motta
(See De La Motta)

Augustus Lamoyne (c. 1816)
Philadelphia, Pa.
Bibl. 3

John Lampe(y)
Annapolis, Md. (c. 1779)
Baltimore, Md. (c. 1780-1787)

Bibl. 36, 38, 44

I L   ?

J. Lamson (c. 1790)
Location unknown
Bibl. 28, 29, 36, 44

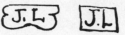

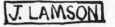

L. Lamson (c. 1800)
Location unknown
Bibl. 24

L Lamson

Augustus Lamvine (Lemvine)
(c. 1811-1816)
Philadelphia, Pa.
Bibl. 3

Americus Lancaster (c. 1842-1850)
Philadelphia, Pa.
Bibl. 3

Arman Lancaster(c. 1837)
Philadelphia, Pa.
Bibl. 3

M. Lancaster (c. 1839)
Philadelphia, Pa.
Bibl. 3

Richard Lancaster (c. 1818-1822)
Philadelphia, Pa.
Rickards & Lancaster
(c. 1817)
Bibl. 3

Lander
Location unknown
Bibl. 15, 44

LANDER

Tobias D. Lander (c. 1826-1833)
Newburgh, N.Y.
Bibl. 20

Lane, Bailey & Co. (c. 1850)
Madison, N.Y.
Bibl. 20

Lane & Bros. (c. 1840)
Clarks Mills, N.Y.
Bibl. 20

Aaron Lane (b. 1753-d. 1819)
Elizabeth, N.J. (c. 1775-1780)
Bibl. 24, 25, 28, 36, 44, 46, 54

James Lane (c. 1803-1818)
Philadelphia, Pa.
Bibl. 3

William Lane (c. 1772-1790)
Nixonton, N.C.
Pasquotank County, N.C.
Bibl. 21

Abraham Lang (c. 1850)
Philadelphia, Pa.
Bibl. 3

Edward Lang (b. 1742-d. 1830)
Salem, Mass.
Bibl. 2, 21, 24, 29, 36, 44, 54

E L   LANG

Jeffrey Lang (b. 1707-d. 1758)
Salem, Mass.
Bibl. 2, 15, 23, 24, 25, 28, 29,
   44, 54, 70

I. LANG   I L
LANG

Lewis W. Lang (c. 1837-1844)
Philadelphia, Pa.
Bibl. 3

Nathaniel Lang (b. 1736-d.
   1826)
Salem, Mass.
Bibl. 15, 25, 44

N. LANG

Richard Lang (b. 1733-d. 1820)
Salem, Mass.
Bibl. 2, 15, 23, 24, 29, 36, 44

R. LANG

William Lange (c. 1844)
New York, N.Y.
Bibl. 23, 24, 25, 29, 44

·LANGE·

Joseph Langer (c. 1811)
Philadelphia, Pa.
Bibl. 3, 23, 36, 44

E. P. Langworthy & Son
   (c. 1814)
Ballston Spa, N.Y.
Elisha Perkins Langworthy
Bibl. 20

Elisha Perkins Langworthy
   (b. 1766-d. 1827)
Ballston Spa, N.Y.
E. P. Langworthy & Son
   (c. 1814)
Bibl. 20, 21

Lyman B. Langworthy (c. 1808-
   1814)
Ballston Spa, N.Y.
Bibl. 20

William Andrews Langworthy
   (c. 1822)
Ballston Spa, N.Y.
Saratoga Springs, N.Y.
Bibl. 20

Gerrit Lansing (b. 1812)
Albany, N.Y. (c. 1838)
Bibl. 20

Jacob Gerritse (Gerrittze)
   Lansing
Albany, N.Y. (b. 1681-d. 1767)
Bibl. 29, 54

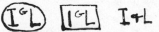

Jacob H. Lansing (c. 1847)
Rochester, N.Y.
Bibl. 20

John (Jacob) Gerrit Lansing
   Jr. (b. 1736-d. 1803)
Albany, N.Y. (c. 1765-1790)
Bibl. 15, 20, 23, 24, 25, 28,
   36, 44, 54

I G L

I^G L   I^G L   I+L

John B. Laperouse (c. 1822)
New Orleans, La.
Bibl. 23, 36, 44

Charles La Place (c. 1795-
   1796)
Wilmington, N.C.
Bibl. 21

———— La Pointe (c. 1795)
Baltimore, Md.
Bibl. 38

Francis Laquain (c. 1794)
Philadelphia, Pa.
Bibl. 3

F. Larchambault (c. 1830)
Location unknown
Bibl. 89

F. LARCHAMBAULT

Alexander E. Larer (c. 1846-
   1850)
Philadelphia, Pa.
Bibl. 3

Laret & Brechémin (c. 1816-
   1818)
Philadelphia, Pa.
Michael Laret
Louis Brechémin
Bibl. 3

Michael Laret (Larit) (c. 1814-
   1818)
Philadelphia, Pa.
Michael Laret
Louis Brechémin
Bibl. 3

Peter Larousse(bierre)
   (c. 1797)
New York, N.Y.
Bibl. 23, 36, 44

Peter L. LaRousselier
   (La Roussitur)
Charleston, S.C. (c. 1803-1809)
Bibl. 5

Elias Larson (c. 1850)
Rochester, N.Y.
Bibl. 20

William La Rue (c. 1847-1849)
Philadelphia, Pa.
Bibl. 3

Larzelere & Moffat (c. 1835)
Buffalo, N.Y.
Abraham Larzelere
William Moffat
Bibl. 20

Abraham Larzelere (c. 1815-
   1835)
Buffalo, N.Y.
Larzelere & Moffat (c. 1835)
Bibl. 20

James E. Lasell (c. 1844-1846)
Troy, N.Y.
Bibl. 20

Luther R. Lasell (c. 1831-
1846)
Troy, N.Y.
Bibl. 20

Peter Lashing (c. 1805)
New York, N.Y.
Bibl. 24, 36, 44

John Latchow (c. 1829)
Baltimore, Md.
Bibl. 38

James Latham (c. 1795)
Albany, N.Y.
Bibl. 20

Rufus Lathrop (b. 1731-d.
1805)
Norwich, Conn.
Bibl. 16, 28, 36, 44

James Latimer (c. 1813-1822)
Philadelphia, Pa.
Bibl. 3

John B. M. La(e)tourn(e)au
(Letourneaux) (b. 1796-d.
1853)
Baltimore, Md.
Bibl. 17, 38

John P. Latruite (c. 1807-1834)
Washington, D.C.
Baltimore, Md.
Alexandria, Va.
Bibl. 19, 36, 44

A. Latta (c. 1837)
Philadelphia, Pa.
Bibl. 3

Orson Lattimer (c. 1832)
Jefferson, Ohio
Bibl. 34

A. Lauder (c. 1840)
Location unknown
Bibl. 24

A LAUDER

George Laval (c. 1842-1843)
Philadelphia, Pa.
Bibl. 3

Peter Laval (c. 1842)
Philadelphia, Pa.
Bibl. 3

William P. Law (c. 1837-1850)
Philadelphia, Pa.
Bibl. 3

Lawing & Brewer (c. 1842-
1843)
Charlotte, N.C.
Samuel Lawing
N. Alexander F. Brewer
Bibl. 21

Samuel Lawing (b. 1807-d.
1865)
Charlotte, N.C.
Lawing & Brewer (c. 1842-
1843)
Bibl. 21

Lawrence
(See Judson & Lawrence)

William Lawler, Carondolet &
Marion (c. 1842)
St. Louis, Mo.
Bibl. 54

William Lawler (c. 1842)
St. Louis, Mo.
Bibl. 54

———— Lawrence (c. 1835)
Philadelphia, Pa.
Bibl. 3

John Lawrence (d. 1798)
Philadelphia, Pa.
Bibl. 3

Joseph Lawrence (c. 1818-
1822)
Philadelphia, Pa.
Bibl. 3

Joseph Lawrence (c. 1839-
1850)
Philadelphia, Pa.
Bibl. 3

Joseph H. Lawrence (c. 1823-
1825)
Philadelphia, Pa.
Bibl. 3

Josiah Lawrence (c. 1817-
1837)
Philadelphia, Pa.
Bibl. 3

Josiah H. Lawrence (c. 1817-
1824)
Philadelphia, Pa.
Bibl. 23, 36, 44

L. U. Lawrence (c. 1812)
Augusta, Ga.
Bibl. 17

Martin M. Lawrence (c. 1832-
1840)
New York, N.Y.
Bibl. 15, 25, 44

M M LAWRENCE

Robert D. Lawrie (c. 1840-
1850)
Philadelphia, Pa.
Taylor & Lawrie (c. 1837-1850)
Taylor, Lawrie & Wood
(after 1841)
Bibl. 3, 4, 28

Robert O. Lawrie (c. 1840)
Philadelphia, Pa.
Bibl. 23, 36, 44

John Lawrison (c. 1791)
Alexandria, Va.
Bibl. 19, 54

John Laws (c. 1818-1830)
Philadelphia, Pa.
Bibl. 3

Alexander Lawson (c. 1794-
1799)
Philadelphia, Pa.
Bibl. 3

Peter Laycock (c. 1750)
Philadelphia, Pa.
Bibl. 44

Moses Lazarus (c. 1830)
Philadelphia, Pa.
Bibl. 3

Francis Lea (w. 1789, d. 1805)
Fayette County, Ky.
Lexington, Ky.
Bibl. 32, 54, 68

Samuel I. (J.) Lea (Lee)
Baltimore, Md. (c. 1814-1822)
Bibl. 15, 24, 25, 29, 44

Leach & Bennett (c. 1856-1858)
Utica, N.Y.
Almon Leach
L. M. Bennett
Bibl. 18

Leach & Bradley (c. 1832-1835)
Utica, N.Y.
Ebenezer Leach
Horace S. Bradley
Bibl. 18, 20, 23, 28, 36, 44

Leach & Davies (c. 1835-1840)
Utica, N.Y.
Ebenezer Leach
Thomas Davies
Bibl. 18, 20

Almon Leach (b. 1823)
Utica, N.Y. (c. 1845-1858)
Hawley & Leach (c. 1853-1856)
Leach & Bennett
L. M. Bennett
Bibl. 18, 20

Charles Leach (b. 1765-d. 1814)
Boston, Mass.
Bibl. 23, 24, 25, 28, 29, 36, 44

Charles B. Leach (c. 1843-1847)
Utica, N.Y.
Bibl. 18, 20

Ebenezer Leach (c. 1797)
Utica, N.Y. (c. 1832-1840)
Leach & Bradley (c. 1832-1835)
Leach & Davies (c. 1832-1840)
Bibl. 18, 20

George Leach (c. 1854-1857)
Utica, N.Y.
Hawley & Leach (c. 1853-1856)
Bibl. 18

John Leach (c. 1780)
Boston, Mass.
Bibl. 23, 36, 44

Leonard D. Leach (c. 1850)
Auburn, N.Y.
Haight & Leach
Bibl. 20

Nathaniel Leach (c. 1789)
Boston, Mass.
Bibl. 4, 15, 23, 25, 28, 36, 44

N. L

Samuel Leach (c. 1741-1780)
Philadelphia, Pa.

Bibl. 3, 23, 24, 28, 29, 36, 44

S. L

John I. Leacock (c. 1748-1799)
Philadelphia, Pa.
Bibl. 3, 15, 23, 24, 25, 28, 29, 30, 36, 39, 44, 54, 81

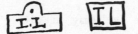

I Leacock

Peter Leacock (c. 1750)
Philadelphia, Pa.
Bibl. 36

William League (b. 1798)
Baltimore, Md. (c. 1815)
Bibl. 38

Leavenworth, Brown & Co. (c. 1836)
Binghamton, N.Y.
Bibl. 20

John Lebeau (c. 1848)
St. Louis, Mo.
Bibl. 54

Christian David Lebey (c. 1787-1827)
Savannah, Ga.
McConky & Lebey (c. 1811-1812)
Bibl. 17

Lewis Le Blanc (c. 1818)
Philadelphia, Pa.
Bibl. 3, 23, 36, 44

Henry Leclere (c. 1791-1826)
Savannah, Ga.
Bibl. 17

Joseph J. Leddel (c. 1752)
New York, N.Y.
Bibl. 28

Joseph Ledell (c. 1797)
Philadelphia, Pa.
Bibl. 23, 36, 44

S. E. Ledman (19th century)
Louisville, Ky.
Bibl. 32, 54

———— Le Dore (c. 1797)
Philadelphia, Pa.
Bibl. 3, 23, 36, 44

Lee
(See Roberts & Lee)

Samuel I. (J.) Lee
(See Lea)

George Lee (c. 1837-1850)
Philadelphia, Pa.
Bibl. 3, 38

John A. Lee (c. 1840-1850)
Mansfield, Ohio
Bibl. 34

Samuel W. Lee (b. 1785-d. 1861, c. 1815-1822)
Providence, R.I. (c. 1815)
Rochester, N.Y. (c. 1822)
Burr & Lee (c. 1815)
Scofield & Lee (c. 1822)
Bibl. 15, 20, 23, 24, 25, 29, 36, 41, 44

S W L   S. LEE

S. W. LEE

Samuel W. Lee Jr. (c. 1849-1850)
Rochester, N.Y.
Bibl. 20, 41, 44

Thomas Lee (b. 1717-d. 1806)
Farmington, Conn.
Martin Bull
Bibl. 28

Thomas Lee (c. 1799-1807-   )
Savannah, Ga.
Bibl. 17

Gideon H. Leeds (c. 1841-1842)
Philadelphia, Pa.
Bibl. 3

Howard G. Leeds (c. 1840)
Philadelphia, Pa.
Bibl. 3

Peter Leevell (c. 1841)
Philadelphia, Pa.
Bibl. 3

Lefevre & Gravelle (c. 1811)
Philadelphia, Pa.
John Felix Lefevre
Bibl. 3, 23, 36, 44

F. Lefevre (c. 1818)
Philadelphia, Pa.
Bibl. 3, 23, 36, 44

John Felix Lefevre (d. 1813)
Philadelphia, Pa. (c. 1806-1813)
Lefevre & Gravelle (c. 1811)
Bibl. 3, 23, 36, 44

Theodore Lefevre (c. 1820-1822)
Philadelphia, Pa.
Bibl. 3

Lefferts & Hall (c. 1818-1822)
Philadelphia, Pa.
Charles Lefferts
——— Hall
Bibl. 3

Charles Lefferts (c. 1818-1822)
Philadelphia, Pa.
Lefferts & Hall
Bibl. 3

Charles Lefferts (c. 1827)
Ovid, N.Y.
Bibl. 20

Daniel Legare (b. 1688-d. 1724)
Boston, Mass.
Bibl. 28, 44

Francis Legare (b. 1636-d. 1711)
Boston, Mass.
Bibl. 23, 28, 36, 44

Solomon Legare (b. 1674-1760)
Charleston, S.C. (c. 1696-1740)
Bibl. 5

Louis Andrew Legay (c. 1842-1845)
Columbus, Ga.
Bibl. 17

John F. Legoux (c. 1797-1811)
Savannah, Ga.
Bibl. 17

John Francis Le Gras (c. 1796)
Baltimore, Md.
Philippe & Le Gras
Bibl. 38

Nicholas Le Huray (c. 1809-1831)
Philadelphia, Pa.
Bibl. 3, 15, 44

N. LE HURAY

Nicholas J. Le Huray Jr. (c. 1821-1846)
Philadelphia, Pa.

Bibl. 3, 15, 25, 44

N. LE HURAY JR

Theodore Le Huray (c. 1843-1850)
Philadelphia, Pa.
Bibl. 3

Nathaniel Augustine Leinbach (c. 1850-1860)
Salem, N.C.
Bibl. 21

Traugott Leinbach (b. 1796-d. 1863)
Salem, N.C. (c. 1821-1860)
Bibl. 21

Joseph Leland (c. 1846)
Philadelphia, Pa.
Bibl. 3

Joseph Lelurge (c. 1817-1822)
Philadelphia, Pa.
Bibl. 3

Baptiste Lemaire (Lemar) (c. 1804)
Philadelphia, Pa.
Bibl. 3, 23, 36

Benjamin Lemaire (Lemar) (Lamar) (d. 1785)
Philadelphia, Pa.
Bibl. 15, 23, 25

BL   LAMAR

Mathias Lemaire (Lemar) (Lamar)
(See Matthias Lamar)
Bibl. 36

Matthew Le Merre (c. 1781)
Philadelphia, Pa.
Bibl. 3

Lemist & Tappan (c. 1818-1819)
Philadelphia, Pa.
William Lemist
William B. Tappan
Bibl. 3

William Lemist (c. 1816-1819)
Philadelphia, Pa.
Lemist & Tappan (c. 1818-1819)
Bibl. 3

A. Lemoine (Limone) (c. 1810-1817)
Philadelphia, Pa.
Bibl. 3

Lemon & Kendrick (c. 1831-1842)
Louisville, Ky.
James Innes Lemon
William Kendrick
Bibl. 32, 54, 68

Lemon & Son (after 1861)
Louisville, Ky.
James Innes Lemon
Bibl. 68

James I. Lemon & Co. (c. 1859-1861)
Louisville, Ky.
James Innes Lemon
Edmund J. Daumont
Bibl. 32

James Innes Lemon (b. 1804-d. 1869)
Louisville, Ky. (c. 1828-1869)
Lexington, Ky.
Lemon & Kendrick (c. 1831-1842)
James I. Lemon & Co. (c. 1859-1861)
Lemon & Son (after 1861)
Bibl. 32, 54, 68

Lemvine
(See Lamvine)

Peter Lench (c. 1805-1809)
New York, N.Y.
Bibl. 23, 36

M. Lendigree (c. 1814)
New York, N.Y.
Bibl. 23, 36, 44

Lendner
(See Lindner)

G. Lenhart (19th century)
Bowling Green, Ky.
Bibl. 15, 25, 32, 44, 54, 68

G Lenhart

Raimond Lenoir (c. 1818)
Savannah, Ga.
Bibl. 17

William Lenoir (Lenon)
Philadelphia, Pa. (c. 1843-
1850)
Bibl. 3

Andrew Lenormant
(Lenorment)
Charleston, S.C. (c. 1801-1810)
Bibl. 5

John Lent (c. 1751-1791)
New York, N.Y.
Philadelphia, Pa.
Bibl. 23, 25, 28, 36, 44

Lentner
(See Lindner)

George K. Lentz (c. 1825)
Philadelphia, Pa.
Bibl. 3, 15, 44

Leonard & Rogers (c. 1831-
1833)
New York, N.Y.
Allen Leonard
———— Rogers
Bibl. 15

Leonard & Wilson (c. 1847-
1850)
Philadelphia, Pa.
Allen Leonard
———— Wilson
Bibl. 3, 23, 25, 44

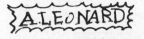

Allen Leonard (c. 1827-1840)
New York, N.Y.
Bibl. 15, 23, 25, 44

Allen Leonard (c. 1844-1850)
Philadelphia, Pa.
Bibl. 3, 36

D. Gillis Leonard (c. 1841-
1847)
Newburgh, N.Y.
Haight & Leonard (c. 1847)
Bibl. 20

J. Leonard
Location unknown
Bibl. 15, 44

Jacob Leonard (c. 1828)
Fredericksburg, Va.
Bibl. 19

Samuel T. Leonard (b. 1786-d.
1848, c. 1805-1848)
Baltimore, Md.
Chestertown, Md.
Lynch & Leonard (c. 1805-
1840)
Bibl. 24, 25, 29, 38

Alexander Le Page (c. 1818)
Philadelphia, Pa.
Bibl. 3

Edward Leppleman (c. 1836-
1839)
Buffalo, N.Y.
Bibl. 20

Peter Leret (Le Ret) (c. 1787-
1802)
Baltimore, Md.
Carlisle, Pa.
Philadelphia, Pa.
Bibl. 15, 23, 24, 28, 29, 36, 38,
44, 50

Bartholomew Le Roux (b.
1663)
New York, N.Y. (c. 1689-
1713)
Bibl. 2, 15, 23, 24, 25, 28, 29, 35,
36, 44, 54

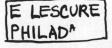

Bartholomew Le Roux II (b.
1720-d. 1763)
New York, N.Y.

Bibl. 4, 15, 23, 25, 35, 44

Charles Le Roux (b. 1689-d.
1745)
New York, N.Y. (c. 1713-1745)
Bibl. 2, 4, 15, 23, 24, 25, 28, 29,
30, 35, 36, 44, 54

John Le Roux (c. 1716-1725)
Albany, N.Y.
New York, N.Y.
Bibl. 4, 15, 20, 23, 24, 25, 28,
29, 30, 36, 44, 54

Alexander Le Row (c. 1827)
Flycreek, N.Y.
Bibl. 20

Abraham Le Roy (c. 1757, d.
1763)
Lancaster, Pa.
Bibl. 3

John Leroy (c. 1827-1832)
New York, N.Y.
Bibl. 15

Edward P. Lescare (Lescure)
Philadelphia, Pa. (c. 1822-1850)
Bibl. 3, 15, 23, 24, 25, 36, 44

Louis Leschot (d. 1838)
Charlottesville, Va. (c. 1836)
Bibl. 19

John Lesfauries (c. 1800)
Baltimore, Md.
Bibl. 38

Francis Lesfro (c. 1802)
Baltimore, Md.
Bibl. 38

Leslie & Parry (c. 1803)
Philadelphia, Pa.

Robert Leslie
———— Parry
Bibl. 3

Leslie & Price (c. 1793-1800)
Philadelphia, Pa.
Robert Leslie
Isaac Price
Abraham Patton
Bibl. 3

Robert Leslie (d. 1804)
Philadelphia, Pa. (c. 1788-
1803)
Baltimore, Md. (c. 1795-1796)
(?)
Leslie & Price (c. 1793-1800)
Leslie & Parry (c. 1803)
Robert Leslie & Co. (c. 1795-
1796) (?)
Bibl. 3, 38

Robert Leslie & Co. (c. 1795-
1796)
Baltimore, Md.
Robert Leslie (?)
Abraham Patton
Bibl. 38

William Lesser (c. 1859)
Orangeburg, S.C.
Bibl. 5

J. U. Lester (c. 1843-1845)
Oswego, N.Y.
Bibl. 20

Talbot G. Lester (c. 1831-1840)
Portsmouth, Va.
Bibl. 19

John (I.) Letelier (Letellier)
Philadelphia, Pa. (c. 1770-
1793)
Bibl. 3, 15, 23, 24, 25, 28, 29,
36, 81

I L T   I LETELLER

John (I.) Letelier (Le Telier)
Wilmington, Del. (c. 1793)
Bibl. 30

I L T   LeTeLier

I. LETELIER

John Letelier (Le Telier) (c.
1800-1810)
Washington, D.C.
Alexandria, Va.
Richmond, Va.
Bibl. 54

J L T

Letourneau & Pearson (c. 1802-
1803)
Savannah, Ga.
John Letourneau
John Pearson
Bibl. 17

John Letourneau (d. 1803)
Savannah, Ga.
Letourneau & Pearson (c. 1802-
1803)
Bibl. 17

M. Letourneau(x) (c. 1797)
Quebec, Canada
New York, N.Y.
Bibl. 17, 23, 36, 44

Letourneaux
(See preceding entry)
(See La[e]tourn[e]au)

Henry Leuba (19th century)
Lexington, Ky.
Bibl. 54

George Levely (c. 1774-1796)
Baltimore, Md.
Philadelphia, Pa.
Bibl. 3, 23, 36, 38, 44

Knight Leverett (c. 1703-1753)
Boston, Mass.
Bibl. 2, 4, 15, 23, 24, 25, 28, 29,
36, 78

K L   K Leverett

K LEVERETT

Lewis Levering (c. 1835)
Philadelphia, Pa.
Bibl. 3

Garretson Levi (c. 1840-1843)
Philadelphia, Pa.
Bibl. 3

Isaac Levi (c. 1780)
Philadelphia, Pa.
Bibl. 3

Jeremiah Levi (c. 1750)
Pickawaxon, Md.
Bibl. 38

William Levis (c. 1810-1814)
Philadelphia, Pa.
Bibl. 3, 23, 36

Abraham Levy (c. 1813)
Charleston, S.C.
Bibl. 5

Henry A. Levy (c. 1841-1850)
Philadelphia, Pa.
Bibl. 3

John I. Levy (c. 1818-1822)
Norfolk, Va.
Bibl. 19

Jona(e)s Levy (c. 1835-1838)
New York, N.Y.
Bibl. 15, 25, 44, 89

J. LEVY   ?

Joseph Levy (c. 1824)
Cincinnati, Ohio
Bibl. 34

Lewis B. Levy (c. 1841-1845)
Philadelphia, Pa.
Bibl. 3

M. Levy & Co. (c. 1816-1817)
Philadelphia, Pa.
Bibl. 3

Martin Levy (c. 1814-1817)
Philadelphia, Pa.
Bibl. 3

Michael Levy (c. 1802-1816)
Philadelphia, Pa.
Bibl. 3

Michael & Isaac Levy (c. 1785)
Maryland
Bibl. 38

Gabriel Lewin (c. 1773)
Baltimore, Md.
Bibl. 4, 23, 24, 28, 36

G L

Lewis
(See Sterret & Lewis)

———— Lewis (c. 1796)
Philadelphia, Pa.
Bibl. 3

Lewis & Co. (c. 1854-1856)
York, S.C.
J. N. Lewis
Bibl. 5

Lewis & Smith (c. 1805-1811)
Philadelphia, Pa.
Bibl. 3, 4, 23, 24, 25, 28, 29, 36,
39, 44, 80

Lewis & Smith

LEWIS + SMITH

C. C. Lewis (c. 1844-1847)
Staunton, Va.
Bibl. 19

Frederick H. Lewis (c. 1850)
Rochester, N.Y.
Bibl. 20

Harvey Lewis (c. 1811-1826)
Philadelphia, Pa.
Bibl. 3, 4, 15, 23, 24, 25, 28, 29,
36, 39, 54, 72

{ H LEWIS }
[H. LEWIS]

Isaac Lewis (b. 1773-d. 1860)
Huntington, Conn.
Ridgefield, Conn.
Bibl. 15, 16, 23, 24, 25, 28, 29,
36, 44, 46

[I LEWIS]

Isaac Lewis (c. 1782)
Newark, N.J.
Bibl. 46, 54

J. H. Lewis (c. 1810)
Albany, N.Y.
Bibl. 25, 44

J. N. Lewis
York, S.C.
J. N. Lewis & Co. (c. 1854)
Lewis & Co. (c. 1854-1856)
Bibl. 5

J. N. Lewis & Co. (c. 1854)
York, S.C.
J. N. Lewis
Jordan Bennett (?)
D. W. Wilson
Bibl. 5

John M. (I.) Lewis (c. 1830-
1850)
Philadelphia, Pa.
Johnson & Lewis (c. 1837-1842)
(?)
Bibl. 3, 15

[J I LEWIS]

John V. Lewis (1847-1852)
Utica, N.Y.
Bibl. 18, 20

Jonathan Lewis (c. 1797)
Poughkeepsie, N.Y.
Bibl. 20

Tunis Lewis (c. 1805)
New York, N.Y.
Bibl. 23, 36, 44

William Lewis (c. 1813)
Batavia, N.Y.
Bibl. 20

Gabriel Lewyn (c. 1768-1780)
Baltimore, Md.
Bibl. 25, 29, 38, 44, 54

John A. L'Hommedieu (d.
1867)
Mobile, Ala. (c. 1830)
William T. L'Hommedieu (c.
1830)
Bibl. 54

[L'Hommedieu]
[J. A. L'Hommedieu]

John A. & William T.
L'Hommedieu
Mobile, Ala. (c. 1830)
Bibl. 54

[L'H. Bros]

William T. L'Hommedieu (c.
1830, d. 1834)
Mobile, Ala.
John A. L'Hommedieu (c.
1830)
Bibl. 54

Lhulier (Luhlier) (Lunier) &
Co. (c. 1846)
Philadelphia, Pa.
Bibl. 3

Cassimer (Cashmere) Lhulier
(Luhlier) (Lunier) (c. 1825-
1850)
Philadelphia, Pa.
Bibl. 3

Lewis Lhulier (Luhlier)
(Lunier) (c. 1829-1849)
Philadelphia, Pa.
Bibl. 3

Jacob G. L. Libby (c. 1820-
1846)
Boston, Mass.
Bibl. 24, 25, 28, 29, 44
[J G Libby] [Libby]
[J. G. L. Libby]

John Lidden (c. 1850)
St. Louis, Mo.

Bibl. 24, 25, 44
[LIDDEN]

James Lightfoot (b. 1726)
New York, N.Y. (c. 1749)
Bibl. 23, 36, 44

J. H. Lillie (c. 1837)
Elmira, N.Y.
Badger & Lillie
Bibl. 20

John Limeburner (c. 1790-
1791)
Philadelphia, Pa.
Bibl. 3

Limone
(See Lemoine)

Peter Linch (c. 1805)
New York, N.Y.
Bibl. 23, 36, 44

Lincoln & Foss (c. 1850)
Boston, Mass.
A. L. Lincoln
——— Foss
Bibl. 15, 23, 24, 25, 29, 36, 44,
54, 89

[LINCOLN & FOSS]

Lincoln & Green (c. 1790-
1810)
Boston, Mass.
Bibl. 24, 25, 28, 29, 44

{ L&G }

Lincoln and Reed (Read) (c.
1835-1846)
Boston, Mass.
Bibl. 15, 23, 24, 25, 28, 29, 36,
44, 89

[LINCOLN & READ]

A. L. Lincoln (c. 1820-1850)
Boston, Mass. (c. 1850-1865)
St. Louis, Mo.
Lincoln & Foss (c. 1850)
Haddock, Lincoln & Foss (c.
1850-1865)
Bibl. 15, 24, 25, 44

[A L Lincoln]

Elijah Lincoln (c. 1818-1833)
(b. 1794-d. 1861)
Hingham, Mass.

Bibl. 15, 23, 25, 28, 29, 36

E. Lincoln

John Lind (Linn) (c. 1775-
1805)
Philadelphia, Pa.
Bibl. 3

Charles Linder (c. 1811)
Geneva, N.Y.
Bibl. 20

George Lindner (Lendner)
(Lentner) (c. 1837-1850)
Philadelphia, Pa.
Bibl. 3, 23, 36, 44

William Lindsay (c. 1839-1841)
Portsmouth, Ohio
Bibl. 34

William K. Lindsay (c.
1839-   )
Wheeling, Va.
Bibl. 19

Thomas Lindsey (c. 1799)
Philadelphia, Pa.
Bibl. 3

Clark Lindsley (c. 1843-1850)
Hartford, Conn.
Bibl. 23, 25, 44

C. LINDSLEY

Ben Linebaugh (c. 1825)
Russellville, Ky.
Bibl. 32, 54

John Linerd (c. 1816)
Philadelphia, Pa.
Bibl. 3

James Lines (c. 1839)
Charleston, S.C.
Bibl. 5

Henry Lingley (c. 1810)
New York, N.Y.
Bibl. 23, 36, 44

Peter Link (c. 1811-1822)
Philadelphia, Pa.
Bibl. 3, 23, 36, 44

Linn
(See Lind)

Robert Linn (c. 1831)
Pendleton, S.C.
Bibl. 5

——— Lintot (c. 1762)
New York, N.Y.
Bibl. 28, 36, 44

Lipincott
(See Lippincott)

Abraham Lipman
Charleston, S.C. (c. 1816-
1821)
Columbia, S.C. (c. 1822-1830)
Bibl. 5

Joseph Lippincott (Lipincott)
Haddonfield, N.J. (c. 1768-
1788)
Bibl. 46, 54

Robert Lisenbee (c. 1860)
Abbeville, S.C.
Bibl. 5

——— Lisset (c. 1819)
Philadelphia, Pa.
Bibl. 3

List & Smith (Smith & List) (c.
1847)
Philadelphia, Pa.
John List (?)
——— Smith
Bibl. 3

John List (c. 1837-1850)
Philadelphia, Pa.
List & Smith (c. 1847) (?)
Bibl. 3

Archibald Little (c. 1839-1840)
Camden, N.J.
Philadelphia, Pa.
Bibl. 3

John Little (c. 1823-1838)
Martinsburg, Va.
Bibl. 19

Paul Little (b. 1740, c. 1761-
1776)
Windham, Conn.
Portland, Me.
Butler & Little (c. 1759-1765)
Bibl. 15, 23, 25, 36, 44

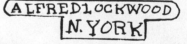

Peter Little (b. 1775-d. 1830)
Baltimore, Md. (c. 1796-1816)
Bibl. 38

Thomas Little (c. 1813-1819)
Philadelphia, Pa.
Bibl. 3

William Little (c. 1775)
Newbury, Mass.
Bibl. 14, 15, 24, 25, 28, 29, 36,
44

William Little (c. 1813-1819)
Philadelphia, Pa.
Bibl. 3

T. Hodgman Littleton (after
1800)
Location unknown
Bibl. 28

Henry Livingston (c. 1731)
Charleston, S.C.
Bibl. 5

H. Lloyd (c. 1836-1842)
Cooperstown, N.Y.
Bibl. 20

W. A. Lloyd (c. 1810)
Philadelphia, Pa.
Bibl. 54

L. or I. Lockward
Location unknown
Bibl. 15, 44

LOCKWARD

——— Lockwood (c. 1841)
Newburgh, N.Y.
Pratt & Lockwood
Bibl. 20

Alfred (A.) Lockwood (c.
1817-1837)
New York, N.Y.
Bibl. 15, 23, 24, 25, 29, 36, 44

ALFRED LOCKWOOD
N. YORK

A · LOCKWOOD

Charles Lockwood (c. 1817)
New York, N.Y.
Bibl. 15

Frederick Lockwood (c. 1828-
1845)
New York, N.Y.

Bibl. 4, 23, 24, 25, 28, 29, 44

[F LOCKWOOD]

James Lockwood (c. 1799-
1838)
New York, N.Y.
Bibl. 15, 23, 24, 25, 36, 44

[J. LOCKWOOD]

[LOCKWOOD]

Laetitia Locton (c. 1811)
Philadelphia, Pa.
Bibl. 3

Lewis Lodds (c. 1836-1837)
Buffalo, N.Y.
Bibl. 20

Peter Lodds (c. 1836-1837)
Buffalo, N.Y.
Bibl. 20

John J. Loew (c. 1816-1848)
Philadelphia, Pa.
Bibl. 3

Purnel Lolland (d. 1825)
Philadelphia, Pa. (c. 1810)
Bibl. 3, 23, 36, 44

Adam Logan (c. 1803-1823)
New York, N.Y.
Bibl. 23, 24, 25, 29, 36, 44

[A. LOGAN]

James Logan (c. 1769)
Philadelphia, Pa.
Bibl. 3, 23, 36, 44

Richard Logan (c. 1837)
Albany, N.Y.
Bibl. 20

Robert Logan (c. 1819)
St. Louis, Mo.
Bibl. 54

Lohse & Kayser (c. 1831-1835)
Philadelphia, Pa.
Bibl. 3

Barthelemy Edouard Lombard
(c. 1800-1830)
Charleston, S.C.
Bibl. 5, 25, 44

LOMBARD

Asa Lond
(See Asa Loud)

Andrew K. Long (c. 1837-
1844)
Philadelphia, Pa.
Bibl. 3, 23, 36, 44

George W. Long (c. 1837-
1850)
Philadelphia, Pa.
Bibl. 3

N. Long
Location unknown
Bibl. 15, 44

[N LONG]

Robert Long (b. 1753, c. 1774)
Maryland
Bibl. 28, 38

Robert M. Long (c. 1832-
1837)
Buffalo, N.Y.
Bibl. 20

Samuel R. Long (c. 1842-1846)
Philadelphia, Pa.
Bibl. 3

William Long (c. 1807-1822)
Philadelphia, Pa.
Bibl. 3, 23, 36, 44

Longley & Dodge (c. 1810)
Charleston, S.C.
Bibl. 5, 25, 44

Henry Longl(e)y (c. 1810)
New York, N.Y.
Bibl. 23, 24, 25, 29, 36, 44

[H. Longley]

Loomis and Ralph (c. 1819-
1838)
Frankfort, Ky. (c. 1819)
Bibl. 32, 54, 68

G. Loomis & Co. (c. 1850)
Erie, Pa.
Bibl. 24, 25, 44

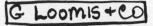

W. P. Loomis
Louisville, Ky.
Bibl. 54

Worham P. Loomis (c. 1819-
1854)
Frankfort, Ky.
Bibl. 32, 54

W P Loomis

John Lorange (c. 1837-1850)
Philadelphia, Pa.
Bibl. 3

———— Lord (c. 1792)
Fayetteville, N.C.
Lord & Gale
Bibl. 21

Lord & Gale (c. 1792)
Fayetteville, N.C.
———— Lord
Joseph Gale
Bibl. 21

Lord & Goddard (c. 1797-
1807)
Rutland, Vt.
Benjamin Lord
Nicholas Goddard
Bibl. 54

Lord & Smith (c. 1824-1829)
New York, N.Y.
Jabez C. Lord
George Smith
Bibl. 15, 36, 44

B. B. Lord & Co. (c. 1830-
1839)
Athens, Ga.
Benjamin B. Lord
Ebenezer Lord
Joel White
Bibl. 17

Benjamin Lord (b. 1770-d.
1843)
Pittsfield, Mass. (1796)
Rutland, Vt. (c. 1797-1807)
Athens, Ga. (c. 1831)
Norwich, Conn.
Lord & Goddard (c. 1797-
1807)
B. B. Lord & Co. (c. 1830-
1839)
William P. Sage
Bibl. 15, 17, 23, 24, 25, 36, 44

[B. LORD]

Ebenezer Lord (c. 1801-1838)
Athens, Ga.
B. B. Lord & Co. (c. 1830-1839)
Bibl. 17

H. Lord & Co. (c. 1805-)
Savannah, Ga.
Hezekiah Lord
Cornelius Paulding
Isaac Marquand
Bibl. 17

Hezekiah Lord (c. 1805)
Savannah, Ga.
H. Lord & Co.
Bibl. 17

Jabez C. Lord (c. 1825-1840)
New York, N.Y.
Lord & Smith (c. 1824-1829)
Bibl. 15, 23, 24, 25, 29, 36, 44

J. LORD   J. LORD

Joseph Lord (d. 1795)
Philadelphia, Pa.
Bibl. 3

Joseph Lord (c. 1815)
Philadelphia, Pa.
Bibl. 23, 36, 44

T. Lord (c. 1825)
Location unknown
Bibl. 15, 49

T. LORD

Peter Lorin (c. 1751)
New York, N.Y.
Bibl. 44

Eliphalet (Elijah) Loring (b. 1740, c. 1744-1782)
Barnstable, Mass.
Boston, Mass.
Bibl. 15, 23, 24, 25, 28, 29, 36, 44

E. Loring

Henry Loring (b. 1773-d. 1818)
Boston, Mass. (c. 1794)
Bibl. 2, 15, 23, 24, 28, 36

H L

Joseph Loring (b. 1743-d. 1815, c. 1785-1796)
Boston, Mass.
Hull, Mass.

Bibl. 2, 15, 23, 24, 25, 28, 29, 36, 39, 44, 54

J. Loring

I. Loring

J. Loring   J. L.

J. Loring

Lormger
Lorronge
Lorronger
(See Lorange)

Benson John Lossing (b. 1813-d. 1891)
Poughkeepsie, N.Y.
Henderson & Lossing (c. 1835)
Bibl. 2, 20, 28

Benjamin C. Lotier (c. 1846-1847)
Philadelphia, Pa.
Bibl. 3, 23

Asa Loud (Lond) (b. 1765-d. 1823)
Hartford, Conn. (c. 1792)
Bibl. 16, 23, 28, 36, 44

Benjamin Louderback (c. 1830-1845)
Philadelphia, Pa.
Bibl. 3

George Loughlin (c. 1849-1850)
Philadelphia, Pa.
Bibl. 3

Lawrence Loughlin (c. 1848)
Philadelphia, Pa.
Bibl. 3

A. D. Louiset (c. 1816-1817)
Philadelphia, Pa.
Bibl. 3

Daniel Love (c. 1817-1840)
Liberty, Va. (now Bedford)
Lynchburg, Va.
Bibl. 19

James Love (c. 1832-1836)
Louisville, Ky.
Bibl. 32, 54, 68

John Love (c. 1801-1809)
Charleston, S.C.
Bibl. 5

Lovell & Smith (c. 1841-1843)
Philadelphia, Pa.
Bibl. 3

A. E. Lovell (c. 1844-1849)
Philadelphia, Pa.
Bibl. 3

Peter Lovell (c. 1837)
Philadelphia, Pa.
Bibl. 3

Robert Lovett (c. 1818-1838)
New York, N.Y.
Philadelphia, Pa.
Bibl. 3, 15, 25, 44

LOVETT

Robert Lovett Jr. (c. 1840-1850)
Philadelphia, Pa.
Bibl. 3

Low(s), Ball & Co. (c. 1840)
Boston, Mass.
John B. Jones
S. S. Ball(?)
——— Low
Bibl. 2, 15, 23, 25, 28, 36, 44

LOWS, BALL & COMPANY

Francis Low (b. 1806-d. 1855)
Boston, Mass.
John J. Low & Co. (c. 1828)
Bibl. 15, 23, 28, 36, 44

John J. Low & Co. (c. 1828)
Boston, Mass.
John J. Low
Francis Low
Bibl. 15, 24, 25, 28, 29, 36, 44, 54

J J LOW & CO   LOW & CO

John J. (S.) Low (b. 1800-d. 1876, c. 1821-1828)
Boston, Mass.
Salem, Mass.
Bibl. 23, 25, 28, 36, 44

J. J. LOW

Joseph J. Low (c. 1843-1850)
Philadelphia, Pa.
Bibl. 3

Mark Low (c. 1847-1850)
Philadelphia, Pa.
Bibl. 3

Peter Low (c. 1832-1837)
Buffalo, N.Y.
Bibl. 20

Joshua Lowe (c. 1828-1833)
New York, N.Y.
Bibl. 15, 25, 44

Lowell & Senter (c. 1830)
Portland, Me.
Bibl. 25, 28, 44

A. Lowell (c. 1830)
Location unknown
Bibl. 24, 89

| A LOWELL |

Lowens
(See Lownes)

Isaac Lower (c. 1844-1846)
Philadelphia, Pa.
Bibl. 3

Jacob Lower (c. 1833-1850)
Philadelphia, Pa.
Bibl. 3

Joseph Lower (c. 1803-1831)
Philadelphia, Pa.
Bibl. 3, 23, 24, 25, 29, 36, 44

| LOWER |

Theodore O. Lower (c. 1844)
Philadelphia, Pa.
Bibl. 3

William Lower (c. 1837-1848)
Philadelphia, Pa.
Bibl. 3

F. N. Lown
Location unknown
Bibl. 89

Isaac Lowner (c. 1844)
Philadelphia, Pa.
Bibl. 23

Jacob Lowner (c. 1833)
Philadelphia, Pa.
Bibl. 23, 36, 44

William Lowner (c. 1837)
Philadelphia, Pa.
Bibl. 23, 36, 44

Lownes & Erwin (c. 1816)
Philadelphia, Pa.
Joseph Lownes
John Erwin
Bibl. 3, 23, 36, 44

Caleb Lownes (c. 1779)
Philadelphia, Pa.
Bibl. 3

David Lownes (d. 1810)
Philadelphia, Pa. (c. 1785-
1807)
Bibl. 3

Edward Lownes (d. 1834)
Philadelphia, Pa. (c. 1806-
1833)
Bibl. 3, 4, 15, 23, 24, 25, 28, 29,
36, 39, 44

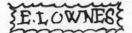

Hyatt Lownes (c. 1792)
Hagerstown, Md.
Bibl. 38

J. & J. H. Lownes (c. 1816-
1819)
Philadelphia, Pa.
Joseph Lownes
Josiah H. Lownes
Bibl. 3, 4, 23, 28, 36, 44

Joseph Lownes (b. 1754-d.
1816)
Philadelphia, Pa.
Lownes & Erwin (c. 1816)
J. & J. H. Lownes (c. 1816-
1819)
Bibl. 3, 4, 15, 23, 24, 25, 28,
29, 36, 39, 44, 54, 81

| J Lownes |

Joseph & Josiah Lownes
(c. 1816-1822)
(See J. & J. H. Lownes)

Josiah H. Lownes (d. 1822)
Philadelphia, Pa. (c. 1820-
1822)
J. & J. H. Lownes (c. 1816-
1819)
Bibl. 3, 23, 24, 25, 29, 36, 44

I H L   J H L

J. J. Lowrey (c. 1840-1844)
Pendleton, S.C.
Bibl. 5

R. B. Lowrie (c. 1847-1849)
Philadelphia, Pa.
Bibl. 3, 23

Salvador Lowry (c. 1824)
Baltimore, Md.
Bibl. 38

Adrian Loyer (d. 1781)
Savannah, Ga. (c. 1756-1760)
Bibl. 17, 23, 36, 44

Ivory Lucas (c. 1732-1748)
New London, Conn.
Oglestown (New Castle), Del.
Bibl. 2

James Lucet (c. 1802-1805)
New York, N.Y.
Bibl. 23, 36, 44

John P. Lucke (c. 1849)
Philadelphia, Pa.
Bibl. 3

John Ludwig (c. 1790-1791)
Philadelphia, Pa.
Bibl. 3

Luhlier
(See Lhulier)

G. W. Lukens (c. 1830)
Philadelphia, Pa.
Bibl. 39

G. W. LUKENS

Isaiah Lukens (c. 1823-1831)
Philadelphia, Pa.
Bibl. 3

J. Lukens (c. 1837)
Philadelphia, Pa.
Bibl. 3

William Lukens (c. 1847)
Philadelphia, Pa.
Bibl. 3

J. Lukey
Location unknown
Bibl. 15, 44

| J. LUKEY |

Lambert Luls (Lulis) (c. 1804)
New York, N.Y.
Bibl. 23, 36, 44

C. Lumsden & Co. (c. 1834)
Petersburg, Va.

Susanna E. Nichols
Charles Lumsden
Bibl. 19

Charles Lumsden
Petersburg, Va. (c. 1834)
Richmond, Va.
C. Lumsden & Co. (c. 1834)
Bibl. 19

CHAS. LUMSDEN

Thomas Lumsden (c. 1801-
1806)
Norfolk, Va.
Bibl. 19

Lunier
(See Lhulier)

John M. Lunquest (c. 1835-
1846)
Charleston, S.C.
Edgefield, S.C.
Bibl. 5

Charles Lupp (b. 1788-d.
1825)
New Brunswick, N.J. (c. 1810-
1825)
Bibl. 46, 54

Henry Lupp (b. 1760-d. 1800)
New Brunswick, N.J. (c. 1783-
1800)
Bibl. 24, 25, 44, 46, 54

H Lupp

Henry Lupp (c. 1790-1845)
New Brunswick, N.J.
Bibl. 54

John Lupp (b. 1734-d. 1805)
New Brunswick, N.J. (c. 1782-
1805)
Bibl. 46, 54

Lawrence K. Lupp(e) (b. 1783)
(Lewis) (Louis)
New Brunswick, N.J. (c. 1804-
1806)
Bibl. 15, 24, 25, 44, 46, 54

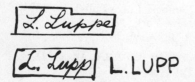
L. LUPP

Peter Lupp (c. 1760-1827)
New Brunswick, N.J.
Bibl. 15, 24, 39, 44, 46, 54

P.L.   PL

Samuel Vickers Lupp
(b. 1789-d. 1809)
New Brunswick, N.J. (c. 1809)
Bibl. 25, 44, 46, 54

S V LUPP

William Lupp (b. 1766-d. 1845)
New Brunswick, N.J. (c. 1790-
1845)
Bibl. 46, 54

Benjamin Lusada (c. 1797)
New York, N.Y.
Bibl. 23, 36

John G. Luscomb (c. 1813-
1823)
Boston, Mass.
Bibl. 4, 23, 28, 36, 44

John Lussaur (c. 1791)
New York, N.Y.
Bibl. 23, 36, 44

Benjamin Luzerder (c. 1796)
New York, N.Y.
Bibl. 28, 44

John Lyburn (c. 1820-1822)
Philadelphia, Pa.
Bibl. 3

John Lycett (c. 1818-1822)
Philadelphia, Pa.
Bibl. 3

John C. Lycett (c. 1821)
St. Louis, Mo.
Bibl. 54

David Lyell (b. 1670-d. 1725)
Matawan, N.J. (c. 1717-1725)
Bibl. 4, 23, 28, 36, 44, 46, 54

Lyman
(See Savage & Lyman)

R. Lyman
Location unknown
Bibl. 15

R. LYMAN

Lynch & Leonard (c. 1805-
1840)
Baltimore, Md.

Chestertown, Md.
———— Lynch
Samuel T. Leonard
Bibl. 29, 38, 44, 89

LYNCH &
LEONARD

F. Lynch
Petersburg, Va.
Bibl. 19

John Lynch (b. 1761-d. 1848)
Baltimore, Md. (c. 1786-1848)
Bibl. 23, 24, 25, 28, 29, 36,
38, 39, 44

I L   I L   J L
I LYNCH   J LYNCH   LYNCH

F. LYNCH   J.L.

L. George Lynch
(c. 1840-   )
Hillsboro, N.C.
Bibl. 21

Lemuel Lynch (b. 1808-d.
1893)
Hillsboro, N.C. (c. 1828)
Greensboro, N.C. (c. 1829)
Concord, N.C. (c. 1834)
Hillsboro, N.C. (c. 1834)
Huntington & Lynch (c. 1834)
Bibl. 21

Seaborn Lynch (c. 1840-   )
Hillsboro, N.C.
Bibl. 21

Thomas M. Lynch (c. 1840)
Oxford, N.C.
Bibl. 21

William Lyndall (c. 1844)
Philadelphia, Pa.
Bibl. 3

Thomas Lynde (b. 1748-d.
1812)
Malden, Mass.
Worcester, Mass.
Bibl. 23, 24, 25, 28, 29, 36,
44, 72

T LYNDE   T LYNDE

John Lyng (c. 1734)
Philadelphia, Pa.
Bibl. 23, 28, 36, 44

I + L

John Burt Lyng (d. 1785)
New York, N.Y. (c. 1761)
Bibl. 4, 15, 23, 25, 28, 29, 35,
  36, 44, 54

Philip Lyng (c. 1778-1785)
Philadelphia, Pa.
Bibl. 3, 23

Adam Lynn (b. 1775-d. 1836)
Alexandria, Va. (c. 1795-1835)
Coryton & Lynn (c. 1795-1796)
Bibl. 15, 19, 25, 29, 44

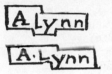

George Lyon (c. 1819-1844)
Wilmington, N.C.
Bibl. 21

R. A. Lytle (c. 1825)
Baltimore, Md.
Bibl. 24, 25, 44

R A LYTLE

Mabrid & Co. (Malrid & Co.)
New York, N.Y. (c. 1787)
Bibl. 23, 36, 44

George James Macauley
  (c. 1802)
Charleston, S.C.
Bibl. 5

MacFarlane
(See John McFarlane)

Alexander MacHarey (c. 1842)
Albany, N.Y.
Bibl. 23

Thomas W. Machen (c. 1812-
  1830)
New Bern, N.C.
Bibl. 21

Austin Machon (c. 1759)
Philadelphia, Pa.
Bibl. 3, 23, 36, 44

James Mackey (c. 1816-1818)
Baltimore, Md.
Bibl. 38

John Mackey (c. 1841-1842)
Philadelphia, Pa.
Bibl. 3, 23

Edward Mackinder (c. 1839)
St. Louis, Mo.
Bibl. 54

James Madock (c. 1796)
Martinsburg, Va.
Bibl. 19

F. W. Maffit (c. 1846)
Syracuse, N.Y.
Bibl. 20

Simon M. Magnus
  (c. 1849-   )
Albany, N.Y.
Bibl. 20

Matthew Maher (Mahue)
  (c. 1761)
Philadelphia, Pa.
Bibl. 81

Thomas S. Mahin (b. 1819-d.
  1880)
Franklin, Ky.
Bibl. 32, 68

Robert Maholland (c. 1850)
Philadelphia, Pa.
Bibl. 81

John Mahony (c. 1847-1849)
Utica, N.Y.
Bibl. 18

William A. Mahony (c. 1837-
  1849)
Philadelphia, Pa.
Bibl. 3

Mahue
(See Maher)

Peter A. Maille (c. 1819-1831)
Charleston, S.C.
Bibl. 5

David Main (b. 1752-d. 1843)
Stonington, Conn. (c. 1773)
Bibl. 16, 23, 28, 36, 44

Thomas Mainwaring (c. 1664)
New Jersey
Bibl. 23, 36, 44

Jean Claude Mairot (c. 1822)
New Orleans, La.
Bibl. 23, 36

Francois Paul Malcher
  (c. 1790, d. 1810)
Detroit, Mich.
Gallipolis, Ohio
Bibl. 58

P. M.   ?

John A. Mallory (c. 1839)
Delhi, N.Y.
Bibl. 20

Samuel Mallory (c. 1842)
Catskill, N.Y.
Bibl. 20

Malrid & Co.
(See Mabrid & Co.)

Henry Mander (c. 1848-1850)
Philadelphia, Pa.
Bibl. 3, 23

Horace Manley (c. 1836)
Canandaigua, N.Y.
Bibl. 20

James Manley (c. 1790)
Philadelphia, Pa.
Bibl. 3

Matthew Manley (c. 1843)
Philadelphia, Pa.
Bibl. 3

Mann
(See Brown & Mann)

Alexander Mann (b. 1777)
Middletown, Conn. (c. 1804)
Brewer & Mann (c. 1803-1805)
Bibl. 16, 23, 28, 36, 44

L. Mannerback (c. 1820)
Reading, Pa.
Bibl. 23, 36

William Mannerback (c. 1825)
Reading, Pa.
Bibl. 25, 29, 44, 54

W MANNERBACK   READING

Manning
(See Evans & Manning)

Daniel Manning (c. 1823)
Boston, Mass.
Bibl. 28, 36, 44

Ezra L. Manning (b. 1838)
Utica, N.Y. (c. 1858-
1860-   )
Bibl. 18

John Manning (c. 1819-1822)
Philadelphia, Pa.
Bibl. 3

Joseph Manning (c. 1823-1840)
New York, N.Y.
Bibl. 15, 23

Samuel Manning (c. 1823)
Boston, Mass.
Bibl. 23, 36, 44

Elisha Hyde Mansfield
(b. 1795)
Norwich, Conn. (c. 1816)
Coit & Mansfield (c. 1816-
1819)
Bibl. 16, 23, 28, 36

John Mansfield (b. 1601-d.
1674)
Charlestown, Mass. (c. 1634)
Boston, Mass. (c. 1650)
Bibl. 2, 23, 28, 36, 44

Samuel A. Mansfield (c. 1848-
1850)
Philadelphia, Pa.
Bibl. 3

Thomas Mansfield (c. 1804)
Philadelphia, Pa.
Bibl. 3, 23, 36, 44

John Mansure (c. 1844-1850)
Philadelphia, Pa.
Bibl. 3

Jules Manuel (c. 1849-1850)
Philadelphia, Pa.
Bibl. 3

Joseph Marand (c. 1804)
Baltimore, Md.
Bibl. 38

Benjamin Marble (c. 1840-
1850)
Albany, N.Y.
Bibl. 25, 44

Simeon Marble (b. 1776-d.
1856)
New Haven, Conn.
Sibley & Marble (c. 1801-1806)
Bibl. 16, 23, 24, 25, 28, 29, 36,
44

S MARBLE

Marce
(See Maree)

Isaac Marceloe (c. 1735)
Philadelphia, Pa.
Bibl. 3

Louis Marchalle (Marchelle)
(Marshall)
Norfolk, Va. (c. 1793-
1806-   )
Bibl. 19

Evariste Marchand (c. 1822)
New Orleans, La.
Bibl. 23, 36, 44

Marchelle
(See Marchalle)

Frank W. W. Marchisi
(b. 1832)
Utica, N.Y. (c. 1855-1860)
Bibl. 18

Joseph Marchisi (b. 1802-d.
1874, c. 1845-1868)
Chittenango, N.Y.
Utica, N.Y.
Bibl. 18, 20

Marcus
(See Starr & Marcus)

Henry Maree (Marce)
(c. 1845-1850)
Philadelphia, Pa.
Bibl. 3

L. Mario (c. 1825)
Location unknown
Bibl. 13

Jacob Marius Groen
(Morrisgreen)
(See Groen)   I·M

Isaac Marks (c. 1795-1799)
Philadelphia, Pa.
Bibl. 3

Michael Marmigan (c. 1814-
1815)
Baltimore, Md.
Bibl. 38

Marquand & Brother (c. 1815-
1831)
New York, N.Y.
Isaac Marquand
Frederick Marquand
Bibl. 23, 36, 44

Marquand & Co. (c. 1834-
1839)

New York, N.Y.
Frederick Marquand
Josiah P. Marquand
Erastus O. Tompkins
Bibl. 15, 23, 25, 28, 36, 44, 72

Marquand, Harriman & Co.
(c. 1809-1812)
New York, N.Y.
Isaac Marquand
Orlando Harriman
Cornelius Paulding
Bibl. 17, 46

Marquand & Paulding (c. 1801-
1810)
Savannah, Ga.
Isaac Marquand
Cornelius Paulding
Bibl. 17

Marquand, Paulding & Penfield
(c. 1810-1816)
Savannah, Ga.
Isaac Marquand
Cornelius Paulding
——— Penfield
Bibl. 17

Frederick Marquand (b. 1799-d.
1882)
New York, N.Y. (c. 1815)
Savannah, Ga. (c. 1820-1828)
Marquand & Brother (c. 1815-
1831)
J. Penfield & Co. (c. 1820-1828)
Marquand & Co. (c. 1834-1839)
Bibl. 15, 17, 23, 24, 25, 28, 29,
35, 36, 44, 72, 83

F. M.   F MARQUAND

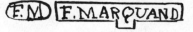

Isaac Marquand (b. 1766-d.
1838)
Fairfield, Conn. (c. 1787)
Edenton, N.C. (c. 1791-1796)
Savannah, Ga. (c. 1800)
New York, N.Y. (1805-1839)
Marquand & Paulding (c. 1801-
1810)
H. Lord & Co. (c. 1805)
E. Barton & Co.
Marquand & Brother
Marquand, Harriman & Co.
Bibl. 15, 17, 21, 23, 36, 44

Josiah P. Marquand (c. 1834)
New York, N.Y.

Marquand & Co. (c. 1834-1839)
Bibl. 15

Marrs & Stewart (c. 1802)
Philadelphia, Pa.
Robert Marrs
———— Stewart
Bibl. 3

Robert Marrs (c. 1803-1818)
Philadelphia, Pa.
Marrs & Stewart (c. 1802)
Bibl. 3

S. Mars (c. 1770)
Location unknown
Bibl. 28, 29, 44, 72

Benedict Beal Marsh
    (b. 1804-d. 1875)
Flemingsburg, Ky.
Paris, Ky.
Richmond, Ky.
Bibl. 32, 68

B B MARSH

Benjamin Marsh (c. 1840-1850)
Albany, N.Y.
Bibl. 20, 28

B MARSH
ALBANY

Edwin A. Marsh (c. 1847-
    1850-   )
Rochester, N.Y.
Bibl. 20

Edwin A. Marsh (c. 1832-1840)
Buffalo, N.Y.
Bibl. 20

Eli P. Marsh (b. 1815)
Utica, N.Y. (c. 1858-
    1859-   )
Bibl. 18

Thomas King Marsh (b. 1804)
Paris, Ky. (c. 1831-1850)
Bibl. 24, 25, 32, 44, 54, 68

T K MARSH

Louis Marshall
(See Louis Marchalle)

Marshall
(See Spencer & Marshall)

———— Marshall (c. 1833)
Philadelphia, Pa.
Bibl. 3

Marshall & Smith (c. 1837)
Philadelphia, Pa.
Bibl. 3

Marshall & Tempest (c. 1813-
    1830)
Philadelphia, Pa.
———— Marshall
Robert Tempest
Bibl. 3, 23, 24, 25, 44

MARSHALL &
TEMPEST

Marshall & White (c. 1817-   )
Petersburg, Va.
G. Marshall
Andrew White
Bibl. 19

Alexander D. Marshall
    (c. 1847-1848)
Philadelphia, Pa.
Bibl. 3

G. Marshall (c. 1816)
Petersburg, Va. (c. 1817-   )
Richmond, Va.
Marshall & White (c. 1817-   )
G. Marshall & Co.
Bibl. 19

John Marshall (c. 1838-1840)
Troy, N.Y.
Bibl. 20

John C. Marshall (c. 1899)
Louisville, Ky. (c. 1836-1849)
Bibl. 32, 54

Joseph Marshall (c. 1818-1850)
Philadelphia, Pa.
Bibl. 3, 4, 23, 28, 36, 44

Louis Marshall
(See Louis Marchalle)

Thomas Henry Marshall
Albany, N.Y. (c. 1832-1836)
Troy, N.Y. (c. 1836)
Rochester, N.Y. (c. 1838-1852)
Bibl. 15, 20, 23, 25, 36, 41, 44

T. H. MARSHALL

———— Martin (c. 1811)
Philadelphia, Pa.
Bibl. 3

Abraham W. Martin (c. 1835-
    1840)
New York, N.Y.
Bibl. 15, 23, 36, 44

Ambrose Martin (c. 1840-1850)
Philadelphia, Pa.
Bibl. 3

John Martin (c. 1823-1835)
Philadelphia, Pa.
Bibl. 3

John (J. L.) J. Martin (c. 1844-
    1850)
Philadelphia, Pa.
Bibl. 3

Lewis Martin (c. 1811)
Philadelphia, Pa.
Bibl. 3

M. Martin (c. 1790)
Location unknown
Bibl. 24

Patrick Martin (c. 1820-1850)
Philadelphia, Pa.
Bibl. 3, 44

Peter Martin (c. 1756)
New York, N.Y.
Bibl. 4, 15, 23, 24, 25, 28,
    29, 36, 44

P. M.   P MARTIN

P. MARTIN

Peter Martin II (c. 1825)
New York, N.Y.
Bibl. 25, 44

P. MARTIN

Thomas Martin (c. 1764)
Philadelphia, Pa.
Baltimore, Md.
Bibl. 38

Valentine Martin (c. 1842-
    1859)
Boston, Mass.
Bibl. 25, 28, 29, 44

V. MARTIN

Warner Martin (c. 1836)
New York, N.Y.
Bibl. 15

Zebedee Martin (c. 1806)
Baltimore, Md.
Bibl. 38

Peter Martinet (c. 1811)
Savannah, Ga.
Bibl. 17

John Martini (c. 1859)
Charleston, S.C.
Bibl. 5

J. Martiniere (c. 1820)
Augusta, Ga.
Morand, Alleoud & Co.
Bibl. 17

John F. Mascher (c. 1845-1850)
Philadelphia, Pa.
Bibl. 3

Samuel Masham (b. 1738,
    c. 1774)
Maryland
Bibl. 38

Seraphim Masi (c. 1832)
Washington, D.C.
Bibl. 28, 44

Mason
(See Masson)

Charles T. Mason (d. 1893)
Sumter, S.C. (c. 1851-   )
F. Hoyt & Co. (c. 1850-1851)
Bibl. 5

J. D. Mason (c. 1830)
Philadelphia, Pa.
Bibl. 24, 25, 44

J D MASON

Levant L. Mason
Rochester, N.Y. (c. 1847-1850)
Jamestown, N.Y. (c. 1850)
Bibl. 20

Richard Mason (c. 1814-1824)
Baltimore, Md.
Bibl. 38

Samuel Mason Jr. (c. 1820-
    1830)
Philadelphia, Pa.
Bibl. 3

Thomas Mason (c. 1795-1797)
Alexandria, Va.
Bibl. 19

Charles R. Massey (c. 1837-
    1839)
Philadelphia, Pa.
Bibl. 3

Charles A. Masson (Mason)
Philadelphia, Pa. (c. 1829-1850)
Bibl. 3

Masterman & Son
    (c. 1870-   )
Charleston, S.C.
William Masterman
Bibl. 5

William Masterman (c. 1852-
    1870)
Charleston, S.C.
Masterman & Son
    (c. 1870-   )
Bibl. 5

Mather & North (c. 1827-1829)
New Britain, Conn. (c. 1827)
New York, N.Y. (1827-1829)
Thaddeus Mather
Thomas Mather
William B. North (?)
Bibl. 15, 23, 24, 25, 29, 36, 44,
    89

MATHER & P. NORTH

MATHER & NORTH

Mather & Pitkin (c. 1844-1848)
Buffalo, N.Y.
Theodore Mather
Joseph F. Pitkin
Bibl. 20

Thaddeus Mather (c. 1831)
New Britain, Conn. (c. 1827)
Columbia, S.C.
New York, N.Y. (c. 1827-
    1829?)
Mather & North (c. 1827-1829)
Bibl. 5

Theodore Mather (c. 1844-
    1848)
Buffalo, N.Y.
Mather & Pitkin
Bibl. 20

Thomas Mather (c. 1825)
New York, N.Y.
Mather & North (c. 1827-1829)
Bibl. 15

F. Mathew (b. 1825)
Mobile, Ala. (c. 1850)
Bibl. 54

Harriet Mathews (b. 1807-d.
    1882)

Charlottesville, Va. (c. 1850)
Bibl. 19

Richard Mathews (c. 1836-
    1848)
Charlottesville, Va.
Bibl. 19

Thomas Mathews (d. 1852)
Charleston, Va. (c. 1810-   )
Bibl. 19

Aime Mathey (c. 1824-1835)
New York, N.Y.
Aime Mathey & Co. (c. 1836)
Bibl. 15

A. MATHEY

Aime Mathey & Co.
    (c. 1836-   )
New York, N.Y.
Aime Mathey
Augustus Mathey
Bibl. 15

Augustus Mathey (c. 1824-
    1828)
New York, N.Y.
Aime Mathey & Co.
    (c. 1836-   )
Bibl. 15, 25, 44, 89

A MATHEY

Lewis Mathey (c. 1797-1803)
Philadelphia, Pa.
Brandt & Mathey (c. 1795-
    1799)
Bibl. 3

Peter Mathiew (c. 1837-1843)
Philadelphia, Pa.
Bibl. 3

White Matlack (c. 1777)
Philadelphia, Pa.
William Matlack (c. 1780)
Bibl. 3

White & William Matlack
    (c. 1780)
Philadelphia, Pa.
Bibl. 3

William Matlack (c. 1797)
Philadelphia, Pa.
Bibl. 3

William Matlack (c. 1828-1833)
Philadelphia, Pa.
Bibl. 3, 23, 36, 44

Newell Matson (b. 1817-d. 1887)
Owego, N.Y. (c. 1845)
Bibl. 15, 20, 25, 44

N MATSON

H. E. Matteson (c. 1840)
Location unknown
Bibl. 89

L. Matthews (c. 1852)
Paris, Ky.
Alonzo Corwin Hallack
  (c. 1840-1853)
Bibl. 32, 54, 68

Peter Matthews (c. 1845)
Philadelphia, Pa.
Bibl. 3

Charles Matthias (c. 1849)
Philadelphia, Pa.
Bibl. 3

John Maull (c. 1848-1849)
Philadelphia, Pa,
Bibl. 3

Joseph E. Maull (c. 1830-1837)
Philadelphia, Pa.
Clausen & Maull (c. 1830-
  1833) (?)
Bibl. 3

———— Maurel (c. 1810)
Charleston, S.C.
Maurel & Boudo
Bibl. 5

Maurel & Boudo (c. 1810)
Charleston, S.C.
———— Maurel
Louis Boudo
Bibl. 5

Frederick Maus (c. 1782-1793)
Philadelphia, Pa.
Bibl. 3

E. Maussenet (c. 1841-1845)
Macon, Ga.
Bibl. 17

John Mautz (c. 1841)
Philadelphia, Pa.
Bibl. 3

D. Maverick (c. 1828)
New York, N.Y.
Bibl. 28, 29

Peter Rushton (C.) Maverick
  (c. 1755-1811)
New York, N.Y.
Bibl. 23, 28, 36, 44

John Mawdsley (c. 1846-1847)
Philadelphia, Pa.
Bibl. 3

A. Maxwell (c. 1805-1811)
Philadelphia, Pa.
Bibl. 3

May & Clark (c. 1765)
Philadelphia, Pa.
Samuel May
Richard Clark
Bibl. 3

Samuel May (c. 1765)
Philadelphia, Pa.
May & Clark
Bibl. 3

Elias Mayer (c. 1831-1833)
Philadelphia, Pa
Bibl. 3

Gotlieb A. Mayer (c. 1840-
  1868)
Norfolk, Va.
Minton & Mayer (c. 1840-1842)
Bibl. 19

G. MAYER

Jacob Mayer (Meier) (Myre)
  (Myers)
Cleveland, Ohio (c. 1830-1846)
Bibl. 23, 34, 54

Maynard & Taylor (c. 1852-
  1858)
Utica, N.Y.
Thomas Maynard
William S. Taylor
Bibl. 18, 20

R. H. Maynard (c. 1825-1829)
Black Rock, N.Y.
Buffalo, N.Y.
Bibl. 15, 20, 25, 44

R. H. MAYNARD

Thomas Maynard (d. 1860)
Utica, N.Y. (c. 1841-1859)
Cleveland, Ohio
Maynard & Taylor (c. 1852-
  1858)
Dana & Maynard (c. 1841)
Bibl. 18

Charles Maysenhoelder
  (Maysenhaelder)

Philadelphia, Pa. (c. 1810-1825)
Bibl. 3, 23, 36, 39, 44

(Note that Mc on following
  pages was sometimes listed
  as M'.)

William McAdams (c. 1846-
  1850)
Philadelphia, Pa.
Bibl. 3

James McAllister (c. 1840-
  1850)
Philadelphia, Pa.
Bibl. 3

Charles McAuky (c. 1831-
  1833)
New York, N.Y.
Bibl. 15

McBride & Gardner (c. 1807)
Charlotte, N.C.
Andrew McBride
Barzillai Gardner
Bibl. 21

Andrew McBride (c. 1807)
Charlotte, N.C.
McBride & Gardner
Bibl. 21

Henry McBride (c. 1810)
Macklenburg County, N.C.
Bibl. 21

McBryde & Patton (c. 1819-
  1822)
Clinton, Ga.
Andrew McBryde
———— Patton
Bibl. 17

Andrew McBryde
Clinton, Ga. (c. 1819-1822)
Monticello, Ga. (c. 1822)
McBryde & Patton (c. 1819-
  1822)
Bibl. 17

McCabe & Walker (c. 1805-
  1806)
Richmond, Va.
William McCabe
James Walker
Bibl. 19

John McCabe (c. 1773)
Baltimore, Md.
Bibl. 3

William McCabe (c. 1804-
  1819)

Richmond, Va.
McCabe & Walker (c. 1805-
1806)
Bibl. 19

S. & M. McCain (c. 1824)
Genesee, N.Y.
Bibl. 20

S. McCain (c. 1830)
Batavia, N.Y.
Bibl. 20

John McCalse (c. 1774)
Baltimore, Md.
Bibl. 44

McCall
(See Van Voorhis, Schank &
McCall)

Daniel McCalvey (c. 1837)
Philadelphia, Pa.
Bibl. 3

Michael McCann (c. 1839-
1845)
Philadelphia, Pa.
Bibl. 3

John McCarter (McCarty)
Philadelphia, Pa. (c. 1845-1850)
Bibl. 3

Edward McCarty (c. 1845-
1850)
Philadelphia, Pa.
Bibl. 3, 23

Charles McCauley (c. 1834)
New York, N.Y.
Bibl. 15

James McCauley (c. 1833)
New York, N.Y.
Bibl. 15

John A. McCaulley (c. 1840)
Lexington, Ky.
Richmond, Ky.
Bibl. 32, 54, 68

McCay & Cowan (c. 1805-
1807)
Richmond, Va.
William McCay
William Cowan
Bibl. 19

William McCay (b. 1753-d.
1829)
Richmond, Va. (c. 1805-1807)
Petersburg, Va. (c. 1811)

McCay & Cowan (c. 1805-
1807)
Bibl. 19

William McClain (c. 1848)
Philadelphia, Pa.
Bibl. 3

James McClanan (c. 1836-
1837)
Buffalo, N.Y.
Myer & McClanan
Bibl. 20

W. S. McClean Jr. (c. 1837)
Philadelphia, Pa.
Bibl. 3

Daniel McCleary (c. 1837-
1841)
Philadelphia, Pa.
Bibl. 3

James McClever (c. 1828-1833)
Philadelphia, Pa.
Bibl. 3

John McClinch (c. 1760)
Boston, Mass.
Bibl. 28

F. McCloskey (c. 1850)
Philadelphia, Pa.
Bibl. 3

Samuel McClure (c. 1808)
Fredericksburg, Va.
Bibl. 19

John McClyman (c. 1805-1819)
New York, N.Y.
Bibl. 15

John (I.) C. McClymo(a)n
(c. 1805-1840)
New York, N.Y.
Bibl. 4, 15, 23, 24, 25, 28, 29,
36, 44

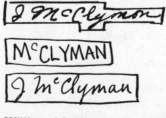

William McClymon (c. 1800-
1815)
Schenectady, N.Y.

Bibl. 20, 25, 44

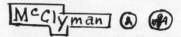

John McCollin (c. 1823-1824)
Philadelphia, Pa.
Bibl. 3

Thomas McCollin (c. 1824-
1833)
Philadelphia, Pa.
Bibl. 3, 15, 44

T. MCCOLLIN

McConky & Lebey (c. 1811-
1812)
Savannah, Ga.
David Marion McConky
Christian David Lebey
Bibl. 17

David Marion McConky
(c. 1808-1820, d. 1820)
Savannah, Ga.
Jackson & McConky (c. 1808-
1809)
McConky & Lebey (c. 1811-
1812)
Bibl. 17

———— McConnaghy (before
1850)
Wayne County, Ky.
Bibl. 32, 68

Hugh McConnel(l) (c. 1811-
1813)
Philadelphia, Pa.
Bibl. 3, 23, 24, 25, 29, 36, 44, 54

MCCONNEL   MCCONNELL

John McConnell (d. 1858)
Richmond, Va. (c. 1827-
1850-)
Bibl. 19

Thomas McConnell (b. 1768-d.
1825, c. 1790-1818)
Richmond, Va.
Wilmington, Del.
Bibl. 19, 25, 30, 44

MCCONNELL   T. MCCONNELL

H. McConnelly (c. 1811)
Philadelphia, Pa.
Bibl. 3, 23, 36

Milton McConothy (c. 1843-
1848)

Louisville, Ky.
Bibl. 32, 54, 68

Bernard McCormick (c. 1844-
1850)
Philadelphia, Pa.
Bibl. 3

Henry McCormick (c. 1833)
Philadelphia, Pa.
Bibl. 3

John McCormick (c. 1837)
Philadelphia, Pa.
Bibl. 3, 23, 36, 44

Patrick McCosker (c. 1842-
1846)
Philadelphia, Pa.
Bibl. 3

Coles McCoun (c. 1840-1841)
Whitehall, N.Y.
Bibl. 20

Henry T. McCoun (c. 1837-
1840)
Troy, N.Y.
Bibl. 20

George W. McCoy (c. 1837-
1850)
Philadelphia, Pa.
Bibl. 3

Robert McCrea (c. 1785)
Philadelphia, Pa.
Schenectady, N.Y.
Bibl. 3, 23, 36

R. A. McCredie (d. 1839)
Savannah, Ga. (c. 1836)
Bibl. 17

Thomas McCrow (c. 1767)
Annapolis, Md.
Bibl. 38

George H. McCulley (c. 1829-
1850)
Philadelphia, Pa.
Bibl. 3

William McCulley (c. 1841-
1850)
Philadelphia, Pa.
Bibl. 3

Francis McCutchen (c. 1844-
1846)
Philadelphia, Pa.
Bibl. 3

John McDaniel (c. 1848-1849)
Philadelphia, Pa.
Bibl. 3, 23

Peter McDaniel (c. 1743)
New York, N.Y.
Bibl. 23, 36, 44

William H. McDaniel (c. 1825)
Philadelphia, Pa.
Bibl. 3

——— McDannold (19th
century)
Winchester, Ky.
Bibl. 32, 54, 68

MCDANNOLD

Charles C. McDermott (c.
1850)
Philadelphia, Pa.
Bibl. 3

Edward McDermott (c. 1848)
Philadelphia, Pa.
Bibl. 3

James McDermott (c. 1835)
Philadelphia, Pa.
Bibl. 3

Charles McDonald (19th
century)
Lexington, Ky.
Bibl. 32, 54

Daniel McDonald (McDonell)
Philadelphia, Pa. (c. 1828-
1837)
Bibl. 3, 23, 36, 44

Jacob McDonald (c. 1833-
1834)
Troy, N.Y.
Bibl. 20

Richard McDonald (Mc-
Donnell)
Philadelphia, Pa. (c. 1820-
1824)
Bibl. 3

William T. McDonald
Shepherdstown, Va. (c. 1845)
Alexandria, Va. (c. 1846)
Harpers Ferry, Va. (c. 1850)
Bibl. 19

John McDonough
(McDonnough)
Philadelphia, Pa. (c. 1775)
Bibl. 3, 23, 36, 44

Patrick McDonough
(McDonnough)
Philadelphia, Pa. (c. 1811)
Bibl. 3, 23, 36, 44

William McDougall (c. 1825)
Meredith, N.H.
Bibl. 25, 28, 44

WM MCDOUGALL

James McDowell (c. 1794-
1808)
Philadelphia, Pa.
Bibl. 3

John McDowell (c. 1817)
Philadelphia, Pa.
Bibl. 3

William Hanse McDowell (b.
1795-d. 1842)
Philadelphia, Pa.
Bibl. 25, 44

WM H. MCDOWELL

I. McE.
Alexandria, Va.
Bibl. 54

James McElwee (c. 1813-1814)
Philadelphia, Pa.
Ferris & McElwee (c. 1813)
Bibl. 3

John McEwen (c. 1830-1833)
Philadelphia, Pa.
Bibl. 3

J. B. McFadden (c. 1840)
Pittsburgh, Pa.
Bibl. 24, 25, 44, 78

J. B. MCFADDEN

John McFarlane (MacFarland)
(MacFarlane)
Boston, Mass. (c. 1796)
Bibl. 4, 23, 24, 25, 28, 29, 36, 44

J. McF

William McFarlane (c. 1805)
Philadelphia, Pa.
Bibl. 3

John McFee (c. 1797-1800)
Philadelphia, Pa.
McFee & Reeder (c. 1793-
1796)

Bibl. 3, 23, 28, 36, 44, 46

McFee & Reeder (c. 1793-
1796)
Philadelphia, Pa.
John McFee
Abner Reeder
Bibl. 3, 15, 24, 25, 29, 36, 44,
46, 54

M & R

M. McFee (c. 1769)
Philadelphia, Pa.
Bibl. 3, 23, 36, 44

Patrick McGann (c. 1799-
1831)
Charleston, S.C.
Bibl. 5

John McGlensey (c. 1845-
1850)
Philadelphia, Pa.
Bibl. 3

I. D. McGoodwin (c. 1870-
1885)
Bowling Green, Ky.
Fuselli & McGoodwin (c. 1873-
1885)
Bibl. 54

Daniel McGraw (c. 1772)
Chester, Pa.
Bibl. 3, 23, 36, 44

McGrew and Beggs (c. 1850)
Louisville, Ky.
——— McGrew
William Beggs
Bibl. 32, 89

Alexander McGrew (c. 1817-
1819)
Cincinnati, Ohio
Bibl. 34

W. McGrew & Son (c. 1829-
1864)
Cincinnati, Ohio
Wilson McGrew (?)
Bibl. 54

Wilson McGrew (c. 1824)
Cincinnati, Ohio
Bibl. 34

Robert McGuire (c. 1803)
Martinsburg, Va.
Bibl. 19

McHarg & Selkirk (c. 1815)
Albany, N.Y.
Alexander McHarg
——— Selkirk
Bibl. 20

Alexander McHarg (c. 1817-
1849)
Albany, N.Y.
McHarg & Selkirk (c. 1815)
Bibl. 20, 28, 44

Dennis McHenry (c. 1827-
1830)
Baltimore, Md.
Bibl. 38

William T. McHenry (c. 1833)
Hawkinsville, Ga.
Bibl. 17

McIlhenney & West (c. 1818-
1822)
Philadelphia, Pa.
Joseph McIlhenney
Thomas G. West(?)
Bibl. 3

Joseph McIlhenney (c. 1818-
1825)
Philadelphia, Pa.
Bibl. 3

John K. McIlvaine (McIlwain)
(c. 1823-1837)
Philadelphia, Pa.
Bibl. 3

James McIntire (c. 1840)
Philadelphia, Pa.
Bibl. 3, 23, 36, 44

John McIntosh (c. 1761)
Ft. Stanwix, Pa.
Bibl. 3, 23, 36, 44

Colin (?) McIver (c. 1785)
Alexandria, Va.
Dawe & McIver
Bibl. 19

Murdo McIvor (c. 1844)
Rochester, N.Y.
Bibl. 20

J. R. McKay (c. 1837)
New York, N.Y.
Bibl. 15

William McKean (c. 1819)
Charleston, S.C.
Bibl. 5

A. B. McKee
Kentucky (?)
Bibl. 54

John McKee (c. 1816)
Chester, S.C.
Bibl. 5

Henry McKeen (c. 1823-1850)
Philadelphia, Pa.
Bibl. 3, 15, 24, 25, 44

H. MCKEEN

James McKeever (c. 1829-1850)
Philadelphia, Pa.
Bibl. 3

Edward McKinley (c. 1830-
1837)
Philadelphia, Pa.
Bibl. 3

C. F. McKinney (c. 1825)
Location unknown
Bibl. 24

C. F. MCKINNEY

John McKliment (c. 1804)
New York, N.Y.
Bibl. 23, 36, 44

John McLawrence (c. 1818)
New York, N.Y.
Bibl. 23, 36, 44

Daniel J. McLean (c. 1850)
Philadelphia, Pa.
Bibl. 3

O. P. McLean (c. 1840)
Columbus, Ga.
Bibl. 17

William S. McLean (c. 1845-
1850)
Philadelphia, Pa.
Bibl. 3

McLure and Fuselli (19th
century)
Bowling Green, Ky.
Bibl. 32, 54

McLure & Valenti (c. 1867)
Bowling Green, Ky.
James McLure
Philip Valenti
Bibl. 54

James McLure (c. 1840-1881)
Bowling Green, Ky.
McLure & Valenti (c. 1867)
Bibl. 32, 54

John McMahon (c. 1803-1804)
Philadelphia, Pa.
Bibl. 3, 23, 36, 44

John McManus (c. 1840)
Philadelphia, Pa.
Bibl. 3

Michael McManus (c. 1839)
New York, N.Y.
Bibl. 15

Hugh A. McMaster (c. 1839-
1850)
Philadelphia, Pa.
Bibl. 24, 25, 44

H. A. MCMASTER

John McMaster (c. 1805)
Philadelphia, Pa.
Bibl. 3, 23, 36

Hugh A. McMasters (c. 1839-
1850)
Philadelphia, Pa.
Bibl 3

John McMillen (c. 1820)
Cambridge, Ohio
Bibl. 34

James McMinn (c. 1846-1850)
Philadelphia, Pa.
Bibl. 3

McMullen
(See John McMullin)
(See William McMullin)

Edward McMullen (c. 1846-
1848)
Philadelphia, Pa.
Bibl. 3

James McMullen (c. 1814)
Philadelphia, Pa.
Bibl. 3, 23, 36

McMullin & Black (c. 1811)
Philadelphia, Pa.
John McMullin
John Black
Bibl. 3, 4, 23, 24, 25, 28, 29, 36,
44, 80

MCMULLIN AND BLACK

John McMullin (McMullen)
(b. 1765-d. 1843)
Philadelphia, Pa. (c. 1795-1841)
McMullin & Black (c. 1811)

Bibl. 3, 4, 23, 24, 25, 28, 29, 36,
39, 44, 54, 72, 81

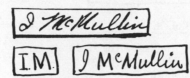

William McMullin (McMullen)
Philadelphia, Pa. (c. 1791-
1794)
Bibl. 3, 23, 36, 44

Thomas McMurrey (Mc-
Murray)
Frankfort, Ky. (c. 1810)
Louisville, Ga. (c. 1811)
Bibl. 17, 32, 54, 68

John McMurry (c. 1809)
Athens, Ga
Bibl. 17

John McMyers (c. 1799)
Baltimore, Md.
Bibl. 38

McN & S (c. 1830)
Pennsylvania (?)
Bibl. 89

McNamara (c. 1765)
Philadelphia, Pa.
Bibl. 3

William McNeare (c. 1828-
1833)
Philadelphia, Pa.
Bibl. 3

———— McNeeley (c. 1814)
Paris, Ohio
Bibl. 34

D. McNeil (c. 1818)
Greensboro, Ga.
Bibl. 17

E. McNeil (c. 1813-1839)
Binghamton, N.Y.
Troy, N.Y.
Bibl. 15, 20, 25, 44

E MCNEIL

William McNeir (c. 1835-
1848)
Philadelphia, Pa.
Bibl. 3

Ezra McNutt (c. 1848)
Philadelphia, Pa.
Bibl. 3

William McParlin (b. 1780-d.
1850)
Annapolis, Md. (c. 1803-1850)
Bibl. 24, 25, 29, 38, 44

W. McP

John McPherson (c. 1846-
1850)
Philadelphia, Pa.
Bibl. 3

Robert McPherson (c. 1828-
1850)
Philadelphia, Pa.
Bibl. 3, 23, 36, 44

Hugh McQuarters (c. 1819)
Cincinnati, Ohio
Bibl. 34

William McQuilkin (c. 1045-
1853)
Philadelphia, Pa.
Bibl. 54

Solomon McQuivey (c. 1832-
1841)
Utica, N.Y.
Bibl. 18, 20

James McRea (c. 1805)
Mecklenburg County, N.C.
Bibl. 21

Francis McStocker (c. 1831-
1850)
Philadelphia, Pa.
Bibl. 3

A. McVicker (c. 1821)
Winchester, Va.
Bibl. 19

Mead
(See Phinney & Mead)

Mead & Adriance (c. 1838-
1842)
St. Louis, Mo.
Ithaca, N.Y.
Edward Edmund Mead
Edwin Adriance
Bibl. 15, 20, 24, 25, 29, 36, 44,
54

MEAD & ADRIANCE

Mead, Adriance & Co. (c. 1831-
1832)
Ithaca, N.Y.

St. Louis, Mo.
Edward Edmund Mead
Edwin Adriance
Bibl. 20, 23, 28, 36

B. Mead
Massachusetts (?)
Bibl. 28

Daniel Mead (c. 1845-1848)
Louisville, Ky.
Bibl. 32, 54, 68

Edward Edmund Mead (c. 1831-1842)
Ithaca, N.Y. (c. 1831-1832)
St. Louis, Mo. (c. 1838-1842)
DeRiemer & Mead (c. 1830-1831)
Mead, Adriance & Co. (c. 1831-1832)
Mead & Adriance (c. 1838-1842)
Bibl. 20, 24, 25, 44, 54

E MEAD

John O. Mead (c. 1850)
Philadelphia, Pa.
Filley, Mead & Caldwell
Bibl. 3

Meadows & Co. (c. 1831)
Philadelphia, Pa.
Bibl. 24, 25, 44, 54

MEADOWS & CO.

Charles Mears (c. 1828-1835)
Philadelphia, Pa.
Bibl. 3

Lewis Mears (c. 1848)
Philadelphia, Pa.
Bibl. 3

Lewis J. Mears (c. 1839)
Philadelphia, Pa.
Bibl. 3

John Mecke (c. 1837-1850)
Philadelphia, Pa.
Bibl. 3

John Mecom (d. 1770)
New York, N.Y.
Bibl. 23, 28, 36, 44

George Mecum (c. 1825-1836)
Boston, Mass.

G MECUM

Bibl. 4, 15, 23, 25, 28, 36, 44

J. Medberry (c. 1831)
Rochester, N.Y.
Bibl. 20

John Medenhall (c. 1841-1846)
Philadelphia, Pa.
Bibl. 3

Jacob Mediary Jr. (b. 1791, c. 1808)
Location unknown
Bibl. 38

Andrew G. Medley (c. 1832-1850)
Louisville, Ky.
Bibl. 32, 54, 68

Meek and Milam (c. 1850-1852)
Frankfort, Ky.
Jonathan Fleming Meek
Benjamin F. Meek
Benjamin Cave Milam
Bibl. 32

Benjamin F. Meek (b. 1816-d. 1901)
Danville, Ky. (1832-1834)
Frankfort, Ky. (1834-1882)
Louisville, Ky. (1882-1901)
J. F. and B. F. Meek (c. 1837-1846)
Meek & Milam (c. 1850-1852)
Bibl. 32, 54

J. F. Meek and Co. (c. 1837-1852)
Frankfort, Ky.
Jonathan Fleming Meek
Bibl. 32

J. F. and B. F. Meek (c. 1837-1846)
Frankfort, Ky.
Jonathan Fleming Meek
Benjamin F. Meek
Bibl. 32

Jonathan Fleming Meek (b. 1809)
Frankfort, Ky. (c. 1837-1852)
Louisville, Ky.
J. F. and B. F. Meek (c. 1837-1846)
J. F. Meek and Co. (c. 1837-1852)

Meek and Milam (c. 1850-1852)
Bibl. 32, 54

Thomas J. Megear (Megar) (c. 1830-1850)
Philadelphia, Pa.
Wilmington, Del.
Bibl. 3, 15, 25, 30, 44

T.J.MEGEAR

F. Megonegal (c. 1841-1842)
Philadelphia, Pa.
Bibl. 3

W. H. Megonegal (c. 1844)
Philadelphia, Pa.
Bibl. 3

Meier
(See Jacob Mayer)

Michael Melhorn (c. 1830-1832)
Harpers Ferry, Va.
Bibl. 19

Henry Melville (c. 1798)
Wilmington, N.C.
Bibl. 21

Alexander Menard (c. 1828-1829)
Macon, Ga.
Garland & Menard
Bibl. 17

Stephen Menard (c. 1817)
Philadelphia, Pa.
Bibl. 3

John Mendenhall (c. 1841)
Philadelphia, Pa.
Bibl. 23

Thomas Mendenhall (c. 1772)
Lancaster, Pa.
Bibl. 3

Benjamin Mends (Mens)
Philadelphia, Pa. (c. 1796-1797)
Bibl. 3

James Mends (Mens)
Philadelphia, Pa. (c. 1795)
Bibl. 3

Menkens & Recordon (c. 1842)
St. Louis, Mo.
Bibl. 24, 54

MENKENS

Mens
(See Mends)

John Menzies (c. 1804-1850)
Philadelphia, Pa.
Bibl. 3

John Menzies Jr. (c. 1835-
1850)
Philadelphia, Pa.
Bibl. 3

J. Merchant (c. 1795)
New York, N.Y.
Bibl. 23, 24, 25, 36, 44, 78

| J MERCHANT | J M |

Meredith & Johnston (c. 1827)
Winchester, Va.
James Meredith
William Johnston
Bibl. 19

J. Meredith & Son (c. 1850)
Winchester, Va.
James Meredith
Bibl. 19

James Meredith (d. 1860)
Winchester, Va.
Meredith & Johnston (c. 1827)
J. Meredith & Son
Bibl. 19

Joseph P. Meredith (c. 1824-
1848)
Baltimore, Md.
Bibl. 15, 24, 25, 38, 44

| J MEREDITH |

J. Merick (c. 1800)
Location unknown
Bibl. 54

| J. MERICK |

J. B. Merick
Location unknown
Bibl. 28, 29

| J. B. MERICK |

Perry (Parry) Merkle (c.
1840-1848)
Philadelphia, Pa.
Bibl. 3

John H. Merkler (c. 1780-
1791)
New York, N.Y.
Bibl. 23, 24, 25, 28, 36, 44

| I H M |

Merrick (c. 1815-1820)
Location unknown
Bibl. 15, 44

| MERRICK |

John P. Merrie (c. 1833)
Utica, N.Y.
Bibl. 18, 20

James Merrifield (c. 1850)
New York, N.Y.
Bibl. 23

Thomas V. Z. Merrifield (d.
1845)
Albany, N.Y. (c. 1817-1845)
Hall, Hewson & Co. (c. 1836-
1842)
Hall, Hewson & Merrifield (c.
1840)
Bibl. 20, 23, 28, 36, 44

J. A. Merrill (19th century)
Location unknown
Bibl. 89

Merriman & Bradley (c. 1817-
1820)
New Haven, Conn.
Marcus Merriman
Zebul Bradley
Bibl. 15, 16, 23, 24, 25, 28, 36,
61

| M&B |

| M&B |

Merriman & Tuttle (c. 1802)
New Haven, Conn.
Marcus Merriman
Bethuel Tuttle
Bibl. 16, 28, 23, 36, 44

C. Merriman (c. 1825)
New York, N.Y.
Bibl. 23, 36, 44

Marcus Merriman (b. 1762-d.
1850, c. 1787-1817)
New Haven, Conn. (c. 1802-
1820)

Cheshire, Conn.
Merriman & Tuttle (c. 1802)
Marcus Merriman & Co. (c.
1802-1817)
Merriman & Bradley (c. 1817-
1820)
Bibl. 15, 16, 23, 24, 25, 28, 36,
44, 54

| MERRIMAN | M M | M |

Marcus Merriman & Co. (c.
1802-1817)
New Haven, Conn.
Marcus Merriman
Zebul Bradley
Bethuel Tuttle
Bibl. 16, 21, 23, 24, 25, 28, 36,
44, 61, 72

| M:M&CO |

Marcus Merriman Jr. (c. 1826)
New Haven, Conn.
Bradley & Merriman (c. 1826-
1847)
Bibl. 19, 23, 28, 54

Reuben Merriman (b. 1783-d.
1866)
Cheshire, Conn.
Litchfield, Conn.
Bibl. 16, 24, 25, 28, 36, 44, 61

| R.M |

| R.MERRIMAN |

Samuel Merriman (b. 1769-d.
1805)
New Haven, Conn.
Bibl. 15, 16, 23, 24, 25, 28, 29,
36, 44, 61

| S. MERRIMAN | S M |
| S MERRIMAN |

Silas Merriman (b. 1734-d.
1805)
Cheshire, Conn.

New Haven, Conn.
Bibl. 15, 16, 23, 28, 36, 44, 61

S: M

Nathan Merrow (b. 1758-d.
1825)
East Hartford, Conn.
Bibl. 16, 23, 28, 36, 44

F. Merry (c. 1799)
Philadelphia, Pa.
Bibl. 3

Mesker
(See Mexter)

S. Messinger (c. 1800)
Location unknown
Bibl. 15, 44

S MESSINGER

B. Mestier (c. 1817)
Philadelphia, Pa.
Bibl. 3

Metten and Muller (c. 1839)
St. Louis, Mo.
Bibl. 54

John G. D. Meurset (c. 1778-
1810)
Charleston, S.C.
Monk & Meurset (c. 1804-
1807)
Bibl. 5

J Meurset

Godfrey Mexter (Mesker) (c.
1837-1840)
Philadelphia, Pa.
Bibl. 3

Gottlieb Meyer
(See Gottlieb Myer)

Joseph Meyer (c. 1840)
Canton, Ohio
Bibl. 34, 44

Matthew Meyer (c. 1858-1859)
Utica, N.Y.
Bibl. 18

Maurice Meyer (c. 1849)
Philadelphia, Pa.
Bibl. 3

Albert G. Meyers (c. 1837-
1846)
Philadelphia, Pa.
Bibl. 3

Elijah Meyers (c. 1829-1830)
Philadelphia, Pa.
Bibl. 3

T. Meyers (c. 1802-1807)
Norfolk, Va.
Bibl. 19

Richard Meyrick (c. 1729)
Philadelphia, Pa.
Bibl. 3, 28

James Michaels (c. 1820-1826)
New York, N.Y.
Bibl. 15, 23, 36, 44

Adrian L. Michel (c. 1820-
1858)
Charleston, S.C.
Bibl. 5

John E. Michel (c. 1819-1844)
Charleston, S.C.
Bibl. 5

Lewis C. Michel (c. 1822)
Charleston, S.C.
John Michel
Bibl. 5

William B. Middlebrook (c.
1842)
Middletown, N.Y.
Bibl. 20

Thomas F. Midlam (b. 1828)
Utica, N.Y. (c. 1850-1860)
Bibl. 18, 20

P. Miedzielski (c. 1837)
Columbus, Ga.
Bibl. 17

Lewis Mignard (c. 1829-1835)
Philadelphia, Pa.
Bibl. 3

James Mikles (c. 1828-1841)
New York, N.Y.
Bibl. 15

John Matthew Miksch (b.
1754-d. 1823)
Bethlehem, Pa.
Bibl. 3, 23, 24, 25, 29, 36, 44

I M MIKSCH

Benjamin Cave Milam (b.
1821-d. 1904)
Frankfort, Ky.
Meek & Milam (c. 1850-1852)
Bibl. 32

John Miler (19th century)
Cincinnati, Ohio
Bibl. 34

John Miles (c. 1785-1796)
Philadelphia, Pa.
Bibl. 3, 23, 28, 36, 44

Robert Miles (c. 1828-1850)
Philadelphia, Pa.
Bibl. 3

John Miley (c. 1829-1850)
Philadelphia, Pa.
Bibl. 3

Stephen Milhe (d. 1798)
Philadelphia, Pa. (c. 1780)
Bibl. 3, 23, 36, 44

Thomas Milk (b. 1753)
Maryland (c. 1775)
Bibl. 38

R. P. Milks (c. 1840)
Mansfield, Ohio
Bibl. 34

James Millar (c. 1825, 1832)
Boston, Mass.
Bibl. 23, 28, 36, 44

George Millard (c. 1816)
Philadelphia, Pa.
Bibl. 3, 23, 36, 44

Miller & Powers (c. 1799-1801)
Savannah, Ga.
Francis S. Miller
William Powers
Bibl. 17

Miller & Son (c. 1833)
Philadelphia, Pa.
Bibl. 36, 44

Miller & Son (c. 1833-1835)
Philadelphia, Pa.
Bibl. 3, 23

A. Miller (19th century)
Location unknown
Bibl. 15, 44

D. B. Miller (c. 1850)
Boston, Mass.
Bibl. 24, 25, 44

D. B. MILLER

Francis S. Miller (c.
1798-   )
Savannah, Ga.
Miller & Powers (c. 1799-1801)
Bibl. 17

George Miller (c. 1809)
Philadelphia, Pa.
Bibl. 3

George Miller (c. 1829-1853)
Philadelphia, Pa.
Bibl. 3

H. Miller (c. 1815)
Schenectady, N.Y.
I. S. & H. Miller
Bibl. 20

I. R. Miller (c. 1810)
Philadelphia, Pa.
Bibl. 24, 25, 44

I. S. Miller (c. 1813-1822)
Schenectady, N.Y.
I. S. & H. Miller (c. 1815)
I. S. Miller & Co. (c. 1822-
1826) (?)
Bibl. 20

I. S. Miller & Co. (c. 1822-
1826)
Schenectady, N.Y.
Bibl. 20

I. S. & H. Miller (c. 1815)
Schenectady, N.Y.
Bibl. 20

James Miller (c. 1812)
Cadiz, Ohio
Bibl. 34

John Miller (c. 1834)
Bellefontaine, Ohio
Bibl. 34

John Miller (c. 1840-1841)
New York, N.Y.
Bibl. 15

John David Miller (c. 1780-
1815)
Charleston, S.C.
Bibl. 5, 25, 44, 54

| J D Miller | | I D M |

Joseph Miller (c. 1837)
Milledgeville, Ga.
Bibl. 17

Julius Miller (c. 1850)
Prattsville, N.Y.
Bibl. 20

L. H. Miller & Co. (c. 1840)
Baltimore, Md.
Bibl. 25, 44

Martha Miller (c. 1807-1819)
Charleston, S.C.
Bibl. 5, 54

Matthew Miller (b. 1780-d.
1840)
Charleston, S.C. (c. 1805-1840)
Bibl. 5, 25, 44, 54

| M MILLER |

Mordecai Miller (b. 1763-d.
1832)
Alexandria, Va. (c. 1791-1795)
Bibl. 19, 54

P. Miller (c. 1810)
Philadelphia, Pa.
Bibl. 24

| P MILLER |

Pardon Miller (d. 1800)
Providence, R.I.
Bibl. 15, 28, 44, 56

Philip Miller (c. 1763)
New York, N.Y.
Bibl. 3

S. W. Miller (c. 1843)
Philadelphia, Pa.
Bibl. 3

Thomas Miller (c. 1819-1841)
Philadelphia, Pa.
Bibl. 3

William Miller (c. 1758)
Winchester, Va.
Bibl. 19

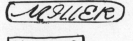

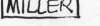

William Miller (c. 1810-1847)
Philadelphia, Pa.
Ward & Miller (c. 1822-1824)
Bibl. 3, 23, 24, 25, 29, 36, 44

William Miller (c. 1819)
Charleston, S.C.
Bibl. 5, 44

William S. Miller (c. 1844-
1848)
Philadelphia, Pa.
Bibl. 3

Thomas Millner (b. 1690-d.
1745)
Boston, Mass.
Bibl. 2, 15, 23, 24, 25, 28, 29,
36, 72

Thomas Millner (c. 1825)
Ashtabula, Ohio
Bibl. 34

Peter Millon (c. 1820)
New York, N.Y.
Bibl. 23, 36

Phillippe Milloudon (c. 1811)
Philadelphia, Pa.
Bibl. 3, 23, 36

Edmund Mills (c. 1785)
Philadelphia, Pa.
Bibl. 3, 23, 36

Edward Mills (c. 1794)
Philadelphia, Pa.
Bibl. 3, 23, 36

George F. Mills (c. 1834-1837)
New York, N.Y.
Bibl. 15

John Mills (c. 1793-1815)
Philadelphia, Pa.
Bibl. 3

John Bryant Mills (c. 1830)
Fayetteville, N.C.
Bibl. 21

Robert Mills (c. 1790)
Winchester, Va.
Bibl. 19

Moses Millum (c. 1819)
Baltimore, Md.
Bibl. 38

Edmund (Edward) Milne (b.
1757-d. 1813)
Philadelphia, Pa.
Bibl. 2, 3, 15, 24, 25, 28, 29, 39,
44, 54, 81

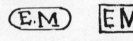

F. Milne (c. 1800)
New York, N.Y.
Bibl. 23, 36, 44

John Milne (c. 1817)
Morristown, Ohio
Bibl. 34

Robert Milne (c. 1817)
Philadelphia, Pa.
Bibl. 3

Stephen Milne (c. 1817)
Morristown, Ohio
Bibl. 34

Thomas Milne (c. 1795-1815)
New York, N.Y.
Bibl. 15, 23, 25, 36, 44

T. MILNE

Gustavus Mindel (c. 1850)
Philadelphia, Pa.
Bibl. 3

Joseph Miner (c. 1840)
Burton, Ohio
Bibl. 34

Minott & Austin (c. 1760-
1769)
Boston, Mass.
Samuel Minott

Josiah John Austin
Bibl. 15, 23, 24, 25, 29, 44

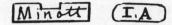

IA

Minott & Simpkins (c. 1750-
1760)
Boston, Mass.
Bibl. 23, 24, 25, 29, 36, 44

Minott   W S

Samuel Minott (b. 1732-d.
1803)
Boston, Mass.
Minott & Simpkins (c. 1750-
1760)
Minott & Austin (c. 1760-1769)
Bibl. 2, 15, 24, 25, 28, 29, 36,
44, 54

Minott   Minott

Minott

William Minshall (c. 1773)
Philadelphia, Pa.
Bibl. 3, 23, 36, 44

Vermont Mint (c. 1785-1788)
Rupert, Vt.
Bibl. 54

Minton & Mayer (c. 1840-
1842)
Norfolk, Va.
Joseph B. Minton
Gotlieb A. Mayer
Bibl. 19

MINTON & MAYER

Joseph B. Minton (c. 1840-
1847)
Norfolk, Va.
Minton & Mayer (c. 1840-
1842)
Bibl. 15, 19, 44

MINTON

John Miot (Myot) (b. 1740-d.
1791)
Charleston, S.C. (c. 1773-1791)
Bibl. 5, 54

Charles Missing (c. 1847)
Philadelphia, Pa.
Bibl. 3

Mitchell & Tyler (c. 1845-
1866)
Richmond, Va.
Samuel Phillips Mitchell
William Mitchell Jr.
John Henry Tyler
Bibl. 19, 54

MITCHELL & TYLER

Benjamin Mitchell (c. 1799-
1800)
Alexandria, Va.
Bibl. 19

Henry Mitchell (c. 1837-1841)
New York, N.Y.
Gunn & Mitchell (c. 1832) (?)
Bibl. 15

Henry Mitchell (c. 1844-1850)
Philadelphia, Pa.
Bibl. 3, 23, 24, 25, 44

MITCHELL

James Mitchell (c. 1799)
Baltimore, Md.
Bibl. 38

James Mitchell (c. 1845-1846)
Philadelphia, Pa.
Bibl. 3, 23

Jesse C. Mitchell (c. 1835-
1836)
Buffalo, N.Y.
Bibl. 20

John Mitchell (c. 1816)
Charleston, S.C.
Bibl. 5

Phineas Mitchell (c. 1812)
Boston, Mass.
Bibl. 23, 28, 36, 44

MITCHELL

Samuel Phillips Mitchell (b.
1815-d. 1866)
Richmond, Va.

Mitchell & Tyler (c. 1845-1866)
Bibl. 19

William Mitchell (c. 1820)
Boston, Mass.
Bibl. 15, 23, 24, 25, 29, 36, 44

W MITCHELL

William Mitchell Jr. (b. 1795-d. 1852)
Richmond, Va.
Taft & Mitchell (c. 1818-1819)
Bibl. 19, 44

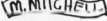

WM. JR

James Mix (b. 1793)
Albany, N.Y. (c. 1817-   )
Bibl. 4, 20, 23, 28, 36, 44

James Mix Jr. (c. 1846-   )
Albany, N.Y.
Bibl. 20

Thomas Mix (c. 1803)
Philadelphia, Pa.
Bibl. 3

Vischer (Visscher) Mix (c. 1840-1848)
Albany, N.Y.
Bibl. 20, 23, 28, 44

William Mobbs (c. 1835-1838)
Albany, N.Y.
Black Rock, N.Y.
Buffalo, N.Y.
Bibl. 20, 23, 36, 44

Peter Moeller (c. 1849)
Cleveland, Ohio
Bibl. 54

Moellinger
(See Mollinger)

Moffat & Chase (c. 1839)
Buffalo, N.Y.
Bibl. 20

Charles H. Moffat (c. 1830-1835)

New York, N.Y.
Bibl. 15, 36, 44

F. W. Moffat (c. 1853)
Albany, N.Y.
Bibl. 4, 28

John L. Moffat (c. 1815-1835)
New York, N.Y.
Bibl. 15, 23, 24, 25, 36, 44

J.L.MOFFAT

J.L. MOFFAT

William Moffat (c. 1832-1848)
Buffalo, N.Y.
Larzelere & Moffat (c. 1835)
Bibl. 20

Benjamin Moffett (c. 1839)
Philadelphia, Pa.
Bibl. 3

Jacob Mohler (b. 1744-d. 1773)
Baltimore, Md.
Bibl. 29, 38, 44

I M   ?

David Molan (c. 1835-1841)
Troy, N.Y.
Albany, N.Y.
Bibl. 20

Henry Mollinger (Moellinger) (Moollinger)
Philadelphia, Pa. (c. 1794-1804)
Bibl. 3

Lawrence Mollyneux (c. 1830)
New York, N.Y.
Bibl. 23

Daniel Molyneaux (c. 1828-1832)
New York, N.Y.
Bibl. 15

Monell & Williams (c. 1825)
New York, N.Y.
John I. (J.) Monell
Charles M. Williams
Bibl. 25, 44

J J Monell

John I. (J.) Monell (c. 1824-1829)

New York, N.Y.
Bibl. 15, 23, 35, 83

Benedict Monfay (c. 1828-1835)
Philadelphia, Pa.
Bibl. 3

Benjamin Monger (c. 1806)
Poughkeepsie, N.Y.
Field & Monger (c. 1805-1806)
Bibl. 20

David Mongin Sr. (c. 1765-1767)
Purysburgh, Ga.
Bibl. 17

Daniel Monier (c. 1825-1850)
Philadelphia, Pa.
Bibl. 3

I. Monil & M. Williams (c. 1835)
Location unknown
Bibl. 24

Monk & Co. (c. 1805)
Charleston, S.C.
James Monk
Bibl. 5

MONK & CO.

Monk & Meurset (c. 1804-1807)
Charleston, S.C.
James Monk
John G. D. Meurset
Bibl. 5

James Monk (c. 1797-1808)
Charleston, S.C. (c. 1797-1799, c. 1804-1807)
Manchester, S.C.
Atmar & Monk (c. 1797-1799)
Monk & Meurset (c. 1804-1807)
Monk & Co. (c. 1805)
Bibl. 5, 25, 44, 54

MONK

E. P. Monroe (c. 1830's)
Mogadore, Ohio
Bibl. 34

J. S. Monroe (c. 1830's)
Mogadore, Ohio
Bibl. 34

James F. Monroe (c. 1848)
St. Louis, Mo.
Bibl. 54

C. J. Monson (c. 1815)
Location unknown
Bibl. 24

| C. J. MONSON |

Albert Montandon (c. 1824)
Clarksburg, Va.
Bibl. 19

William R. Montcastle (c. 1844-
1856)
Warrenton, N.C.
Bibl. 21

Monteith & Co. (c. 1845)
Philadelphia, Pa.
Bibl. 3

Monteith & Shippen (c. 1817)
Philadelphia, Pa.
—— Monteith
William A. Shippen
Bibl. 3

Benjamin Monteith (c. 1847-
1848)
Philadelphia, Pa.
Bibl. 3

Charles Monteith (c. 1847-
1848)
Philadelphia, Pa.
Bibl. 3

I. & R. Monteith (c. 1814-
1849)
Baltimore, Md.
John Monteith
Robert Monteith
Bibl. 38, 44

John Monteith (c. 1814-1849)
Baltimore, Md.
I. & R. Monteith
Bibl. 38, 44

John & Robert Monteith (c.
1814-1849)
Baltimore, Md.
I. & R. Monteith
Bibl. 15, 38, 44

Robert Monteith (c. 1814-
1849, d. 1849)
Baltimore, Md.
I. & R. Monteith
Bibl. 3, 25, 29, 44

| R M |

Andrew Montgomery (c. 1822-
1830)
Norfolk, Va. (c. 1822-1823)
Baltimore, Md. (c. 1824-1830)
Bibl. 19, 38

Edwin Montgomery (c. 1850)
Syracuse, N.Y.
Bibl. 20

Summerfield Montgomery (c.
1856-1872, d. 1872)
Newberry, S.C.
Bibl. 5

Mood & Ewan (c. 1824)
Charleston, S.C.
—— Mood
John Ewan
Bibl. 44

| MOOD & EWAN |

Christian Adam Mood (b.
1799-d. 1858)
Charleston, S.C. (w. 1819-
1831)
Bibl. 5

J. & P. Mood (c. 1834-1841)
Charleston, S.C.
John Mood
Peter Mood Jr.
Bibl. 5, 15, 25, 44, 54

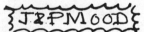

John (I.) Mood (b. 1792-d.
1864)
Charleston, S.C. (c. 1810, c.
1834-1841)
Athens, Ga.
Peter Mood & Son (c. 1816-
1819)
Peter Mood & Sons (c.
1819-   )
J. & P. Mood (c. 1834-1841)
Bibl. 5, 17, 25, 28, 44, 54, 89

Joseph Mood (c. 1806)
Charleston, S.C.
Philadelphia, Pa.
Bibl. 23, 24, 29, 44

| I MOOD   J MOOD |

P. Mood & Co. (c. 1823-1834)
Charleston, S.C.
Peter Mood Jr.
John Ewan
Bibl. 5

Peter Mood Sr. (b. 1766-d.
1821)
Charleston, S.C. (c. 1785-
1821)
Peter Mood & Son (c. 1810)
Peter Mood & Sons (c. 1819)
Bibl. 5, 15, 24, 25, 44, 54

Peter Mood Jr. (b. 1796-d.
1879)
Charleston, S.C.
Peter Mood & Sons (c.
1819-   )
P. Mood & Co. (c. 1823-1834)
J. & P. Mood (c. 1834-1841)
Bibl. 5, 15, 54

| P. Mood Jr |

Peter Mood & Son (c. 1816-
1819)
Charleston, S.C.
Peter Mood Sr.
John Mood
Bibl. 5

| P MOOD & SON |

Peter Mood & Sons (c.
1819-   )
Charleston, S.C.
Peter Mood Sr.
Peter Mood Jr.
John Mood
Bibl. 5

Thomas S. Mood (d. 1871)
Athens, Ga. (c. 1821)
Charleston, S.C. (1824)
Orangeburg, S.C. (c. 1849)
Sumter, Ga. (c. 1857)
Columbia, Ga. (c. 1860)
Augusta, Ga.
Bibl. 5, 17

Moollinger
(See Mollinger)

Moore & Brewer (c. 1824-
1844)
New York, N.Y.
Jared L. Moore
Charles Brewer
Bibl. 15, 23, 25, 36, 44

MOORE & BREWER

Moore & Brown (c. 1832-1835)
New York, N.Y.
Jared L. Moore (?)
Francis Brown (?)
Bibl. 4, 15, 23, 28, 36, 44

Moore & Ferguson (c. 1801-
1805)
Philadelphia, Pa.
Charles Moore
John Ferguson
Bibl. 3, 23, 24, 25, 28, 36, 39,
44

MOORE & FERGUSON

Moore & Hibbard
Location unknown
Bibl. 15, 44

M & H

Apollos Moore (c. 1842)
Albany, N.Y.
Bibl. 20

Charles Moore (c. 1801-1809)
Philadelphia, Pa.
Moore & Ferguson (c. 1801-
1805)
Bibl. 3, 15, 23, 25, 36, 44

C. MOORE

E. C. Moore (c. 1850)
New York, N.Y.
Bibl. 23, 28

H. Moore
Philadelphia, Pa.
Bibl. 15, 44

H. MOORE

Jared (John) L. Moore (c.
1825-1844)
New York, N.Y.
Moore & Brewer (c. 1824-
1844)
Jared L. Moore & Co. (c.
1837-1844)

Bibl. 4, 15, 23, 24, 25, 30, 35,
36, 44, 83

J. L. MOORE   MOORE
J L MOORE   MOORE

Jared L. Moore & Co. (c.
1837-1844)
New York, N.Y.
Jared L. Moore
Charles Brewer
Francis Brown
Bibl. 15, 23

John C. Moore (c. 1832-1844)
New York, N.Y.
Eoff & Moore (c. 1835)
Bibl. 15, 23, 24, 28, 36, 44

J. C. M

John L. Moore (c. 1810)
Philadelphia, Pa.
Bibl. 28, 29

J. L. MOORE

Robert Moore (b. 1736)
Baltimore, Md. (c. 1774-1778)
Bibl. 23, 28, 36, 38

Robert Moore (c. 1829-1840)
Philadelphia, Pa.
Bibl. 3

Sylvanus Moore (c. 1847)
Oxford, N.Y.
Bibl. 20

Thomas Moore (c. 1805)
Philadelphia, Pa.
Bibl. 3, 23, 36, 44

Morand, Alleoud & Co.
(c.   -1820)
Augusta, Ga.
J. Morand
Marc Alleoud
J. Martiniere
Bibl. 17

J. Morand (c. 1820)
Augusta, Ga.
Morand, Alleoud & Co.
Bibl. 17

Thomas F. Moreland (c. 1850)
Philadelphia, Pa.
Bibl. 3, 23

Nicholas Morell (c. 1816)
Charleston, S.C.
Bibl. 5

Morgan
(See Hooker & Morgan)

Morgan (c. 1860)
Location unknown
Bibl. 15, 28, 44

MORGAN

Morgan & Cook (c. 1806-
1807)
Poughkeepsie, N.Y.
Elijah Morgan
——— Cook
Bibl. 20, 25

Morgan & Gibson (c. 1841-
1843)
Camden, N.J.
John Morgan
——— Gibson
Bibl. 3

Morgan & Kennedy (c. 1807)
Poughkeepsie, N.Y.
Elijah Morgan
——— Kennedy
Bibl. 20

Aaron Morgan (c. 1842-1850)
Philadelphia, Pa.
Bibl. 3

Arthur Morgan (c. 1849)
Philadelphia, Pa.
Bibl. 3

Chauncey Morgan (c. 1850)
Hartford, Conn.
Bibl. 23

E. Morgan & Son (c. 1832-
1835)
Poughkeepsie, N.Y.
Elijah Morgan (?)
Bibl. 20

Elijah Morgan (b. 1783-d.
1857)
Poughkeepsie, N.Y.
Sadd & Morgan (c. 1806)
Morgan & Cook (c. 1806-1807)
Morgan & Kennedy (c. 1807)
E. Morgan & Son (c. 1832-
1835) (?)
Bibl. 15, 20, 24, 25, 44

E. MORGAN

Jeremiah Morgan (c. 1743-
1744)
Charleston, S.C.
Bibl. 5, 54

John Morgan (Morin) (c. 1808-1831)
Philadelphia, Pa.
Bibl. 3, 23, 36, 38, 44

John Morgan (c. 1844-1848)
Camden, N.J.
Morgan & Gibson (c. 1841-1843)
Bibl. 3

Lewis Morgan (c. 1847)
Hartford, Conn.
Bibl. 23

Thomas Morgan (c. 1771-1782)
Baltimore, Md.
Philadelphia, Pa.
Bibl. 3, 38

William S. Morgan (c. 1837-1847)
Poughkeepsie, N.Y.
Bibl. 20

John Morin
(See John Morgan, Philadelphia)

Alexander C. Morin (c. 1813-1850)
Philadelphia, Pa.
Bibl. 3

Anthony Morin (c. 1849-1850)
Philadelphia, Pa.
Bibl. 3

Augustus Morin (c. 1835)
Philadelphia, Pa.
Bibl. 3

Pierre Morin (c. 1796)
Baltimore, Md.
Bibl. 38

Michael Mormagea (c. 1817)
Philadelphia, Pa.
Bibl. 3, 23, 36, 44

Angelo Morozzi (c. 1839-1842)
Philadelphia, Pa.
Bibl. 3

John Morrell (c. 1822-1823)
Baltimore, Md.
Bibl. 38

Joseph Morrell (c. 1840-1844)
Buffalo, N.Y.
Castle & Morrell
Bibl. 20

William M. Morrell (c. 1828-1834)
New York, N.Y.
Bibl. 14, 15, 25

{W·M ORRELL}

Morrie
(See Eagles & Morrie)

S. S. Morrill (c. 1850)
Fulton, N.Y.
Bibl. 20

Benjamin Morris (c. 1800-1802)
Petersburg, Va.
Bibl. 19

James Morris (b. 1754)
Maryland (c. 1775)
Bibl. 28, 38

James Morris (c. 1844)
Philadelphia, Pa.
Bibl. 3

John Morris (c. 1796)
New York, N.Y.
Bibl. 23, 28, 36, 44

John Morris (c. 1817, 1842)
Philadelphia, Pa.
Bibl. 3

Sylvester Morris (c. 1759-1783)
New York State
Bibl. 4, 23, 24, 25, 28, 36, 44

(SM)

William Morris (c. 1832-1833)
Utica, N.Y.
Bibl. 18, 20

William Morris (c. 1837-1850)
Philadelphia, Pa.
Bibl. 3

William Morris Jr. (c. 1844-1850)
Philadelphia, Pa.
Bibl. 3

William C. Morris (c. 1850)
Penn Yan, N.Y.
Bibl. 20

William Henry Morris (c. 1801-1805)
New York, N.Y.
Bibl. 23, 36, 44

Wollaston Morris (b. 1753)
Maryland (c. 1774)
Bibl. 38

Morrisgreen
(See Jacob Marius Groen)

Israel Morrison (c. 1823-1824)
Philadelphia, Pa.
Bibl. 3, 23, 36, 44

Norman Morrison (c. 1783)
Hartford, Conn.
Bull & Morrison (c. 1780)
Bibl. 23

William Morrison (c. 1834-1835)
New York, N.Y.
Bibl. 15

C. R. Morrissey (c. 1837)
Philadelphia, Pa.
Bibl. 3

Morrow & Barnard (c. 1805)
Philadelphia, Pa.
B. Morrow
———— Barnard
Bibl. 3

B. Morrow (c. 1806-1808)
Philadelphia, Pa.
Morrow & Barnard (c. 1805)
Bibl. 3

Obadiah Mors(e) (c. 1733)
Boston, Mass.
Bibl. 15, 44, 70

[MORS]

Morse & Mosely (c. 1823)
Albany, N.Y.
Bibl. 20

David Morse (c. 1798)
Boston, Mass.
Bibl. 4, 23, 28, 36, 44

Hazen Morse (c. 1813-1815)
Boston, Mass.
Bibl. 4, 23, 28, 36, 44

J. H. Morse (c. 1792-1820)
Boston, Mass.
Bibl. 23, 24, 29, 36, 44, 88

[J H MORSE]

Moses Morse (c. 1813-1825)
Boston, Mass.
Bibl. 4, 15, 23, 24, 28, 29, 36, 44

| M. Morse | Morse |

Nathaniel Morse (b. 1685-d.
1748)
Boston, Mass.
Bibl. 2, 15, 23, 24, 25, 28, 29,
36, 44, 54, 69

Stephen Morse (b. 1743, c.
1764-1796)
Boston, Mass.
Newbury, Mass.
Portsmouth, N.H.
Bibl. 23, 28, 29, 36, 44, 54

| MORSE |

George Morton (c. 1829-1850)
Philadelphia, Pa.
Bibl. 3

David Moseley (b. 1753-d.
1812)
Boston, Mass.
Bibl. 15, 23, 24, 25, 28, 29, 36,
44, 69, 88

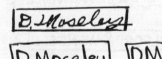

Joseph Moseley (c. 1828-1838)
New York, N.Y.
Gale & Moseley (c. 1828-1833)
Bibl. 15, 23, 36, 44

———— Moses (c. 1821)
Richmond, Va.
Bibl. 19

Isaac N. Moses (c. 1781)
Derby, Conn.
Bibl. 44

Jacob Moses (d. 1785)
Savannah, Ga. (c. 1768-1769)
Birmingham, Ga.
Baltimore, Md.
Sime & Moses (c. 1768-1769)
Bibl. 17, 24, 25, 29, 36, 44

| MOSES |

Jacob Moses (c. 1817-1822)
Baltimore, Md.
Philadelphia, Pa.
Bibl. 3, 38

M. Moses (c. 1830)
Boston, Mass.
Bibl. 36

O. H. Moses
Location unknown
Bibl. 21

S. Moses (c. 1830)
Boston, Mass.
Bibl. 23

Mosher & Davis (c. 1834)
Hamilton, N.Y.
S. Mosher
———— Davis
Bibl. 20

S. Mosher (c. 1830)
Hamilton, N.Y.
Mosher & Davis (c. 1834)
Bibl. 20

John Moshore (c. 1805)
New York, N.Y.
Bibl. 23, 36

Jacob Mosiman (c. 1810-1812)
Baltimore, Md.
Bibl. 38

Barnet Moss (c. 1840)
Warrenton, Va.
Bibl. 19

(B. MOSS)

Isaac Nichols Moss (b. 1760-d.
1840)
Derby, Conn.
Bibl. 16, 23, 28, 36

George Moton (c. 1849-1850)
Philadelphia, Pa.
Bibl. 3

Mott Bros. (c. 1840)
New York, N.Y.
Bibl. 15

J. & W. Mott
(See John S. & William Mott)

James S. Mott (c. 1829-1835)
New York, N.Y.
Bibl. 15, 24, 25

| J S MOTT |
| COR. PEARL & FULTON ST NY |

John S. Mott (c. 1790)
New York, N.Y.
Bibl. 23, 24, 25, 28, 29, 36, 44

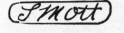

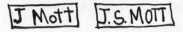

John S. & William Mott (c.
1789)
New York, N.Y.
J. & W. Mott
W. & J. S. Mott
Bibl. 15, 23, 24, 25, 28, 29, 36,
44

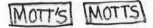

| MOTT'S | MOTTS |

Jordan Mott (c. 1815-1835)
New York, N.Y.
Bibl. 15, 44

| J. MOTT |

Jordan Mott Jr. (c. 1836)
New York, N.Y.
Bibl. 15

W. & J. S. Mott
(See John S. & William Mott)

Benjamin Motteux
(c. -1725)
Charleston, S.C.
Bibl. 5

E. L. Mottley & Co. (c. 1857)
Bowling Green, Ky.
Bibl. 54

John Moulinar (b. 1722, c.
1761)
Albany, N.Y.
New York, N.Y.
Bibl. 4, 15, 23, 24, 25, 28, 29, 30,
35, 36, 44, 78

| I. M |
| I M |

Moulton & Bradbury (c. 1830)
Newburyport, Mass.
Joseph Moulton IV
Theophilus Bradbury

Bibl. 23, 28, 36, 44

Moulton & Davis (c. 1824-1830)
Newburyport, Mass.
Abel Moulton
John D. (W. ?) Davis
Bibl. 15, 23, 25, 36, 44

M & D   B

Moulton & Lunt (c. 1870)
Newburyport, Mass.
William Moulton V
———— Lunt
Bibl. 28

Abel Moulton (b. 1784-d.
1840)
Newburyport, Mass.
Moulton & Davis (c. 1824-1830)
Bibl. 15, 23, 24, 25, 28, 29, 36

A. MOULTON

Ebenezer (Eben Noyes) S.
Moulton (b. 1768-d. 1824)
Boston, Mass.
Newburyport, Mass.
Bibl. 24, 25, 28, 29, 44, 54

Edmund Moulton (c. 1780)
Marietta, Ohio
Bibl. 34

Edward Moulton (b. 1846-d.
1907)
Newburyport, Mass.
Bibl. 28

Edward S. Moulton (b. 1778-d.
1855)
Rochester, N.H. (c. 1800)
Bibl. 25, 44

Enoch Moulton (b. 1780-d.
1815)
Portland, Me. (c. 1801)
Bibl. 15, 23, 24, 25, 28, 29, 36,
44

E. MOULTON

Joseph Moulton I (b. 1694-d.
1756)
Newburyport, Mass.
Bibl. 2, 28, 29, 36

J. M

Joseph Moulton II (b. 1724-d.
1795)
Newburyport, Mass.
Marietta, Ohio (?)

Joseph M. Moulton III (b.
1740-d. 1818)
Newburyport, Mass.
Bibl. 2, 15, 23, 24, 25, 28, 29,
36, 44, 54

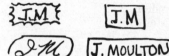

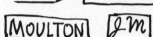

Joseph Moulton IV (b. 1814-d.
1903)
Newburyport, Mass.
Bibl. 15, 23, 24, 25, 28, 29, 36,
44

J MOULTON
J M

William Moulton I (b. 1617-d.
1664)
Hampton, N.H. (c. 1638)
Bibl. 15, 28

William Moulton II (b. 1664-d.
1732)
Newburyport, Mass.
Bibl. 15, 23, 24, 28, 36

William Moulton III (b. 1720-d.
1793)
Newburyport, Mass.
Marietta, Ohio (c. 1788)
Bibl. 15, 23, 25, 28, 34, 36, 44

W M   W MOULTON

William Moulton IV (b.
1772-d. 1861)
Newburyport, Mass.
Bibl. 15, 23, 28, 29, 36

W MOULTON   W M   ?
MOULTON   MOULTON

William Moulton V (b. 1851)
Newburyport, Mass.

Moulton & Lunt (c. 1870)
Bibl. 28

Samuel P. Mountain (c. 1842)
Philadelphia, Pa.
Bibl. 3

John Mountford (c. 1818-1819)
Philadelphia, Pa.
Bibl. 3

John Hugan Moyston (b.
1772-d. 1844)
Schenectady, N.Y. (c. 1798)
Bibl. 20

Mudge & Co. (c. 1848)
New York, N.Y.
Bibl. 23

M. A. Mudge (c. 1837)
Philadelphia, Pa.
Bibl. 3

Mulen
(See Mullin)

Mulford & Wende(a)ll
(c. 1843-1850)
Albany, N.Y.
John H. Mulford
William Wendell
Bibl. 15, 20, 23, 24, 25, 28, 44

MULFORD&WENDALL

MULFORD& WENDELL

John H. Mulford (c. 1841-1843)
Albany, N.Y.
Boyd & Mulford (c. 1832-1842)
Mulford & Wendell (c. 1843-1850)
Bibl. 20, 23, 28, 36, 44

William Mulholland (c. 1837-1844)
Philadelphia, Pa.
Bibl. 3

William Mulhollen (c. 1817-1818)
Philadelphia, Pa.
Bibl. 3

Robert Mullan (c. 1764)
Baltimore, Md.
Bibl. 38

Muller
(See Metten & Muller)

Charles Muller (19th century)
Winnsboro, S.C.
Bibl. 5

Ferdinand Muller (c. 1844)
New York, N.Y.
Bibl. 23

Fred Will Muller (c. 1739)
Ebenezer, Ga.
Bibl. 17

H. Mulligan (c. 1840)
Philadelphia, Pa.
Bibl. 24, 25, 44

William (W. J.) Mullin
(Mulen) (c. 1829-1833)
Philadelphia, Pa.
Bibl. 3

Mumford
(See Barker & Mumford)

Henry (G.) (B.) Mumford
(c. 1813)
Providence, R.I.
Frost & Mumford (c. 1810) (?)
George C. (G.) Clark (c. 1813-
1824)
Bibl. 15, 23, 25, 28, 36

J. T. Munds (c. 1855-1859)
Sumter, S.C.
Bibl. 5

Munger & Benedict (c. 1826-
1828)
Auburn, N.Y.
Asa Munger
——— Benedict
Bibl. 20, 25

Munger & Dodge (c. 1824-
1825)
Ithaca, N.Y.
——— Munger
Abraham Dodge Jr.
Bibl. 20

Munger & Pratt (c. 1832)
Ithaca, N.Y.
——— Munger
Daniel Pratt
Bibl. 20

A. Munger & Son (c. 1840)
Auburn, N.Y.
Asa Munger (?)
Bibl. 15, 20, 25, 44

A. MUNGER & SON

Asa Munger (b. 1778-d. 1851)
Herkimer, N.Y. (c. 1810-1818)
Auburn, N.Y. (c. 1818-   )
Munger & Benedict (c. 1826-
1828)
A. Munger & Son (c. 1840) (?)
Bibl. 15, 20, 25, 44

A. MUNGER

Austin E. Munger (c. 1847)
Syracuse, N.Y.
Bibl. 20

James E. Munger (c. 1839-
1845)
Ithaca, N.Y.
Bibl. 20

Sylvester Munger
Onondaga, N.Y. (c. 1822)
Elmira, N.Y. (c. 1835)
Ithaca, N.Y. (c. 1835-1845)
Bibl. 20

John Munro (c. 1785-1809)
Charleston, S.C.
Bibl. 5, 15

Munro

Munroe & Holman (c. 1826-
1829)
Baltimore, Md.
Nathaniel Munroe
D. Holman
Bibl. 38

C. A. Munroe
Location unknown
Bibl. 28

D. Munroe
Location unknown
Bibl. 28

D. MUNROE

James Munroe (b. 1784-d.
1879)
Barnstable, Mass.

Bibl. 15, 23, 24, 25, 28, 29,
36, 44

John Munroe
(See James Munroe; he is
James Munroe)

Nathaniel Munroe (b. 1777-d.
1861)
Norfolk, Va. (c. 1805)
Massachusetts (before 1815)
Baltimore, Md. (c. 1815-1840)
Munroe & Holman (c. 1826-
1829)
Bibl. 19, 24, 25, 29, 38, 44

G. C. Munsell (c. 1835-
1836-   )
Northampton, Mass.
Bibl. 15, 44, 84

G.C. MUNSELL COIN   PURE

Amos Munson (b. 1753-d.
1785)
New Haven, Conn.
Bibl. 16, 23, 28, 36, 44

Cornelius Munson (b. 1742-d.
1776)
Wallingford, Conn.
Bibl. 16, 23, 28, 36, 44

A. H. Munyan (c. 1848)
Northampton, Mass.
Bibl. 84

Murdoch
(See Murdock)

Murdock & Andrews (c. 1822-
1826, c. 1838-1849)
Utica, N.Y.
James Murdock
Elon Andrews
Selden Collins Jr.

Bibl. 18, 20, 25, 44

MURDOCK & ANDREWS

Murdock & Collins (c. 1849-
1850)
Utica, N.Y.
James Murdock
Selden Collins Jr.
Bibl. 18, 20

David A. Murdock (c. 1812)
New Bern, N.C.
Bibl. 21

H. & S. Murdock & Co.
(c. 1830)
Philadelphia, Pa. (?)
Bibl. 89

H & S MURDOCK

James Murdock (b. 1792-d.
1850)
Utica, N.Y.
Murdock & Andrews (c. 1822-
1826, c. 1838-1849)
James Murdock & Co. (c. 1826-
1838)
Murdock & Collins (c. 1849-
1850)
Bibl. 15, 18, 20

James Murdock & Co. (c. 1826-
1838)
Utica, N.Y.
James Murdock
Elon Andrews
Selden Collins Jr.
Julius A. Spencer
Bibl. 15, 18, 20, 44

JAMES MURDOCK & CO

James Murdock of Philadelphia
(See next entry; he is
John Murdock)

John Murdock (b. 1748-d.
1786)
Philadelphia, Pa. (c. 1779-1785)
Woodbury, N.J. (c. 1785-1786)
Bibl. 3, 15, 23, 24, 25, 29, 36,
39, 44, 46, 54, 81

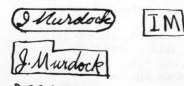

John Murdock & Co. is
James Murdock & Co.,
Philadelphia, Pa.

Murphy & Pollard (c. 1818-
1820)
Norfolk, Va.
John Murphy
Lewis R. Pollard
Bibl. 19

James Murphy
Boston, Mass. (c. 1816)
Philadelphia, Pa. (c. 1828-1846)
Bibl. 3, 15, 23, 24, 25, 29, 36, 44

J. MURPHY

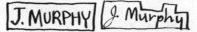

John Murphy (c. 1798-1810)
Norfolk, Va.
Bibl. 19

John B. Murphy
Norfolk, Va. (c. 1830-1833)
Augusta, Ga. (c. 1834-1845)
Bibl. 17, 19

J. B. Murphy

Robert (R. E.) Murphy
(c. 1849-1850)
Philadelphia, Pa.
Bibl. 3

Murray, Draper, Fairman &
Co. (c. 1830)
Philadelphia, Pa.
Jacob Perkins
Gideon Fairman (?)
Bibl. 28

Alexander Murray (c. 1814-
1816)
Philadelphia, Pa.
Bibl. 3

Elijah Murray (c. 1829)
Sandy Hill, N.Y.
Bibl. 20

John Murray (c. 1776)
New York, N.Y.
Bibl. 28

William Murray (c. 1850)
Louisville, Ky.
Bibl. 32

John N. Murrell (c. 1816)
Charleston, S.C.
Bibl. 5

Robert Murrey (c. 1805)
Baltimore, Md.
Bibl. 38

Perry Murtel (c. 1839)
Philadelphia, Pa.
Bibl. 3

Musgrave & James (c. 1797-
1811)
Philadelphia, Pa.
(Could be incorrect listing for
James Musgrave.)
Bibl. 28, 89

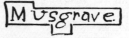

Musgrave & Kelly (c. 1812)
Buffalo, N.Y.
Bibl. 20

James Musgrave (c. 1793-1813)
Philadelphia, Pa.
Parry & Musgrave (c. 1793-
1796)
Bibl. 3, 4, 23, 24, 25, 29, 36, 39,
44, 81

Musgrave   Musgrave

S. Musgrove (c. 1800-1850)
Location unknown
Bibl. 72

S. MUSGROVE

Myer & McClanan (c. 1836-
1837)
Buffalo, N.Y.
Henry B. Myer
James McClanan
Bibl. 20

Gottlieb Myer (Meyer)
Norfolk, Va.
Bibl. 28

H. B. Myer (c. 1810)
New York, N.Y.
Bibl. 23, 24, 36

H B MYER   H B MYER

H. B. Myer & Co. (c. 1832-
1835)
Newburgh, N.Y.
Henry B. Myer
Bibl. 20

Henry B. Myer
Newburgh, N.Y. (c. 1818-1835)
Buffalo, N.Y. (c. 1836-1848)

H. B. Myer & Co. (c. 1832-1835)
Myer & McClanan (c. 1836-1837)
Bibl. 15, 20, 25, 29, 44

H B MYER

John A. Myer (c. 1832)
Charleston, S.C.
Bibl. 5

Jacob Myers
(See Jacob Mayer)

Myers and Holsted
New York, N.Y. (?)
Myer Myers (b. 1723-d. 1795)
———— Holsted
Bibl. 2, 15, 23, 24, 25, 29, 30, 35, 36, 40, 44, 54, 61

Myers & Jacob (c. 1839)
Philadelphia, Pa.
Albert G. Myers
Celestin Jacob (?)
Bibl. 3, 23, 36, 44

Albert G. Myers
Philadelphia, Pa. (c. 1837)
Camden, N.J. (c. 1847)
Bibl. 3, 23, 36, 44

Christalar Myers (c. 1844)
Philadelphia, Pa.
Bibl. 3

John Myers (c. 1785-1804)
Philadelphia, Pa.
Bibl. 3, 4, 15, 23, 24, 25, 28, 29, 36, 39, 44, 54, 81

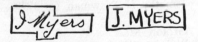

Myer Myers (b. 1723-d. 1795)
Norwalk, Conn.
Stamford, Conn.
Underhill, Vt.
New York, N.Y. (c. 1770)
Hays & Myers (c. 1770)
Myers & Holsted
Bibl. 2, 15, 23, 24, 25, 29, 30, 35, 36, 40, 44, 54, 61

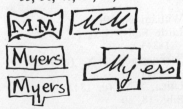

Comfort Starr Mygatt
(b. 1763-d. 1823)
Danbury, Conn. (c. 1804)
Canfield, Ohio (c. 1807)
Bibl. 16, 28, 36, 44

David Mygatt (b. 1777-d. 1822)
Danbury, Conn.
South East, N.Y.
Bibl. 16, 23, 24, 25, 28, 29, 36, 44, 61

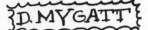

DM

Eli Mygatt (b. 1742-d. 1807)
Danbury, Conn.
Daniel Noble Carrington
(c. 1793)
Najah Taylor (c. 1793)
Bibl. 16, 23, 28, 36, 44

Noadiah Mygatt
New Milford, Conn.
Isaac Beach (c. 1788-1794)
Bibl. 89

J. P. Mylius (c. 1838)
St. Louis, Mo.
Bibl. 54

John P. Mylius (c. 1835-1836)
Harpers Ferry, Va.
Bibl. 19

Myot
(See Miot)

Myre
(See Jacob Mayer)

Joseph Myring (c. 1811-1825)
Philadelphia, Pa.
Bibl. 3

———— Mysendhender
(c. 1813)
Philadelphia, Pa.
Bibl. 23, 36, 44

Jacob Mytinger
Newtown, Va. (c. 1827)
Warrenton, Va. (c. 1848-1860)
Bibl. 19

J. MYTINGER

N. & Pratt
Location unknown

Bibl. 15

N & PRATT

Nagel
(See Nagle)

William Nagel (c. 1865)
Paducah, Ky.
Bibl. 54

George P. Nagle (c. 1823-1850)
Philadelphia, Pa.
Bibl. 3

R. Nagle (c. 1828)
Philadelphia, Pa.
Bibl. 3

R. C. Nagle (c. 1828-1833)
Philadelphia, Pa.
Bibl. 3

John Naglee (Nagles)
(d. 1780)
Philadelphia, Pa. (c. 1748-1755)
Bibl. 3, 23, 28, 36, 44

Martin Nangle (c. 1842)
Philadelphia, Pa.
Bibl. 3, 23

William Nangle (c. 1833-1837)
Philadelphia, Pa.
Bibl. 3

John F. Nardler (c. 1819-1822)
Philadelphia, Pa.
Bibl. 3

F. J. Nardin (c. 1823-1824)
Philadelphia, Pa.
Bibl. 3

Coleman Nash (c. 1820)
Cincinnati, Ohio
Bibl. 34

Martin Naugh (c. 1833)
New York, N.Y.
Bibl. 15

Joseph Neagt (c. 1816)
Philadelphia, Pa.
Bibl. 3

Daniel Neall (b. 1784-d. 1846)
Milford, Del.
Bibl. 15, 25, 30, 44

D. NEALL   D. N

Needels
(See Needles)

Joseph Needham
Richmond, Va. (c. 1799)
Lynchburg, Va. (c. 1814)
Bibl. 19, 54

William Needles (Needels)
Easton, Md. (c. 1798-1818)
Bowdle & Needles (c. 1798)
Bibl. 25, 29, 38, 44

W. NEEDELS

Samuel Neely (c. 1842)
Philadelphia, Pa.
Bibl. 3

Paul Negrin (c. 1820-1823)
Charlottesville, Va.
Bibl. 19

Daniel Neill (c. 1823-1833)
Philadelphia, Pa.
Bibl. 3

George Neilson (d. 1736)
Annapolis, Md. (c. 1716-1736)
Bibl. 3, 38

Neise
(See Kneass)

George Neiser (c. 1823-1824)
Philadelphia, Pa.
Bibl. 3

Augustine Neisser (c. 1764-
1772, d. 1780)
Philadelphia, Pa.
Bibl. 3

George B. Neisser (c. 1829-
1839)
Philadelphia, Pa.
Bibl. 3

Joseph Neitt (c. 1813)
Philadelphia, Pa.
Bibl. 3

Ambrose Nelson
Charleston, S.C. (c. 1795)
Savannah, Ga. (c. 1795-1801)
Bibl. 5, 17

John Nelson (d. 1795?)
Portsmouth, N.H. (c. 1755)
Bibl. 25, 44, 54

R. & J. Nelson (c. 1850)
Dunkirk, N.Y.
Bibl. 20

Richard W. Nelson (c. 1829-
1837)

Philadelphia, Pa.
Bibl. 3

Neuill
(See Nevill)

Jan Neuss (Nys) (Nice) (d.
1719)
Philadelphia, Pa. (c. 1698)
Bibl. 3, 23, 44

Richard Nevill (Neuill)
Boston, Mass. (c. 1674)
Bibl. 4, 23, 28, 36, 44

Rufus Nevins
New York, N.Y.
Hyde & Nevins (c. 1798-1819)
Bibl. 15, 23, 24, 25, 28, 29,
36, 44

Edwin C. Newberry
Brooklyn, N.Y. (c. 1828)
Bibl. 16, 23, 28, 44

J. & R. Newberry (c. 1816)
Philadelphia, Pa.
Bibl. 3

James Newberry (c. 1748)
Annapolis, Md.
Bibl. 38

James W. Newberry (c. 1819-
1850)
Philadelphia, Pa.
Bibl. 3

Newcomb
(See Palmer & Newcomb)

H. K. Newcomb (c. 1821-1850)
Watertown, N.Y.
Bibl. 20, 25, 44

Henry Newcomb (d. 1843)
Cooperstown, N.Y. (c. 1842-
1843)
Bibl. 20

J. N. Newell (c. 1834)
Petersburg, Va.
Bibl. 19

James J. Newell (c. 1834)
Utica, N.Y.
Bibl. 18, 20

Norman Newell (c. 1844)
Rochester, N.Y.
Bibl. 20

Dudley Newhall (c. 1730)
Salem, Mass.
Bibl. 23, 28, 36, 44

Joseph Newkirke (Van
Niewkirke) (Van Nieukirke)
New York, N.Y. (c. 1716)
Bibl. 23, 28, 29, 36, 44

Newland & Jones (c. 1825-
1827)
Albany, N.Y.
Luke F. Newland
———— Jones
Bibl. 20

Luke F. Newland (c. 1824-
1847)
Albany, N.Y.
Newland & Jones (c. 1825-
1827)
Bibl. 20

Edward G. Newlin (c. 1848)
Philadelphia, Pa.
Warner & Newlin (c. 1848-
1850)
Bibl. 3

John Newman (c. 1833-1837)
Philadelphia, Pa.
Bibl. 3

John A. Newman (c. 1833-
1850)
Philadelphia, Pa.
Witham & Newman (c. 1837-
1850)
Bibl. 3

Timothy H. Newman (c. 1778-
1812)
Groton, Mass.
Bibl. 15, 24, 25, 28, 29, 36, 44

William Newth
Little Falls, N.Y. (c. 1832-
1834)
Schenectady, N.Y. (c. 1837-
1842)
Utica, N.Y. (c. 1842-1843)
Bibl. 18, 20

Newton & Reed (c. 1850)
Location unknown
Bibl. 15, 44

NEWTON & REED

Neys
(See Johannis Nys)

Nice
(See Jan Neuss)
(See Johannis Nys)

Nicherson
(See Nickerson)

Casper Nicholas (c. 1837)
Philadelphia, Pa.
Bibl. 3

Michael Nicholas (c. 1793)
Philadelphia, Pa.
Bibl. 3

Nichols
(See Graves & Nichols)

———— Nichols (c. 1840)
Albany, N.Y. (?)
Bibl. 28

NICHOLS

Nichols and Salisbury (c. 1844-
1846)
Charleston, S.C.
Bibl. 5, 44, 54

N & S   Nichols & Salisbury

Basset(t) Nichols (c. 1815)
Providence, R.I.
Bibl. 15, 23, 24, 25, 28, 29,
36, 39, 44, 54

NICHOLS

D. B. Nichols & Co. (c. 1820-
1830)
Savannah, Ga.
David B. Nichols
John P. Smith
Bibl. 17

David B. Nichols (b. 1791-d.
1860)
Savannah, Ga. (c. 1815)
D. B. Nichols & Co. (c. 1820-
1830)
Bibl. 17

H. Nichols (c. 1850)
Location unknown

Bibl. 15, 44

H. NICHOLS

H. M. Nichols (Nickols)
(c. 1840)
Location unknown
Bibl. 15, 24, 72

H. M. NICHOLS

James Nichols (b. 1750)
Charleston, S.C. (c. 1774)
Bibl. 5

Nathaniel B. Nichols (d. 1831)
Petersburg, Va. (c. 1817-
1831-   )
Bibl. 19

N. B. Nichols

Susanna E. Nichols
Petersburg, Va.
C. Lumsden & Co. (c. 1834)
Bibl. 19

William Nichols (c. 1819-1832)
Cooperstown, N.Y.
Bibl. 20

William Stoddard Nichols
(b. 1785-d. 1871)
Newport, R.I. (c. 1808)
Bibl. 6, 23, 24, 25, 28, 29, 36,
39, 44, 54

NICHOLS

W S N   W. S. NICHOLS

Casper Nickels (c. 1823-1824)
Philadelphia, Pa.
Bibl. 3

Baty Nickerson (Nicherson)
Harwich, Mass. (c. 1825)
Bibl. 23, 28, 36

Nickols
(See H. M. Nichols)

Julian Nicolet (c. 1819-1831)
Baltimore, Md.
Bibl. 38

Julian Nicolet (c. 1842-1848)
St. Louis, Mo.
Bibl. 54

Joseph Marce Nicollett
(c. 1797)
Philadelphia, Pa.
Bibl. 3

Joseph W. Nicollett (c. 1798)
Philadelphia, Pa.
Bibl. 3

Mary Nicollett (c. 1799)
Philadelphia, Pa.
Bibl. 3

———— Nicolette (c. 1793)
Philadelphia, Pa.
Bibl. 3

Henry Niel (c. 1811)
Edenton, N.C.
Bibl. 21

Jan Niewkerk (Van Nieukirke)
(Van Niewkirke)
New York, N.Y. (c. 1708-
1716)
Bibl. 15, 25, 35, 54

Joseph Nihet (Nitch) (c. 1817-
1819)
Philadelphia, Pa.
Bibl. 3

James Ninde (c. 1799-1835)
Baltimore, Md.
Bibl. 38

Nitch
(See Nihet)

Richard Nixon (c. 1820-1835)
Philadelphia, Pa.
Bibl. 3, 15, 23, 25, 36, 44

R. NIXON

George Noble (c. 1846-1850)
Philadelphia, Pa.
Bibl. 3

Joseph Noble (c. 1823)
Portland, Me.
Wyer & Noble
Bibl. 23, 36, 44

Alpheus (Alpherrs) Noe
(c. 1850)
Philadelphia, Pa.
Bibl. 3, 23

Beverly Noel (c. 1838-1839)
Louisville, Ky.
Bibl. 32, 54

Washington Noel (c. 1836)
Louisville, Ky.
Bibl. 32

William Noggle (c. 1822)
Baltimore, Md.
Bibl. 38

Nehemiah Norcross (c. 1765-1804)
Boston, Mass.
Bibl. 4, 23, 24, 25, 28, 29, 36, 44, 72

Charles Nordmeyer (c. 1845-1850)
Richmond, Va.
Bibl. 19

Chas Nordmeyer

Norman & Bedwell (c. 1779)
Philadelphia, Pa.
John Norman
—————— Bedwell
Bibl. 3

Norman & Ward (c. 1774)
Philadelphia, Pa.
John Norman
—————— Ward
Bibl. 3

James S. Norman (c. 1840)
Lincolnton, N.C.
Bibl. 21

John Norman (d. 1817)
Philadelphia Pa. (c. 1748-1817)
Boston, Mass.
Norman & Ward (c. 1774)
Norman & Bedwell (c. 1779)
Bibl. 3, 28

George Norris (b. 1752)
Philadelphia, Pa. (c. 1775)
Bibl. 3, 23, 28, 36, 44

Patrick Norris (c. 1844-1845)
Philadelphia, Pa.
Bibl. 3

North & Co.
(See W. B. North & Co.)

Linus North (c. 1830)
Palmyra, N.Y.
Bibl. 20

Owen North (c. 1827-1829)
New York, N.Y.
Bibl. 15

William B. North (b. 1787-d. 1838)
New Haven, Conn. (c. 1810)
New York, N.Y. (c. 1818-1826)

New Britain, Conn. (c. 1827-1831)
William B. North & Co. (c. 1824-1826)
Mather & North (c. 1827-1829)
Bibl. 15, 23, 24, 25, 28, 29, 36, 44

W B N

W(illiam). B. North & Co. (c. 1824-1826)
(North & Co.)
New York, N.Y.
Bibl. 15, 24, 25, 28, 35, 44, 83

W B NORTH & CO

David I. Northee (Northey) (d. 1778)
Salem, Mass. (c. 1748)
Bibl. 15, 24, 25, 28, 29, 36, 44, 55, 72

D. N.

D. NORTHEE   D I NORTHEE

Abijah Northey (d. 1817)
Salem, Mass. (c. 1775)
Bibl. 28, 29, 36, 44

A N   ?

Elijah Northey (c. 1844-1850)
Philadelphia, Pa.
Bibl. 3

Norton & Hotchkiss (c. 1849-   )
Syracuse, N.Y.
Benjamin R. Norton
David Hotchkiss
Bibl. 20

Norton & Pitkin (Pitkin & Norton) (c. 1825)
Hartford, Conn.
C. C. Norton
Walter M. Pitkin
Bibl. 23, 24, 25, 29, 36, 44

C C NORTON & PITKIN

Norton & Seymour (c. 1850)
Syracuse, N.Y.
Benjamin R. Norton
Joseph Seymour
Bibl. 15, 20, 44

NORTON & SEYMOUR

Norton, Seymour & Co. (c. 1850)
Syracuse, N.Y.

Benjamin R. Norton
Joseph Seymour
Bibl. 15, 20, 44

Andrew Norton (b. 1765-d. 1838)
Goshen, Conn.
Bibl. 16, 23, 25, 28, 36, 44

B. R. Norton & Co. (c. 1844-1849)
Syracuse, N.Y.
Benjamin R. Norton
Bibl. 20, 44

Benjamin Norton (c. 1810-1813)
Boston, Mass.
Bibl. 4, 23, 28, 36, 44

Benjamin R. Norton
Palmyra, N.Y. (c. 1841)
Syracuse, N.Y. (c. 1845-1850)
Hotchkiss & Norton (c. 1841)
B. R. Norton & Co. (c. 1844-1849)
Norton & Hotchkiss (c. 1849-   )
Norton & Seymour (c. 1850)
Norton, Seymour & Co. (c. 1850)
Bibl. 15, 20, 25, 44

B R NORTON

C. C. Norton
Hartford, Conn. (c. 1820-1825)
Norton & Pitkin (c. 1825)
(Pitkin & Norton)
Bibl. 23, 24, 25, 28, 29, 36, 44

C C NORTON

John F. Norton (c. 1820-1822)
Philadelphia, Pa.
Bibl. 3

Jonathan Norton (c. 1783)
Savannah, Ga.
Papot & Norton (c. 1790-   )
Bibl. 17

Samuel Norton (c. 1790)
Hingham, Mass.
Bibl. 23, 28, 36, 44

Thomas Norton (b. 1773-d. 1834)
Farmington, Conn.
Albion, N.Y.

Bibl. 16, 23, 24, 25, 28, 29,
36, 44

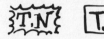

Thomas Norton (c. 1786-1811)
Philadelphia, Pa.
Waage & Norton (c. 1798)
Bibl. 3

Thomas Norton (b. 1773-d.
1834)
Morrisville, N.Y. (-1827)
Albion, N. Y. (c. 1827-1834)
Bibl. 20

Richard Norwood (c. 1774)
New York, N.Y.
Bibl. 23, 36, 44

Nowlan & Co. (c. 1866-1908)
Richmond, Va.
Thomas Nowlan
Bibl. 19

NOWLAN & CO

Thomas Nowlan
Petersburg, Va. (c. 1848-1865)
Richmond, Va. (c. 1866-1908)
Nowlan & Co. (c. 1866-1908)
Bibl. 19

Thomas Nowland (c. 1806-
1808)
Philadelphia, Pa.
Bibl. 3

Martin Noxon (c. 1780-1814)
Edenton, N.C. (c. 1800-   )
Oswego, N.Y.
Bibl. 21, 25, 28, 29, 44

NOXON

John Noyes (b. 1674-d. 1749)
Boston, Mass.
Bibl. 2, 15, 23, 25, 28, 29, 36, 44,
54, 66, 69, 72

Joseph Noyes (d. 1719)
Philadelphia, Pa.
Bibl. 24

N. & T. F. Noyes
Norwich, Conn. (?)
Bibl. 36

Samuel Noyes (b. 1747-d. 1781)
Norwich, Conn.
Bibl. 16, 23, 28, 36, 44

Frederick Nusz (c. 1819)
Fredericktown, Md.
Bibl. 25, 29, 38, 44

F NUSZ

——— Nutman (c. 1818)
Lexington, Ky.
January & Nutman
Bibl. 32, 54

Joseph Nuttall (b. 1738)
Maryland (c. 1774)
Bibl. 23, 28, 36, 38, 44

Jan Nys
(See Jan Neuss)

Johan Nys
(See John Denise)

Johannis Nys (Neys) (Nice)
(Dennis) (De Noys)
(b. 1671-d. 1734)
Philadelphia, Pa. (c. 1700-1723)
Bibl. 3, 15, 24, 25, 30, 39, 44, 81

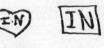

Oakes & Spencer (c. 1814)
Hartford, Conn.
Frederick Oakes
James Spencer
Bibl. 15, 16, 23, 24, 25, 28, 29,
36, 44

O & S

Frederick Oakes (c. 1804-1825)
Hartford, Conn.
Oakes & Spencer (c. 1814)
David Greenleaf Jr.
Bibl. 15, 16, 23, 24, 25, 28, 29,
36, 44

H. Oakes
Location unknown
Bibl. 15, 44

H Oakes

John Oathret (c. 1843)
Philadelphia, Pa.
Bibl. 3

James O'Brien (c. 1850)
Philadelphia, Pa.
Bibl. 3

John O'Brien (c. 1844-1849)
Philadelphia, Pa.
Bibl. 3

M. Isabella O'Brien (d. 1808)
Charleston, S.C. (c. 1802-1808)
Bibl. 5

Patrick O'Brien (c. 1848-1850)
Philadelphia, Pa.
Bibl. 3

Joseph Obrihim (c. 1784)
Annapolis, Md.
Bibl. 36

Narcis O'Clair (c. 1819)
Albany, N.Y.
Bibl. 20

Perry O'Daniel (c. 1837-1850)
Philadelphia, Pa.
Bibl. 3

Lawrence Odell (c. 1827-1835)
New York, N.Y.
Bibl. 15, 23, 36, 44

Charles E. Oertelt (O'Ertell)
Philadelphia, Pa. (c. 1830-
1850)
Bibl. 3, 23, 36, 44

Charles G. Oertelt (c. 1847-
1849)
Philadelphia, Pa.
Bibl. 3, 44

E. C. Oertelt (c. 1833)
Philadelphia, Pa.
Bibl. 3, 44

John Ogier (b. 1761-d. 1814)
New York, N.Y. (c. 1791)
Baltimore, Md. (c. 1796-1799)
Norfolk, Va. (c. 1799-1806)
Savannah, Ga. (c. 1808-1814)
Bibl. 17, 19, 23, 28, 38, 44

Gabriel Ogilvie (c. 1791-1802)
New York, N.Y.
Bibl. 23, 36

John Ogilvie (c. 1732-1764)
New York, N.Y.
Bibl. 25, 44

William Ogle (c. 1828-1829)
Philadelphia, Pa.
Bibl. 3

Charles O'Hara (c. 1799-1800)
Philadelphia, Pa.
Bibl. 3

John O'Hara (c. 1844-1849)
Philadelphia, Pa.
Bibl. 3

Franklin Olds (c. 1842)
Providence, R.I.
Bibl. 23

D. F. Olendorf (c. 1849-   )
Cooperstown, N.Y.
Bibl. 20

Oliphant & Henderson
   (c. 1767)
Charleston, S.C.
James Oliphant
Logan Henderson
Bibl. 5

James Oliphant (c. 1767-1777)
Charleston, S.C.
Oliphant & Henderson
   (c. 1767)
Bibl. 5

Oliver & Graham (c. 1823-
1824)
Philadelphia, Pa.
Bibl. 3

Andrew Oliver (c. 1722)
Boston, Mass.
Bibl. 15, 25, 28, 29, 36, 44

| A. OLIVER | A O |

Daniel Oliver (c. 1805)
Philadelphia, Pa.
Bibl. 23, 24, 25, 29, 36, 44

| D. OLIVER |

Frederick Oliver (c. 1840-1842)
Buffalo, N.Y.
Bibl. 20

Griffith Oliver (c. 1785)
Philadelphia, Pa.
Bibl. 3

Peter Oliver (b. 1682-d. 1712)
Boston, Mass.
Bibl. 2, 15, 23, 24, 25, 28, 29,
   36, 39, 44, 54

William G. Oliver (c. 1839-
1848)
Buffalo, N.Y.
Bibl. 20

Peter Olivier (d. 1798)
Philadelphia, Pa. (c. 1797)
Bibl. 3, 15, 23, 24, 25, 28, 29, 36,
44

| P O |

Gideon Olmstead (c. 1832)
Charlotte, N.C.
Bibl. 21

N. Olmstead & Son (c. 1847)
Farmington, Conn.
New Haven, Conn.
Nathaniel Olmsted
Bibl. 16, 23, 28, 44

| N. OLMSTED & SON |

P. H. Olmstead (c. 1830)
Columbus, Ohio
Bibl. 34

Nathaniel Olmste(a)d
   (b. 1785-d. 1860)
Farmington, Conn. (c. 1808)
New Haven, Conn. (c. 1826)
N. Olmstead & Son (c. 1847)
Bibl. 15, 16, 23, 24, 25, 28, 29,
   36, 44

| N. OLMSTED |

Henry Olwine (c. 1840-1850)
Philadelphia, Pa.
Bibl. 3

Gerrit (Garrett) Onclebagh
   (Onkelbag) (b. 1670-d.
   1732)
New York, N.Y.
Bibl. 2, 4, 15, 23, 24, 25, 28,
   29, 30, 35, 36, 44, 54

N. & D. Onderdonk
New York, N.Y. (?)
Bibl. 28

N & D O

Charles O'Neil (c. 1823)
New Haven, Conn.
Bibl. 28

Thomas O'Neil (c. 1837-1842)
Philadelphia, Pa.
Bibl. 3

John O'Neill (c. 1841)
Philadelphia, Pa.
Bibl. 3

Antoine Oneille (b. 1764-d.
   1820)
(Oneil) (Oneal) (Onelle)
   (Onel)
Detroit, Mich. (c. 1797)
Vincennes, Ind. (c. 1803-1817)
Missouri Territory (c. 1820)
Bibl. 54, 58

A O | A O |

Onel
Onelle
(See Oneille)

Onkelbag
(See Onclebagh)

John Oram (Ouram)
Philadelphia, Pa. (c. 1809-1811)
Bibl. 3

Joseph Orbrihim (c. 1784)
Annapolis, Md.
Bibl. 23

Ordway (c. 1840)
Location unknown
Bibl. 89

ORDWAY

Francis Oretle (c. 1832)
New York, N.Y.
Bibl. 15

Daniel D. R. Ormsby
   (c. 1812-   )
Cortland, N.Y.
Boon & Ormsby (c 1832-1834)
Bibl. 20

Henry Ormsby (c. 1839-1850)
Philadelphia, Pa.
Bibl. 3

James Ormsby (c. 1771)
Baltimore, Md.
Bibl. 3

Thomas Orr (c. 1809-1817)
Philadelphia, Pa.
Bibl. 3

Thomas Orr (c. 1848-1849)
Louisville, Ky.
Bibl. 32, 54, 68

C. E. Ortelett (c. 1828-1831)
Philadelphia, Pa.
Bibl. 3

Osborn & Hammond
 (c. 1804-   )
Utica, N.Y.
John Osborn
Seneca Hammond
Bibl. 20

John Osborn (c. 1805-1807)
Utica, N.Y.
Rugg & Osborn (c. 1804)
Osborn & Hammond
 (c. 1804-   )
Butler & Osborn (c. 1805-1807)
Bibl. 18, 20

OSBORN   OSBORN

Robert Osborn (c. 1847)
Rochester, N.Y.
Bibl. 20

W. R. Osborn (c. 1850)
Watertown, N.Y.
Bibl. 20

William Osborn (c. 1840)
Providence, R.I.
Bibl. 15, 25, 44

William Osborn

Henry J. Osborne
Milledgeville, Ga. (c. 1848)
Augusta, Ga. (c. 1860)
Bibl. 17

Orlando C. Osborne (c. 1827)
Baltimore, Md.
Bibl. 38

Osburn
(See Stone & Osburn [Osborn])

Clement Oscamp (c. 1849-
 1865)
Cincinnati, Ohio
Bibl. 54

John Osgood (Jr.) (c. 1795-
 1817)
Boston, Mass.
Haverhill, Mass.
Salem, Mass.
New Hampshire
Bibl. 15, 23, 25, 28, 29, 36, 44

J: OSGOOD

Andrew Osthoff (c. 1809-1814)
Pittsburgh, Pa. (c. 1815)
Baltimore, Md.
Bibl. 23, 24, 25, 36, 38, 44

A. OSTHOFF

Ralph Ostrom
Troy, N.Y. (c. 1830)
Schenectady, N.Y. (c. 1838-
 1842)
Bibl. 20

John Otis (c. 1706)
Barnstable, Mass.
Bibl. 23, 36, 44

Jonathan Otis (b. 1723-d. 1791)
Middletown, Conn. (c. 1775)
Newport, R.I. (c. 1778)
Bibl. 2, 15, 16, 23, 24, 25, 28,
 36, 39, 44, 61, 69

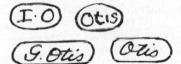

Ott & Cluff (c. 1803-1806)
Norfolk, Va.
George Ott
Matthew Cluff
Bibl. 19

Daniel Ott (c. 1792)
New York, N.Y.
Bibl. 23, 36, 44

Daniel Ott (c. 1812)
Chillicothe, Ohio
Bibl. 34

David Ott (Otto)
Philadelphia, Pa. (c. 1797-
 1809)
Bibl. 3

George Ott (d. 1831)
Norfolk, Va. (c. 1801-1822)
Ott & Cluff (c. 1803-1806)
Bibl. 19, 23, 24, 25, 29, 36, 44

G. Ott   Ott

H. & S. M. Ott (c. 1845-1848)
Harrisonburg, Va.
Bibl. 19

Henry Ott (c. 1837-1850)
Harrisonburg, Va.
Bibl. 19

Jacob Ott (c. 1812)
Chillicothe, Ohio
Bibl. 34

Michael Ott (c. 1812)
Chillicothe, Ohio
Bibl. 34

Philip Ott (c. 1792)
Fayetteville, N.C.
Bibl. 21

Otto
(See David Ott)

Joseph Oudin (c. 1814)
Philadelphia, Pa.
Bibl. 3

Ouram
(See Oram)

Ephraim Outten (d. 1825)
Maysville, Ky. (c. 1816-1825)
Bibl. 32, 54, 68

Richard Overin (c. 1702)
New York, N.Y.
Bibl. 4, 23, 28, 36, 44

Owen and Read (Reed)
 (c. 1840)
Cincinnati, Ohio
Bibl. 34

Owen
(See Palmer & Owen)

Ann Owen (c. 1837)
Philadelphia, Pa.
Bibl. 3

Griffith Owen (c. 1790-1814)
Philadelphia, Pa.
Bibl. 3

I. Owen
(See John Owen)

J. Owen & Co. (c. 1839-1840)
Philadelphia, Pa.
Bibl. 3

J. T. Owen (c. 1859-1860)
Abbeville, S.C.
M. T. & J. T. Owen
Bibl. 5

Jesse E. Owen (d. 1794)
Philadelphia, Pa. (c. 1790)
Bibl. 3, 15, 23, 24, 29, 36, 39,
44, 54, 79

| OWEN | JSE. E. OWEN |

Jesse Owen (c. 1801-1816)
Philadelphia, Pa.
Bibl. 3, 23, 25, 29

| JSE. OWEN |

Jesse Owen (c. 1841-1848)
Philadelphia, Pa.
Bibl. 3

John Owen (I. Owen) (c. 1804-
1831)
Philadelphia, Pa.
Bibl. 3, 15, 23, 24, 25, 28, 29,
36, 44, 89

| I. OWEN | OWEN |

M. T. Owen (c. 1848-1860)
Abbeville, S.C.
Bailey & Owen (c. 1848-1850)
M. T. & J. T. Owen (c. 1859-
1860)
Bibl. 5

M. T. & J. T. Owen (c. 1859-
1860)
Abbeville, S.C.
M. T. Owen
J. T. Owen
Bibl. 5

Owens & Currin (c. 1846-1850)
Philadelphia, Pa.
Samuel W. Owens
James W. Currin
Bibl. 3

Jesse Owens (c. 1836)
Philadelphia, Pa.
Bibl. 3

Samuel H. Owens (c. 1857)
Anderson, S.C.
Bibl. 5

Samuel W. Owens (c. 1846-
1850)
Philadelphia, Pa.
Bibl. 3

William Owens (c. 1839-1860)
Utica, N.Y.
Bibl. 18, 20

Aloysius Owings (c. 1800)
Baltimore, Md.
Bibl. 38

P. B. & C. (c. 1815)
(See Pelletreau, Bennett, &
Cooke)

F. W. Pachmann (c. 1850-1865)
Location unknown
Bibl. 54

William Pack (b. 1817)
Utica, N.Y. (c. 1850-
1860-   )
Bibl. 18, 20

Packard & Brown (c. 1815)
Albany, N.Y.
Jonathan Packard
——— Brown
Bibl. 20, 41

Packard & Scofield (c. 1818-
1819)
Rochester, N.Y.
Jonathan Packard
Salmon Scofield
Bibl. 20, 41

Jonathan Packard (b. 1789-d.
1854)
Springfield, Mass. (c. 1811)
Albany, N.Y. (c. 1815)
Rochester, N.Y. (c. 1818-
1854)
Huntington & Packard
(c. 1811)
Packard & Brown (c. 1815)
Packard & Scofield (c. 1818-
1819)
Bibl. 20, 41

L. H. Packard (c. 1847)
Potsdam, N.Y.
Bibl. 20

Samuel Paddy (b. 1659)
Boston, Mass. (c. 1679)
Bibl. 23, 28, 36, 44

Lewis Pagaud
Norfolk, Va. (c. 1815)
Petersburg, Va. (c. 1815-1846)
Bibl. 19

Charles Page (c. 1801-1802)
Staunton, Va.
Bibl. 19

Jacob Pain (c. 1793)
Philadelphia, Pa.
Bibl. 3

(James?) Paine (c. 1835-   )
Waynesboro, Va.
Bibl. 19

Washington Paine (c. 1841-
1850)
Philadelphia, Pa.
Bibl. 3

Isaac Painter (c. 1837-1842)
Philadelphia, Pa.
Bibl. 3

Isaac Painter Jr. (c. 1845-
1850)
Philadelphia, Pa.
Bibl. 3

John Painter (c. 1735)
Philadelphia, Pa.
Bibl. 23, 36, 44

John S. Painter (c. 1835-1848)
Philadelphia, Pa.
Bibl. 3

Palmer & Batchelder
(Bachelder) (Bachlader)
(Bachlander)
Boston, Mass. (c. 1850)
New York, N.Y. (?)
James Palmer
——— Batchelder
Bibl. 23, 24, 25, 28, 29, 36, 44

| PALMER & BACHELDER |

Palmer & Clapp (c. 1823)
New York, N.Y.
James Palmer
——— Clapp
Bibl. 23, 36, 44

Palmer, Davis & Co.
(See Davis, Palmer & Co.)

Palmer & Hinsdale (c. 1815)
New York, N.Y.
James Palmer
Horace Hinsdale
Bibl. 23, 36, 44,

Palmer & Newcomb
Location unknown
Bibl. 15, 44

Palmer & Owen (c. 1851)
Cincinnati, Ohio
Bibl. 54

Palmer & Ramsay (c. 1847-
1855)
Raleigh, N.C.
John C. Palmer
Walter J. Ramsay
Bibl. 21

Abraham Palmer (c. 1849)
Cincinnati, Ohio
Bibl. 54

E. H. P. Palmer (c. 1865)
Richmond, Va.
Bibl. 54

James Palmer (c. 1815-1823,
    c. 1850)
New York, N.Y. (c. 1815-1823)
Boston, Mass. (c. 1850)
Palmer & Hinsdale (c. 1815)
Palmer & Clapp (c. 1823)
Palmer & Batchelder (c. 1850)
Bibl. 23, 36, 44

James Palmer (c. 1831-1835)
Philadelphia, Pa.
Bibl. 3

John Palmer (c. 1795-1796)
Philadelphia, Pa.
Bibl. 3

John C. Palmer (b. 1806-d.
    1893)
Salisbury, N.C. (c. 1830-1832)
Raleigh, N.C. (c. 1840-   )
Hampton & Palmer (c. 1830-
    1832)
Palmer & Ramsay (c. 1847-
    1855)
Bibl. 21

Thomas Palmer (c. 1845)
Rochester, N.Y.
Bibl. 20

William H. Palmer (c. 1837-
    1840)
Philadelphia, Pa.
Bibl. 3

Samuel Pancoast (c. 1785-1795)
Philadelphia, Pa.
Bibl. 3, 23, 25, 36, 39, 44, 81

[S P]

Stacy Pancoast (c. 1835)
Philadelphia, Pa.
Bibl. 3

Pangborn & Brinsmaid
    (c. 1833)
Burlington, Vt.
Bibl. 25, 29, 44, 62

P & B

Papot & Norton (c. 1790-   )
Savannah, Ga.
——— Papot

Jonathan Norton
Bibl. 17

William Anthony Paradice
    (c. 1799)
Philadelphia, Pa.
Bibl. 3, 23, 36, 44

William Paraset (c. 1811)
Philadelphia, Pa.
Bibl. 3, 23, 36, 44

William V. Pardee (c. 1834)
Albany, N.Y.
Bibl. 20

William Parham (d. 1794)
Philadelphia, Pa. (c. 1785-1794)
Bibl. 3, 15, 23, 25, 36, 44, 81

W P

Joseph Parie (c. 1811)
Philadelphia, Pa.
Bibl. 3, 23, 36, 44

David (de) Parisien (o. 1780-
    1817)
New York, N.Y.
Bibl. 28, 72

[PARISIEN]

Otto de Parisien (w. 1789-1791)
New York, N.Y.
Otto Paul de Parisien & Son
    (c. 1789-1791)
Bibl. 23, 25, 28, 29, 36, 44

Otto Paul de Parisien (de
    Perrizang)
New York, N.Y. (c. 1763-1789)
Otto Paul de Parisien & Son
    (c. 1789-1791)
Bibl. 4, 15, 23, 24, 25, 28, 29,
    35, 36, 44, 54, 83

[O P] [O P D P]
[PARISIEN]

Otto Paul de Parisien & Son
    (c. 1789-1791)
New York, N.Y.
Otto de Parisien
Paul de Parisien
Bibl. 23, 25, 28, 29, 36, 44

[O P D P]

Paul de Parisien (c. 1780-1817)
New York, N.Y.
Otto Paul de Parisien & Son
    (c. 1789-1791)
Bibl. 23, 25, 28, 29, 36, 44

John Francis Parisot (c. 1828-
    1836)
Savannah, Ga.
Bibl. 17

Park
(See Vernon & Park)

John Park (d. 1858)
Louisville, Ky. (c. 1848)
Bibl. 32

Jonas Park (c. 1785-1786)
Bennington, Vt.
Bibl. 54

Parke, Solomon & Co. (c. 1797-
    1801)
Philadelphia, Pa.
Bibl. 3

Parke & Son (c. 1806)
Philadelphia, Pa.
Bibl. 3

Augustus W. Parke (c. 1817-
    1822)
Philadelphia, Pa.
Bibl. 3

Charles B. Parke (c. 1806-1810)
Philadelphia, Pa.
Bibl. 3

Solomon Parke (c. 1791-1822)
Philadelphia, Pa.
Southampton, Bucks County,
    Pa. (c. 1782)
Bibl. 3

Parker & Co. (c. 1818-1819)
Philadelphia, Pa.
Isaac Parker (?)
Bibl. 3

Allen Parker (c. 1817-1819)
New York, N.Y.
Bibl. 15, 25, 44

[A PARKER]   ?

Caleb Parker (c. 1731-1770)
Boston, Mass.
Bibl. 28

Charles H. Parker (c. 1793-
    1819)
Salem, Mass.
Philadelphia, Pa.
Bibl. 28

Daniel Parker (b. 1726-d. 1785)
Boston, Mass.

Bibl. 2, 15, 23, 24, 25, 28, 29,
36, 44, 55

D: PARKER

D: P

George Parker (c. 1804-1831)
Baltimore, Md.
Bibl. 23, 24, 25, 28, 29, 36,
38, 44

G. PARKER

George Parker (c. 1828-1834)
Utica, N.Y.
Bibl. 18, 20

G. PARKER

Isaac Parker (c. 1780)
Deerfield, Mass.
Bibl. 23, 24, 25, 28, 29, 36, 44

I PARKER

Isaac Parker (c. 1818-1850)
Philadelphia, Pa.
Parker & Co. (c. 1818-1819) (?)
Bibl. 3

J. Parker
Location unknown
Bibl. 54

James Parker
(See George Parker)

John Parker (b. 1750)
Maryland (c. 1774)
Bibl. 38

Joseph Parker (c. 1785)
Princeton, N.J.
Bibl. 44, 46, 54

Richard Parker (c. 1785)
Philadelphia, Pa.
Bibl. 3, 23, 36, 44

T. E. Parker (c. 1840?)
Location unknown
Bibl. 89

T. E. Parker

T. H. Parker (c. 1833)
Philadelphia, Pa.
Bibl. 3

Thomas Parker (c. 1785-1817)
Philadelphia, Pa.
Bibl. 3

Thomas Parker Jr. (c. 1817-
1822)
Philadelphia, Pa.
Bibl. 3

William Parker (c. 1733)
Savannah, Ga.
Bibl. 17

William Parker (c. 1777)
Newport, R.I.
Bibl. 28

William Parker (c. 1778)
Lewes, Del.
Bibl. 30

William Parker (c. 1823-1824)
Philadelphia, Pa.
Bibl. 3

William Parker (c. 1834)
New York, N.Y.
Bibl. 15, 44

William Parker Jr. (c. 1835)
Philadelphia, Pa.
Bibl. 3

William B. Parker (c. 1821)
Camden, S.C.
Bibl. 5

William H. Parker
New York, N.Y. (c. 1835)
Brooklyn, N.Y. (c. 1837-1843)
Bibl. 23, 36

Nelson Parkes (c. 1846-1847)
Utica, N.Y.
Bibl. 18

Joseph Parkins (c. 1837)
Philadelphia, Pa.
Bibl. 3

Charles Parkman (c. 1790)
Boston, Mass.
Bibl. 23, 25, 29, 36, 44

C PARKMAN

Henry D. Parkman (c. 1820-
1823)
Hudson, N.Y.
Bibl. 20

John Parkman (c. 1716-1748)
Boston, Mass.
Bibl. 15, 23, 24, 25, 28, 29,
36, 44

PARKMAN

Thomas Parkman (c. 1793)
Boston, Mass.
Bibl. 23, 24, 25, 29, 36, 44

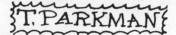

A. Parks (c. 1845)
Oswego, N.Y.
Bibl. 20

John Parks (c. 1791)
New York, N.Y.
Bibl. 23, 36, 44

James Parmele (b. 1763-d.
1828)
Durham, Conn.
Bibl. 16, 23, 28, 36

Samuel Parmele (b. 1737-d.
1803)
Guilford, Conn.
Bibl. 15, 16, 24, 25, 28, 29,
36, 44, 61

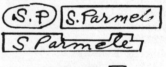

Parmenter
(See Bailey & Parmenter)

John Peter Parmier (c. 1793)
Philadelphia, Pa.
Bibl. 3

Frederick W. Parrot (Perrott)
Philadelphia, Pa. (c. 1847-1850)
Bibl. 3

Joseph Parrot (Perrot)
Philadelphia, Pa. (c. 1835-1843)
Bibl. 3

T. Parrot(t)
Philadelphia, Pa. (c. 1770)
Boston, Mass. (c. 1760) (?)
Bibl. 15, 25, 28, 29, 44, 50

T. PARROT

Parry
(See Leslie & Parry)

Parry & Musgrave (c. 1793-
1796)
Philadelphia, Pa.
Rowland Parry
James Musgrave
Bibl. 3, 15, 23, 24, 25, 36, 39,
44, 54

 P & M

Francis Parry (c. 1846-1850)
Philadelphia, Pa.
Bibl. 3, 23

John Parry (c. 1795-1797)
Philadelphia, Pa.
Bibl. 3

John F. Parry (c. 1824)
Philadelphia, Pa.
Bibl. 3

John J. Parry (c. 1810)
Philadelphia, Pa.
Bibl. 46

Martin Parry (b. 1737-d. 1807)
Portsmouth, N.H. (c. 1760)
Philadelphia, Pa. (c. 1793-
1796)
Kittery, Me.
Parry & Musgrave (c. 1793-
1796)
Bibl. 15, 23, 24, 25, 28, 29,
36, 44

PARRY

Rowland Parry (c. 1790-1796)
Philadelphia, Pa.
Parry & Musgrave (c. 1793-
1796)
Bibl. 3, 23, 25, 36, 39, 44

Thomas Parry (c. 1848-1850)
Philadelphia, Pa.
Bibl. 3

———— Parsons (c. 1770)
Philadelphia, Pa.
Bibl. 28, 29, 36

PARSONS

Henry R. Parsons (c. 1840-
1850)
Philadelphia, Pa.
Bibl. 3

John Parsons (c. 1780)
Boston, Mass.

Bibl. 15, 24, 25, 44

I. PARSONS

Peterson Partin
Richmond, Va. (c. 1819-1828)
Norfolk, Va. (c. 1819)
Bibl. 19

William Paschall (Pascall)
(Pascal) (d. 1696)
Philadelphia, Pa. (c. 1675)
Bibl. 3, 23, 36, 44

Joseph Passano (c. 1827)
Location unknown
Bibl. 38

Blovet Pasteur (c. 1759-
1782-   )
Williamsburg, Va.
Bibl. 19

T. A. Patchin (c. 1846)
Syracuse, N.Y.
Bibl. 20

George Paterson (c. 1835)
New York, N.Y.
Bibl. 23, 36

A. Paton (c. 1850)
Boston, Mass.
Bibl. 4, 23, 28, 44

George Patterson (c. 1835)
New York, N.Y.
Bibl. 44

James Patterson (c. 1837-1848)
Philadelphia, Pa.
Bibl. 3

I. P   ?

James Patterson (d. 1773)
Williamsburg, Va. (c. 1767)
Richmond, Va. (c. 1772-1773)
Bibl. 19

John Patterson (c. 1751)
Annapolis, Md.
Bibl. 28, 38, 44

I. P   ?

John Patterson (c. 1814)
Alexandria, Va.
Pittsburgh, Pa.
Potter & Patterson (c. 1814-
1815)
Bibl. 19, 54

Wilson M. Patterson (c. 1840)
Mansfield, Ohio
Bibl. 34

Joseph Pattison (c. 1751)
Philadelphia, Pa.
Bibl. 3

Pattit
(See Pettit)

Patton
(See McBryde & Patton)

Patton & Jones (c. 1799-1815)
Baltimore, Md. (c. 1799-1815)
Philadelphia, Pa. (c. 1804-1814)
Abraham Patton
Samuel G. Jones
Bibl. 3, 38

Abraham Patton (c. 1795-1815)
Baltimore, Md. (c. 1795-1796)
Philadelphia, Pa. (c. 1799-1819)
Leslie & Price (c. 1793-1800)
Robert Leslie & Co. (c. 1795-
1796)
Patton & Jones (c. 1799-1815)
Bibl. 3, 38

Thomas Patton (c. 1824)
Philadelphia, Pa.
Bibl. 3, 23, 36, 44

Philip Paul (c. 1835-1840)
Philadelphia, Pa.
S. & P. Paul (c. 1839-1840)
Bibl. 3

S. & P. Paul (c. 1839-1840)
Philadelphia, Pa.
Simon & Philip Paul
Bibl. 3

Simon Paul (c. 1839-1840)
Philadelphia, Pa.
S. & P. Paul
Bibl. 3

Cornelius Paulding
New York, N.Y. (c. 1801-1802)
Savannah, Ga. (c. 1802-1810)
New Orleans, La. (c. 1810)
Marquand & Paulding (c. 1801-
1810)
Marquand, Paulding & Co.
(c. 1809-1812)
H. Lord & Co. (c. 1805-   )
Marquand, Harriman & Co.
(c. 1809-1812)
Cornelius Paulding & Co.
(c. 1810)

Marquand, Paulding &
  Penfield (c. 1810-1816)
Bibl. 17

Cornelius Paulding & Co.
  (c. 1810)
New Orleans, La.
Cornelius Paulding
Bibl. 17

Paulgreen
(See Polgrain)

Anthony R. Paulin (c. 1778-
  1824)
Savannah, Ga.
Bibl. 17

Peter Paulson (c. 1800)
Wilmington, Del.
Bibl. 30

John A. (J. I.) Paxson
  (Paxton)
Philadelphia, Pa. (c. 1807-1811)
Bibl. 3, 23, 36, 44

Isaac Paxton (c. 1821)
Hamilton, Ohio
Bibl. 34

John A. Paxton
(See John A. Paxson)

John W. Paxton (c. 1814-   )
Danville, Va.
John W. Paxton & Son
  (c. 1815)
Bibl. 19

John W. Paxton & Son
  (c. 1815)
Danville, Va.
Bibl. 19

William D. Paylor (c. 1823)
Macon, Ga.
Bibl. 17

Payn & Heroy (c. 1813)
Albany, N.Y.
Bibl. 20

C. S. Payn (c. 1815)
Albany, N.Y.
Bibl. 20

Hiram Payn (c. 1815-1818)
Albany, N.Y.
Bibl. 20

Chauncey S. Payne (b. 1795-d.
  1877)
Detroit, Mich.

Levi Brown (c. 1866)
Bibl. 58

Asa Peabody (c. 1821)
Wilmington, N.C.
Bibl. 21

John Peabody (c. 1823-   )
Fayetteville, N.C.
Bibl. 21

John Tyng Peabody (b. 1756-d.
  1822)
Enfield, Conn. (c. 1779)
Wilmington, N.C. (c. 1787)
Bibl. 16, 21, 23, 24, 25, 28, 29,
  36, 44

Nathaniel Prentiss Peabody
  (b. 1806-d. 1883)
Bennettsville, S.C. (c. 1830-
  1870)
Bibl. 5

Richard G. Peacock Jr.
  (c. 1819)
Fredericksburg, Va.
Weidemeyer & Peacock
Bibl. 19

Thomas Peacock (b. 1818)
Lancaster, Ky. (c. 1845-1879)
Louisville, Ky.
Bibl. 32, 54

Peak
(See Walter & Peak)

Daniel Peake (c. 1837-1840)
Philadelphia, Pa.
Bibl. 3

Daniel Peake Jr. (c. 1839-1850)
Philadelphia, Pa.
Bibl. 3

Edward Peake (c. 1829-1850)
Philadelphia, Pa.
Bibl. 3

Thomas Peake (c. 1850)
Philadelphia, Pa.
Bibl. 3

Charles Willson Peale
  (b. 1741-d. 1827)
Annapolis, Md. (c. 1761-1764)
Philadelphia, Pa. (c. 1765)
Bibl. 2, 3, 23, 28, 36, 38, 44

James Peale (c. 1814-1817)
Philadelphia, Pa.
Bibl. 3

Pear & Bacall (c. 1850)
Boston, Mass.
Edward Pear
Thomas Bacall
Bibl. 4, 23, 28, 44

PEAR & BACALL

Edward Pear (c. 1836-1850)
Boston, Mass.
Pear & Bacall (c. 1850)
Bibl. 4, 23, 24, 25, 28, 29, 36

Pearce & Spratley (c. 1833)
Norfolk, Va.
Walter Pearce
James H. Spratley
Bibl. 19

Hamett A. Pearce (c. 1845-
  1850)
Richmond, Va.
Kersey & Pearce
Bibl. 19

Hart Pearce (c. 1833-1835)
New York, N.Y.
Bibl. 15

Samuel Pearce (c. 1783)
New York, N.Y.
Bibl. 28, 44

Walter (William) Pearce
  (c. 1831-1833)
Norfolk, Va.
Pearce & Spratley (c. 1833)
Bibl. 19, 23, 25, 29, 36, 44

William Pearman
Petersburg, Va. (c. 1832)
Williamsburg, Va. (after 1832)
Richmond, Va.
Bibl. 19

Pearse
(See Hunter & Pearse)

Samuel Pearse (c. 1783)
New York, N.Y.
Bibl. 23, 36

Isaac Pearson (b. 1685-d. 1749)
Burlington, N.J. (c. 1710-1749)
Bibl. 46, 54

John Pearson
New York, N.Y. (c. 1791)
Savannah, Ga. (c. 1802)
Letourneau & Pearson (c. 1802-1803)
Bibl. 17, 23, 24, 25, 28, 29, 36, 39, 44

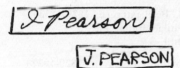

John Pearson (c. 1815-1817)
New York, N.Y.
Bibl. 15

Widow of John Pearson (c. 1819-1824)
New York, N.Y.
Bibl. 15

M. & T. Pearson (c. 1825)
Portland, Me.
Bibl. 15, 44

M & T. PEARSON

Peck & Porter (c. 1827)
Bridgeport, Conn.
Bibl. 23

A. G. Peck (c. 1823)
Ashtabula, Ohio
Bibl. 15, 24, 34, 44

A. G. PECK

B. Peck (c. 1820)
Connecticut (?)
Bibl. 28, 29, 44

B. PECK

George Peck Jr. (c. 1850)
New York, N.Y.
Bibl. 23

Lawrance M. Peck (c. 1837)
Philadelphia, Pa.
Bibl. 3, 23, 36, 44

Moses Peck (c. 1789)
Boston, Mass.
Bibl. 3

Timothy Peck (b. 1765-d. 1818)
Middletown, Conn. (c. 1791)
Litchfield, Conn. (after 1791)
Boston, Mass. (c. 1810?)
Bibl. 16, 23, 28, 36, 44

James Peckham (c. 1830-1847)
Charleston, S.C.
Peckham & George
Bibl. 5

S. Pedosy (c. 1810)
Philadelphia, Pa.
Bibl. 3, 23, 36, 44

Peebles & Wils——? (c. 1840)
Location unknown
Bibl. 89

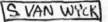

Allen T. Peebles
Charlottesville, Va. (before 1837)
Staunton, Va. (c. 1839)
Leesburg, Va. (c. 1843-1848)
Richmond, Va. (c. 1849-1857)
Bibl. 19

John Pegg (c. 1830)
Albany, N.Y.
Bibl. 20

John Peirce
(See John Pierce)

William S. Peirce (c. 1841)
Philadelphia, Pa.
Bibl. 3

Joseph Peiri (c. 1811)
Philadelphia, Pa.
Bibl. 3, 23, 36, 44

William Pelham (c. 1846)
Fishkill, N.Y.
Bibl. 20

Emmett (Emmet) T. Pell (c. 1824-1841)
New York, N.Y.
Bibl. 15, 25, 44

E. T. PELL

Pelletrau
(See William Smith Pelletreau)

Pelletreau & Richards (c. 1825)
New York, N.Y.
William Smith Pelletreau
Thomas Richards (?)
Bibl. 24, 25, 44

W S P   T R

Pelletreau & Upson (c. 1818)
New York, N.Y.
William Smith Pelletreau
——— Upson
Bibl. 23, 24, 25, 44

P & U

Pelletreau & Van Wyck (c. 1815)
New York, N.Y.
William Smith Pelletreau
Stephen Van Wyck
Bibl. 24, 25, 44

S VAN WYCK

W.S. PELLETREAU

Pelletreau, Bennett & Co. (c. 1827-1829)
New York, N.Y.
John Bennett Sr.
D. C. Cooke
Maltby Pelletreau
Bibl. 15

Pelletreau, Bennett & Cooke (c. 1815)
New York, N.Y.
John Bennett Sr.
D. C. Cooke
Maltby Pelletreau
Bibl. 15, 25, 44

Elias Pelletreau (b. 1726-d. 1810, c. 1776-1782)
Southampton, L.I., N.Y.
Simsbury, Conn.
Saybrook, Conn.
Bibl. 4, 15, 20, 23, 24, 25, 28, 29, 30, 35, 44, 54, 61, 64

John Pelletreau (b. 1755-d.
 1822)
Southampton, N.Y.
Bibl. 20, 23, 36, 44

Maltby Pelletreau (c. 1815-
 1840)
Charleston, S.C
New York, N.Y.
Pelletreau, Bennett & Cooke
 (c. 1815-1827)
Clark & Pelletreau (c. 1819)
Bennett, Cooke & Co. (1823-
 1827)
Pelletreau, Bennett & Co.
 (c. 1827-1829)
Bibl. 15, 23, 25, 36, 44, 89

William Smith Pelletreau
 (Pelletrau) (b. 1786-d. 1842)
Southampton, N.Y.
Pelletreau & Van Wyck
 (c. 1815)
Pelletreau & Upson (c. 1818)
Pelletreau & Richards (c. 1825)
(Richards & Pelletreau)
Bibl. 15, 20, 23, 24, 25, 28,
 29, 36, 44

| W S PELLETRAU |

| W S P | | W. S. PELLETREAU |

Jean Baptiste Pellissier
 (b. 1792)
Charleston, S.C. (c. 1815)
Bibl. 5

James S. Pemberton
 (c. 1842-)
Albany, N.Y.
Bibl. 20

William F. Pendrell (Pendren)
Philadelphia, Pa. (c. 1843-1846)
Bibl. 3, 23

Penfield (Pennfield) (c. 1810)
Location unknown
Bibl. 89

J. Penfield & Co. (c. 1820-1828)
Savannah, Ga.
Josiah Penfield
Moses Eastman
Frederick Marquand
Bibl. 17

| PENFIELD &CO. |

Josiah Penfield (b. 1785-d.
 1828)
Savannah, Ga.

Marquand, Paulding & Penfield
 (c. 1810-1816)
J. Penfield & Co. (c. 1820-1828)
Bibl. 17

John Pennefather (Penny-
 feather) (d. 1745)
Charleston, S.C. (c. 1736-1740)
Bibl. 5

Charles D. Pennell (c. 1847)
Providence, R.I.
Bibl. 23

Pennfield
(See ——— Penfield)

A. C. Pennington (c. 1849)
Wellsburg, Va.
Bibl. 19

Joshua S. Pennington (c. 1825-
 1834-)
Eatonton, Ga.
Bibl. 17

Harvey Pennoyer (c. 1818)
Sing Sing, N.Y.
Bibl. 20

Pennyfeather
(See Pennefather)

Penot & Brother (c. 1821)
Charleston, S.C.
Bibl. 5

S. Pentecost (c. 1829)
Henderson, Ky.
Bibl. 32, 54, 68

H. S. Pepper (c. 1837)
Philadelphia, Pa.
Bibl. 3

Henry J. Pepper (c. 1766)
Philadelphia, Pa.
Henry J. Pepper & Son
 (c. 1846-1850)
Bibl. 28, 29, 30, 44, 79

H. I. PEPPER   H. J. PEPPER

Henry J. (I.) Pepper
Wilmington, Del. (before
 1814)
Philadelphia, Pa. (c. 1828-1850)
Bibl. 3, 15, 23, 24, 25, 30, 36,
 39, 44

| H. J. PEPPER | | H. I. PEPPER |

Henry I. Pepper & Son
 (c. 1846-1850)
Philadelphia, Pa.
Bibl. 3, 15, 25, 44

Joel S. Pepper (c. 1850)
Philadelphia, Pa.
Bibl. 3

S. W. Pepper (c. 1848-1850)
Philadelphia, Pa.
Bibl. 3

Thomas Percival (c. 1840)
Albany, N.Y.
Bibl. 20

S. Perdriaux (c. 1829-1833)
Philadelphia, Pa.
Bibl. 3

William Peres (c. 1820-1822)
Philadelphia, Pa.
Bibl. 3

Houghton Perkins (b. 1735-d.
 1778)
Boston, Mass.
Taunton, Mass.
Bibl. 23, 25, 28, 36, 44, 54

Isaac Perkins (c. 1707-1737,
 d. 1737)
Boston, Mass.
Charlestown, Mass.
Bibl. 23, 28, 29, 36, 44

Jacob Perkins (b. 1766-d.
 1849)
Newburyport, Mass. (c. 1781-
 1815)
Philadelphia, Pa. (c. 1816-
 1819)
Bibl. 14, 15, 23, 24, 25, 28,
 29, 36, 44

Jacob Perkins (d. 1841)
Philadelphia, Pa.
Bibl. 3

Joseph Perkins (b. 1749)
South Kingston, R.I. (c. 1789)
Bibl. 15, 24, 25, 28, 44, 56

J PERKINS

Leonard Perkins (b. 1796)
Sparta, Ga. (c. 1818-1820)
Milledgeville, Ga. (c. 1820-
1831)
Wilcox & Perkins (c. 1818-
1820)
Bibl. 17

T. Perkins (c. 1810)
Boston, Mass.
Bibl. 24, 25, 44

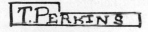

T.PERKINS

T PERKINS

Thomas Perkins (c. 1705-1799)
Philadelphia, Pa.
Bibl. 3

Isaac Peronneau (c. 1743)
Charleston, S.C.
Bibl. 5

I P

James Perot (c. 1753)
Bermuda
Bibl. 3

Peter Perpignan (c. 1809-1825)
Philadelphia, Pa.
Bibl. 3, 23, 36, 44

S. Perpignan & J. Varnier
(c. 1800-1801)
Philadelphia, Pa.
Bibl. 3, 23

Peter Perraux (Perreaux)
(c. 1797)
Philadelphia, Pa.
Bibl. 3, 4, 15, 23, 24, 25, 28,
29, 36, 44, 54

PP

Perret & Sandoz (Sander)
(c. 1810-1811)

New York, N.Y.
Augusta Perret
——— Sandoz
Bibl. 23, 36, 44

August(a)(e) Perret (c. 1811-
1819)
New York, N.Y.
Perret & Sandoz (c. 1810-1811)
Bibl. 15, 23, 36, 44

Phillip H. Perret (c. 1820)
Cincinnati, Ohio
Bibl. 34

W. D. Perrine (c. 1850)
Lyons, N.Y.
Bibl. 20

Perrot
(See Joseph Parrot)

Perrott
(See Frederick W. Parrot)

Elias Perry (c. 1804)
Philadelphia, Pa.
Bibl. 3

Felicity Perry (c. 1820-1822)
Philadelphia, Pa.
Bibl. 3

J. J. Perry (19th century)
Location unknown
Bibl. 54

Thomas Perry (b. 1814-d. 1898)
Westerly, R.I. (c. 1828-1865)
Bibl. 15, 28, 36, 44, 74

T. PERRY

Jefferson Peterman (c. 1841)
Rochester, N.Y.
Boss & Peterman
Bibl. 20

William Peterman (c. 1837)
Philadelphia, Pa.
Bibl. 3

——— Peters (c. 1813)
Philadelphia, Pa.
Bibl. 3

J. Peters & Co. (c. 1830)
Philadelphia, Pa.
James Peters
Bibl. 15, 25, 44

J. PETERS & CO

James Peters (c. 1821-1850)
Philadelphia, Pa.
J. Peters & Co. (c. 1830)
Bibl. 3, 15, 23, 25, 36, 44

J. PETERS

R. Peters (c. 1807-1809)
Philadelphia, Pa.
Bibl. 3, 23, 36, 44

William S. Peters (c. 1833-
1850)
Philadelphia, Pa.
Bibl. 3

Henry Peterson (c. 1783)
Philadelphia, Pa.
Bibl. 25, 28, 44

H P   ?

Henry Peterson Jr. (c. 1787)
Alexandria, Va.
Bibl. 19

Matthew Petit (c. 1811)
New York, N.Y.
Bibl. 23, 24, 25, 29, 36, 44

M P

Alexander Petrie (c. 1745-1765,
d. 1768)
Charleston, S.C.
Bibl. 5, 25, 44, 54, 74

A P

E. P. Pettes (c. 1850)
Location unknown
Bibl. 89

E. P. Pettes

Pettit
(See Borde & Pettit)

Thomas Pettit (Petit) (Pattit)
New York, N.Y. (c. 1796)
Bibl. 23, 28, 36, 44

——— Pettit (c. 1803)
Charleston, S.C.
Borde & Pettit (c. 1803)
Bibl. 5

Henry Petty (c. 1829-1833)
Philadelphia, Pa
Bibl. 3

Lewis Peyssou (c. 1807-1810)
South Carolina (c.   -1810?)
Bibl. 5

Widow Peyssou (c. 1810)
South Carolina
Bibl. 5

Peter Pezant (b. 1786-d. 1843)
Charleston, S.C. (c. 1816)
Bibl. 5

August Pfaff (c. 1829-1833)
Philadelphia, Pa.
Bibl. 3

Henry Pfaff (c. 1829-1833)
Philadelphia, Pa.
Bibl. 3

John William Pfaltz (c. 1800-
1812)
Baltimore, Md. (c. 1800-1806)
Alexandria, Va.
Sadtler & Pfaltz (c. 1800-1806)
Bibl. 19, 38

F. Pfeiffer (c. 1839-1847)
St. Louis, Mo.
Bibl. 54

Hermann Pfluefer (c. 1849-
1850)
Philadelphia, Pa.
Bibl. 3

David Pheil (File) (c. 1798-
1817)
Philadelphia, Pa.
Bibl. 3

Phelps & Holland (c. 1827-
1828)
Northampton, Mass.
E. S. Phelps
Nelson Holland
Bibl. 84

Phelps & Strong (c. 1823-1826)
Northampton, Mass.
Ebenezer S. Phelps
——— Strong
Bibl. 44

Phelps & White (c. 1828-1830)
Northampton, Mass.
Ebenezer S. Phelps
G. W. White
Bibl. 84

Phelps
(See Bowles & Phelps)

Charles H. Phelps (c. 1825)
Bainbridge, N.Y.
Bibl. 25, 44

C H PHELPS

Ebenezer S. Phelps (c. 1815-
1831)
Northampton, Mass.
Phelps & Strong (1823-1826)
Phelps & Holland 1827)
Phelps & White (1828-1830)
Bibl. 84

Jedediah Phelps (c. 1781)
Great Barrington, Vt.
Bibl. 23, 28, 36, 44

Samuel F. Phelps (c. 1834-
1838)
Troy, N.Y.
Bibl. 20

Silas Phelps (b. 1788-d. 1825)
Newark, N.J. (c. 1815)
New York, N.Y. (c. 1825)
Downing & Phelps (c. 1815,
c. 1825)
Bibl. 46, 54

Philibert
(See Philobad)

Philip & Yver (c. 1796)
Philadelphia, Pa.
Bibl. 36, 44

Ranard Guyeon & Yver
Philip (c. 1796)
Philadelphia, Pa.
Bibl. 23

——— Philipe (c. 1794)
Philadelphia, Pa.
Georgeon & Philipe
Bibl. 3

Philippe & Le Gras (c. 1796)
Baltimore, Md.
Joseph Phillippe
John Francis LeGras
Bibl. 38

James D. Philips (Phillips)
Cincinnati, Ohio (c. 1824-
1829)
Bibl. 24, 25, 29, 34, 36, 44

JAS. D. PHILIPS

Jasper D. Philips
(Incorrect name for James
D. Philips)

Edward Philley (c. 1846)
Philadelphia, Pa.
Bibl. 3

Joseph Phillippe (Phillyss)
(Phillips) (Philippe)
Baltimore, Md. (c. 1796-1802,
c. 1819-1823)
Philippe & LeGras (c. 1796)
Bibl. 29, 38, 44

Phillips
(See Richard & Phillips)

James D. Phillips
(See James D. Philips)

Joseph Phillips
(See Joseph Philippe)

——— Phillips (c. 1817)
Winchester, Va.
Phillips & Foster
Bibl. 19

Phillips & Foster (c. 1817)
Winchester, Va.
——— Phillips
John Foster
Bibl. 19

Phillips and Frazer (c. 1799)
Paris, Ky.
Thomas Phillips
Alexander Frazer
Robert Frazer
Bibl. 32, 54, 68

A. Phillips (c. 1829)
Cincinnati, Ohio
Bibl. 54

James Phillips (c. 1839)
Philadelphia, Pa.
Bibl. 3

James D. Phillips (c. 1829)
Cincinnati, Ohio
Bibl. 23

John W. Phillips (c. 1842-
1850)
Philadelphia, Pa.
Bibl. 3, 15

J. W. P   ?

Samuel Phillips (b. 1658-d.
1722)
Boston, Mass.
Salem, Mass.

Bibl. 23, 25, 28, 29, 36, 44

S P   ?

Thomas Phillips
Paris, Ky. (c. 1792-1818,
  c. 1820-1827)
Hopkinsville, Ky. (c. 1818-
  1820)
Lawrenceburg, Ky. (c. 1827-
  1831)
Phillips and Frazer (c. 1799)
Bibl. 32, 54, 68

Phillyss
(See Joseph Phillippe)

Augustus Philobad (Philibert)
  (c. 1839)
St. Louis, Mo.
Bibl. 54

William H. C. Philpot (c. 1846-
  1849)
Philadelphia, Pa.
Bibl. 3, 23

Phinney & Mead (c. 1825)
Location unknown
Bibl. 28, 29, 44

P & M

Gotthold Benjamin Phole
  (b. 1812)
Columbus, Ga. (c. 1842)
Bibl. 17

William Phyfe
Boston, Mass. (c. 1830)
New York, N.Y. (c. 1840-
  1850)
Eoff & Phyfe (c. 1844-1850)
Bibl. 15, 23, 36, 44

W. A. Piatt & Co. (c. 1840-
  1847)
Columbus, Ohio
Bibl. 34

Richard Pickadick (c. 1770-
  1776)
Norfolk, Va.
Bibl. 19

Charles Pickering (b. 1683-d.
  1749)
Philadelphia, Pa.
Bibl. 3, 23, 36, 44

John Pickering (c. 1823-1824)
Philadelphia, Pa.
Bibl. 3

Joseph Pickering (c. 1816-
  1846)
Philadelphia, Pa.
Bibl. 3

J. L. Pickrell (c. 1851)
Greenville, S.C.
Bibl. 5

Hart Pierce (c. 1835)
New York, N.Y.
Bibl. 23, 36, 44

John Pierce (Peirce) (Peirse)
Boston, Mass. (c. 1810)
Bibl. 23, 24, 25, 28, 29, 36, 44

Peirce

O. Pierce (c. 1824)
Boston, Mass.
Bibl. 15, 23, 25, 29, 36, 44

O.PIERCE

G. PIERCE   ?

Benjamin Pierpont (b. 1730-d.
  1797)
Boston, Mass.
Roxbury, Mass.
Bibl. 2, 4, 15, 23, 24, 25, 28, 29,
  36, 44

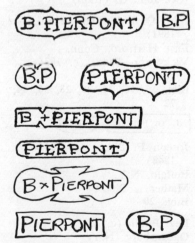

Matthey Pierret (c. 1795-1796)
Philadelphia, Pa.
Bibl. 3

Phillip Pierson (c. 1798)
New York, N.Y.
Bibl. 23, 35, 36, 44, 83

John Peter Pignolet (c. 1814-
  1816)
Philadelphia, Pa.
Bibl. 3

John Pigott (c. 1798)
Savannah, Ga.
Bibl. 17

H. Pike (19th century)
Location unknown
Bibl. 15, 44

H. PIKE

George P. Pilling (c. 1845)
Philadelphia, Pa.
Bibl. 3, 23

Stephen Pilly (c. 1816)
Raleigh, N.C.
Bibl. 21

Amos Pilsbury (b. 1772-d.
  1812, c. 1798)
Location unknown
Bibl. 5

Pincheon
(See Pinchon)

William Pinchin (c. 1818-1824)
Philadelphia, Pa.
Bibl. 3, 23, 28, 36, 44

William Pinchon (Pincheon)
  (c. 1779-1809)
Philadelphia, Pa.
Bibl. 3

Charles Pine (c. 1844-1850)
Philadelphia, Pa.
Bibl. 3

David Pine (c. 1772)
Strasburg, Pa.
Bibl. 3

Edwin Pine (c. 1850)
Philadelphia, Pa.
Bibl. 3

H. S. Pine (c. 1849)
Philadelphia, Pa.
Bibl. 3

Edward Pink (c. 1843)
Philadelphia, Pa.
Bibl. 3

Pinkerd & Brown (c. 1774)
Savannah, Ga.
Jonathan Thomas Pinkerd
Robert Brown
Bibl. 17

Jonathan Thomas Pinkerd
Philadelphia, Pa. (c. 1773)
Savannah, Ga. (c. 1774-1776)
Pinkerd & Brown (c. 1774)
Bibl. 3, 17

Charles Pinkney (c. 1795)
Richmond, Va.
Bibl. 19

George Pinney (c. 1849)
Philadelphia, Pa.
Bibl. 3

E. J. Pinson (c. 1856)
Greenville, S.C.
Bibl. 5

Joseph Pinto (c. 1758)
New York, N.Y.
Bibl. 4, 23, 28, 36, 44

James Piper (b. 1749-d. 1802)
Chestertown, Md.
Baltimore, Md. (c. 1772-1791)
Bibl. 38

John Piper (c. 1791)
Alexandria, Va.
Bibl. 19, 54

John H. Pippen (c. 1855-)
Mobile, Ala.
Bibl. 54

Joseph N. Piquet (c. 1835-
1850)
Philadelphia, Pa.
Bibl. 3

Charles Piquette (c. 1813-1859)
Detroit, Mich.
Bibl. 58

Jean-Baptiste Piquette (c.
1803-1813)
Montreal, Canada (b. 1781)
Detroit, Mich. (d. 1813)
Bibl. 58

Jean Baptiste Piquette (c.
1809-1851)
Detroit, Mich.
Bibl. 58

Henry Pitcher (c. 1833-1834)
Troy, N.Y.
Bibl. 20

Pitkin & Norton (c. 1825)
(Norton & Pitkin)
Hartford, Conn.
Walter M. Pitkin
C. C. Norton

Bibl. 24, 25, 29, 36, 44

W PITKIN   C C NORTON

Henry Pitkin (b. 1811)
Hartford, Conn. (c. 1834)
Bibl. 15, 24, 25, 28, 29, 36, 44

Henry Pitkin (c. 1832-1834)
Troy, N.Y.
Bibl. 20, 23

Horace E. Pitkin (b. 1832)
Hartford, Conn.
Bibl. 28, 44

J. O. & W. Pitkin
Philadelphia, Pa. (c. 1811-1831)
East Hartford, Conn. (c. 1826-
1840)
John O. Pitkin
Walter Pitkin
Bibl. 15, 23, 24, 25, 28, 29, 36,
44

J O & W PITKIN

James F. Pitkin (c. 1834)
East Hartford, Conn.
Bibl. 15, 23, 36

Job O. Pitkin
(See John O. Pitkin)

John O. Pitkin (b. 1803-d.
1891)
East Hartford, Conn.
Vicksburg, Tenn. (c. 1834-
1837)
Bibl. 15, 16, 24, 25, 28, 36, 44,
72

J. O. PITKIN   PITKIN

Joseph F. Pitkin (c. 1844-
1848)
Buffalo, N.Y.
Mather & Pitkin
Bibl. 20

Levi Pitkin (c. 1811)
Ogdensburg, N.Y.
Bibl. 20

Walter M. Pitkin (b. 1808-d.
1885)
East Hartford, Conn. (c. 1825)
Vicksburg, Tenn. (c. 1834-
1837)

Pitkin & Norton (c. 1825)
(Norton & Pitkin)
Bibl. 15, 16, 23, 24, 25, 28, 29,
36, 44, 72

W. PITKIN

William J. Pitkin (c. 1820)
East Hartford, Conn.
Bibl. 23, 24, 29, 36, 44

WM J. PITKIN

William L. Pitkin (c. 1825)
East Hartford, Conn.
Bibl. 23, 24, 25, 28, 29, 36, 44

WM L PITKIN

James F. Pitkins (b. 1812)
Hartford, Conn.
Bibl. 28, 44

Pitman & Dodge (c. 1790)
Providence, R.I.
Sanders Pitman
Nehemiah Dodge
Bibl. 23, 36, 44

Pitman & Dorrance (c. 1795-
1800)
Providence, R.I.
Saunders Pitman
——— Dorrance
Bibl. 23, 28, 36, 44

B. Pitman (c. 1810-1840)
Providence, R.I.
Benjamin Pitman
Bibl. 15, 24, 25, 28, 29, 36, 44

B. PITMAN

I. Pitman
(See John Pitman)

John K. Pitman (c. 1805)
Providence, R.I.
Bibl. 28, 36, 44

Sa(u)nders Pitman (b. 1732-d.
1804)
Providence, R.I.
Pitman & Dodge (c. 1790)
Pitman & Dorrance (c. 1795-
1800)
Bibl. 2, 15, 24, 25, 28, 29, 36, 44,
54, 56

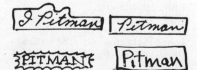

TEAPOTS

When teapots were first introduced into Europe they were very small. Since tea was very expensive, the teapot was designed to hold only one cup of tea. As tea became cheaper and easier to buy, the size of the teapot increased until it reached its present size. The shape of the teapot changed from round to pear-shaped, to the inverted pear shape, finally to the classical straight-sided designs, and still later to the bulbous belly pots made in the nineteenth century. Coffee pots went through very similar changes of size and shape.

1730-1760

1730-1760

1750

1760-1775

1760

1780

TEAPOTS

1790

1790

1800

1810

1820

1825

1835

COFFEEPOTS

1700

1715

1720

1730

1730

1730-1760

1735

1750

1760

1770

1790-1800

1790-1800

1790

1790-1800

1790-1800

1815-1825

CREAMERS

Creamers were very small in the eighteenth century. They began to increase in size, and by 1825 were as large as the early eighteenth-century teapots. The most famous creamer shape is the Queen Anne (1755), with three small feet. This shape has been copied ever since its introduction.

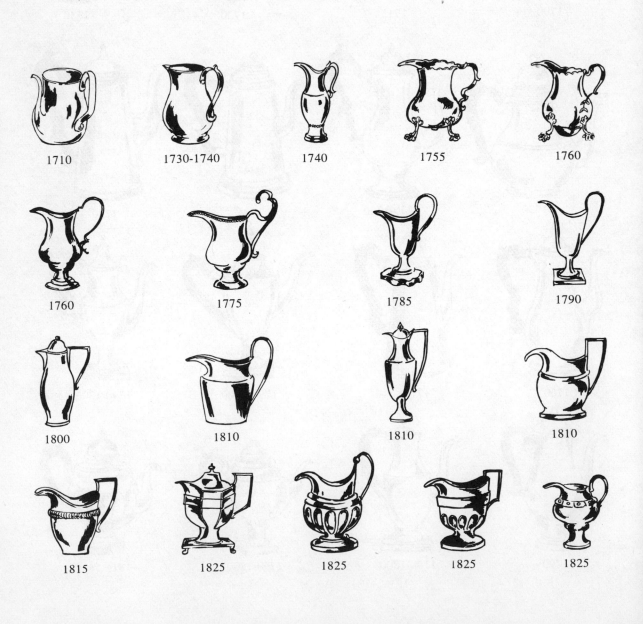

1710

1730-1740

1740

1755

1760

1760

1775

1785

1790

1800

1810

1810

1810

1815

1825

1825

1825

1825

William R. Pitman (c. 1835)
New Bedford, Mass.
Bibl. 15, 23, 25, 28, 36, 44

Richard Pitt(s) (c. 1744)
Philadelphia, Pa.
Bibl. 23, 44

John Pittman
Falmouth, Va. (c. 1792)
Alexandria, Va. (c. 1797)
Philadelphia, Pa. (c. 1801-
1818)
Bibl. 3, 19, 25, 28, 29, 44

A. Pitts (c. 1790)
Philadelphia, Pa.
Bibl. 23, 36, 44

Abner Pitts
Berkeley, Mass.
Bibl. 28

Albert Pitts
Berkeley, Mass.
Bibl. 28

Richard Pitts
Philadelphia, Pa. (c. 1732-
1745)
Charleston, S.C. (c. 1746)
Bibl. 3, 24, 25, 28, 29, 30, 36,
44

Daniel Place
Rochester, N.Y. (c. 1827)
Ithaca, N.Y. (c. 1832-1845)
Bibl. 20, 41, 44

Edward Plain
New York, N.Y. (c. 1836-
1838)
Philadelphia, Pa. (c. 1841-
1850)
Bibl. 3, 15, 23, 36, 44

Gregory Planquet (c. 1797)
New York, N.Y.
Bibl. 23, 36, 44

Platt & Brother (c. 1825)
New York, N.Y.
Bibl. 15, 24, 25, 36, 44, 89

Platt & Brother   Platt & Bro.

George W. Platt (c. 1820)
New York, N.Y.
Bibl. 23, 36, 44

George W. & N. C. Platt (c.
1816-1820)
New York, N.Y.
Bibl. 29, 35, 36, 44, 83, 88

GW.NC PLATT

PLATT & BROTHER

James Platt (c. 1834-1837)
New York, N.Y.
Bibl. 15, 23, 36, 44

John Platt (c. 1843)
Philadelphia, Pa.
Bibl. 3

Nathan C. Platt (c. 1820)
New York, N.Y.
Bibl. 23, 36, 44

William Platt (c. 1817)
Columbus, Ohio
Bibl. 34

John Frederick Plint (c. 1839)
Philadelphia, Pa.
Bibl. 3

P. S. Plowman (c. 1838)
Wheeling, Va.
Bibl. 19

J. F. Plummer
Location unknown
Bibl. 15, 44

J F PLUMMER

Francis Poincignon (c. 1794-
1799)
Philadelphia, Pa.
Bibl. 3, 23, 36, 44

Peter Poincy (d. 1815)
Philadelphia, Pa. (c. 1813-
1814)
Bibl. 3, 23, 36, 44

W. Poindexter and Son (c.
1838-1839)
Lexington, Ky.
Bibl. 32, 54

William A. Poindexter (b.
1818-d. 1884)

Lexington, Ky. (c. 1838-1859)
Bibl. 32

William P. Poindexter (b.
1792-d. 1869)
Lexington, Ky. (c. 1820-1859)
Bibl. 32

Pointe & Tanguy (c. 1811)
Philadelphia, Pa.
James Pointe (?)
———— Tanguy
Bibl. 3, 23, 36, 44

James Pointe (c. 1811-1814)
Philadelphia, Pa.
Pointe & Tanguy (c. 1811) (?)
Bibl. 3, 23, 36, 44

N. J. Poissenot (c. 1806)
Philadelphia, Pa.
Bibl. 3, 23, 36, 44

F. Poissonier (c. 1797)
Philadelphia, Pa.
Bibl. 3, 23, 28, 36, 44

Peter Poltevin (c. 1813)
Philadelphia, Pa.
Bibl. 3

D. R. Poland (c. 1837)
Philadelphia, Pa.
Bibl. 3

P. Poland (c. 1837)
Philadelphia, Pa.
Bibl. 3, 23, 36, 44

Quom Polgrain (Polegreen)
(Paulgreen)
Philadelphia, Pa. (c. 1797-
1799)
Bibl. 3, 23, 28, 36

John Polhemus (Polhamus) (c.
1833-1837)
New York, N.Y.
Bibl. 4, 15, 23, 28, 36, 44

Robert Isaac Watts Polk (b.
1818-d. 1861)
Winchester, Va.
Campbell & Polk (c. 1850-
1858)
Bibl. 19

POLK

H. N. Pollard (19th century)
Location unknown
Bibl. 15

H. N. POLLARD

H. N. Pollard & Co. (19th
century)
Location unknown
Bibl. 15, 44

H. N. POLLARD & CO.

Lewis R. Pollard (c. 1818-
1832)
Norfolk, Va.
Murphy & Pollard (c. 1818-
1820)
Freeman & Pollard (c. 1832-
1834)
Bibl. 19

William Pollard (d. 1740)
Charleston, S.C. (c. 1738-
1740)
Bibl. 5

W.P

Jonas Polley (c. 1823)
Steubenville, Ohio
Bibl. 34

Hyman Pollock (c. 1841-1850)
Philadelphia, Pa.
Bibl. 3

Hunt Pomeroy
Ithaca, N.Y. (c. 1828-1829)
Elmira, N.Y. (c. 1832)
Bibl. 20

Lewis Joseph Poncet (c. 1800-
1822)
Baltimore, Md.
Bibl. 24, 25, 28, 29, 36, 38, 44

L. PONCET

William Pollard (b. 1687-d.
1746)
Boston, Mass.
Bibl. 2, 15, 23, 24, 25, 29, 36,
44, 54

Thomas Pons (b. 1757-d. 1817)
Boston, Mass. (c. 1789)
Bibl. 4, 23, 24, 25, 28, 29, 36,
44

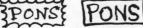

Peter Ponson (c. 1796)
Philadelphia, Pa.
Bibl. 3

John Baptiste Pontier (c. 1801)
Baltimore, Md.
Bibl. 38

Abraham Pontran (c. 1727)
New York, N.Y.
Bibl. 28

David L. Pool (b. 1810-d. 1861)
Philadelphia, Pa. (before 1832)
Salisbury, N.C.
Bibl. 21

James Pool (c. 1837-1844)
Philadelphia, Pa.
Bibl. 3

James M. Pool (c 1846)
Washington, N.C.
Bibl. 21

Thomas Pool (c. 1842-1850)
Philadelphia, Pa.
Bibl. 3

Charles Poole (c. 1819-1835)
New York, N.Y.
Bibl. 35, 83

Henry Poole (c. 1775, b. 1754)
Maryland
Bibl. 28, 38

J. Poole (c. 1850)
Leesburg, Va.
Bibl. 19

Nicholas Poole (c. 1770-1776)
Norfolk, Va.
Bibl. 19

Thomas Poole (c. 1776)
Norfolk, Va.
Bibl. 19

William Poole (b. 1764-d.
1846)
Wilmington, Del.
Bibl. 25, 30, 44, 54

W P　WP

William W. Poole (c. 1828-
1843)
Philadelphia, Pa.
Bibl. 3

Nathaniel C. Poor (b. 1808-d.
1895)
Boston, Mass.
Bibl. 23, 28, 36, 44

Porter
(See Peck & Porter)

Porter & White (c. 1808-1809)
Canandaigua, N.Y.
Joseph S. Porter
——— White
Bibl. 20

F. W. Porter (c. 1820)
New York, N.Y.
Bibl. 23, 24, 25, 29, 36, 44

F. W. PORTER

George E. Porter
Utica, N.Y. (c. 1834-1840)
Syracuse, N.Y. (c. 1841)
Bibl. 18, 20

Henry C. Porter (c. 1820)
New York, N.Y.
Henry C. Porter & Co. (c.
1830)
Bibl. 23, 36, 44

Henry C. Porter & Co. (c.
1830)
New York, N.Y.
Bibl. 15, 23, 24, 25, 28, 29, 36,
44

H PORTER & CO

H Porter & Co

John Porter (c. 1842)
Philadelphia, Pa.
Bibl. 3

Joseph S. Porter (b. 1783-d.
1862)
Utica, N.Y. (c. 1805-1849)
Barton & Porter (c. 1811-
1816)
Doolittle, Norris, & Co. (1842-
1846)
Nicholas N. Weaver
Bibl. 15, 18, 20, 25, 28, 44, 72

I. S. PORTER　　I. S. PORTER

Joseph S. Porter (c. 1810)
Canandaigua, N.Y.
Porter & White (c. 1808-1809)
Bibl. 20

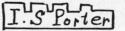

M. S. Porter (c. 1830)
Location unknown
Bibl. 28

(M S PORTER)

William S. Porter (c. 1835)
Philadelphia, Pa.
Bibl. 3

Abraham Portram (c. 1727)
New York, N.Y.
Bibl. 23, 29, 36

Frederick J. Posey
Hagerstown, Md. (c. 1820-
1842)
Shepherdstown, Va. (c. 1842)
Bibl. 19, 25, 29, 38, 44

F. J. POSEY

J. Post (before 1800)
Location unknown
Bibl. 28

Samuel Post (b. 1736, c. 1783)
New London, Conn.
Norwich, Conn.
Cleveland & Post (c. 1799)
Bibl. 16, 23, 28, 36, 44

Potter
(See Redman & Potter)

Potter & Patterson (c. 1814-
1815)
Alexandria, Va.
John Potter
John Patterson
Bibl. 19

J. O. & J. R. Potter (c. 1810-
1824)
Providence, R.I.
Bibl. 23, 24, 25, 36, 44

John Potter (c. 1813-1821)
Alexandria, Va. (c. 1814-1815)
Norfolk, Va. (c. 1818-   )
Redman & Potter (c. 1819-
1821)
Potter & Patterson (c. 1814-
1815)
Bibl. 19, 54

J. POTTER

Niles Potter (18th century)
Westerly, R.I.
Bibl. 28, 44

William Potter (c. 1827)
New York, N.Y.
Bibl. 15

Francis Pottier (b. 1794-d.
1818)
Savannah, Ga.
Avice & Pottier (c. 1818)
Bibl. 17

Potwine & Whiting (c. 1735-
1762)
Hartford, Conn.
John Potwine
Captain Charles Whiting
Bibl. 23, 28, 36, 44

John Potwine (b. 1698-d. 1792)
Hartford, Conn. (c. 1735-
1762)
Coventry, Conn.
East Windsor, Conn.
Boston, Mass.
Potwine & Whiting (c. 1735-
1762)
Bibl. 2, 4, 15, 16, 23, 24, 25,
28, 29, 36, 54, 61

I.P   I Potwine

I. Potwine

IP   I. Potwine

James Poupard (Poussard) (c.
1772-1814)
Boston, Mass. (?)
Philadelphia, Pa.
Bibl. 3, 23, 28, 36, 44

Auguste Poupon (c. 1813-
1814)
Philadelphia, Pa.
Bibl. 3

Poussard
(See Poupard)

Abraham Poutrau (b. 1701)
New York, N.Y. (c. 1726)
Bibl. 15, 25, 44, 71

Christopher Frederick Powell
(c. 1764)
Philadelphia, Pa.
Boston, Mass. (?)
Bibl. 3, 23, 36, 44

John Powell (c. 1745)
Annapolis, Md.
Bibl. 38

John B. Powell (c. 1850)
Philadelphia, Pa.
Bibl. 3

W. S. Powell (c. 1839)
Honeoye Falls, N.Y.
Bibl. 20

Charles Powelson (c. 1840)
Albany, N.Y.
Bibl. 23

Charles Powelson (c. 1841)
Albany, N.Y.
Bibl. 20, 36, 44

Henry Power (c. 1822-
1850-   )
Poughkeepsie, N.Y.
Bibl. 20

Gilbert Powers (c. 1832-   )
Utica, N.Y.
Bibl. 18, 20

Titus Powers (c. 1832)
Utica, N.Y.
Bibl. 18, 20

William Powers (c. 1799-1801)
Savannah, Ga.
Miller & Powers
Bibl. 17

John Praefelt (c. 1797-1798)
Philadelphia, Pa.
Bibl. 3

Pratt & Lockwood (c. 1841)
Newburgh, N.Y.
George W. Pratt
————— Lockwood
Bibl. 20

Pratt & Reath
Location unknown
Bibl. 54

Azariah Pratt (c. 1788)
Marietta, Ohio
Bibl. 34

Daniel Pratt (c. 1832-
1839-   )
Ithaca, N.Y.

Munger & Pratt (c. 1832)
Bibl. 20, 41

E. P. Pratt (19th century)
Location unknown
Bibl. 54

E. W. Pratt (c. 1820)
Chillicothe, Ohio
Bibl. 34

Elisha Pratt (c. 1828)
Marietta, Ohio
Bibl. 34

George W. Pratt (c. 1839-
1845)
Newburgh, N.Y.
Pratt & Lockwood (c. 1841)
Bibl. 20

Henry Pratt (c. 1709-1749)
Philadelphia, Pa.
Bibl. 3, 23, 25, 36, 44, 81

Nathan Pratt (b. 1772-d. 1842)
Essex, Conn.
Bibl. 16, 23, 24, 25, 28, 29, 36,
44

N. PRATT

Nathan Pratt Jr. (b. 1802)
Essex, Conn. (c. 1823)
Bibl. 16, 23, 28

Phineas Pratt (b. 1747-d.
1813)
Lyme, Conn. (c. 1772)
Westbrook, Conn.
Bibl. 16, 23, 28, 36, 44

Seth Pratt (b. 1741-d. 1802)
Lyme, Conn.
Bibl. 16, 23, 28, 36, 44

W. T. Pratt (c. 1826)
Black Rock, N.Y.
Bibl. 20

William T. Pratt (c. 1828)
New York, N.Y.
Bibl. 15

William T. Pratt (c.
1834-   )
Washington, N.C.
Bibl. 21

Charles Pree (c. 1818-1822)
Philadelphia, Pa.
Bibl. 3

———— Prentice (w. 1788)
Baltimore, Md.
Joseph Morgan Bowene
Bibl. 38

A. T. Prentice (c. 1821)
Buffalo, N.Y.
Bibl. 20

Alanzo T. Prentice (c. 1826-
1850-   )
Lockport, N.Y.
Bibl. 20

W. W. Prentice (c. 1827-
1831)
Lockport, N.Y.
Bibl. 20

John H. Prentiss (c. 1832)
Utica, N.Y.
Bibl. 18, 20

John H. Prentiss (c. 1838)
Little Falls, N.Y.
Bibl. 20

Henry Prescot (c. 1828)
Keeseville, N.Y.
Bibl. 25

Henry Prescott (c. 1828-1831)
Keeseville, N.Y.
Bibl. 20, 44

———— Preston (c. 1825-1831)
Philadelphia, Pa.
Curry & Preston
Bibl. 3

James B. Preston (c. 1819)
Baltimore, Md.
Bibl. 38

James Bond Preston (b. 1790-d.
1833)
Alexandria, Va. (c. 1817-   )
Baltimore, Md. (c. 1819)
Bibl. 19

Stephen L. Preston (c. 1849)
Newburgh, N.Y.
Bibl. 13, 20, 25, 44

S. L. PRESTON

Prevear & Harrington (c. 1841-
1842)
Amherst, Mass.
Edward Prevear

Samuel Harrington
Bibl. 84

Edward Prevear (c. 1841)
Amherst, Mass.
Prevear & Harrington (c. 1841-
1842)
Bibl. 84

Benjamin Price (c. 1767)
Philadelphia, Pa.
Bibl. 23, 28, 36, 44

Henry P. Price (c. 1810)
Philadelphia, Pa.
Bibl. 44

Isaac Price (c. 1793-1800)
Philadelphia, Pa.
Leslie & Price
Bibl. 3

John Price (c. 1764)
Lancaster, Pa.
Bibl. 23, 28, 36, 44

Joseph Price (Rice?)
Baltimore, Md. (c. 1799)
Bibl. 38

Philip Price (c. 1824)
Philadelphia, Pa.
Bibl. 3

Philip Price Jr. (c. 1813-1825)
Philadelphia, Pa.
Bibl. 3

William Price (c. 1806)
Cincinnati, Ohio
Bibl. 34

William H. Price (c. 1818-
1822)
Philadelphia, Pa.
Bibl. 3

Prichard
(See Burger & Prichard)

P. Prie (c. 1780)
Location unknown
Bibl. 10, 28, 29, 44

Joseph Priest (b. 1756)
Maryland (c. 1775)
Bibl. 38

Prime & Roshore (Roshore & Prime) (c. 1825)
New York, N.Y.
———— Prime
John Roshore
Bibl. 15

Peter Primrose (c. 1811-1816)
Augusta, Ga.
Bibl. 17

A. Prince (c. 1825)
Location unknown
Bibl. 24

A. PRINCE

Job Prince (b. 1680-d. 1704)
Milford, Conn.
Boston, Mass.
Hull, Mass. (b. 1680)
Bibl. 16, 23, 24, 25, 28, 29, 36, 44, 61

I. P

Samuel Prioleau (b. 1690-d. 1752)
Charleston, S.C. (c. 1721)
Bibl. 5

John N. Prior
Fayetteville, N.C.
Warren Prior & Son (after 1887)
Bibl. 21

Warren Prior (b. 1811-d. 1909, c. 1833-1887)
Fayettcville, N.C. (c. 1834-1836, after 1887)
Northfield, Mass.
Campbell & Prior (c. 1834-1836)
Warren Prior & Son (after 1887)
Bibl. 21

Warren Prior & Son (after 1887)
Fayetteville, N.C.
Warren Prior
John N. Prior
Bibl. 21

Jacob Probasco (c. 1822)
Philadelphia, Pa.
Bibl. 3

G. Promise (c. 1816-1817)
Philadelphia, Pa.
Bibl. 3

William Promise (c. 1810-1818)
Philadelphia, Pa.
Bibl. 3

Charles Pryse (c. 1824)
Baltimore, Md.
Bibl. 38

Jonathan H. Pugh (c. 1845-1850)
Philadelphia, Pa.
Bibl. 3

Richard Pugh (c. 1845)
Cleveland, Ohio
Bibl. 54, 65

Robert Pullen (c. 1798-1811)
Philadelphia, Pa.
Bibl. 3

Charles Purcell (d. 1815)
Richmond, Va. (c. 1791-1795-   )
Bibl. 19

Charles Purcell II (c. 1819-1820)
Richmond, Va.
Bibl. 19

Elisha Purdy (c. 1803-1804)
Kingston, N.Y.
Bibl. 20

J. H. Purdy (19th century)
Location unknown
Bibl. 54

John Purkis (c. 1732, d. 1741)
Charleston, S.C.
Bibl. 5

Samuel B. Purple (b. 1813-d. 1857)
Columbus, Ga.
Foster & Purple (c. 1844-1845)
Bibl. 17

John Purse (c. 1803)
Philadelphia, Pa.
Bibl. 3

Thomas Purse (b. 1776-d. 1823)
Baltimore, Md. (c. 1795, c. 1812)
Winchester, Va. (c. 1801)
Charleston, S.C. (c. 1813)
Bibl. 19, 38

T P

William Purse (b. 1760-d. 1844)
Charleston, S.C. (c. 1785-1825)
Bibl. 5, 25, 44

Purse   PURSE

Henry Pursell (c. 1775)
New York, N.Y.
Bibl. 28, 29, 44

H. P.

Henry Pursell (c. 1783-1785)
Philadelphia, Pa.
Bibl. 3

Putnam & Low (c. 1822)
Boston, Mass.
Edward Putnam
John J. Low
Bibl. 15, 28, 44

Putnam & Low

Edward Putnam
Salem, Mass. (c. 1810)
Boston, Mass. (c. 1822-1825)
Putnam & Low (c. 1822)
Bibl. 23, 25, 28, 29, 36

E. P

F. H. Putnam (c. 1830)
Worcester, Mass.
Bibl. 89

F. H. PUTNAM

George Washington Putnam (b. 1820)
Roxbury, Mass. (c. 1842)
Bibl. 23

John Putnam (c. 1835)
Albany, N.Y.
Bibl. 20

John S. Putnam (c. 1836-1848)
Buffalo, N.Y.
Wright & Putnam (c. 1836)
Bibl. 20

Rufus Putnam (c. 1815)
Albany, N.Y.
Bibl. 20, 23, 36

Putney & Howe (c. 1816-1817)
Sackets Harbor, N.Y.
Reuben H. Putney
Otis Howe
Bibl. 20

Reuben H. Putney
Sackets Harbor, N.Y. (c. 1816)
Watertown, N.Y. (c. 1821-
1828)
Putney & Howe (c. 1816-1817)
Bibl. 20, 25, 44

R PUTNEY

Benjamin Pyle (d. 1812)
Washington, N.C.
Bibl. 21

Benjamin Pyle II (c. 1837-
1841)
Fayetteville, N.C.
Selph & Pyle (c. 1837-1838)
Bibl. 21

George Pyle (c. 1850)
Philadelphia, Pa.
Bibl. 3

Lewis Quandale (c. 1813-1845)
Philadelphia, Pa.
Bibl. 3

Frederick Quaritus (c. 1833-
1835)
New York, N.Y.
Bibl. 15, 23, 36

J. V. D. Quereau (Quercau) (c.
1841-1845)
Philadelphia, Pa.
Bibl. 3

M. Quimby (19th century)
Location unknown
Bibl. 15, 44

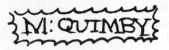

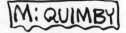

QUIMBY

Abrilla Quinby (early 19th
century)
Warren, Ohio
Bibl. 34

Captain Ephraim Quinby (c.
1799)
Warren, Ohio
Bibl. 34

Daniel Quincy (c. 1651-1690)
Braintree, Mass.
Quincy, Mass.
Bibl. 2, 23, 28, 36, 44

Joseph Quinn (c. 1849-1850)
Philadelphia, Pa.
Bibl. 3

F. F. Quintard (c. 1843)
New York, N.Y.
Bibl. 23

Peter Quintard (b. 1699-d.
1762)
New York, N.Y. (c. 1731)
Norwalk, Conn. (c. 1737-
1762)
Bibl. 4, 15, 16, 23, 24, 25, 28, 29,
30, 35, 36, 44, 61

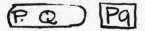

James Rabbeth (Rabeth)
New York, N.Y. (c. 1836-
1838)
Bibl. 15, 23, 36, 44

James Rabbith (c. 1834)
Albany, N.Y.
Bibl. 20

Rabeth
(See Rabbeth)

Rach
(See Anthony Rasch)

Daniel Racine (c. 1799)
Baltimore, Md.
Bibl. 38

George Rackett (d. 1852)
Augusta, Ga.
Clark, Rackett & Co. (c. 1840-
1852)
Bibl. 17

Radcliffe & Guignard (c. 1856-
1858)
Columbia, S.C.
Thomas W. Radcliffe
James S. Guignard
Bibl. 5

Thomas W. Radcliffe (d. 1870)
Columbia, S.C. (c. 1827-1833,
c. 1848-1870)

Camden, S.C. (c. 1833)
Glaze & Radcliffe (c. 1848-
1851)
Thomas W. Radcliff(e) & Co.
(c. 1852-1856)
Radcliffe & Guignard (c. 1856-
1858)
Bibl. 5

Thomas W. Radcliffe & Co.
(c. 1852-1856)
Columbia, S.C.
Bibl. 5

Nathaniel Raine (c. 1773)
Philadelphia, Pa.
Bibl. 3

David Rait (c. 1835-1850)
New York, N.Y.
Bibl. 23, 36, 44

Robert Rait (c. 1830-1855)
New York, N.Y.
Bibl. 15, 23, 24, 25, 29, 35, 36,
83

R RAIT

Ralph
(See Loomis & Ralph)

William Ralston (c. 1840-1850)
Ashland, Ohio
Bibl. 34

John Rambo (c. 1837)
Philadelphia, Pa.
Bibl. 3

Peter Rambo (c. 1837-1841)
Philadelphia, Pa.
Bibl. 3

William Rambo (c. 1837)
Philadelphia, Pa.
Bibl. 3

John Rampp (c. 1848-1849)
Louisville, Ky.
Bibl. 32

William Rampp (c. 1848-1859)
Louisville, Ky.
Bibl. 32

Ramsay & Beckwith (c. 1840-
1843)
New Bern, N.C.
Raleigh, N.C.
Walter J. Ramsay
Robert W. Beckwith
Bibl. 21

W. J. Ramsay & Co. (c. 1833-1836)
Raleigh, N.C.
Walter J. Ramsay
Bibl. 21

Walter J. Ramsay (b. 1802-d. 1856)
Raleigh, N.C. (c. 1826, c. 1833-1855)
New Bern, N.C. (c. 1840-1843)
W. J. Ramsay & Co. (c. 1833-1836)
Ramsay & Beckwith (c. 1840-1843)
Palmer & Ramsay (c. 1847-1855)
Bibl. 21

C. A. Rand (c. 1846)
Haverstraw, N.Y.
Bibl. 20

Joseph Rand (b. 1762-d. 1836)
Medford, Mass.
Bibl. 28

Randle & Harwell (c. 1833)
Eatonton, Ga.
Bibl. 17

James H. Randolph (c. 1827-1857)
Greensville, S.C.
Bibl. 5

Alexander Rankin (c. 1829-1833)
Philadelphia, Pa.
Bibl. 3

Elijah Ranney (c. 1804-1805-)
Utica, N.Y.
Bibl. 18, 20

Asa Ransom (b. 1767-d. 1837)
Buffalo, N.Y. (c. 1797-1812)
Bibl. 20

Solomon Raphael (c. 1796)
Philadelphia, Pa.
Bibl. 3

William D. Rapp (c. 1828-1850)
Philadelphia, Pa.
Bibl. 3, 15, 25, 44

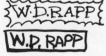

Rasch (Rach) (Roush) & Willig (Jr.) (c. 1819)
Philadelphia, Pa.
Anthony Rasch
George Willig Jr.
Bibl. 3, 4, 23, 28, 36, 44

Anthony Rasch (Rach) (Roush) (c. 1807-1819)
Philadelphia, Pa. (c. 1815-1820)
New Orleans, La.
Chaudron & Rasch (c. 1812-1820)
Rasch & Willig (c. 1819)
Anthony Rasch & Co. (c. 1820)
Bibl. 3, 4, 15, 23, 24, 25, 28, 29, 36, 44, 54

ANTY RASCH   A R
A RASCH

Anthony Rasch & Co. (c. 1820)
Philadelphia, Pa.
Bibl. 24, 25, 28, 44

A. RASCH & CO.

W. A. Rasch (c. 1830)
New Orleans, La.
Bibl. 25, 44

W A RASCH

Frederick Rath (c. 1840)
New York, N.Y.
Bibl. 15, 25, 44

F. RATH

Anthony R. Raulin (d. 1824)
Savannah, Ga. (c. 1818-1824)
Avice & Raulin (c. 1818-1819)
Bibl. 17

Francis Raulin (c. 1805-1822)
Savannah, Ga.
Bibl. 17

Xavier Ravee (Ravel) (c. 1796-1797)
Philadelphia, Pa.
Bibl. 3, 23, 36, 44

Benjamin Rawls (b. 1772-d. 1866)
Columbia, S.C. (c. 1816-1866)
Bibl. 5

E. Raworth (c. 1783)
Location unknown
Bibl. 28

E. RAWORTH

Asa Rawson (c. 1808)
Charlton, N.Y.
Bibl. 20

Newton Rawson (c. 1850-1854)
Utica, N.Y.
Bibl. 18

Henry Raymond (c. 1833-1840)
Albany, N.Y.
Bibl. 20

John Raymond (d. 1775)
Boston, Mass.
Bibl. 28, 44

Peter Elizabeth Benjamin Raynal (c. 1806-1831)
Charleston, S.C.
Bibl. 5

William Thomas Raynal (c. 1831)
Columbia, S.C.
Bibl. 5

Joseph Raynes (c. 1835)
Lowell, Mass.
Bibl. 15, 44, 25

JOSEPH RAYNES

Read (and Owen?) (c. 1840)
Cincinnati, Ohio
Bibl. 34

Daniel I. Read (c. 1798)
Philadelphia, Pa.
Bilbl. 3

Isaac Read (c. 1819-1822)
Philadelphia, Pa.
Bibl. 3

Jacob Read (b. 1741-d. 1783)
Burlington, N.J. (1763-1783)
Bibl. 46

John Read (c. 1835-1848)
Buffalo, N.Y.
Bibl. 20

Thomas (Culbert) Read (c. 1759)
Annapolis, Md.
Bibl. 38

William H. J. Read (c. 1831-
1850)
Philadelphia, Pa.
Bibl. 3

———— Reade
New York, N.Y.
Gibney & Reade (c. 1847)
Bibl. 23

Thomas Reak (c. 1835)
Philadelphia, Pa.
Bibl. 3

John Reasnors (c. 1841)
Rochester, N.Y.
Bibl. 20

James Reat (b. 1782-d. 1815)
Richmond, Va.
Johnson & Reat (c. 1810-
1815)
James Reat & Co.
Bibl. 19

James Reat & Co.
Richmond, Va.
Bibl. 19

Reath
(See Pratt & Reath)

———— Recordon (c. 1838-
1842)
St. Louis, Mo.
Menkens & Recordon (c. 1842)
Bibl. 54

Redfield & Rice
Location unknown
Bibl. 54

Jacob Redifer (c. 1844-1850)
Philadelphia, Pa.
Bibl. 3

Redman & Potter (c. 1819-
1821)
Norfolk, Va.
Henry H. Redman
John Potter
Bibl. 19

R & POTTER

Henry H. Redman (d. 1840)
Norfolk, Va.
Redman & Potter (c. 1819-
1821)
Bibl. 19

REDMAN

Claudius Redon (c. 1828)
New York, N.Y.
Bibl. 15, 25, 44

C. REDON

Reed
(See Bleasom & Reed)
(See Lincoln & Reed)
(See Newton & Reed)

Reed & Slater (c. 1830?)
Nashua, N.H.
Bibl. 28

A. G. Reed & Co. (c. 1835)
Nassau, N.H.
Bibl. 36, 44

Frederick Reed (c. 1814-1823)
Philadelphia, Pa.
Bibl. 3

G. Washington Reed (c. 1839-
1850)
Philadelphia, Pa.
Bibl. 3

Isaac Reed (b. 1746)
Stamford, Conn. (c. 1776)
Bibl. 16, 28, 36, 44

Isaac Reed (c. 1820-1846)
Philadelphia, Pa.
Bibl. 3, 15

Isaac Reed & Son (c. 1830-
1850)
Philadelphia, Pa.
Bibl. 3, 15, 24, 25, 29, 36, 44

I REED & SON   I R & S

John W. Reed (c. 1846-1847)
Philadelphia, Pa.
Bibl. 3

Jonathan Reed (c. 1725-1740)
Boston, Mass.
Bibl. 29, 54

I · R

Joseph Reed (c. 1847)
St. Louis, Mo.
Bibl. 54

Lewis Reed (c. 1810)
New York, N.Y.
Bibl. 23, 36, 44

Osmon Reed (c. 1831-1841)
Philadelphia, Pa.
Osmon Reed & Co. (c. 1841-
1850)
Bibl. 3, 23, 24, 28, 29, 36, 44

O REED

Osmon Reed & Co. (c. 1841-
1850)
Philadelphia, Pa.
Bibl. 3, 15, 23, 24, 25, 29, 44

O REED & CO

REED & CO

Robert W. Reed
Winchester, Va. (c. 1837)
Baltimore, Md. (c. 1849-1852)
Bibl. 19

Samuel Reed (c. 1827)
New York, N.Y.
Bibl. 15

Stephen Reed (b. 1805)
Philadelphia, Pa. (c. 1846-
1850)
Bibl. 3, 15, 23, 24, 25, 44

S. REED

Abner Reeder (b. 1766-d.
1841)
Philadelphia, Pa. (c. 1793-1800)
Trenton, N.J. (c. 1798-1830)
McFee & Reeder (c. 1793-
1796)
Bibl. 3, 4, 23, 24, 25, 28, 29,
36, 46, 54

A. REEDER

John Reeder (c. 1835)
Philadelphia, Pa.
Bibl. 3, 23, 36, 44

P. L. Reese (c. 1857-1897)
Mt. Sterling, Ky.
Bibl. 54

William Reese (c. 1802, b.
1786)
Baltimore, Md.
Bibl. 38

Reeve & Clark (c.   -1818)
Newburgh, N.Y.
Bibl. 20

Reeve & Heroy (c. 1813-1815)
Newburgh, N.Y.
Bibl. 20

Charles Reeve (c. 1826-1840)
Newburgh, N.Y.
Charles Reeve & Co. (c. 1835-1837)
Bibl. 20

Charles Reeve & Co. (c. 1835-1837)
Newburgh, N.Y.
Bibl. 20

G. Reeve (c. 1825)
Location unknown
Bibl. 28, 29, 44

George Reeve (c. 1804-1805)
Philadelphia, Pa.
Richard & George Reeve (c. 1804)
Bibl. 3

J. Reeve
(See James Reeves)

Joseph Reeve (d. 1828)
Newburgh, N.Y. (c. 1813)
New York, N.Y. (c. 1828)
Bibl. 20, 24, 25

Richard Reeve (c. 1803-1807)
Philadelphia, Pa.
Richard & George Reeve (c. 1804)
Bibl. 3

Richard & George Reeve (c. 1804)
Philadelphia, Pa.
Bibl. 3

Y. Reeve (c. 1808)
Philadelphia, Pa.
Bibl. 3

Abner Reeves (c. 1832-1838)
Louisville, Ky.
Bibl. 32

David S. Reeves (c. 1830-1835)
Philadelphia, Pa.
Bibl. 3

Enos Reeves (b. 1753-d. 1807)
Charleston, S.C. (c. 1784-1807)
Bibl. 5, 24, 25, 28, 29, 36, 46

J. F. Reeves (c. 1835-1840)
Baltimore, Md.
Bibl. 15, 25, 44

James Reeves (J. Reeve) (c. 1837-1838)
New York, N.Y.
Bibl. 15, 44

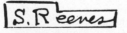 ?

Joseph James Reeves (c. 1831-1837)
New York, N.Y.
Bibl. 15

 ?

Stephen Reeves (b. 1738)
Bridgeton, N.J. (before 1754-) (?)
Philadelphia, Pa. (c. 1754-1774)
Burlington, N.J. (1766)
Georgetown, Md. (c. 1775)
New York, N.Y. (c. 1776-)
Bibl. 24, 25, 28, 29, 36, 44, 46, 54, 72

M. A. Regensburg (c. 1821)
Lovingston, Va.
Bibl. 19

Abraham Regin (c. 1820-1822)
Philadelphia, Pa.
Bibl. 3

Joseph Reibley (Rively)
Philadelphia, Pa. (c. 1845-1846)
Bibl. 3

John Reich (c. 1803-1808)
Philadelphia, Pa.
Bibl. 3

Frederick Reicke (Richie) (Ritchie)
Philadelphia, Pa. (c. 1794-1798)
Bibl. 3

Elisha Reid (c. 1814-1816)
Milledgeville, Ga.
T. & E. Reid (c. 1814-1815)
Bibl. 17

Elisha Reid (c. 1836)
Columbus, Ga.
Bibl. 17

Jacob Reid (c. 1763-1783)
Burlington, N.J.
Bibl. 54

James Reid (c. 1825)
Philadelphia, Pa.
Bibl. 3

Josephus Reid (c. 1821)
Milledgeville, Ga.
Bibl. 17

T. & E. Reid (c. 1814-1815)
Milledgeville, Ga.
Templeton Reid
Elisha Reid
Bibl. 17

Templeton Reid (b. 1765-d. 1851)
Milledgeville, Ga. (c. 1813-1815)
Columbus, Ga. (c. 1836-1851)
T. & E. Reid (c. 1814-1815)
Bibl. 17

J. C. Reilly and Co. (c. 1816)
Louisville, Ky.
Bibl. 32, 54, 68

John Reilly (c. 1783-1818)
Philadelphia, Pa.
Bibl. 3

John Reilly
Richmond, Va. (c. 1785)
Bibl. 19

John C. Reilly (c. 1833)
Philadelphia, Pa.
Bibl. 3

J. H. & R. J. Relay (c. 1848)
Albany, N.Y.
Bibl. 20

P. de Remier
(See DeRemier)

John Renaud (Renowd)
Philadelphia, Pa. (c. 1811-
1817)
Bibl. 3

John M. Renaud (Renowd)
Philadelphia, Pa. (c. 1811)
Bibl. 3

William Renville (c. 1837)
New York, N.Y.
Bibl. 15

Revere & Son (c. 1796)
Boston, Mass.
Paul Revere (II)
Paul Revere (III)
Bibl. 4, 15, 23, 28, 36, 44

Edward Revere (b. 1768-d.
1803)
Boston, Mass.
Bibl. 4, 23, 28, 36, 44

J. W. Revere
Boston, Mass. (c. 1796)
Canton, Ohio (c. 1801)
Joseph Warren Revere
Bibl. 23, 28, 36, 44

Paul Revere Sr. (Apollos
Rivoire)
Boston, Mass. (c. 1702-1754)
Bibl. 4, 15, 23, 24, 25, 26, 28,
29, 36, 43, 44, 54, 77

Paul Revere (II) (b. 1735-d.
1807)
Boston, Mass.
Revere & Son (c. 1796)

Bibl. 4, 15, 23, 24, 25, 26, 28, 29,
36, 43, 54, 77

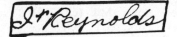

Paul Revere (III) (b. 1760-d.
1813)
Boston, Mass.
Revere & Son (c. 1796)
Bibl. 4, 15, 23, 28, 29, 36, 44

Thomas Revere (b. 1738-1817)
Boston, Mass.
Bibl. 4, 23, 24, 25, 28, 29, 36,
44

Henry Reymond (c. 1842)
St. Louis, Mo.
Bibl. 54

George W. Reynolds (c. 1837-
1843)
Philadelphia, Pa.
Bibl. 3

Henry A. Reynolds (c. 1847)
Rochester, N.Y.
Bibl. 20

John Reynolds (b. 1770-1832)
Hagerstown, Md. (c. 1790-
1832)
Bibl. 25, 29, 38, 44

S. R. Reynolds (c. 1800)
Boston, Mass.
Bibl. 28

Theodore J. Reynolds (c. 1830-
1833)
Philadelphia, Pa.
Bibl. 3, 23, 24, 44

Theodore J. Reynolds (c. 1837)
New York, N.Y.
Bibl. 15

Theodore J. Reynolds (b. 1806)
Utica, N.Y. (c. 1850-1851)
Bibl. 18, 20

Thomas Reynolds (c. 1784, d.
1785)
Philadelphia, Pa.
Bibl. 3, 28

William Reynolds (c. 1770)
Rhode Island
Bibl. 54

John Rheinhart (c. 1839)
Buffalo, N.Y.
Bibl. 20

———— Rhodes (c. 1837)
Cincinnati, Ohio
Bibl. 34

Thomas F. Rhodes (c. 1836)
Cincinnati, Ohio
Bibl. 54

Isaac Riboulau (c. 1726)
Location unknown
Bibl. 2

———— Rice (c. 1780)
Location unknown
Bibl. 28, 29

Rice & Barry (c. 1785-1787)
Baltimore, Md.
Joseph Rice
Standish Barry
Bibl. 38

Rice & Burnett (c. 1860)
Cleveland, Ohio
Bibl. 89

Rice & Rutter (c. 1794)
Baltimore, Md.
Joseph Rice
Richard Rutter
Bibl. 38

A. W. Rice (c. 1850)
Hamilton, N.Y.
Bibl. 20

Arthur Rice (b. 1785-1808)
Savannah, Ga.
Bibl. 17

H. P. Rice (c. 1815-1830)
Saratoga Springs, N.Y. (c.
1827-1830)
Albany, N.Y.
Bibl. 15, 20, 23, 24, 25, 36, 44

J. J. Rice (c. 1849)
Auburn, N.Y.
Bibl. 20

Joseph Rice (b. 1761-d. 1808)
Baltimore, Md. (c. 1784-1787,
c. 1794)
Savannah, Ga. (c. 1799-1801)
Augusta, Ga. (c. 1802)
Rice & Barry (c. 1785-1787)
Rice & Rutter (c. 1794)
Bibl. 3, 17, 23, 24, 25, 36, 38,
39, 44

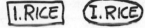

Joseph T. Rice (c. 1813-1850)
Albany, N.Y.
Bibl. 4, 15, 20, 23, 24, 25, 28,
29, 44

William C. Rice (c. 1835-1850)
Philadelphia, Pa.
Bibl. 3

William H. Rice (c. 1839)
Albany, N.Y.
Bibl. 20

Joseph Rich (c. 1790)
Philadelphia, Pa.
Bibl. 28

Obadiah Rich (c. 1832-1850)
Boston, Mass.
Ward & Rich (c. 1832-1835)
Bibl. 4, 23, 24, 25, 28, 29, 36,
44

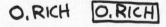

Richard & Phillips (c. 1832-
1836)
New York, N.Y.
Bibl. 15

Richard & Williamson
(See Richards & Williamson)

Augustus Richard (c. 1818-
1819)
Philadelphia, Pa.
Bibl. 3, 23, 36

George E. Richard & Co. (c.
1828-1832)
New York, N.Y.
Bibl. 15

Stephen Richard (c. 1815-1829)
New York, N.Y.
Bibl. 4, 28, 29, 35, 83

Richards
(See Rickards)

———— Richards (c. 1819)
Baltimore, Md.
Richards & Campbell
Bibl. 38

Richards & Campbell (c. 1819)
Baltimore, Md.
———— Richards
Robert Campbell
Bibl. 25, 38

Richards & Pelletreau (c. 1825)
(Pelletreau & Richards)
New York, N.Y.
Thomas Richards (?)
William S. Pelletreau
Bibl. 25

Richards & Williamson (c.
1797-1800)
Philadelphia, Pa.
Samuel R. Richards Jr.
Samuel Williamson
Bibl. 3, 4, 15, 23, 24, 25, 28, 29,
36, 39, 44

A. Richards (c. 1809)
Philadelphia, Pa.
Bibl. 3

George Richards (c. 1829-
1840)
Philadelphia, Pa.
Bibl. 3

Hervey M. Richards (c. 1839-
1842)

Philadelphia, Pa.
Bibl. 3

John Richards
(See John Rickards)

Samuel R. Richards Jr. (c.
1791-1818)
Philadelphia, Pa.
Richards & Williamson (c.
1797-1800)
Bibl. 3, 24, 25, 28, 36, 39, 44, 46,
81

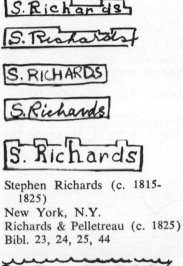

Stephen Richards (c. 1815-
1825)
New York, N.Y.
Richards & Pelletreau (c. 1825)
Bibl. 23, 24, 25, 44

Thomas Richards (c. 1815-
1834)
New York, N.Y.
Sayre & Richards (1802-1811)
Foster & Richards (c. 1815)
Pelletreau & Richards (c. 1825)
Bibl. 15, 24, 25, 28, 30, 36, 44

W. & S. Richards (c. 1818-
1829)
Philadelphia, Pa.
Bibl. 3, 23, 36

William Richards (c. 1823-
1824)
Philadelphia, Pa.
Bibl. 3

William Richards (c. 1842-
1843-   )
Utica, N.Y.
Bibl. 18, 20

William Richards Jr. (c. 1813)
Philadelphia, Pa.
Bibl. 3, 23, 36

Richardson & Delleker
(Delleker & Richardson) (c.
1819)
Philadelphia, Pa.
John Richardson
Samuel Delleker
Bibl. 3

Colin Richardson (c. 1819)
Charleston, S.C.
Bibl. 5

Francis Richardson (b. 1681-d.
1729)
Philadelphia, Pa.
Bibl. 3, 4, 23, 24, 25, 28, 29, 36,
39, 44, 54, 81

Francis Richardson II (Jr.) (b.
1708)
Philadelphia, Pa. (c. 1736-1745)
Bibl. 3, 25, 39, 44, 81

FR

George Richardson (b. 1761,
c. 1782-1790-   )
Richmond, Va.
William & George Richardson
(c. 1782-1793)
Bibl. 19

George Richardson (c. 1818-
1828)
Boston, Mass.
Bibl. 54

G RICHARDSON

George Richardson (c. 1845-
1848)
Louisville, Ky.
Bibl. 32

James Richardson (c. 1840-
1850)
Mansfield, Ohio
Bibl. 34

John Richardson (c. 1793-
1831)
Philadelphia, Pa.
Richardson & Delleker (c.
1819)
Bibl. 3

Joseph Richardson Sr. (b.
1711-d. 1784)
Philadelphia, Pa.
Bibl. 3, 4, 15, 23, 24, 25, 28, 29,
39, 54, 81

Joseph Richardson Jr. (b.
1752-d. 1831)
Philadelphia, Pa. (c. 1777-
1805)
Bibl. 3, 15, 23, 24, 25, 28, 29, 36,
39, 54, 81

I R   J R

Joseph & Nathaniel Richardson
(c. 1785-1791)
Philadelphia, Pa.
Joseph Richardson Jr.
Nathaniel Richardson
Bibl. 3, 15, 24, 25, 29, 36, 39,
44, 54, 72, 81

I N R   I NR

Martin Richardson (c. 1837-
1839)
Little Falls, N.Y.
Bibl. 20

Nathaniel Richardson (c. 1785-
1791)
Philadelphia, Pa.
Joseph & Nathaniel Richardson
(c. 1785-1791)
Bibl. 44

Richard Richardson (c. 1793-
1796)
Philadelphia, Pa.
Bibl. 23, 36, 44

Richards
(See Boyd & Richards)

Thomas Richardson (c. 1769)
New York, N.Y.
Bibl. 28

Capt. William Richardson
(b. 1757-d. 1809)
Richmond, Va.
William and George
Richardson (c. 1782-1793)
Bibl. 19

W. R.   W R

William Richardson (c. 1782-
1789-   )
Winchester, Va.
Bibl. 19

William Richardson (c. 1796)
Norfolk, Va.
Bibl. 19

William Richardson Jr.
(c. 1808)
Richmond, Va.
Bibl. 19

William & George Richardson
(c. 1782-1793)
Richmond, Va.
Captain William Richardson
George Richardson
Bibl. 19

W & G R

Richie
(See Reicke)

Isaac Richman (c. 1850)
Philadelphia, Pa.
Bibl. 3

Franklin Richmond (c. 1815-
1820)
Providence, R.I.
Bibl. 23, 24, 25, 29, 36

F. RICHMOND

G. & A. Richmond (c. 1815)
Providence, R.I.
Bibl. 28, 36, 44

Horace Richmond (c. 1814-
1825)
Canandaigua, N.Y.
Bibl. 20

Thomas Richmond (c. 1806-
1808)
Waterford, N.Y.
Bibl. 15, 20, 44

RICHMOND   ?

Thomas Richmond (c. 1817)
New York, N.Y.
Bibl. 15, 44

RICHMOND ?

William Richmond (c. 1835-
1848)
Philadelphia, Pa.
Bibl. 3

Charles William Richter
(c. 1842-1867)
Madison, Ga.
Bibl. 17

Joseph Rickard (Rickardus)
(c. 1796-1797)
Philadelphia, Pa.
Bibl. 3

Rickards & Dubosq (c. 1828-
1833)
Philadelphia, Pa.
Bibl. 3

Rickards & Lancaster (c. 1817)
Philadelphia, Pa.
—— Rickards
Richard Lancaster
Bibl. 3

Rickards & Snyder (c. 1842)
Philadelphia, Pa.
Bibl. 3

John Rickards (Richards)
(c. 1841-1850)
Philadelphia, Pa.
Bibl. 3

Nutter Rickards (Rickett)
Philadelphia, Pa. (c. 1829-1850)
Bibl. 3

William Rickards (c. 1825-
1845)
Philadelphia, Pa.
William Rickards & Son
(c. 1850)
Bibl. 3

William Rickards & Son (c.
1850)
Philadelphia, Pa.
William Rickards
William D. Rickards
Bibl. 3

William D. Rickards (c. 1841-
1850)
Philadelphia, Pa.

William Rickards & Son
(c. 1850)
Bibl. 3

Rickardus
(See Rickard)

Rickett
(See Nutter Rickards)

Israel Ricksecker (c. 1834-
1872)
Dover, Ohio
Bibl. 34

Arthur Rider (c. 1822-1824)
Baltimore, Md.
Bibl. 38

J. J. Rider (c. 1830)
Salem, Mass.
Bibl. 89

James (John) Ridg(e)way
(b. 1780-d. 1851)
Boston, Mass. (1789)
Groton, Mass. (1793)
Worcester, Mass.
Bibl. 15, 23, 24, 25, 28, 29,
36, 39, 44, 89

John Ridgway Jr. (c. 1813-
1869)
Boston, Mass.
Bibl. 28

George Ridout (Rydout)
(c. 1745)
New York, N.Y.
Bibl. 4, 15, 23, 24, 25, 28, 29,
30, 35, 36, 44, 54

G R

Johan Ried (b. 1784)
Philadelphia, Pa. (1810)
Bibl. 23, 36, 44

George Riehl (c. 1805)
Philadelphia, Pa.
Bibl. 3

Bernard Rielly (c. 1835)
New York, N.Y.
Bibl. 23, 36, 44

—— Riggs (d. 1819)
Philadelphia, Pa.
Bibl. 28

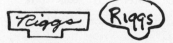

Riggs & Griffith (c. 1816-1818)
Baltimore, Md.
George W. Riggs
Henry Griffith or C. Green-
berry Griffith
Bibl. 24, 25, 29, 38, 44, 54

R&G

Benjamin McKenny Riggs
(b. 1799-d. 1839)
Paris, Ky.
Bibl. 15, 25, 32, 44, 54, 68

BM RIGGS

David H. Riggs (c. 1840)
Paris, Ky.
Bibl. 32, 54, 68

George W. Riggs (b. 1777-d.
1864)
Baltimore, Md.
Georgetown, Va.
Washington, D.C.
Riggs & Griffith (c. 1816-1818)
Bibl. 15, 29, 38, 39, 44, 54

RIGGS   RIGGS   G R

Riggs

Richard Riggs (d. 1819)
Philadelphia, Pa.
Bibl. 15, 23, 24, 25, 36, 44

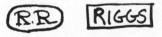

William H. C. Riggs (c. 1819-
1850)
Philadelphia, Pa.
Bibl. 3

Albert M. Rihl (c. 1849-1850)
Philadelphia, Pa.
Bibl. 3

—— Rikeman
Savannah, Ga.

Horton & Rikeman (c. 1850-
1856)
Bibl. 17

Riker & Alexander (Alexander
& Riker) (c. 1797-1798)
New York, N.Y.
Peter Riker
———— Alexander
Bibl. 4, 23, 25, 28, 36, 44

Peter Riker (c. 1797-1814)
New York
Riker & Alexander (c. 1798)
Clapp & Riker (c. 1802-1808)
Bibl. 4, 23, 25, 28, 29, 36, 44, 54

———— Riley (c. 1786)
Baltimore, Md.
Johnson & Riley
Bibl. 38

Bernard Riley (c. 1845-1850)
Philadelphia, Pa.
Bibl. 3, 23

Conrad Riley (c. 1837-1841)
Philadelphia, Pa.
Bibl. 3

Robert Riley (c. 1806)
Philadelphia, Pa.
Bibl. 3

William Riley (c. 1818-1822)
Philadelphia, Pa.
Bibl. 3

Rily
(See Reily)

Ritchie
(See Reicke)

Benjamin Ritchie (b. 1751)
Maryland (c. 1774)
Bibl. 38

George Ritchie (b. 1785-1811)
Philadelphia, Pa.
Bibl. 3

Benjamin Rittenhouse (c. 1760)
Norriton, Pa.
Bibl. 3

David Rittenhouse (c. 1768,
d. 1796)
Philadelphia, Pa.
Bibl. 3

Michael Ritter (c. 1786-1800)
New York, N.Y.
Bibl. 4, 23, 28, 36, 44

Peter Ritter (c. 1786)
New York, N.Y.
Bibl. 23

Richard Ritter (c. 1790-1800)
New York, N.Y.
Bibl. 15, 23, 44

Rively
(See Reibley)

Apollos Rivoire (c. 1702-1754)
Boston, Mass.
Changed name to Paul Revere
Sr.

Roswell Walston (Walsten)
Roath (b. 1805)
Norwich, Conn. (c. 1826)
Denver, Col.
Bibl. 16, 28, 36, 44

Amos Robbins (c. 1846-1849)
Philadelphia, Pa.
Bibl. 3

E. Robbins (c. 1846-1848)
Camden, N.J.
Bibl. 3

Elisha Robbins (c. 1831-1843)
Philadelphia, Pa.
Bibl. 3, 23, 36, 44

George Robbins (Robins)
Philadelphia, Pa. (c. 1833-
1850)
Bibl. 3

Jeremiah Robbins (Robins)
Philadelphia, Pa.
(c. 1847-1850)
Bibl. 3

John Robbins (Robins)
Philadelphia, Pa. (c. 1835-
1850)
Bibl. 3

———— Robbs (c. 1788)
New York, N.Y.
Bibl. 28

Robert
(See James S. H. Robert[s])

Christopher Robert (b. 1708-d.
1783)

New York, N.Y.
Bibl. 4, 23, 24, 25, 28, 29, 33,
35, 36, 44, 54, 56, 83

James Robert
(See next entry)

James S. H. Robert(s)
Lexington, Ky. (c. 1806)
Frankfort, Ky. (c. 1807)
Bibl. 32, 54, 68

Roberts
(See Wendell & Roberts)

Roberts & Atmore (c. 1850)
Philadelphia, Pa.
Bibl. 3

Roberts & Lee (c. 1772-1775)
Boston, Mass.
Frederick Roberts (?)
———— Lee
Bibl. 23, 24, 25, 36, 44

Daniel F. Roberts & Co.
(c. 1840-1850)
Philadelphia, Pa.
Daniel F. Roberts & Co.
(c. 1850)
Bibl. 3

Daniel F. Roberts & Co. (c.
1850)
Philadelphia, Pa.
Bibl. 3

Enoch Roberts (c. 1816)
Philadelphia, Pa.
Bibl. 3

F. Roberts (c. 1828-1829)
Philadelphia, Pa.
Bibl. 3

Frederick Roberts (c. 1770)
Boston, Mass.
Roberts & Lee (c. 1772-
1775) (?)
Bibl. 23, 28, 36, 44

George Roberts (c. 1835-1843)
Philadelphia, Pa.
Bibl. 3

John Roberts (c. 1797-1799)
Philadelphia, Pa.
Bibl. 3

John Roberts (c. 1841-1849)
Philadelphia, Pa.
Bibl. 3

L. D. Roberts (c. 1850)
Hartford, Conn.
Chapell & Roberts
Bibl. 89

Michael Roberts (c. 1786)
New York, N.Y.
Bibl. 28, 44

Michael Roberts (c. 1791-1796)
Philadelphia, Pa.
Bibl. 3, 23

N. H. Roberts (c. 1848-1850)
Philadelphia, Pa.
Bibl. 3

S. & E. Roberts (c. 1830)
Location unknown
Bibl. 28

Samuel Roberts (c. 1833-1850)
Fredericksburg, Va.
Bibl. 19

Thomas Roberts (b. 1744)
Philadelphia, Pa. (c. 1774)
Bibl. 28

Thomas Roberts (c. 1842)
Philadelphia, Pa.
Bibl. 3

William Roberts (c. 1745)
Annapolis, Md.
Bibl. 38

William Roberts (c. 1802)
Charleston, S.C.
Bibl. 5

William Roberts (c. 1821)
Philadelphia, Pa.
Bibl. 3

Alexander Robertson (d. 1751)
Philadelphia, Pa. (c. 1740-
1750)
Bibl. 3, 23, 36, 44

Robert Robertson (c. 1777)
Philadelphia, Pa.
Bibl. 3, 23, 36, 44

Isaac Robeson (Robinson)
Philadelphia, Pa. (c. 1843-
1846)
Bibl. 3

J. C. Robie (c. 1835)
Binghamton, N.Y.
Bibl. 20

John Robie (c. 1817)
Plattsburg, N.Y.
Bibl. 20

Robins
(See George Robbins)
(See Jeremiah Robbins)
(See John Robbins)

Robinson
(See Robeson)

Robinson & Dixon (c. 1845-
1846)
Portsmouth, Va.
Andrew Robinson
D. L. Dickson
Bibl. 19

Robinson & Harwood (c. 1814-
1822)
Philadelphia, Pa.
John Harwood
———— Robinson
Bibl. 3, 4, 23, 28, 36, 44

A. Robinson & Co. (c. 1839-
1842)
Charlottesville, Va.
Staunton, Va.
Alexander Robinson
J. C. La Grange
Bibl. 19

Alexander Robinson (c. 1839-
1842)
Charlottesville, Va.
Staunton, Va.
A. Robinson & Co.
Bibl. 19

Andrew Robinson (c. 1845-
1846)
Portsmouth, Va.
Robinson & Dixon
Bibl. 19

Anthony W. Robinson (c. 1788-
1803)
Trenton, N.J.
Philadelphia, Pa.
Bibl. 3, 23, 24, 25, 29, 36, 39,
44, 46, 54

[A ROBINSON]

Benjamin Robinson (c. 1818-
1844)
Philadelphia, Pa.
Bibl. 3, 23, 36, 44

E. Robinson (c. 1780?,
c. 1820?)
Rhode Island (?)
Bibl. 15, 28, 29, 44

[E. ROBINSON]

G. E. Robinson (c. 1850)
Nashua, N.Y.
Bibl. 89

[G E. ROBINSON]

Hannah Robinson (b. 1803)
Wilmington, Del. (c. 1865)
Bibl. 25, 30, 44

[H. ROBINSON]

Isaac Robinson (c. 1829-1835)
Philadelphia, Pa.
Bibl. 3

Israel Robinson (c. 1840)
Philadelphia, Pa.
Bibl. 23, 36, 44

James Robinson (c. 1827)
Montgomery, N.Y.
Bibl. 20

James Robinson (c. 1831-1833)
Philadelphia, Pa.
Bibl. 3

John F. Robinson (b. 1812-d.
1867)
Wilmington, Del.
Bibl. 15, 25, 30

[J. F. ROBINSON]

O. Robinson (c. 1790-
1800-   )
New Haven, Conn.
Bibl. 24, 25, 44, 61

[O. ROBINSON]

William Robinson (c. 1810)
Chillicothe, Ohio
Bibl. 34

William Robinson (c. 1840)
Baltimore, Md. (1844)
Portsmouth, Va.
North Carolina (?)
Bibl. 19

William D. Robinson (c. 1846-1850)
Philadelphia, Pa.
Bibl. 3

William F. Robinson (c. 1835)
Philadelphia, Pa.
Bibl. 3

William F. Robinson (c. 1850)
Wilmington, Del.
Bibl. 30

William K. Robinson (c. 1828)
Brownville, N.Y.
Bibl. 20

William K. Robinson (c. 1834)
Fayetteville, N.Y.
Bibl. 20

Thomas Rochead (c. 1833-1844)
Albany, N.Y.
Bibl. 20

William B. Rock (c. 1850)
Philadelphia, Pa.
Bibl. 3, 23

——— Rockwell (c. 1839)
Bridgeport, Conn. (?)
Bibl. 28

ROCKWELL

Rockwell & Garland (c. 1829)
Macon, Ga.
Peter P. Rockwell
John R. Garland
Bibl. 17

Rockwell, Smith & Whitney
(c. 1788-1789)
Lansingburgh, N.Y.
John Rockwell
David Smith
Henry Whitney
Bibl. 20

Edward Rockwell (c. 1807-1825)
New York, N.Y.
Edward & Samuel Rockwell
(c. 1815-1841)
Bibl. 15, 23, 24, 25, 29, 35, 36, 44, 54, 83

ROCKWELL

ROCKWELL

Edward & Samuel Rockwell
(c.1815-1841)
New York, N.Y.
Edward Rockwell
Samuel D. Rockwell
Bibl. 15

John Rockwell (c. 1789-1795)
Lansingburgh, N.Y.
Yates & Rockwell (c. 1787-1788)
Rockwell, Smith & Whitney
(c. 1788-1789)
Bibl. 20

Peter P. Rockwell (c. 1826-1833)
Macon, Ga.
Rockwell & Garland (c. 1829)
Bibl. 17

R. Rockwell (c. 1825)
New York, N.Y.
Bibl. 23

Samuel D. Rockwell (c. 1815-1841)
New York, N.Y.
Edward & Samuel Rockwell
Bibl. 15, 24, 25, 44

S. D. ROCKWELL

Thomas Rockwell (c. 1775, d. 1795)
New London, Conn.
Norwalk, Conn.
Bibl. 15, 16, 24, 28, 29, 36, 44

ROCKWELL

William Rode (c. 1795)
Philadelphia, Pa.
Bibl. 3

William Rodgers (c. 1824)
Philadelphia, Pa.
Bibl. 3

Peter C. (G.) Rodier (c. 1810-1825)
New York, N.Y.
Bibl. 15, 23, 36, 44

(W.) Roe & Stollenwerck
(c. 1805)
Kingston, N.Y.
William Roe

——— Stollenwerck
Bibl. 20, 23, 25, 29, 36, 44, 72

Stollenwerck

W ROE

James Roe (c. 1770)
Kingston, Ky.
Bibl. 25

I·ROE

I·ROE

William Roe (c. 1795-1805)
Kingston, Ky.
Roe & Stollenwerck (c. 1805)
Bibl. 15, 20, 21, 23, 25, 28, 29, 44, 54, 78

W·R   W·R

W·ROE

——— Roff (c. 1813)
New York, N.Y.
Bibl. 23, 44

Rogers
(See Leonard & Rogers)

Rogers & Wendt (c. 1850)
Boston, Mass.
Bibl. 4, 23, 28, 44

Augustus Rogers (c. 1831-1832)
New York, N.Y.
Bibl. 15

Augustus (Aug.) Rogers
(c. 1840-1850)
Boston, Mass.
Bibl. 4, 15, 23, 28, 36, 44

Daniel Rogers (c. 1753-1792)
Newport, R.I.
Bibl. 2, 5, 15, 23, 25, 29, 36, 39, 44, 54, 72, 80

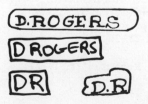

Henry Rogers (c. 1838-
1850-   )
Troy, N.Y.
Bibl. 20

James M. Rogers (c. 1836-
1840)
Troy, N.Y.
Bibl. 20

Joseph Rogers (b. 1753-d.
1825)
Newport, R.I. (c. 1760)
Hartford, Conn. (c. 1808-1825)
Church & Rogers (c. 1825-
1828)
Bibl. 15, 16, 23, 24, 25, 28, 29,
36, 44, 54, 89

S. B. Rogers (b. 1800-d. 1855,
c. 1840-1855)
Charleston, S.C.
Bibl. 5

William Rogers (b. 1801-d.
1873)
Hartford, Conn.
Church & Rogers (c. 1825-
1828)
Bibl. 15, 16, 24, 25, 28, 29,
36, 44

| WM ROGERS |

William Rogers & Son (c. 1850)
Hartford, Conn.
Bibl. 15, 24, 25, 44

| WM. ROGERS & SON |

John A. Rohr (c. 1807-1813)
Philadelphia, Pa.
Bibl. 3, 24, 25, 44

| I ROHR |

William Rollin(g)son
(b. 1762-d. 1842)
New York, N.Y.
Bibl. 23, 28, 36, 44

John Romney (Rominie)
New York, N.Y. (c. 1770)
Bibl. 4, 23, 28, 36, 44

Nicholas Roosevelt (b. 1715-d.
1769)
New York, N.Y. (c. 1735-
1763)
Bibl. 2, 4, 15, 23, 24, 28, 29,
35, 44, 54

Root & Chaffee (c. 1826-1880)
Hartford, Conn.
Bibl. 72

Charles Boudinot Root
(b. 1818-d. 1903)
Raleigh, N.C.
Bibl. 25, 44

| C. B. ROOT |

L. M. & A. C. Root (c. 1830)
Pittsfield, Mass.
Bibl. 15, 25, 44

| L M & A C ROOT |

W. M. Root (c. 1840)
Pittsfield, Mass.
Bibl. 25

W. N. Root & Brother (c. 1850)
New Haven, Conn.
Bibl. 25, 44

| W. N. ROOT & BROTHER |

Anthony Rose (b. 1731)
New York, N.Y. (c. 1755)
Bibl. 23, 36, 44

William E. Rose (c. 1844)
New York, N.Y.
Bibl. 23

William Rosenteel (c. 1801)
Baltimore, Md.
Bibl. 38

Roshore & Prime (Prime &
Roshore) (c. 1825)
New York, N.Y.
John Roshore
———— Prime
Bibl. 23, 36, 44

John Roshore (c. 1792-1835)
New York, N.Y.
Roshore & Prime (c. 1825)
Bibl. 15, 23, 28, 36, 44

Alexander Coffin Ross (c.
1812)
Zanesville, Ohio
Bibl. 34

James Ross (c. 1829)
Zanesville, Ohio
Bibl. 34

John Ross (b. 1756-d. 1798)
Baltimore, Md. (c. 1790-1798)
Bibl. 25, 29, 38, 44

| I R |

Robert Ross (c. 1789)
Frederica, Del.
Bibl. 25, 30, 36, 44

| R. ROSS | | R R |

William Ross (c. 1838-1839)
Troy, N.Y.
Bibl. 20

Bartholomew Roswell
Hartford, Conn.
(See Roswell Bartholomew)
Bibl. 25, 44

Nelson Roth (c. 1837-1853)
Utica, N.Y.
Bibl. 15, 18, 20, 25, 44

N ROTH UTICA

Volkert Roth (c. 1846-1847)
Utica, N.Y.
Bibl. 18, 20

John Round (c. 1634)
Portsmouth, N.H.
Bibl. 36, 44

Victor Rouquette (c. 1817-
1824)
Detroit, Mich.
Bibl. 58

V. R.

Anthony Rouse (c. 1807)
Philadelphia, Pa.
Bibl. 23, 36, 44

Emanuel Rouse (c. 1747-1768)
Philadelphia, Pa.
Bibl. 3

Michael Rouse (b. 1687)
Boston, Mass. (c. 1711)
Bibl. 23, 28, 36

Sidney Rouse (c. 1849-1850)
Rochester, N.Y.
Bibl. 20, 41, 44

William Rouse (Rowse)
(b. 1639-d. 1705)
Boston, Mass.
Bibl. 15, 23, 25, 28, 29, 36,
44, 54, 69, 70

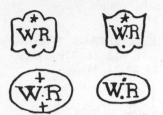

William Madison Rouse
(b. 1812-d. 1888)
Charleston, S.C.
Bibl. 5, 25, 44

W. M. ROUSE

Roush
(See Rasch)

Rowan
(See Holmes & Rowan)

Thomas T. Rowe (c. 1832-
1834)
Utica, N.Y.
Bibl. 18, 20

David S. Rowland
(c. 1832-   )
Utica, N.Y.
Storrs & Cooley (c. 1831-1839)
Bibl. 18, 20

John & William Rowsay
(c. 1774-   )
Williamsburg, Va.
Bibl. 19

William Rowse
(See William Rouse)

John (I.) Royalston (c. 1725-
1770)
Boston, Mass.
Bibl. 23, 28, 29, 36, 44, 50

J R   I R

Harvey Royce (c. 1834-1850)
Morrisville, N.Y.
Bibl. 20

J. Rudd & Co. (c. 1831-1841)
New York, N.Y.
Bibl. 15, 25, 44

J. RUDD & CO

William Rudell (c. 1844-1848)
Buffalo, N.Y.
Bibl. 20

Samuel Rudolph (c. 1803)
Philadelphia, Pa.
Bibl. 3

Henry Rue (c. 1835)
Philadelphia, Pa.
Bibl. 3

William E. Ruff (c. 1829-   )
Halifax, N.C.
Bibl. 21

Rugg & Osborn (c. 1804)
Utica, N.Y.
Samuel Rugg
John Osborn
Bibl. 20

Samuel Rugg (c. 1800-1811)
Utica, N.Y.
Rugg & Osborn (c. 1804)
Bibl. 18, 20

Israel Ruland (c. 1772)
Detroit, Mich.
Bibl. 58

——— Rule (c. 1780)
Massachusetts (?)
Bibl. 28, 29, 44

Rule

Rule

A. Rumrill & Co. (c. 1831-
1832)
New York, N.Y.
Alexander Rumrill
Bibl. 15, 44

A. RUMRILL & CO.

Alexander Rumrill (c. 1831-
1832)
New York, N.Y.
A. Rumrill & Co.
Bibl. 15

Alexander Rumrill Jr. (c. 1840)
New York, N.Y.
Bibl. 15

Lucius Rumrill (c. 1832-
1833-   )

Utica, N.Y.
Bibl. 18, 20

Charles Rumsey (d. 1841)
Salem, N.J.
Bibl. 15, 44, 46, 54

C RUMSEY   C RUMSEY

Rusher
(See Brower & Rusher)

John H. Russel (c. 1792-1798)
New York, N.Y.
Bibl. 23, 25, 28, 29, 36, 44

I. H. R.

Jonathan Russel (c. 1807-
1817)
Auburn, N.Y.
Geneva, N.Y.
Bibl. 20

Jonathan Russel(l) (b. 1770,
c. 1807)
Ashford, Conn.
Bibl. 16, 24, 25, 28, 29, 36, 44

RUSSEL

RUSSEL

Moody Russel(l) (b. 1694-d.
1761)
Barnstable, Mass.
Bibl. 2, 15, 24, 25, 28, 29, 36,
44, 55, 72, 78

MR

Arthur Russell (19th century)
Bardstown, Ky.
Bibl. 32, 54

Daniel Russell (b. 1698-d.
1771)
Newport, R.I.
Bibl. 2, 15, 23, 24, 25, 28, 29,
36, 44, 54, 55, 56, 72

Eleazer Russell (c. 1663-1691)
Boston, Mass.
Bibl. 15, 28

George Russell (c. 1831-1850)
Philadelphia, Pa.
Bibl. 3, 28, 44

John H. Russell (c. 1795)
New York, N.Y.
Bibl. 44

[I·H·R]

Joseph Russell (b. 1702-d.
1780)
Barnstable, Mass.
Bristol, R.I.
Bibl. 15, 44, 72

(J R)

Thomas Russell (c. 1855-1856)
Charleston, S.C.
Columbia, S.C.
Bibl. 5

William Russell (c. 1830)
Columbus, Ga.
Bibl. 17, 68

William Russell (19th century)
Nelson County, Ky.
Bibl. 32

William Russell & Son (c. 1840-
1865)
Bardstown, Ky.
Bibl. 32, 54

William A. Russell (c. 1842-
1843)
Utica, N. Y.
Bibl. 18, 20

Peter Russellier (c. 1794)
New York, N.Y.
Bibl. 23, 36, 44

James Rutherford (c. 1751-
1752)
Charleston, S.C.
Bibl. 5, 54

Benjamin Rutledge (c. 1809)
Charleston, S.C.
Bibl. 5

Moses Rutter (c. 1811)
Denton, Md.
Bibl. 38

Peter Rutter (c. 1837-1850)
Philadelphia, Pa.
Bibl. 3

Richard Rutter (c. 1790-1798)
Baltimore, Md.
Rice & Rutter (c. 1794)
Bibl. 24, 25, 29, 38, 44, 78

(Rutter)

(Rutter)

Samuel Rutter (c. 1807-1812)
Baltimore, Md.
Bibl. 38

Rydout
(See Ridout)

Low Ryerson (b. 1771-d. 1855)
Manchester (Hawthorne), N.J.
York, Pa.
Bibl. 15, 18, 23, 24, 25, 28, 29,
36, 54

[L. Ryerson]

John Sacheverel(l) (c. 1732-
1733)
Philadelphia, Pa.
Bibl. 3, 28

Sackett & Willard (c. 1815-
1823)
Providence, R.I.
Adnah Sackett
———— Willard
Bibl. 23, 28, 36, 44

Adnah Sackett (c. 1815-1823)
Providence, R.I.
Sackett & Willard
Bibl. 23

Sadd & Morgan (c. 1806)
Poughkeepsie, N.Y.
———— Sadd
Elijah Morgan
Bibl. 20

Hervey Sadd (b. 1776-d. 1840)
New Hartford, Conn.
(c. 1776-1829)
Austinburg, Ohio (after 1829)

Bibl. 16, 23, 24, 25, 28, 29,
36, 44

[H. SADD]

Sadtler (c. 1790)
Baltimore, Md.
Bibl. 54

Sadtler & Pfaltz (c. 1800-1806)
Baltimore, Md.
Philip Benjamin Sadtler
John William Pfaltz
Bibl. 38, 44

Philip Sadtler & Son (b. 1860-d.
1923)
Baltimore, Md.
Bibl. 24, 25, 38, 44

[P B SADTLER & SON]

Philip Benjamin Sadtler
(b. 1771-d. 1860)
Baltimore, Md.
Sadtler & Pfaltz (c. 1800-1806)
Bibl. 4, 15, 23, 25, 28, 29, 36,
38, 44

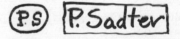

[P.S.]

H. (Henry) Harry Safford
(c. 1800-1812)
Gallipolis, Ohio
Marietta, Ohio
Zanesville, Ohio
Bibl. 15, 25, 34, 44

[H SAFFORD]

H. Sage (c. 1840)
Location unknown
Bibl. 89

William P. Sage (c. 1833-1852)
Athens, Ga.
Benjamin B. Lord
Bibl. 17

Washington Sailor (c. 1825-
1833)
Philadelphia, Pa.
Bibl. 3

S. L. St. Cyr (c. 1822)
New Orleans, La.
Bibl. 23, 36, 44

C. G. St. John (c. 1834)
Saratoga Springs, N.Y.
Bibl. 20

Charles Grandison St. John
(c. 1811-1846)
Macon, Ga.
Bibl. 17

Gould St. John (c. 1817)
Sing Sing, N.Y.
Bibl. 20

De St. Leger (c. 1790)
New Bern, N.C.
Bibl. 21

Anthony Saint-Martin (c. 1794-
1796)
Philadelphia, Pa.
Bibl. 3, 23, 28, 36

James Saint-Maurice (c. 1748)
Philadelphia, Pa.
Bibl. 3

Salisbury
(See Nichols & Salisbury)

Salisbury & Co. (c. 1835)
New York, N.Y.
Bibl. 25, 28

Henry Salisbury (c. 1830-1838)
New York, N.Y.
Salisbury & Co. (c. 1835)
Bibl. 15, 24, 25, 28, 44

H SALISBURY	SALISBURY

Owen Salisbury (c. 1847)
Providence, R.I.
Bibl. 23

Alfred Salmon
Cincinnati, Ohio
Bibl. 34

William H. Salmon (c. 1830-
1850)
Cazenovia, N.Y.
Morrisville, N.Y.
Troy, N.Y.
Bibl. 20

Henry Salsbury (c. 1831-1838)
New York, N.Y.
Bibl. 78

Nathaniel Saltonstall (c. 1821)
Eatonton, Ga.
Daniel B. Hempsted & Co.
Bibl. 17

S. A. Salstonstall (c. 1830)
Augusta, Ga.
Victor Crepu
Bibl. 17

William Sampson (c. 1802-
1803)
Philadelphia, Pa.
Bibl. 3

Hyman Samuel (c. 1791-1809)
Petersburg, Va. (c. 1791)
Norfolk, Va. (c. 1803)
Charleston, S.C. (c. 1806-1809)
Richmond, Va.
Baltimore, Md. (?)
Bibl. 5, 19

A. Sanborn (c. 1850)
Lowell, Mass.
Bibl. 15, 23, 24, 25, 28, 44

A.SANBORN

A. Sanborn

Jacob Sandbuhler (Jacobi
Cembuhler)
Utica, N.Y. (c. 1854-1860)
Bibl. 18

Edward Sandell (d. 1822)
Baltimore, Md. (c. 1816-1822)
Bibl. 25, 29, 38, 44

E. S

Charles Sanders (c. 1833-1845)
Schenectady, N.Y.
Bibl. 20

James Sanders (c. 1850)
Schenectady, N.Y.
Bibl. 20

Benjamin Sanderson (c. 1649-
1678)
Boston, Mass.
Bibl. 2, 15, 23, 24, 25, 28, 29,
36, 44, 69

B S

Joseph Sanderson (c. 1642-
1687)
Boston, Mass.
Bibl. 2, 15, 28

Robert Sanderson (b. 1608-d.
1693)

Boston, Mass.
Hull & Sanderson (c. 1652-
1683)
Bibl. 15, 23, 24, 25, 28, 29, 36,
44, 69

Robert Sanderson Jr. (b. 1652-d.
1714)
Boston, Mass.
Watertown, Mass.
Bibl. 2, 15, 23, 28, 36, 54

William Sanderson (c. 1799-
1801)
New York, N.Y.
Bibl. 23, 36, 44

Sandford
(See Frederick C. Sanford)
(See William Sanford)

F. S. Sandford (c. 1830)
Location unknown
Bibl. 89

F. A. Sandon (c. 1809)
Charleston, S.C.
Bibl. 5

Peter Sandose (Sandoz)
(c. 1824)
Baltimore, Md.
Bibl. 38

Sandoz & Brother (c. 1811)
New York, N.Y.
Bibl. 36, 44

Charles H. Sandoz (c. 1800-
1802)
Philadelphia, Pa.
Bibl. 3

Louis Sandoz (c. 1845)
Philadelphia, Pa.
Bibl. 3

Philip Augustus Sandoz
(c. 1814-1822)
Philadelphia, Pa.
Bibl. 3, 23, 36, 44

D. Sands (c. 1840)
Location unknown
Bibl. 89

Stephen Sands (c. 1771-1774)
New York, N.Y.
Bibl. 23, 36, 44

Sanford & Beach
(See Beach & Sanford)

Abel Sanford (b. 1798-d. 1843)
Hamilton, N.Y.
Bibl. 20

Edward Sanford (d. 1814)
Alexandria, Va. (c. 1773)
Bibl. 19, 54

Edward N. Sanford (c. 1855-
1859)
Utica, N.Y.
B. F. & T. M. Davies
Bibl. 18

Frederick C. (S.) Sanford
(Sandford) (d. 1890)
Nantucket Island, Mass.
(c. 1828-1830)
Easton & Sanford (c. 1830-
1838)
Bibl. 12, 23, 24, 25, 28, 36, 44

F. S. Sandford

Isaac Sanford (c. 1783-1824)
Hartford, Conn.
Providence, R.I.
Beach & Sanford (c. 1785-1788)
Bibl. 15, 16, 23, 28, 44

Isaac Sanford (c. 1785)
Hartford, Conn.
Bibl. 36

Judson Sanford (c. 1843-1844)
Hamilton, N.Y.
Bibl. 20

William Sanford (Sandford)
(c. 1817-1818)
Nantucket Island, Mass.
Bibl. 12, 15, 23, 24, 25, 44

W Sandford

Sanger
(See Hall & Sanger)
(See Hull & Sanger)

Michael Sardo (c. 1817)
Baltimore, Md.
Bibl. 23, 28, 36, 44

Ensign Sargeant (b. 1761-d.
1843)
Hartford, Conn.
Mansfield, Conn.

Boston, Mass.
Bibl. 23, 24, 25, 28, 29, 36, 44

H. Sargeant (c. 1825)
Hartford, Conn. (?)
Bibl. 15, 25, 44

H. Sargent

H. Sargeant

Jacob Sargeant (b. 1761-d.
1843, c. 1785-1838)
Hartford, Conn.
Mansfield, Conn.
Springfield, Mass.
Bibl. 2, 15, 16, 23, 24, 25, 28,
29, 36, 44, 61, 88

J SARGEANT

Thomas Sargeant (c. 1810-
1816)
Springfield, Mass.
Connecticut
Bibl. 15, 25, 28, 44

Sargent & Gaylord
(c. 1822-)
Batavia, N.Y.
Bibl. 20

A. G. Sargent (c. 1830's)
Milan, Ohio
Bibl. 34

John Sargent (c. 1821-)
Wilmington, N.C.
Bibl. 21

Sarrazin & Wright (c. 1746)
Charleston, S.C.
Moreau Sarrazin
William Wright
Bibl. 54

Jonathan Sarrazin (c. 1754-
1790)
Charleston, S.C.
Moreau & Jonathan Sarrazin
(c. 1754-1761)
Bibl. 5, 44, 54

I S

Moreau Sarrazin (b. 1710-d.
1761)
Charleston, S.C.

Sarrazin & Wright (c. 1746)
Moreau & Jonathan Sarrazin
(c. 1754-1761)
Bibl. 5, 25, 44, 54

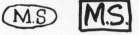

Moreau & Jonathan Sarrazin
(c. 1754-1761)
Charleston, S.C.
Bibl. 54

Christopher Saur (c. 1724)
Philadelphia, Pa.
Bibl. 3

William S. Saurman (c. 1829)
Philadelphia, Pa.
Bibl. 3

Richard Sause (c. 1778)
Philadelphia, Pa.
Bibl. 3

Savage and Eubank (c. 1805-
1820)
Glasgow, Ky.
William M. Savage
James Eubank
Bibl. 32, 54

Savage & Kunsman (c. 1823)
Salisbury, N.C.
——— Savage
Henry Kunsman
Bibl. 21

Savage & Lyman
Location unknown
Bibl. 15, 44

SAVAGE & LYMAN

Savage & Stedman (c. 1819-
1820)
Raleigh, N.C.
John Y. Savage
John C. Stedman
Bibl. 21

Benjamin Savage (b. 1699-d.
1750)
Boston, Mass.
Charleston, S.C. (?)
Bibl. 5

Edward Savage (c. 1761-1817,
d. 1817)
Philadelphia, Pa.
New York, N.Y.
Bibl. 3, 23, 28, 36, 44

John Y. Savage (c. 1818-1820)
Raleigh, N.C.
Savage & Stedman (c. 1819-
1820)
Bibl. 21, 25, 44

Thomas Savage (b. 1664-d.
1749)
Boston, Mass.
Bibl. 2, 15, 23, 24, 28, 29, 36, 44

Thomas Savage Jr. (b. 1692)
Boston, Mass.
Bibl. 23, 36, 44

William Savage (c. 1808)
Liberty, Va. (now Bedford,
Va.)
Bibl. 19

William M. Savage (c. 1805-
1820)
Glasgow, Ky.
Savage & Eubank
Bibl. 15, 25, 32, 44, 54, 68

William Savil (Saville)
Philadelphia, Pa. (c. 1820-
1837)
Bibl. 3

Silas Sawin (c. 1811)
Boston, Mass.
Bibl. 2, 15, 23, 24, 28, 29, 36

Silas W. Sawin (c. 1825-1838)
New York, N.Y.
Bibl. 23, 25, 36, 44

H. L. Sawyer (c. 1840)
New York, N.Y.
Hartford, Conn. (?)
Coe & Upton
Bibl. 15, 23, 24, 25, 28, 29,
36, 44

H. L. SAWYER

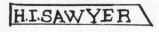

Joseph Saxton (c. 1823-1824)
Philadelphia, Pa.
Bibl. 3

Saya
Southampton, L.I., N.Y.
Bibl. 54

Sayre & Richards (c. 1802-
1811)
New York, N.Y.
John Sayre
Thomas Richards
Bibl. 15, 23, 24, 25, 29, 35,
44, 54

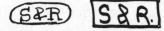

David A. (E.) Sayre (b. 1793-d.
1870)
Lexington, Ky.
Bibl. 32, 68

Joel Sayre (c. 1778-1818)
New York, N.Y.
Bibl. 15, 23, 24, 25, 28, 29, 30,
35, 36, 44, 54

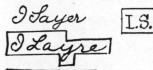

John Sayre (b. 1771-d. 1852)
New York, N.Y.
Sayre & Richards (c. 1802-
1811)
Bibl. 2, 3, 4, 15, 23, 24, 25,
35, 36, 54

I SAYRE		SAYRE

L. Sayre (19th century)
Lexington, Ky.
Bibl. 32, 68

L. Sayre

Paul Sayre (b. 1762)
Southampton, N.Y. (c. 1785)
Bibl. 15, 20, 25, 44

P SAYRE

Scarret
(See Skerret)

Scerad
(See Serad)

Bartholomew Schaats (Skaats)
(b. 1670-d. 1758)
New York, N.Y.
Bibl. 2, 4, 15, 23, 24, 25, 28,
30, 35, 36, 44, 50

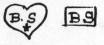

M. Schafer (c. 1840)
Location unknown
Bibl. 89

Jeremiah Schaffield (c. 1785)
Philadelphia, Pa.
Bibl. 3, 23, 36, 44

Schank
(See Van Voorhis, Schank
& McCall)

Garret Schank (d. 1795)
New York, N.Y. (c. 1791)
Van Voorhis & Schank
(c. 1791-1792)
Bibl. 15, 23, 24, 25, 29, 35,
44, 72

G SCHANK

John A. Schank (c. 1792-1797)
New York, N.Y.
Bibl. 15, 23, 24, 25, 28, 29, 36,
44, 72

J SCHANK		SCHANK
I SCHANK		W

Bartholomew Schatts (Staats)
(Skaats)
New York, N.Y. (c. 1784-1796)
Bibl. 4, 15, 23, 28

Bernard Scheer (c. 1855)
Charleston, S.C.
Bibl. 5

John C. Scheer (c. 1835-1850)
Philadelphia, Pa.
Bonsall & Scheer (c. 1845-
1847) (?)
Dubosq & Scheer (c. 1849-
1850) (?)
Bibl. 3

Samuel F. Schell (c. 1829-1835)
Philadelphia, Pa.
Bibl. 3

Frederick Schern (Shehum)
(c. 1848-1850)
Philadelphia, Pa.
Bibl. 3, 23

Lewis Scherr (c. 1843-1850)
Philadelphia, Pa.
Bibl. 3

Jonas (Joseph) Schindler
(c. 1776-1792)
Montreal, Canada
Detroit, Mich.
Bibl. 58

I S

John Schinkle (c. 1810)
Philadelphia, Pa.
Bibl. 3

John G. Schmid (c. 1850)
Philadelphia, Pa.
Bibl. 3

Christian Schmidt (Smith)
(c. 1819-1840)
New Philadelphia, Ohio
Winesburg, Ohio
Bibl. 34

John Schmitt (Smith)
(c. 1846-1850)
Philadelphia, Pa.
Bibl. 3, 23

Solomon Schofield (c. 1815-
1827)
Albany, N.Y.
Rochester, N.Y.
Bibl. 36

Schoolfield (c. 1855)
Location unknown
Bibl. 15, 44

SCHOOLFIELD

Gerrit Van Schoonhoven
(c. 1830)
Albany, N.Y.
Bibl. 20

H. Schoonmater (c. 1810)
Location unknown
Bibl. 24

F. V. Schrader & Co. (c. 1837)
Philadelphia, Pa.
Bibl. 3

Charles W. Schreiner (c. 1813-
1833)
Philadelphia, Pa.
Bibl. 3

Andrew B. Schreuder
(Schroeder) (b. 1828,
c. 1852-1853-   )
Utica, N.Y.
Syracuse, N.Y. (after 1850)
Hotchkiss & Schreuder (after
1850)
Bibl. 18, 20

Schroeder & Wangelin (c. 1844-
1850)
Cleveland, Ohio
A. Schroeder
Edward Wangelin
Lewis Wangelin
Bibl. 54

A. Schroeder (c. 1844)
Cleveland, Ohio
Schroeder & Wangelin (c. 1844-
1850)
Bibl. 54

Andrew B. Schroeder
(See Schreuder)

J. Schuller (c. 1845-1846)
Philadelphia, Pa.
Bibl. 3

G. A. Schultz
Location unknown
Bibl. 54

Gottlieb Schultz (Shultz)
(c. 1821-1844)
Philadelphia, Pa.
Bibl. 3

Thomas Schumo (c. 1824-1825)
Philadelphia, Pa.
Bibl. 3

Jodocus Schutte (c. 1800)
Baltimore, Md.
Bibl. 38

Michael Schwartz (c. 1824-
1825)
Philadelphia, Pa.
Bibl. 3

Peter Schwartz (c. 1770)
York, Pa.
Bibl. 3

B. Schwekert (c. 1842)
Philadelphia, Pa.
Bibl. 3

Godfrey Schwing
(See Shiving)

John G. Schwing (b. 1783-d.
1868)
Louisville, Ky.
Bibl. 32, 54, 68

Scofield & Lee (c. 1822)
Rochester, N.Y.
Salmon Scofield
Samuel W. Lee
Bibl. 20, 41

Salmon Scofield (b. 1792-d.
1831, c. 1815-1831)
Rochester, N.Y. (c. 1818-1822)
Albany, N.Y.
Packard & Scofield (c. 1818-
1819)
Scofield & Lee (c. 1822)
Bibl. 4, 20, 23, 28, 41

Jehu Scot(t) (c. 1806, d. 1819)
Raleigh, N.C.
Bibl. 21, 24, 25, 44

J Scott

Robert Scot (c. 1775-1779)
Fredericksburg, Va.
Bibl. 19

Robert Scot (c. 1781-1822)
Philadelphia, Pa.
Bibl. 3

Scott & Anderson (c. 1829)
Greensboro, N.C.
David Scott
——— Anderson
Bibl. 21

Scott and Kitts (c. 1843-1845)
Louisville, Ky.
William D. Scott
John Kitts
Bibl. 32, 68

Charles Scott (c. 1839)
Penn Yan, N.Y.
Bibl. 20

David Scott (b. 1797-d. 1875)
Greensboro, N.C.
Scott & Anderson (c. 1829)
Bibl. 21

David Scott (c. 1819-1823)
Martinsburg, Va.
Bibl. 19

I. Scott (c. 1750)
Albany, N.Y.
Bibl. 25, 44

Jehu Scott
(See Jehu Scot)

John Scott (c. 1803-1809)
Charleston, S.C.
Bibl. 5

John Scott (c. 1838-1847)
St. Louis, Mo.
Bibl. 54

John B. Scott (c. 1820)
New York, N.Y.
Bibl. 36

John B. Scott (c. 1820-1850)
New York, N.Y.
Bibl. 23, 24, 25, 28, 44

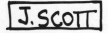

Samuel Scott (c. 1825)
Concord, N.C.
Bibl. 21

W. D. Scott and Co. (c. 1848-
1849)
Louisville, Ky.
William D. Scott
Bibl. 32

William D. Scott (c. 1841-1849)
Louisville, Ky.
Scott and Kitts (c. 1843-1845)
W. D. Scott and Co. (c. 1848-
1849)
Bibl. 32, 54

———— Scotthorn (c. 1799)
Shelby County, Ky.
Bibl. 32, 54, 68

Scovil & Co. (c. 1836)
Cincinnati, Ohio
Bibl. 54

Scovil & Kinsey (c. 1830)
Cincinnati, Ohio
Bibl. 15, 25, 29, 44, 54

Scovil, Willey & Co. (c. 1818)
Cincinnati, Ohio
Bibl. 54

Scovil-Willey & Co. (c. 1815-
1836)
Cincinnati, Ohio
Bibl. 54, 78

Edward Scranton (c. 1847)
Philadelphia, Pa.
Bibl. 3, 23

James Scrymageour (c. 1835)
New York, N.Y.
Bibl. 23, 36

Andrew Scudder (c. 1850-1851)
Utica, N.Y.
Bibl. 18, 20

Egbert Scudder (c. 1827-1837)
New York, N.Y.
Benedict & Scudder
Bibl. 15

Thomas Scummo (c. 1823-
1824)
Philadelphia, Pa.
Bibl. 3

John Scwind (c. 1790)
New York, N.Y.
Bibl. 23, 36

Charles Seager (c. 1840-
1841-   )
Utica, N.Y.
Tanner & Cooley (c. 1840-1842)
Bibl. 18, 20

William Seal(e) (Jr.) (c. 1810-
1819)
Philadelphia, Pa.
Browne & Seal(e) (c. 1810-
1811)
Bibl. 3, 4, 15, 24, 25, 29, 36, 44

W SEAL

J. W. Sealey (Suley) (c. 1846-
1849)

Charleston, S.C.
Bibl. 5

Thomas Seaman (c. 1790-1802)
Edenton, N.C.
Bibl. 21

J. M. Seamans (c. 1848-
1850-   )
Troy, N.Y.
Bibl. 20

Joseph Searl (c. 1840-1850)
Philadelphia, Pa.
Bibl. 3

John Sears (c. 1805-1817)
Cambridge, Ohio
Chillicothe, Ohio
Bibl. 34

Mathew Sears (c. 1835)
New York, N.Y.
Bibl. 23, 36, 44

Samuel Sears (c. 1839-1850)
Philadelphia, Pa.
Bibl. 3

Jeanne L. Sebastien (c. 1814)
New York, N.Y.
Bibl. 23, 36, 44

John Seccombe (c. 1850)
Cobleskill, N.Y.
Bibl. 20

John D. Seckle (Seckler)
(c. 1837-1850)
Philadelphia, Pa.
Bibl. 3

Margaret Seddinger (c. 1846)
Philadelphia, Pa.
Bibl. 3

Matthias Seddinger (c. 1819-
1850)
Philadelphia, Pa.
Bibl. 3

Conrad F. (Frederick C.)
Seeger (c. 1823-1850)
Philadelphia, Pa.
Bibl. 3

H. Seely & Co. (c. 1830)
Staunton, Va.
Horace Seely
Bibl. 19

Horace Seely (c. 1830)
Staunton, Va.
H. Seely & Co.
Bibl. 19, 28

——— Seewald (eighteenth century)
Seneca, Huron, Muskingum Counties, Ohio
Bibl. 34

Philip B. Segee (c. 1840)
Location unknown
Bibl. 24

George Segn (c. 1820-1822)
Philadelphia, Pa.
Bibl. 3, 23, 36, 44

Sehro
(See Sekro)

Lawrence Sekel (c. 1841)
Philadelphia, Pa.
Bibl. 3

William C. Sekro (Sehro)
(c. 1837-1850)
Philadelphia, Pa.
Bibl. 3

Lemuel T. Selby (c. 1842-1850)
Philadelphia, Pa.
Bibl. 3, 23

Samuel Selby (c. 1841)
Philadelphia, Pa.
Bibl. 3, 23

——— Selkirk
Albany, N.Y.
Selkirk & Putnam (c. 1814)
McHarg & Selkirk (c. 1815)
Bibl. 20

Selkirk & Putnam (c. 1814)
Albany, N.Y.
Bibl. 20

William Selkirk (c. 1817-1819)
New York, N.Y.
Bibl. 15, 23, 36, 44

J. Sell (c. 1800)
New York, N.Y.
Bibl. 23, 36, 44

Joseph Sellers (c. 1828-1850)
Philadelphia, Pa.
Bibl. 3

Selph & Campbell (c. 1827-1829)
Fayetteville, N.C.
John Selph
John Campbell
Bibl. 21, 25

Selph & Pyle (c. 1837-1838)
Fayetteville, N.C.

John Selph
Benjamin Pyle II
Bibl. 21

John Selph (c. 1807-1836, d. 1838)
Fayetteville, N.C.
Selph & Campbell (c. 1827-1829)
Selph & Pyle (c. 1837-1838)
Bibl. 21, 54

John B. Sénémaud (Sénémand)
Philadelphia, Pa. (c. 1798-1822)
Bibl. 3, 23, 36

Louis Senneshac (c. 1804)
Baltimore, Md.
Bibl. 38

E. Sepes (c. 1851-1852)
Utica, N.Y.
Bibl. 18, 20

John Serad (Scerad) (c. 1835-1850)
Philadelphia, Pa.
Bibl. 3

Thomas Serre (c. 1810-1812)
Baltimore, Md.
Bibl. 38

J. Serrill (c. 1837)
Philadelphia, Pa.
Bibl. 3

Charles Servoss (c. 1849)
Philadelphia, Pa.
Bibl. 3

Joseph S. Servoss (c. 1850)
Philadelphia, Pa.
Bibl. 3

Lewis Sestie (c. 1796-1800)
Richmond, Va.
Philadelphia, Pa. (?)
Bibl. 19

Benjamin Settle (c. 1867)
Russellville, Ky.
Bibl. 54

——— Setzler (date unknown)
Newberry, S.C.
Bibl. 5

Jacques Seveignes (c. 1822)
New Orleans, La.
Bibl. 23, 36, 44

Lewis Sevrin (Sivrin) (c. 1837-1840)
Philadelphia, Pa.
Bibl. 3, 23, 36, 44

Simon Sexnine (c. 1772)
New York, N.Y.
Bibl. 23, 28, 29, 36, 44, 78

S S ?

Pliny Sexton (c. 1819-1820)
Palmyra, N.Y.
Bibl. 20

Joseph Seydell (c. 1848-1849)
Philadelphia, Pa.
Bibl. 3

Seymour & Holister (Hollister)
(c. 1843-1850)
Hartford, Conn.
Oliver D. Seymour
Julius Hol(l)ister
Bibl. 15, 23, 24, 25, 44

SEYMOUR & HOLLISTER

S & H

Edward Seymour (c. 1839-1850)
Philadelphia, Pa.
Bibl. 3

H. P. Seymour (c. 1840)
Location unknown
Bibl. 15, 44

H. P. Seymour

Holister A. Seymour (c. 1843)
Hartford, Conn.
Bibl. 23

Jeffrey Seymour (c. 1818)
Cincinnati, Ohio
Bibl. 34

Joseph Seymour (c. 1835-1863)
Syracuse, N.Y. (c. 1850)
New York, N.Y.
Utica, N.Y.
Joseph Seymour & Co.
(c. 1850)
Norton & Seymour (c. 1850)
Norton, Seymour & Co.
(c. 1850)
Bibl. 15, 18, 20, 23, 36, 44

Joseph Seymour & Co.
(c. 1850)
Syracuse, N.Y.

Bibl. 15, 20, 25, 44

J. S. & Co.

Oliver D. Seymour (c. 1850)
Hartford, Conn.
Seymour & Hol(l)ister
(c. 1843-1850)
Bibl. 15, 23, 25, 29, 44

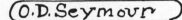

O. D. Seymour

John V. Shade (c. 1845-1847)
Philadelphia, Pa.
Bibl. 3

Whitaker Shadforth (b. 1754-d.
1802)
Petersburg, Va. (c. 1791)
Richmond, Va. (c. 1795-   )
Georgia
Folwell, Shadforth & Co.
(c. 1795-   )
Bibl. 19

J. Shakespeare (c. 1850)
Nyack, N.Y.
Bibl. 20

Francis Shallus (c. 1797-1822)
Philadelphia, Pa.
Bibl. 3

Robert Shannon (c. 1841-1842)
Philadelphia, Pa.
Ashburn & Shannon (c. 1841)
Hattrick & Shannon (c. 1844)
Bibl. 3

George Sharp(e) (c. 1850-
1870)
Danville, Ky.
Philadelphia, Pa.
Bibl. 32, 44, 54, 68

G SHARP   G S

George B. Sharp (c. 1844-
1850)
Philadelphia, Pa.
William & George Sharp
Bibl. 3, 15, 23

Ⓢ

William Sharp (c. 1835-1850)
Philadelphia, Pa.
William & George Sharp
(c. 1848-1850)
Bibl. 3, 23, 36, 44

William & George Sharp
(c. 1848-1850)
Philadelphia, Pa.
William Sharp
George B. Sharp
Bibl. 3, 4, 23, 25, 28, 29, 44

W. & G. SHARP

William H. Sharpe (c. 1843)
Philadelphia, Pa.
Bibl. 3

R. Sharpley (c. 1855)
Location unknown
Bibl. 15, 44

R SHARPLEY

Sharrard and Ewing (c. 1840)
Shelbyville, Ky.
Warren B. Ewing
James S. Sharrard
Bibl. 32, 54

James S. Sharrard (c. 1836-
1842)
Scott County, Ky. (1836)
Paris, Ky. (1841)
Shelbyville, Ky. (c. 1840-1861)
Henderson, Ky.
Owensboro, Ky.
Paducah, Ky.
Sharrard and Ewing (c. 1840)
Bibl. 24, 25, 32, 44, 54, 68

J S SHARRARD

Judson Sharrard (c. 1848)
Shelbyville, Ky.
Bibl. 25, 32

William M. Sharrard (c. 1839-
1850)
Harrodsburg, Ky.
Bibl. 32, 54

Jacob A. Shartle (c. 1844)
Philadelphia, Pa.
Bibl. 3

Charles C. Shaver (d. 1900)
Utica, N.Y. (c. 1854)
Bibl. 15, 18, 20, 44

C C S   C C SHAVER
Ⓒ Ⓒ Ⓢ

Michael Shaver (b. 1775-d.
1859)
Abingdon, Va.
Bibl. 19

M. SHAVER

Shaw & ———rk (c. 1840)
Location unknown
Bibl. 89

Shaw & Dunlevy (c. 1833)
Philadelphia, Pa.
——— Shaw
Robert Dunlevy (?)
Bibl. 3, 15, 23, 24, 25, 36, 44

SHAW & DUNLEVY   SHAW & DUNLEVY

Benjamin Shaw (c. 1828-1829)
New York, N.Y.
Bibl. 15

Edward Shaw (c. 1837)
Philadelphia, Pa.
Bibl. 3

Edward G. Shaw (c. 1825-1830)
Philadelphia, Pa.
Bibl. 3, 23, 36, 44

Foster Shaw (c. 1793)
Fair Haven, Vt.
Bibl. 54

James Shaw (c. 1839-1841)
Philadelphia, Pa.
Bibl. 3

James W. Shaw (c. 1854)
Winnsboro, S.C.
Bibl. 5

John Shaw (c. 1819)
Philadelphia, Pa.
Bibl. 3

John Shaw & Co. (c. 1842-
1851)
St. Louis, Mo.
Bibl. 54

J SHAW & CO

John A. Shaw (c. 1802-1819)
Newport, R.I.
Bibl. 15, 23, 24, 25, 28, 29, 36,
44

Shearman
(See Robert Sherman)

Walter Sheed (c. 1831-1833)
Philadelphia, Pa.
Bibl. 3

William W. Sheed (c. 1840)
Philadelphia, Pa.
Bibl. 3

―――― Sheets (c. 1697)
Henrico, Va.
Bibl. 28

Shehum
(See Schern)

Alonzo D. Sheldon (c. 1851-
1852)
Utica, N.Y.
Bibl. 18, 20

Alpheus Xavier Francis
Shepard (b. 1795)
Georgetown, Ky. (c. 1815-
1831)
Bibl. 32, 68

G. Shepard (c. 1831-1832)
Lockport, N.Y.
Bibl. 20

Thomas Jefferson Shepard
(b. 1801-d. 1875)
Georgetown, Ky. (c. 1817-
1828)
Louisville, Ky. (c. 1828-1831)
Georgetown, Ky. (c. 1831-
1875)
Beard & Ayres (c. 1828-1831)
(Ayres & Beard)
Bibl. 32, 54, 68

| T J SHEPARD GEORGETOWN KY |

Timothy B. Shepard
(c. 1834-   )
Utica, N.Y.
Bibl. 18, 20

Sheperd (Shepherd) & Boyd
(c. 1810-1830)
Albany, N.Y.
Robert Sheperd
William Boyd
Bibl. 15, 20, 23, 24, 28, 29,
36, 44, 54

| •SHEPHERD & BOYD | | S & B |

Cumberland Sheperd (c. 1850)
Philadelphia, Pa.
Bibl. 3

Ephraim Sheperd (c. 1834-
1836)
Newport, Ky.
Bibl. 32

―――― Shepherd
(See Goff & Shepard)

Robert Sheperd (Shepherd)
(c. 1800-1810)
Albany, N.Y.
Sheperd & Boyd (c. 1810-1830)
Bibl. 20, 23, 24, 25, 28, 29,
36, 44, 72

Humphrey M. Shepherd
(c. 1824-1826)
New York, N.Y.
Bibl. 15

George L. Sheppard (c. 1846-
1848)
Philadelphia, Pa.
Bibl. 3, 23

George M. Sheppard (c. 1837)
Philadelphia, Pa.
Bibl. 3

John Sheppard (c. 1798)
Easton, Me.
Bibl. 38

| I S | ?

John D. Shepper (c. 1818-
1819)
Philadelphia, Pa.
Bumm & Shepper (c. 1818-
1823)
Bibl. 3, 4, 23, 28, 36, 44

Edward Sherman (c. 1850)
Hartford, Conn.
Bibl. 23

James Sherman (c. 1770)
Boston, Mass.
Bibl. 28

Robert Sherman (Shearman)
(c. 1799)
Philadelphia, Pa.
Bibl. 3

John Shermer (c. 1803-1813)
Philadelphia, Pa.
Bibl. 3

John Sherwood (c. 1832)
Buffalo, N.Y.
Bibl. 20

Smith J. Sherwood (c. 1835-
1836)
Buffalo, N.Y.
Bibl. 20

Sheth(e)ar & Gorham
(c. 1806-   )
New Haven, Conn.
Samuel Sheth(e)ar
Richard Gorham
Bibl. 15, 16, 23, 36, 44

Sheth(e)ar & Thom(p)son
(c. 1801)
Litchfield, Conn.
Samuel Sheth(e)ar
Isaac Thompson
Bibl. 15, 16, 23, 25, 36, 44

| S & T |

Samuel Sheth(e)ar (c. 1800-
1810)
Litchfield, Conn. (c. 1801)
New Haven, Conn.
(c. 1806-   )
Shethar & Thom(p)son
(c. 1801)
Shethar & Gorham
(c. 1806-   )
Bibl. 15, 16, 23, 36, 44

Walter D. Shewell (c. 1829-
1840)
Philadelphia, Pa.
Bibl. 3

Caleb Shields (c. 1773-1782)
Baltimore, Md.
Bibl. 3, 23, 24, 36, 38, 44, 54

| C S |

Francis Shields (c. 1818)
Cincinnati, Ohio
Bibl. 34

Jesse C. Shields (c. 1845)
Philadelphia, Pa.
Bibl. 3

Thomas Shields (c. 1765-1794)
Philadelphia, Pa.
Bibl. 3, 15, 23, 24, 25, 28, 29,
36, 39, 44, 54, 81

| T S | | T S |

Anthony Shimer (c. 1850)
Auburn, N.Y.
Bibl. 20

John Shimer (c. 1811)
Philadelphia, Pa.
Bibl. 3

John T. Shinkle (c. 1824-1825)
Philadelphia, Pa.
Bibl. 3

Shinn (?) and Baldwin
(c. 1860)
Location unknown
Bibl. 79

Arthur Shipherd (c. 1764)
New York, N.Y.
Bibl. 3

Nathaniel Shipman (b. 1764-d.
1853)
Norwich, Conn. (c. 1790)
Bibl. 15, 16, 23, 24, 25, 28,
29, 36, 44

N SHIPMAN   N S

Shipp & Collins (c. 1850)
Cincinnati, Ohio
Bibl. 15, 25, 44

Shipp & Woodbridge (c. 1842)
St. Louis, Mo.
Bibl. 54

SHIPP & WOODBRIDGE

S. A. M. Shipp (c. 1820)
Cincinnati, Ohio
Bibl. 34

William A. Shippen (c. 1818-
1824)
Philadelphia, Pa.
Monteith & Shippen (c. 1817)
Bibl. 3

Godfrey Shiving (Schwing)
(c. 1779)
Philadelphia, Pa.
Bibl. 3, 23, 25, 36, 39, 44, 81

G S

Abraham Shoemaker (c. 1846)
Philadelphia, Pa.
Bibl. 3

Charles Shoemaker (c. 1825-
1832)
New York, N.Y.
Bibl. 15, 23, 36, 44

Joseph Shoemaker (c. 1793-
1839)
Philadelphia, Pa.
New York State (?)
Bibl. 3, 4, 15, 23, 24, 25, 28,
29, 36, 39, 44, 54, 81

J. SHOEMAKER   J S

George Shonnard (c. 1797)
New York, N.Y.
Bibl. 23, 36, 44

Shopshire
(See Shropshire)

Robert Shopshire (c. 1778)
Baltimore, Md.
Bibl. 38

John Short (c. 1792)
Halifax, N.C.
Bibl. 21

John Short (c. 1783-1792)
Alexandria, Va.
Norfolk, Va.
Bibl. 19

Martin Shreiner (b. 1767-d.
1866)
Lancaster, Pa.
Bibl. 3

Philip Shreiner (c. 1760)
Lancaster, Pa.
Bibl. 3

Shreve, Brown & Co. (c. 1857)
Boston, Mass.
Benjamin Shreve
——— Brown
Bibl. 15

Shreve, Crump & Low
(c. 1869-present)
Boston, Mass.
Benjamin Shreve
——— Crump
John J. Low
Bibl. 15

Shreve, Stanwood & Co.
(c. 1860)
Boston, Mass.
Benjamin Shreve
——— Stanwood
Bibl. 15

Benjamin Shreve (b. 1813;
to 1896)
Boston, Mass. (c. 1834, c. 1854)
Salem, Mass.

Jones, Shreve, Brown & Co.
(c. 1854)
Shreve, Brown & Co. (c. 1857)
Shreve, Stanwood & Co.
(c. 1860)
Shreve, Crump & Low
(c. 1869-present)
Bibl. 23, 28, 36, 44

Thomas H. Shriver (c. 1837-
1843)
Philadelphia, Pa.
Baker & Shriver (c. 1837-1841)
Bibl. 3

Charles Shroeter (c. 1807-1818)
Baltimore, Md.
Bibl. 38

Robert Shropshire (Shopshire)
(b. 1748)
Baltimore, Md. (c. 1774-1778)
Bibl. 28

——— Shuber (c. 1837)
Philadelphia, Pa.
Gregory & Shuber
Bibl. 3

Shuire
(See Suire)

John Shuler (c. 1849)
Philadelphia, Pa.
Bibl. 3

Shultz
(See Gottlieb Schultz)

Gustavus Shultz (c. 1825-1833)
Philadelphia, Pa.
Bibl. 3

John Shultz (c. 1813-1822)
Philadelphia, Pa.
Bibl. 3

Frederick Shuman (c. 1818)
Philadelphia, Pa.
Bibl. 3

John Shuman (c. 1818-1837)
Philadelphia, Pa.
Bibl. 3

John Shurley (c. 1839-1840)
Albany, N.Y.
Bibl. 20

Sibley & Adams (c. 1847-1848)
Buffalo, N.Y.
O. E. Sibley
Nathaniel W. Adams
Bibl. 20

Sibley & Marble (c. 1801-1806)
New Haven, Conn.
Clark Sibley
Simeon Marble
Bibl. 16, 23, 24, 25, 28, 29, 36, 44

S & M

Asa Sibley (b. 1764)
Woodstock, Conn. (c. 1787)
Walpole, N.H. (c. 1807-1808)
Rochester, N.Y. (c. 1827)
Bibl. 41, 44

Clark Sibley (b. 1778-d. 1808)
New Haven, Conn.
Sibley & Marble (c. 1801-1806)
Bibl. 15, 16, 23, 24, 25, 28, 36, 44

SIBLEY

James Sibley (b. 1779-d. 1865)
Great Barrington, Mass.
 (c. 1799-1801)
Albany, N.Y. (c. 1801-1803)
Canandaigua, N.Y. (c. 1803-1836)
Ann Arbor, Mich. (c. 1843-1846)
Rochester, N.Y. (c. 1847-1850)
Detroit, Mich. (?)
Bibl. 20, 40, 41

John Sibley (c. 1810)
New Haven, Conn.
Bibl. 23, 24, 25, 29, 36, 44

J. SIBLEY

O. E. Sibley (c. 1836-1848)
Buffalo, N.Y. (c. 1847-1848)
Canandaigua, N.Y.
Sibley & Adams (c. 1847-1848)
Bibl. 20, 79

R. J. Sibley (c. 1850)
Genesee, N.Y.
Bibl. 20

Stephen Sibley (c. 1795)
Great Barrington, Mass.
Bibl. 41

Joseph Siddall (c. 1846-1847)
Philadelphia, Pa.
Bibl. 3

John Siddons (c. 1841-1850)
Philadelphia, Pa.
Bibl. 3

Josiah C. Siddons (c. 1835-1837)
Philadelphia, Pa.
Bibl. 3

Lawrence L. Siddons (c. 1852-1855)
Charleston, S.C.
Bibl. 5

Michael Siebenlist (c. 1846-1850)
Camden, N.J.
Bibl. 3

Amos Sigler (c. 1847-1850)
Philadelphia, Pa.
Bibl. 3, 23

Sigourncy & Hitchcock (after 1850)
Watertown, N.Y.
Bibl. 20

Sigourney & Turner (c. 1838-1842)
Watertown, N.Y.
——— Sigourney
Alonzo B. Turner
Bibl. 20

Alanson P. Sigourney (c. 1839-)
Watertown, N.Y.
W. H. & A. P. Sigourney
Bibl. 20

W. H. Sigourney & Co. (c. 1851-)
Watertown, N.Y.
William H. Sigourney
Bibl. 20

W. H. & A. P. Sigourney (c. 1839-)
Watertown, N.Y.
Alanson P. Sigourney
William H. Sigourney
Bibl. 20

William H. Sigourney (c. 1842-after 1850)
Watertown, N.Y.
W. H. & A. P. Sigourney (c. 1839-)
W. H. Sigourney & Co. (c. 1851-)
Bibl. 20

William Sikler (c. 1850)
Philadelphia, Pa.
Bibl. 3

H. Sill (c. 1840-1850)
New York, N.Y.
Bibl. 15, 25, 44

H. & R. W. Sill (c. 1840-)
New York, N.Y.
Bibl. 15, 25, 44

H.&R.W.SILL

Hezekiah Silliman (b. 1738-d. 1804)
New Haven, Conn.
Cutler, Silliman, Ward & Co.
 (c. 1767)
Bibl. 15, 16, 23, 24, 25, 28, 36, 44, 61

H S

Silverthorn & Clift (c. 1857-1860-)
Lynchburg, Va.
Henry Silverthorn
Josiah Clift
Bibl. 19

Silverthorn & Clift

Henry Silverthorn (b. 1810-d. 1900)
Baltimore, Md. (1832-1837)
Lynchburg, Va. (1842-1897)
Silverthorn & Clift (c. 1857-1860)
Bibl. 19, 54

SILVERTHORN

H SILVERTHORN

Henry T. Silverthorn (c. 1850)
Lynchburg, Va.
Bibl. 19

Sime & Moses (c. 1768-1769)
Savannah, Ga.
Birmingham, Ga. (?)
William Sime
Jacob Moses
Bibl. 17, 23, 36

William Sime (c. 1768-1778)
Savannah, Ga.
Birmingham, Ga. (?)
Sime & Moses (c. 1768-1769)

Wright & Sime (c. 1774)
Bibl. 17, 23, 44

William Simes (b. 1773-d.
1824)
Portsmouth, N.H.
Bibl. 15, 23, 24, 25, 28, 29, 36,
44

Simmon(s) & Alexander (c.
1798-1804)
Philadelphia, Pa.
Anthony Simmons
Samuel Alexander
Bibl. 15, 23, 24, 25, 29, 36, 54

Simmonds
(See Andrew Simmons)

Simmons & Williamson (c.
1797-1798)
Philadelphia, Pa.
Anthony Simmons
Samuel Williamson (?)
Bibl. 25, 44

Abel Simmons (c. 1836)
Buffalo, N.Y.
Bibl. 20

Andrew Simmons (Simmonds)
(c. 1795-1798)
Philadelphia, Pa.
Bibl. 3, 23, 28, 36

Anthony Simmons (c. 1797-
1808)
Philadelphia, Pa.
Simmons & Williamson (c.
1797-1798)

Simmon(s) & Alexander (c.
1798-1804)
Bibl. 3, 4, 15, 23, 24, 28, 29, 36,
39, 44, 54, 81

J. & A. Simmons (c. 1805-
1813)
New York, N.Y.
Bibl. 15, 23, 24, 28, 29, 36, 44,
46, 54

James Simmons (c. 1815-1820)
New York, N.Y.
Bibl. 15, 23, 24, 25, 28, 29, 36,
44

Joseph Simmons (c. 1765)
Philadelphia, Pa.
Bibl. 3, 44

Joseph Simmons (c. 1828-1833)
Philadelphia, Pa.
Bibl. 3, 23, 36, 44

Peter Simmons (c. 1817)
New York, N.Y.
Bibl. 15, 23, 36, 44

Robert H. Simmons (c. 1837-
1850)
Philadelphia, Pa.
Bibl. 3

S. Simmons (c. 1797)
Philadelphia, Pa.
Simmons & Alexander (c. 1798-
1804)
Bibl. 23, 24, 25, 28, 36, 44

John Simnet (c. 1783)
Albany, N.Y.
Bibl. 20

Elijah Simons (c. 1804-1810)
Sag Harbor, N.Y.
Bibl. 20

George W. Simons (c. 1844-
1850)
Philadelphia, Pa.
Bibl. 3, 23

Simpkins
(See Minott & Simpkins)

James Simpkins (c. 1845-1846)
Louisville, Ky.
Bibl. 32

Thomas Barton Simpkins (b.
1728-d. 1804)
Boston, Mass.
Bibl. 2, 4, 15, 23, 24, 25, 28, 29,
36, 44

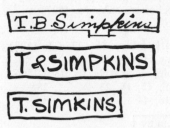

William Simpkins (b. 1704-d.
1780)
Boston, Mass.
Minott and Simpkins (c. 1750-
1760)
Bibl. 2, 15, 23, 24, 25, 28, 29,
36, 44, 54, 70

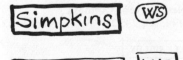

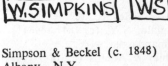

Simpson & Beckel (c. 1848)
Albany, N.Y.
Moses Simpson
Moses Beckel
Bibl. 20, 23, 28, 44

Simpson & Bro. (c. 1846-1850)
Philadelphia, Pa.
Bibl. 3

Alexander Simpson (c. 1799-
1805-   )
Hagerstown, Md.
Bibl. 38

David Simpson (c. 1807-1850)
Philadelphia, Pa.
Bibl. 3

J. Alexander Simpson (c. 1848-1850)
Philadelphia, Pa.
Bibl. 3

James Simpson (c. 1840)
Philadelphia, Pa.
Bibl. 3

John W. Simpson (c. 1832)
Charleston, S.C.
Bibl. 5

John W. Simpson (c. 1839-1850)
Philadelphia, Pa.
Bibl. 3

Jonathan Simpson
Bardstown, Ky. (c. 1830-1861)
Madison, Ind. (c. 1861-1863)
Bardstown, Ky. (c. 1863)
Bibl. 32, 54, 68

Moses Simpson (c. 1848-   )
Albany, N.Y.
Simpson & Beckel (c. 1848)
Bibl. 20

S. Simpson (19th century)
Hopkinsville, Ky
Bibl. 32, 54

Thomas W. Simpson (c. 1839-1841)
Philadelphia, Pa.
Bibl. 3

William Simpson (c. 1801)
Philadelphia, Pa.
Bibl. 3

William Simpson (c. 1830-1844)
Philadelphia, Pa.
Bibl. 3

William Sinclair (c. 1837)
Philadelphia, Pa.
Bibl. 3

Louis Singer (c. 1846)
New York, N.Y.
Bibl. 23

Singleton & Young (c. 1800)
New York, N.Y.
Bibl. 23, 36, 44

Anthony Singleton (b. 1750-d. 1795)
Richmond, Va. (c. 1787-1795)
Newport, R.I.
Williamsburg, Va.
Bibl. 19

Ripley Nichols Singleton (b. 1754-d. 1799)
Charleston, S.C. (c. 1779-1787)
Bibl. 5

Robert Singleton (c. 1839)
Greensboro, N.C.
Bibl. 21

Patrick Sinnott (c. 1761)
Baltimore, Md.
Bibl. 38

Sivrin
(See Sevrin)

Joseph A. Sixte (c. 1837-1850)
Philadelphia, Pa.
Bibl. 3, 23, 36, 44

Vincent B. Sixte (c. 1837-1840)
Philadelphia, Pa.
Bibl. 3, 23, 36, 44

Skaats
(See Schaats)
(See Schatts)

John Skates (c. 1668-1680)
Boston, Mass.
Bibl. 28

Skeplinger
(See S[amuel] Keplinger)

Joseph Skerret (Scarret) (c. 1797-1798, d. 1804)
Philadelphia, Pa.
Bibl. 3, 28, 44

Joseph Skerret (Scarret) (c. 1804-1850)
Philadelphia, Pa.
Bibl. 3, 23, 36, 44

George W. Skerry (c. 1837)
Boston, Mass.
Bibl. 23, 28, 36, 44

Thomas Skidmore (c. 1767)
Lancaster, Pa.
Bibl. 3

Skinker & Ballantine (c. 1772-   )
Norfolk, Va.
William Skinker
James Ballantine
Bibl. 19

William Skinker (b. 1741, c. 1766-1776-   )
Norfolk, Va. (c. 1772-   )

Easton, Md.
Skinker & Ballantine (c. 1772-   )
Bibl. 19

Abraham Skinner (c. 1756)
New York, N.Y.
Bibl. 4, 15, 23, 24, 25, 28, 29, 36, 44

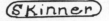

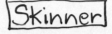

Benjamin Skinner
Easton, Md. (c. 1801)
Baltimore, Md. (c. 1804)
Norfolk, Va. (c. 1804)
Bibl. 19, 38

Elizer Skinner (d. 1858)
Hartford, Conn. (c. 1826-   )
Bibl. 16, 23, 28, 36, 44

Matt Skinner (c. 1752)
Philadelphia, Pa.
Bibl. 23, 29, 36, 44

| MATT SKINNER |

Thomas Skinner (b. 1712-d. 1761)
Marblehead, Mass.
New York, N.Y.
Bibl. 2, 15, 23, 24, 25, 28, 29, 36, 44, 72, 83

| Skinner | T S | ?

William Skinner (c. 1789-1790)
Easton, Md.
Bibl. 38

Josiah U. Slack (c. 1837-1839)
Norfolk, Va.
Bibl. 19

William Slack (c. 1850)
Philadelphia, Pa.
Bibl. 3

Joseph P. Slade (b. 1784)
Augusta, Ga. (c. 1794-1805)
Bibl. 17

William Slater (c. 1792)
Baltimore, Md.
Bibl. 38

John Slattery (c. 1850)
Hartford, Conn.
Bibl. 23

Sleeper & Jeannert (c. 1850)
Philadelphia, Pa.
Bibl. 3

Joshua Slidell (Slydell) (c.
1765)
New York, N.Y.
Bibl. 4, 23, 24, 25, 28, 36, 44

SLIDELL

SLIDELL

William Sloan (c. 1794)
Hartford, Conn.
Bibl. 23, 36, 44

Slydell
(See Slidell)

Williams Small (c. 1795-1796)
Philadelphia, Pa.
Bibl. 3

George Smart (c. 1794)
Lexington, Ky.
Bibl. 32, 54, 68

John Smart (c. 1839-1850)
Philadelphia, Pa.
Bibl. 3

Elisha Smartt (c. 1810)
Mecklenburg County, N.C.
Bibl. 21

Peter Smick (c. 1846-1848)
Philadelphia, Pa.
Bibl. 3

Smith
(See List & Smith)
(See Lovell & Smith)
(See Hull & Smith)
(See Hattrick & Smith)

———— Smith (c. 1815)
Batavia, N.Y.
Hull & Smith (c. 1815-1816)
Bibl. 20

Smith & Bean (c. 1844)
Skaneateles, N.Y.
S. Smith
H. L. Bean (?)
Bibl. 20

Smith and Beggs (Beggs &
Smith) (c. 1840?)

Louisville, Ky.
———— Smith
William Beggs (?)
Bibl. 32, 54

Smith & Bro. (c. 1843-1844)
Philadelphia, Pa.
Bibl. 3

Smith & Chamberlain (19th
century)
Location unknown
Bibl. 89

SMITH & CHAMBERLAIN

Smith & Goodrich (c. 1850)
Philadelphia, Pa.
Bibl. 3

Smith & Grant (Grant &
Smith) (c. 1827-1831)
Louisville, Ky.
Richard Ewing Smith
William Grant (?)
Bibl. 24, 25, 32, 44, 54, 68

Smith & Grant

Smith & Kitts (c. 1844-1845)
Louisville, Ky.
———— Smith
John Kitts
Bibl. 32

Smith & List (c. 1848-1850)
Philadelphia, Pa.
———— Smith
John List
Bibl. 3

Smith & Patterson (c. 1860)
Boston, Mass.
Bibl. 89

Smith & Whitney (c. 1787-
1793)
Lansingburgh, N.Y.
David Smith
Henry Whitney
Bibl. 20

A. Smith (19th century)
Location unknown
Bibl. 89

A Smith

Allen Smith (c. 1841)
Philadelphia, Pa.
Bibl. 3

Alvin Smith (c. 1846)
Port Chester, N.Y.
Bibl. 20

B. Smith (c. 1835)
Philadelphia, Pa.
Bibl. 3

Benjamin C. Smith (c. 1850)
Philadelphia, Pa.
Bibl. 3

B. H. Smith & Co. (c. 1836-
1838)
Fredericksburg, Va.
Benjamin H. Smith
William K. Smith
William H. White
Bibl. 19

Benjamin H. Smith (c. 1834)
Fredericksburg, Va.
B. H. Smith & Co. (c. 1836-
1838)
Bibl. 19

C. C. Smith (c. 1841-1843)
Fayetteville, N.C.
Bibl. 21

Charles Smith (c. 1848-1850)
Philadelphia, Pa.
Bibl. 3

Charles Smith
Pendleton, S.C. (c. 1848)
Laurens, S.C. (c. 1849)
Spartanburg, S.C. (c. 1851)
Greenville, S.C. (c. 1852-1857)
Lancaster, Pa. (c. 1853)
Bibl. 5

Charles A. Smith (c. 1850)
Auburn, N.Y.
Harbottle & Smith
Bibl. 20

Charles R. Smith (c. 1837-1850)
Philadelphia, Pa.
Bibl. 3, 23

Christian Smith (Ohio)
(See Christian Schmidt)

Christian Smith (c. 1820-1833)
Philadelphia, Pa.
Bibl. 3, 23, 36, 44

D. S. Smith (c. 1831)
Columbus, Ga.
Bibl. 17

David Smith (b. 1751)
Virginia (c. 1774)
Bibl. 15, 23, 28, 29, 36

D. SMITH

David Smith
Philadelphia, Pa. (c. 1778-
1793)
Lansingburgh, N.Y. (c. 1787-
1793)
Smith & Whitney (c. 1787-
1793)
Rockwell, Smith & Whitney (c.
1788-1789)
Bibl. 20, 24, 25, 44

D S   D. SMITH

Ebenezer Smith (c. 1775-1790)
Brookfield, Conn.
Bibl. 16, 23, 28, 36, 44

Edwin Smith (c. 1837)
Albany, N.Y.
Bibl. 20

Ernest Smith (c. 1830-1833)
Philadelphia, Pa.
Bibl. 3

F. C. Smith (c. 1844)
Philadelphia, Pa.
Bibl. 3

Floyd Smith (c. 1815-1836)
New York, N.Y.
Bibl. 15, 25, 44

FLOYD SMITH

Francis Smith (b. 1720, c.
1743)
Location unknown
Bibl. 23

Francis W. Smith (c. 1837)
Philadelphia, Pa.
Bibl. 3

George Smith (c. 1823-1849)
Philadelphia, Pa.
Bibl. 3, 23, 36, 44

George Smith (c. 1827-1829)
New York, N.Y.
Bibl. 15

George C. Smith (c. 1839-
1845)

Philadelphia, Pa.
Bibl. 3

George E. Smith (c. 1848-
1849)
Louisville, Ky.
Bibl. 32

George H. Smith (c. 1850)
Watertown, N.Y.
Bibl. 20

George M. Smith (c. 1845-
1849)
Philadelphia, Pa.
Bibl. 3

George O. Smith (c. 1825-
1850)
New York, N.Y.
Bibl. 23, 36

Gerritt Smith (c. 1840)
New York, N.Y.
Bibl. 15

Hartley T. Smith (c. 1850-
1860)
Bowling Green, Ky.
Bibl. 32, 54

Hezekiah Smith (c. 1845)
Philadelphia, Pa.
Bibl. 3

I. Smith (c. 1742, d. 1789)
Boston, Mass.
Bibl. 23, 36

I S   ?

I. Smith (c. 1842)
Boston, Mass.
Bibl. 4, 15, 23, 25

I. SMITH

Isaac Smith (c. 1840-1843)
Philadelphia, Pa.
Bibl. 3

J. & T. Smith (c. 1817)
Baltimore, Md.
John & Thomas Smith
Bibl. 36

J. W. W. Smith (c. 1847)
Shelbyville, Ky.
Bibl. 32, 54, 68

Jacob Smith (c. 1809-1822)
Philadelphia, Pa.
Bibl. 3, 23, 36, 44

Jacob C. Smith (c. 1839-1850)
Philadelphia, Pa.
Bibl. 3

James Smith (c. 1794-1797)
New York, N.Y.
Bibl. 23, 28, 36, 44

James Smith (c. 1807-1808)
Philadelphia, Pa.
Bibl. 3, 36, 44

James E. Smith (c. 1839)
Albany, N.Y.
Bibl. 20

James S. Smith (c. 1837-1850)
Philadelphia, Pa.
Bibl. 3

John Smith (c. 1814-1825)
Baltimore, Md.
Hart & Smith (c. 1814-1816)
Kirk & Smith (c. 1818-1823)
J. & T. Smith (c. 1817)
John & Thomas Smith (c. 1817-
1818)
Bibl. 25, 29, 38

I SMITH

John Smith (c. 1818-1822)
Philadelphia, Pa.
Bibl. 3, 23, 36

John Smith
Winchester, Va. (c. 1790)
Alexandria, Va. (c. 1792)
Bibl. 19

John Smith (c. 1835-1850)
Philadelphia, Pa.
Bibl. 3

John Smith (c. 1846-1850)
Philadelphia, Pa.
(See John Schmitt)

John Smith (c. 1850)
Camden, N.J.
Bibl. 3

John Creagh Smith (c. 1839-
1850)
Philadelphia, Pa.
Bibl. 3

John E. Smith (c. 1825)
Philadelphia, Pa.
Bibl. 3

John Leonard Smith (c. 1850-
1855)
Syracuse, N.Y.

Bibl. 15, 20, 25, 44

J. L. SMITH

John P. Smith (c. 1799-1820)
Savannah, Ga.
D. B. Nichols & Co. (c. 1820-
1830)
Bibl. 17

John & Thomas Smith (c. 1817-
1818)
Baltimore, Md.
J. & T. Smith
Bibl. 23, 28, 38, 44

Joseph Smith (c. 1742-1789, d.
1789)
Boston, Mass.
Bibl. 2, 4, 23, 24, 25, 28, 29, 36,
44

I. SMITH   I. S.

Joseph Smith (c. 1804-1810)
Philadelphia, Pa.
Bibl. 3, 23, 36, 44

Joseph E. Smith (c. 1839-1850)
Philadelphia, Pa.
Bibl. 3

Levin H. Smith (c. 1837-1843)
Philadelphia, Pa.
Bibl. 3, 23, 36, 44

Nathaniel W. Smith
Wheeling, Va. (c. 1829-1838)
Clarksburg, Va. (c. 1846)
Bibl. 19

Nathaniel W. Smith (c. 1814)
Columbus, Ohio
Bibl. 34

Nicholas Smith (c. 1762-1782)
Charleston, S.C.
Bibl. 5

Philip Smith (c. 1847-1850)
Philadelphia, Pa.
Bibl. 3

Richard Ewing Smith (b.
1800-d. 1849)
Louisville, Ky. (c. 1821-1849)
Peter Daumont (c. 1843-1846)
Smith & Grant (c. 1827-1831)
Bibl. 25, 32, 44, 54, 68

R E SMITH

Robert Smith (c. 1818-1822)
Philadelphia, Pa.
Bibl. 3, 23

Robert E. Smith (c. 1820-1831)
Philadelphia, Pa.
Bibl. 3, 24, 29, 36

R E SMITH

Roderick D. Smith (c. 1846-
1850)
Philadelphia, Pa.
Bibl. 3

Rufus R. Smith (c. 1823-1833)
Troy, N.Y. (c. 1823-1826)
Macon, Ga. (c. 1829-1833)
Bibl. 17, 20

S. Smith (c. 1844)
Skaneateles, N.Y.
Smith & Bean
Bibl. 20

S. Smith (c. 1846)
Saratoga Springs, N.Y.
Bibl. 20

Samuel Smith (c. 1785)
Philadelphia, Pa.
Bibl. 3, 23, 36, 44

Samuel Smith (c. 1845)
Philadelphia, Pa.
Bibl. 3, 23

Thomas Smith (b. 1790-d.
1850)
Lexington, Ky. (c. 1818)
Bibl. 32

Thomas Smith (c. 1817-1818)
Baltimore, Md.
J. & T. Smith (c. 1817)
John & Thomas Smith (c. 1817-
1818)
Bibl. 38

Truman Smith (c. 1815)
Utica, N.Y.
Nathaniel Butler
Bibl. 89

W. C. Smith (c. 1850-1860)
Bowling Green, Ky.
Bibl. 32, 54, 68

William Smith (c. 1770)
New York, N.Y.
Bibl. 23, 25, 28, 44

William Smith (c. 1817-1840)
New York, N.Y.

Bibl. 15, 44

WM SMITH

William Smith (c. 1818-1825)
Philadelphia, Pa.
Bibl. 3

William Smith (c. 1837)
Philadelphia, Pa.
Bibl. 3

William Smith & Co. (c. 1837)
Wellsburg, Va.
Bibl. 19

William A. Smith (c. 1840)
Leesburg, Va.
Bibl. 19

William K. Smith
Fredericksburg, Va.
B. H. Smith & Co. (c. 1836-
1838)
Bibl. 19

Zebulon Smith (b. 1786-d.
1865)
Maine (c. 1820-1830)
Bibl. 15, 25, 44

James Smither (c. 1768-1819)
Philadelphia, Pa. (c. 1768-
1777)
New York, N.Y. (?)
Bibl. 3, 28

George Smithson (c. 1775-
1778)
Charleston, S.C.
Bibl. 5

R. T. Smitten (c. 1844-1847)
Philadelphia, Pa.
Bibl. 3

John Smoker (c. 1846-1847)
Philadelphia, Pa.
Bibl. 3, 23

John L. Snedeker (c. 1837-
1841)
New York, N.Y.
Bibl. 15

Lewis Snell (c. 1831-1835)
Philadelphia, Pa.
Bibl. 3

Henry Snelling (c. 1776-1777)
Philadelphia, Pa.
Bibl. 3

Philip Snider (c. 1831-1833)
New York, N.Y.
Bibl. 15

I. Snow (c. 1810)
(See Jeremiah Snow Jr.)
Bibl. 15, 28, 39

Jeremiah Snow Jr. (c.
1808-   )
Williamsburg, Mass.
Bibl. 15, 25, 29, 44, 84

| I. Snow | J: SNOW |

William H. Snow
Cleveland, Ohio (c. 1833 1839)
Troy, N.Y. (c. 1840-1842)
Hall & Snow (c. 1835)
Bibl. 20, 54

Snyder
(See Rickards & Snyder)

Snyder & Bros. (c. 1847-1850)
Philadelphia, Pa.
Bibl. 3

Charles F. Snyder (c. 1801)
Philadelphia, Pa.
Bibl. 3

George Snyder (c. 1801)
Philadelphia, Pa.
Bibl. 3, 44

George (H.) Snyder (c. 1816-
1818)
Philadelphia, Pa.
Bibl. 3, 23, 36

George W. Snyder Sr. (c. 1803-
1813, d. 1813)
Paris, Ky.
Bibl. 32, 54, 68

George W. Snyder Jr. (c. 1821-
1848)
Paris, Ky.
J. C. and G. W. Snyder (c.
1845-1848)
Bibl. 32

J. C. and G. W. Snyder (c.
1845-1848)
Paris, Ky.
James C. Snyder

George W. Snyder Jr.
Bibl. 32

James C. Snyder (b. 1815-d.
1852)
Paris, Ky. (1845-1852)
J. C. and G. W. Snyder (c.
1845-1848)
Bibl. 32, 54, 68

Joseph H. Snyder (c. 1848-
1850)
Philadelphia, Pa.
Bibl. 3

Robert Snyder (c. 1850)
Philadelphia, Pa.
Bibl. 3

Abner Solcher (c. 1819)
Cincinnati, Ohio
Bibl. 34

Daniel H. Solliday (c. 1829-
1850)
Philadelphia, Pa.
Bibl. 3

Solomon
(See Parke, Solomon, & Co.)

Lewis Solomon (c. 1840-1841)
Philadelphia, Pa.
Bibl. 3

Samuel Solomon (c. 1800)
Baltimore, Md.
Bibl. 38

Samuel Solomon (c. 1811)
Philadelphia, Pa.
Bibl. 3, 23, 36, 44

Robert Somerby (c. 1794-
1821)
Boston, Mass.
Bibl. 28, 44

William Somerdike (c. 1848-
1850)
Philadelphia, Pa.
Bibl. 3

Somers & Crowley (c. 1828-
1833)
Philadelphia, Pa.
———— Somers
E. Crowley (?)
Bibl. 3

Albertus Somers (d. 1863)
Woodstown, N.J. (c. 1820)

Gloucester County, N.J. (c.
1821)
Bibl. 3, 46, 54

John Somerville (Sommerville)
(c. 1844-1846)
Philadelphia, Pa.
Bibl. 3

Joseph Sonnece (c. 1816)
Philadelphia, Pa.
Bibl. 3

Joseph Sonnier (c. 1811-1818)
Philadelphia, Pa.
Lagazze & Sonnier (c. 1814-
1816)
Bibl. 3, 23, 36, 44

Samuel Soumain (Soumaine)
(b. 1718-d. 1765)
Annapolis, Md. (c. 1740-
1754)
Philadelphia, Pa. (c. 1754-
1765)
Bibl. 2, 3, 23, 24, 25, 28, 36,
38, 81

Simeon Soumaine (b. 1685-d.
1750)
New York, N.Y.
Bibl. 2, 15, 23, 24, 25, 28, 29,
30, 35, 36, 44, 54

| S S |

(S S)

Peter Sounalet
Norfolk, Va. (c. 1806-1822)
Richmond, Va. (c. 1812)
Bibl. 19

Michael Soque (c. 1794-1819)
New York, N.Y.
Bibl. 15, 23, 36, 44

George South (c. 1823-1824)
Philadelphia, Pa.
Bibl. 3

William South (c. 1828-1850)
Philadelphia, Pa.
Bibl. 3

Elijah Southworth (c. 1788)
Kingston, N.Y.
Bibl. 20

A. Souty (c. 1811)
Philadelphia, Pa.
Bibl. 3

Samuel Souza (c. 1819)
Philadelphia, Pa.
Bibl. 3, 44

Anthony Sowerall (Sowerlt)
(c. 1811-1824)
Philadelphia, Pa.
Bibl. 3, 23, 36, 44

George Spackman (c. 1824-
1825)
Philadelphia, Pa.
Bibl. 3

John Spalding (c. 1801)
Baltimore, Md.
Bibl. 38

Rudolph Spangler (c. 1774)
York, Pa.
Bibl. 3

Henry Sparrow (c. 1811)
Philadelphia, Pa.
Bibl. 3, 23, 36, 44

Thomas Sparrow (b. 1746-
c. 1764-1784?)
Philadelphia, Pa. (before 1765)
Annapolis, Md.
Bibl. 25, 29, 38, 44, 54

Spear & Co. (c. 1849)
Charleston, S.C.
James E. Spear
J. Charles Wood
Bibl. 5

Spear & Jones (c. 1841)
Savannah, Ga.
——— Spear
James M. Jones
Bibl. 17

Isaac Spear (Speer)
Boston, Mass. (c. 1836)
Newark, N.J. (c. 1837)
Bibl. 2, 23, 25, 36, 44

James E. Spear (b. 1817-d.
1871, c. 1846-1871)
Charleston, S.C.
Spear & Co. (c. 1849)
Bibl. 5, 54

J. E. SPEAR

Thomas S. Spear (c.
1858-   )
Columbus, Ga.
Bibl. 17

T S SPEAR | T Spear

David H. Spears (before 1850)
Washington County, Ky.
Springfield, Ky. (?)
Bibl. 32, 54, 68

Speer
(See Isaac Spear)

Speigelhalder & Sons (c. 1865-
1867)
Louisville, Ky.
John F. Speigelhalder
Bibl. 32

Speigelhalder and Werne (c.
1836-1858)
(Werne and Speigelhalder)
Louisville, Ky.
Ferdinand Speigelhalder
Joseph Werne Sr.
Bibl. 32

Ferdinand Speigelhalder (c.
1836-1858)
Louisville, Ky.
Speigelhalder & Werne
Bibl. 32, 68

John F. Speigelhalder (c. 1844-
1867)
Louisville, Ky.
Speigelhalder & Sons (c. 1865-
1867)
Bibl. 32

G. Spence (c. 1830-1840)
Newark, N.J.
Bibl. 15, 25, 44

G. Spences
Newark, N.J.

Spencer & Hand (c. 1843)
Philadelphia, Pa.
Oliver Spencer
Joseph S. K. Spencer
Bibl. 3

Spencer & Marshall (c. 1829-
1833)
Philadelphia, Pa.
Oliver Spencer
——— Marshall
Bibl. 3

George Spencer (b. 1787-d.
1878)
Essex, Conn.
Bibl. 16, 23, 28, 44

George W. Spencer (b. 1824-d.
1876)
Charleston, S.C. (c. 1860)
Bibl. 5

James Spencer (c. 1793)
Hartford, Conn.
Oakes & Spencer (c. 1814)
Bibl. 16, 23, 28, 36, 44

James Spencer Jr. (c. 1843)
Hartford, Conn.
Bibl. 23, 44

Julius A. Spencer (b. 1802-d.
1874)
Utica, N.Y.
James Murdock & Co. (c. 1826-
1838)
Bibl. 15, 18, 20

Oliver Spencer (c. 1833-1843)
Philadelphia, Pa.
Spencer & Marshall (c. 1829-
1833)
Spencer & Hand (c. 1843)
Bibl. 3

William Sperry (c. 1843-1849)
Philadelphia, Pa.
Bibl. 3

H. S. Sprague (c. 1825)
Location unknown
Bibl. 24

H. S. Sprague

James H. Spratley (c. 1833-
1835)
Norfolk, Va.
Pearce & Spratley (c. 1833)
Bibl. 19

John Spring (c. 1807, d. 1827)
Charleston, S.C.
Bibl. 5

John Sprogell (c. 1764-   , d.
1794)
Philadelphia, Pa.
Bibl. 3

John Sprogell Jr. (c. 1771)
Philadelphia, Pa.
Bibl. 3

Peter Spurck (c. 1794-1806)
Philadelphia, Pa.
Bibl. 3

David M. Spurgin (b. 1814)
Mt. Sterling, Ky. (c. 1829)
Carlisle, Ky. (c. 1833-1847)
Winchester, Ky. (c. 1847-1852)
Greencastle, Ind. (c. 1852)
Bibl. 32, 54, 68

Peter Spurk (c. 1812)
Chillicothe, Ohio
Bibl. 34

Moses Spyers (c. 1830)
Philadelphia, Pa.
Bibl. 3

Squire & Bros. (c. 1846)
New York, N.Y.
Bibl. 23, 25, 28, 44, 89

SQUIRE & BROS

Squire & Lander (c. 1840)
New York, N.Y.
Bibl. 23, 25, 29, 36, 44

SQUIRE & LANDER

Bela S. Squire Jr. (c. 1839)
New York, N.Y.
Benedict & Squire (c. 1825-
1839)
Bibl. 15

S. P. Squire (c. 1835)
New York, N.Y.
Bibl. 25, 29, 36, 44

S. P. SQUIRE

R. Squires (c. 1845)
Binghamton, N.Y.
Bibl. 20

Staats
(See Schatts)

Jacob Stackel (c. 1825)
Philadelphia, Pa.
Bibl. 3

Philemon Stacy Jr. (c. 1798-
1829)
Boston, Mass.
Bibl. 4, 23, 24, 25, 28, 29, 36,
44

P. STACY

Joseph Stall (c. 1802-1812)
Baltimore, Md.
Bibl. 23, 28, 36, 38, 44

John Staniford (b. 1737-d.
1811)
Windham, Conn.
Elderkin & Staniford (c. 1790-
1792)
Bibl. 15, 16, 23, 24, 25, 28, 29,
36, 44, 61

——— Stanley (c. 1807)
Chillicothe, Ohio
Bibl. 34

Joseph E. Stanley
Zanesville, Ohio (c. 1804-
1848)
Cleveland, Ohio (c. 1848)
Probably Joseph M. Stanley
Bibl. 54

Joseph M. Stanley
Zanesville, Ohio (c. 1804-
1848)
Cleveland, Ohio (c. 1848)
Bibl. 34, 65

Salmon Stanley (c. 1831)
Cazenovia, N.Y.
Bibl. 20

I. Stanniford (c. 1788)
Bennington, Vt.
Bibl. 54

Stanton & Brother (c. 1845-
1850-   )
Rochester, N.Y.
William P. Stanton (?)
Henry Stanton (?)
Bibl. 20

D. E. & Z. Stanton (c. 1775-
1780)
Stonington, Conn.
Daniel Stanton
Enoch Stanton
Zebulon Stanton
Bibl. 44

Daniel Stanton (b. 1755-d.
1781)

Stonington, Conn.
D. E. & Z. Stanton (c. 1775-
1780)
Bibl. 16, 23, 24, 25, 28, 36, 44

D. Stanton

Enoch Stanton (b. 1745-d.
1781)
Stonington, Conn.
D. E. & Z. Stanton (c. 1775-
1780)
Bibl. 16, 25, 28, 36, 44

Henry Stanton (b. 1803-d.
1872)
Rochester, N.Y. (c. 1825-
1850-   )
W. P. & H. Stanton (c. 1826-
1841)
Stanton & Brother (c. 1845-
1850-   ) (?)
Bibl. 20, 41

W. P. & H. Stanton (c. 1826-
1841)
Rochester, N.Y.
William P. Stanton
Henry Stanton
Bibl. 15, 20, 25, 41, 44

W. P. & H. STANTON

William Stanton (b. 1772)
Hudson, N.Y. (c. 1801-1802)
Providence, R.I. (?)
Bibl. 20, 28, 41, 44

William P. Stanton (c. 1821)
Nantucket Island, Mass.
Bibl. 12

William P. Stanton (b. 1794-d.
1878)
Rochester, N.Y.
W. P. & H. Stanton (c. 1826-
1841)
Stanton & Brother (c. 1845-
1850-   ) (?)
Bibl. 20, 41

Zebulon Stanton (b. 1753-d.
1828)
Stonington, Conn.
D. E. & Z. Stanton (c. 1775-
1780)
Bibl. 6, 23, 24, 25, 28, 29, 36,
44

Z S   STANTON

Stanwood & Halstrick (c. 1850)
Boston, Mass.
——— Stanwood
Joseph Halstrick
Bibl. 4, 23, 28, 44

Stanwood
(See Shreve, Stanwood & Co.)

Henry B. Stanwood (b. 1818-d. 1869)
Boston, Mass.
Harris & Stanwood (c. 1835)
Bibl. 15, 23, 24, 25, 28, 29, 36, 44

| Henry B. Stanwood |

J. E. Stanwood (c. 1850)
Philadelphia, Pa.
Bibl. 23, 24, 25, 44

| J E STANWOOD |

James D. Stanwood (c. 1846)
Boston, Mass.
Bibl. 4, 23, 28, 44

George Staple (Staples) (c. 1848-1850)
Philadelphia, Pa.
Bibl. 3, 23

John J. Staples Jr. (c. 1788)
New York, N.Y.
Bibl. 23, 24, 25, 28, 29, 36, 44

| I I S | | I I S | | J.J.S |

E. F. Starbuck (c. 1833, d. 1848)
Nantucket Island, Mass.
Bibl. 12

Erastus Charles Starin (c. 1832-1834-   )
Utica, N.Y.
Storrs & Cooley (c. 1831-1839)
Bibl. 18, 20

W. T. Stark (c. 1832)
Xenia, Ohio
Bibl. 34

Starr & Marcus (19th century)
Location unknown
Bibl. 89

| Starr & Marcus |

Jasper Starr (b. 1709-d. 1792)
New London, Conn.
Bibl. 28, 44

Richard Starr (c. 1807-1813)
Boston, Mass.
Bibl. 24, 25, 28, 29, 44

| R STARR |

Richard Starr (c. 1813)
Philadelphia, Pa.
Bibl. 3

Theodore B. Starr (c. 1900)
New York, N.Y.
Bibl. 89

James Starrett (c. 1796)
Brandywine, Mass.
Bibl. 3

P. M. Statzell (c. 1845-1850)
Philadelphia, Pa.
Bibl. 3

Stebbins & Co. (c. 1836-1841)
New York, N.Y.
Edwin Stebbins
Bibl. 15, 78

| STEBBINS & CO |

Stebbins & Howe (c. 1830-1832)
New York, N.Y.
——— Stebbins
George C. Howe (?)
Bibl. 24, 25, 29, 36, 44, 54

| STEBBINS & HOWE |

E. Stebbins & Co. (c. 1810)
New York, N.Y.
Edwin Stebbins (?)
Bibl. 4, 23, 24, 28, 29, 35, 36, 83

| E. STEBBINS & CO |

Edwin Stebbins (c. 1828-1835)
New York, N.Y.
Stebbins & Co. (c. 1836-1841)
Bibl. 15

N. W. Stebbins (c. 1848)
Seneca, Huron, Muskingum Counties, Ohio
Bibl. 34

Thomas E. Stebbins (c. 1828-1833)

New York, N.Y.
Thomas E. Stebbins & Co. (c. 1810-1835)
Bibl. 15, 24, 29, 44

| T STEBBINS | | T. E. S. |
| STEBBINS |

Thomas E. Stebbins & Co. (c. 1810-1835)
New York, N.Y.
Bibl. 23, 24, 25, 36, 44

| Stebbins |

Valentine Steckell (Stickell) (d. 1796)
Fredericktown, Md. (c. 1793)
Bibl. 38

Alexander Stedman (c. 1793-1814)
Philadelphia, Pa.
Bibl. 3, 23, 36, 44

John C. Stedman (c. 1819-1822, d. 1833)
Raleigh, N.C.
Savage & Stedman (c. 1819-1820)
Bibl. 21

John Stedmetz (c. 1829-1833)
Philadelphia, Pa.
Bibl. 3

Steel & Field (c. 1814-1825)
Philadelphia, Pa.
Robert Steel
Samuel Field
Bibl. 3, 23

James Steel (c. 1812)
Baltimore, Md.
Bibl. 3

Robert Steel (c. 1811-1831)
Philadelphia, Pa.
Steel & Field (c. 1814-1825)
Bibl. 3

Steele and Carr (c. 1836)
Louisville, Ky.
Robert Steele
——— Carr
Bibl. 32, 54

Steele & Hocknell (c. 1830)
Location unknown
Bibl. 89

| STEELE & HOCKNELL |

James P. Steele (b. 1811-d. 1893)
Rochester, N.Y. (c. 1838-1855)
Bibl. 20, 41, 44

John Steele (c. 1720-1722, d. 1722)
Annapolis, Md.
Bibl. 23, 36, 38, 44

Robert Steele (c. 1832-1848)
Louisville, Ky.
Steele and Carr (c. 1836)
Bibl. 32, 54

Samuel Steele (c. 1829-1850)
Baltimore, Md.
Bibl. 38

T. Steele & Co. (c. 1840)
Location unknown
Bibl. 88

| T. Steele & Co |

T. S. Steele (c. 1800)
Hartford, Conn.
T. S. Steele & Co. (c. 1815)
Bibl. 24, 25, 44

(T. Steele)

| T. Steele |

T. S. Steele & Co. (c. 1815)
Hartford, Conn.
Bibl. 24, 25, 44

| T Steele & Co |

The Rev. William Steele (c. 1780-1844)
Henderson County, Ky.
Bibl. 32, 54, 68

Haldor S. Steen (c. 1844-1850-   )
Rochester, N.Y.
Bibl. 20

Ole S. Steen (c. 1847)
Rochester, N.Y.
Bibl. 20

John Steeper (c. 1762)
Philadelphia, Pa.
Bibl. 3

I. Steer (c. 1835)
Location unknown
Bibl. 24

| I STEER |

John Steikleader (c. 1791-1793-   )
Hagerstown, Md.
Bibl. 38

Abraham Stein (c. 1795-1828)
Philadelphia, Pa.
Bibl. 3

Charles K. Stellwagen (c. 1840-1848)
Philadelphia, Pa.
Bibl. 3

W. S. Stenson
Location unknown
Bibl. 28

Gothelf Stephanis (c. 1791-1795)
New York, N.Y.
Bibl. 23, 36

Stephen
(See Thomas H. Stevens)

Stephens & Doud (c. 1841-   )
Utica, N.Y.
David Stephens
William Gaylord Doud
Bibl. 18, 20

David Stephens (c. 1840)
Utica, N.Y.
T. C. & D. Stephens (c. 1840-1841)
Stephens & Doud (c. 1841-   )
Bibl. 18, 20

George Stephens (c. 1790)
New York, N.Y.
(may be Gothelf Stephanis)
Bibl. 23, 24, 25, 28, 29, 35, 36, 44, 83

§ G.S § | GS |

Joseph Lawrence Stephens (b. 1764-d. 1848)
Paris, Ky. (c. 1810-1827)
Bibl. 32

J STEPHENS   PARIS

T. C. & D. Stephens (c. 1840-1841)
Utica, N.Y.
Thomas C. Stephens

David Stephens
Bibl. 18, 20

Thomas C. Stephens (b. 1819)
Utica, N.Y.
T. C. & D. Stephens (c. 1840-1841)
Bailey & Brothers
Bibl. 18, 20

William Stephens (c. 1840-1842)
Albany, N.Y.
Bibl. 20

Thomas Stephenson (c. 1835-1848)
Buffalo, N.Y.
Bibl. 20, 25, 44

Thomas Stephenson & Co. (c. 1839-1848)
Buffalo, N.Y.
Bibl. 20, 24

STEPHENSON

Sterling
(See Haight & Sterling)

——— Sterling
Newburgh, N.Y.
Haight & Sterling (c. 1841-1843)
Bibl. 20

William Stern (c. 1820-1822)
Philadelphia, Pa.
Bibl. 3

Sterne Brothers (c. 1850)
Syracuse, N.Y.
Baruch Sterne
Abraham Sterne
Bibl. 20

Abraham Sterne (c. 1850)
Syracuse, N.Y.
Sterne Brothers
Bibl. 20

Baruch Sterne (c. 1850)
Syracuse, N.Y.
Sterne Brothers
Bibl. 20

Sterret & Lewis (c. 1822)
Leesburg, Va.
Samuel Sterret
——— Lewis
Bibl. 19

Samuel Sterret (c. 1822-1834-   )

Leesburg, Va.
Sterret & Lewis (c. 1822)
Bibl. 19

T. W. Sters (c. 1850)
Location unknown
Bibl. 24

George Steven (c. 1719)
New York, N.Y.
Bibl. 23, 36, 44

———— Stevens (c. 1815)
Chillicothe, Ohio
Bibl. 34

Stevens & Lakeman (c. 1825)
Salem, Mass.
John Stevens
Ebenezer Knowlton Lakeman
Bibl. 15, 23, 24, 25, 28, 29, 36, 44

[STEVENS+LAKEMAN]

B. F. Stevens (19th century)
Location unknown
Bibl. 89

George Stevens (c. 1845-1848)
Philadelphia, Pa.
Bibl. 3

J. C. Stevens (c. 1837-1838)
Utica, N.Y.
Bibl. 18, 20

John Stevens (c. 1819-1830)
Salem, Mass.
Stevens & Lakeman (c. 1825)
Bibl. 15

Joseph Stevens (c. 1810)
Paris, Ky.
Bibl. 54, 68

Robert Stevens (c. 1808)
Petersburg, Va.
Cohen & Stevens
Bibl. 19

Thomas H. Stevens (Stephen)
   (c. 1839-1846)
Philadelphia, Pa.
Bibl. 3, 23, 44

Charles Stevenson (c. 1823-
   1825)
Philadelphia, Pa.
Bibl. 3

John Stevenson (c. 1850)
Location unknown
Bibl. 89

John Stevenson (c. 1777)
New Bern, N.C.
Bibl. 21

Steward
(See James Stuart)
(See Thomas Stuart)

Aaron Steward (c. 1843)
Philadelphia, Pa.
Bibl. 3

Stewart
(See James Stuart)
(See Thomas Stuart)
(See Marrs & Stewart)

———— Stewart (c. 1830)
(may be mark of John
   Stewart)
Bibl. 15, 44

[STEWART]

Stewart & Co. (c. 1824)
Philadelphia, Pa.
George Stewart (?)
Bibl. 3

Alexander Stewart (c. 1850)
New York, N.Y.
Bibl. 23

C. Stewart (19th century)
Location unknown
Bibl. 79

C. W. Stewart (c. 1840)
New York, N.Y.
Bibl. 23, 36

C. W. Stewart (c. 1850)
Lexington, Ky.
Bibl. 24, 25, 44, 54

C W STEWART

Charles Stewart (b. 1805)
Albany, N.Y. (c. 1837-1848)
Utica, N.Y. (c. 1848-1851)
Bibl. 18, 20

Charles G. Stewart (c. 1820-
   1849)
Charles Town, Va.
Bibl. 19

Charles G. Stewart & Son (c.
   1847-1849)
Charles Town, Va.
Charles G. Stewart

George L. Stewart
Bibl. 19

George Stewart (c. 1837)
Philadelphia, Pa.
Stewart & Co. (c. 1824) (?)
Bibl. 3

George L. Stewart
Charles Town, Va.
Charles G. Stewart & Son (c.
   1847-1849)
Bibl. 19

George W. Stewart (c. 1846-
   1852)
Lexington, Ky.
Garner & Stewart (c. 1850)
Bibl. 32, 68

James Stewart (c. 1787-1811)
Savannah, Ga.
Bibl. 17

James D. Stewart (c. 1836-
   1841)
New York, N.Y.
Bibl. 15

John Stewart
New York, N.Y. (c. 1791)
Baltimore, Md. (c. 1810)
Bibl. 23, 25, 36, 44

[STEWART]

Warner W. Stewart (c. 1837-
   1838)
Utica, N.Y.
Bibl. 18, 20

William Stewart (c. 1790-1851)
Russellville, Ky.
Bibl. 32

William Stewart (c. 1845)
St. Louis, Mo.
Bibl. 54

Worthington Stewart (c. 1842-
   1847)
St. Louis, Mo.
Bibl. 54

Stickell
(See Steckell)

John Stickler (c. 1823)
New York, N.Y.
Gale & Stickler
Bibl. 23, 36, 44

Stickles
(See Connor & Stickles)

Jonathan Stickney (Jr.) (c. 1770-1798)
Newburyport, Mass.
Bibl. 23, 24, 25, 28, 29, 36, 44

I. STICKNEY

M. P. Stickney (c. 1820)
Newburyport, Mass.
Bibl. 23, 24, 25, 29, 36, 44

M P STICKNEY

Stiles & Baldwin (c. 1791-1792)
Northampton, Mass.
Samuel Stiles
Bibl. 41, 84

Benjamin Stiles (c. 1825)
Woodbury, Conn.
Curtis(s), Candee & Stiles (c. 1831-1835)
Bibl. 16, 23, 28, 36, 44

George K. Stiles (b. 1805, c. 1834-1844)
Cortland, N.Y.
Bibl. 20

John Stiles (c. 1792-1798)
Augusta, Ga.
John & Joseph Stiles
Bibl. 17

John & Joseph Stiles (c. 1792-   )
Augusta, Ga.
Bibl. 17

Joseph Stiles (d. 1838)
Augusta, Ga.
John & Joseph Stiles
Bibl. 17

Samuel Stiles (c. 1785-1795)
Northampton, Mass.
Stiles & Baldwin (c. 1791-1792)
Bibl. 41, 84

John Stillas (c. 1784-1793, d. 1793)
Philadelphia, Pa.
Bibl. 3

Stillman
(See Wilmot & Stillman)

Alexander Stillman (c. 1806)
Philadelphia, Pa.
Bibl. 3, 23, 36, 44

Barton Stillman (b. 1767-d. 1858)

Westerly, R.I.
Bibl. 28, 44

E. Stillman (c. 1800-1825)
Stonington (?), Conn.
Bibl. 23, 24, 25, 28, 29, 36, 44

E Stillman

E.Stillman

Paul Stillman
Westerly, R.I.
Bibl. 28, 44

Richard Stillman (c. 1805)
Philadelphia, Pa.
Bibl. 23, 24, 25, 29, 36, 44

R STILLMAN

Samuel W. Stillman (c. 1850)
Hartford, Conn.
Bibl. 23, 44

Willet Stillman (c. 1804)
Utica, N.Y.
Bibl. 20

William Stillman
(See Stilman)

Mortimer F. Stillwell (c. 1845-1859)
Rochester, N.Y.
Cook & Stillwell (c. 1847-1859)
Bibl. 20, 41

William Stilman (b. 1767-d. 1858)
Hopkinton, R.I.
Bibl. 2, 28, 36, 44

George F. (A.) Stinger (c. 1845)
Cincinnati, Ohio
Bibl. 34

S. J. Stinger (c. 1850)
Cincinnati, Ohio
Bibl. 34

William Stinson (c. 1813-1815)
New York, N.Y.
Bibl. 23, 36, 44

Stockerman & Pepper
(See Stockman & Pepper)

Stocking & Kipp (c. 1833)
Wheeling, Va.
Philo W. Stocking

R. M. Kipp
Bibl. 19

Philo W. Stocking (c. 1833-1839)
Wheeling, Va.
Stocking & Kipp (c. 1833)
Forking & Kipp (c. 1835-1839)
Bibl. 19

Reuben Stocking (c. 1831)
Batavia, N.Y.
Keyes & Stocking
Bibl. 20

Stock(er)man & Pepper (c. 1828-1831)
Philadelphia, Pa.
Bibl. 3, 24, 25, 28, 29, 36, 44

STOCKERMAN & PEPPER

Jacob Stockman (c. 1828-1850)
Philadelphia, Pa.
Bibl. 3, 15, 23, 25, 36, 44

J. STOCKMAN

J. STOCKMAN

S. Stockman (c. 1837)
Philadelphia, Pa.
Bibl. 3

Samuel W. Stockton (c. 1823-1831)
Philadelphia, Pa.
Bibl. 3

Stodder & Frobisher (c. 1816-1825)
Boston, Mass.
——— Stodder
Benjamin C. Frobisher (?)
Bibl. 4, 15, 23, 25, 28, 29, 36, 39, 44

Stodder & Frobisher

Jonathan Stodder (Jr.) (c. 1826-1829)
New York, N.Y.
Bibl. 15, 25, 44

J. STODDER

George Stokeberry (c. 1837)
Philadelphia, Pa.
Bibl. 3

T. Stokes (c. 1832)
Cazenovia, N.Y.
Willard & Stokes (c. 1833)
Bibl. 20

Stollenwerck & Bros. (c. 1805)
New York, N.Y.
Bibl. 23, 24, 25, 36, 44

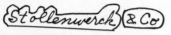

Stollenwerck & Co. (c. 1800)
New York, N.Y.
Bibl. 23, 25, 29, 36, 44

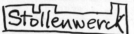

Stollenwerck & Roe
(See Roe & Stollenwerck)
Bibl. 20, 23

P. M. Stollenwerck (c. 1813-1814)
Philadelphia, Pa.
Bibl. 3

Stone & Ball (c. 1850)
Syracuse, N.Y.
Seymour H. Stone
Calvin S. Ball Jr.
Bibl. 20

Stone & Osburn (Osborn)
(c. 1796)
New York, N.Y.
Bibl. 23, 28, 36, 44

Adam Stone (c. 1803-1812)
Baltimore, Md.
Bibl. 23, 25, 28, 36, 44

A S

John Stone (c. 1831)
Baltimore, Md.
Bibl. 38

John A. Stone (c. 1817)
Baltimore, Md.
Bibl. 38

Seymour H. Stone (c. 1850)
Syracuse, N.Y.
Stone & Ball
Bibl. 20

William G. Stone (c. 1809)
Somers, N.Y.
Bibl. 20

William R. Stone (c. 1845-1846)
Louisville, Ky.
Bibl. 32

Rudy Stoner (c. 1764)
Lancaster, Pa.
Bibl. 3

A. Stoops (c. 1825)
Location unknown
Bibl. 24

A STOOPS

Storer & Wilmot (c. 1796-1800)
Rutland, Vt.
William Storer
Thomas Wilmot
Bibl. 54

William Storer (c. 1792-1796)
Rutland, Vt.
Storer & Wilmot (c. 1796-1800)
Bibl. 54

Storm & Son (c. 1830)
Albany, N.Y. (?)
Abraham G. Storm (?)
Bibl. 15

Storm & Wilson (c. 1802-1818)
Poughkeepsie, N.Y.
James Wilson
Abraham G. Storm
Bibl. 15, 20, 25, 44

A. G. Storm & Son (c. 1823-1826)
Poughkeepsie, N.Y.
Abraham G. Storm
Bibl. 20, 25, 44

Storm & Son

Abraham G. Storm (b. 1779-d. 1836)
Albany, N.Y. (c. 1830)

Poughkeepsie, N.Y.
Storm & Wilson (c. 1802-1818)
A. G. Storm & Son (c. 1823-1826)
Storm & Son (c. 1830) (?)
Fellows & Storm (c. 1839)
Bibl 15, 20, 23, 24, 25, 29

A. G. STORM

E. C. Storm (c. 1815)
Rochester, N.Y.
Bibl. 25, 44

E. C. STORM

Storrs & Chubbuck (c. 1847-1849-)
Utica, N.Y.
Henry S. Storrs
Samuel W. Chubbuck
Bibl. 18, 20

STORRS & CHUBBUCK

Storrs & Cook (c. 1827-1833)
Amherst, Mass.
Northampton, Mass.
Nathan Storrs
Benjamin E. Cook
Bibl. 25, 44, 84

Storrs & Cook

Storrs & Cooley (c. 1831-1839)
Utica, N.Y.
Charles Storrs
Oliver B. Cooley
Horace P. Bradley
David S. Rowland
Erastus Charles Starin
Bibl. 15, 18, 20, 23, 25, 28, 29, 36, 89

Storrs & Davies (c. 1829-1830)
Utica, N.Y.
Charles Storrs
Thomas Davies
Bibl. 18, 20

Storrs & Davies Utica

Storrs & Parker (c. 1828)
Utica, N.Y.
Charles Storrs
George Parker
Bibl. 18, 20

Charles Storrs (c. 1828,
d. 1839)
Utica, N.Y.
Storrs & Parker (c. 1828)
Storrs & Davies (c. 1829-1830)
Storrs & Cooley (c. 1831-1839)
Bibl. 18, 20

Eli A. Storrs (c. 1832-1833)
Utica, N.Y.
Bibl. 18, 20

Henry S. Storrs (c. 1846-1849)
Utica, N.Y.
Storrs & Chubbuck (c. 1847-
1849-   )
Bibl. 18, 20

Nathan Storrs (b. 1768-d.
1839)
Amherst, Mass.
Northampton, Mass.
New York, N.Y. (?) (c. 1825)
Baldwin & Storrs (c. 1792-1794)
Storrs & Cook (c. 1827-1833)
Bibl. 15, 23, 24, 25, 28, 29,
41, 44, 84

| N. STORRS |

Shubael Storrs (d. 1847)
Utica, N.Y. (c. 1803-1828)
Bibl. 18, 20

| STORRS |

E. F. Story (c. 1872)
Wilmington, N.C.
T. W. Brown & Sons
Bibl. 21

S. N. Story (c. 1845)
Worcester, Mass.
Bibl. 15, 25, 44

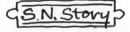

S.N.Story

Edwin Stott (c. 1850)
Philadelphia, Pa.
Bibl. 3

John Stott (d. 1749)
Williamsburg, Va. (c. 1737)
Bibl. 19

Samuel Stott (c. 1846-1850)
Philadelphia, Pa.
Bibl. 3

Stout
(See Brown & Stout)

James D. Stout (c. 1817-1836)
New York, N.Y.
Bibl. 15, 24, 25, 28, 44, 72

(J D STOUT)   { J D STOUT }

Samuel Stout (b. 1756-d. 1795)
Princeton, N.J. (c. 1779-1795)
Bibl. 3, 23, 36, 44, 46, 54

Luke (Lucas) Stoutenburgh
Sr. (b. 1691-d. 1743)
Charleston, S.C. (c. 1718-1743)
Bibl. 5, 25, 44

Luke (Lucas) Stoutenburgh Jr.
(c. 1765)
Charleston, S.C.
Bibl. 5

Tobias Stoutenburgh (b. 1700-d.
1759)
New York, N.Y.
Bibl. 2, 4, 23, 24, 25, 28, 29,
35, 36, 44, 54, 87

(T.S.B) | TS |

John Stow (b. 1748-d. 1802,
c. 1772)
Wilmington, Del.
Bibl. 3, 23, 25, 30, 36, 39, 44

J Stow

Frederick Stowee (c. 1802-
1803)
Philadelphia, Pa.
Bibl. 3

A. Stowell Jr.
Baltimore, Md. (c. 1855)
Charlestown, Mass.
Gould, Stowell & Ward
(c. 1855-1858)
Bibl. 24, 28, 44

(A. STOWELL JR)

Avery W. Stowell (d. 1844)
Syracuse, N.Y.
Bibl. 20

David C. Stoy (c. 1844-1849)
Louisville, Ky.
Kitts & Stoy (c. 1851-1852)
Bibl. 32

Frederick Stoy (c. 1807-1822)
Augusta, Ga.
(may be Frederick Stowee of
Philadelphia, Pa.)
Bibl. 17

Pierce Stoy (c. 1803-1827)
Savannah, Ga.
Bibl. 17

C. Strade (c. 1838)
Richmond, Va.
Bibl. 19

Samuel Stradley (c. 1857)
Greenville, S.C.
Bibl. 5

Jacob Strembeck (c. 1820-1822)
Philadelphia, Pa.
Bibl. 3

Isaac Stretch (c. 1732-1752)
Philadelphia, Pa.
Bibl. 3

Peter Stretch (c. 1708-1738,
d. 1746)
Philadelphia, Pa.
Bibl. 3

Samuel Stretch (c. 1715,
d. 1732)
Philadelphia, Pa.
Bibl. 3

Thomas Stretch (c. 1754-1764,
d. 1765)
Philadelphia, Pa.
Bibl. 3

George W. Striker (c. 1825-
1833)
New York, N.Y.
Bibl. 15, 25, 44

(GWSTRIKER)

George A. Stringer (c. 1849)
Cincinnati, Ohio
Bibl. 54

Samuel Stringfellow (c. 1816-
1837)
Augusta, Ga.
Bibl. 17

Edmund Strock (c. 1850)
Philadelphia, Pa.
Bibl. 3

Strom & Son (c. 1835)
Albany, N.Y.
(may be Storm & Son)
A. G. Strom
Bibl. 36

STROM & SON

A. G. Strom (c. 1830)
Albany, N.Y.
(may be A. G. Storm)
Strom & Son (c. 1835)
Bibl. 36

Strong
(See Phelps & Strong)

John Strong (b. 1749,
c. 1774)
Maryland
Bibl. 23, 28, 36, 38, 44

Peter Strong (b. 1764-d. 1797)
Fayetteville, N.C.
Bibl. 21

William Strong (c. 1807-1811)
Philadelphia, Pa.
Bibl. 3, 23, 36, 44

———— Strother
Cincinnati, Ohio
Bibl. 54

A. Strub (c. 1847)
St. Louis, Mo.
Bibl. 54

Alexander C. Stuart (c. 1834-
1841)
New York, N.Y.
Bibl. 15

H. Stuart (c. 1800-1808)
New York, N.Y.
Bibl. 23, 36, 44

I. (J.) Stuart (c. 1700)
(probably John Stuart)
Bibl. 28

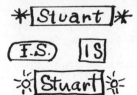

James Stuart (Steward)
(Stewart) (c. 1837-1850)
Philadelphia, Pa.
Bibl. 3

John Stuart (c. 1720, d. 1737)
Providence, R.I.
Bibl. 23, 24, 25, 29, 36, 44

J. S.   J. S.
Stuart

Thomas Stuart (Steward)
(Stewart)
Philadelphia, Pa. (c. 1839-
1850)
Bibl. 3

Isaac Stuckert (c. 1809)
Philadelphia, Pa.
Bibl. 3, 23, 36, 44

D. F. Studley (c. 1830)
Location unknown
Bibl. 28, 29, 44

D. F. STUDLEY

L. Studley (19th century)
Location unknown
Bibl. 89

Joseph Gordon Bonner Stukes
(c. 1788)
Charleston, S.C.
Bibl. 5

Thomas Sturgeon (c. 1830)
Lancaster, Ohio
Bibl. 34

Timothy Sturgeon (c. 1812)
Lancaster, Ohio
Bibl. 34

Joseph Sturgis (c. 1813-1817)
Philadelphia, Pa.
Bibl. 3

James Stutson (c. 1838)
Rochester, N.Y.
Bibl. 20

James Styles (c. 1780)
Rhinebeck, N.Y.
Bibl. 20

James Styles (c. 1784)
Kingston, N.Y.
Bibl. 20

William J. Styles (c. 1823)
Rhinebeck, N.Y.
Bibl. 20

Suire & Deloste (c. 1822-1826)
Baltimore, Md.
Joseph Suire
Francis Deloste
Bibl. 38

Joseph Suire (Shuire) (Suiro)
Baltimore, Md. (c. 1799-1826)
Suire & Deloste (c. 1822-1826)
Bibl. 38

Suley
(See Sealey)

John Suley (c. 1810-1812)
Baltimore, Md.
Bibl. 38

Cornelius D. Sullivan (c. 1842-
1868)
St. Louis, Mo.
Bibl. 24, 25, 54

C D Sullivan

D. Sullivan & Co. (c. 1820)
New York, N.Y.
Bibl. 3, 23, 24, 29, 36, 44

D.SULLIVAN&CO

D. SULLIVAN & Co

Enoch Sullivan (c. 1800-1816)
Richmond, Va.
Bibl. 19

E SULLIVAN

George Sullivan (c. 1802-1806)
Lynchburg, Va.
Bibl. 19, 54

Owen Sullivan (c. 1748)
Boston, Mass.
Bibl. 54

Sunderlin & Weaver (before 1864)
Brooklyn, N.Y. (?)
Rochester, N.Y. (?)
Bibl. 41

Jacob Supplee (c. 1790)
Philadelphia, Pa.
Bibl. 3, 23, 36, 44

George Sutherland (c. 1810)
Boston, Mass.
Bibl. 4, 23, 28, 36, 44

Robert Sutton (c. 1800-1825)
New Haven, Conn.
Bibl. 16, 23, 28, 36, 44

Swaine
(See Robert Swan)

B. Swan (c. 1825)
Location unknown
Bibl. 23, 29

Caleb Swan (b. 1754-d. 1816)
Boston, Mass.
Charlestown, Mass.
Bibl. 2, 23, 28, 36, 44

Robert Swan (Swaine)
Worcester, Mass. (c. 1775)
Andover, Mass. (c. 1795)
Philadelphia, Pa. (c. 1799-1831)
Bibl. 3, 15, 23, 24, 25, 28, 29, 36, 39, 44, 54, 78, 81

R Swan   R SWAN

William Swan (b. 1715-d. 1774)
Boston, Mass.
Worcester, Mass.
Bibl. 2, 15, 23, 24, 25, 28, 29, 36, 44, 54, 72

John Sweeney (c. 1814-1827)
Geneva, N.Y.
Giffing & Sweeney (c. 1809-1814) (?)
Bibl. 15, 20, 24, 25, 44

Henry Philips Sweetser (b. 1742)
Worcester, Mass. (c. 1768)
Bibl. 23, 36, 44

Swift & Jones (c. 1810)
Canandaigua, N.Y.
John D. Swift
Harlow Jones (?)
Bibl. 20

Amos B. Swift (c. 1846)
Earlville, N.Y.
Bibl. 20

John D. Swift (c. 1810)
Canandaigua, N.Y.
Swift & Jones
Bibl. 20

John D. Swift (c. 1811-1813)
Manlius, N.Y.
Bibl. 20

John D. Swift (c. 1816-1821)
Cazenovia, N.Y.
Bibl. 20

George J. Swortfiguer (c. 1840-1842)
Schenectady, N.Y.
Bibl. 20

Christopher Syberry (c. 1769-   )
Savannah, Ga.
Bibl. 17

Philip Syderman (c. 1785)
Philadelphia, Pa.
Bibl. 3

J. Sylvester (c. 1838-1861)
St. Louis, Mo.
Bibl. 54

William Sylvester (19th century)
Nixonton, N.C.
Bibl. 21

Celadon (Cleadon) Symmes (b. 1770, c. 1789-1790)

Cincinnati, Ohio
Bibl. 34, 46

Daniel Symmes (b. 1772-d. 1827, c. 1792-1793)
Cincinnati, Ohio (c. 1793)
Newton, N.J.
Bibl. 46, 54

John Symmes (c. 1766)
Boston, Mass.
Bibl. 15, 23, 25, 28, 36, 44

(Judge) Timothy Symmes (b. 1744-d. 1797)
Newton, N.J.
Walpack, N.J.
Bibl. 46, 54

Daniel Syng (b. 1713-d. 1745)
Lancaster, Pa. (c. 1734)
Bibl. 15, 23, 25, 36, 44

John Syng (c. 1738?)
Philadelphia, Pa. (c. 1734)
Wilmington, Del. (c. 1772) (?)
Bibl. 3, 15, 25, 44

Philip Syng Sr. (b. 1676-d. 1739)
Philadelphia, Pa. (c. 1714-1730)
Cape May, N.J. (after 1723-1728)
Annapolis, Md. (c. 1728-1739)
Bibl. 2, 3, 4, 15, 23, 24, 25, 28, 29, 38, 44, 54, 74, 81

Philip Syng Jr. (b. 1703-d. 1789)
Philadelphia, Pa. (c. 1726-1785)

Bibl. 2, 3, 4, 15, 23, 25, 28, 29, 36, 44, 54, 74, 81

S. M. Taber (c. 1835)
Location unknown
Bibl. 89

S. M. Taber & Co. (c. 1835)
Location unknown
Bibl. 15, 44

William Taber (c. 1835)
Philadelphia, Pa.
Bibl. 3, 23, 36, 44

John James Taf (c. 1794)
Philadelphia, Pa.
Bibl. 3

Taft & Mitchell (c. 1818-1819)
Richmond, Va.
Elisha Taft
William Mitchell Jr.
Bibl. 19

Elisha Taft (c. 1817)
Richmond, Va.
Taft & Mitchell (c. 1818-1819)
Bibl. 19

R. Taft (19th century)
Location unknown
Bibl. 15, 44

R. TAFT

Thomas E. Taggart (c. 1839)
Columbus, Ga.
Bibl. 17

W. H. Talbot
Indianapolis, Md. (c. 1855-1865)
Kentucky (?)
Bibl. 32

A. G. Talcott (c. 1840)
Oswego, N.Y.
Bibl. 20

C. Talcott (19th century)
Location unknown
Bibl. 89

Tanguy
(See Desquet & Tanguy)

John Tanguy (Tanguey)
(Tanguay)
Philadelphia, Pa. (c. 1801-1822)
John & Peter Tanguy (c. 1808)
Bibl. 3, 15, 23, 24, 25, 28, 36, 39, 44, 80

John & Peter Tanguy
(Tanguey) (Tanguay)
Philadelphia, Pa. (c. 1808)
Bibl. 3, 23, 44

J & P TANGUY

Peter Tanguy (Tanguey)
(Tanguay) (c. 1810-1819)
Philadelphia, Pa.
John & Peter Tanguy (c. 1808)
Bibl. 3, 23, 44

Rebiton Tanguy (c. 1806)
Philadelphia, Pa.
Bibl. 3, 23

Theodore Tankey (b. 1841)
Utica, N.Y. (c. 1859-1860)
Bibl. 18

Tanner & Cooley (c. 1840-1842)
Utica, N.Y.
Perry G. Tanner
Oliver B. Cooley
Horace P. Bradley
Nathan M. Christian
William Gaylord Doud
Charles Seager
Bibl. 18, 20

TANNER & COOLEY

Tanner & Rogers (c. 1750)
Newport, R.I.
John Tanner
Joseph & Daniel Rogers
Bibl. 25, 44

T & R

Benjamin Tanner (c. 1800)
Philadelphia, Pa.
Bibl. 3

John Tanner (b. 1713-d. 1785)
Newport, R.I.
Bibl. 15, 24, 28, 36, 44, 54, 56

Perry G. Tanner
Utica, N.Y. (c. 1840-1844)
Cooperstown, N.Y.
(c. 1844-   )
Tanner & Cooley
Oliver B. Cooley
Bibl. 18, 20, 24, 25, 44

Richard Tape (c. 1844)
Rochester, N.Y.
Bibl. 20

Tappan & Whitney (c. 1809)
Northampton, Mass.
Benjamin Tappan
——— Whitney
Bibl. 84

Benjamin Tappan (b. 1742-d. 1831)
Northampton, Mass. (c. 1768-1809)
Tappan & Whitney (c. 1809)
Bibl. 84

William Tappan (c. 1806)
Geneva, N.Y.
Bibl. 20

William B. Tappan (c. 1818-1819)
Philadelphia, Pa.
Lemist & Tappan
Bibl. 3

E. Tarbell (c. 1830)
Location unknown
Bibl. 24, 28, 44

E. TARBELL

John Targee (c. 1797-1841)
New York, N.Y.
John & Peter Targee (c. 1798-1811)

Bibl. 15, 23, 24, 25, 26, 36, 44

[I T]

John & Peter Targee (c. 1798-1811)
New York, N.Y.
Bibl. 4, 15, 23, 24, 25, 28, 29, 30, 35, 36, 39, 44, 83, 89

[I & P T]

[I & P TARGEE]

Peter Targee (c. 1811)
New York, N.Y.
John & Peter Targee (c. 1798-1811)
Bibl. 23, 36, 44

William Targee (c. 1807)
New York, N.Y.
Bibl. 23, 36, 44

Taylor
(See Fairchild & Taylor)

Taylor & Baldwin (c. 1825)
Newark, N.J.
John Taylor
Isaac Baldwin
Bibl. 46, 54

Taylor & Gilpin (c. 1843)
Philadelphia, Pa.
Bibl. 3

Taylor & Hinsdale (c. 1801-1829)
Newark, N.J.
New York, N.Y.
John Taylor
Horace Seymour Hinsdale
Bibl. 15, 23, 24, 25, 29, 35, 36, 44, 46, 78, 83

[T & H]

Taylor & Lawrie (Lowrie) (c. 1837-1850)
Philadelphia, Pa.
——— Taylor
Robert D. Lawrie
Bibl. 3, 4, 23, 24, 25, 28, 36, 44

[TAYLOR & LAWRIE]

Taylor, Lawrie & Wood (after 1841)
Philadelphia, Pa.
——— Taylor
Robert D. Lawrie
——— Wood
Bibl. 23

E. A. Taylor (c. 1810-1820)
New Orleans, La.
Bibl. 54

Edward Taylor (c. 1828-1837)
New York, N.Y.
Bibl. 15

George Taylor (b. 1825)
Mobile, Ala. (c. 1850)
Bibl. 54

George W. Taylor (c. 1823-1850)
Philadelphia, Pa.
Bibl. 3, 23, 36, 44

John Taylor
Philadelphia, Pa. (c. 1786) (?)
Charleston, S.C. (c. 1790)
Bibl. 3, 5

John Taylor (c. 1801-1829)
New York, N.Y.
Newark, N.J.
Hempstead, L.I., N.Y.
Taylor & Hinsdale (c. 1801-1829)
E. Hinsdale & Co. (before 1810)
Taylor & Baldwin (c. 1825)
Bibl. 36, 44, 54

John G. Taylor (c. 1837-1843)
Philadelphia, Pa.
Bibl. 3

Luther Taylor (c. 1823-1835)
Philadelphia, Pa.
Bibl. 3

N. Taylor & Co. (c. 1825)
New York, N.Y.
Bibl. 24, 25, 44

[N TAYLOR & CO]

Najah Taylor (c. 1793)
Danbury, Conn.
New York, N.Y.
Eli Mygatt
Daniel Noble Carrington
Bibl. 23, 28, 36, 44

Noah C. Taylor (c. 1844)
Salisbury, N.C.
Bibl. 21

Richard Taylor (c. 1834-1841)
New York, N.Y.
Bibl. 15

Robert Taylor (c. 1839-1850)
Philadelphia, Pa.
Bibl. 3

Samuel Taylor (c. 1798-1799)
Philadelphia, Pa.
Bibl. 3

Thomas Taylor (d. 1727)
Providence, R.I.
Bibl. 23, 36, 44

W. S. Taylor (c. 1847-1849)
Troy, N.Y.
Bibl. 20

W. S. Taylor & Co. (c. 1858-)
Utica, N.Y.
William S. Taylor
Theodore M. Timms
Bibl. 20

[W. S. TAYLOR & CO.]

William Taylor (c. 1772-1778)
Philadelphia, Pa.
Bibl. 3, 15, 23, 25, 28, 44, 54, 81

[W T]

William Taylor (c. 1829-1850)
Philadelphia, Pa.
Bibl. 3

William Taylor (c. 1835)
Buffalo, N.Y.
Bibl. 20

William S. Taylor (c. 1829-)
Utica, N.Y.
Davies & Taylor (c. 1851-1852)
Maynard & Taylor (c. 1852-1858)
W. S. Taylor & Co. (c. 1858-)
Bibl. 18, 20

[WM S. TAYLOR]

Robert Tempest (c. 1814-1816, d. 1816)
Philadelphia, Pa.
Marshall & Tempest (c. 1813-1830)
Bibl. 3, 23, 44

Robert Tempest (c. 1814-1850)
Philadelphia, Pa.
Bibl. 3, 36

John Templeman (b. 1746, c. 1774)

Carolinas
Bibl. 62

William Templeman (b. 1746)
Charleston, S.C. (c. 1774)
Bibl. 5

Barent Ten Eyck (b. 1714-d.
1795)
Albany, N.Y.
Bibl. 15, 20, 44, 54

B. E

Jacob Ten Eyck (b. 1705-d.
1793)
Albany, N.Y.
Bibl. 2, 15, 20, 23, 24, 25, 28,
29, 36

Koenraet Ten Eyck (b. 1678-d.
1753)
Albany, N.Y. (c. 1703-1753)
Bibl. 4, 15, 20, 23, 24, 28, 29,
30, 35, 36, 44, 54

K E

William I. Tenney (c. 1831-
1852)
New York, N.Y.
Bibl. 15, 24, 25, 29, 44

TENNEY   W I TENNEY

Geer Terry (b. 1775-d. 1858)
Enfield, Conn.
Worcester, Mass.
Bibl. 15, 16, 23, 24, 25, 28, 36,
44, 54

G TERRY   TERRY

John Terry
Savannah, Ga. (c. 1741-
1745-   )
Frederick, Va. (c. 1742)
Charleston, Va. (c. 1746)
Bibl. 5, 17

John Terry (c. 1819)
New York, N.Y.
Bibl. 15, 23, 36, 44

L. B. Terry (c. 1810)
Enfield, Conn.
Bibl. 23, 29, 36, 44

L. B. TERRY

Lucien B. Terry (c. 1830-1835)
Albany, N.Y.
Bibl. 20

Wilbert Terry (c. 1785-1810)
Enfield, Conn.
Bibl. 23, 24, 25, 29, 36, 44

W. TERRY   WM TERRY

William Terry (c. 1799)
Mechanic Town, N.Y.
Bibl. 20

David Tew (c. 1785)
Philadelphia, Pa.
Bibl. 3

George Tharp (c. 1807-1820)
Baltimore, Md.
Bibl. 38

Joseph Blake Thaxter
(b. 1791-d. 1863)
Hingham, Mass.
Bibl. 15, 23, 25, 28, 36, 44

J B THAXTER

Amos Thayer (c. 1809)
Troy, N.Y.
Bibl. 20

William Theofile (c. 1822)
New Orleans, La.
Bibl. 23, 36, 44

Thibarult
(See Thibault & Co.)
(See Felix Thibault)

Thibault & Brothers (c. 1810-
1835)
Philadelphia, Pa.
Bibl. 3, 23, 24, 25, 29, 36, 44

THIBAULT
BROTHERS

Thibault & Co. (Thibarult
& Co.)
Philadelphia, Pa. (c. 1797-
1798)
Bibl. 3, 23, 28, 36, 44

Felix Thibault (Thibarult)
Philadelphia, Pa. (c. 1814-
1837)
Bibl. 3, 15, 23, 36, 44

Francis Thibault (Thibout)
(d. 1802?)

Philadelphia, Pa. (c. 1800-
1802)
Bibl. 3, 15, 23

Francis Thibault (c. 1816-1850)
Philadelphia, Pa.
Bibl. 3, 15

Francis, Frederick & Felix
Thibault
Philadelphia, Pa. (c. 1813)
Bibl. 3, 15

Frederick Thibault (c. 1818-
1835)
Philadelphia, Pa.
Bibl. 3, 15, 23, 36, 44

Frederick (Francis) & Felix
Thibault (c. 1813)
Philadelphia, Pa.
Bibl. 15, 23, 24, 25, 29, 36,
44, 54

F & F THIBAULT   THIBAULT

Thibout
(See Francis Thibault)

John Thiele (c. 1847)
St. Louis, Mo.
Bibl. 54

Thirion & Hinkle (c. 1850)
Philadelphia, Pa.
Lewis Thirion
Benjamin Hinkle
Bibl. 3

Lewis Thirion (c. 1828-1850)
Philadelphia, Pa.
Thirion & Hinkle (c. 1850)
Bibl. 3

August Thomas (c. 1838)
Piqua, Ohio
Bibl. 34

Benjamin Thomas (c. 1813-
1850)
Philadelphia, Pa.
Bibl. 3

Ebenezer Thomas (c. 1802-
1819)
Petersburg, Va.
Bennett & Thomas (c. 1812-
1819)
John W. Thomas & Co.
(c. 1819)
Bibl. 19

John W. Thomas & Co.
(c. 1819)

Petersburg, Va.
John Warren Thomas
Ebenezer Thomas
John Bennett
Bibl. 19

John Warren Thomas (c. 1817-
   1820-   )
Petersburg, Va.
Bennett & Thomas (c. 1812-
   1819)
John W. Thomas & Co.
   (c. 1819)
Bibl. 19

Joseph Thomas (c. 1805-1808)
Philadelphia, Pa.
Bibl. 3

Richard Thomas (c. 1802-1808)
Philadelphia, Pa.
Bibl. 3

Thomas Thomas (c. 1784)
New York, N.Y.
Bibl. 23, 36, 44

Walter Thomas (c. 1769)
New York, N.Y.
Bibl. 4, 23, 24, 25, 28, 36, 44

W·T

William Thomas
Elizabethtown, N.J. (before
   1780)
Trenton, N.J. (c. 1780)
Bibl. 23, 36, 44, 46, 54

Peter Thomeguex (c. 1802)
Northampton, Mass.
Bibl. 84

Peter Thomison (c. 1817)
Boston, Mass.
Bibl. 36, 44

Thompson & Benjamin
   (c. 1803)
Canandaigua, N.Y.
Seth Thompson
Luther W. Benjamin
Bibl. 20

Thompson & Griffith (c. 1785-
   1786)
Savannah, Ga.
John Thompson
Edward Griffith
Bibl. 17

D. B. Thompson (c. 1825)
Litchfield, Conn.
Bibl. 23, 25, 36, 44

D B THOMPSON

Henry Thompson (c. 1847-
   1850)
Philadelphia, Pa.
Bibl. 3

Isaac Thompson (c. 1801-   )
(See Isaac Thomson)
Litchfield, Conn.
Shethar & Thom(p)son
   (c. 1801)
Bibl. 15, 23, 36, 44

I THOMPSON

Isaac Thompson Jr. (c. 1831-
   1833)
Kingston, N.Y.
Bibl. 20

Isaac P. Thompson (c. 1857)
Orangeburg, S.C.
Bibl. 5

James Thompson (c. 1796)
Baltimore, Md.
Bibl. 38

James Thompson (c. 1834)
Brooklyn, N.Y.
Bibl. 36

James S. Thompson (c. 1832)
Louisville, Ky.
Bibl. 54

Jeremiah Thompson (c. 1840-
   1841)
Philadelphia, Pa.
Bibl. 3

John Thompson (b. 1741)
Maryland, (c. 1774)
Bibl. 44

John Thompson (c. 1786)
Savannah, Ga.
Thompson & Griffith (c. 1785-
   1786)
Bibl. 17

John P. Thompson (c. 1819-
   1824)
Philadelphia, Pa.
Bibl. 3

Joseph S. Thompson (c. 1832)
Louisville, Ky.
Bibl. 32

Peter Thompson (c. 1835-1850)
Philadelphia, Pa.
Bibl. 3, 23

Robert Thompson (c. 1840-
   1841)
Philadelphia, Pa.
Bibl. 3

Seth Thompson (c. 1803)
Canandaigua, N.Y.
Thompson & Benjamin
Bibl. 20

William Thompson
Abingdon, Md. (before 1774)
Port Tobacco, Md. (c. 1762-
   1772)
Bibl. 29, 38

W T

William Thompson (c. 1795-
   1824)
Baltimore, Md.
Bibl. 23, 38, 44

W T

William Thompson (c. 1810)
New York State
Bibl. 54

Thomson & Beckwith (c. 1837-
   1839)
Raleigh, N.C.
William Thomson
Robert W. Beckwith
Bibl. 21

F. Thomson
Location unknown
Bibl. 15, 44

F THOMSON

H. Thomson
Location unknown
Bibl. 89

Isaac Thomson (c. 1801-1805)
(See Isaac Thompson)
Litchfield, Conn.
Shethar & Thom(p)son
   (c. 1801)
Bibl. 16, 24, 25, 28, 29, 44

I THOMSON

James Thomson (c. 1834-1841)
New York, N.Y.
Bibl. 4, 15, 23, 24, 25, 28, 36, 44

Jas Thomson

John L. Thomson (c. 1849)
Philadelphia, Pa.
Bibl. 3

Peter Thomson (c. 1817)
Boston, Mass.
Bibl. 23, 28

Peter Thomson (c. 1835)
Philadelphia, Pa.
Bibl. 36, 44

W. Thomson (c. 1804)
New York, N.Y.
Bibl. 54

William Thomson (c. 1810-
1834)
New York, N.Y.
Bibl. 4, 15, 24, 25, 28, 29, 35,
36, 39, 44, 78, 83

William Thomson (b. 1800-d.
1850, c. 1834)
Raleigh, N.C. (c. 1837-1839)
Wilmington, N.C.
Thomson & Beckwith (c. 1837-
1839)
Bibl. 21

C. B. Thorn (c. 1834-1835)
Troy, N.Y.
Bibl. 20

John Thorn (c. 1837)
Philadelphia, Pa.
Bibl. 3

Andrew Thornton (c. 1811)
Philadelphia, Pa.
Bibl. 3

Henry Thornton (c. 1824)
Providence, R.I.
Bibl. 23, 36

Henry Thornton (c. 1824)
Providence, R.I.
Bibl. 44

John Thornton Jr. (c. 1825-
1847)
Philadelphia, Pa.
Bibl. 3

Joseph Thornton (c. 1819)
Philadelphia, Pa.
Bibl. 3

Joseph Thornton (c. 1824)
Cincinnati, Ohio
Bibl. 34

Thran
(See Trahn)

Charles Thum (c. 1828-1833)
Philadelphia, Pa.
Bibl. 3

Thurber
(See Gorham & Thurber)

Robert Thurmer (d. 1758)
Yorktown, Va.
Bibl. 19

Jacob Thurston (c. 1797-1815)
Schenectady, N.Y.
Bibl. 20

William N. Tibbets (c. 1837-
1838)
Utica, N.Y.
Bibl. 18, 20

William Tibbits (c. 1842)
Buffalo, N.Y.
Bibl. 20

Tibolt
(See Thibault)

Philip Tidyman (d. 1780)
Charleston, S.C. (c. 1764-1776)
Bibl. 5

Cornelius Tiebout (c. 1770-
1830)
New York, N.Y.
Bibl. 28

John Tierney (c. 1820-1824)
Philadelphia, Pa.
Bibl. 3

A. Tiers (c. 1790)
Location unknown
Bibl. 24

A. TIERS

Tiffany & Co. (c. 1853-   )
New York, N.Y.
Bibl. 35

Tiffany & Young (c. 1837-1853)
New York, N.Y.
Bibl. 35, 88

James Tiley (b. 1740-d. 1792)
Hartford, Conn.
Norfolk, Va.

Bibl. 16, 23, 24, 25, 28, 29, 36,
44, 61

I TILEY   TILEY

Theodore M. Timms
Utica, N.Y.
W. S. Taylor & Co.
(c. 1858-   )
Bibl. 20

Charles Tinges (b. 1765-d.
1816)
Annapolis, Md. (c. 1788-1794)
Baltimore, Md. (1794-1816)
Bibl. 38

Samuel Tingley (c. 1765-1790)
New York, N.Y
Philadelphia, Pa.
Bibl. 15, 23, 24, 25, 28, 35, 36,
44, 50, 54, 83

F. Tinkham & Co. (c. 1840-
1850)
New York, NY.
Foster Tinkham
Bibl. 15, 25

F. TINKHAM & CO.

B. H. Tisdale (c. 1825)
Newport, R.I.
Providence, R.I.
Bibl. 15, 23, 24, 25, 28, 29,
36, 39, 44, 56

Nathan Tisdale (c. 1795-1829)
New Bern, N.C.
Bibl. 21

William Tisdale I (c. 1771-
1796)
New Bern, N.C.
Bibl. 21

William Tisdale II (b. 1791-d.
    1861)
New Bern, N.C.
Bibl. 21

Francis Titcomb (b. 1790-d.
    1832, c. 1815)
Newburyport, Mass.
Bibl. 14, 23, 24, 25, 28, 29,
    36, 44

| F TITCOMB | TITCOMB |

Titlow & Fry (c. 1844-1847)
Philadelphia, Pa.
J. Titlow
N. L. Fry
Bibl. 3, 23

J. Titlow (c. 1844-1850)
Philadelphia, Pa.
Titlow & Fry (c. 1844-1847)
Bibl. 3, 23

Charles T. Tittle (c. 1841-1847)
Philadelphia, Pa.
Bibl. 3, 23

James Titus (c. 1833)
Philadelphia, Pa.
Bibl. 3, 25, 44

| I TITUS |

Peter N. Titus (c. 1843)
Albany, N.Y.
Bibl. 20

Robert Titus (c. 1817)
Petersburg, Va.
Bibl. 19

Tobey
(See Hood & Tobey)

William Tod(d) (c. 1794,
    d. 1836)
Lexington, Ky.
Bibl. 32, 54, 68

Richard Todd (c. 1769)
Strasburg, Pa.
Bibl. 3

Elijah Tollotson Jr. (c. 1815)
West Bloomfield, N.Y.
Bibl. 20

C. Tompkins (c. 1822)
Clarksville, Ga.
Monticello, Ga.
Bibl. 17

Edmund Tompkins (b. 1757)
Waterbury, Conn. (c. 1779)
Bibl. 16, 23, 28, 36, 44

Erastus O. Tompkins (c. 1836)
New York, N.Y.
Marquand & Co. (c. 1834-1839)
Ball, Tompkins & Black
    (c. 1839-1851)
Bibl. 15

Daniel Toncry (c. 1799)
Martinsburg, Va.
Bibl. 19

Silas Tonkrey (c. 1812)
Shelbyville, Ky.
Bibl. 32, 68

James Took (c. 1842-1847)
St. Louis, Mo.
Bibl. 54

Benjamin Toppan (c. 1760)
Northampton, Mass.
Bibl. 28

Peter Torlay (c. 1813-1819)
Charleston, S.C.
Bibl. 5

Tounshendt
(See Thomas Townsend)

John Touzell (Towzell)
    (b. 1726-d. 1785)
Salem, Mass.
Bibl. 15, 23, 24, 25, 28, 29, 36

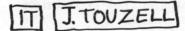

| IT | J. TOUZELL |

Towle & Jones (c. 1857-1873)
Newburyport, Mass.
Bibl. 89

H. Towle (c. 1835)
Location unknown
Bibl. 24

Town & Witherall (c. 1825)
Location unknown
Bibl. 89

Ira S. Town (c. 1825)
Montpelier, Vt.
Bibl. 15, 25, 44

| IRA S TOWN |

Townsend (c. 1775)
Location unknown
Bibl. 24

Charles Townsend (c. 1799-
    1850)
Philadelphia, Pa.
Bibl. 3

Charles Townsend Jr. (c. 1829-
    1850)
Philadelphia, Pa.
Bibl. 3

Elisha Townsend (c. 1828-
    1829)
Philadelphia, Pa.
Bibl. 3

James Townsend (b. 1750,
    c. 1774)
Maryland
Bibl. 38

John Townsend (c. 1849)
Philadelphia, Pa.
Bibl. 3

John Townsend (before 1820)
Lancaster, Ohio
Bibl. 34

John Townsend Jr. (c. 1813-
    1833)
Philadelphia, Pa.
Bibl. 3

S. Townsend (c. 1775)
Delaware (?)
Bibl. 24, 28, 29, 30, 44

Thomas Townsend (Town-
    shend) (Tounshendt)
    (b. 1701-d. 1777)
Boston, Mass. (c. 1725)
Bibl. 25, 44

James Townsley (c. 1772-
    1790)
Salisbury, N.C.
Bibl. 21

Obadiah W. Towson (b. 1791)
Baltimore, Md. (c. 1813-1819)
Philadelphia, Pa. (c. 1819-
    1824)

Bibl. 3, 23, 24, 25, 29, 36, 38, 44

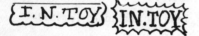

Philemon Towson (b. 1769-d. 1843)
Baltimore, Md. (c. 1790-)
Bibl. 38

Towzell
(See Touzell)

Toy & Wilson (c. 1790)
Abingdon, Md.
Joseph Toy
William Wilson
Bibl. 25, 44

Isaac Nicholas Toy (b. 1771-d. 1830)
Abingdon, Md. (c. 1790-1795)
Bibl. 24, 25, 29, 38, 44

Joseph Toy (b. 1748-d. 1826, c. 1776-1795)
Hartford, Conn.
Abingdon, Md.
Candy, Md.
Toy & Wilson (c. 1790)
Bibl. 25, 29, 38, 44, 54

J. F. Tozer (c. 1850)
Binghamton, N.Y.
Bibl. 20

Junius F. Tozer (c. 1847-1850-)
Binghamton, N.Y. (c. 1850)
Rochester, N.Y.
Bibl. 20, 41, 44

Tracy & Hawley (c. 1848)
Cazenovia, N.Y.
A. Fayette Tracy
Bibl. 20

A. Fayette Tracy
Oswego, N.Y. (c. 1844)
Cazenovia, N.Y. (c. 1848)
Tracy & Hawley (c. 1848-)
Bibl. 20

C. & E. Tracy (c. 1847-1850)
Philadelphia, Pa.
Charles Tracy
E. Tracy
Bibl. 3

Charles Tracy (c. 1842-1850)
Philadelphia, Pa.
C. & E. Tracy (c. 1847-1850)
Bibl. 3

E. Tracy (c. 1841-1850)
Philadelphia, Pa.
C. & E. Tracy (c. 1847-1850)
Bibl. 3

Elisha C. Tracy (c. 1810)
Cooperstown, N.Y.
Bibl. 20

Erastus Tracy (b. 1768-d. 1795)
New London, Conn.
Norwich, Conn.
Bibl. 16, 23, 28, 36, 44

Gurdon (Gordon) Tracy (b. 1767-d. 1792)
Norwich, Conn. (1781-1791)
New London, Conn. (after 1791)
Bibl. 16, 23, 24, 25, 28, 36, 44, 67

William Tracy (c. 1843-1850)
Philadelphia, Pa.
Bibl. 3

Peter C. Trahn (Thran) (c. 1843-1849)
Philadelphia, Pa.
Bibl. 3

J. Trast (c. 1850)
Syracuse, N.Y.
Bibl. 20

Traux
(See Henry R. Truax)

Samuel Treadway (c. 1848)
St. Louis, Mo.
Bibl. 54

—— Treadwell
Boston, Mass.
Churchill & Treadwell (c. 1805-1813)
Bibl. 4, 24, 25, 28, 29, 36, 44

—— Treadwell
New York, N.Y.
Gelston & Treadwell (c. 1836)
Bibl. 23, 25, 28, 35, 36, 44, 83

Oren B. Treadwell (c. 1847-1849)
Philadelphia, Pa.
Bibl. 3

Arthur Trench (d. 1838)
Raleigh, N.C. (c. 1833-1838)
Bibl. 21

Trenchard & Watson (c. 1800)
Philadelphia, Pa.
James Trenchard (?)
—— Watson
Bibl. 3

James Trenchard (c. 1777-1793)
Philadelphia, Pa.
Trenchard & Watson (c. 1800) (?)
Bibl. 3

John Trenson (c. 1817)
Philadelphia, Pa.
Bibl. 3

Daniel Trezevant (Trezvant) (d. 1768)
Charleston, S.C. (c. 1757-1768)
Bibl. 5, 28, 44, 54

Christian Tripler (c. 1794-1797)
New York, N.Y.
Bibl. 23, 36, 44

William Troll (c. 1810-1811)
Philadelphia, Pa.
Bibl. 3, 23, 36, 44

Peter Trone (c. 1844)
Philadelphia, Pa.
Bibl. 3

James Troth
Easton, Md. (c. 1802)
Pittsburgh, Pa.
Bibl. 3, 23, 36, 38, 44

William Troth (c. 1804-1819)
Philadelphia, Pa.
Bibl. 3, 23

William Troth (c. 1833-1835)
Philadelphia, Pa.
Bibl. 3

Trott & Brooks (c. 1798-)
New London, Conn.
John Proctor Trott

—— Brooks
Bibl. 16, 23, 25, 28, 29, 36, 44

T & B

Trott & Cleveland
   (c. 1792-   )
New London, Conn.
John Proctor Trott
William Cleveland
Bibl. 16, 23, 25, 28, 29, 36, 44

T. & C.

George Trott (c. 1765)
Boston, Mass.
Bibl. 28, 44

John P. Trott & Son (c. 1820)
New London, Conn.
Bibl. 23, 24, 25, 36, 44

J. P. T. & SON

John Proctor Trott (b. 1769-d.
   1852)
New London, Conn.
Trott & Cleveland
   (c. 1792-   )
Trott & Brooks (c. 1798-   )
John P. Trott & Son (c. 1820)
Currier & Trott (c. 1836)
Bibl. 2, 15, 23, 24, 25, 28, 29,
   36, 44

J: P. TROTT   J. P. T.

   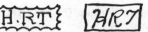

Jonathan Trott (b. 1730-d.
   1815)
Boston, Mass. (before 1772)
Norwich, Conn. (after 1772)
New London, Conn. (c. 1790-
   1815)
Bibl. 2, 15, 16, 23, 24, 25, 28,
   29, 36, 44

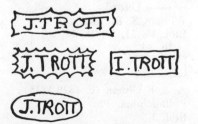

Jonathan Trott Jr. (b. 1771-d.
   1813)
New London, Conn. (c. 1800)
Bibl. 15, 16, 23, 25, 28, 29, 36,
   44

I. T.

Thomas Trott (b. 1701-d. 1777)
Boston, Mass.
Bibl. 23, 24, 28, 29, 44

T. T

Trotter & Alexander (c. 1837-
   1838)
Charlotte, N.C.
Thomas Trotter
Samuel P. Alexander
Bibl. 21

Trotter & Huntington (c. 1828-
   1832)
Charlotte, N.C.
Thomas Trotter
John Huntington
Bibl. 21

Jeremiah Trotter (c. 1831-
   1844)
Cincinnati, Ohio
Bibl. 34

Thomas Trotter (b. 1800-d.
   1865)
Charlotte, N.C.
Thomas Trotter & Co. (c. 1827-
   1828)
Trotter & Huntington (c. 1828-
   1832)
Trotter & Alexander (c. 1837-
   1838)
Bibl. 21

Thomas Trotter & Co. (c. 1827-
   1828)
Charlotte, N.C.
Bibl. 21

A. W. Trou (b. 1818-d. 1854)
Charleston, S.C. (c. 1846-1854)
Bibl. 5

George Trout (c. 1837-1843)
Philadelphia, Pa.
Bibl. 3

Truax & Clench (c. 1813-   )
Albany, N.Y.
Henry R. Truax (?)
Benjamin Clench
Bibl. 20

Dewitt Truax (c. 1842-1843)
Utica, N.Y.
Bibl. 18, 20

Henry R. Truax (Traux)
   (b. 1760-d. 1834)
Albany, N.Y. (c. 1815-
   1819-   )
Truax & Clench (c.
   1813-   ) (?)
Bibl. 4, 15, 20, 23, 24, 25, 28,
   29, 36, 44

H.RT   HRT

Isaac Truax
Albany, N.Y.
Isaac & Henry Truax (c. 1796)
Bibl. 20

Isaac & Henry Truax (c. 1796)
Albany, N.Y.
Bibl. 20

Richard Trumbul (Trumbull)
   (b. 1742-d. 1815)
Boston, Mass.
Bibl. 23, 36, 44

Armistead Truslow (c. 1813-
   1825)
Lynchburg, Va.
Bibl. 19, 54

A. T.

Benoni Tucker (c. 1858-1860)
Utica, N.Y.
Bibl. 18

Daniel Tucker (c. 1781)
Portland, Me.
Bibl. 23, 36, 44

John Walter Tucker (c. 1803)
New York, N.Y.
Bibl. 21, 44

J W TUCKER

M. Tucker (c. 1840)
Location unknown
Bibl. 24

Tuells
(See Johonnot & Tuells)

B. Tuells (c. 1818)
Palmyra, N.Y.
Bibl. 20

Alonzo B. Turner (c. 1838-1844)
Watertown, N.Y.
Sigourney & Turner (c. 1838-1842)
Bibl. 20

Ansel Turner (b. 1789-d. 1814)
Savannah, Ga.
Bibl. 17

Charles Turner (d. 1776)
Alexandria, Va. (c. 1760-1766)
Bibl. 19, 54

Franklin Turner (c. 1812-1823)
Cheraw, N.C.
Fayetteville, N.C.
Wadesboro, N.C.
Clark & Turner (c. 1820-1823)
Bibl. 5, 21, 44, 54

TURNER

J. A. S. Turner & Co. (c. 1833)
Columbus, Ga.
Bibl. 17

James Turner (d. 1759)
Boston, Mass. (c. 1748)
Philadelphia, Pa. (c. 1758)
Bibl. 3, 24, 25, 28, 29, 44

William Turner (c. 1847-1850)
Philadelphia, Pa.
Bibl. 3

Thomas M. Turpin (c. 1813)
Richmond, Va.
Bibl. 19

A. B. Turrell (c. 1827-1828)
Penn Yan, N.Y.
Bibl. 20

Septimus Tustin (c. 1814)
Baltimore, Md.
Bibl. 38

Christopher Tuthill (c. 1730)
Philadelphia, Pa.
Bibl. 3, 23, 28, 36, 44

John Tuthill (c. 1831)
New York, N.Y.
Bibl. 15

Bethuel Tuttle (b. 1779-d. 1813)
New Haven, Conn. (c. 1802-1818)
Merriman & Tuttle (c. 1802)
Marcus Merriman & Co. (c. 1802-1817)
Bibl. 16, 23, 28, 36, 44

William Tuttle (b. 1800-d. 1849)
New Haven, Conn.
Suffield, Conn.
Bibl. 16, 23, 28, 36, 44

Weston Weed Tuxford (c. 1837)
Clarksville, Ga.
Bibl. 17

Twedy & Barrowss
Location unknown
Bibl. 15, 44

TWEDY & BARROWSS

M. Twelbib (c. 1828-1833)
Philadelphia, Pa.
Bibl. 3

Spencer Twitchel (c. 1832)
New York, N.Y
Bibl. 15

Marcus Twitchell (c. 1829-   )
Utica, N.Y.
Bibl. 18, 20

William Twybill (c. 1841)
Philadelphia, Pa.
Bibl. 3

Andrew Tyler (b. 1682-d. 1741)
Boston, Mass.
Bibl. 2, 4, 15, 23, 24, 25, 28, 29, 33, 36, 44, 50, 54, 70

D. M. Tyler (c. 1810)
Boston, Mass.
Bibl. 23, 24, 25, 29, 36, 44

D. M. TYLER

David Tyler (b. 1760-d. 1804)
Boston, Mass.
Bibl. 4, 15, 23, 24, 25, 28, 29, 36, 44, 54

DT   DT

George Tyler (b. 1740-d. 1785)
Boston, Mass.
Bibl. 15, 23, 24, 25, 28, 29, 36, 44

GT

John H. Tyler & Co. (c. 1840)
Boston, Mass.
John Henry Tyler
Bibl. 24, 25, 44

JOHN H. TYLER & CO.

John Henry Tyler (d. 1883)
Richmond, Va.
John H. Tyler & Co. (c. 1840)
Mitchell & Tyler (c. 1845-1866)
Bibl. 19

John H. Tyler & Co.

A. B. Tyrrel(l)
Location unknown
Bibl. 15, 44

Leech Tyson (c. 1823-1831)
Philadelphia, Pa.
Bibl. 3

Frederick Ubelin (c. 1773)
Philadelphia, Pa.
Bibl. 3, 23, 36, 44

————— Udall (early 19th century)
Garrettsville, Ohio
Hiram, Ohio
Bibl. 34

Ufford & Burdick (c. 1812-1814-   )
New Haven, Conn.
————— Ufford
William S. Burdick
Bibl. 16, 23, 24, 25, 28, 29, 36, 44

U & B

A. & J. Ulman (c. 1829-1835)
Philadelphia, Pa.
Bibl. 3

J. Ulman (c. 1829-1830)
Philadelphia, Pa.
A. & J. Ulman (c. 1829-1835)
Bibl. 3

Jacob Ulman (c. 1843)
Philadelphia, Pa.
Bibl. 3

Underhill & Vernon (c. 1786)
New York, N.Y.
Thomas Underhill
John Vernon
Bibl. 4, 15, 24, 25, 28, 29,
   36, 44, 54

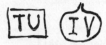

Andrew Underhill (c. 1780-
   1788)
New York, N.Y.
Bibl. 15, 23, 24, 28, 29, 35,
   36, 44, 72

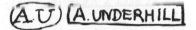

Thomas Underhill (c. 1787)
New York, N.Y.
Underhill & Vernon (c. 1786)
Bibl. 4, 15, 23, 24, 25, 28, 29,
   35, 36, 44, 83

T U

John Underwood (c. 1797-
   1798)
Philadelphia, Pa.
Bibl. 3, 23, 36, 44

George M. Updike (c. 1848)
Philadelphia, Pa.
Bibl. 3

Upson
(See Pelletreau & Upson)

George Urwiler (c. 1814-1844)
Philadelphia, Pa.
Bibl. 3

J. Urwiler (c. 1831)
Philadelphia, Pa.
Bibl. 3

Austin Usher (c. 1842)
Philadelphia, Pa.
Bibl. 3

Elijah M. Vail (c. 1835-
   1850-   )
Albany, N.Y.

Troy, N.Y.
Bibl. 20, 23, 36, 44

Victor Vaissiere (c. 1816-1819)
New York, N.Y.
Bibl. 15, 23, 36, 44

Philip Valenti (c. 1860-1879)
Bowling Green, Ky.
Fuselli & Valenti
McLure & Valenti (c. 1867)
Bibl. 54

Dennis Valentine (c. 1850)
Syracuse, N.Y.
Barney & Valentine
Bibl. 20

Peter Valet (c. 1787)
New York, N.Y.
Bibl. 23, 36, 44

William Vallant (c. 1752)
Philadelphia, Pa.
Bibl. 44

Vallee & Co. (c. 1817)
New York, N.Y.
Bibl. 15

Antonie Valleé (c. 1822)
New Orleans, La.
Bibl. 23, 36, 44

F. D. Vallee (c. 1835)
Philadelphia, Pa.
Bibl. 3

Benjamin F. Vallet (c. 1833-
   1850)
Kingston, N.Y.
Bibl. 20

John Vanall (c. 1749-1752)
Charleston, S.C.
Bibl. 5, 25, 44

I VANALL

James Vanarsdale (c. 1849)
Philadelphia, Pa.
Bibl. 3

John Van Bergen (c. 1813-
   1822)
Albany, N.Y.
Bibl. 4, 20, 23, 28, 36, 44

Peter Van Beuren (c. 1795-
   1798)
New York, N.Y.

Bibl. 4, 23, 24, 25, 28, 29, 36,
   44

William Van Beuren (c. 1790-
   1796)
Newark, N.J.
New York, N.Y.
Bibl. 15, 23, 24, 28, 29, 36, 44,
   46

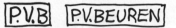

Peter Van Bomell (c. 1792-
   1803)
Poughkeepsie, N.Y.
Bibl. 20

Cornelius Vander Burgh
   (Vanderbrugh) (b. 1653-d.
   1699)
New York, N.Y.
Bibl. 15, 23, 24, 25, 29, 35, 44,
   54

J. Vanderhan (Venderhaul) (c.
   1740)
Philadelphia, Pa.
Bibl. 23, 24, 28, 29, 36

I V

John G. Vanderleyden
   (c. 1842-1845)
Utica, N.Y
Bibl. 18, 20

Vanderslice & Co. (c. 1860-
   1906)
San Francisco, Cal.
Bibl. 54

W. Vanderslice (c. 1840)
Philadelphia, Pa.
Bibl. 3

Jacobus Vanderspiegel (b.
1668-d. 1708)
Albany, N.Y.
New York, N.Y.
Bibl. 2, 3, 15, 23, 24, 25, 28, 29,
30, 35, 36, 39, 44, 54

Johannes Vander Spiegel (b.
1666-d. 1716)
New York, N.Y.
Bibl. 4, 23, 28, 29, 30, 36

Peter Van Dyck (Van Dyke)
(b. 1684-d. 1750)
New York, N.Y.
Bibl. 2, 4, 15, 23, 24, 25, 28, 29,
30, 35, 36, 44, 50, 54

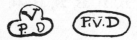

Richard Van Dyck (b. 1717-d.
1770)
New York, N.Y.
Bibl. 15, 23, 24, 25, 28, 29, 30,
35, 36

Van Dyke
(See Van Dyck)

George Vane (c. 1752-1781)
Charleston, S.C.
Bibl. 5, 54

John Van Hook Jr. (c. 1816-
1820)
Hillsboro, N.C.
William Huntington & Co.
Bibl. 21

David Vanhorn (c. 1801)
Philadelphia, Pa.
Bibl. 3, 23, 36, 44

Shelby Van Hoy (19th century)
Shelbyville, Ky.
Bibl. 54

Peter Van Inburgh (b. 1689-d.
1740)
New York, N.Y.
Bibl. 25, 35, 44, 83

James Vanlone (c. 1775)
Philadelphia, Pa.
Bibl. 3

Jan Van Loon (c. 1678)
Albany, N.Y.
Bibl. 54

Van Ness & Bwistrand
(c. 1844)
New York, N.Y.
Peter Van Ness
——— Bwistrand
Bibl. 23

Van Ness & Waterman
(c. 1835)
(Waterman & Van Ness)
New York, N.Y.
Peter Van Ness
——— Waterman
Bibl. 23, 24, 25, 28, 29, 36, 44

V & W

Van Ness, Wood & Co.
(c. 1846)
New York, N.Y.
Peter Van Ness
——— Wood
Bibl. 23

Peter Van Ness (Vanness)
(c. 1833-1841)
New York, N.Y.
Van Ness & Waterman
(c. 1835)
Van Ness & Bwistrand
(c. 1844)
Van Ness, Wood & Co.
(c. 1846)
Bibl. 15, 23

Van Nieukirke
Van Niewkirke
(See Newkirke)
(See Niewkerk)

Kiliaen van Rensselaer
(b. 1663-d. 1719)
Albany, N.Y.
Watervliet, N.Y.
Bibl. 20, 54

Nicholas Van Rensselaer
(c. 1760-1770)
New York, N.Y.
Albany, N.Y. (?)
Bibl. 15, 25, 44

N V

Tunis Van Riper (c. 1813-
1829)
New York, N.Y.
Bibl. 15, 23, 25, 36, 44

T V R

Van Sanford & Cluet (c. 1725)
Albany, N.Y.
John Cluet
Bibl. 20

Richard Vansant
(See Richard Vincent)

Vansant & Company (c. 1850-
1880)
Philadelphia, Pa.
Bibl. 15, 25, 44

V&CO

G. Van Schaick (c. 1800-
1840)
Albany, N.Y.
Bibl. 25, 28, 29, 44

G V" Schaick

James Vanstavoren (c. 1818)
Philadelphia, Pa.
Bibl. 3

John Van Steenbergh (Jr.)
(c. 1772-1782)
Kingston, N.Y.
Bibl. 15, 20, 25, 44

John S. Van Steenbergh
(c. 1820)
Kingston, N.Y.
Bibl. 20

Peter Van Steenbergh (c. 1780)
Kingston, N.Y.
Bibl. 20

John L. Vantine (c. 1829-1847)
Philadelphia, Pa.
Bibl. 3

Henry Van Veghten (c. 1760,
d. 1787)
Albany, N.Y.
Bibl. 20, 23, 25, 36, 44

Van Vliet & Cromwell
(c. 1844)
Poughkeepsie, N.Y.
B. C. Van Vliet
——— Cromwell
Bibl. 20

B. C. Van Vliet (c. 1830-1847)
Poughkeepsie, N.Y.
Van Vliet & Cromwell
(c. 1844)
Bibl. 20, 23, 29, 36

| B VAN VLEIT |

Van Voorhis & Coley (c. 1786)
New York, N.Y.
Daniel Van Voorhis
William Coley
Reuben Harmon
Bibl. 4, 23, 24, 25, 28, 36

| V & C |

Van Voorhis & Schanck
(c. 1791-1792)
New York, N.Y.
Daniel Van Voorhis
Garret Schanck
Bibl. 23, 24, 25, 29, 35, 36

| V V & S | | V & S |

Van Voorhis, Schanck &
McCall (c. 1800)
Albany, N.Y.
Bibl. 25, 44

Van Voorhis & Son (c. 1798)
New York, N.Y.

Bibl. 23, 24, 25, 29, 35, 36

| V. V. & S |

——— Van Voorhis (c. 1843)
Utica, N.Y.
Brooks & Van Voorhis
(c. 1843)
Bibl. 18, 20

Daniel Van Voorhis (b. 1751-d.
1824)
Princeton, N.J.
New York, N.Y.
Philadelphia, Pa.
Burlington, Vt.
Rupert, Vt.
Underhill, Vt.
Daniel Van Voorhis & William
Coley (c. 1785-1786)
Van Voorhis & Coley (c. 1786)
Van Voorhis & Schanck
(c. 1791-1792)
Bibl. 3, 4, 15, 23, 28, 29, 30, 35,
36, 46, 54, 74, 81

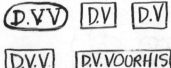

Daniel Van Voorhis & William
Coley (c. 1785-1786)
New York, N.Y.
Bibl. 54

Van Wyck & Pelletreau
(See Pelletreau & Van Wyck)

Stephen Van Wyck (c. 1825)
New York, N.Y.
Pelletreau & Van Wyck
Bibl. 24, 25, 44

| S VAN WYCK |

John Van Zandt (c. 1842-
1848)
Albany, N.Y.
Bibl. 20

Joseph Varley (b. 1809)
Utica, N.Y. (c. 1858-1860)
Bibl. 18

John Varney (d. 1802)
Philadelphia, Pa.
Bibl. 3, 23, 36, 44

J. Varnier (c. 1800-1801)
Philadelphia, Pa.

S. Perpignan & J. Varnier
Bibl. 3, 23

Robert Varrick (c. 1844-1845)
Philadelphia, Pa.
Bibl. 3, 23

D. Vaughan (c. 1695)
Philadelphia, Pa.
Bibl. 3

George C. Vaughn (c. 1840-
1844)
Buffalo, N.Y.
Chase & Vaughn (c. 1842)?
Bibl. 20

Vautroit and Meyers (c.
1860-   )
Warren, Ohio
Bibl. 89

Vautroma (Vautroit) &
Ackley (c. 1850)
Warren, Ohio
Bibl. 89

Vautrot (Vautroit) (c. 1850)
Warren, Ohio
Bibl. 89

Veal and Glaze (c. 1838-1841)
Columbia, S.C.
John Veal (Sr.)
William Glaze
Bibl. 5, 44, 54

| VEAL & GLAZE |

John Veal (Sr.) (c. 1827-1857)
Columbia, S.C.
Veal & Glaze (c. 1838-1841)
Bibl. 5, 44

| J. VEAL |

Joseph E. Veal (c. 1848-
1853-   )
Madison, Ga.
Bibl. 17

Joseph Veazie (c. 1774)
Boston, Mass.
Bibl. 2

Joseph Veazie (c. 1815-1824)
Providence, R.I.
Samuel & Joseph Veazie
(c. 1820)
Bibl. 23, 28, 36, 44

Samuel & Joseph Veazie
(c. 1820)

Providence, R.I.
Bibl. 28

Anthony Veeter (c. 1825)
Shelbyville, Ky.
Bibl. 32, 54, 68

Venderhaul
(See Vanderhan)

Emanuel Vener (c. 1826)
Madison, Ga.
Bibl. 17

Bordo Vensal (c. 1850)
Philadelphia, Pa.
Bibl. 3

Vent (c. 1810)
Location unknown
Bibl. 24

Peter Vergereau (b. 1700-d.
   1755)
New York, N.Y.
Bibl. 4, 15, 24, 25, 28, 29, 35,
   36, 44, 54, 83

Vernon & Co. (c. 1806-1807)
Charleston, S.C.
Nathaniel Vernon
Bibl. 25

Vernon & Park (c. 1815)
Pittsburgh, Pa.
Nathaniel Vernon
—————— Park
Bibl. 23, 36, 44

Daniel Vernon (b. 1716)
Newport, R.I.
Bibl. 28

John (I.) Vernon (c. 1768-
   1815)
New York, N.Y.
Underhill & Vernon (c. 1786)
John Vernon & Co. (c. 1796)
Bibl. 4, 15, 23, 24, 25, 28, 29,
   35, 36, 39, 44, 54, 83

John Vernon & Co. (c. 1796)
New York, N.Y.
Bibl. 23, 28, 36

Nathaniel Vernon (b. 1777-d.
   1843)
Charleston, S.C. (w. 1808-
   1835)
Nathaniel Vernon & Co. (c.
   1802-1808)
Vernon & Co. (c. 1806-1807)
Bibl. 5, 23, 24, 25, 28, 29, 54

| N VERNON | | VERNON |

| N V |

Nathaniel Vernon & Co.
   (c. 1802-1808)
Charleston, S.C.
Bibl. 5, 23, 24, 25, 36, 44

| N VERNON & CO |

| N VERNON & CO |

Samuel Vernon (b. 1683-d.
   1737)
Newport, R.I.
Bibl. 2, 15, 23, 25, 28, 29, 36,
   39, 44, 50, 54, 69

Samuel Verree (c. 1804-1816)
Charleston, S.C.
Bibl. 5

Edward William Victor
   (b. 1819, c. 1844-1849)
Lynchburg, Va. (c. 1844-1850)
Bibl. 19

John Victor (b. 1793-d. 1845)
Lynchburg, Va.
Williams & Victor (c. 1814-
   1845)
Bibl. 9, 54

John Vignes (c. 1820)
Kingston, N.Y.
Bibl. 20

| J. VIGNES |

Vilant
(See Vivant)

R. H. L. Villard (c. 1833-
   1835)
Washington, D.C.
Georgetown, Md.

Bibl. 15, 23, 24, 25, 29, 36, 44

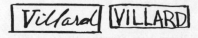

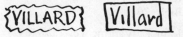

L. Villenjer (c. 1845)
St. Louis, Mo.
Bibl. 54

(Monsieur) Antoine Claude
   Vincent (c. 1790)
Gallipolis, Ohio
Bibl. 34

Richard Vincent (Vansant)
   (c. 1799)
Baltimore, Md.
Bibl. 23, 25, 28, 29, 36, 38, 44

| R: V |

David Vinton (c. 1790-1792)
Boston, Mass.
Providence, R.I.
Bibl. 23, 24, 25, 28, 36, 54

| D. V | ?

J. A. & S. S. Virgin (c. 1834-
   1837)
Macon, Ga.
Jonathan Ambrose Virgin
Samuel Stanley Virgin
Bibl. 17

| J A & S S VIRGIN |

Virgin(s) & Stringfellow
   (c. 1837)
Macon, Ga.
Samuel Stanley Virgin(s)
Samuel Stringfellow (?)
Bibl. 17

Jonathan Ambrose Virgin
   (b. 1808-d. 1881)
Macon, Ga.
J. A. & S. S. Virgin (c. 1834-
   1837)
Bibl. 17

Samuel Stanley Virgin(s)
   (b. 1810-d. 1887)
Macon, Ga. (c. 1833, c. 1840-
   1849)
Columbus, Ga.
J. A. & S. S. Virgin (c. 1834-
   1837)

Bruno & Virgins (c. 1840-
1849)
Virgins & Stringfellow
Bibl. 17

W. M. Virgin (c. 1830)
Location unknown
Bibl. 24, 28, 44

W. M. VIRGIN

———— Virney (c. 1844-1845)
Louisville, Ky.
Bibl. 32

William Vivant (Vilant)
(c. 1725)
Philadelphia, Pa.
Bibl. 3, 15, 23, 24, 25, 28, 29,
36, 39, 44, 54, 78, 81

Elias Alexander Vogler
(b. 1825-d. 1876)
Salem, N.C.
Bibl. 21

John Vogler (b. 1783-d. 1881)
Salem, N.C.
Bibl. 21, 25, 44

J. VOGLER

John Utzmann Vogler (c. 1812-
1856)
Salisbury, N.C.
Bibl. 21

Ignatius Christian Vogt (c.
1764)
New York State
Bibl. 3

Henry Voight (Voigt) (c. 1785-
1791, d. 1814)
Philadelphia, Pa.
Bibl. 3

Sebastian Voight (c. 1793-1800)
Philadelphia, Pa.
Bibl. 3

Henry Voigt
(See Henry Voight)

Thomas H. Voigt (c. 1811-
1835)

Philadelphia, Pa.
Bibl. 3

Frederick C. Van Borstel
(d. 1876)
Anderson, S.C. (c. 1848-1876)
Athens, Ga.
Bibl. 5, 17

Hermanus Vondyk (c. 1820-
1822)
Philadelphia, Pa.
Bibl. 3

Jacob Vonneida (c. 1837-
1840)
Philadelphia, Pa.
Bibl. 3

Abraham Voorhees (c. 1840)
New Brunswick, N.J.
Bibl. 15, 44, 46

A. VOORHEES

John O. Vorse (c. 1841)
Palmyra, N.Y.
Bibl. 20

John Hobart Vosburgh (b.
1830)
Utica, N.Y. (c. 1852-1860)
Bibl. 18

Lewis C. Voute (Vouty)
(c. 1826-1850)
Bridgeton, N.J.
Philadelphia, Pa.
Bibl. 3, 46, 54

Jacob I. Vrooman (c. 1814)
Ithaca, N.Y.
Bibl. 20

Alexander Vuille (c. 1766)
Baltimore, Md.
Bibl. 3

Waage & Norton (c. 1798)
Philadelphia, Pa.
———— Waage
Thomas Norton
Bibl. 3

F. W. Wachner (c. 1791-1819)
New York, N.Y.
Bibl. 23, 36, 44

Noel Waddill (b. 1753-d.
1833)
Petersburg, Va.
Hill & Waddill (c. 1780-1782)
Bibl. 19, 23, 36

William Waddill
Williamsburg, Va. (c. 1767-
1772)
Richmond, Va. (c. 1785-   )
Petersburg, Va. (c. 1785-1795)
Bibl. 19

Wade
(See Hogan & Wade)

Jacob B. Wade (c. 1820-1822)
Philadelphia, Pa.
Bibl. 3

Nathaniel Wade (c. 1793)
Newfield, Conn.
Bibl. 61

Thomas Waglin (c. 1818-1819)
Philadelphia, Pa.
Bibl. 3, 23, 36

Thomas Wagstaff (c. 1791)
New York, N.Y.
Bibl. 36, 44

Isaiah Wagster (c. 1776-1793)
Baltimore, Md.
Bibl. 25, 29, 38, 44

I W

Wait & Wright (c. 1837)
Philadelphia, Pa.
Bibl. 3, 23, 36, 44

Edgar S. Wait (c. 1848)
Louisville, Ky.
Bibl. 32

L. D. Wait (c. 1838-1847)
Skaneatcles, N.Y.
Bibl. 20

Alva Waite (c. 1840)
Ravenna, Ohio
Bibl. 34

Edwin F. Waite (c. 1840)
Ravenna, Ohio
Bibl. 34

George Waite (c. 1847-1850)
Philadelphia, Pa.
Bibl. 3

John Waite (b. 1742-d. 1817)
Kingston, R.I.
Bibl. 24, 25, 28, 29, 39

I. WAITE

J WAITE   J W

Jonathan Waite (b. 1730-d.
1822)

Wickford, R.I.
Bibl. 28

William Waite (b. 1730-d.
1826)
Cambridge, N.Y.
Little Rest, R.I.
Wickford, R.I.
Bibl. 21, 24, 25, 28, 29, 44

W: WAITE

Frederick Waitt (c. 1843-1850)
Philadelphia, Pa.
Bibl. 3

Wakefield & Woodward
Great Falls, N.H.
Bibl. 15, 44

WAKEFIELD & WOODWARD

Charles Wakefield (c. 1835)
Philadelphia, Pa.
Bibl. 3

Thomas Wakefield (c. 1837)
Philadelphia, Pa.
Bibl. 3

Walcott & Gelston
(See Wolcott & Gelston)

Henry D. Walcott (Wolcott)
(c. 1797-1830)
Boston, Mass.
Walcott & Gelston (c. 1824)
Bibl. 28

D. Waldron (c. 1789)
New York, N.Y.
Bibl. 23, 24, 25, 29, 36, 44

D. WALDRON

Walker & Peak (c. 1843)
Philadelphia, Pa.
Bibl. 3

Walker
(See Barnhurst & Walker)

Albert Walker
Brockport, N.Y. (c. 1831)
Rochester, N.Y. (c. 1834)
Bibl. 20

Calvin Walker (c. 1831)
Philadelphia, Pa.
Bibl. 3

George Walker (c. 1797-1822)
Philadelphia, Pa.
William & George Walker
(c. 1795-1796)

Bibl. 3, 15, 23, 24, 25, 28, 29,
36, 44, 46

G. WALKER

Hannah Walker (c. 1816-
1817)
Philadelphia, Pa.
Bibl. 3, 23, 24, 25, 29, 36, 44

H.WALKER

James Walker
Fredericksburg, Va. (c. 1791-
1802)
Richmond, Va. (c. 1805)
McCabe & Walker (c. 1805-
1806)
Bibl. 19

John Walker Jr. (c. 1798-1833)
Philadelphia, Pa.
Bibl. 3, 23, 36

Jonathan Walker (b. 1797,
c. 1812)
Baltimore, Md.
Bibl. 38

Julius Walker (c. 1840-1848)
Buffalo, N.Y.
Bibl. 20

L. (I.) Walker (c. 1825)
Boston, Mass.
Bibl. 24, 25, 44

L. Walker   Joys Building

Richard Walker (c. 1837-1846)
Philadelphia, Pa.
Bibl. 3

W. & G. Walker (c. 1795)
Philadelphia, Pa.
Bibl. 44

William Walker (c. 1793-1816)
Philadelphia, Pa.
William & George Walker
(c. 1795-1796)
Bibl. 3, 15, 23, 24, 25, 28, 29,
36, 44, 80

W WALKER

William & George Walker
(c. 1795-1796)
Philadelphia, Pa.
Bibl. 3, 15, 23, 36

James Wallace Jr. (c. 1739)
Edenton, N.C.
Bibl. 21

William F. Wallace
Westerly, R.I.
Bibl. 28, 44

John Wallen (c. 1763)
Philadelphia, Pa.
Bibl. 25, 44

J. WALLEN

John Waller (c. 1763)
Philadelphia, Pa.
Bibl. 3, 23, 36

Robert Wallin (c. 1845-1850)
Philadelphia, Pa.
Freeman & Wallin (c. 1850)
Bibl. 3

Thomas Wallis (c. 1804-1808)
Philadelphia, Pa.
Bibl. 3, 23, 36, 44

Richard Waln (c. 1837)
Philadelphia, Pa.
Bibl. 3

John Walraven (b. 1771-d.
1814)
Baltimore, Md.
Bibl. 15, 24, 25, 28, 29, 38, 44

J Walraven

JW

Walsh (c. 1780)
Location unknown
Bibl. 24, 28

WALSH

Abm. Walter (c. 1849-1850)
Philadelphia, Pa.
Bibl. 3

H. N. Walter (c. 1833-
1850-   )
Norwich, N.Y.
Bibl. 20

Jacob Walter (b. 1782-d. 1865)
Baltimore, Md. (c. 1815)
Bibl. 15, 24, 25, 29, 38

J. WALTER

John J. Walter (c. 1837)
Canton, Ohio
Bibl. 34

Joseph M. Walter (c. 1835)
Baltimore, Md.
Bibl. 15, 44

JOS M. WALTER

Edward Walters (c. 1847)
Philadelphia, Pa.
Bibl. 3

John Walters (c. 1779-1784)
Philadelphia, Pa.
Bibl. 3

John J. Walto (c. 1849-1850)
Philadelphia, Pa.
Bibl. 3

Daniel Walton (c. 1816-1817)
Philadelphia, Pa.
Bibl. 3, 23, 36, 44

Daniel Walworth (b. 1760-d. 1830)
Middletown, Conn. (c. 1785)
Bibl. 16, 23, 28, 36, 44

Edward Wangelin
Cleveland, Ohio
Schroeder & Wangelin (c. 1844-1850)
Bibl. 89

Lewis Wangelin
Cleveland, Ohio
Schroeder & Wangelin (c. 1844-1850)
Bibl. 89

Edward Wanton (c. 1799-1810, d. 1811)
Richmond, Va.
Bibl. 19

Nathaniel Waples (c. 1816-1819)
Philadelphia, Pa.
Bibl. 3

Ward
(See Foster & Ward)
(See Norman & Ward)

Ward & Bartholomew (c. 1804-1809)
Hartford, Conn.
James Ward
Roswell Bartholomew

Bibl. 15, 16, 23, 24, 25, 28, 29, 36, 39, 61

Ward, Bartholomew & Brainard (c. 1809-1830)
Hartford, Conn.
James Ward
Roswell Bartholomew
Charles Brainard
Bibl. 16, 23, 25, 28, 36, 44

Ward & Cox (c. 1811-1818)
Philadelphia, Pa.
John Ward
John Cox
Bibl. 3, 4, 23, 28, 36, 44, 54

Ward & Cox

Ward & Govett (Gavett) (c. 1813-1814)
Philadelphia, Pa.
John Ward
—— Govett
Bibl. 3, 23, 36, 44

Ward & Hughes (c. 1806)
Middletown, Conn.
John Ward
Edmund Hughes
Bibl. 16, 23, 36, 44

Ward & Jones (19th century)
Location unknown
Bibl. 28

Ward & Miller (c. 1822-1824)
Philadelphia, Pa.
John Ward
William Miller
Bibl. 3, 23, 44

Ward & Rich (c. 1832-1835)
Boston, Mass.
—— Ward
Obadiah Rich
Bibl. 4, 23, 25, 28, 36

—— Ward (c. 1774-1810)
Philadelphia, Pa.
Bibl. 15, 28

WARD

Ambrose Ward (b. 1735-d. 1808)
New Haven, Conn.
Cutler, Silliman, Ward & Co. (c. 1767)
Bibl. 16, 23, 25, 28, 36, 44

A W

Anthony Ward (c. 1717)
Philadelphia, Pa.
Bibl. 3

Benjamin Ward
Pasquotank County, N.C.
Bibl. 21

Benjamin Ward (c. 1845-1846)
Troy, N.Y.
Bibl. 20

Bil(l)ious Ward (b. 1729-d. 1777)
Guilford, Conn.
Middletown, Conn.
Bibl. 2, 15, 16, 23, 24, 25, 28, 29, 36, 44

Charles Ward (c. 1824)
Philadelphia, Pa.
Bibl. 3

Charles Ward (c. 1839-1840)
Philadelphia, Pa.
Bibl. 3

Edward H. Ward (c. 1839-1842)
Philadelphia, Pa.
Bibl. 3

Isaac Ward (c. 1811-1818)
Philadelphia, Pa.
Bibl. 3

J. Ward & Co. (c. 1843)
Philadelphia, Pa.
Bibl. 3

James Ward (b. 1768-d. 1856)
Guilford, Conn.
Hartford, Conn.
Beach & Ward (c. 1790-1797)
Ward & Bartholomew (c. 1804-1809)

Ward, Bartholomew &
Brainard (c. 1809-1830)
Bibl. 15, 16, 23, 24, 25, 28, 29,
36, 44, 61, 78

Jehu Ward (c. 1808-1848)
Philadelphia, Pa.
Jehu & W. L. Ward & Co.
(c. 1839-1850)
Bibl. 3, 80

J. WARD

Jehu & W. L. Ward & Co.
(c. 1839-1850)
Philadelphia, Pa.
Bibl. 3, 15, 25, 79

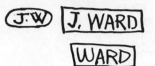

John Ward
Middletown, Conn (c. 1805)
Ward & Hughes (c. 1806)
Bibl. 16, 23, 25, 28, 36

John Ward (c. 1803-1839)
Philadelphia, Pa.
Ward & Cox (c. 1811-1818)
Ward & Govett (c. 1813-1814)
Ward & Miller (c. 1822-1824)
Bibl. 3, 23, 28, 29, 36, 39, 44

WARD, 67 MARKET ST.

Joshua Ward (c. 1826-1828)
Auburn, N.Y.
Bibl. 20

Macock Ward (b. 1705)
Wallingford, Conn.
Bibl. 28

Richard Ward (c. 1815)
Boston, Mass.
Jones & Ward (c. 1809)
Bibl. 23, 28, 36, 44, 72

R W

Samuel L. Ward (c. 1830-1835)
Boston, Mass.
Ward & Rich (c. 1832-1835)
Bibl. 23, 28, 36, 44

Thomas Ward (c. 1755)
Baltimore, Md.
Bibl. 38

Timothy Ward (b. 1742-d.
1768)
Middletown, Conn.
Bibl. 16, 23, 28, 36, 44

W. W. Ward (c. 1841)
Winnsboro, S.C.
Bibl. 5

William Ward (b. 1678-d.
1767)
Wallingford, Conn.
Bibl. 2, 28, 29

William Ward (b. 1705-d.
1761)
Guilford, Conn.
Bibl. 2, 15, 16, 23, 24, 28, 36,
44

W. W. | W. WARD

W. Ward

William Ward (c. 1797-1798)
New Windsor, N.Y.
Bibl. 20

William Ward (Jr.) (b. 1736-d.
1826)
Litchfield, Conn. (c. 1757)
Bibl. 15, 16, 23, 25, 28, 29, 36,
44, 54, 61

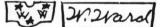

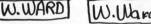

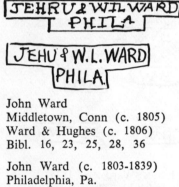

William H. Ward
Baltimore, Md.
Gould & Ward (c. 1850)
Gould, Stowell & Ward
(c. 1855-1858)
Bibl. 23, 36, 38, 44

William L. Ward (c. 1831-
1850)

Philadelphia, Pa.
Bibl. 3

Warden
(See Ayres & Warden)

——— Warden
Philadelphia, Pa.
Ayres & Warden (c. 1817)
Bibl. 3

Abijah B. Warden (c. 1842-
1850)
Philadelphia, Pa.
Bibl. 3, 15, 25, 44

WARDEN

Daniel Wardin (c. 1811)
Bridgeport, Conn.
Bibl. 16, 23, 28, 36, 44

J. Wardwool (c. 1791)
New York State
Bibl. 4

J. H. Warfield (c. 1827)
Baltimore, Md.
Bibl. 38

Warford
(See Bassett & Warford)

Joseph Warford (c. 1810)
Albany, N.Y.
Bibl. 15, 20, 25, 44

WARFORD

G. Waring (c. 1848)
Hudson, N.Y.
Bibl. 20

William Wark (c. 1848-1850)
Philadelphia, Pa.
Bibl. 3

Warner & Fellows (c. 1824)
Portsmouth, N.H.
Caleb Warner
——— Fellows
Bibl. 23, 36, 44

Warner & Keating (c. 1840-
1843)
Philadelphia, Pa.
Bibl. 3

Warner & Newlin (c. 1848-
1850)
Philadelphia, Pa.

—— Warner
Edward G. Newlin
Bibl. 3

A. E. & T. H. Warner (c. 1805-1812)
Baltimore, Md.
Andrew Ellicott & Thomas H. Warner
Thomas & A. E. Warner
Bibl. 4, 23, 24, 28, 29, 36, 38, 39, 44, 48

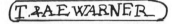

Andrew Ellicott Warner (b. 1786-d. 1870)
Baltimore, Md.
A. E. & T. H. Warner (c. 1805-1812)
Bibl. 4, 15, 23, 24, 25, 28, 29, 36, 38, 44, 54, 72, 78

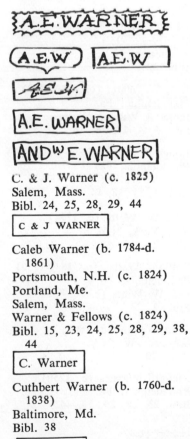

C. & J. Warner (c. 1825)
Salem, Mass.
Bibl. 24, 25, 28, 29, 44

Caleb Warner (b. 1784-d. 1861)
Portsmouth, N.H. (c. 1824)
Portland, Me.
Salem, Mass.
Warner & Fellows (c. 1824)
Bibl. 15, 23, 24, 25, 28, 29, 38, 44

C. Warner

Cuthbert Warner (b. 1760-d. 1838)
Baltimore, Md.
Bibl. 38

C. WARNER   ?

Cuthbert Warner (c. 1837-1850)
Philadelphia, Pa.
Bibl. 3, 15

D. Warner (c. 1810-1820)
Salem, Mass.
Ipswich, Mass. (?)
Bibl. 23, 24, 25, 28, 29, 36

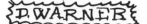

J. Warner
Norfolk, Va. (before 1801)
Richmond, Va. (c. 1801-1803)
Bibl. 19

John S. Warner (c. 1825-1846)
Philadelphia, Pa.
Baltimore, Md. (b.c. 1795)
Bibl. 3, 38

Joseph Warner (b. 1742-d. 1800)
Wilmington, Del.
Bibl. 3, 15, 23, 24, 25, 30, 36, 44

J. WARNER   I W

I WARNER

Joseph Warner (c. 1811-1850)
Philadelphia, Pa.
Bibl. 3, 4, 23, 28, 29, 36, 72

J WARNER

Joseph P. Warner (b. 1811-d. 1862)
Baltimore, Md. (c. 1830-1862)
Bibl. 24, 25, 29, 38, 44

J P W

Joseph P. Warner (c. 1839)
Philadelphia, Pa.
Bibl. 3

Philip Warner (c. 1835)
Philadelphia, Pa.
Bibl. 3

Robert P. Warner (c. 1839-1850)
Philadelphia, Pa.
Bibl. 3

Samuel Warner
Philadelphia, Pa. (c. 1797)
Baltimore, Md. (c. 1812)
Bibl. 3, 23, 24, 25, 28, 29, 44

S W   S. Warner

WARNER

T. Warner (nineteenth century)
Location unknown
Bibl. 28

T WARNER

Thomas & A. E. Warner
(See A. E. & T. H. Warner)

Thomas H. Warner (c. 1780-1828)
Baltimore, Md.
A. E. & T. H. Warner (c. 1805-1812)
Bibl. 15, 23, 24, 25, 28, 29, 36, 38, 54, 86

T W

T. WARNER

William Warner (c. 1814-1850)
Philadelphia, Pa.
William Warner & Co. (c. 1844-1850)
Bibl. 3

William Warner & Co. (c. 1844-1850)
Philadelphia, Pa.
Bibl. 3

Benjamin Warren (c. 1809-1817)
Philadelphia, Pa.
Bibl. 3, 23, 36, 44

S. W. Warriner (c. 1845-1848)
Louisville, Ky.
J. N. Alrich & S. W. Warriner (c. 1848)
Bibl. 32, 54, 68

—— Warrington (c. 1840)
Philadelphia, Pa.
Bibl. 15

WARRINGTON

John Warrington (c. 1811-1833)
Philadelphia, Pa.
John Warrington & Co. (c. 1828-1831)
Bibl. 3

John Warrington & Co.
(c.1828-1831)
Philadelphia, Pa.
Bibl. 3

John & S. R. Warrington
(c. 1841-1850)
Philadelphia, Pa.
John Warrington
Samuel R. Warrington
Bibl. 3

Samuel R. Warrington (c. 1841-
1850)
Philadelphia, Pa.
John & S. R. Warrington
Samuel R. Warrington & Co.
Bibl. 3

Samuel R. Warrington & Co.
(c. 1841-1850)
Philadelphia, Pa.
Bibl. 3

William Warrock (c. 1795-
1804)
Richmond, Va. (c. 1803)
Norfolk, Va.
Brooks & Warrock (c. 1795-
1796-   )
Bibl. 19

Warrock

F. A. Wart (c. 1841)
Philadelphia, Pa.
Bibl. 3

William Warwick (c. 1837)
Philadelphia, Pa.
Bibl. 3

Charles Washburn (c. 1844-
1850-   )
Rochester, N.Y.
Bibl. 20

Charles H. Waterhouse (c.
1847)
Providence, R.I.
Bibl. 23

Waterman & Van Ness
(See Van Ness & Waterman)

Waterman & Whalen (c. 1849)
Albany, N.Y.
George Waterman
James Whalen
Bibl. 20

George Waterman (c. 1848-
1850)

Albany, N.Y.
Waterman & Whalen (c. 1849)
Bibl. 20, 23, 28, 44

Henry Waters (c. 1738)
Yorktown, Va.
Bibl. 19

Samuel Waters (c. 1790-1805)
Boston, Mass.
Bibl. 2, 15, 23, 24, 25, 28, 29,
36

S.WATERS

James Watkins (c. 1819)
New York, N.Y.
Bibl. 23, 36, 44

John Watkins (c. 1831-1837)
Philadelphia, Pa.
Bibl. 3, 44

O. C. Watkins (c. 1850)
Unadilla, N.Y.
Bibl. 20

James Watling (c. 1837-1850)
Philadelphia, Pa.
Bibl. 3, 23, 36

Watson & Brown (c. 1820-
1830)
Philadelphia, Pa.
Boston, Mass. (?)
Bibl. 23, 24, 25, 28, 29, 36, 44

WATSON & BROWN

Watson & Hildeburn (Hildeburn & Watson) (c. 1833-
1849)
Philadelphia, Pa.
Bibl. 3`

Edward E. (J.) Watson
(d. 1839)
Boston, Mass.
Davis & Watson (c. 1815)
Davis, Watson & Co.
(c. 1820)
Bibl. 2, 15, 23, 24, 25, 28, 29, 36,
39, 54

E. WATSON   E. Watson

Isaac S. Watson (c. 1843-1846)
Philadelphia, Pa.
Bibl. 3, 23

James Watson (c. 1820-1850)
Philadelphia, Pa.
Bibl. 3, 23, 24, 25, 29, 36, 39,
54

J. WATSON

Joseph H. Watson (c. 1844-
1878)
Warrenton, Va.
Bibl. 19

WATSON

Joshua Watson (c. 1819-1824)
Philadelphia, Pa.
Bibl. 3

L. Watson (19th century)
Location unknown
Bibl. 54

Robert Watson (c. 1842-1850)
Philadelphia, Pa.
Bibl. 3

William Watt (c. 1767-1789)
Savannah, Ga.
Bibl. 17

Charles Watts (c. 1844-
1850-   )
Rochester, N.Y.
Bibl. 20

J. & W. Watts (c. 1839-1845)
Philadelphia, Pa.
James & William Watts
Bibl. 3, 4, 23, 28, 36

James Watts (c. 1835-1850)
Philadelphia, Pa.
J. & W. Watts (c. 1839-1845)
Bibl. 3, 23, 36, 44

John W. Watts (c. 1794)
New York, N.Y.
Bibl. 23, 36, 44

William Watts (c. 1841-1850)
Philadelphia, Pa.
J. & W. Watts (c. 1839-1845)
Bibl. 3, 23

John Waugh (c. 1803)
Schenectady, N.Y.
Bibl. 20

Richard Waynes (c. 1750)
Philadelphia, Pa.
Bibl. 23, 28, 29, 36, 44

William Wearer (c. 1825)
Augusta, Ga.
Brelet, Wearer & Co.
Bibl. 17

David Weatherly (c. 1805-
1850)
Philadelphia, Pa.
Bibl. 3

Michael Weathers (c. 1794)
New York, N.Y.
Bibl. 23, 36, 44

Weaver
(See Sundelin & Weaver)

Emmor T. Weaver (b. 1786-
d. 1860)
Philadelphia, Pa.
Bibl. 3, 23, 24, 25, 29, 36, 39,
44

Joseph S. Weaver (c. 1846-
1849-   )
Utica, N.Y.
N. N. Weaver & Son (c. 1846-
1847)
Bibl. 18, 20

Joshua Weaver (b. 1753-d.
1827)
West Chester, Pa.
Bibl. 24, 25, 39

I·W

N. N. Weaver & Son (c. 1846-
1847)
Utica, N.Y.
Nicholas N. Weaver
William N. Weaver
Bibl. 18, 20

N. N. & W. Weaver (c. 1817)
Utica, N.Y.
Nicholas N. Weaver
William Weaver
Bibl. 18, 20

Nicholas N. Weaver (b. 1791-d.
1853)
Utica, N.Y.
Cleveland, Ohio

N. N. Weaver & Son (c. 1846-
1847)
N. N. & W. Weaver
Joseph S. Porter
William N. Weaver
Bibl. 15, 18, 20, 25, 44

N. N. WEAVER

William Weaver (c. 1794-
1817)
Utica, N.Y.
N. N. & W. Weaver
Bibl. 18, 20

William N. Weaver (b. 1822)
Utica, N.Y.
N. N. Weaver & Son (c. 1846-
1847)
Bibl. 18, 20

Webb & Boon (c. 1785)
Philadelphia, Pa.
Bibl. 3, 23, 36, 44

Webb & Cowell (c. 1739)
Boston, Mass.
Edward Webb
Bibl. 70

WEBB & COWELL

Webb & Johannes (c. 1827-
1835)
Baltimore, Md.
James Webb
John M. Johannes
Bibl. 38

Barnabas (Barnebus) Webb
(c. 1756-1786)
Thomaston, Me.
Boston, Mass.
Bibl. 15, 23, 25, 28, 29, 36

B W

Charles Webb (c. 1738)
Philadelphia, Pa.
Bibl. 3, 23, 36, 44

Charles Webb (c. 1850)
Philadelphia, Pa.
Bibl. 3

Christopher Webb (c. 1737)
Charleston, S.C.
Bibl. 5

Edward Webb (b. 1665-d.
1718)
Boston, Mass.

Bibl. 15, 24, 25, 44, 54, 55, 69,
70

E W   WEBB

George W. Webb (b. 1812-d.
1890)
Baltimore, Md.
Bibl. 4, 15, 23, 24, 25, 28, 38,
44

G W WEBB

GEO W WEBB

James Webb (c. 1788-d. 1844)
Baltimore, Md. (w. 1817)
Webb & Johannes (c. 1827-
1835)
James Webb & Son
Bibl. 15, 23, 24, 25, 28, 29, 38

J WEBB

James Webb & Son (c. 1835)
Baltimore, Md.
Bibl. 38

John Webb (c. 1827-1842)
Baltimore, Md.
Bibl. 38

Lewis Webb (c. 1827-1830)
Baltimore, Md.
Bibl. 38

Robert Webb (c. 1791-1817)
Philadelphia, Pa.
Bibl. 3, 23, 36

Thomas Webb (c. 1818-1819)
Philadelphia, Pa.
Bibl. 3

William Webb (c. 1801)
Philadelphia, Pa.
Bibl. 3

Henry L. Webster (c. 1831-
1841)
Providence, R.I. (c. 1831-
1841)
Boston, Mass.
Gorham & Webster (c. 1831-
1841)
Henry L. Webster & Co.
(c. 1831-1841)
Gorham, Webster & Price
(c. 1835)
Bibl. 15, 23, 24, 25, 28, 44

H L WEBSTER

Henry L. Webster & Co.
(c. 1831-1841)
Providence, R.I.
Bibl. 15, 23, 24, 25, 29, 36

| H L W & Co |

| H L Webster & Co |

P. M. Weddell (c. 1845)
Cleveland, Ohio
Bibl. 89

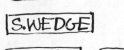

S. WEDGE

S. Wedge   S. W

Simon Wedge Sr. (b. 1774-d.
1823)
Baltimore, Md. (c. 1798-1823)
Bibl. 15, 23, 25, 28, 29, 36, 38,
44

Simon Wedge Jr. (b. 1799-d.
1887)
Baltimore, Md. (c. 1823-1869)
Bibl. 15, 38

George Weedaman (c. 1807)
Philadelphia, Pa.
Bibl. 3

Peleg Weeden (c. 1803)
North Kingston, R.I.
Bibl. 23, 28, 36, 44

John Weeks (c. 1835)
Philadelphia, Pa.
Bibl. 3

Solomon Weida (c. 1847)
Rochester, N.Y.
Bibl. 20

Weidemeyer & Peacock (c.
1819)
John M. Weidemeyer
Richard G. Peacock Jr.
Bibl. 19

John M. Weidemeyer (c. 1800-
1819)
Baltimore, Md. (c. 1800-1801)
Fredericksburg, Va. (c. 1806-
1819)
Bibl. 19

John M. Weidemeyer (c. 1823)
Charlottesville, Va.
Bibl. 19

Lewis Weidemeyer (c. 1828-
1829)
New York, N.Y.
Bibl. 15

Louis Weidemeyer
(c. 1817-   )
Lynchburg, Va.
Bibl. 19, 54

John Wein (c. 1811)
Philadelphia, Pa.
Bibl. 3

George Weiss (c. 1847)
Philadelphia, Pa.
Bibl. 3, 23

Jedediah Weiss (c. 1777-1815)
Bethlehem, Pa.
Philadelphia, Pa.
Bibl. 3

John Welch
Boston, Mass.
Bibl. 44

John Welch (c. 1823)
Fincastle, Va.
Bibl. 19

Francis Weller (c. 1777-1778)
Philadelphia, Pa.
Bibl. 3

James M. Welles
(See James M. Wells)

Welles & Co. (c. 1800-1821)
Boston, Mass.
George Welles
Hugh Gelston
Bibl. 2, 23, 24, 25, 28, 29, 36,
44

| WELLES & CO. |

Welles & Gelston (c. 1840)
New York, N.Y.
Bibl. 24, 25, 28

| Welles & Gelston |

| WELLES & GELSTON |

Alfred George Welles (c. 1804-
1810)
Boston, Mass.

Bibl. 23, 24, 25, 28, 29, 39, 44,
72

| A + G WELLES |

| A. & G. W. |

Andrew (Alfred) Welles
(b. 1783-d. 1860)
Hebron, Conn. (c. 1804)
Bibl. 15, 16, 25, 28, 36, 44

| A. Welles |

George I. Welles (c. 1784-
1827)
Boston, Mass.
Hebron, Conn.
Bibl. 2, 4, 15, 23, 25, 28, 29, 36,
44, 54

| WELLES |

| WELLES |

Wells & Horace
(See Lemuel & Horace Wells)

Wells, Tain & Hall (after 1800)
Location unknown
Bibl. 28

| L T Welles |

| A S Tain |

| D G Hall |

D. Wells (c. 1813)
Ogdensburg, N.Y.
Bibl. 20

D. A. Wells (c. 1833)
Medina, Ohio
Bibl. 34

Horace Wells (c. 1790)
New York, N.Y.
Lemuel & Horace Wells
(c. 1794)
Wells & Horace
Lemuel Wells & Horace
Bibl. 36, 44

James M. Wells (Welles)
(c. 1827-1835)
New York, N.Y.
Bibl. 15, 23, 36

L. & C. Wells (c. 1794-1798)
New York, N.Y.
Bibl. 36, 44

Lemuel Wells (c. 1790)
New York, N.Y.
Lemuel Wells & Co. (c. 1794)
Lemuel & Horace Wells
(c. 1794)
Wells & Horace
Lemuel Wells & Horace
Bibl. 23, 24, 25, 29, 44

L W

Lemuel Wells & Co. (c. 1794)
New York, N.Y.
Bibl. 23, 24, 25, 44

L W & Co

Lemuel Wells & Horace
(See next entry)

Lemuel & Horace Wells
(c. 1794)
New York, N.Y.
Wells & Horace
Lemuel Wells & Horace
Bibl. 23, 25, 36

Richard Wells (c. 1775)
Sunbury, Ga.
Bibl. 17

Robert Wells (c. 1787-
1804-   )
Winchester, Va.
Bibl. 19

William Wells (b. 1766,
c. 1828)
Hartford, Conn.
Bibl. 16, 23, 28, 36, 44

John Wellwood (c. 1751-   )
Edenton, N.C.
Bibl. 21

William Welscher (c. 1783-
1789)
Savannah, Ga.
Bibl. 17

Alexander Welsh (c. 1800-
1801)
Baltimore, Md.
Bibl. 38

Bela Welsh (c. 1808)
Northampton, Mass.
Bibl. 84

David Welsh (c. 1848-1851)
Lincanton, N.C.
Bibl. 21

John Welsh (b. 1730-d. 1812)
Boston, Mass.
Bibl. 28

Wendell & Roberts (c. 1850)
Albany, N.Y.
William Wendell
———— Roberts
Bibl. 23

William Wendell (c. 1839-
1842)
Albany, N.Y.
Mulford & Wendell (c. 1843-
1850)
Wendell & Roberts (c. 1850)
Bibl. 20, 23

John Wendover (d. 1727,
c. 1694)
New York, N.Y.
Bibl. 23, 24, 25, 28, 29, 30, 36,
44

Wendt
(See Rogers & Wendt)

J. R. Wendt & Co.
Location unknown
Bibl. 28

Bernard Wenman (c. 1789-
1805)
New York, N.Y.
Bibl. 4, 15, 23, 24, 25, 28, 29,
35, 36, 39, 44, 54, 72, 83

B. WENMAN   B W

Widow of Bernard Wenman
(c. 1834-1835)
New York, N.Y.
Bibl. 15

Wentworth & Co. (c. 1850)
New York, N.Y.
Bibl. 24, 25, 44

WENTWORTH & CO.

C. K. Wentworth & Co.
(c. 1847)
Macon, Ga.
Cyrus King Wentworth
B. L. Burnett
Bibl. 17

Cyrus King Wentworth (c.
1816-1847)
Milledgeville, Ga. (c. 1840)
Macon, Ga. (c. 1847)
Boston, Mass.
New York, N.Y.
C. K. Wentworth & Co.
(c. 1847)
Bibl. 17

Jason Wentworth (c. 1846)
Boston, Mass.
Bibl. 25, 44

J. WENTWORTH

Hilary (Henry) Wentz (c. 1822-
1824)
Philadelphia, Pa.
Bibl. 3

Benjamin Wenzell (Winzel)
(Winson) (c. 1839-1850)
Philadelphia, Pa.
Bibl. 3

Werne & Speiglehalder (c. 1836-
1858)
(Speiglehalder & Werne)
Louisville, Ky.
Joseph Werne Sr.
———— Speiglehalder
Bibl. 54

Joseph Werne Sr. (c. 1808-
1858)
Louisville, Ky.
Werne & Speiglehalder
(c. 1836-1858)
Bibl. 32, 54, 68

Joseph Werne Jr. (b. 1837-d.
1903)
Louisville, Ky.
Kitts & Werne (c. 1865-1874)
Bibl. 32, 54, 68

Werner & Fellows (c. 1824)
Portsmouth, N.H.
———— Werner
John F. Fellows
Bibl. 23, 36

I. Wescoat (c. 1830)
Location unknown
Bibl. 15, 24, 44

Benjamin West (c. 1770-1830)
Boston, Mass.
Bibl. 23, 25, 28, 29, 36

B. WEST

Charles West (c. 1830)
Boston, Mass.
Bibl. 23, 28, 36, 44

Edward West Sr. (c. 1765)
Stafford County, Va.
Bibl. 19

Edward West Jr. (b. 1757-d. 1827)
Stafford County, Va. (c. 1785-1788)
Lexington, Ky. (c. 1788-1827)
Bibl. 19, 32, 54, 68

James L. West (c. 1829-1833)
Philadelphia, Pa.
Bibl. 3

Joseph West (d. 1780, c. 1776)
Philadelphia, Pa.
Bibl. 3, 23, 36, 44

Josiah West (c. 1798-1808)
Philadelphia, Pa.
Bibl. 3

S. W. West (c. 1859)
Laurens, S.C.
Bibl. 5

Thomas G. West (c. 1819-1822)
Philadelphia, Pa.
McIlhenney & West (c. 1818-1822) (?)
Bibl. 3

William E. West (nineteenth century)
Lexington, Ky.
Bibl. 54

Andrew Westermeyer (c. 1790-1807)
Charleston, S.C.
Bibl. 5

Henry Westermeyer (c. 1790)
Charleston, S.C.
Bibl. 5, 44

H W

John L. Westervelt (Westervell) (c. 1826-1850)
Newburgh, N.Y.
Bibl. 20, 23, 24, 25, 28, 29, 44

J. L. W.

Benjamin Weston (c. 1797)
Philadelphia, Pa.
Bibl. 3, 19, 36, 44

Charles Westphall (c. 1801)
Philadelphia, Pa.
Bibl. 3

Charles William Westphall (c. 1802-1822)
Philadelphia, Pa.
Bibl. 3, 23, 24, 25, 28, 29, 44

C. WESTPHAL

C. WESTPHAL

C. WESTPHAL

Ferdinand Westphall (c. 1814-1824)
Philadelphia, Pa.
Bibl. 3

Wetmore & Dikeman (c. 1817)
Bath, N.Y.
Bibl. 20

Edward A. Wetmore (c. 1839-1843)
Troy, N.Y.
Bibl. 20

Jacob G. Weyman (c. 1844-1846)
Philadelphia, Pa.
Bibl. 3

James Whalen (c. 1849)
Albany, N.Y.
Waterman & Whalen
Bibl. 20

Joseph Wharfe (c. 1804)
Baltimore, Md.
Bibl. 38

Joseph Wharfe (b. 1789, c. 1819)
Fredericktown, Md.
Bibl. 38

Whartenby and Bumm (c. 1816-1818)
Philadelphia, Pa.
Thomas Whartenby
Peter Bumm (?)
Bibl. 3, 36, 39, 44

James Whartenby (c. 1847-1848)
Philadelphia, Pa.
Bibl. 3, 23

John Whartenby (c. 1829-1835)
Philadelphia, Pa.
Bibl. 3, 4, 23, 28, 36, 44

Thomas Whartenby (c. 1811-1850)
Philadelphia, Pa.
Whartenby & Bumm (c. 1816-1818)
Thomas Whartenby & Co. (c. 1847-1850)
Bibl. 3, 4, 23, 24, 25, 28, 29, 44, 54

WHARTENBY

Thomas Whartenby & Co. (c. 1847-1850)
Philadelphia, Pa.
Bibl. 3, 4, 23, 28, 44

William Whartenby (c. 1844)
Philadelphia, Pa.
Bibl. 3, 23

Frederick G. Wheatley (c. 1805-1824)
New York, N.Y.
Fourniquet & Wheatley (c. 1815)
Bibl. 15, 23, 36, 44

Benjamin Wheaton (c. 1835)
Philadelphia, Pa.
Bibl. 3

Calvin (Caleb) Wheaton (c. 1784-1827)
Providence, R.I.
Bibl. 23, 24, 25, 28, 29, 36, 56

C. WHEATON

Joseph Whedbee (c. 1771-1779)
Edenton, N.C.
Bibl. 21

I. Wheeler (Wheelen) (c. 1810)
Location unknown
Bibl. 15, 24, 44

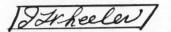

Wheeler(s) & Brooks (c. 1830)
Livonia, N.Y.
Bibl. 15, 25, 44

WHEELERS & BROOKS

Wheeler, Brooks & Co.
(c. 1835)
Livonia, N.Y.
Bibl. 20

Ralph Wheeler (c. 1838)
Hudson, N.Y.
Bibl. 20

Richard C. Wheeler (c. 1800-
1831)
Savannah, Ga.
Bibl. 17

Samuel Wheeler Jr. (c. 1844)
Rochester, N.Y.
Bibl. 20

Wheelers & Brooks
(See Wheeler & Brooks)

Samuel H. Wheritt (c. 1860)
Richmond, Va.
Bibl. 54

Whetcroft & Higginson
(c. 1774)
Annapolis, Md.
William Whetcroft
Samuel Higginson
Bibl. 38

William Whetcroft (b. 1735-d.
1799) (c. 1766-1769)
Annapolis, Md. (c. 1774)
Baltimore, Md.
Whetcroft & Higginson
(c. 1774)
Bibl. 24, 25, 28, 29, 38, 44

W W

William G. Whilden (c. 1855)
Charleston, S.C.
Gregg, Hayden & Whilden
(c. 1855)
Hayden & Whilden (c. 1855-
1863) (?)
Bibl. 54

Arnold Whipple (c. 1825)
Providence, R.I.
Bibl. 28, 44

Whit(t)aker & Green(e)
(c. 1825)
Providence, R.I.
Bibl. 23, 28, 36, 44

John Whitaker (c. 1814-1822)
Philadelphia, Pa.
Bibl. 3

White & Cooke (c. 1829-1833)
Petersburg, Va.
Andrew White
William A. Cooke
Bibl. 19

White
(See White & William Matlock)
(See Porter & White)

Alfred White (c. 1807-1809)
Boston, Mass.
Philadelphia, Pa.
Bibl. 3, 23, 36, 44

Alphine White (c. 1805)
Philadelphia, Pa.
Bibl. 3

Amos White (b. 1745-d. 1825)
East Haddam, Conn.
Meriden, Conn.
Maryland
Bibl. 16, 23, 24, 25, 28, 29, 36,
44, 54

WHITE   A WHITE

Andrew White (c. 1817-1833)
Lynchburg, Va. (c. 1817-1818)
Petersburg, Va. (after 1818-
c. 1833)
Norfolk, Va. (c. 1829-1833)
Marshall & White (c.
1817-   )
White & Cooke (c. 1829-1833)
Cooke & White (c. 1833)
Bibl. 15, 19, 25, 72

C. White (c. 1830-1840)
Mobile, Ala.
Bibl. 15, 25, 72

C WHITE   C WHITE MOBILE

Edward White (c. 1757)
Ulster County, N.Y.
Bibl. 23, 24, 25, 28, 29, 44

E W   E: WHITE

Francis White (c. 1849)
Philadelphia, Pa.
Bibl. 3

G. W. White (c. 1828-1830)
Northampton, Mass.
Phelps & White
Bibl. 84

George L. (A.) White (c. 1822-
1843)
Cincinnati, Ohio
Woodruff & White (c. 1829)
Bibl. 23, 34, 36, 54

H. White & Son (c. 1818-1822)
Fredericksburg, Va.
Henry White
William H. White
Bibl. 19

Henry White (d. 1827)
Fredericksburg, Va. (c. 1788)
H. White & Son (c. 1818-1822)
Bibl. 19

H. W   H. WHITE

J. White & Co. (c. 1830-1831)
Athens, Ga.
Joel White
Bibl. 17

Joel White (c. 1830-1831)
Athens, Ga.
J. White & Co. (c. 1830-1831)
B. B. Lord & Co. (c. 1830-1839)
Bibl. 17

Joseph White (c. 1808-1818)
Philadelphia, Pa.
Bibl. 3

Moses White (c. 1811)
Buffalo, N.Y.
Bibl. 20

Peregrine White (b. 1747-d.
1834)
Woodstock, Conn.
Bibl. 16, 23, 24, 25, 28, 29, 36,
41, 44, 61

P WHITE   ?

Peter White (b. 1718-d. 1803)
Norwalk, Conn.
Bibl. 16, 23, 28, 36, 44

P. WHITE   ?

Peter White (c. 1832)
Louisville, Ky.
Bibl. 32, 54, 68

Philo White (c. 1843-1844)
Utica, N.Y.
Bibl. 18, 20

S. White
Delaware (?)
Bibl. 30

S. WHITE	S W

S. White & Co. (c. 1830)
New York, N.Y.
Samuel White
Bibl. 15, 44

Samuel White (c. 1805-1833)
New York, N.Y.
S. White & Co. (c. 1830)
Bibl. 15, 23, 36, 44

Sebastian White (c. 1795-1796)
Philadelphia, Pa.
Bibl. 3

Silas White (b. 1754-d. 1816)
New York, N.Y. (c. 1791)
Bibl. 23, 24, 25, 29, 35, 36, 54,
83

S W	S	W

S WHITE

Stephen White (c. 1805-1815)
New York, N.Y.
Bibl. 15, 23, 36

Thomas White (c. 1810)
Philadelphia, Pa.
Bibl. 3

Thomas Sturt White (c. 1734)
Boston, Mass.
Bibl. 28

William H. White (c. 1822-
1838, d. 1859)
Philadelphia, Pa. (c. 1835-1837)
Fredericksburg, Va. (c. 1836-
1838)
H. White & Son (c. 1818-1822)
William H. White & Co.
(c. 1835-1837)
B. H. Smith & Co. (c. 1836-
1838)
Bibl. 19

W. H. WHITE

William H. White & Co.
Philadelphia, Pa. (c. 1835-1837)
Fredericksburg, Va. (c. 1836-
1838)
William H. White
Benjamin H. Smith
Bibl. 19

William J. White (c. 1833-1838)
New York, N.Y.
Bibl. 15, 23, 36, 44

William Wilson White
New York, N.Y. (c. 1827-1841)
Philadelphia, Pa. (c. 1805-
1806)
Bibl. 3, 15, 23, 24, 25, 29, 36,
44, 54

W. W. WHITE

WM. W. WHITE

John Whitehead (b. 1791-d.
1875)
Haddenfield, N.J. (c. 1821-
1830)
Bibl. 46, 54

John Whitehead (c. 1848-1849)
Philadelphia, Pa.
Bibl. 3

William W. Whitehead
(c. 1850)
Philadelphia, Pa.
Bibl. 3

Ira Whiteman (c. 1761,
b. 1740)
New York, N.Y.
Bibl. 23, 36, 44

Nelson Whiteside (c. 1832)
Wheeling, Va.
Bibl. 19

Samuel Whiteside (c. 1802)
Staunton, Va.
Bibl. 19

Samuel H. Whiteside (c. 1819-
1831)
Cincinnati, Ohio
Bibl. 34

Whiting & Marquand (c. 1787)
Fairfield, Conn.
———— Whiting
Isaac Marquand
Bibl. 89

B. Whiting (c. 1755-1765)
Norwich, Conn.

Bibl. 15, 23, 25, 29, 36, 44

B: WHITING

Captain Charles Whiting
(b. 1725-d. 1765)
Norwich, Conn.
Bibl. 15, 16, 17, 23, 24, 25, 28,
29, 36, 44, 54, 61

C W	WHITING	C W

Ebenezer Whiting (b. 1735-d.
1794)
Savannah, Ga. (c. 1786-1788)
Bibl. 17

E Whiting

S. Whiting (c. 1700)
Norwich, Conn.
New York, N.Y.
Bibl. 23, 36, 44

Spencer Whiting
Rhinebeck, N.Y. (c. 1816)
Hudson, N.Y. (c. 1819-1820)
Waterford, N.Y. (c. 1824)
Bibl. 20

Frederick A. Whitlock
Augusta, Ga.
Woodstock & Whitlock
(c. 1850-1851)
Bibl. 17

Thomas B. Whitlock (c. 1796)
New York, N.Y.
Bibl. 23, 24, 25, 28, 29, 36, 44

Whitlock

William H. Whitlock (c. 1805-
1827)
New York, N.Y.
Bibl. 15, 23, 24, 25, 29, 36, 44

Wm. H. Whitlock

Whitnery (c. 1846)
New York, N.Y.
Bibl. 89

Whitney
(See Tappan & Whitney)

Whitney & Hoyt (c. 1827-1836)
New York, N.Y.
Bibl. 15, 23, 24, 25, 29, 36, 44

WHITNEY & HOYT

Amos Whitney (c. 1800-1810)
New York, N.Y.
Bibl. 15, 23, 24, 25, 35, 36,
   44, 83

A WHITNEY

Eben (W.) Whitney (c. 1805-
   1828)
New York, N.Y.
Bibl. 15, 23, 24, 25, 29, 36, 44

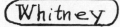 Whitney

E. WHITNEY

Whitney

Edward T. Whitney (c. 1847)
Rochester, N.Y.
Bibl. 20

Henry Whitney (c. 1793-1798)
Lansingburgh, N.Y.
Smith & Whitney (c. 1787-
   1793)
Rockwell, Smith & Whitney
   (c. 1788-1789)
Bibl. 20

John Whitney (c. 1839-1845)
Albany, N.Y.
Bibl. 20

Lemuel Whitney (b. 1764-d.
   1847)
Newfane, Vt. (c. 1785-1790)
Brattleboro, Vt. (c. 1790-1847)
Bibl. 54

Leonard Whitney (c. 1841-
   1842)
Philadelphia, Pa.
Bibl. 3

M. F. Whitney (c. 1823-1824)
Schenectady, N.Y.
Bibl. 15, 20, 25, 28, 29, 44

M. WHITNEY

William H. Whitney
Rochester, N.Y. (c. 1845)
Binghamton, N.Y.
Bibl. 20

Ezra (Ebed) Whiton (b. 1813-d.
   1879)
Boston, Mass.

Bibl. 4, 15, 23, 24, 25, 28, 29,
   36, 44

E. Whiton

―――― Whitteker
Charleston, Va.
Anderson & Whitteker (c. 1831-
   1835)
Bibl. 19

Edward Whittemore (d. 1772)
Boston, Mass.
Bibl. 28

William Whittemore (b. 1710-d.
   1770)
Portsmouth, N.H.
Bibl. 2, 13, 23, 25, 28, 29, 36

Whittemore

WW

Whittemore

Whittlesey (c. 1808)
Vincennes, Ind.
Bibl. 28

Daniel H. Wickham Jr.
   (c. 1832-1841)
New York, N.Y.
Bibl. 15, 23, 36, 44

Widdifield & Gaw (c. 1820-
   1822)
Philadelphia, Pa.
William Widdifield Jr.
William P. Gaw
Bibl. 3

William Widdifield (c. 1817)
Philadelphia, Pa.
Bibl. 3

William Widdifield Jr.
Philadelphia, Pa. (c. 1820-
   1822)
Fayetteville, N.C. (c. 1820-
   1840)
Widdifield & Gaw (c. 1820-
   1822)
Bibl. 21

Frederick W. Widman (c. 1817-
   1848)

Philadelphia, Pa.
Bibl. 3

Henry P. Wiedemeyer (c. 1830)
Lynchburg, Va.
Bibl. 19

J. M. Wiedemeyer (c. 1800-
   1801)
Baltimore, Md.
Bibl. 38

Frederick Wieland (c. 1848)
Philadelphia, Pa.
Bibl. 3

T. Wieland (c. 1835)
Philadelphia, Pa.
Bibl. 3

Thomas Wiggins & Co.
   (c. 1833)
Philadelphia, Pa.
Bibl. 3

William Wightman (c. 1700-
   1825, d. 1835)
Charleston, S.C.
Bibl. 5, 44, 54

W W

John Wilbank (c. 1839-1841)
Philadelphia, Pa.
Bibl. 3

―――― Wilcke (c. 1810)
Location unknown
Bibl. 28

WILCKE

Wilcox & Perkins (c. 1818-
   1820)
Sparta, Ga.
Cyprian Wilcox
Leonard Perkins
Bibl. 17

Alanson D. Wilcox (c. 1843-
   1850-   )
Albany, N.Y. (c. 1844)
Troy, N.Y. (c. 1847-1850)
Harris & Wilcox (?)
Bibl. 20, 25, 44

A.O. WILCOX

Alvan Wilcox (Willcox)
   (b. 1783-d. 1870)
Norwich, Conn. (1805-1807)
Fayetteville, N.C. (c. 1819-
   1823)

New Haven, Conn. (1824-
1870)
New Jersey
Hart & Wilcox (c. 1805-1807)
Bibl. 16, 17, 21, 23, 28, 36, 44

Cyprian Wilcox (Willcox)
(b. 1795-d. 1875)
Sparta, Ga. (c. 1818-1821)
Berlin, Conn.
New Haven, Conn.
Wilcox & Perkins (c. 1818-
1820)
Bibl. 15, 16, 17, 23, 25, 28,
36, 44

C. WILCOX

Michael Wilcox (c. 1772-1799)
Dorchester County, Md.
Bibl. 29, 38, 44

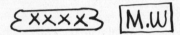

L. H. Wilder & Co. (c. 1845)
Philadelphia, Pa.
Bibl. 3

Samuel Wilham(s) (c. 1795-
1796)
Philadelphia, Pa.
Bibl. 3, 23, 28, 36

William Wilkings (c. 1749-
1751)
Charleston, S.C.
Bibl. 5

Wilkinson & Horah (c. 1820-
1821)
Salisbury, N.C.
Curtis Wilkinson
Hugh Horah
Bibl. 21

Curtis Wilkinson (c. 1820-1823)
Salisbury, N.C.
Wilkinson & Horah (c.1820-
1821)
Bibl. 21

E. Wilkinson (c. 1840)
Mansfield, Ohio
Bibl. 34

Wilson Wilkinson (c. 1840)
Mansfield, Ohio
Bibl. 34

Willard
(See Willard & Sackett)

Willard & Hawley (c. 1844-
1851)
Syracuse, N.Y.
William W. Willard
John Dean Hawley
Bibl. 15, 20, 44

WILLARD&HAWLEY

Willard & Stokes (c. 1833)
Cazenovia, N.Y.
William W. Willard
T. Stokes
Bibl. 20

A. Willard (c. 1810)
Utica, N.Y.
Bibl. 24, 25

A. WILLARD

B. Willard (c. 1838)
Schenectady, N.Y.
Bibl. 20

H. Willard (c. 1818)
Catskill, N.Y.
Bibl. 20

James Willard (c. 1815)
East Windsor, Conn.
Bibl. 24, 25, 44

WILLARD

William W. Willard
Cazenovia, N.Y. (c. 1833-
1834)
Syracuse, N.Y. (c. 1841-1844)
Willard & Stokes (c. 1833)
Willard & Hawley (c. 1844-
1851)
Bibl. 20

Willcox
(See Alvan Wilcox)
(See Cyprian Wilcox)

Curtis R. Willett (c. 1799-
1820)
Savannah, Ga.
Bibl. 17

Willey
(See Scovil, Willey & Co.)

Willey & Blakesley (19th
century)
Cincinnati, Ohio
Bibl. 54

Willey & Co. (c. 1836)
Cincinnati, Ohio
Bushnell Willey
Bibl. 54

Bushnell Willey (c. 1836)
Cincinnati, Ohio
Willey & Co.
Bibl. 29, 44, 54

B. WILLEY

George William (c. 1843-1848)
Philadelphia, Pa.
Bibl. 3

———— Williams
Winchester, Va.
Bibl. 19

Williams & Son
Lynchburg, Va.
Jehu Williams Sr.
Bibl. 19

Williams & Victor (c. 1814-
1845)
Lynchburg, Va.
Jehu Williams Sr.
John Victor
Bibl. 19, 54

WILLIAMS & VICTOR

A. & R. Williams (c. 1812)
Philadelphia, Pa.
Bibl. 3

Alexander Williams (c. 1807-
1813)
Philadelphia, Pa.
Bibl. 3, 23, 36, 44

Andrew Williams
Location unknown
Bibl. 28

ANDREW WILLIAMS

Benjamin Williams (c. 1788-
1794)
Elizabeth, N.J.
New Brunswick, N.J.
Trenton, N.J.
Bibl. 46, 54

Charles Williams (c. 1827)
New York, N.Y.
Bibl. 15

Charles M. Williams (c. 1837)
New York, N.Y.
Monell & Williams (c. 1825)
Bibl. 15, 23, 44

Deodat Williams (d. 1781)
Hartford, Conn. (c. 1776)
Bibl. 16, 23, 28, 36

E. Williams (c. 1829-1830)
Augusta, Ga.
Bibl. 17

Henry Williams (c. 1804)
Philadelphia, Pa.
Bibl. 3

J. Williams (c. 1795)
Alexandria, Va.
Philadelphia, Pa. (?)
Bibl. 15, 19

Jehu Williams Sr. (b. 1788-d.
  1859)
Lynchburg, Va.
Williams & Victor (c. 1814-
  1845)
Williams & Son
Bibl. 19, 54

John Williams (c. 1793)
Philadelphia, Pa.
Bibl. 44

John Williams (c. 1818)
Philadelphia, Pa.
Bibl. 3, 23, 25, 36

John Williams (c. 1836)
New York, N.Y.
Bibl. 15

John Williams (c. 1858-
  1860-   )
Utica, N.Y.
Bibl. 18

Joseph Williams (c. 1816)
Philadelphia, Pa.
Bibl. 3

Margery & Mary Williams
  (c. 1823-1824)

Philadelphia, Pa.
Bibl. 3

Nicholas Williams (c. 1792)
Liberty Town, Md.
Bibl. 38

Oliver S. Williams (c. 1850)
Hartford, Conn.
Bibl. 23

Stephen Williams (c. 1799)
Providence, R.I.
Bibl. 23, 25, 28, 36, 44, 56

W. H. Williams (c. 1839-1844)
Hamilton, N.Y.
Bibl. 20

W. W. Williams (c. 1829)
Alexandria, Va.
Bibl. 23, 36

William A. Williams (b. 1787-d.
  1846)
Alexandria, Va. (c. 1809-1835)
Washington, D.C. (c. 1829)
Bibl. 19, 24, 25, 29, 36, 44,
  54, 78

Henry Williamson (c. 1808)
Baltimore, Md.
Bibl. 38

Samuel Williamson (c. 1794-
  1813)
Philadelphia, Pa.
Simmons & Williamson
  (c. 1797-1798) (?)
Richards & Williamson (c. 1797-
  1800)
Bibl. 2, 3, 15, 23, 24, 25, 29,
  36, 39, 44, 54, 72, 81

George Willig Jr. (c. 1819-
  1822)
Philadelphia, Pa.
Rasch & Willig (c. 1819)
Bibl. 3, 4, 23, 28, 36

Willis
(See Willis & Billis)

Andrew Willis (c. 1842)
Boston, Mass.
Bibl. 15, 25, 44

J. Willis (c. 1820)
Boston, Mass.
Bibl. 23, 36, 44

Stillman Willis (c. 1813-1825)
Boston, Mass.
Bibl. 15, 23, 24, 25, 28, 29,
  36, 44

William S. Willis (c. 1830)
Boston, Mass.
Bibl. 24, 25

Othniel Williston (c. 1816-
  1819)
Cincinnati, Ohio
Bibl. 34

Seymour Williston (c. 1816-
  1819)
Cincinnati, Ohio
Bibl. 34

Benjamin Willmott (c. 1797-
  1816-   )
Easton, Md.
Bibl. 38

James Willock (b. 1793,
  c. 1811)
Baltimore, Md.
Bibl. 38

Henry Wills (c. 1774)
New York, N.Y.
Bibl. 23, 36, 44

Joseph Wills (c. 1753, d. 1759)
Philadelphia, Pa.
Bibl. 3

J. Wilmer (c. 1849)
Philadelphia, Pa.
Bibl. 3

Wilmot & Richmond
Charleston, S.C.
Samuel Wilmot
—— Richmond
Bibl. 25

Wilmot & Stillman (Stilliman)
(c. 1800-1808)
New Haven, Conn.
Samuel Wilmot
——— Stillman
Bibl. 16, 23, 28, 36, 44

Samuel Wilmot (b. 1777-d.
1846)
New Haven, Conn. (c. 1800-
1808)
Georgetown, S.C. (c. 1825)
Charleston, S.C. (c. 1837)
Wilmot & Stillman (c. 1800-
1808)
Wilmot & Richmond
Bibl. 5, 15, 16, 17, 23, 24, 25,
28, 29, 36, 54, 61

S. WILMOT

Samuel & Thomas T. Wilmot
(c. 1837)
Charleston, S.C.
Bibl. 25

S. & T. T. WILMOT

T. T. Wilmot (c. 1810)
New Haven, Conn.
Bibl. 23, 24, 29, 36

T. T. WILMOT

Thomas Wilmot (b. 1774-d.
1813, c. 1801-1813)
Rutland, Vt. (c. 1796-1800)
Fairhaven, Vt.
Storer & Wilmot (c. 1796-1800)
Bibl. 54

Thomas T. Wilmot
Charleston, S.C. (c. 1837-1838)
Savannah, Ga. (c. 1843-1850)
Columbus, Ga. (c. 1844)
Bibl. 5, 17, 25, 44

T T WILMOT

Wilson
(See Leonard & Wilson)

Wilson & Toy
(See Toy & Wilson)

Albert Wilson (c. 1833-
1850-   )
Albany, N.Y. (c. 1834)
Troy, N.Y.
Bibl. 4, 20, 23, 28, 36, 44

Alfred Wilson (c. 1842)
St. Louis, Mo.
Bibl. 54

Andrew Wilson (c. 1844-1847)
Philadelphia, Pa.
Bibl. 3

D. W. Wilson
York, S.C.
J. N. Lewis & Co. (c. 1854)
Bibl. 25

Edwin Franklin Wilson
(b. 1813-d. 1904)
Rochester, N.Y. (c. 1838)
Bibl. 20, 41, 44

George Wilson (c. 1848-1850)
Philadelphia, Pa.
Bibl. 3, 4, 23, 28, 44

Hosea Wilson
Philadelphia, Pa. (c. 1812)
Baltimore, Md. (c. 1814-1819)
Hosea Wilson & Co. (c. 1814-
1816)
Bibl. 15, 23, 24, 25, 28, 29, 38,
44

H. WILSON

H. WILSON

Hosea Wilson & Co. (c. 1814-
1816)
Baltimore, Md.
Bibl. 15, 24, 29, 38, 44

H WILSON & CO

J. Wilson (b. 1804-d. 1889)
Lexington, Ky. (c. 1838-1839)
Bibl. 32, 54

James Wilson (b. 1745,
c. 1768)
Trenton, N.J.
Bibl. 3, 23, 36, 44, 46, 54

James Wilson (c. 1802-1818)
Poughkeepsie, N.Y.
Storm & Wilson
Bibl. 20

John Wilson (c. 1770, d. 1787)
Philadelphia, Pa.
Bibl. 3, 23, 36

John Wilson (c. 1784-1791,
d. 1795)
Richmond, Va.
Bibl. 19

P. G. Wilson (c. 1840)
Philadelphia, Pa.
Bibl. 3

Robert Wilson
New York, N.Y. (c. 1805)
Philadelphia, Pa. (c. 1814-1846)
Robert & William Wilson
(c. 1825-1846)
Bibl. 3, 4, 15, 24, 25, 28, 29, 36

R·W

Robert & William Wilson
(c. 1825-1846)
Philadelphia, Pa.
Bibl. 3, 4, 15, 23, 24, 28, 29,
36, 39, 44, 54, 72

R & W. W   R & W W

R & W. WILSON

S. Wilson (c. 1805)
Philadelphia, Pa.
Bibl. 23, 36, 44

S. N. Wilson (c. 1800)
Connecticut
Bibl. 28

S. N. WILSON

S. & S. Wilson (c. 1805)
Philadelphia, Pa.
Bibl. 24, 25, 29, 36, 72

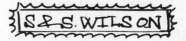

S & S. WILSON

Thomas Wilson (c. 1837-1839)
Philadelphia, Pa.
Bibl. 3, 23, 36, 44

William Wilson (b. 1755-d.
1829)

Abingdon, Md. (c. 1781-1829)
Toy & Wilson (c. 1790)
Bibl. 38

W W

William Wilson (c. 1829-1850)
Philadelphia, Pa.
Robert & William Wilson
    (c. 1825-1846)
Bibl. 3, 4, 23, 28, 36

William Rowan Wilson
    (b. 1821-d. 1866)
Salisbury, N.C.
Boger & Wilson (c. 1846-1853)
Bibl. 21

Wiltberger & Alexander
    (c. 1797-1808)
Philadelphia, Pa.
Christian Wiltberger
Samuel Alexander
Bibl. 3, 23, 25, 36, 44

Christian Wiltburger (Wilt-
    berger) (Jr.) (b. 1766-d.
    1851)
Philadelphia, Pa. (o. 1793-
    1819)
Wiltberger & Alexander
Bibl. 3, 4, 15, 24, 25, 28, 29,
    36, 54, 72

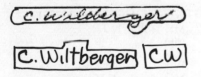

Frances Wilte (c. 1839)
St. Louis, Mo.
Bibl. 54

Andrew Wimer (c. 1818-1819)
Philadelphia, Pa.
Bibl. 3

V. Winchell
Location unknown
Bibl. 15, 44

V. Winchell

———— Winchester
Lexington, Ky.
Garner & Winchester (c. 1813-
    1861)
Bibl. 32, 54

Daniel F. Winchester (c. 1841)
Louisville, Ky.
Bibl. 32

James Edwin Winckler
    (b. 1824-d. 1910)
Charleston, S.C. (c. 1761-1763)
Mecklenburg County, Va.
    (c. 1778-1801)
Bibl. 19

John Winckler (b. 1730-1803)
Charleston, S.C. (c. 1761-1763)
Mecklenburg County, Va.
    (c. 1778-1801)
Bibl. 5, 19, 54

John Winckler Jr. (b. 1775-d.
    1854)
Mecklenburg County, Va.
Bibl. 19

John Windover (c. 1694-1727)
New York, N.Y.
Bibl. 44, 72

I W   ?

Moses Wing (b. 1760-d. 1809)
Windsor, Conn.
Worcester, Mass.
Bibl. 15, 25, 44

M WING

S. Wing & Co. (c. 1850-1851)
Utica, N.Y.
Stephen Wing
Bibl. 18, 20

Stephen Wing (b. 1828,
    c. 1845)
Utica, N.Y.
S. Wing & Co. (c. 1850-1851)
Bibl. 18, 20

George W. Wingate (c. 1816)
Baltimore, Md.
Bibl. 38

Edward Winslow (b. 1669-d.
    1753)
Boston, Mass.
Bibl. 2, 15, 23, 24, 25, 28, 29,
    36, 39, 44, 54, 55, 69, 70

E W E·W   E·W   E·W
E·W

Isaac Winslow (c. 1847-1848)
Philadelphia, Pa.
Bibl. 3

Winson
(See Wenzell)

William Winsor (b. 1723,
    c. 1759)
Boston, Mass.
Bibl. 23, 36, 44

Stephen Winter (c. 1740)
Boston, Mass.
Bibl. 70

Stephen Winter (b. 1753,
    c. 1774)
Maryland
Bibl. 38

Isaac Winters (c. 1844-1848)
Philadelphia, Pa.
Bibl. 3

Winzel
(See Wenzell)

Wirship
(See Burwell & Wirship)

John Wirt (c. 1818)
Lexington, Ky.
Bibl. 32, 54

William Wirth (c. 1839)
St. Louis, Mo.
Bibl. 54

George K. Wise (c. 1842-1850)
Philadelphia, Pa.
Butler, Wise & Keim (c. 1843-
    1850)
Dunlevy & Wise (c. 1847-
    1850) (?)
Bibl. 3, 23

W. M. Wise (c. 1800)
Brooklyn, N.Y.
Bibl. 28

Alexander Wishart (c. 1808-
    1810)
New York, N.Y.
Bibl. 23, 44

B. Wishart (c. 1839-1840)
Philadelphia, Pa.
Bibl. 3

Daniel Wishart (c. 1825)
New York, N.Y.
Bibl. 23, 36, 44

Hugh Wishart (c. 1784-1819)
New York, N.Y.
Bibl. 4, 23, 24, 25, 29, 30, 35,
    36, 44, 54

H WISHART   WISHART

William Wishart (c. 1800)
New York, N.Y.
Bibl. 23, 36, 44

Witham & Newman (c. 1837-
1850)
Philadelphia, Pa.
———— Witham
John A. Newman
Bibl. 3

A. Witham (c. 1828-1831)
Philadelphia, Pa.
Bibl. 3

Ebenezer Witham (c. 1833-
1850)
Philadelphia, Pa.
Bibl. 3

William Witham (c. 1846-1850)
Philadelphia, Pa.
Bibl. 3

James Withers (b. 1753-d.
1778)
Maryland (c. 1774)
Bibl. 28, 38

Daniel Withington (c. 1840)
Ashland, Ohio
Bibl. 34

James Withington (c. 1823-
1824)
Philadelphia, Pa.
Bibl. 3

Marlin A. Withington (c. 1830)
Massillon, Ohio
Bibl. 34

Samuel Withington (c. 1820-
1841)
Philadelphia, Pa.
Bibl. 3

Wittich & Beaver (c. 1793)
Augusta, Ga.
John Wittich
Mathias Beaver
Bibl. 17

Charles & Frederick Wittich
(c. 1802-1807)
Charleston, S.C.
Bibl. 5, 25, 44, 54

| C F WITTICH |

Christian Charles Lewis Wittich
(c. 1785-1804)
Charleston, S.C.

Charles & Frederick Wittich
(c. 1802-1807)
Bibl. 5, 54

| C W |

Frederick Wittich (c. 1802-
1807)
Charleston, S.C.
Charles & Frederick Wittich
(c. 1802-1807)
Bibl. 89

John Wittich (c. 1791-
1793-   )
Augusta, Ga.
Wittich & Beaver (c. 1793)
Bibl. 17

Wolcott & Gelston (c. 1824-
1830)
Boston, Mass.
Henry D. Wolcott
George P. Gelston
Maltby Gelston
Bibl. 24, 25, 28, 29, 44

| WOLCOTT & GELSTON |

Henry D. Wolcott
(See Henry D. Walcott)

S. B. Wolcott (c. 1840)
Massachusetts (?)
Bibl. 15, 44

Wolf(e) & Wriggins (c. 1837)
Philadelphia, Pa.
Bibl. 3, 23, 24, 25, 29, 36, 44

| WOLFE & WRIGGINS |

Francis H. Wolf(e) (c. 1829-
1849)
Philadelphia, Pa.
Bibl. 3, 23, 24, 25, 36, 44

| F. H. WOLFE |

General James Wolf
Wilmington, Del. (c. 1822)
Philadelphia, Pa. (c. 1830-
1833)
Bibl. 3, 15, 23, 25, 30, 36, 89

| G. J. WOLF | I. WOLF |

I. Wolf (c. 1828-1833)
Philadelphia, Pa.
Bibl. 15, 44

| I. WOLF |

J. Wolf(f) (b. 1775, c. 1828-
1833)
Philadelphia, Pa.
Bibl. 3

| I. WOLFF |

George Wolfe (c. 1870-1895)
Louisville, Ky.
Bibl. 54

George Woltz (c. 1775?-1813,
d. 1813)
Hagerstown, Md.
Bibl. 38

John Woltz (c. 1811-1814)
Shepherdstown, Va.
Bibl. 19

| I. B WOLTZ |

Wood & Dodge (c. 1816-1817)
Philadelphia, Pa.
———— Wood
Daniel H. Dodge
Bibl. 3

Wood & Force (c. 1839-1841)
New York, N.Y.
———— Wood
Jabez W. Force
Bibl. 15

Wood & Hudson (c. 1773)
Mt. Holly, N.J.
Bibl. 3

Wood & Hughes (c. 1845)
New York, N.Y.
Jacob Wood
Jasper W. Hughes
Bibl. 4, 23, 24, 25, 28, 29, 44

Wood
(See Taylor, Lawrie & Wood)
(See Van Ness, Wood & Co.)

A. H. Wood
Location unknown

Bibl. 89

A. & W. Wood (c. 1850)
New York, N.Y.
Bibl. 23, 24, 25, 44

A & W WOOD

Abraham C. Wood (c. 1822)
Newburgh, N.Y.
Bibl. 20

Alfred Wood (c. 1800)
New England (?)
Bibl. 28, 29, 44

WOOD

Bazel Wood (c. 1823-1833)
Philadelphia, Pa.
Bibl. 3

Benjamin B. Wood (c. 1794-
 1846)
New York, N.Y.
Ebenezer Cole (c. 1818-1826)
Bibl. 15, 23, 24, 25, 28, 29, 36,
 44, 54

B.WOOD

BBWOOD

Charles Wood (c. 1829-1830)
Philadelphia, Pa.
Bibl. 3

J. Charles Wood (c. 1849)
Charleston, S.C.
Spear & Co.
Bibl. 5

J. E. Wood (c. 1845)
New York, N.Y.
(May be Jacob Wood)
Bibl. 4, 15, 24, 25, 28, 29, 44

J.E. WOOD

Jacob Wood (c. 1834-1841)
New York, N.Y.
Dale, Wood & Hughes (c. 1833-
 1844)
Wood & Hughes (c. 1845)

Bibl. 44

J. WOOD

John Wood (d. 1761, c. 1734)
Philadelphia, Pa.
Bibl. 3

John Wood (c. 1762-1793)
Philadelphia, Pa.
Bibl. 3

John Wood
New York, N.Y. (c. 1770)
Schenectady, N.Y. (c. 1780-
 1792)
Bibl. 25, 44

J Wood

Landais Wood (c. 1832-1834)
Utica, N.Y.
Bibl. 18, 20

T. S. Wood (c. 1849)
Laurens, S.C.
Bibl. 5

Thomas Wood (c. 1837-1848)
Philadelphia, Pa.
Bibl. 3

William Wood (c. 1799)
Newport, R.I.
Bibl. 56

William S. Wood (c. 1810-
 1815)
Skaneateles, N.Y.
Bibl. 20

———— Woodbridge (c. 1842)
St. Louis, Mo.
Shipp & Woodbridge
Bibl. 54

Woodbury, Dix & Hartwell
 (c. 1836)
Location unknown
Bibl. 28

WOODBURY, DIX & HARTWELL

Woodcock & Byrnes (c. 1793)
Wilmington, Del.
Bancroft Woodcock
Thomas Byrnes
Bibl. 25, 44

Bancroft Woodcock (b. 1732-d.
 1817)
Wilmington, Del. (c. 1735-
 1820)
Woodcock & Byrnes (c. 1793)

Bibl. 3, 15, 23, 24, 25, 28, 29,
 30, 36, 39, 44, 54

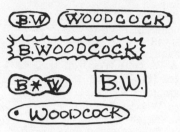

Isaac Woodcock (b. 1765-d.
 1817)
Hagerstown, Md. (c. 1795)
Wilmington, Del.
Bibl. 15, 25, 30, 38, 44

I.WOODCOCK

William Woodcock (c. 1819-
 1829)
Baltimore, Md.
Bibl. 38

Woodford & Kimball (c. 1850)
Dunkirk, N.Y.
Bibl. 20

S. D. Woodhill (b. 1831)
Utica, N.Y. (c. 1852-
 1853-)
Bibl. 18, 20

Woodruff & Deterly (c. 1819)
Cincinnati, Ohio
Enos Woodruff
———— Deterly
Bibl. 54

Woodruff & White (c. 1829)
Cincinnati, Ohio
Enos Woodruff
George L. White
Bibl. 23, 36, 44, 54

Enos Woodruff (c. 1820-1831)
Cincinnati, Ohio
Woodruff & Deterly (c. 1819)
Woodruff & White (c. 1829)
Bibl. 23, 34, 36, 44

Ezra Woodruff (c. 1815)
Lexington, Ky.
L. & W. (E.) Woodruff
 (c. 1811-1815)
Bibl. 54

Jesse Woodruff (b. 1744-d.
 1797)

Bridgeton, N.J.
Bibl. 46, 54

L. Woodruff (c. 1843)
Cincinnati, Ohio
Bibl. 34

L. & W. (E.) Woodruff
   (c. 1811-1815)
Lexington, Ky.
Ezra Woodruff
Bibl. 32, 68

Freeman Woods
New York State (c. 1791-1794)
New Bern, N.C. (c. 1794-1827)
Bibl. 2, 15, 21, 23, 24, 25, 28,
   29, 30, 35, 36, 44, 54

I. Woods (c. 1790)
Location unknown
Bibl. 15, 44

I. Woods

David Woodson (b. 1735)
Petersburg, Va. (c. 1766)
Salisbury, N.C. (c. 1774-1807)
Bibl. 21

Richard Woodson (c. 1736-
   1766)
Petersburg, Va.
Bibl. 19, 21

Woodstock & Whitlock (c.
   1850-1851)
Augusta, Ga.
William G. Woodstock
Frederick A. Whitlock
Bibl. 17

William G. Woodstock (c.
   1840-1853)
Augusta, Ga.
Woodstock & Whitlock
   (c. 1850-1851)
Bibl. 17

Woodward
(See Wakefield & Woodward)

Woodward & Grosjean (c. 1847-
   1852)
Boston, Mass.
Hartford, Conn.
Eli Woodward
────── Grosjean
Bibl. 4, 15, 23, 24, 25, 28, 29, 44

W & G

Antipas Woodward (b. 1763-d.
   1812)
Middletown, Conn.
Bibl. 16, 23, 24, 25, 28, 29, 36,
44

A W   Woodward

Charles Woodward (c. 1825)
New York, N.Y.
Bibl. 23, 36, 44

Eli Woodward (c. 1812)
Boston, Mass.
Hartford, Conn.
Woodward & Grosjean (c. 1847-
   1852)
Bibl. 23, 28, 36

Thomas Woodward (c. 1828)
New York, N.Y.
Bibl. 15

William Woodward (b. 1700-d.
   1774)
Annapolis, Md. (c. 1759)
Bibl. 38

E. Woodworth (c. 1800)
Location unknown
Bibl. 29, 44

E. WOODWORTH

Jeremiah Ward Wool (c. 1791)
New York, N.Y.
Bibl. 23, 25, 28, 36, 44

Charles Woolley (c. 1848-
   1849)
Philadelphia, Pa.
Bibl. 3

John W. Woolridge (Woold-
   ridge) (c. 1819)
Frankfort, Ky.
Bibl. 32, 54, 68

Woolworth & Anderson
   (c. 1829-1830)
Greensboro, N.C.

Aaron Woolworth
────── Anderson
Bibl. 21

Aaron Woolworth (b. 1801-d.
   1856)
Salisbury, N.C. (c. 1825-1826)
Greensboro, N.C. (c. 1829)
Woolworth & Anderson
   (c. 1829-1830)
Bibl. 21

Charles Woolworth (c. 1829)
Philadelphia, Pa.
Bibl. 3

Danforth Woolworth (c. 1823-
   1824)
Philadelphia, Pa.
Bibl. 3

R. C. Woolworth (c. 1816-
   1817)
Philadelphia, Pa.
Bibl. 3

R. C. Woolworth (c. 1835)
Philadelphia, Pa.
Bibl. 3

Richard Woolworth (c. 1830-
   1839)
Philadelphia, Pa.
Bibl. 3

W. W. Wormwood (c. 1850)
Lyons, N.Y.
Bibl. 20, 89

W. W. WORMWOOD

James W. Worn (c. 1849-1850)
Philadelphia, Pa.
Bibl. 3

Goodwin Worrell (c. 1837-
   1849)
Philadelphia, Pa.
Bibl. 3

John Worrell (c. 1837)
Philadelphia, Pa.
Bibl. 3

Samuel Worthington (c. 1833)
Philadelphia, Pa.
Bibl. 3

Robert Worton (c. 1849)
Philadelphia, Pa.
Bibl. 3

Wriggins
(See Wolfe & Wriggins)

Wriggin(s) & Co. (c. 1831-1833)
Philadelphia, Pa.
Thomas Wriggins
Bibl. 3, 23, 36, 44

T. Wriggins & Co. (c. 1842-1846)
Philadelphia, Pa.
Thomas Wriggins
Bibl. 3

Thomas Wriggins (c. 1837-1846)
Philadelphia, Pa.
Wriggin(s) & Co. (c. 1831-1833)
T. Wriggins & Co. (c. 1842-1846)
Bibl. 3, 4, 23, 28, 36, 44

Wright & Putnam (c. 1836)
Buffalo, N.Y.
William S. Wright
John S. Putnam
Bibl. 20

Wright & Sime (c. 1774)
Savannah, Ga.
———— Wright
William Sime
Bibl. 17

Wright
(See Wait & Wright)

Alexander Wright (b. 1748, c. 1775)
Maryland
Bibl. 23, 28, 36, 38, 44

George B. Wright (c. 1849)
Staunton, Va.
Bibl. 19

H. C. Wright (c. 1850)
Cleveland, Ohio (?)
Bibl. 89

James Wright (c. 1841-1844)
Philadelphia, Pa.
Bibl. 3

James R. Wright (c. 1846)
Lynchburg, Va.
Bibl. 19, 54

James R. Wright (c. 1849-1856-   )
Lexington, Va.
Bibl. 19

WRIGHT

John Wright (c. 1845-1850)
Philadelphia, Pa.
Bibl. 3

John Austin Wright (c. 1844-1846)
Leesburg, Va.
Bibl. 19

John F. Wright (c. 1830-1833)
Philadelphia, Pa.
Bibl. 3, 23, 36, 44

John F. Wright (c. 1841-1848)
Louisville, Ky.
Bibl. 32

Joseph Wright (d. 1793)
Philadelphia, Pa.
Bibl. 3

M. Wright (c. 1815)
New York, N.Y.
Bibl. 15

Mary Ann Wright (c. 1847-1850)
Leesburg, Va.
Bibl. 19

William Wright (c. 1802-1803)
Baltimore, Md.
Bibl. 29, 38

William Wright (d. 1746)
Charleston, S.C. (before 1740)
Sarrazin & Wright (c. 1746)
Bibl. 5, 19, 28, 54

W WRIGHT   W Wright

William Wright (c. 1777-1799)
Petersburg, Va.
Bibl. 19

William S. Wright (c. 1836)
Buffalo, N.Y.
Wright & Putnam
Bibl. 20

John Wyand (c. 1847)
Philadelphia, Pa.
Bibl. 3

John Wyant (c. 1829-1833)
Philadelphia, Pa.
Bibl. 3

Joseph Wyatt (c. 1797-1798)
Philadelphia, Pa.
Bibl. 3, 23, 24, 25, 28, 36, 44

J·W   J.W.

Wyer & Farley (c. 1828-1830)
Portland, Me.
Eleazer Wyer (Sr.)
Eleazer Wyer Jr.
Charles Farley
Bibl. 15, 23, 24, 25, 28, 29, 36

WYER & FARLEY

Wyer & Noble (c. 1823)
Portland, Me.
Eleazer Wyer (Sr.)
Eleazer Wyer Jr.
Joseph Noble
Bibl. 23, 25, 36, 44

Eleazer Wyer (Sr.) (b. 1752-d. 1848)
Charlestown, Mass.
Boston, Mass.
Wyer & Noble (c. 1823)
Wyer & Farley (c. 1828-1830)
Bibl. 15, 23, 28, 36, 44

Eleazer Wyer Jr. (b. 1786-d. 1848)
Portland, Me.
Wyer & Noble (c. 1823)
Wyer & Farley (c. 1828-1830)
Bibl. 15, 24, 25, 28, 29, 44

E. WYER

E WYER.

Benjamin Wynkoop (b. 1675-d. 1751)
New York, N.Y. (c. 1740)
Bibl. 4, 15, 24, 25, 28, 30, 35, 36, 44, 54

Benjamin Wynkoop Jr.
(b. 1705-d. 1766)
Fairfield, Conn.

New Haven, Conn.
New York, N.Y.
Bibl. 15, 25, 29, 44, 54, 61

Cornelius Wynkoop (b. 1701)
New York, N.Y. (c. 1727-1740)
Bibl. 4, 15, 23, 24, 25, 28, 29,
  35, 36, 44

Jacobus Wynkoop (c. 1765)
Kingston, N.Y.
Bibl. 23, 25, 36, 44

WYNKOOP

Christopher Wynn (b. 1795-d.
  1883)
Baltimore, Md.
Bibl. 24, 25, 29, 38, 44

C. WYNN

Robert Wynne (c. 1827-1830)
Salisbury, N.C.
Huntington & Wynne (c. 1827-
  1828)
Bibl. 21

Yates & Clark (c. 1788-1790)
Lansingburgh, N.Y.
Bibl. 20

Yates & Kent (c. 1798)
Trenton, N.J.
Joseph Yates
——— Kent
Bibl. 46, 54

Yates & Kimball (c. 1842-
  1843)
Elmira, N.Y.
William P. Yates
O. Kimball
Bibl. 20

Yates & Rockwell (c. 1787-
  1788)
Lansingburgh, N.Y.
——— Yates
John Rockwell
Bibl. 20

Henry H. Yates (c. 1822-1831)
Albany, N.Y.
Bibl. 20

Joseph Yates (c. 1798)
Trenton, N.J.
Yates & Kent
Bibl. 46

S. Yates (c. 1825)
Albany, N.Y.
Bibl. 24, 25, 28, 29, 44

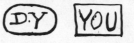

William P. Yates (c. 1841-
  1850)
Elmira, N.Y.
Yates & Kimball (c. 1842-
  1843)
Bibl. 20

Edward Yeager (c. 1844-1850)
Philadelphia, Pa.
Bibl. 3

J. M. Yeager (c. 1839-1846)
Philadelphia, Pa.
Bibl. 3

Joseph Yeager (c. 1816-1847)
Philadelphia, Pa.
Bibl. 3

William Yeager (c. 1837)
Philadelphia, Pa.
Bibl. 3

Frederick Yeiser
Danville, Ky. (c. 1814-1820)
Lexington, Ky. (c. 1857)
Bibl. 32, 54

Philip Yeiser (d. 1859)
Danville, Ky. (c. 1814)
Lexington, Ky. (c. 1859)
Bibl. 32

Alexander Yeoman (c. 1837)
Philadelphia, Pa.
Bibl. 3

Elijah Yeomans (b. 1738-d.
  1794)
Hartford, Conn.
Hadley, Mass. (?)
Bibl. 16, 28, 36, 44

Randal (Randell) Yettons
  (c. 1739)
Philadelphia, Pa.
Bibl. 3, 28, 44

Elijah Yoemans (b. 1738,
  c. 1771-1794)

Hadley, Mass.
Bibl. 23

Robert A. Yongue (c. 1852-
  1857)
Columbia, S.C.
Cooper & Yongue (c. 1852)
Bibl. 5

William Yost (c. 1846-1847)
Wheeling, Va.
Bibl. 19

Daniel You (c. 1743-1750,
  d. 1750)
Charleston, S.C.
Bibl. 5, 15, 24, 25, 44, 54

Thomas You (b. 1753-d.
  1786)
Charleston, S.C. (c. 1775)
Bibl. 5, 15, 24, 25, 44, 54

Young
(See Singleton & Young)
(See Tiffany & Young)

——— Young (c. 1829-1831)
Philadelphia, Pa.
Bibl. 3

Young & Bockius (c. 1798)
Martinsburg, Va.
William Young
Daniel Bockius
Bibl. 19

Young & Co. (c. 1848)
Columbia, S.C.
Edward Young
Bibl. 5, 54

Young & Delleker (c. 1823-
  1824)
Philadelphia, Pa.
——— Young
Samuel Delleker
Bibl. 3

Young & Tiffany
(See Tiffany & Young)

A. Young & Co. (c. 1807)
Camden, S.C.
Alexander Young
Edward Young
Bibl. 5, 25

 A Young & Co.

A. Young & Son (c. 1848)
Camden, S.C.
Alexander Young
Bibl. 54

Alexander Young (b. 1784-d.
 1856, c. 1807-1856)
Baltimore, Md.
Camden, S.C.
A. Young & Co. (c. 1807)
A. Young & Son (c. 1848)
Bibl. 5, 23, 24, 25, 29, 36, 44,
 54

| A. YOUNG | YOUNG |

Daniel D. Young (c. 1841)
Schenectady, N.Y.
Bibl. 20

Ebenezer Young (b. 1756,
 c. 1778-1780)
Hebron, Conn.
Bibl. 16, 23, 24, 25, 28, 36, 44

| YOUNG |

Edward Young (b. 1816-d.
 1848, c. 1848)
Columbia, S.C.
A. Young & Co. (c. 1807)
Young & Co.
A. Young & Son (c. 1848)
Bibl. 5, 54

| A YOUNG & SON |

Francis Young (c. 1777)
Philadelphia, Pa.
Bibl. 3

J. T. Young (c. 1855)
Petersburg, Va.
Bibl. 19

| J T YOUNG |

Jacob Young (b. 1752-d.
 1791)
Hagerstown, Md. (c. 1780-
 1791)
Bibl. 38

James Young (c. 1829-1838)
Troy, N.Y.
Bibl. 20

James H. Young (c. 1817-
 1850)
Philadelphia, Pa.
Bibl. 3

John H. Young (c. 1834)
Rochester, N.Y.
Bibl. 20

John Henry Young (c. 1833)
Albany, N.Y.
Bibl. 20

Levi Young (c. 1827)
Bridgeport, Conn.
Bibl. 16, 23, 28, 36, 44

Nicholas E. Young (c. 1839-
 1846)
Saratoga Springs, N.Y.
Bibl. 20

Philip Young (c. 1792)
Martinsburg, Va.
William & Philip Young
Bibl. 20

S. E. Young (c. 1840)
Laconia, N.H.
Bibl. 4, 25, 44

| S E YOUNG |

Samuel Young (c. 1811-1816)
Charles Town, Va.
Bibl. 19

Thomas Young
Lexington, Ky. (c. 1789-1793)
Danville, Ky. (after 1793)
Bibl. 32, 54, 68

Walter Young (c. 1831-1832,
 c. 1838-1839)
Albany, N.Y.
Bibl. 20

Walter Young (c. 1834)
Rochester, N.Y.
Bibl. 20

William Young (c. 1761-1778)
Philadelphia, Pa.
Bibl. 3, 15, 23, 25, 28, 36, 44,
 81

W. Young

WY

William Young
Martinsburg, Va. (c. 1792,
 c. 1798)

Staunton, Va. (c. 1806-1807)
William & Philip Young
 (c. 1792)
Young & Bockius (c. 1798)
Bibl. 19

William & Philip Young
 (c. 1792)
Martinsburg, Va.
Bibl. 19

Yver
(See Philip & Yver)

Zadek & Caldwell (c. 1867)
Mobile, Ala.
Bibl. 54

Zahm & Jackson (c. 1830)
New York, N.Y.
Bibl. 24, 25, 44

| ZAHM & JACKSON |

G. M. Zahm (c. 1840)
Lancaster, Pa.
Bibl. 24, 25, 44

| G. M. ZAHM |

Isaac Zane (c. 1795)
Zanesfield, Ohio
Bibl. 25, 34, 44

| I. ZANE |

Jacob Zane (c. 1837-1846)
Philadelphia, Pa.
Bibl. 3

Jesse Shenton Zane (c. 1796)
Wilmington, Del.
Bibl. 25, 30, 44

| J. ZANE |

John Zeibler (c. 1848)
St. Louis, Mo.
Bibl. 54

G. A. Zeissler (c. 1848)
Philadelphia, Pa.
Bibl. 3

William Zeller (c. 1835-1850)
Philadelphia, Pa.
Bibl. 3

Samuel Zepp (c. 1842-1850)
Philadelphia, Pa.
Bibl. 3

George A. Zumar (Zuma)
 (Zumer) (Zeuma) (Zeumer)
 (Zoomer)
Louisville, Ky. (c. 1831-1849)
E. C. Beard & Co. (c. 1831-
 1852-)
Bibl. 32, 54

PART TWO:
PEWTER

Pewter has been known since the Bronze Age, and its basic composition (copper, tin, lead, antimony or bismuth) has changed little over the years. The history of pewter in America began in Salem, Massachusetts, in 1635, when Richard Graves opened the first pewter shop. Few other pewterers are known to have worked in the colonies during the seventeenth century. Less than ten of them are recorded, and it is only recently that any seventeenth-century pewter has been located. One small spoon, made by Joseph Copeland sometime before 1691, was discovered in Jamestown, Virginia. Pewter was very important to the colonists. Not only was it inexpensive and attractive, but food was more palatable from a pewter dish. A middle-class family was usually equipped with plates, spoons, cups, and a few serving dishes and tankards for stronger drinks.

Pewter is a soft metal and it wore out with constant use. The colonist who brought his pewter with him from Europe found many pieces wearing out, and those were taken to a local pewter maker who melted and remade the pewter plates and spoons.

The pewterers of the colonies arrived with molds made in England. The expensive bronze molds were not made on this side of the ocean. There were only a limited number of molds, so it is logical to assume that all American pewter was made from the English molds. It must also be remembered that the English guilds did not want the colonists to make their own pewter. The raw materials were not available in the colonies and the guilds were in a position to force the colonist to buy British-made pewter. A high duty was placed on bar tin, while there was no duty on finished pewter. It was cheaper for the colonists to buy the guild product.

The pewter made in America in the eighteenth and nineteenth centuries was of a generally good quality. The added strength given by hammering the metal and the simplicity yet ingenuity of design, showed that the maker was attempting to produce an attractive, long-wearing item. The old-world tradition was evident in each type of pewter made. English and central European designs were preferred, reflecting the origin of most of the colonists.

The American pewterer made every type of ware needed by his customers. This included eating and drinking utensils, church vessels, candlesticks, and lamps. The need for pewter lessened as other tablewares of pottery and glass became available. The pewterers in England solved this problem by developing a slightly harder pewter that could be cast or worked on a lathe. The new metal was called "britannia," and it could be sold at a lower price because the hand finishing was omitted. Hiram Yale started to make britannia ware in Wallingford, Conn., in 1825, with the help of several English workmen.

Silver-plating was discovered about the same time britannia was developed, and the inevitable silver-plated britannia ware appeared. Silver-plating, and the ornate designs of the Victorian, changed the tastes of the buyer and the simple handmade pewter was no longer desired. The pewter makers of America were unimportant by 1850.

PEWTER PORRINGER HANDLES

American pewter-makers in each area worked in a design characteristic of that area. The handle of a pewter porringer is often the best indication of where it was made. The shapes pictured are typical of porringer handles of the eighteenth and nineteenth centuries.

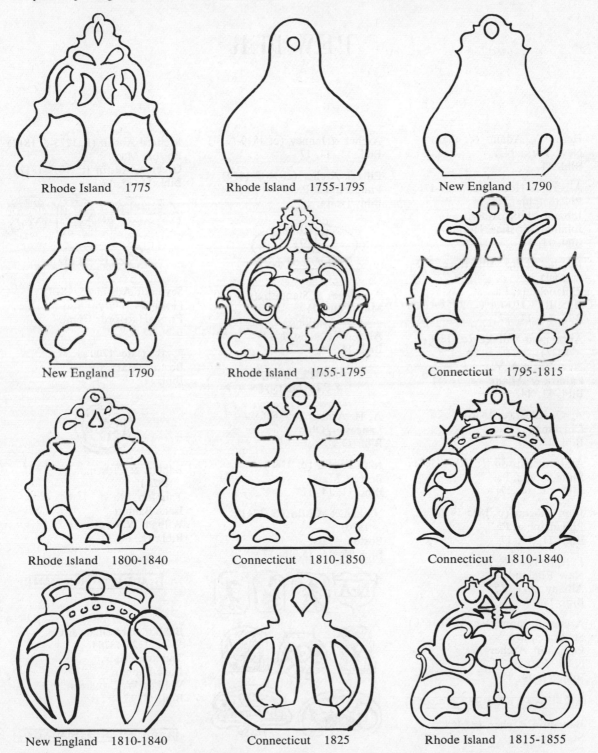

Rhode Island   1775

Rhode Island   1755-1795

New England   1790

New England   1790

Rhode Island   1755-1795

Connecticut   1795-1815

Rhode Island   1800-1840

Connecticut   1810-1850

Connecticut   1810-1840

New England   1810-1840

Connecticut   1825

Rhode Island   1815-1855

PEWTER

Henry W. Adams (c. 1857)
New York, N.Y.
Bibl. 11

Alberti & Horan (c. 1758-1764)
Philadelphia, Pa.
Johann Philip Alberti
Johann Christian Horan
Bibl. 11, 17

Johann Philip Alberti (c. 1754-
1780)
Philadelphia, Pa.
Alberti & Horan (c. 1758-1764)
Bibl. 11, 14, 17

Anthony J. Allaire (c. 1816-
1821)
New York, N.Y.
Lafetra & Allaire (c. 1816)
Bibl. 11, 14, 17

A. C. Allen (c. 1836)
Cincinnati, Ohio
Bibl. 13

Andrew Allison (c. 1835-1841)
Philadelphia, Pa.
Bibl. 11, 14, 17

John Allison (c. 1835-1836)
Philadelphia, Pa.
Bibl. 11, 14, 17

J. Applebee (c. 1820)
New England
Albany, N.Y. (?)
Bibl. 11

Archer & Janney (c. 1840-1850)
St. Louis, Mo.
Benjamin Archer
N. E. Janney
Bibl. 11, 14, 17

Benjamin Archer (c. 1847)
St. Louis, Mo.

Archer & Janney (c. 1840-1850)
Bibl. 11, 14, 17

Ellis S. Archer (c. 1842-1850)
Philadelphia, Pa.
Bibl. 11, 14, 17

Armitages & Standish (c. 1840)
Massachusetts
——— Armitages
Alexander Standish (?)
Bibl. 11, 14, 17

ARMITAGES
& STANDISH

A. H. Arnold (c. 1826)
Lancaster, Ohio
Bibl. 13

John Austin (c. 1785)
Boston, Mass.
Bibl. 11, 14, 17

Nathaniel Austin (b. 1741-d.
1816)
Boston, Mass.
Bibl. 12, 14, 15, 16, 17

Richard Austin (b. 1773-d. 1817)
Boston, Mass.
Green & Austin (c. 1812-1817)
Bibl. 11, 15, 17

Seymour Austin (c. 1810)
Geauga County, Ohio
From Hartford, Conn.
Bibl. 13

R. B. (late 1700's)
Boston, Mass. (?)
Bibl. 11

Babbitt & Crossman (c. 1814-
1828)
Taunton, Mass.
Isaac Babbitt
William W. Crossman
Bibl. 11, 14, 17

BABBITT & CROSSMAN

Babbitt, Crossman & Co.
(c. 1826-1828)
Taunton, Mass.
Isaac Babbitt
William W. Crossman
Bibl. 14, 17

Isaac Babbitt
Taunton, Mass.
Babbitt & Crossman (c. 1814-1828)
Babbitt, Crossman & Co. (c. 1826-1828)
Bibl. 11, 14

Samuel Babcock (c. 1817-1825)
Middletown, Conn.
Nott, Babcock & Johnson
Bibl. 11, 14, 17

Thomas Badcocke
(See Badocke)

Thomas Badger (Jr.) (b. 1735-d. 1815)
Boston, Mass.
Bibl. 6, 11, 14

Thomas Bad(o)ocke (o. 1710)
Philadelphia, Pa.
Bibl. 11, 14, 17

Bailey & Brainard (c. 1840)
Cobalt, Conn.
Bibl. 11

Bailey & Putnam (c. 1830-1835)
Malden, Mass.
Timothy Bailey
James Henry Putnam
Bibl. 11, 14, 17

O & A Bailey (c. 1845)
New York, N.Y.
Bibl. 12

Timothy Bailey (c. 1830-1840)
Malden, Mass.
Bailey & Putnam (c. 1830-1835)
Bibl. 11, 14, 17

John Baker (c. 1676-1696)
Boston, Mass.
Bibl. 11, 14, 17

D. S. Baldwin (c. 1850)
Connecticut
Bibl. 11

L. G. Baldwin (c. 1849)
Meriden, Conn.
Bibl. 11, 14, 17

William Ball (c. 1775-1782)
Philadelphia, Pa.
Bibl. 11, 14, 17

C. Bancks
Chelmsford, Mass. (?)
Bibl. 12

Blak(e)slee Barns (Barnes) (c. 1811-1819)
Philadelphia, Pa.
Bibl. 11, 14, 15, 16, 17

Stephen Barn(e)s (c. 1791-1810)
Middletown, Conn. (?)
Philadelphia, Pa. (?)
Bibl. 11, 12, 14, 15, 16, 17

Barr & Campbell (c. 1827)
Chillicothe, Ohio
Bibl. 13

William Bartholdt (c. 1850-1854)
Williamsburg, N.Y.
Bibl. 9, 11, 14, 17

WM BARTHOLDT

Charles E. Barton (c. 1835-1850)
Taunton, Mass.
Leonard, Reed & Barton (1837-1847)
Reed & Barton (1847 to present)
Bibl. 11, 14, 17

Francis Bassett I (b. 1690-d. 1758)
New York, N.Y.
Bibl. 11, 14, 15, 16, 17

Francis Bassett II (b. 1729-d. c. 1800)
New York, N.Y. (1749-1800)
New Jersey (c. 1780-1783)
Bibl. 6, 11, 14, 16, 17

Frederick Bassett (b. 1740-d. c. 1800)
Hartford, Conn.
New York, N.Y.
Bibl. 6, 11, 14, 15, 16, 17

John Bassett (b. 1696-d. 1761)
New York, N.Y.
Bibl. 11, 14, 15, 16, 17

S. Bast (late 19th century?)
New York, N.Y. (?)
Bibl. 12

Chester Beach (c. 1837)
Chester, Conn.
Russell & Beach (c. 1838)
Bibl. 11, 14

John Valentine Beck (b. 1731-d. 1791)

Winston-Salem, N.C.
Pennsylvania
Bibl. 11

Thomas Beck (c. 1775)
Trenton, N.J.
Bibl. 11

———— Beebe (c. 1830-1840)
St. Louis, Mo.
Sage & Beebe (after 1840)
Bibl. 11, 14

Joseph Belcher (c. 1729-1778)
New London, Conn.
Newport, R.I.
Bibl. 11, 14, 15, 16, 17

Joseph Belcher, Jr.
Newport, R.I. (c. 1769-1784)
New London, Conn. (after 1784)
Green & Belcher (c. 1787) (?)
Bibl. 11, 14, 16, 17

Lewis Benedict (c. 1815-1824)
Albany, N.Y.
Stafford, Spencer & Co. (c. 1815-
1817)
S. Stafford & Co. (c. 1817-1824)
Stafford, Benedict & Co.
(c. 1824)
Bibl. 11, 14, 17

Benham & Whitney (c. 1850)
New York, N.Y.
Bibl. 11, 14, 17

Morris Benham (c. 1849)
West Meriden, Conn.
Frary & Benham
Bibl. 11, 14, 17

Thomas Berkshire (c. 1820-
1840)
Putnam, Ohio
Bibl. 13

———— Bidgood (Bigood)
(c. 1825)
Philadelphia, Pa.

Plumly & Bidgood
Bibl. 11, 14

Billings & Danforth (c. 1798-
1801)
Providence, R.I.
William Billings
Job Danforth
Bibl. 14, 17

William Billings (b. 1768-
d. 1813)
Providence, R.I.
Billings & Danforth (c. 1798-
1801)
Bibl. 11, 14, 15, 16, 17

James Bird (c. 1820)
New York, N.Y.
Bibl. 6, 11, 14, 17

James Bland (Blaun) (c. 1760)
Westchester County, N.Y.
Bibl. 11, 14, 17

Peter Blin (b. 1733, c. 1757-
1759)
Boston, Mass.
Bibl. 11, 14, 17

Boardman
(See Henry S. Boardman)

Boardman & Co. (c. 1825-
1827)
New York, N.Y.
Thomas Danforth Boardman
Sherman Boardman
Bibl. 6, 12, 14, 16

Boardman & Hall (c. 1844-
1845)
Philadelphia, Pa.
Henry S. Boardman

Thomas Danforth Boardman
Franklin D. Hall
Bibl. 12, 14

Boardman & Hart (c. 1828-
1850)
New York, N.Y.
Hartford, Conn. (?)
Thomas Danforth Boardman
Lucius D. Hart
Bibl. 6, 11, 12, 14, 16

Boardman Warranted
(See Luther Boardman)

Henry S. Boardman (c. 1841-
1861)
Hartford, Conn.
Philadelphia, Pa. (c. 1830-
1848)
Hall, Boardman & Co. (c. 1830-
1848)
Boardman & Hall (c. 1844-
1845)
Hall & Boardman (c. 1849-
1857)
Bibl. 11, 14, 16, 17

BOARDMAN
PHILADA

J. D. Boardman (c. 1828)
Hartford, Conn.
Bibl. 11, 14

Luther Boardman
South Reading, Mass. (c. 1836-
1837)
Chester, Conn. (c. 1837-1842)
East Haddam, Conn. (after
1842)
Bibl. 11, 14

Sherman Boardman (b. 1787-d. 1861)
New York, N.Y. (c. 1822-1827)
Hartford, Conn.
T. D. & S. Boardman (c. 1810-1854)
Timothy Boardman & Co. (c. 1822-1824)
Boardman & Co. (c. 1825-1827)
Bibl. 12, 14, 15

T. D. & S. Boardman (c. 1810-1854)
Hartford, Conn.
Thomas Danforth Boardman
Sherman Boardman
Bibl. 12, 14, 16

Thomas Danforth Boardman (b. 1784-d. 1873)
New York, N.Y. (c. 1825-1827)
Philadelphia, Pa. (c. 1844-1845)
Hartford, Conn.
T. D. & S. Boardman (c. 1810-1854)
Timothy Boardman & Co. (c. 1822-1824)
Boardman & Co. (c. 1825-1827)
Boardman & Hart (c. 1828-1850)
Boardman & Hall (c. 1844-1845)
Bibl. 6, 11, 14, 15, 16

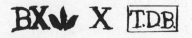

Timothy Boardman (c. 1798-1825)
Hartford, Conn.
Bibl. 15

Timothy Boardman & Co. (c. 1822-1824)
New York, N.Y.
Thomas Danforth Boardman
Sherman Boardman
Bibl. 11, 14

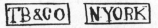

Robert Bonning (Bonnynge) (c. 1731-1739)
Boston, Mass.
Bibl. 11, 14

———— Bonzigues (c. 1800-1810)
Philadelphia, Pa.
Bibl. 11, 14

John Bouis (c. 1829-1834)
Baltimore, Md.
John & Joseph Bouis (c. 1830)
John Bouis & Son (c. 1831-1832)
Bibl. 14

John Bouis & Son (c. 1831-1832)
Baltimore, Md.
Bibl. 14

John & Joseph Bouis (c. 1830)
Baltimore, Md.
Bibl. 11

Joseph Bouis (c. 1834)
Baltimore, Md.
John & Joseph Bouis (c. 1830)
Bibl. 14

———— Bowdith (c. 1814)
Salem, Mass.
Bibl. 11

Samuel Bowles (c. 1787-1788)
Boston, Mass.
Bibl. 11, 14

Nathaniel Bowman (c. 1806-1814)
Charlestown, Mass.
Bibl. 11, 14

Parks Boyd (c. 1795-1819)
Philadelphia, Pa.
Bibl. 11, 14, 15, 16

Robert Boyle (b.c. 1732-d.c. 1780)
New York, N.Y. (c. 1752-1758)
Bibl. 11, 14, 15, 16

Bradford & McEuen (c. 1772-1785)
New York, N.Y.
Cornelius Bradford
Malcolm McEuen
Bibl. 11, 14

Cornelius Bradford (w. 1753-1786)
New York, N.Y. (c. 1772-1785)
Philadelphia, Pa.
Bradford & McEuen (c. 1772-1785)
Bibl. 11, 14, 16

John Bradford (c. 1784-1788)
Boston, Mass.
Bibl. 11, 14

William Bradford (Jr.) (b. 1688-d. 1758)
New York, N.Y.
Bibl. 11, 14, 16

Elijah Braman (c. 1834-1839)
Taunton, Mass.
Warren, R.I.
Bibl. 11

Reese Branson (c. 1802-1806)
St. Clairsville, Ohio
Bibl. 13

Wallace Brattan (c. 1810)
Geauga County, Ohio
Bibl. 13

——— Bretney (c. 1806-1810)
Lebanon, Ohio
Bibl. 13

T. M. Brickley (c. 1835)
Troy, N.Y.
Bibl. 11

Timothy Brigden (c. 1816-1819)
Albany, N.Y.
Bibl. 11, 14, 16

———n Brigh———
(before 1825)
Location unknown
Bibl. 12

Samuel Brillhart (c. 1820)
Coshocton, Ohio
Bibl. 13

Brook Farm (c. 1841-1847)
West Roxbury, Mass.
Bibl. 11, 14, 16

David S. Brooks (c. 1828)
Hartford, Conn.
Bibl. 11, 14

James Broom (c. 1748)
New Castle, Del.
Bibl. 11

Browe & Dougherty (c. 1845)
Newark, N.J.
Bibl. 11, 14

A. Brower (c. 1820)
New York, N.Y.
Bibl. 11

John Andrew Brunstrom
(d. 1793)

Philadelphia, Pa. (c. 1783-1793)
Bibl. 11, 14, 16

Townsend M. Buckley (c. 1854-
1857)
Troy, N.Y.
Bibl. 9, 11, 14

T.M.BUCKLEY

Bull, Lyman, & Couch (c. 1845-
1849)
Meriden, Conn.
——— Bull
William W. Lyman
Ira Couch
Bibl. 11, 14

Thomas Bumste(a)d
Roxbury, Mass. (c. 1640-1643)
Boston, Mass. (c. 1643-1677)
Bibl. 6, 11, 14

Aaron Burdett (c. 1838-1841)
Baltimore, Md.
Bibl. 11, 14

Thomas Byles
Newport, R.I. (c. 1711-1712)
Philadelphia, Pa. (c. 1738-1771)
Bibl. 11, 14, 16

E. C. (c. 1800)
New England (?)
Bibl. 11

I. C. (c. 1725-1760)
New England (?)
Boston, Mass. (?)
Bibl. 11

J. W. Cahill & Co. (c. 1835)
Location unknown
Bibl. 11, 14, 17

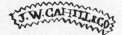

William Calder (b. 1792-d.
1856)
Providence, R.I.
Bibl. 6, 11, 14, 15, 16, 17

John Calverley (c. 1840)
Philadelphia, Pa.
Bibl. 11, 14, 17

William E. Camp (c. 1850)
Middletown, Conn.
Bibl. 11, 14, 17

John Campbell (w. 1749-d.
1774)
Annapolis, Md.
Bibl. 11, 14, 17

Mungo Campbell (c. 1750-1752)
Philadelphia, Pa.
Bibl. 11, 14, 17

Samuel Campbell (Campmell)
(c. 1783-1800)
Middletown, Conn.
Bibl. 11, 14, 16, 17

Capen & Molineux (c. 1848-
1854)
New York, N.Y.
Ephraim Capen
George Molineux
Bibl. 11, 14, 17

Ephraim Capen
Dorchester, Mass. (c. 1844-1847)
New York, N.Y. (c. 1848-1854)
Capen & Molineux (c. 1848-
1854)
Bibl. 11, 14, 17

John Carnes (b. 1698-d. 1760)
Boston, Mass.

Bibl. 11, 14, 16, 17

Samuel Carter (w. 1712-1747)
Boston, Mass.
Bibl. 11, 14, 17

Gideon Casey (b. 1726-d. 1786)
Providence, R.I.
South Kingston, R.I.
Bibl. 11

Hugh Cassidy (c. 1820)
St. Clairsville, Ohio
Bibl. 13

Cincinnati Britannia Co.
(c. 1850)
Cincinnati, Ohio
Bibl. 11

Jonas Clark(e) (b. 1690-d. 1760)
Boston, Mass. (w. 1715-1737)
Bibl. 11, 14, 17

Joshua Clark (c. 1813)
Lancaster, Ohio
Bibl. 13

Thomas Clark(e) (c. 1674-1720)
Boston, Mass.
Bibl. 6, 11, 14, 17

Mathew Clunn (c. 1769)
Trenton, N.J.
Bibl. 11

H. R. Colburn (c. 1830)
Location unknown
Bibl. 11

George Coldwell (c. 1787-d.
1811)
New York, N.Y.
Bibl. 6, 11, 14, 16, 17

Oren Colton (c. 1835-1838)
Philadelphia, Pa.
Woodbury & Colton (c. 1835)
Bibl. 11, 17

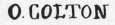

John Comer (b. 1674-d. 1721)
Boston, Mass.
Bibl. 6, 11, 14, 17

John Comer Jr. (c. 1700-1706)
Boston, Mass.
Bibl. 11, 14, 17

Claudius Compaire (c. 1736)
Charleston, S.C.
Bibl. 11

S. L. Cone (c. 1849)
Meriden, Conn.
Bibl. 11, 14, 17

Thomas Connell (c. 1829-1840)
Philadelphia, Pa.
Palethorp & Connell (c. 1820-
1840)
Bibl. 11, 14, 17

———— Conrad (c. 1806-1810)
Lebanon, Ohio
Bibl. 13

———— Cook (after 1830)
Portland, Me.
Woodman, Cook & Co. (c. 1840)
Bibl. 14

Joseph Copeland (c. 1675-1691)
Jamestown, Va. (c. 1688-1691)
Chuckatuck, Va.
Bibl. 11, 14, 16, 17

W. Corbin (c. 1818-1831)
Cincinnati, Ohio
Bibl. 11

Anthony Corne (c. 1735)
Charleston, S.C.
Bibl. 11, 14, 17

Shubel Cottam (c. 1815)
Albany, N.Y.
Bibl. 9

———— Cotton (c. 1840)
Middlefield, Conn.
Hall & Cotton
Bibl. 11, 14

Ira Couch (c. 1830-1845)
Meriden, Conn.
Griswold and Couch (c. 1830)
Lyman & Couch (c. 1844-1845)
Bull, Lyman, & Couch (c. 1845-
1849)
Bibl. 11, 14

George Cowles (c. 1834-1835)
East Meriden, Conn.
Lewis & Cowles (c. 1834-1836)
Bibl. 11, 14

William Cox(e) (c. 1715-1721)
Philadelphia, Pa.
Bibl. 11, 14, 17

Creesy & Lee (c. 1815-1820)
Beverly, Mass.
———— Creesy
Richard Lee Jr.
Bibl. 11

Crossman, West, & Leonard
(c. 1828-1830)
Taunton, Mass.
William W. Crossman
William A. West
Zephaniah A. Leonard
Bibl. 11, 14, 17

CROSSMAN
WEST & LEONARD

Ebenezer Crossman (early
1800's)
Taunton, Mass.
Newport, R.I.
Bibl. 11

William W. Crossman (c. 1824-
1835)
Taunton, Mass.
Babbitt & Crossman (c. 1814-
1828)
Babbitt, Crossman & Co.
(c. 1826-1828)
Crossman, West, & Leonard
(c. 1828-1830)
Bibl. 14

Curtis & Co. (c. 1868)
New York, N.Y.
Stephen Curtis Jr.
Bibl. 12

Curtis & Curtis (c. 1838-1840)
Meriden, Conn.
Edwin E. Curtis
Lemuel J. Curtis
Bibl. 11, 14, 17

Curtis & Lyman (c. 1846)
Meriden, Conn.
Lemuel J. Curtis
William W. Lyman
Bibl. 11, 14, 17

Edwin E. Curtis (c. 1838-1845)
Meriden, Conn.
Curtis & Curtis (c. 1838-1840)
Bibl. 11, 14, 17

Enos H. Curtis (c. 1845-1849)
Meriden, Conn.
Bibl. 11, 14, 17

I. Curtis(s) (c. 1815-1820)
Connecticut
Bibl. 11, 12, 14, 15

Lemuel J. Curtis(s) (c. 1836-
1849)
Meriden, Conn.
Curtis & Curtis (c. 1838-1840)
Curtis & Lyman (c. 1846)
Bibl. 11, 14, 17

Stephen Curtis Jr. (c. 1858-1867)
New York, N.Y.
Yale & Curtis (c. 1858-1867)
Curtis & Co. (c. 1868)
Bibl. 11, 12, 14

Daniel Curtis (c. 1822-1850)
Albany, N.Y.
Bibl. 9, 11, 12, 14, 15, 16, 17

F. Curtiss
Connecticut (?)
Bibl. 11

Joseph Curtiss Jr. (c. 1827-
1859)
Troy, N.Y. (c. 1827-1832)
Albany, N.Y. (c. 1832-1859)
Bibl. 9, 11, 14, 17

David Cutler (b. 1703-d. 1772)
Boston, Mass.
Bibl. 11, 14, 17

James Cutler (c. 1770-179?)
Salem, Mass.
Bibl. 11

Edward Danforth
Middletown, Conn. (c. 1788-
1790)
Hartford, Conn. (c. 1790-1794)
Bibl. 11, 14, 15, 16, 17

Henry G. Danforth (c. 1830)
Richmond, Va.
Bibl. 11

Job Danforth (c. 1798-1801)
Providence, R.I.
Billings & Danforth
Bibl. 11, 14, 17

John Danforth (c. 1741-1799)
Norwich, Conn.
Bibl. 11, 14, 15, 16, 17

John Danforth (c. 1804)
Ellsworth, Ohio
Bibl. 13

Joseph Danforth (c. 1758-1788)
Middletown, Conn.
Bibl. 11, 14, 15, 16, 17

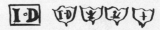

Josiah Danforth (b. 1803-
d. 1872)
Middletown, Conn.
Bibl. 11, 14, 15, 16, 17

Joseph Danforth & Thomas
Danforth II (18th century)
Connecticut
Bibl. 16

Joseph Danforth Jr. (b. 1783-
d. 1844)
Richmond, Va.
Bibl. 11, 14, 16, 17

Samuel Danforth (c. 1772-1827)
Norwich, Conn.
Bibl. 11, 14, 15, 16, 17

Samuel Danforth (b. 1774-
d. 1816)
Hartford, Conn.
Bibl. 6, 11, 14, 15, 16, 17

Samuel Danforth (c. 1804)
Ellsworth, Ohio
Bibl. 13

Thomas Danforth
Taunton, Mass. (c. 1727-1733)
Norwich, Conn. (c. 1733-1773)
Bibl. 11, 14, 15, 17

Thomas Danforth II (b. 1731-
d. 1782)
Middletown, Conn.
Bibl. 11, 14, 15, 16, 17

Thomas Danforth III
Stepney, Conn. (c. 1777-1818)
Philadelphia, Pa. (c. 1807-1813)
Bibl. 11, 12, 14, 16, 17

Thomas Danforth IV (b. 1792-
d. 1836)
Augusta, Ga.
Philadelphia, Pa.
Bibl. 11, 14, 17

William Danforth (b. 1792-
d. 1820)
Middletown, Conn.
Bibl. 11, 14, 15, 16, 17

Edmund Davis (c. 1721)
Philadelphia, Pa.
Bibl. 11

Benjamin Day (b. 1706-d. 1757)
Newport, R.I.
Bibl. 11, 14, 16, 17

Andrew Deemer (c. 1827)
Chillicothe, Ohio
Bibl. 13

Thomas S. Derby (c. 1812-1852)
Middletown, Conn.
Thomas S. Derby & Son
  (c. 1849)
Bibl. 11, 14, 16, 17

Thomas S. Derby Jr. (c. 1840-
1850)
Middletown, Conn.

Thomas S. Derby & Son
  (c. 1849)
Bibl. 11, 14, 17

T.S.DERBY II

Thomas S. Derby & Son
  (c. 1849)
Middletown, Conn.
Bibl. 14, 17

Cornelius B. DeRiemer & Co.
  (c. 1833-1835)
Auburn, N.Y.
Bibl. 9, 11, 14, 17

C.B.DERIEMER&CO.
AUBURN

Dietz Bros. & Co.
New York, N.Y. (?)
Cincinnati, Ohio (?)
Bibl. 11

William Digg(e)s (c. 1701-1702)
New York, N.Y.
Bibl. 11, 17

Dolbeare & Jackson (c. 1725)
Boston, Mass.
John Dolbeare
Jonathan Jackson
Bibl. 11

Edmund Dolbeare (c. 1671-
1705)
Boston, Mass.
Bibl. 11, 14, 17

James Dolbeare (b. 1705-
d. 1775)
Boston, Mass.
Bibl. 14, 17

John Dolbeare (b. 1690-d. 1740)
Boston, Mass.
Dolbeare & Jackson (c. 1725)

Bibl. 11, 14, 17

Joseph Dolbeare (c. 1690-1704)
Boston, Mass.
Bibl. 11, 14, 17

———— Dougherty (c. 1845)
Newark, N.J.
Browe & Dougherty
Bibl. 11, 14

John Dulty (c. 1807)
Zanesville, Ohio
Bibl. 13

E. Dunham (after 1825)
Location unknown
Bibl. 14, 17

E. DUNHAM

Frederick Dunham (c. 1861-
1882)
Portland, Me.
R. Dunham & Sons
Bibl. 11, 14, 17

Joseph Dunham (c. 1861-1882)
Portland, Me.
R. Dunham & Sons
Bibl. 11, 14, 17

R. Dunham & Sons (c. 1861-
1882)
Portland, Me.
Rufus, Joseph and Frederick
Dunham
Bibl. 11, 14, 17

Rufus Dunham (b. 1815-
d. 1882)
Portland, Me. (c. 1861-1882)
Westbrook, Me.
R. Dunham & Sons (c. 1861-
1882)
Bibl. 6, 11, 14, 16, 17

R. DUNHAM

Thomas Dunham (c. 1813)
Lancaster, Ohio
Bibl. 13

H. Dunlop & Co. (c. 1830)
Philadelphia, Pa.
Bibl. 11

Andrew Dunseth (c. 1812-1814)
Cincinnati, Ohio
Bibl. 13

Daniel Durninger (c. 1722-1723)
Boston, Mass.
Bibl. 11, 14, 17

Semper Eadem
(See *Eadem Semper*)
Bibl. 11, 14, 16

Eastabrook
Richard E(a)stabrook(e)
(c. 1720)
Boston, Mass.
Bibl. 11, 14, 17

Eastman & Co.
Albany, N.Y.
Bibl. 12

Simon Edgell (b. 1687-d. 1742)
Philadelphia, Pa.
Bibl. 11, 14, 15, 16, 17

William Edgell (c. 1724)
Boston, Mass.
Bibl. 11, 14, 17

Lemuel Effinger (c. 1813-1816)
Lancaster, Ohio
Bibl. 13

Samuel Effinger (c. 1813-1826)
Lancaster, Ohio
Bibl. 13

Jacob Eggleston
Middletown, Conn. (c. 1795-
1807)
Fayetteville, N.C. (c. 1807-1813)
Bibl. 11, 14, 16, 17

Eli Eldrige (Eldrege)
Boston, Mass. (c. 1849)
Taunton, Mass. (c. 1860)
Bibl. 11, 14, 17

John Ellison (c. 1837)
Philadelphia, Pa.
Bibl. 11, 14, 17

William (J.) El(l)sworth
(b. 1767-d. 1798)
New York, N.Y.
Bibl. 6, 11, 14, 16, 17

Endicott & Sumner (c. 1846-
1851)
New York, N.Y.
Edmund Endicott
William F. Sumner
Bibl. 11, 14, 17

Edmund Endicott (c. 1846-1853)
New York, N.Y.
Endicott & Sumner (c. 1846-
1851)
Bibl. 11, 14, 17

E. ENDICOTT

George Engel (c. 1850)
Philadelphia, Pa.
Bibl. 11

N. England (c. 1755-1793)
Newport, R.I.
May be for New England
Used by David Melville
Bibl. 11

James Everett (c. 1716-1717)
Philadelphia, Pa.

Bibl. 11, 14, 17

James C. Feltman Jr. (c. 1847-
1848)
Albany, N.Y.
Sheldon & Feltman (c. 1847-
1848)
Smith & Feltman (c. 1849-1852)
Bibl. 9, 11, 14, 17

Gaius & Jason Fenn (c. 1831-
1843)
New York, N.Y.
Bibl. 11, 14, 16, 17

Philip Fields (c. 1799)
New York, N.Y.
Bibl. 6, 11, 14, 17

I & T Fischer (late 18th
century)
Pennsylvania
Bibl. 11

John Fischer (late 18th century)
Pennsylvania
Bibl. 11

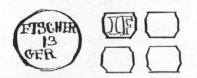

Flagg & Homan (c. 1842-1854)
(Homan & Flagg)
Cincinnati, Ohio
Asa F. Flagg
Henry Homan
Bibl. 11, 14, 17

Asa F. Flagg (c. 1842-1854)
Cincinnati, Ohio
Flagg & Homan (c. 1842-1854)
(Homan & Flagg)
Homan Manufacturing Co.
(c. 1847)
H. Homan & Co. (c. 1847-1864)
Bibl. 11, 13, 14, 17

David Flagg (c. 1750-1772)
Boston, Mass.
Bibl. 11, 14, 17

Thomas Fletcher (c. 1837-1841)
Philadelphia, Pa.
Bibl. 11, 14, 17

Daniel Francis (c. 1833-1842)
Buffalo, N.Y.
Whitmore & Francis (c. 1833-
1835)
Bibl. 11, 14, 17

Thomas Francis
Boston, Mass. (c. 1718)
Bibl. 11, 14, 17

Frary & Benham (c. 1849)
Meriden, Conn.
James A. Frary
Morris Benham
Bibl. 11, 14, 17

James A. Frary (c. 1845-1849)
Meriden, Conn.
Frary & Benham (c. 1849)
Bibl. 11, 14, 17

Nathaniel Frink (c. 1820)
Northampton, Mass.
Bibl. 11

John Fryers (b. 1685-d. 1776)
Newport, R.I.
Bibl. 11, 14, 15, 17

Fuller & Smith (c. 1849-1851)
New London, Conn.

Bibl. 11, 14, 17

H. G.
Boston, Mass.
Henry Green(?)
Bibl. 11

I. G. (18th century)
Virginia
Bibl. 11, 16

I. G. (c. 1800)
New England
Bibl. 11

R. G. (early 19th century)
New England
Roswell Gleason (?)
Bibl. 11

S. G. (c. 1800)
New England
Bibl. 11

———— Gable (c. 1840)
Cadiz, Ohio
Bibl. 13

Lewis G(e)anty (c. 1800-1803)
Baltimore, Md.
Bibl. 11, 12, 14, 17

————y & Gardner (c. 1830-
1840)
Bibl. 11, 14, 17

Y & GARDNER

Anthony George Jr. (c. 1839-
1847)
Philadelphia, Pa.
Bibl. 11, 14, 17

Gerhardt & Co. (c. 1840)
Location unknown

Bibl. 11, 14, 17

Roswell Gleason (b. 1799-
d. 1877)
Dorchester, Mass.
Bibl. 6, 11, 14, 16, 17

Glenmore
(See next entry)

Glennore Co. (c. 1828)
Cranston, R.I.
George Richardson
Bibl. 11, 12, 14, 17

John Gooch (before 1850)
Location unknown
Bibl. 11

J. Gould (c. 1828)
Cincinnati, Ohio
Bibl. 13

Graham & Savage (c. 1837)
(Savage & Graham)
Middletown, Conn.
Jasper Graham
John B. Graham
William H. Savage
Bibl. 14

Jasper Graham (c. 1837)
Middletown, Conn.
Graham & Savage
Bibl. 14

John B. Graham (c. 1835-1838)
Middletown, Conn.
Graham & Savage (c. 1837)
Bibl. 11, 14

Samuel Gr(e)ame(s) (c. 1639-
1645)
Boston, Mass.
Bibl. 11, 14, 17

J. B. & H. H. Graves (c. 1852)
Middletown, Conn.
Joshua B. Graves

Henry H. Graves
Bibl. 14, 17

J.B.&H.H.GRAVES

Joshua B. Graves (c. 1850)
Middletown, Conn.
J. B. & H. H. Graves (c. 1852)
Bibl. 11, 14, 17

J.B.GRAVES

Henry H. Graves (c. 1849-1851)
Middletown, Conn.
J. B. & H. H. Graves (c. 1852)
Bibl. 11, 14, 17

H.H.GRAVES

Richard Gr(e)aves (c. 1635-
1667)
Salem, Mass.
Bibl. 12, 14, 17

Greames
(See Grame)

Greaves
(See Richard Graves)

Green & Austin (c. 1812-1817)
Boston, Mass.
Samuel Green
Richard Austin
Bibl. 14, 17

Green & Belcher (c. 1787)
New London, Conn.
John Green
Joseph Belcher (Jr.?)
Bibl. 89

Green & Richardson (c. 1818)
Boston, Mass.
Samuel Green
George Richardson
Bibl. 14, 17

Andrew Green (c. 1773-1798)
Boston, Mass.
Bibl. 6, 11, 14, 17

John Green (c. 1787)
New London, Conn.
Green & Belcher
Bibl. 89

Jonas Green (c. 1786-1787)
Boston, Mass.
Bibl. 11, 14, 17

Samuel Green (c. 1794-1830)
Boston, Mass.

Green & Austin (c. 1812-1817)
Green & Richardson (c. 1818)
Bibl. 6, 11, 14, 15, 16, 17

Samuel Green Jr. (c. 1821-1835)
Boston, Mass.
Bibl. 11, 14, 17

Thomas Green (b. 1715-d. 1794)
Boston, Mass.
Bibl. 6, 11, 14, 17

Thomas Green Jr. (b. 1746-
d. c. 1790)
Boston, Mass.
Bibl. 11, 14, 17

Timothy Green (c. 1780-1782)
New London, Conn.
Boston, Mass.
Bibl. 11, 14, 17

Grennell
(See Grindell)

Henry Grilley (c. 1790)
Waterbury, Conn.
Bibl. 12

Thomas Grindell (Grennell)
(c. 1789-1791)
New York, N.Y.
Bibl. 11, 14, 17

Griswold & Couch (c. 1830)
Meriden, Conn.
Ashbil Griswold
Ira Couch
Bibl. 11, 14, 17

Ashbil Griswold (b. 1784-
d. 1853)
Meriden, Conn.
Griswold & Couch (c. 1830)
Bibl. 11, 14, 15, 16, 17

Giles Griswold (c. 1818-1820)
Augusta, Ga.

Bibl. 11, 14, 17

Sylvester Griswold (c. 1820)
Baltimore, Md.
Bibl. 11, 14, 16, 17

D. M. H. (c. 1830)
Meriden, Conn.
Bibl. 11, 17

DMH

G. H. (c. 1840)
New York, N.Y.
Bibl. 11

Halden
(See Holden)

Hall, Boardman & Co. (c. 1830-
1848)
Philadelphia, Pa.
Franklin D. Hall
Henry S. Boardman
Bibl. 11, 14, 17

Hall & Boardman (c. 1849-1857)
Philadelphia, Pa.
Franklin D. Hall
Henry S. Boardman
Bibl. 12, 14, 17

Hall & Cotton (c. 1840)
Middlefield, Conn.
Bibl. 11, 14, 16, 17

Hall, Elton, & Co. (1857-1882)
Wallingford, Conn.
Bibl. 11, 17

Franklin D. Hall
Hartford, Conn. (c. 1840)
Philadelphia, Pa. (c. 1842-1857)

Hall, Boardman & Co. (c. 1830-
1848)
Boardman & Hall (c. 1844-1845)
Hall & Boardman (c. 1849-1857)
Bibl. 11, 12, 14, 17

John H. Hall (c. 1815-1817)
Middletown, Conn.
Johnson, Hall & Co.
Bibl. 11, 14, 17

James Hamill (c. 1820)
Portsmouth, Ohio
Bibl. 13

Hamlin & Jones (c. 1774-1781)
Providence, R.I.
Samuel Hamlin
Gershom Jones
Bibl. 11, 14, 17

Samuel Hamlin (b. 1746-
d. 1801)
Hartford, Conn. (c. 1767-1769)
Providence, R.I. (c. 1774-1781)
Henshaw & Hamlin (c. 1767-
1769)
Hamlin & Jones (c. 1774-1781)
Bibl. 11, 12, 15, 16

Samuel E. Hamlin (Jr.)
(b. 1774-d. 1864)
Providence, R.I.
Bibl. 6, 11, 14, 17

William (?) Hamlin (b. 1772-
d. 1869)
Providence, R.I.
Bibl. 12

Milton Hampton (c. 1813)
Lancaster, Ohio
Bibl. 13

———— Harbeson (c. 1800)
Philadelphia, Pa.
Benjamin, Joseph, or Robert
Bibl. 14, 17

Benjamin & Joseph Harbeson
Philadelphia, Pa. (c. 1765-1775)
(c. 1778-1800)
Lancaster, Pa. (c. 1775-1778)
Bibl. 11, 16

Robert Harbeson (c. 1800)
Philadelphia, Pa.
Bibl. 89

George Harner (c. 1760)
New York, N.Y.
Bibl. 11, 14, 17

Joseph Harrison (c. 1829-1852)
Philadelphia, Pa.
Bibl. 11, 14, 17

Lucius Hart & Co. (after 1864)
Hartford, Conn.
New York, N.Y.
Lucius D. Hart
Bibl. 11, 12, 15

Lucius D. Hart (c. 1828-1850)
Hartford, Conn.
New York, N.Y.
Boardman & Hart (c. 1828-1850)
Lucius Hart & Co. (after 1864)
Bibl. 11, 12, 15

Abraham Hasselberg
Wilmington, Del. (c. 1759)
Philadelphia, Pa. (c. 1762-1769)
Bibl. 11, 14, 17

Francis G. Hendricks (c. 1771-
1784)
Charleston, S.C.
Bibl. 11, 14, 17

Andrew Henry (c. 1761)
Orange County, N.Y.
Bibl. 11, 14, 17

Henshaw & Hamlin (c. 1767-
1769)
Hartford, Conn.
Benjamin Henshaw
Samuel Hamlin
Bibl. 11

Benjamin Henshaw (b. 1731-
d. 1793)
Hartford, Conn.
Middletown, Conn.
Henshaw & Hamlin
Bibl. 11

C. & J. Hera (c. 1800-1812)
Philadelphia, Pa.
Christian & John Hera
Bibl. 11, 14, 15, 16, 17

Charlotte Hera (Hero) (c. 1791-
1798)
Philadelphia, Pa.
Bibl. 6, 12

Christian Hera (c. 1791-1817)
Philadelphia, Pa.
C. & J. Hera (c. 1800-1812)
Bibl. 11, 12, 14, 17

John Hera (c. 1800-1812)
Philadelphia, Pa.
C. & J. Hera
Bibl. 11, 14, 17

John Hera II (c. 1817-1821)
Philadelphia, Pa.
Bibl. 11, 14, 17

John Christian Hera
(See Johann Christian Horan)

Charlotte Hero
(See Charlotte Hera)

Christopher Hero (c. 1797-1798)
Philadelphia, Pa.
Bibl. 12

Christiana Herroe (c. 1785)
Philadelphia, Pa.
Bibl. 12

S. S. Hersey (c. 1830)
Belfast, Me.
Bibl. 11, 14, 17

John Christopher Heyne
(b. 1715-d. 1781)
Lancaster, Pa.
Bibl. 11, 14, 16, 17

John Hill (c. 1846-1848)
New York, N.Y.
Bibl. 11, 14, 17

T. Hill (c. 1800)
Location unknown
Bibl. 16

Charles Hillsburgh (c. 1830-
1840)
New York, N.Y.
Bibl. 11, 14, 17

John & Daniel Hinsdale
(c. 1815)
Middletown, Conn.
Bibl. 11, 14, 16, 17

John Holden (Halden)
(c. 1743)
New York, N.Y.
Bibl. 12

Robert Holmes & Sons (c. 1853-
1854)
Baltimore, Md.
Bibl. 11, 14, 17

HOLMES&SONS
BALTIMORE

Thomas R. Holt (c. 1845-1849)
Meriden, Conn.
Bibl. 11, 14, 17

T·R·HOLT

John Holyoke (b. 1693-d. 1775)
Boston, Mass.
Bibl. 11, 14, 17

H. Homan & Co. (c. 1847-1864)
Cincinnati, Ohio
Henry Homan
Asa F. Flagg
Bibl. 14, 16, 17

HOMAN
& INN

HOMAN&CO
CINCINNATI

Homan & Flagg (c. 1842-1854)
(Flagg & Homan)
Cincinnati, Ohio
Henry Homan
Asa F. Flagg
Bibl. 17

Homan Manufacturing Co.
(c. 1847)
Cincinnati, Ohio
Henry Homan
Asa F. Flagg
Bibl. 13

Henry Homan (c. 1847-d. 1864)
Cincinnati, Ohio
Homan & Flagg (c. 1842-1854)
Homan Manufacturing Co.
(c. 1847)
H. Homan & Co. (c. 1847-1864)
Bibl. 11, 13, 14, 17

H·HOMAN

Margaret Homan (Mrs. Henry)
(c. 1865-1887)
Cincinnati, Ohio
Managed Homan firm with sons
Frank, Louis and Joseph T.
Bibl. 13

"Widow" Hooker (c. 1767)
Hartford, Conn.
Bibl. 11

Henry Hopper (c. 1842-1847)
New York, N.Y.
Bibl. 11, 14, 16, 17

H·HOPPER

Johann Christian Horan
(Hera?) (c. 1758-1786)
Philadelphia, Pa.
Alberti & Horan
Bibl. 11, 14, 17

William Horsewell (c. 1705-1708)
New York, N.Y.
Bibl. 11, 14, 17

E. N. Horsford (c. 1830)
Location unknown
Bibl. 11, 14, 17

E.N.HORSFORD'S
PATENT

Houghton & Wallace (c. 1840-1843)
Philadelphia, Pa.
Bibl. 11, 14, 17

HOUGHTON
&
WALLACE

Edwin House (c. 1841-1846)
Hartford, Conn.
Bibl. 11, 14, 17

F. Hubley (c. 1830)
Crawford County, Ohio
Bibl. 13

Michael Humble (c. 1779)
Louisville, Ky.
Bibl. 89

Wlllls Humiston (Huniston)
(c. 1830-1860)
Troy, N.Y.
Bibl. 9, 11, 14, 17

S. Hunt (c. 1840)
Location unknown
Bibl. 11, 14, 17

S. HUNT

George Hunter (c. 1831)
Troy, N.Y.
Bibl. 9, 11, 14, 17

Martin Hyde (c. 1857-1858)
New York, N.Y.
Bibl. 11, 14, 17

M HYDE

T. I. (b. 1727-d. 1773)
Taunton, Mass.

Norwich, Conn.
Thomas Danforth I (?)
Bibl. 11

Joseph Isly (c. 1715)
New York, N.Y.
Bibl. 11, 14, 17

Henry Jack
Chillicothe, Ohio (c. 1816)
Columbus, Ohio (c. 1827)
Bibl. 13

William Jack (c. 1816)
Columbus, Ohio
Bibl. 13

Isaac Jackson (late 18th
century)
Pennsylvania
Bibl. 11

Jonathan Jackson (b. 1672-
d. 1736)
Boston, Mass.
Dolbeare & Jackson (c. 1725)
Bibl. 14, 17

Mary Jackson (early 19th
century)
Boston, Mass.
Bibl. 12

Daniel H. Jagger (c. 1844-1846)
Hartford, Conn.
Bibl. 11, 14, 17

James H. Jagger (c. 1843)
Hartford, Conn.
Bibl. 11, 14, 17

Walter W. Jagger (c. 1839-1846)
Hartford, Conn.
Bibl. 11, 14, 17

N. E. Janney (c. 1846)
St. Louis, Mo.
Archer & Janney (c. 1840-1850)
Bibl. 11, 14

Theodore Jennings (c. 1775)
Maryland
Bibl. 11, 14, 17

Johnson, Hall & Co. (c. 1815-
1817)
Middletown, Conn.
Jehiel and Constant Johnson
John H. Hall
Bibl. 14, 17

Johnson & Nott (Mott)
(c. 1817-1818)
Middletown, Conn.

Jehiel Johnson
William Nott
Bibl. 14, 17

Constant Johnson
(See Johnson, Hall & Co.)

Jehiel Johnson
Middletown, Conn. (c. 1815-
1825)
Fayetteville, N.C. (c. 1818-1819)
Johnson, Hall & Co. (c. 1815-
1817)
Johnson & Nott (c. 1817-1818)
Nott, Babcock, & Johnson
(c. 1817-1825)
Bibl. 11, 14, 16, 17

Daniel Jones (c. 1705-1714)
Boston, Mass.
Bibl. 11, 14, 17

Edward Jones (c. 1837-1850)
New York, N.Y.
Bibl. 11, 14, 17

Gershom Jones (b. 1751-
d. 1809)
Providence, R.I.
Hamlin & Jones (c. 1774-1781)
Gershom Jones & Sons (c. 1806-
1807)
Bibl. 11, 14, 15, 17

Gershom Jones & Sons (c. 1806-1807)
Providence, R.I.
Gershom Jones
James Jones
Samuel Jones
Bibl. 14, 17

James Jones (c. 1806)
Newport, R.I.
Providence, R.I.
Gershom Jones & Sons
Bibl. 15

Samuel Jones (c. 1806)
Providence, R.I.
Gershom Jones & Sons
Bibl. 14, 17

D. H. K. (c. 1840)
Meriden, Conn.
Bibl. 11

D. W. K. (c. 1845-1849)
Meriden, Conn.
DeWitt Kimberly (?)
Bibl. 11

H. Kannerer (c. 1843)
Columbus, Ohio
Bibl. 13

Ernest Kauffman (c. 1850)
Philadelphia, Pa.
Bibl. 11

Josiah Keene (c. 1801-1817)
Providence, R.I.
Bibl. 11, 14, 15, 16, 17

Adam Kehler (c. 1780-1783)
Philadelphia, Pa.
Bibl. 11, 14, 17

Luke Kiersted (c. 1805)
New York, N.Y.
Bibl. 11, 14, 17

Kilbourn & Porter (c. 1814-1816)
Baltimore, Md.
Samuel Kilbourn
Jephtha Porter
Bibl. 11, 14, 17

Samuel Kilbourn (Kilburn)
Hartford, Conn. (c. 1794-1813)
Baltimore, Md. (c. 1814-1839)
Kilbourn & Porter (c. 1814-1816)
Bibl. 11, 14, 15, 16, 17

DeWitt Kimberly (c. 1845-1849)
Meriden, Conn.
Bibl. 11, 14, 17

Peter Kirby (c. 1736-1788)
New York, N.Y.
Bibl. 11, 14, 16, 17

William Kirby (b. 1740-d. 1804)
New York, N.Y.
Bibl. 11, 14, 15, 16, 17

Elisha Kirk (c. 1755-1790)
York, Pa.
Bibl. 11, 14, 15, 16, 17

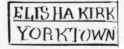

William Kirkby (Kirby)
(c. 1786)
New York, N.Y.
Bibl. 6

Elijah Knapp (c. 1797)
New York, N.Y.
Bibl. 11, 14, 17

Edward Kneeland (c. 1768-1791)
Boston, Mass.
Bibl. 11, 14, 17

W. W. Knight & Co. (c. 1840)
Philadelphia, Pa.
Bibl. 11, 14, 17

Knowles & Ladd
Philadelphia (?), Pa.
Bibl. 12

Lewis Kruiger (c. 1830)
Philadelphia, Pa.
Bibl. 11, 14, 17

David Kyner (c. 1831)
Lancaster, Ohio
Bibl. 13

M. L. (early 19th century)
Pennsylvania
Bibl. 11

T. L. (late 18th century)
Rhode Island
Bibl. 11

Lafetra & Allaire (c. 1816)
New York, N.Y.
Moses Lafetra
Anthony J. Allaire
Bibl. 6, 11, 14, 17

Moses Lafetra (c. 1811-1816)
New York, N.Y.
Lafetra & Allaire (c. 1816)
Bibl. 11, 14, 15, 16, 17

Lawrence Langworthy (c. 1730-1739)
Newport, R.I.
Bibl. 11, 14, 17

Southcote Langworthy (c. 1750)
Newport, R.I.
Bibl. 11

John Lathbury (c. 1655)
Virginia
Bibl. 11, 14, 17

William Lawrence (c. 1830)
Meriden, Conn.
Bibl. 11

——— Lawson
Cincinnati, Ohio
Bibl. 13

James Leddel (c. 1744-1780)
New York, N.Y.
Bibl. 12

Joseph Led(d)ell (c. 1690-1753)
New York, N.Y.
Bibl. 11, 14, 16, 17

Joseph Led(d)ell Jr. (c. 1740-
1754)
New York, N.Y.
Bibl. 11, 14, 16, 17

Lee & Creesy
(See Creesy & Lee)

Richard Lee
Taunton, Mass (c. 1770-1781)
Grafton, N.H. (c. 1788-1790)
Ashfield, Mass. (c. 1791-1793)
Lanesborough, Mass. (c. 1794-
1802)
Springfield, Vt. (c. 1802-1823)
Bibl. 11, 14, 16, 17

Richard Lee Jr. (d. 1858)
Springfield, Vt. (c. 1795-1815)
Beverly, Mass. (c. 1816-1820)
Rhode Island (c. 1820)
Providence, R.I. (c. 1823-1858)
Creesy & Lee (c. 1815-1820)
Bibl. 11, 12, 16, 17

Leonard, Reed & Barton (1837-
1847)
Taunton, Mass.
Gustavus Leonard
Henry G. Reed
Charles E. Barton
Bibl. 11, 14, 17

LEONARD REED & BARTON

Gustavus Leonard (c. 1835-
1840)
Taunton, Mass.
Leonard, Reed & Barton
(1837-1847)
Bibl. 11, 14

Zephaniah A. Leonard (c. 1828-
1830)
Taunton, Mass.
Crossman, West & Leonard
Bibl. 11, 14

Elkins Leslie
Philadelphia, Pa. (c. 1821)
Providence, R.I. (c. 1828)
Bibl. 11, 14, 17

Lewis & Cowles (c. 1834-1836)
East Meriden, Conn.
Isaac C. Lewis
George Cowles
Bibl. 11, 14, 16, 17

Lewis & Curtis (c. 1836-1839)
East Meriden, Conn.
Isaac C. Lewis
Lemuel J. Curtis
Bibl. 11, 14, 17

I. C. Lewis & Co. (c. 1839-1852)
Meriden, Conn.
Isaac C. Lewis
D. B. Wells
Bibl. 11, 14, 17

Isaac C. Lewis (c. 1834-1852)
Meriden, Conn.
Lewis & Cowles (c. 1834-1836)
Lewis & Curtis (c. 1836-1839)
I. C. Lewis & Co. (c. 1839-1852)
Bibl. 11, 14, 17

George Lightner (c. 1790-1815)
Baltimore, Md.
Bibl. 11, 14, 15, 16, 17

John Lightner (c. 1814)
Baltimore, Md.
Bibl. 12

——— Lincoln (c. 1820)
Hingham, Mass. (?)
Bibl. 11

Andrew Lindsay (c. 1816)
Chillicothe, Ohio
Columbus, Ohio
Bibl. 13

William Linthwaite (c. 1736)
Charleston, S.C.
Bibl. 11

Locke & Carter (c. 1837-1845)
New York, N.Y.
Bibl. 11, 14, 17

J. D. Locke (c. 1835-1860)
New York, N.Y.
Bibl. 6, 11, 14, 17

Jacob Loesch (c. 1781-1787)
Winston-Salem, N.C.
Bibl. 11

———— Long (c. 1806-1810)
Lebanon, Ohio
Bibl. 13

Bartholomew Longstreet (c. 1810)
Bucks County, Pa.
Bibl. 12

———— Love (c. 1780-1830)
Philadelphia, Pa.
Bibl. 11

I. Love (c. 1840)
Baltimore, Md.
Bibl. 11, 14, 17

I. Lowe (after 1800)
Location unknown
Bibl. 11, 14, 17

I LOWE

Ivory Lucas
New London, Conn. (c. 1732-1747)
Ogles Town (New Castle), Del. (c. 1747-1748)
Bibl. 11

Lyman & Couch (c. 1844-1845)
Meriden, Conn.
William W. Lyman
Ira Couch
Bibl. 11, 14, 17

William W. Lyman (c. 1844-1852)
Meriden, Conn. (c. 1844-1849)
Wallingford, Conn.
Lyman & Couch (c. 1844-1845)
Bull, Lyman & Couch (c. 1845-1849)
Curtis & Lyman (c. 1846)
Bibl. 11, 14, 17

LYMAN

William Mann (c. 1690-1738)
Boston, Mass.

Bibl. 11, 14, 17

Manning, Bowman & Co. (c. 1850-1875)
Middletown, Conn.
E. B. Manning
———— Bowman
Bibl. 11, 14, 17

MANNING BOWMAN & CO

E. B. Manning (c. 1850-1875)
Middletown, Conn.
Manning, Bowman & Co.
Bibl. 11, 12, 14, 17

EB MANNING PATENT

Thaddeus Manning (c. 1850-1875)
Middletown, Conn.
Bibl. 11, 14, 17

———— Marston (c. 1840)
Baltimore, Md.
Bibl. 11, 14, 17

MARSTON
BALTIMORE

Marcus Maton (c. 1828)
Hartford, Conn.
Bibl. 11, 14, 17

Duncan McEuen (c. 1793-1803)
New York, N.Y.
Malcolm & Duncan McEuen (c. 1793-1798)
Bibl. 11, 14, 17

Malcolm McEuen (McEwen) (c. 1765-1803)
New York, N.Y.
Bradford & McEuen (c. 1772-1785)
Malcolm McEuen & Son (c. 1793-1798)
Malcolm & Duncan McEuen (c. 1793-1798)
Bibl. 11, 12, 17

Malcolm McEuen & Son (c. 1793-1798)
New York, N.Y.
Malcolm McEuen
Duncan McEuen

Bibl. 6, 11, 12, 14

Malcolm & Duncan McEuen (c. 1793-1798)
New York, N.Y.
Bibl. 12, 17

McEuen
(See Malcolm McEuen)

Calom McFall (c. 1818)
Canton, Ohio
Bibl. 13

John McIlmoy (c. 1793)
Philadelphia, Pa.
Bibl. 11, 14, 17

William McQuilkin (c. 1845-1853)
Philadelphia, Pa.
Bibl. 11, 14, 16, 17

MCQUILKIN

PHILADELPHIA

WM McQUILKIN

Daniel Melvil(le) (c. 1788)
Newport, R.I.
Bibl. 12

Andrew Melville (c. 1804-1810)
Newport, R.I.
Bibl. 11, 14, 17

David Melville (Melvil) (c. 1755-1793)
Newport, R.I.

Bibl. 11, 14, 15, 16, 17

S. & T. Melville (Melvil) (c.
1793-1800)
Newport, R.I.
Samuel & Thomas Melville
Bibl. 11, 14, 16, 17

Samuel Melville (c. 1793-1800)
Newport, R.I.
S. & T. Melville
Bibl. 11, 14, 15, 17

Thomas Melville (Melvil) (c.
1793-1796)
Newport, R.I.
S. & T. Melville (c. 1793-1800)
Bibl. 11, 14, 15, 16, 17

Thomas Melville II (c. 1796-
1824)
Newport, R.I.
Bibl. 11, 14, 17

William L. Melville (b. 1786-d.
1857)
Newport, R.I.

Bibl. 11, 14, 17

NEWPORT

Menze
(See Minze)

Meriden Britannia Co. (c. 1852)
Meriden, Conn.
Dennis C. Wilcox
Horace C. Wilcox
Bibl. 11, 14, 17

MERIDEN BRITANNIA CO.

Robert Merryfield (c. 1760)
New York, N.Y.
Bibl. 11, 14, 17

Joshua Metzger (c. 1806-1820)
Germantown, Pa.
Bibl. 12

Joseph Meyer (c. 1840)
Canton, Ohio
Bibl. 13

Andre Michel (c. 1795-1797)
New York, N.Y.
Bibl. 6, 11, 14, 17

Josiah Miller (c. 1750-1775)
New England
Bibl. 11

James Minze (Menze) (c. 1794-
1830)
Schenectady, N.Y. (c. 1794-
1796)
Albany, N.Y. (c. 1794-1830)
Stafford & Minze (c. 1794-1830)
Bibl. 9, 11 ,14

G. I. Mix & Co. (c. 1803)
Wallingford, Conn.
Bibl. 11, 17

William Mix (c. 1820-1840)
East Granby, Conn.
Bibl. 11

George Molineux
Dorchester, Mass. (c. 1844-
1847)
New York, N.Y. (c. 1848-1854)
Capen & Molineux (c. 1848-
1854)
Bibl. 11, 14

Luke Moore (c. 1819-1822)
Philadelphia, Pa.
Bibl. 11, 14, 17

S. Moore (c. 1820-1830)
Kensington, Conn.
Bibl. 12

Morey & Ober (c. 1852-1855)
Boston, Mass.
David B. Morey
R. H. Ober
Bibl. 11, 14, 17

Morey, Ober & Co. (c. 1852-
1857)
Boston, Mass.
David B. Morey
R. H. Ober
Thomas Smith
Bibl. 11, 14, 17

Morey & Smith (c. 1857-1885)
Boston, Mass.
David B. Morey
Thomas Smith
Bibl. 11, 12

David B. Morey (c. 1852-1885)
Boston, Mass.
Smith & Morey (c. 1841-1842)
Thomas Smith & Co. (c. 1842-
1847)
Smith & Co. (c. 1847-1849)
Smith, Ober & Co. (c. 1849-
1852)
Morey & Ober (c. 1852-1855)
Morey, Ober & Co. (c. 1852-
1857)
Morey & Smith (c. 1857-1885)
Bibl. 11, 12, 14, 17

Henry Morgan (c. 1849)
Groton, Conn.
Bibl. 11, 14, 17

Hugh Morrison (c. 1830)
Xenia, Ohio
Bibl. 13

John Munson (c. 1846-1852)
Wallingford, Conn.
Yalesville, Conn.
Bibl. 11, 14, 17

W. N. (c. 1800)
New England
Bibl. 11

I. Neal (c. 1842)
New York, N.Y.
New England
Bibl. 11, 14, 17

O. Nichols (c. 1820)
New England
Bibl. 11

George Norris (c. 1848-1850)
New York, N.Y.
Ostrander & Norris
Bibl. 11, 14

John Norsworth (c. 1771)
Norfolk, Va.
Bibl. 11, 14, 17

North & Rowe (c. 1818-1823)
Augusta, Ga.
John North
Adna S. Rowe
Bibl. 11, 14, 17

John North (c. 1818-1823)
Augusta, Ga.
North & Rowe
Bibl. 14

David Northey (c. 1732-1778)
Salem, Mass.
Bibl. 11, 14, 17

William Northey (b. 1734-d.
1804)
Lynn, Mass.
Bibl. 11, 14, 17

Nott, Babcock, & Johnson (c.
1817-1825)
Middletown, Conn.
William Nott
Samuel Babcock
Jehiel Johnson
Bibl. 11, 14, 17

William Nott
Stepney, Conn. (c. 1812)
Philadelphia, Pa. (c. 1812)
Middletown, Conn. (c. 1813-
1817)
Fayetteville, N.C. (c. 1817-
1825)
Johnson & Nott (c. 1817-1818)
(Philadelphia, Pa.)
Nott, Babcock, & Johnson (c.
1817-1825)
(Middletown, Conn.)
Bibl. 11, 14, 15, 16, 17

R. H. Ober (c. 1849-1857)
Boston, Mass.
Smith, Ober & Co. (c. 1849-
1852)
Smith & Ober (c. 1850)
Morey & Ober (c. 1852-1855)
Morey, Ober & Co. (c. 1852-
1857)
Bibl. 11, 14

J. W. Olcott (early 1800's)
Baltimore, Md.
Bibl. 11, 14, 16, 17

Thomas Orr (c. 1808-1809)
Chillicothe, Ohio
First pewterer in Chillicothe.
Bibl. 13

Ostrander & Norris (c. 1848-
1850)
New York, N.Y.
Charles Ostrander
George Norris
Bibl. 11, 16, 17

Charles Ostrander (c. 1848-
1854)
New York, N.Y.

Bibl. 11, 14, 17

OSTRANDER

C. P. (c. 1800)
New England
Bibl. 11

S. P. (early 18th century)
Location unknown
Bibl. 16

Palethorp & Connell (c. 1820-
1840)
Philadelphia, Pa.
John H. Palethorp
Thomas Connell
Bibl. 11, 14, 17

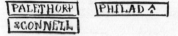

J. H. Palethorp & Co. (c. 1839-
1841)
Philadelphia, Pa.
John H. Palethorp
Bibl. 11, 12, 14

J. H. & Robert Palethorp Jr. (c.
1820-1825)
Philadelphia, Pa.
Bibl. 11, 12, 14, 17

John H. Palethorp (c. 1820-
1845)
Philadelphia, Pa.
J. H. & Robert Palethorp Jr. (c.
1820-1825)
Palethorp & Connell (c. 1820-
1840)
J. H. Palethorp & Co. (c. 1839-
1841)
Bibl. 11, 12, 14, 16, 17

Robert Palethorp (c. 1822-1826)
Philadelphia, Pa.
Bibl. 14, 17

Robert Palethorp Jr. (c. 1817-1822)
Philadelphia, Pa.
J. H. & Robert Palethorp Jr. (c. 1820-1825)
Bibl. 11, 14, 15, 16, 17

Charles G. Parker & Co. (c. 1849)
Meriden, Conn.
New York, N.Y. (?)
Bibl. 11, 12, 14, 17

J. G. Parker (after 1840)
Rochester, N.Y. (after 1840)
New York, N.Y.
Bibl. 11, 14, 17

W. Parkin (c. 1830)
New England
Bibl. 11, 14, 17

W. PARKIN

W. H. Parmenter (c. 1840)
New England
Bibl. 11, 14, 17

Thomas Paschall (c. 1686-1718)
Philadelphia, Pa.
Bibl. 11, 14, 17

Lewis Patterson (c. 1829)
Ravenna, Ohio
Bibl. 13

George Pavey (c. 1733)
Boston, Mass.
Bibl. 11, 14, 17

Robert Pearse (Piercy) (c. 1792)
New York, N.Y.
Bibl. 6, 11, 14

Henry Peel (c. 1822-1833)
Philadelphia, Pa.
Bibl. 11, 14, 17

Simon Pennock
East Marlborough, Pa. (c. 1805-1815)
Lancaster County, Pa. (c. 1817-1845)
Bibl. 11

Robert Pierce (c. 1792-1797)
New York, N.Y.
Bibl. 17

Samuel Pierce (b. 1768-d. 1840)
Greenfield, Mass.
Middletown, Mass. (?)
Bibl. 11, 14, 15, 16, 17

Piercy
(See Pearse)

Plumley
(See Charles Plumly)

Plumly & Bidgood (Bigood) (c. 1825)
Philadelphia, Pa.
Charles Plumly
———— Bidgood
Bibl. 11, 14, 16, 17

Plumly & Felton (c. 1840)
Philadelphia, Pa. (?)
Bibl. 11

Charles Plumly (Plumley)
Philadelphia, Pa. (c. 1822-1833)
Providence, R.I. (c. 1829)
Middletown, Conn. (c. 1844-1848)
Plumly & Bidgood (c. 1825)
Bibl. 11, 14, 17

William Pomeroy (c. 1848)
Cleveland, Ohio
Bibl. 13

William C. Pomroy (c. 1850-1856)
Cincinnati, Ohio
J. H. Stalkamp & Co.
Bibl. 11, 13, 14

Porter Britannia & Plate Co. (c. 1860)
Taunton, Mass.
Bibl. 17

A. & F. Porter (c. 1835-1838)
Westbrook, Me.
Allen and Freeman Porter
Bibl. 11, 14, 17

Allen Porter (o. 1830-1840)
Southington, Conn. (?)
Westbrook, Me.
A. & F. Porter (c. 1835-1838)
Bibl. 11, 12, 14, 16, 17

A. PORTER

Edmund Porter (c. 1847)
Taunton, Mass.
Bibl. 12

Freeman Porter (c. 1835-1860)
Westbrook, Me.
A. & F. Porter (c. 1835-1838)
Bibl. 6, 11, 12, 14, 16, 17

James Porter
Connecticut Valley (c. 1795-1803)
Baltimore, Md. (c. 1803)

Bibl. 9, 11, 14, 16

Jephtha Porter (c. 1814-1816)
Baltimore, Md.
Kilbourn & Porter
Bibl. 11, 14, 17

Lincoln Porter (c. 1800)
Taunton, Mass.
Bibl. 12

Robert Porter (c. 1780)
Caln Township, Chester County,
Pa.
Bibl. 11

P

Samuel Porter (c. 1800)
Taunton, Mass.
Bibl. 11

W. Potter (Porter) (c. 1830)
New England
Bibl. 11, 14

W. POTTER

James Henry Putnam (c. 1830-
1855)
Malden, Mass.
Bailey & Putnam (c. 1830-1835)
Bibl. 11, 14, 16, 17

PUTNAM

George Raisin (c. 1718-1728)
Boston, Mass.
Bibl. 11, 14, 17

Edward Rand (c. 1794-1800)
Newburyport, Mass.
Bibl. 11

John Randle (Randall) (c.
1738-1739)
Boston, Mass.
Bibl. 11, 14, 17

Reed & Barton (1847 to
present)
Taunton, Mass.
Henry G. Reed
Charles E. Barton

Bibl. 14, 17

REED & BARTON

Henry G. Reed (c. 1835-1860)
Taunton, Mass.
Leonard, Reed & Barton (1837-
1847)
Reed & Barton (1847 to
present)
Bibl. 11, 14, 17

John & Philip Reich (c. 1829)
Salem, N.C.
Bibl. 11, 14, 17

John Philip Reich (c. 1820-
1830)
Salem, N.C.
John & Philip Reich (c. 1829)
Bibl. 11, 14, 17

Renton & Co. (c. 1830)
New York, N.Y.
Bibl. 11, 14, 17

RENTON & CO
NEW YORK

Jacob Resore, Sr. (c. 1816)
Cincinnati, Ohio
Bibl. 13

Jacob Resore, Jr. (c. 1841)
Cincinnati, Ohio
Bibl. 13

Paul Revere (b. 1735-d. 1818)
Boston, Mass.
Bibl. 12

B. Richardson & Son (c. 1839)
Philadelphia, Pa.
Bibl. 14, 17

B RICHARDSON & SON
PHILADELPHIA

Francis B. Richardson (c. 1847-
1848)
Providence, R.I.
Bibl. 11, 14, 17

George Richardson (d. 1848)
Boston, Mass. (c. 1818-1828)

Cranston, R.I. (c. 1828-1845)
Green & Richardson (c. 1818)
Glennore Co. (c. 1828)
Bibl. 6, 11, 14, 16, 17

George B. Richardson Jr. (b.
1819-d. 1890)
Providence, R.I. (c. 1847)
Boston, Mass.
Bibl. 11, 14, 17

Thomas Rigden (early 19th
century?)
Philadelphia, Pa. (?)
Bibl. 12

Jacob Rinehart (c. 1818)
Shanesville, Ohio
Bibl. 13

Mathew Roberts (c. 1826)
Steubenville, Ohio
Bibl. 13

——— Rogers (c. 1814)
Albany, N.Y.
Stafford, Rogers & Co.
Bibl. 9, 11, 14, 17

Rogers, Smith & Co. (c. 1850)
Hartford, Conn.
Bibl. 11, 14, 17

John Rogers (c. 1840)
Philadelphia, Pa.
Bibl. 11, 14, 17

Elijah Ross (c. 1812)
Zanesville, Ohio
Bibl. 13

Adna S. Rowe
Augusta, Ga. (c. 1818-1828)

Connecticut
North & Rowe (c. 1818-1823)
Bibl. 11, 14

Russell & Beach (c. 1838)
Chester, Conn.
——— Russell
Chester Beach
Bibl. 11, 14, 17

H. N. Rust (c. 1840)
New York, N.Y. (?)
Bibl. 11

H .N.RUST

John N. Rust & Samuel Rust (c.
1842-1845)
New York, N.Y.
Bibl. 11, 14, 17

Leonard M. Rust (c. 1849)
New York, N.Y.
Bibl. 11, 14, 17

Samuel Rust (c. 1837-1843)
New York, N.Y.
John N. Rust & Samuel Rust (c.
1842-1845)
Bibl. 11, 14, 17

S.RUSTS PATENT NEWYORK

B. G. S. & Co. (c. 1825-1830)
Northeastern Massachusetts.
Bibl. 11

B.G.S&CO.

H. S. (18th century, c. 1750?)
Virginia (?)
Bibl. 11

I. S.
(John Skinner?)
Bibl. 11

T. S. (after 1750)
New England
Bibl. 11, 16

TS

Sage & Beebe (after 1840)
St. Louis (?), Mo.
Timothy Sage
——— Beebe

SAGE & BEEBE

Bibl. 14, 17

T. Sage & Co. (c. 1847)
St. Louis, Mo.
Timothy Sage
Bibl. 14, 17

Timothy Sage (c. 1847-1848)
St. Louis, Mo.
Sage & Beebe (after 1840)
T. Sage & Co. (c. 1847)
Bibl. 11, 14, 16, 17

T.SAGE ST.LOUIS MO.

Savage & Graham (c. 1837)
(Graham & Savage)
Middletown, Conn.
William H. Savage
Jasper Graham
John D. Graham
Bibl. 14, 17

William H. Savage (c. 1837-
1840)
Middletown, Conn.
Savage & Graham (c. 1837)
Bibl. 11, 14, 16, 17

SAVAGE MIDD CT

T. Schmidt (c. 1870)
Connecticut (?)
Bibl. 11

Jacob Schwing (c. 1817)
Cincinnati, Ohio
Bibl. 13

Jacob Seip (c. 1820-1822)
Philadelphia, Pa.
Bibl. 11, 14, 17

Sellew & Co. (c. 1830-1860)
Cincinnati, Ohio
Enos, Osman and William
Sellew

Bibl. 11, 14, 16, 17

SELLEW&CO CINCINNATI

Enos Sellew (c. 1831-1832)
Cincinnati, Ohio
Sellew & Co. (c. 1830-1860)
Bibl. 13

Osman Sellew (c. 1831-1832)
Cincinnati, Ohio
Sellew & Co. (c. 1830-1860)
Bibl. 13

William Sellew (c. 1838)
Cincinnati, Ohio
Sellew & Co. (c. 1830-1860)
Bibl. 13

Abraham Seltzer (c. 1793)
Philadelphia, Pa.
Bibl. 11, 14, 17

Eadem Semper (c. 1750-1780)
Boston, Mass.
Trade mark of several pewterers.
John Skinner may have used
it.
Bibl. 11, 16, 17

William Sharp (c. 1840)
Cadiz, Ohio
Bibl. 13

——— Shaw (c. 1850-1854)
Philadelphia, Pa.
Sickel & Shaw
Bibl. 11, 14

Sheldon & Feltman (c. 1847-
1848)
Albany, N.Y.

Smith Sheldon
James C. Feltman Jr.
Bibl. 11, 14, 17

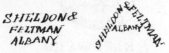

Smith Sheldon (c. 1847-1848)
Albany, N.Y.
Sheldon & Feltman (c. 1847-
1848)
Smith & Co. (c. 1853-1856)
Bibl. 9

William A. Sheriff (c. 1822)
Steubenville, Ohio
Bibl. 13

John I. Shoff (c. 1780-1793)
Lancaster, Pa.
Bibl. 11, 14, 15, 17

Henry Shrimpton (c. 1615-
1666)
Boston, Mass.
Bibl. 11, 14, 17

Henry Shrimpton (c. 1665-1700)
Boston, Mass.
(Nephew of Henry Shrimpton,
c. 1615-1666)
Bibl. 6, 11

Jonathan Shrimpton (d. 1674)
Boston, Mass.
Bibl. 11

Samuel Shrimpton (c. 1700)
Boston, Mass.
Bibl. 11

Sickel & Shaw (c. 1850-1854)
Philadelphia, Pa.
H. G. Sickel
———— Shaw
Bibl. 11, 14, 17

H. G. Sickel (c. 1849-1853)
Philadelphia, Pa.
Bibl. 14, 17

Thomas Simpkins (b. 1702-d.
1766)

Boston, Mass.
Bibl. 11, 14, 16, 17

Simpson & Benham (c. 1845-
1847)
New York, N.Y.
Samuel Simpson
Morris Benham
Bibl. 11, 14, 17

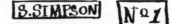

Samuel Simpson
Yalesville, Conn. (c. 1835-1852)
New York, N.Y. (c. 1845-1847)
William & Simpsin (Simpson)
(c. 1837-1838)
Simpson & Benham (c. 1845-
1847)
Bibl. 11, 12, 14, 16, 17

Adam Sites (c. 1816)
Columbus, Ohio
Bibl. 13

Andrew Sites (c. 1826)
Columbus, Ohio
Bibl. 13

John Skinner (b. 1733-d. 1813)
Boston, Mass.
Bibl. 6, 11, 14, 15, 16, 17

Smith & Co.
Boston, Mass. (c. 1847-1849)
Thomas Smith
David B. Morey
Henry White
Bibl. 11, 12, 14, 16, 17

Smith & Co. (c. 1853-1856)
Albany, N.Y.
George W. Smith
Smith Sheldon
James C. Feltman Jr.
Bibl. 11, 14, 17

Smith & Feltman (c. 1849-
1852)
Albany, N.Y.
George W. Smith
James C. Feltman Jr.
Bibl. 11, 12, 14, 17

Smith & Morey (c. 1841-1842)
Boston, Mass.
Thomas Smith
David B. Morey
Bibl. 14, 17

Smith & Ober (c. 1850)
Boston, Mass.
Thomas Smith
R. H. Ober
Bibl. 11

Smith, Ober & Co. (c. 1849-
1852)
Boston, Mass.
Thomas Smith
R. H. Ober
David B. Morey
Bibl. 11, 14, 17

Eben Smith (b. 1773-d. 1856)
Beverly, Mass.
Bibl. 11, 14, 16, 17

George W. Smith (c. 1849-
1856)

Albany, N.Y.
Smith & Feltman (c. 1849-1852)
Smith & Co. (c. 1853-1856)
Bibl. 9, 14, 17

James E. Smith (after 1775)
Maryland (?)
Bibl. 14, 17

Thomas Smith (c. 1700-d.
1742)
Boston, Mass.
Bibl. 11, 14, 17

Thomas Smith (c. 1841-1862)
Boston, Mass.
Smith & Morcy (c. 1841-1842)
Thomas Smith & Co. (c. 1842-
1847)
Smith & Co. (c. 1847-1849)
Smith, Ober & Co. (c. 1849-
1852)
Smith & Ober (c. 1850)
Morey, Ober & Co. (c. 1852-
1857)
Bibl. 14, 17

Thomas Smith & Co. (c. 1842-
1847)
Boston, Mass.
Thomas Smith
David B. Morey
Henry White
Bibl. 11, 17

William Smith & Brother (c.
1774)
Stafford County, Va.
Bibl. 11

William R. Smith (c. 1848)
Middletown, Conn.
Bibl. 11, 14

H. Snyder
Philadelphia, Pa. (?)
Bibl. 12

Ebenezer Southmayd (c. 1775-
1830)
Middletown, Conn. (c. 1790)
Castleton, Vt. (c. 1802-1830)
Bibl. 11, 14, 16, 17

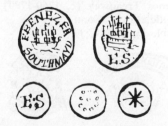

George B. Spencer (c. 1775-
1817)
Albany, N.Y.
Stafford, Rogers & Co. (c. 1814-
1815)
Stafford, Spencer & Co. (c.
1815-1817)
Bibl. 9, 11, 14

Thomas Spencer (c. 1800-1815)
Albany, N.Y.
Stafford, Rogers & Co. (c. 1814-
1815)
Bibl. 9, 11, 14

Stafford, Benedict & Co.
(c. 1824)
Albany, N.Y.
Joab Stafford
Spencer Stafford
Lewis Benedict
Bibl. 9, 11, 17

Stafford & Minze (c. 1794-
1830)
Albany, N.Y.
Spencer Stafford
James Minze
Bibl. 11, 14, 17

Stafford, Spencer & Co. (c.
1815-1817)
Albany, N.Y.
Hallenbake Stafford
Spencer Stafford
George B. Spencer
Lewis Benedict
Sebastian Tymiesen
Bibl. 9, 11, 14, 17

Stafford, Rogers & Co. (c. 1814-
1815)
Albany, N.Y.
John and Spencer Stafford
——— Rogers
Thomas and George B. Spencer
Bibl. 9, 11, 14, 17

Hallenbake Stafford (c. 1815-
1824)
Albany, N.Y.
John, Hallenbake, and Joab
Stafford (c. 1795-1830)
Stafford, Spencer & Co. (c.
1815-1817)
S. Stafford & Co. (c. 1817-1824)
Bibl. 9, 14

Joab Stafford (c. 1824)
Albany, N.Y.
John, Hallenbake, and Joab
Stafford (c. 1795-1830)

Stafford, Benedict & Co. (c.
1824)
Bibl. 9, 14

John Stafford c. 1796-1815)
Albany, N. Y.
John, Hallenbake, and Joab
Stafford (c. 1795-1830)
Stafford, Rogers & Co. (c. 1814-
1815)
Bibl. 9, 14

John, Hallenbake, and Joab
Stafford (c. 1795-1830)
Albany, N.Y.
Bibl. 11

S. Stafford & Co. (1817-1824)
Albany, N.Y.
Spencer Stafford
Spencer Stafford Jr.
Hallenbake Stafford
Lewis Benedict
Bibl. 9, 11, 14, 17

Spencer Stafford (b. 1770-d.
1844)
Albany, N.Y.
Stafford & Minze (c. 1794-1830)
Stafford, Rogers & Co. (c.
1814-1815)
Stafford, Spencer & Co. (c.
1815-1817)
S. Stafford & Co. (c. 1817-
1824)
Stafford, Benedict & Co. (c.
1824)
Bibl. 9, 14, 15, 16, 17

ALBANY

S·STAFFORD

Spencer Stafford Jr. (c. 1817-
1824)
Albany, N.Y.
Spencer & Spencer Stafford Jr.
(c. 1795-1830)
S. Stafford & Co. (c. 1817-1824)
Bibl. 9, 14

Spencer & Spencer Stafford Jr.
(c. 1795-1830)
Albany, N.Y.
———— Spencer
Spencer Stafford Jr.
Bibl. 11

J. H. Stalkamp (c. 1840)
Cincinnati, Ohio (c. 1850-1856)
Cleveland, Ohio
J. H. Stalkamp & Co. (c. 1850-
1856)
Bibl. 13

J. H. Stalkamp & Co. (c. 1850-
1856)
Cincinnati, Ohio
J. H. Stalkamp
John F. Wendelyn
Ezra Woodruf
Bibl. 11, 13, 14, 17

Alexander Standish (c. 1840)
New England
Armitages & Standish (?)
Bibl. 11, 14, 17

ALEX^R STANDISH

William H. Starr (c. 1843-1846)
New York, N.Y.
Bibl. 11, 14, 17

S. Stedman (c. 1800)
Connecticut (?)
Rhode Island (?)
Bibl. 11, 14, 17

S. STEDMAN

John Frederick Steinman (c.
1783-1785)
Lancaster, Pa.
Bibl. 11, 14, 17

Henry Stephenson (c. 1818)
Taunton, Mass.
Bibl. 11

C. Stevens (c. 1760)
Connecticut Valley
Bibl. 11

James Stimpson (c. 1840)
Baltimore, Md.
Bibl. 11

Frederick Stoddard (Stoddart)
(Stoddant) (c. 1833)
Philadelphia, Pa.
Bibl. 11, 14, 17

Jireh Strange (c. 1800)
Taunton, Mass.
Bibl. 12

Joseph Strange (c. 1800)
Taunton, Mass.
Bibl. 11

William F. Sumner (c. 1846-
1851)
New York, N.Y.
Endicott & Sumner
Bibl. 11, 14

———— Sykes (c. 1840)
Connecticut (?)
Bibl. 11, 14, 17

SYKES

Taunton Britannia Manufactur-
ing Co. (c. 1830-1837)
Taunton, Mass.
Bibl. 11, 14, 17

T.B.M.CO

C. S. Taylor (c. 1826)
Brooklyn, Ohio
(near Cleveland)
Bibl. 13

John Thomas (c. 1841)
Trenton, N.J.
Philadelphia, Pa.
Shippen Lane, Pa.
Bibl. 11, 14, 17

Andrew Thompson (c. 1810-
1820)
Albany, N.Y.

Bibl. 11

Jonathan Thompson (c. 1821)
Ashtabula, Ohio
Bibl. 13

John Thornton (c. 1775)
Pennsylvania (?)
Bibl. 11, 14, 17

———— Tillinghast (c. 1810)
Fayetteville, N.C.
Providence, R.I.
Bibl. 11

———— Tomlinson (c. 1843)
Location unknown
Bibl. 11, 14, 17

TOMLINSON'S PATENT 1843

Israel Trask (b. 1786-d. 1867)
Beverly, Mass.
Bibl. 11, 12, 14, 16, 17

John Trask (c. 1822-1826)
Boston, Mass.
Bibl. 6, 11, 12

Oliver Trask (b. 1792-d. 1874)
Beverly, Mass.
Bibl. 11, 14, 16, 17

Amos Treadway (c. 1760-1790)
Middletown, Conn.
Bibl. 11, 14, 16, 17

Joseph Tucker (c. 1845)
New York, N.Y.
Bibl. 12

John Tyler (b. 1695-d. 1757)
Boston, Mass.
Bibl. 11, 14, 17

Sebastian Tymiesen (c. 1795-
1830)
Albany, N.Y.
A partner of Stafford, Spencer
& Co. (c. 1815-1817)
Bibl. 9, 11, 14

J. M. Ufen (18th century)
Pennsylvania (?)
Bibl. 11, 16

M. B. Uven (18th century)
Pennsylvania (?)
Bibl. 11

Peter Van Norden (c. 1782)
Bound Brook, N.J.
Bibl. 11

Vose & Co. (c. 1840)
Albany, N.Y.
Bibl. 11, 14, 17

VOSE & CO
ALBANY

B. W. (c. 1800)
Rhode Island or Massachusetts
Bibl. 11

E. W. (c. 1740)
Virginia
Edward Willett (?)
Bibl. 11

I. W. (c. 1775)
New England (?)
Bibl. 11

Lester Wadsworth (c. 1838)
Hartford, Conn.
Bibl. 11, 14, 17

R. Wallace & Co. (c. 1855)
Wallingford, Conn.
Bibl. 11, 14, 17

R.WALLACE & CO

John J. Walter (c. 1837)
Canton, Ohio
Bibl. 13

H. B. Ward & Co. (c. 1849)
Guilford, Conn.
Bibl. 11, 12, 14, 17

H.B.WARD

James Ward (c. 1795)
Hartford, Conn.
Bibl. 12

———— Warren (c. 1840)
New York State
New England
Bibl. 11, 14, 17

WARREN'S
HARDMETAL

C. P. Wayne & Son (c. 1835)
Philadelphia, Pa.
Bibl. 11, 14, 17

C.P.WAYNE & SON

PHILADA

Weatherly
(See Witherle)

W. Webb (c. 1810-1820)
New York, N.Y.
Bibl. 11

J. Weekes & Co. (c. 1833-1835)
Poughkeepsie, N.Y.
Bibl. 11

J WEEKES & CO

James Weekes
Poughkeepsie, N.Y. (c. 1820-
1835)
New York, N.Y. (c. 1856-1858)
J. Weekes & Co. (c. 1833-1835)
Bibl. 11, 14, 16, 17

J. WEEKES

J.WEEKES NY

Andrew Weissert (c. 1839)
Canton, Ohio
Bibl. 13

John Welch (c. 1789-1803)
Boston, Mass.
Bibl. 6, 12

John Wendelyn (Wendelin) (c.
1807)
Cincinnati, Ohio
Bibl. 13

John F. Wendelyn (Wendelin)
(c. 1853)
Cincinnati, Ohio
J. H. Stalkamp & Co. (c. 1850-
1856)
Bibl. 11, 13, 14

William A. West (c. 1828-1830)
Taunton, Mass.
Crossman, West, & Leonard
Bibl. 11, 14

A. G. Whitcomb (c. 1820-1830)
Boston, Mass.
Bibl. 11, 14, 17

Henry White (c. 1842-1849)
Boston, Mass.
Thomas Smith & Co. (c. 1842-
1847)
Smith & Co. (c. 1847-1849)
Bibl. 11, 14

Whitehouse & Woodbury (c.
1820-1835)
Philadelphia, Pa. (?)
Rhode Island (?)
Bibl. 11

E. Whitehouse (early 1800's)
New York State (?)
Bibl. 11, 14, 16, 17

E WHITEHOUSE

WHITEHOUSE
WARRANTED

WHITEHOUSE

G. & J. Whitfield (c. 1836-1865)
New York, N.Y.
Bibl. 11, 14, 17

G & J WHITFIELD

George B. Whitfield (c. 1828-
1865)
New York, N.Y.
Bibl. 11, 14, 17

John H. Whitlock (c. 1836-1844)
Troy, N.Y.
Bibl. 9, 11, 14, 16, 17

Whitmore & Francis (c. 1833-1835)
Buffalo, N.Y.
Daniel Francis
Bibl. 11, 14, 17

Jacob Whitmore (c. 1758-1790)
Middletown, Conn.
Bibl. 11, 14, 15, 16, 17

Lewis Whitmore (c. 1840)
Rocky Hill, Conn.
Bibl. 11, 14, 17

——— Whitney (c. 1850)
New York, N.Y.
Benham & Whitney
Bibl. 11, 14

Dennis C. Wilcox (c. 1850)
Meriden, Conn.
H. C. Wilcox & Co. (c. 1850)
Meriden Britannia Co. (c. 1852)
Bibl. 11

H. C. Wilcox & Co. (c. 1850)
Meriden, Conn.
Horace C. Wilcox
Dennis C. Wilcox
Bibl. 11

Horace C. Wilcox (c. 1850-)
Meriden, Conn.
H. C. Wilcox & Co. (c. 1850)
Meriden Britannia Co. (c. 1852)
Bibl. 11

George & William Wild (19th century)
Bucks County, Pa.
Bibl. 12

Thomas Wildes (Wilds)
Philadelphia, Pa. (c. 1829-1833)
New York, N.Y. (c. 1833-1840)

Bibl. 6, 11, 14, 17

Christian Will (c. 1770-1789)
New York, N.Y.
Bibl. 14, 17

George Washington Will (c. 1798-1807)
Philadelphia, Pa.
Bibl. 11, 14, 17

Henry Will (b. 1735-d. 1802)
New York, N.Y. (c. 1761-1775)
Albany, N.Y. (c. 1775-1783)
Bibl. 6, 9, 11, 14, 15, 16, 17

John Will (c. 1752-1766)
New York, N.Y.

Bibl. 11, 14, 15, 16, 17

John Will Jr. (c. 1750-1790)
New York, N.Y.
Bibl. 11

John Christian Will (c. 1770-1789)
New York, N.Y.
Bibl. 11

Philip Will (c. 1763-1787)
New York, N.Y.
Philadelphia, Pa.
Bibl. 11, 14, 17

William Will (b. 1742-d. 1798)
Philadelphia, Pa.
Bibl. 6, 11, 14, 15, 16, 17

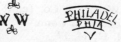

William (Wilhelm) Will Jr. (c.
  1800-1802)
Zanesville, Ohio
From Philadelphia, Pa.
Bibl. 13

Edward Willett (c. 1692-1743)
Charlestown, Md.
Upper Marlboro, Md.
Bibl. 11, 14, 17

Mary Willett (c. 1773)
Upper Marlboro, Md.
Bibl. 11, 14, 17

William Willett (c. 1744-1772)
Upper Marlboro, Md.
Bibl. 11, 14, 17

William & Simpsin (Simpson)
  (c. 1837-1838)
Yalesville, Conn.
Lorenzo L. Williams
Samuel Simpson
Bibl. 11, 14, 17

Lorenzo L. Williams (c. 1838-
  1842)
Yalesville, Conn. (c. 1837-1838)
Philadelphia, Pa.
William & Simpsin (Simpson)
  (c. 1837-1838)
Bibl. 11, 14, 17

Otis Williams (c. 1826-1831)
Buffalo, N.Y.
Bibl. 11, 14, 16, 17

Richard Williams (c. 1771-
  1812)
Stepney, Conn.
Bibl. 11, 14, 17

Thomas Willis (c. 1829-1833)
Philadelphia, Pa.
Bibl. 11, 14, 17

Joshua Witherle (Weatherly)
  (c. 1784-1793)
Boston, Mass.
Bibl. 11, 14, 17

J. Wolcott (c. 1800)
Baltimore, Md.
May be J. W. Olcott
Bibl. 16

John Wolfe (c. 1801)
Philadelphia, Pa.
Bibl. 11, 14, 17

N. G. Wood (c. 1830)
Boston, Mass.
Bibl. 11

Woodbury & Colton (c. 1835)
Philadelphia, Pa.
J. B. Woodbury
Oren Colton
Bibl. 11, 12, 14, 17

J. B. Woodbury
Massachusetts or Rhode Island
  (c. 1820-1835)
Philadelphia, Pa. (c. 1835-1838)
Woodbury & Colton (c. 1835)
Bibl. 11, 12, 14, 16, 17

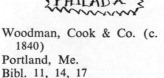

Woodman, Cook & Co. (c.
  1840)
Portland, Me.
Bibl. 11, 14, 17

Ezra Woodruf (c. 1853)
Cincinnati, Ohio
A partner of J. H. Stalkamp &
  Co. in 1853
Bibl. 13

B. Wright (c. 1820)
Columbus, Ohio
Bibl. 13

Simon Wyer (c. 1740-1752)
Philadelphia, Pa.
Bibl. 11, 14, 17

J. Wygle (c. 1810)
Old Washington, Ohio
Bibl. 13

John Wyler (c. 1820)
Norwalk, Ohio
Bibl. 13

Yale & Curtis (c. 1858-1867)
New York, N.Y.
Henry Yale
Stephen Curtis Jr.
Bibl. 11, 14, 17

Burrage Yale (c. 1808-1835)
South Reading, Mass.
Bibl. 11, 14, 17

C. & S. Yale (c. 1817-1823)
Wallingford, Conn.
Richmond, Va.
Charles and Selden Yale
Bibl. 11, 14, 17

Charles Yale (c. 1815-1824)
Wallingford, Conn.
Richmond, Va.
C. & S. Yale (c. 1817-1823)
H. Yale & Co. (c. 1824-1835)
Bibl. 11, 14, 17

Charles Yale (c. 1832)
New York, N.Y.
(May be the man who worked
  in Wallingford, Conn. See
  entry above.)
Bibl. 12, 14

Charles Yale & Co. (c. 1817-
  1823)
Wallingford, Conn.
Bibl. 11

H. Yale & Co. (c. 1824-1835)
Yalesville (Wallingford), Conn.
Hiram Yale
Charles Yale
Bibl. 11, 14, 17

Henry Yale (c. 1858-1867)
New York, N.Y.
Yale & Curtis
Bibl. 14

Hiram Yale (c. 1822-1831)
Wallingford, Conn.
H. Yale & Co. (c. 1824-1835)
Bibl. 11, 14, 16, 17

Samuel Yale (c. 1813-1820)
Meriden, Conn.
W. & S. Yale
Bibl. 14, 17

Selden Yale (c. 1817-1823)
Wallingford, Conn.
Richmond, Va.
C. & S. Yale
Bibl. 14, 17

W. & S. Yale (c. 1813-1820)
Meriden, Conn.
William Yale Jr.
Samuel Yale
Bibl. 11, 14, 15, 17

William Yale (Sr.) (c. 1784-
1810)
Meriden, Conn.
Bibl. 89

William Yale Jr.
Meriden, Conn. (c. 1813-1830)
New York, N.Y. (1830-1832)
W. & S. Yale (c. 1813-1820)
Bibl. 12, 14, 17

George Youle (c. 1793-1828)
New York, N.Y.
Bibl. 6, 11, 14, 17

G.YOULE

Thomas Youle (c. 1813-1819)
New York, N.Y.
Thomas Youle & Co. (w. 1810-
1812)
Bibl. 6, 11, 14, 17

Thomas Youle & Co. (w. 1810-
1812)
New York, N.Y.
Bibl. 6, 12

"Widow" Youle (c. 1821)
(Thomas Youle's wife)
New York, N.Y.
Bibl. 6, 12

Abraham Young (c. 1775-1801)
New York, N.Y.
Bibl. 11, 14, 17

Peter Young
New York, N.Y. (c. 1772-1782)
Albany, N.Y. (c. 1783-1800)
Bibl. 9, 11, 14, 15, 16, 17

PART THREE:
SILVER PLATE

Silver plate has been known since the time of the Aztecs, Incas, and Romans. The art of fusing an expensive metal onto a cheaper one must have been lost, because from the time of the Romans until the time of Thomas Boulsover of Sheffield, England, no silver plate was made. Boulsover rediscovered the method of silver-plating in 1742. At first, only small items were made, but in 1747, when the news of the silver-plating process was released to the world, all types of silver-plated metal pieces were being made. The early wares were made by fusing a layer of silver to a layer of copper. It was called the copper-rolled plate system or Sheffield plate. A new formula was developed for pewter soon after the development of Sheffield plated wares. The new pewter had less lead and could be spun on a lathe. This "new" metal was renamed "britannia" and appeared more like silver than the earlier pewter. Britannia gained world-wide popularity and the Sheffield plate makers were then forced to search for a cheaper method to produce thin silver-plated wares which would enable them to compete with the britannia factories.

The first patent was granted in 1840 for the manufacture of a new kind of silver-plated ware. It was possible with this new process to chemically deposit silver on copper, britannia, or other metals. There were many complaints that the finished electroplated ware was inferior, but it continued to gain in popularity until it completely replaced the earlier Sheffield fusion method. Silver-plate manufacturers used company names and symbols as their trademarks. These names were frequently used in a manner to confuse the buying public. There were many companies called Rogers Bros., since the name Rogers was famous for quality silver. The Sterling Silver Plate Company and other names were designed to mislead the buyer into believing that the article was solid silver and not silver plate.

Manufacturers of silver-plated wares sometimes used a quality stamp. AI meant standard plate, XII meant sectional plate. 4, 6, and 8 appeared on some spoons and forks that were double plated. 6, 9, and 12 was used on some spoons and forks to indicate triple plate.

Silver-plated copper or silver-plated britannia

was commercially developed in America with speed. James O. Mead of Philadelphia went to England in 1837 and learned the process of electroplating. He returned with necessary equipment and began making the first American silver plate. (It was not until 1845 that his wares were commercially acceptable). At that point he joined forces with William Rogers of Hartford, Connecticut, and the firm Rogers and Mead started manufacturing electroplated silver ware.

Their success in the United States can only be measured by the competitive firms that immediately started making electroplated wares. Rogers Brothers, The Meridan Britannia Company (now the International Silver Company), Reed and Barton, and dozens of other companies began making silver plate.

It must be remembered that the electroplated wares were inspired by the solid silver, pewter, and britannia pieces that had preceded them. The designs developed accordingly. As the Victorian era progressed, design in all forms of the decorative arts became more and more elaborate, and the electroplated wares were no exception. Teapots changed from the simple-lined, smooth-surfaced copies of early solid silver pots to ornate, highly decorated fantasies. Victorian design continued and by the twentieth century many pieces of electroplated britannia ware, with their shiny silver finish, were monsters of whimsy and poor design. Toothpick holders, napkin rings, calling-card receivers, caster sets, toilet sets, candy dishes, inkstands, vases, shaving mugs, spoon racks, bells, cardcases, flasks, ice-water pitchers, chafing dishes, crumb-scrapers, knife rests, as well as every type of tableware was made of Victorian silver-plated britannia ware.

The term Sheffield plate has two meanings. It refers to the early rolled copper and silver method, or to electroplated silver currently being made in Sheffield, England.

The term silver plate also has two meanings. Silver plate is solid silver in England, the same as sterling silver in the United States. Silver plate in the United States means a layer of silver on a base metal such as copper or britannia ware, while in England this is called plated silver.

SILVER PLATE

A. 1. Nickel Silver No. 210
(See Oneida Community Silver
Co.)

A & S
(See Adams & Shaw Co.)

EA Co.
(See E. A. Bliss Co.)

Acme Silver Plate Co. (c. 1885)
Boston, Mass.

Acorn
(See Simeon L. & Geo. H.
Rogers Co.)

Adams, Chandler & Co. (c.
1869)
New York, N.Y.

The Adams & Shaw Co. (before
1904)
New York, N.Y.

Adelphi Silver Plate Co. (c.
1890-1920)
New York, N.Y.

Albany Silver Plate Co. (c.
1890-1904)
Location unknown
(See Barbour Silver Co.)

Benjamin Allen & Co. (1887-c.
1900)
Chicago, Ill.

C. A. Allen (c. 1887-1900)
Chicago, Ill.
Also Benjamin Allen & Co.

So. Am.
(See David H. McConnell &
Co.)

The American Silver Co. (1853-
1899)
Bristol, Conn.
Waterbury, Conn.
New York, N.Y.
Merged with International Silver
Co. Mark used by Interna-
tional Silver Co.

THE AMERICAN SILVER CO.

CROWN SILVER PLATE CO.
STERLING PLATE   ◁B▷

EASTERN SILVER CO.

H. & T. MFG. CO.

NEW ENGLAND
SILVER PLATE CO.

PEQUABUCK MFG. CO.

ROYAL PLATE CO.

WELCH SILVER

1857 WELCH-ATKINS

American Silver Plate Co.
(See Simpson, Hall, Miller &
Co.)

Ames Manufacturing Co.
(1870-1885)
Chicopee, Mass.

Anchor Brand
(See next entry)

Anchor Silver Plate Co.
(c. 1904-   )
Muncie, Ind.

St. Paul, Minn.

ANCHOR SILVER PLATE CO.

ANCHOR BRAND

INDIANA BRAND

A. T. Anderson (c. 1884)
Chicago, Ill.

Apollo Silver Co.
New York, N. Y.
(See Bernard Rice's Sons)

Ashbury Paine Manufacturing
Co. (c. 1888)
Philadelphia, Pa.

Aurora Silver Plate Manufacturing Co. (1869-c.
1904-   )
Aurora, Ill.
Became Mulholland Bros., Inc.

1869
AURORA SILVER PLATE M'F'G. CO.

B
(See C. E. Barker Mfg. Co.)

H. B. & H. A. 1.
(See Holmes, Booth &
Haydens)

M B Co
(See Meriden Britannia Co.)

M B & Co.
(See Manning, Bowman & Co.)

PB
(See Merry & Pelton Silver
Co.)

Babbitt & Crossman
(See Crossman & Babbitt)

Babbitt, Crossman & Co.
(1827-1829)
Taunton, Mass.

J. A. Babcock (c. 1884)
New York, N.Y.

Ball, Tompkins & Black
(1839-1851)
New York, N.Y.

C. A. Bamen (c. 1860)
Boston, Mass.

Barbour Brothers (c. 1882-
1898)
New Haven, Conn.
(See next entry)

Barbour Silver Co. (c. 1882-
1898)
Hartford, Conn.
New York, N.Y.
Merged with International
Silver Co. in 1898.

ALBANY SILVER PLATE CO.

James H. Barclay (c. 1869)
New York, N.Y.

C. E. Barker Manufacturing
Co. (c. 1904-   )
New York, N.Y.

J. Barton Jr.
(See Meriden Britannia Co.)

Benedict Silver Co.
(See John Hurly Silver Co.)

M. S. Benedict Manufacturing
Co. (c. 1890-1922)
Syracuse, N.Y.
Became Benedict Manufactur-
ing Co. (1922-present)

M. S. BENEDICT MFG. CO.
QUADRUPLE PLATE

Biggins-Rodgers Company, Inc.
(c. 1870-1904)
Wallingford, Conn.

D

James E. Blake Co. (c. 1904)
Attleboro, Mass.

E. A. Bliss Co. (c. 1904)
Meriden, Conn.

L. Boardman & Son (1884-c.
1904-   )
East Haddam, Conn.

L. BOARDMAN & SON

Bradley & Hubbard (c. 1876)
West Meriden, Conn.

Brazil Silver
(See Weinman Co.)

Bristol.
(See American Silver Co.)

Bristol Brass & Clock Co.
(c. 1857-1901)
Bristol, Conn.
Became American Silver Co.

Bristol Plate Co.
(See Pairpoint Mfg. Co.)

Britannia Metal Co.
(See Van Bergh Silver Plate
Co.)

Brodgers Silver Co. (c. 1880-
1885-   )
Taunton, Mass.

Brooklyn Plate Co.
(See M. Schade)

Brooklyn Silver Co. (before
1887-   )
(See M. Schade)

Brown & Bros. (c. 1884-1904)
Waterbury, Conn.
New York, N.Y.

Buck Silver Co. (c. 1900-   )
Location unknown

M S C
(See Maltby, Stevens &
Curtiss Co.)

Jno Carrow (c. 1884)
Philadelphia, Pa.

Case & Co. (c. 1884)
New York, N.Y.

Cattaraugus Cutlery Co.
(c. 1904-1922)
Little Valley, N.Y.

YUKON SILVER

Cincinnati Silver Co. (before
1904)
Cincinnati, Ohio

Clark Silver Co. (c. 1890-1900)
Ottawa, Ill.
Became M. C. Benedict & Co.

S. Cohen & Son (c. 1855)
Boston, Mass.

R. Coin
(See A. Davis & Co.)

Albert Coles & Co. (c. 1869)
New York, N.Y.
Albert Coles
E. W. Manchester

Colonial Plate Co.
(See Melrose Silver Co.)

Colonial Silver Co. (mark only)
(See Melrose Silver Co.)

Columbia
(See Middletown Plate Co.)

The Columbia
(See G. I. Mix & Co.)

Columbian Quadruple Plate Co.
(1893-before 1904)
New York, N.Y.

COLUMBIAN QUADRUPLE PLATE

Connecticut Plate Co.
(See Adelphi Silver Plate Co.)
(See J. W. Johnson)

P. A. Coon Silver Manufacturing Co.
(See Albert G. Finn Silver Co.)

Crescent Silver Co.
(See Albert G. Finn Silver Co.)

The Cromwell Plate Co.
(1884-before 1900)
Cromwell, Conn.

Crossman & Babbitt (1824-
1839)
(Babbitt & Crossman)
Taunton, Mass.
(See Reed & Barton)

Crossman, West & Leonard
(1829-1830)
Taunton, Mass.

Crown Guild
(See Rockford Silver Plate Co.)

Crown Prince
(See G. I. Mix & Co.)

Crown Silver Plate Co.)
(See American Silver Co.)
(See J. W. Johnson)

J. F. Curran & Co. (c. 1860-
1869-before 1904)
New York, N.Y.

D
(See Biggins-Rodgers Co., Inc.)

A. Davis & Co. (c. 1904-before
1922)
Chicago, Ill.
Purchased M. C. Eppenstein &
Co.

R. COIN   R. SPECIAL

James J. Dawson Co. (c. 1904-
before 1922)
New York, N.Y.

NORTH AMERICA

Derby Silver Co. (1873-1898)
Birmingham, Conn.
Derby, Conn.
Merged with International
Silver Co.

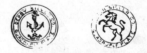

Diamond Brand.
(See American Silver Co.)

Ducimus
(See C. E. Barker Mfg. Co.)

Dutch Silver Novelties
(See Johnson, Hayward &
Piper Co.)

E
(See Holmes & Edwards
Silver Co.)

HE
(See Hall Elton & Co.)
(See Holmes & Edwards Silver
Co.)

T E
(See A. F. Towle & Son Co.)

"Eagle Brand"
(See Simpson, Hall, Miller & Co.)

Eagle Sterling Co. (before 1904)
Glastonbury, Conn.

Geo. Elkins (c. 1884-before 1904)
Philadelphia, Pa.

Eastern Silver Co.
(See American Silver Co.)

Edwards
(See Holmes & Edwards Silver Co.)

Empire Silver Plate Co.
(c. 1890-1922-   )
Brooklyn, N.Y.

M. C. Eppenstein & Co.
(See A. Davis & Co.)

Eureka Silver Co.
(See Meriden Silver Plate Co.)

F
(See Albert G. Finn Silver Co.)

S-F
(See Sheldon & Feltman

Willam Faber & Sons (1828-c. 1887)
Philadelphia, Pa.
Not Farber Brothers (w. 1922), New York, N.Y.

Filley, Mead & Caldwell
(c. 1850)
Philadelphia, Pa.

Harvey Filley & Sons (c. 1859-1884-before 1904)
Philadelphia, Pa.

Albert G. Finn Silver Co.
(c. 1904-before 1922)
Syracuse, N.Y.
Became P. A. Coon Silver Manufacturing Co.

ALBERT G. FINN SILVER CO.

CRESCENT SILVER CO.

Flat 1880 Ware.
(See Pairpoint Mfg. Co.)

Forbes Silver Co. (c. 1890-1898)
Meriden, Conn.
Became Meriden Britannia Co.

Gem Silver Co. (c. 1899-   )
Location unknown
Merged with International Silver Co.

German Silver
(See Holmes & Edwards Silver Co.)
(See Rogers & Brother)

B. Gleason & Sons (c. 1860-1870)
Dorchester, Mass.

The Globe
(See S. F. Myers & Co.)

Gorham Manufacturing Co.
(1863 present)
San Francisco, Cal.
Chicago, Ill.
New York, N.Y.

Providence, R.I.
Made coin silver before 1863.

H
(See Homan Silver Plate Co.)

H. & T. Mfg. Co.
(See American Silver Co.)

Hall, Boardman Co. (c. 1830-1848)
New York, N.Y.
Philadelphia, Pa.

Hall Elton & Co. (1857-1882)
Wallingford, Conn.
New York, N.Y.
Merged Meriden Britannia Co.

Chas. A. Hamill & Co. (c. 1884)
Baltimore, Md.

Hamilton
(See Rogers & Hamilton Co.)

J. L. Harlem & Co. (c. 1869)
New York, N.Y.

Lucius Hart (c. 1856)
Philadelphia, Pa.

Hartford Silver Plate Co.
(c. 1884-1887)
Hartford, Conn.

Hicks Silver Co.
(See A. R. Justice Co.)

George A. Higgins (before 1900)
New York, N.Y.

Holmes, Booth & Haydens (c. 1853-before 1922)
Waterbury, Conn.

New York, N.Y.

H. B. & H. A. 1.

SHEFFIELD PLATED CO.

STERLING SILVER PLATE CO.

UNION SILVER PLATE CO.

Holmes Bros. & Co. (c. 1884)
Baltimore, Md.

The Holmes & Edwards Silver
Co. (1851-present)
Bridgeport, Conn.
Stratford, Conn.
Merged International Silver
Co. in 1898.
Mark used to present.

EDWARDS

ORIENTAL

Holmes & Tuttle (1851-1857)
Bristol, Conn.
Became Bristol Brass & Clock
Co.

Homan & Co. (1847-1900)
Cincinnati, Ohio

Homan Silver Plate Co. (c.
1900)
Cincinnati, Ohio
Became Homan Manufacturing
Co. by 1922.

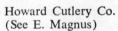

Howard Cutlery Co.
(See E. Magnus)

Howard's Nickel Silver
(See E. Magnus)

John Hurly Silver Co.
(c. 1890-   )

Scriba, N.Y.
Became Benedict Silver Co. in
1894.

Imperial Silver Plate Co.
(See Reichenberg-Smith Co.)

Indiana Brand
(See Anchor Silver Plate Co.)

International Silver Co. (1898-
present)
Meriden, Conn.

J
(See A. R. Justice Co.)

Johnson, Hayward & Piper Co.
(c. 1904-before 1922)
New York, N.Y.

DUTCH SILVER NOVELTIES

J. W. Johnson (1869-c. 1904)
New York, N.Y.
Retail outlet?

CONNECTICUT PLATE CO.

CROWN SILVER PLATE CO.

ROYAL PLATE CO.

A. R. Justice Co. (1900-c. 1922)
Philadelphia, Pa.

HICKS SILVER CO.

MEDFORD CUTLERY CO.

RIVERTON SILVER CO.

K
(See Knickerbocker Mfg. Co.)

C K & S
(See C. Klank & Sons)

L.K
(See Leonard Krower)

Ernest Kaufman (1857 a. 1870)
Philadelphia, Pa.

C. Klank & Sons (c. 1904-before
1922)
Baltimore, Md.

Knickerbocker Manufacturing
Co. (c. 1904-1922-   )
Port Jervis, N.Y.

Leonard Krower (c. 1904-before
1922)
New Orleans, La.

S. Kultana Co. (c. 1880)
Location unknown

L&W Royal Silver
(See Ledig Mfg. Co.)

S. L. & G. H. R. Co.
(See Simeon L. & Geo. H.
Rogers Co.)

LaPierre Manufacturing Co.
(1895-c. 1930)
Newark, N.J.
Merged International Silver Co.

Ledig Manufacturing Co.
(c. 1900-before 1922)
Philadelphia, Pa.

Leonard, Reed & Barton (1837-1847)
Taunton, Mass.
Became Reed & Barton

Lincoln Silver Plate Co. (c. 1840-1870)
Brooklyn, N.Y.

Lippiatt Silver Plate & Engraving Co. (before 1904-)
New York, N.Y.

Lyons Silver Co. (c. 1890-)
Lyons, N.Y.
(See Manhattan Silver Plate Co.)

M
(See Melrose Silver Co.)

M & B Sterling
(See Derby Silver Co.)

G M Co
(See Gorham Mfg. Co.)

Madison Silver Plate Co. (1887-before 1904)
Madison, Ind.

E. Magnus (before 1904)
New York, N.Y.
Became Howard Cutlery Co.

Malacca Plated
(See G. I. Mix & Co.)

Maltby, Stevens & Curtiss Co. (c. 1879)
Wallingford, Conn.
Became Watrous Manufacturing Co. (1896).

Merged with International Silver Co. in 1898.
Mark still used.

Maltby, Stevens & Curtis Shelton (1879-1898)
Location unknown
Merged International Silver Co.

Manhattan Silver Plate Co. (1850-1898)
Brooklyn, N.Y.
Merged International Silver Co.

Manning, Bowman & Co. (1869-1904)
Meriden, Conn.
Middletown, Conn.
New York, N.Y.

Manning Brothers (c. 1860)
Location unknown

Jos. B. Mayo (c. 1884)
Newark, N.J.

McConnell New York
(See next entry)

David H. McConnell & Co. (c. 1895-1904-before 1922)
New York, N.Y.

SO. AM.

Mead Phila
(See next entry)

John O. Mead (1840-1859-)
Philadelphia, Pa.
Became Mead & Sons
Filley, Mead & Caldwell

MEAD
PHILA

Medford Cutlery Co.
(See A. R. Justice Co.)

Medford, Wardell & Company (c. 1855)
Albany, N.Y.

The Melrose Silver Co. (c. 1904-before 1922)
Hartford, Conn.

COLONIAL PLATE CO.

Meriden B. Company
Meriden Brita Co.
(See next entry)

Meriden Britannia Co. (1852-1898)
New York, N.Y.
Meriden, Conn.
Merged International Silver Co.

J.BARTON JR.

M B Co

1847 ROGERS BROS.
MBCo NICKEL SILVER W. M. MOUNTS

MERIDEN BRITA CO.

The Meriden Silver Plate Co.
(1869-1898)
Meriden, Conn.
Merged International Silver Co.

Merry & Pelton Silver Co.
(c. 1904-before 1922)
St. Louis, Mo.

STANDARD PLATE 4

SECTIONAL PLATE XII

TRIPLE PLATE 12

Metropolitan Silver Co.
(c. 1904-before 1922)
New York, N.Y.

Mexican Silver
(See Holmes & Edwards Silver
Co.)

Meyer & Warne (c. 1859)
Philadelphia, Pa.

Miami Silver Co. (c. 1904-
before 1922)
Cincinnati, Ohio

The Middletown Plate Co.
(1864-1899)
Middletown, Conn.
New York, N.Y.

Merged International Silver Co.

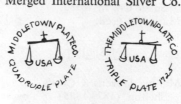

SUPERIOR

COLUMBIA

G. I. Mix & Co. (before 1904)
Yalesville, Conn.

CROWN PRINCE

THE COLUMBIA

MALACCA PLATED

Montauk Silver Company
(See J. W. Johnson)

M. E. Moore (c. 1884)
New York, N.Y.

Morgan Silver Co. (c. 1884)
Boston, Mass.

Mulford, Wendell & Co.
(1855-c. 1865)
Albany, N.Y.

Mulholland Bros. Inc.
Aurora, Ill.
(See Aurora Silver Plate Mfg.
Co.

S. F. Myers & Co. (c. 1860-
before 1922)
New York, N.Y.

.N.B
(See Rogers Silver Plate Co.)

*N. F. Nickel Silver
(See Oneida Community Silver
Co.)

N. F. Silver Co. (1877)
(See Oneida Community Silver
Co.)

National Cutlery Co.
(See Rockford Silver Plate Co.)

210 Nearsilver
(See Oneida Community Silver
Co.)

New Amsterdam Silver Co.
(c. 1890)
New York, N.Y.

New England Silver Plate Co.
(See American Silver Co.)

The New England Silver Plate
Co.
(See Adelphi Silver Plate Co.)

New Haven Silver Plate Co.
(c. 1890)
Location unknown

Niagara Silver Co. (before
1904)
New York, N.Y.
Became William A. Rogers, Ltd.

R. S. MFG. CO.

Non-corrosive
(See Pope's Island Mfg. Corp.)

North America
(See James J. Dawson Co.)

Norwich Cutlery Co. (c. 1890-
1898)
Location unknown
Merged International Silver Co.

NOTXLD
(See Wallingford Ware)

O. C.—A 1 X
(See Oneida Community Silver
Co.)

Ohio Silver Plate Co. (c. 1884)
Cincinnati, Ohio

Old Colony Pewter
Late mark of International
Silver Co.

Old Company Plate
Mark of International Silver
Co.

Oneida Community A. 1.
(See below)

Oneida Community Silver Co.
(1877-1904)
Oneida, N.Y.

A. 1. NICKEL SILVER NO. 210

*N. F. NICKEL SILVER

N. F. SILVER CO., 1877

O. C.—A 1 X

ONEIDA COMMUNITY A. 1.

SILVER METAL

TRIPLE PLUS

210 NEARSILVER

U. S. SILVER CO.

J. ROGERS & CO.

Oneida Silverware Manufacturing Co., Ltd. (c. 1904-1922-present)
William A. Rogers Ltd.
Oneida, N.Y.

Oriental
(See Holmes & Edwards Silver Co.)

Outfit.
(See Homan Silver Plate Co.)

Oxford Cutlery Co.
(See Wm. A. Rogers Ltd.)

P
(See Pairpoint Mfg. Co.)

EP
(See Gorham Mfg. Co.)

Pairpoint Best
(See next entry)

The Pairpoint Manufacturing Co. (1880-present)
Chicago, Ill.
New Bedford, Mass.

New York, N.Y.

PAIRPOINT
FLAT 1880 WARE.
BEST

BRISTOL PLATE CO.

Parker & Casper (1867-1898)
Meriden, Conn.
Merged International Silver Co.

Parker & Casper Britannia Co.
(1860-1869)
West Meriden, Conn.
Merged Middletown Silver Plate Co.

The Charles Parker Co. (c. 1887)
West Meriden, Conn.

Pelton Bros. & Co. (c. 1884)
St. Louis, Mo.

Pequabuck Mfg. Co.
(See American Silver Co.)

Philadelphia Plate Co. (c. 1890)
Location unknown
Merged International Silver Co.

Pittsburgh Silverware Co.
(c. 1887)
Pittsburgh, Pa.

Poole Silver Co. (1893-present)
Taunton, Mass.

Pope's Island Manufacturing Corp. (c. 1904-before 1922)
New Bedford, Mass.

Porter Britannia & Plate Co.
(1859-1870)
Taunton, Mass.

Providence Silver Plate Co.
(See Aurora Silver Plate Mfg. Co.)

Puritan Pewter
Mark of International Silver Co.

Queen City Silver Co. (c. 1888-1922-   )
Cincinnati, Ohio

R
(See Bernard Rice's Sons)
(See Wm. A. Rogers)
(See Wm. G. Rogers)
(See Wm. H. Rogers)

R & B
(See Rogers & Brother)

R. Special
(See A. Davis & Co.)

CMR
(See Charles M. Robbins Co.)

W. R.
(See Wm. A. Rogers Ltd.)

Redfield & Rice (c. 1867-   )
New York, N.Y.
(See Bernard Rice's Sons)

Reed & Barton (1847-present)
Taunton, Mass.

REED & BARTON

Reichenberg-Smith Co. (c. 1904-
before 1922)
Omaha, Nebr.

IMPERIAL SILVER PLATE CO.

Bernard Rice's Sons (c. 1904-
present)
New York, N.Y.
Merger of Apollo Silver Co.;
Redfield & Rice; Shepard &
Rice.

Richfield Plate Co.
(See Homan Silver Plate Co.)

Riverton Silver Co.
(See A. R. Justice Co.)

Charles M. Robbins Co. (c.
1904-1922-　　　)
Attleboro, Mass.

E. M. Roberts & Son (c. 1884)
Hartford, Conn.

Rockford Silver Plate Co.
(1873-1926-　　　)
Rockford, Ill.
Became Sheets Rockford
Silverplate Co.

G. Rodgers
(See Standard Silver Co. Ltd.)

Roger Manufacturing Co.
(c. 1887)
Philadelphia, Pa.

Rogers
(See Simeon L. & Geo. H.
Rogers Co.)
(See Wm. Rogers Mfg. Co.)
(See Wm. A. Rogers Ltd.)

Rogers. A.1.
(See Wm. H. Rogers)

Rogers & Brittin (before 1904)
West Stratford, Conn.

Rogers & Brother (1858-1898)
Waterbury, Conn.
Merged International Silver Co.
Rogers & Bro., A 1
Mark used by International
Silver Co.

★ R & B

R. & B.

★ ROGERS & BROTHER,

★ ROGERS & BRO., A 1.

★ ROGERS & BROTHER, 12

ROGERS & BRO.—GERMAN SILVER

Rogers Bros. (1847-before 1870)
Hartford, Conn.
Merged Meriden Britannia Co.

1847 Rogers Bros.
(See Meriden Britannia Co.)

1847 Rogers Bros. AI (c. 1882-
1902-　　　)
Meriden Britannia Co.
International Silver Co.

1847 Rogers Bros. XII (c. 1882)
Meriden Britannia Co.

The Rogers Cutlery Co. (c.
1871-1898)
The William Rogers Manufacturing Co.
Hartford, Conn.

New York, N.Y.
Merged International Silver Co.

Rogers & Hamilton Co. (1886-
1898)
Waterbury, Conn.
Merged International Silver Co.
Mark used from 1886 to present.

Rogers, Lunt & Bowlen Co.
(See A.F. Towle & Son Co.)

Rogers & Mead (1845-1850)
Hartford, Conn.

Rogers Silver Plate Co.
(c. 1904-1922-　　　)
Danbury, Conn.

Rogers, Smith & Co. (1856-
1902)
Hartford, Conn.
Merged Meriden Britannia Co.
Merged International Silver Co.
Factory moved to Meriden,
Conn. in 1884.

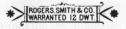

C. Rogers & Bros. (1866-1900)
Meriden, Conn.

Merged International Silver Co.

C. ROGERS & BROS., A 1.

C. B. Rogers & Co.
(See preceding entry)

F. B. Rogers Silver Co. (before
1922)
Taunton, Mass.
(See West Silver Co.)

F. B. Rogers Silverware &
Cutlery Co. (c. 1884)
Boston, Mass.
Shelburne Falls, Mass.

Frank W. Rogers (before 1904)
Hartford, Conn.

J. Rogers & Co.
(See Oneida Community Silver
Co.)

S. L. & G. H. Rogers Co.
(See next entry)

Simeon L. & George H. Rogers
Co. (c. 1902-present)
Hartford, Conn.
Wallingford, Conn.

 ROGERS

ACORN
*

SIMEON L. & GEO. H. ROGERS CO.

S. L. & G. H. ROGERS CO.

S. L. & G. H. R. CO.

Wm. Rogers.
(See Simpson, Hall, Miller
& Co.)

Wm. Rogers & Son.
(See William Rogers Mfg. Co.)

Wm. Rogers' Son
(See Frank W. Rogers)
William Rogers Manufacturing
Co. (1865-1898)
Hartford, Conn.

Merged International Silver Co.
Mark used after merger.

 ROGERS

WM. ROGERS & SON.

1865. WM. ROGERS M'F'G. CO.

1865. Wm. Rogers M'f'g. Co.
(See preceding entry)

William A. Rogers Ltd. (c.
1904-present)
New York, N.Y.

William G. Rogers (c. 1904-
before 1922)
New York, N.Y.

William H. Rogers (before
1904)
Hartford, Conn.
Plainfield, N.J.

Royal Manufacturing Co.
(See Weinman Co.)

Royal Plate Co.
(See American Silver Co.)
(See J. W. Johnson)

Royal Silver
(See Ledig Mfg. Co.)

S
(See E. H. H. Smith Silver Co.)
(See Stevens Silver Co.)

S-F
(See Sheldon & Feltman)

AS Co.
(See American Silver Co.)

R. S. Mfg. Co.
(See Niagara Silver Co.)

SS&Co.
(See S. Sternau & Co.)

W.S.&Co.
(See William Schimper & Co.)

St. Louis Silver Co. (c. 1880)
St. Louis, Mo.

Salamanca Plate
(See Buck Silver Co.)

Henry Schade (c. 1884)
New York, N.Y.

M. Schade (c. 1887)
Brooklyn, N.Y.
Probably became Schade & Co.
(c. 1904-before 1922)

BROOKLYN PLATE CO.

William Schimper & Co. (c.
1904-after 1922)
Hoboken, N.J.

Schultz & Fischer (1868-c.
1884)
San Francisco, Cal.

Sectional Plate XII
(See Merry & Pelton Silver
Co.)

Joseph Seymour Sons & Co.
  (c. 1887)
Syracuse, N.Y.

C. C. Shaver (c. 1887)
Utica, N.Y.

Sheets Rockford Silverplate Co.
  (1926-   )
Rockford, Ill.
(See Rockford Silver Plate Co.)

Sheffield Plated Co.
(See Holmes, Booth &
  Haydens)
Do not confuse with Sheffield
  Silver Co., a present-day
  New York City firm.

Sheldon & Feltman (c. 1850)
Albany, N.Y.

Shepard & Rice
(See Bernard Rice's Sons)

Sick-Call
(See Homan Silver Plate Co.)

Sillimans Silver Ring
(See Meriden Britannia Co.)

Silver City Plate Co. (c. 1850)
Meriden, Conn.

Silver Metal
(See Oneida Community Silver
  Co.)

Silver Plate
(See Oneida Community Silver
  Co.)

Simpson, Hall, Miller & Co.
  (1866-1899)
Wallingford, Conn.
Merged International Silver Co.

Simpson Nickel Silver Co.
  (1871-1899)
Wallingford, Conn.
Merged International Silver Co.

Skultana Silver Co.
(See S. Kultana)

E. H. H. Smith Silver Co.
  (c. 1904)
Bridgeport, Conn.
Purchased by Albert Pick & Co.,
  Chicago, by 1922.

G. W. Smith (c. 1850-   )
Albany, N.Y.
Joined William Rogers in 1856,
  forming Rogers, Smith & Co.,
  Hartford, Conn.

Walter M. Smith (c. 1869)
New York, N.Y.

Southington & Co. (c. 1880)
Location unknown
Merged with International
  Silver Co.

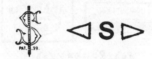

D. S. Spaulding (c. 1904-before
  1922)
Mansfield, Mass.

Special Metal
(See Homan Silver Plate Co.)

R. Special
(See A. Davis & Co.)

Springfield Silver Plate Co.
  (c. 1870)
Springfield, Mass.

Standard of the World.
(See American Silver Co.)

Standard Plate 4
(See Merry & Pelton Silver
  Co.)

Standard Silver Co. Ltd. (1895-
  1898)
Toronto, Canada
Merged International Silver Co.

Standard Silverware Co.
  (c. 1870-   )
Boston, Mass.

Steane, Son & Hall (c. 1884)
New York, N.Y.

SterlinE
(See James E. Blake Co.)

Sterling Inlaid
(See Holmes & Edwards Silver
  Co.)

Sterling Plate
(See American Silver Co.)

Sterling Silver Plate Co.
(See Holmes, Booth &
  Haydens)

Sterling Top
(See D. S. Spaulding)

S. Sternau & Co. (c. 1904-
  1922-   )
New York, N.Y.

Stevens Silver Co. (before 1904)
Portland, Me.

Stratford Silver Co.
Location unknown
Merged International Silver Co.

R. Strickland & Co. (1857-1884)
Albany, N.Y.

Strong Manufacturing Co.
 (c. 1887)
Winsted, Conn.

Superior
(See Middletown Plate Co.)

Superior S.P. Co.
International Silver mark after
 1920.

T
(See Towle Mfg. Co.)
(See James W. Tufts)

Taunton Britannia Co.
 (1830-1833)
Taunton, Mass.

Taunton Britannia Manufacturing Co. (1833-1834)
Taunton, Mass.

Taunton Britannia Manufacturing Co. (new concern)
 (1835-1836)
Taunton, Mass.

Toothill & McBean Silver Co.
 (before 1904)
Ottawa, Ill.

QUADRUPLE PLATE

Toronto Silver Plate Co.
 (c. 1887-1922-　　　)
Toronto, Canada

TORONTO SILVER PLATE CO. A1.

Towle Manufacturing Co.
 (c. 1904-present)
Newburyport, Mass.

A. F. Towle & Son Co. (c. 1904)
Greenfield, Mass.
Became Rogers, Lunt & Bowlen
 Co. before 1922.

Triple Plate 12
(See Merry & Pelton Silver Co.)

Triple-Plus
(See Oneida Community Silver
 Co.)

James W. Tufts (c. 1877-1904)
Boston, Mass.
New York, N.Y.
Incorporated 1881.

Union Silver Plate Co.
(See Holmes, Booth &
 Haydens)

U. S. Silver Co.
(See Oneida Community Silver
 Co.)

Valentine Linsley Silver Co.
 (before 1904)
Wallingford, Conn.
Became The Wallingford
 Company, Inc.

Van Bergh Silver Plate Co.
 (c. 1892-1925)
Rochester, N.Y.

Sold to Oneida Community
 Silver Co.

BRITANNIA METAL CO.

W. K. Vanderslice & Co.
 (c. 1859-1887-before 1904)
San Francisco, Cal.

Victor Silver Co.
Mark of Derby Silver Co.
Variation used after 1922 by
 International Silver Co.

W
(See Oneida Community Silver
 Co.)
(See Wallingford Co., Inc.)
(See Watrous Mfg. Co.)
(See E. G. Webster & Son)
(See Williams Bros. Mfg. Co.)
(See Wm. Wilson & Son Silver
 smiths Co.)

W Silver Plate
(See Oneida Community Silver
 Co.)

The Waldo Foundry (1894-
 1905)
Bridgeport, Conn.

 WALDO

Wallace Bros. Silver Co.
(See Wallingford Co., Inc.)

Wallace M'f'g Co.
(See R. Wallace & Sons Mfg.
 Co.)

"1835 R.Wallace"
(Mark used c. 1900. See below)

R. Wallace & Sons Manufacturing Co. (1871-present)
Wallingford, Conn.

The Wallingford Company, Inc.
   (c. 1904-present)
Wallingford, Conn.
Mark changed after 1904.

Wallingford Ware (c. 1870)
Wallingford, Conn.
Joined Simpson, Hall, Miller,
   & Co.

Warner Silver Manufacturing
Co. (c. 1904-before 1922)
Chicago, Ill.

Warren Silver Plate Co.
   (c. 1890)
New York, N.Y.
(See Wm. A. Rogers Ltd.)

Watrous Manufacturing Co.
   (1896-1898)
Wallingford, Conn.
Merged International Silver
   Co.

Webster Manufacturing Co.
   (c. 1859-1863)
Brooklyn, N.Y.
References to firm made in
   trade periodicals to 1900.

E. G. Webster & Bro. (1863-
1886)
Brooklyn, N.Y.
Became E. G. Webster & Son.

E. G. Webster & Son (1886-
1928)
Brooklyn, N.Y.
Merged International Silver Co.

Weinman Co. (c. 1900)
Philadelphia, Pa.

1857 Welch-Atkins
(See American Silver Co.)

Welch Silver
(See American Silver Co.)

West Silver Co. (c. 1883-1904)
Taunton, Mass.
Became F. B. Rogers Silver Co.
   before 1922.

Wilcox Britannia Co. (1865)
West Meriden, Conn.
Became Wilcox Silver Plate Co.,
   Meriden, Conn. (1867-　　)

Wilcox & Evertsen (1892-1898)
New York, N.Y.
Merged International Silver Co.

Wilcox Silver Plate Co. (1867-
   1898)
Meriden, Conn.
Merged International Silver Co.

The Williams Bros. Manufacturing Co. (c. 1904-1922-　　)
Naubuc, Conn.

William Wilson & Son (c. 1904-
before 1922)
Philadelphia, Pa.

William Wilson & Son Silver-
smiths Co.
(Est. 1812; Incorp. 1883)
Philadelphia, Pa.

Windsor Table Spoons
(See American Silver Co.)

The Winsted Silver Plate Co.
   (c. 1884)
West Winsted, Conn.

"World Brand"
(See American Silver Co.)

Yukon Silver
(See Cattaraugus Cutlery Co.)

BIBLIOGRAPHY

Bibliography—Pewter

1. Cotterell, Howard Herschel. *National Types of Old Pewter*. Boston, Mass.: Antiques, Inc., 1925.
2. Dow, George Francis. *Arts and Crafts in New England*. Massachusetts: The Wayside Press, 1927.
3. Dyer, Walter Alden. *Early American Craftsmen*. New York: The Century Co., 1915.
4. Eberlein, Harold Donaldson, and Abbot McClure. *The Practical Book of Early American Arts and Crafts*. Philadelphia and London: J. B. Lippincott Co., 1916.
5. Evans, J. J. "I.C.H. Lancaster Pewterer." Lancaster, Pa.: Lancaster County Historical Society, 1931.
6. Gale, Edward J. *Pewter and the Amateur Collector*. New York: Scribner's, 1909.
7. Graham, John Meredith. *American Pewter*. Brooklyn, New York: Brooklyn Institute of Arts and Sciences Museum, 1949.
8. Guild, Lurelle Van Arsdale. *Geography of American Antiques*. Garden City, New York: Doubleday, Doran, and Co., 1935.
9. Hatch, ———. *Albany Pewter and its Makers*. Albany, N.Y.: Albany Institute of History and Art, April, 1942.
10. Hayes, Doris. *A Brief Handbook of American Crafts*. Boston: n.d.
11. Jacobs, Carl. *Guide to American Pewter*. New York: McBride, 1957.
12. Kerfoot, John Barrett. *American Pewter*. Boston and New York: Houghton Mifflin Co., 1924.
13. Knittle, Rhea Mansfield, *Early Ohio Silversmiths and Pewterers*. Cleveland: Calvert-Hatch Company, 1943.
14. Laughlin, Ledlie Irwin. *Pewter in America*. Boston: Houghton Mifflin Co., 1940.
15. Myers, Louis Guerineau. *Some Notes on American Pewterers*. Garden City, New York: Country Life Press, 1926.
16. *American Pewterers and Their Marks*. New York: New York Metropolitan Museum of Art, 1940.
17. Thorn, C. Jordan. *Handbook of Silver and Pewter Marks*. New York: Tudor, 1949.

Other sources: private collectors, *Antiques, Hobbies*, early city directories and newspapers.

Bibliography—Silver Plate

Books:

Freeman, Larry and Beaumont, Jane. *Early American Plated Silver*. Watkins Glen, New York: Century House, 1947.

Gibb, George S. *The Whitesmiths of Taunton, A History of Reed and Barton*. Cambridge, Mass.: Harvard University Press, 1946.

Gorham Silver Co. *The Gorham Manufacturing Company Silversmiths*. New York: Cheltenham Press, 1900.

May, Earl Chapin. *A Century of Silver 1847-1947*. New York: Robert McBride Co., 1947.

Trade Marks of Jewelry and Kindred Trades. New York: Jewelers Circular Publishing Co., 1904, 1922, 1940.

A Century of Silversmithing, Reed and Barton. Reed and Barton. 1924.

Magazines, Pamphlets, etc.:

"Illustrated Catalogue and Price List Meriden Britannia Co." West Meriden, Conn., 1867.
"Illustrated Catalogue and Price List of Meriden Britannia Company's Electro Gold and Silver Plate on Nickel Silver and White Metal." 1882.
"Jewelers Mercantile Agency List, Directory of Jobbing Trade Only." 1884.
"The Jewelers Review." 1887, 1888, 1901, 1902.
"Jewelers Silversmith and Watchmaker." Monthly magazine, 1877.
"New York Jeweler Illustrated." 1887.
"1900 Illustrated Catalogue B.A. and Co." Chicago, Illinois.
"The Watchdial" (Jewelers Magazine). Cincinnati, Ohio, 1887.
"Watchmaker and Jeweler." 1869, 1870, 1872, 1874.

Other sources: other pamphlets, advertisements, information furnished by companies still working.

Bibliography—Silver

Books:

1. Avery, Clara Louise. *Early American Silver*. New York: The Century Company, 1930.
2. Bigelow, Francis Hill. *Historic Silver of the Colonies and Its Makers*. New York: Tudor Publishing Company, 1948.
3. Brix, Maurice. *List of Philadelphia Silversmiths and Allied Artificers, 1682-1850*. Philadelphia: Privately Printed, 1920.
4. Buck, J. H. *Old Plate, Its Makers and Marks*. New York: Gorham Manufacturing Company, 1914.
5. Burton, E. Milby. *South Carolina Silversmiths 1690-1860*. Charleston: The Charleston Museum, 1942.
6. Carpenter, Ralph E. Jr. *The Arts and Crafts*

of Newport, Rhode Island 1640-1820. Newport, Rhode Island: Preservation Society of Newport County, Pittshead Tavern, 1954.

7. Clarke, Hermann Frederick. *John Coney, Silversmith 1655-1722.* Boston: Houghton Mifflin Company, 1932.

8. Clarke, Hermann Frederick and Foote, Henry Wilder. *Jeremiah Dummer, Colonial Craftsman and Merchant 1645-1718.* Boston: Houghton Mifflin Company, 1935.

9. Clarke, Hermann Frederick. *John Hull, Builder of the Bay Colony.* Portland, Me.: The Southworth-Anthoensen Press, 1940.

10. Clearwater, Alphonso T. *American Silver, List of Unidentified Makers and Marks.* New York, 1913.

11. Crosby, Everett Uberto. *Books and Baskets, Signs and Silver of Old Time Nantucket.* Nantucket, Mass.: Inquirer and Mirror Press, 1940.

12. Crosby, Everett Uberto. *95% Perfect.* Nantucket Island, Mass.: Tetaukimmo Press, 1953.

13. Crosby, Everett Uberto. *The Spoon Primer.* Nantucket, Mass.: Inquirer and Mirror Press, 1941.

14. Currier, Ernest M. *Early American Silversmiths, The Newbury Spoonmakers.* New York, 1929.

15. Currier, Ernest M. *Marks of Early American Silversmiths, List of New York City Smiths 1815-1841.* Portland, Me.: The Southworth-Athoensen Press, 1938.

16. Curtis, George Munson. *Early Silver of Connecticut and Its Makers.* Meriden, Conn.: International Silver Company, 1913.

17. Cutten, George Barton. *Silversmiths of Georgia.* Savannah, Ga.: Pigeonhole Press, 1958.

18. Cutten, George Barton, and Cutten, Minnie Warren. *The Silversmiths of Utica.* Hamilton, N.Y., 1936.

19. Cutten, George Barton. *Silversmiths of Virginia.* Richmond, Va.: The Dietz Press, 1952.

20. Cutten, George Barton. *The Silversmiths, Watchmakers, and Jewelers of The State of New York outside New York City.* Hamilton, New York: Privately printed, 1939.

21. Cutten, George Barton. *Silversmiths of North Carolina.* Raleigh, N.C.: State Department of Archives & History, 1948.

22. Ensko, Robert. *Makers of Early American Silver.* New York: Trow Press, 1915.

23. Ensko, Stephen. *American Silversmiths and Their Marks.* New York: Privately printed, 1927.

24. Ensko, Stephen G. C. *American Silversmiths and Their Marks II.* New York: Robert Ensko, Inc., Privately printed, 1937.

25. Ensko, Stephen G. C. *American Silversmiths and Their Marks III.* New York: Robert Ensko, Inc., Privately printed, 1948.

26. Forbes, Esther. *Paul Revere and the World He Lived in.* Boston: Houghton Mifflin Co., 1942.

27. French, Hollis. *Jacob Hurd and His Sons Nathaniel and Benjamin, Silversmiths.* Printed by the Riverside Press for the Walpole Society, 1939.

28. French, Hollis. *A List of Early American Silversmiths and Their Marks.* New York: Walpole Society, 1917.

29. Graham, James Jr. *Early American Silver Marks.* New York: James Graham Jr., 1936.

30. Harrington, Jessie. *Silversmiths of Delaware 1700-1850.* Delaware: National Society of Colonial Dames of America, 1939.

31. Heller, David. *History of Cape Silver, 1700-1750.* D. Heller, 1949.

32. Hiatt, Noble W. and Lucy F. *The Silversmiths of Kentucky.* Louisville, Ky.: The Standard Printing Co., 1954.

33. Jones, E. Alfred. *Old Silver of Europe and America.* Philadelphia: Lippincott Company, 1928.

34. Knittle, Rhea Mansfield. *Early Ohio Silversmiths and Pewterers 1787-1847.* (Ohio Frontier Series.) Cleveland, Ohio: Calvert-Hatch Company, 1943.

35. Miller, V. Isabelle. *Silver by New York Makers, Late Seventeenth Century to 1900.* New York: Women's Committee of the Museum of The City of New York, 1938.

36. Okie, Howard Pitcher. *Old Silver and Old Sheffield Plate.* New York: Doubleday, Doran and Company, 1928.

37. Phillips, John Marshall. *American Silver.* New York: Chanticleer Press, 1949.

38. Pleasants, J. Hall and Sill, Howard. *Maryland Silversmiths, 1715-1830.* Baltimore: The Lord Baltimore Press, 1930.

39. Prime, Mrs. Alfred Coxe. *Three Centuries of Historic Silver,* Philadelphia: Pennsylvania Society of Colonial Dames of America, 1938.

40. Rosenbaum, Jeanette. *Myer Myers, Goldsmith.* Philadelphia: Jewish Publication Society of America, 1954.

41. Schild, Joan Lynn. *Silversmiths of Rochester.* Rochester, N.Y.: Rochester Museum of Arts and Sciences, 1944.

42. Semon, Kurt M. *A Treasury of Old Silver.* New York: McBride Company, 1947.

43. Taylor, Emerson. *Paul Revere.* New York: Dodd, Mead & Co., 1930.

44. Thorn, C. Jordan. *Handbook of American Silver and Pewter Marks.* New York: Tudor Publishing Company, 1949.

45. Wenham, Edward. *Practical Book of American Silver.* New York and Philadelphia: J. B. Lippincott Co., 1949.

46. Williams, Carl Mark. *Silversmiths of New Jersey 1700-1825.* Philadelphia: G. S. MacManus Co., 1949.

47. Wroth, Lawrence C. *Abel Buell of Connecticut, Silversmith, Typefounder, and Engraver.* 1926.
48. Wyler, Seymour B. *The Book of Old Silver.* New York: Crown Publishers, 1937.

Articles, Magazines, Newspapers, Museum Bulletins, etc.:

49. *American Church Silver of 17th and 18th Centuries exhibited at the Museum of Fine Arts, July to December, 1911.* Boston: Boston Museum of Fine Arts, 1911.
50. *A Collection of Early American Silver.* Tiffany and Company, 1920.
51. *American Collector.* New York, 1933.
52. "American Silver." *American Magazine of Art,* August 1919, v. 10, p. 400.
53. *Antiquarian Magazine.* 1924-1933.
54. *Antiques Magazine.* 1922-1959.
55. *Boston Museum of Fine Arts Philip Leffingwell Spalding Collection of Early American Silver.* E. J. Hipkiss. Cambridge, Mass.: Harvard University Press, 1943.
56. *Catalog of an Exhibition of Paintings by Gilbert Stuart, Furniture by the Goddards and Townsends, Silver by Rhode Island Silversmiths.* Rhode Island School of Design, Providence, R.I., 1936.
57. *Descriptive Catalogue of Various Pieces of Silver Plate forming Collection of The New York Farmers 1882-1932.*
58. *Detroit Historical Society Bulletin.* November, 1952.
59. "Early American Silver," H. D. Eberlein. *Arts and Decoration,* XI (August 1919), 166.
60. "Early American Silver," W. A. Dyer. *Arts and Decoration,* VII (May 1917), 365.
61. *Early Connecticut Silver 1700-1830.* Gallery of Fine Arts, Yale University, New Haven, Conn., Connecticut Tercentenary Commission, 1935.
62. *Early New England Silver lent from the Mark Bortman Collection.* Northampton, Mass.: Smith College Museum of Art, 1958.
63. "Early Philadelphia Silversmiths," H. F. Jayne and S. W. Woodhouse, Jr. *Art in America,* IX (October 1921), 248.
64. *Elias Pelletreau, Long Island Silversmith and his sources of Design.* Brooklyn, N.Y.: Brooklyn Institute of Arts and Sciences, Brooklyn Museum, 1959.
65. *Early Cleveland Silversmiths.* Muriel Cutten Hoitsma. Cleveland, Ohio: Gates Publishing Co., 1953.
66. *From Colony to Nation exhibit.* Chicago Art Institute, 1949.
67. "Jacob Boelen, Goldsmith of New York and his family circle." Howard S. F. Randolph. *New York Genealogical and Biographical Record,* October, 1941.
68. "Kentucky Silversmiths before 1850." M. M. Bridwell. *Filson Club History Quarterly,* XVI, No. 2 (April 1942), 111-126.
69. *Masterpieces of New England Silver 1650-1800.* Gallery of Fine Arts, Yale University, 1939.
70. "New England Silversmiths, news items gleaned from Boston newspapers, 1704-1705." G. F. Dow. *Art in America,* X (February 1922), 75.
71. "New York Metropolitan Museum of Art Exhibition of Early American Silver." C. Louise Avery. *Metropolitan Museum of Art Bulletin,* December 1931.
72. "New York Metropolitan Museum of Art American Silver of the 17th and 18th centuries." C. L. Avery. *Metropolitan Museum of Art Bulletin,* 1920.
73. "New York Metropolitan Museum Catalogue of Exhibition of Silver Used in New York, New Jersey, and the South." R. T. Haines Halsey. Metropolitan Museum of Art, 1911.
74. *New York Sun,* antiques section, 1938-1959.
75. "Old American Silver," *Country Life in America.* February 1913-January 1915.
76. "Old Silver." Prof. Theodore S. Woolsey. *Harper's Magazine,* 1896.
77. *Outline of the Life and Works of Col. Paul Revere (partial catalogue of silverware bearing his name).* Newburyport, Mass.: Towle Manufacturing Co., 1901.
78. *Parke-Bernet Galleries catalogue.* January 1938-December 1959.
79. *Pennsylvania Museum and School of Industrial Art Exhibition of Old American and English Silver.* 1917.
80. "Pennsylvania Museum and School of Industrial Art Loan exhibition of Colonial Silver, special catalogue." *Pennsylvania Museum Bulletin,* No. 68, June 1921.
81. "Philadelphia Silver 1682-1800." *Philadelphia Museum Bulletin,* LI, No. 249 (Spring 1956).
82. "Silver." H. E. Gillingham. *Pennsylvania Magazine of History and Biography,* 1930-1935.
83. "Silver by New York Makers." *Museum of the City of New York.* New York, 1937. December 7, 1937-January 17, 1938.
84. *Silversmiths of Northampton, Massachusetts and Vicinity down to 1850.* George Barton Cutten. Pamphlet.
85. *The Story of Sterling.* New York: Sterling Silversmiths Guild of America, 1937.
86. *The Story of the House of Kirk.* Baltimore: Samuel Kirk and Son Co., 1914.
87. "Three Centuries of European and American Silver." San Francisco: *M. H. de Young Memorial Museum Bulletin.* October 1938.
88. *Your Garden and Home.* 1931-1932.
89. Ralph M. and Terry H. Kovel.

INDEX
OF INITIALS USED AS MARKS
BY SILVER MAKERS

A

C P A—Charles Platt Adriance

E A—See Ebenezer Austin

F M A—Francis M. Ackley

G A—George Aiken

H A—Henry Andrews

I A—John Adam Jr., John Allen, Isaac Anthony, Joseph Anthony Jr., Josiah Austin, John Avery, Allen & Edwards, Jeronimus Alstyne

J A—John Adam Jr., Jeronimus Alstyne, Joseph Anthony Jr., John Avery, Joseph Anthony & Son

J A & J A—Joseph Anthony & Son

L*A—unknown c. 1770-1810

N A—Nathaniel Austin

P A—Pygan Adams

S A—Samuel Alexander, Samuel Avery, unknown c. 1770-1810

T A—Thomas Arnold

W A—William Anderson

A & G W—A. & G. Welles

A & R—Andras & Richard

A & O—unknown

B

B—Theophilus Bradbury

A B—Adrian Bancker, Andrew Billings, Abel Buel, Asa Blanchard

B B—Barzillai Benjamin, Benjamin Benjamin, Benjamin Brenon, Benjamin Brenton, Benjamin Bunker, Benjamin Bussey

C A B—Charles A. Burnett

C B—Caleb Beal, Clement Beecher, Charles Brewer, C. Brigden

C B & Co.—unknown

C O B—Charles Oliver Bruff

C P B—Charles Butler

C V B—Cornelius Vanderburgh

D B—Duncan Beard, Daniel Boyer

D B & A D—Bayley & Douglas

E B—Eleazer Baker, Ephraim Brasher, Everadus Bogardus, Elias Boudinot, Ezekiel Burr

E B & Co.—E. Benjamin & Co., Erastus Barton & Co.

F S B & Co.—Frederick S. Blackman & Co.

G B—George Bardick, Geradus Boyce

H B—Henry Bailey, Henry Biershing, Henricus Boelen

I B—John Bayly, James Barret, John Benjamin, Jurian Blanck, Jacob Boelen III, Jacob Braelen II, Jacob Boelen, Joseph Bruff, John Burger, John Burt, James Butler, John Bering, Isaac Brunson, John Butler

J B—John Bedford, James Black, John Boyce, John Brown, James Barret, John Black

J S B—John Stiles Bird

J C B & Co.—J. C. Blackman & Co.

J W B—Joseph W. Boyd

L B—Loring Bailey, Luther Bradley, Lewis Buichle

L S B—Lucas Stoutenburgh

M B—Miles Beach

N B—Nathaniel Bartlett, Nicholas Burdock, Nathaniel Burr

P B—Phillip Becker, Phineas Bradley

P B & C—Pelletreau, Bennett & Cooke

P V B—Peter Van Inburgh

R B—Roswell Bartholomew, Robert Brookhouse

R J B & Co.—unknown

S B—Standish Barry, Samuel Bartlett, Stephen Bourdet, Samuel Buel, Samuel Burrill, Samuel Burt

T B—Thauvet Besley, Timothy Bontecou, Timothy Bontecou Jr., Theophilus Bradbury, Timothy Brigden, Thomas Burger, Thomas Bentley

W B—William Bartram, William Ball Jr., William Breed, William Ball, William Byrd

W B & T—unknown

Z B—Zalman Bostwick, Zachariah Brigden

B & C—unknown

B & D—Barrington & Davenport, unknown

B & H—Brinsmaid & Hildreth

B & I—Boyce & Jones

B & J—Boyce & Jones

B & K—Bailey & Kitchen

B & L—unknown

B & M—Bradley & Merriman

B & P—unknown, Barton & Porter

B & R—Brower & Rusher, Burnet & Ryder

B & S—Beach & Sanford

B & W—Beach & Ward

C

C—unknown, J. H. Clark, John A. Coles

A C—Alexander Camman, Aaron Cleveland, Arnold Collins, Albert Cole, Abraham Carlisle, A. Cuyler

B C—Beriah Chittenden

C C—Charles Candell, Christian Cornelius, Charles Carpenter

C C & D—Charters, Cunn, & Dunn

C C & S—Curtis, Candee & Stiles

D C—Daniel Coan

E C—Elias Camp, Ebenezer Chittenden, Ephraim Cobb

F W C—Francis W. Cooper

G C—George Canon, Gideon Casey
I C—John Carman, John Champlin, Jonathan Clarke, Joseph Carpenter, John Coburn, John Coddington, John Coney, James Chalmers, John Chalmers, I. Clark, Joseph Clark, Jacob Cuyler
J C—Joseph Clark, Jonathan Crosby, Jonathan Clarke, John Coburn, Joseph Coolidge
J C & Co.—unknown
J H C—John H. Connor
K C & J—Kidney, Cann & Johnson
N C—Nathaniel Coleman
R C—Robert Campbell
R E C—unknown
S C—Samuel Casey
S C & Co.—Simon Chaudrons & Co., Stephen Castan & Co.
S S C—unknown
T C—Thomas Carson
T B C—Thomas Boyle Campbell
T C C—Thomas Chester Coit
T C & H—Thomas Carson & Hall, Thomas Chadwick & Heims
W C—William Clark, William Cross, William Cleveland, William Cowell
C & C—Colton & Collins
C & D—unknown
C & M—Cot & Mansfield
C & P—Cleveland & Post, Curry & Preston, Clark & Pelletreau
C & Y—unknown

D

A D—Amos Doolittle, Abraham Dubois, Antoine Danjen
D D—Daniel Deshon, Daniel Dupuy
D D D—Dupuy & Sons
E D—Edward David
G D—George Drewry, George Dowig
G R D—George R. Downing
I D—Jeremiah Dummer, John David, John Dixwell, Jonathan Davenport, John David Jr.
J D—John Denise, John David Jr., John David, James Duffel

J & T D—John & Tunis Denise
P D—Phillip Dally, Peter David, Peyton Dana
R D—Robert Douglas
S D—Samuel Drowne, Shem Drowne
T D—Timothy Dwight
T D D—Tunis D. Dubois
D & B—Downing & Baldwin
D & P—Downing & Phelps
D & W—Davis & Watson
D & Co.—DeForest & Co.

E

A E—John Aaron Elliott
C E E—Charles Edward Evard
E M E—Edgar M. Eoff
I E—Joseph Edwards, John Edwards, Allen & Edwards, Jeremiah Elfreth Jr.
J E—Jeremiah Elfreth Jr., James Elliott
R E—Robert Evans
S E—Stephen Emery
T E—Thomas Knox Emery, Thomas Edwards, Thomas Stevens Eayres
T K E—Thomas Knox Emery
E & H—Eoff & Howell
E & P—Eoff & Phyfe
E & S—Easton & Sanford, Eoff & Shepherd

F

A F—Abraham Forbes
A G F—Abraham G. Forbes
C U G F—Colin V. G. Forbes
D C F—Daniel C. Fueter
D F—Daniel C. Fueter
E F—Ebenezer Frothingham
G F—George Fielding
I W F—John W. Forbes
H—101. American Silver
J F—Foster & Richards, John Fitch, John Fite, Josiah Flagg
J W F—John W. Faulkner
L F—Lewis Fueter
R F—Rufus Farnam, Robert Fairchild
S F—Samuel Ford
T F—Thomas Fletcher
W F—William Forbes, William Faris
F & G—Fletcher & Gardiner
F & H—Farrington & Aunnewell
F & M—Frost & Mumford

G

B G—Baldwin Gardiner
B G & Co.—B. Gardiner & Co.
B C G—Benjamin Clark Gilman
C G—Caesar Ghiselin
D G—David Greenleaf Jr.
D T G—D. T. Goodhue
E G—Eliakim Garretson
G G—Greenberry Griffith
I G—John Gardiner, Joseph Goldwaithe, John Gray, John D. Germon, James Geddy
I W G—John Ward Gilman, John W. Gethen
J G—John Gardiner, John Gibbs, James Gough, James Geddy
J L G—John L. Gale
M G—Michael Gibney, Miles Gorham
P G—Philip Goelet
R G—Rufus Greene, Rene Grignon, Robert Gray
S G—Samuel Gray, Samuel Gilbert, S. Garne, S. Garre
T G—Timothy Gerrish
W G—William Gale, William Ghiselin, William W. Gilbert, William Gowen, William Grant Jr., William Gurley
W W G—William Waddell Geddy, W. W. Gaskins
G & D—Goodwin & Dodd
G & H—Gale & Hayden
G & M—Gale & Mosely
G & S—Gale & Stickler

H

A H—Ahasuerus Hendricks
B H—Benjamin Hurd
C H—Charles Hall, Charles Hequenbourg, Christopher Hughes
D B H & Co.—D. B. Hindman & Co.
D H—David Hall, Daniel Henchman
E H—Eliphaz Hart, Eliakim Hitchcock
G H—George Hanners Jr.
I H—Jacob Hurd, John Strangeways Hutton
J H—John Heath, John Husband
L H—Ludwig Lewis Heck, Littleton Holland
M H—Marguerite Hastier
N H—Nathaniel Helme, Nich-

P & M—Parry & Musgrave, Phinney & Mead
P & U—Pelletreau & Upson
J—101—American Silver

Q

P Q—Peter Quintard

R

A R—Anthony Rasch
C R—Christopher Robert
D R—Daniel Rogers, Daniel Russell
E R—Enos Reeves
F R—Francis Richardson, Francis Richardson II
G R—George Ridout, George W. Riggs
I R—Jonathan Reed, John Reynolds, Joseph Richardson Sr., Joseph Richardson Jr., Joseph Rogers, John Ross, John Royalston
I R & S—Isaac Reed & Son
I H R—John H. Russel
I N R—J. & N. Richardson
J T R—Joseph T. Rice
J R—Joseph Richardson Sr., Joseph Richardson Jr., John Royalston, Joseph Russell
M R—Moody Russell
N R—Nicholas Roosevelt
P R—Paul Revere Sr., Paul Revere
R R—Richard Riggs, Richard Ritter, Robert Ross
S R—Samuel Richards Jr.
T R—Thomas Revere, Thomas Richards
T V R—Tunis Van Riper
V R—Victor Rouquette
W R—Capt. William Richardson, William Roe, William Rouse
W & G R—William & George Richardson
R & G—Riggs & Griffith
R & L—Roberts & Lee

S

S—George B. Sharp
J & A S—J. & A. Simmons
A S—Anthony Simmons, Adam Stone
B S—Benjamin Sanderson, Bartholomew Schaats
C C S—Charles C. Shaver

C S—Caleb Shields
D S—David Smith, Daniel Syng
E S—Edward Sandell
G S—George Sharpe, Godfrey Shiving, George Stephens
H S—Hezekiah Silliman
I S—Jonathan Sarrazin, Joel Sayre, Jonas Schindler, John Sheppard, I. Smith, Joseph Smith, I. Stuart, John Syng
I I S—John J. Staples Jr.
J S—Joseph Shoemaker, John Staniford
J J S—John J. Staples Jr.
L B S—Lucas Stoutenburgh Sr.
M S—Moreau Sarrazin
N S—Nathaniel Shipman
P S—Philip Benjamin Sadtler, Philip Syng Sr., Philip Syng Jr.
S S—Silas Sawin, Simon Sexnine, Samuel Soumain, Simeon Soumaine
T S—Thomas Savage, Thomas Shields, Thomas Skinner, Thomas Sparrow, Tobias Stoutenburgh
T E S—Thomas E. Stebbins
I V S—Jacobus Vanderspiegel, Johannes Vanderspiegel, John Van Steenbergh Jr., John Stuart
W S—William Simes, William Simpkins, William Swan
Z S—Zebulon Stanton
J S & Co.—Joseph Seymour & Co.
S & A—Simmon & Alexander
S & B—Sheperd & Boyd
S & C—Storrs & Cooley
S & H—Seymour & Hollister
S & M—Sibley & Marble
S & R—Sayre & Richards
S & T—Shethar & Thomson

T

A T—Armistead Truslow, Andrew Tyler
D T—David Tyler
G T—George Tyler
I T—John Targee, Jacob Ten Eyck, John Touzell, Joseph Toy, Jonathan Trott Jr., James Turner
I & P T—John & Peter Targee
I L T—John Letelier
J P T—John Proctor Trott
S T—Samuel Tingley, S. Townsend
T T—Thomas Townsend, Thomas Trott
W T—William Taylor, Walter Thomas, William Thompson
T & B—Trott & Brooks
T & C—Trott & Cleveland
T & H—Taylor & Hinsdale
T & R—Tanner & Rogers
J P T & Son—John P. Trott & Son
K—101—American Silver

U

A U—Andrew Underhill
T U—Thomas Underhill
U & B—Ufford & Burdick

V

D V—Daniel Van Voorhis, David Vinton
D V V—Daniel Van Voorhis
I V—J. Vanderhan, John Vernon
N V—Nicholas Van Rensselaer, Nathaniel Vernon
P V—Peter Vergereau
R V—Richard Vincent
S V—Samuel Vernon
W V—William Vivant
V & Co.—Vansant & Co.
V & C—Van Voorhis & Cooley
V & S—Van Voorhis & Schanck
V V & S—Van Voorhis & Schanck
V & W—Van Ness & Waterman

W

A W—Ambrose Ward, Antipas Woodward
A E W—Andrew Ellicott Warner
B W—Billious Ward, Barnabas Webb, Barnard Wenman, Bancroft Woodcock, Benjamin Wynkoop Jr.
C W—Captain Charles Whiting, Christian Wiltburger Jr., Christian Charles Lewis Wittich
E W—Edward Webb, Edward White, Edward Winslow
H W—Henry Westermeyer, Henry White
I W—Isaiah Wagster, Joseph Warner, John Wendover, John